Efficiency and Scalability Methods for Computational Intellect

Boris Igelnik
BMI Research, Inc., USA

Jacek M. Zurada
University of Louisville, USA

Information Science
REFERENCE

Managing Director:	Lindsay Johnston
Editorial Director:	Joel Gamon
Production Manager:	Jennifer Yoder
Publishing Systems Analyst:	Adrienne Freeland
Development Editor:	Myla Merkel
Assistant Acquisitions Editor:	Kayla Wolfe
Typesetter:	Lisandro Gonzalez
Cover Design:	Jason Mull

Published in the United States of America by
Information Science Reference (an imprint of IGI Global)
701 E. Chocolate Avenue
Hershey PA 17033
Tel: 717-533-8845
Fax: 717-533-8661
E-mail: cust@igi-global.com
Web site: http://www.igi-global.com

Library of Congress Cataloging-in-Publication Data

Efficiency and scalability methods for computational intellect / Boris Igelnik and Jacek M. Zurada, editors.
    pages cm
  Summary: "This book presents various theories and methods for approaching the problem of modeling and simulating intellect in order to target computation efficiency and scalability of proposed methods"-- Provided by publisher.
  Includes bibliographical references and index.
  ISBN 978-1-4666-3942-3 (hardcover) -- ISBN 978-1-4666-3943-0 (ebook) -- ISBN 978-1-4666-3944-7 (print & perpetual access) 1. Computational intelligence-- Simulation methods. 2. Machine learning--Mathematical models. I. Igelnik, Boris, 1940- II. Zurada, Jacek M.
  Q342.E36 2013
  006.3--dc23
                                    2012051535

British Cataloguing in Publication Data
A Cataloguing in Publication record for this book is available from the British Library.

All work contributed to this book is new, previously-unpublished material. The views expressed in this book are those of the authors, but not necessarily of the publisher.

Editorial Advisory Board

List of Reviewers

Table of Contents

Section 1
Efficient and Scalable Methods in Machine Learning, Data Mining, and Medicine

Section 2
Efficient and Scalable Methods in Image Processing, Robotics, Control, Computer Networks Defense, Human Identification, and Combinatorial Optimization

Detailed Table of Contents

Section 1
Efficient and Scalable Methods in Machine Learning, Data Mining, and Medicine

Amparo Alonso-Betanzos, University of A Coruña, Spain
Verónica Bolón-Canedo, University of A Coruña, Spain
Diego Fernández-Francos, University of A Coruña, Spain
Iago Porto-Díaz, University of A Coruña, Spain
Noelia Sánchez-Maroño, University of A Coruña, Spain

This chapter reviews the most up-to-date feature selection methods focusing on their scalability properties. Besides, the enhancement of learning methods when these methods are applied on large scale datasets are presented and, finally, some examples of the application of feature selection to real world databases are shown.

Óscar Fontenla-Romero, University of A Coruña, Spain
Bertha Guijarro-Berdiñas, University of A Coruña, Spain
David Martinez-Rego, University of A Coruña, Spain
Beatriz Pérez-Sánchez, University of A Coruña, Spain
Diego Peteiro-Barral, University of A Coruña, Spain

In this chapter, online learning's general framework and methods since its inception are discussed and its applicability in current application areas is explored.

This chapter focuses on providing the foundations for defining imprecise hierarchies and the generalization process with crisp and rough data and hierarchies. Scaling and efficiency issues here involve the problems of creation of appropriate concept hierarchies and the scaling of the generalization process to deal with large databases.

This chapter presents two new feature selection methods used in cancer detection problems. The first method focuses on the introduction of a new algorithm for selecting features with high stability, while the second method is prewired into a specific class of projective classifiers and is based on compressive sensing (CS). The efficiency of the methods is demonstrated on cancer detection in Chest X-ray (CXR) and mammographic images.

Section 2
Efficient and Scalable Methods in Image Processing, Robotics, Control, Computer Networks Defense, Human Identification, and Combinatorial Optimization

This chapter proposes a robust embedding of authentication data (represented by a watermark) into an image using the 1D space of univariate functions based on the Kolmogorov superposition theorem and its efficient and scalable computational implementation by the Kolmogorov's Spline Network described in Igelnik and Parikh (2003). Using a key, the watermark can be removed to restore the original image.

This chapter closely examines the problem of real-time autonomous robot navigation, exhibiting target pursuit and obstacle avoidance behaviors in a dynamic environment. Three complete real-time systems are described addressing the navigation problem, using a highly reconfigurable architecture that allows for the different component algorithms to engage or disengage. A fuzzy system design approach, which takes advantage of symmetry in the input space, is introduced. As was shown, that it is actually possible to define fuzzy sets and fuzzy rules covering only half of the input space range, without sacrificing control precision. All algorithms are demonstrated by employing them in a simulation of a real-world system: the robot soccer game.

Chapter 7

This chapter discusses closed-loop control development and simulation results for a semi-active above-knee prosthesis. A closed-loop control using artificial neural networks (ANNs), trained with biogeography-based optimization (BBO), which is an evolutionary algorithm. It was shown that ANNs are able to improve average performance over open-loop control by up to 8%, and that they show the greatest improvement in performance when there is high risk of stumbles.

Chapter 8

This chapter explores intrusion detection systems (IDSs) which are the traditional tool for cyber-attack detection, and attack graphs which are a formalism used to model cyber-attacks. The time required to detect an attack can be reduced by classifying the attacker's knowledge about the system to determine the traces or signatures for the IDS to look for in the audit logs. The adversary's knowledge of the system can then be used to identify their most likely next steps from the attack graph. A computationally efficient technique to compute the likelihood and impact of each step of an attack is presented. The chapter concludes with a discussion describing the next steps for implementation of these processes in specialized hardware to achieve real-time attack detection.

The ability to recognize network traffics plays an important role in securing modern computer network infrastructures. In this chapter, we propose a machine learning approach that is based on statistical features of communication flow between two end-points. The statistical features are then used to develop and test a Parallel Neural Network Classifier Architecture (PNNCA), which is trained to recognize specific HTTP session patterns in a controlled environment, and then used to classify general traffic. The classifier's performance and scalability measures have been compared with other neural network based approaches. The classifier's correct classification rate (CCR) is calculated to be 96%.

Chapter 10

This chapter addresses the solution of combinatorial problems based on BBO combined with five techniques: (1) nearest neighbor algorithm (NNA), (2) crossover methods designed for traveling salesman problems (TSPs), (3) local optimization methods, (4) greedy methods, and (5) density-based spatial clustering of applications with noise (DBSCAN). The chapter also provides a discussion about the advantages and disadvantages for each of these five techniques when used with BBO, and describes the construction of a combinatorial solver based on BBO. A framework for large scale combinatorial problems based on hybrid BBO is proposed. Based on four benchmark problems, the experimental results demonstrate the quality and efficiency of this framework.

Section 3
Concepts

Chapter 11

Kolmogorov's superpositions enable the representation of every real-valued continuous function f defined on the Euclidean n-cube in the form , with continuous functions that compute f, and fixed continuous functions dependent only on n. The functions specify space-filling curves that determine characteristics that are not suitable for efficient computational algorithms. Reversing the process, the suitable space-filling curves that enable new functions that give a computational algorithm better adaptable to applications are specified. Detailed numerical constructions are worked out for the case n = 2.

This chapter discusses the origins of some of the scalability issues and suggest the types of models that may address these limitations. The steps are described towards modeling both recognition and a form attention called biased competition while maintaining scalability. The models that are both static and dynamic during recognition are explored.

Chapter 13

The chapter focuses on the analysis of scaling constants when constructing a utility function over multi-dimensional prizes. Due to fuzzy rationality, those constants are elicited in an interval form. It is assumed that the decision maker has provided additional information describing the uncertainty of the scaling constants' values within their uncertainty interval. The non-uniform method is presented to find point estimates of the interval scaling constants and to test their unit sum. An analytical solution of the procedure to construct the distribution of the interval scaling constants is provided, along with its numerical realization. A numerical procedure to estimate pvalue of the statistical test is also presented. The method allows making an uncertainty description of constants through different types of probability distributions and fuzzy sets.

Chapter 14

This chapter reviews the widely linear estimation for complex numbers, quaternions, and geometric algebras (or Clifford algebras) and their application examples. It was proved effective mathematically to add , the complex conjugate number of , as an explanatory variable in estimation of complex-valued data in 1995. Thereafter, the technique has been extended to higher-dimensional algebras. The widely linear estimation improves the accuracy and the efficiency of estimation, then expands the scalability of the estimation framework, and is applicable and useful for many fields including neural computing with high-dimensional parameters.

Foreword

Already for quite a time researchers strive to provide machines with unique human ability to cope with complex problems in an effective and efficient way. These efforts may be seen as an attempt to computationally model, simulate and even mimic intellectual activities. In the recently most popular data-oriented approach this requires vast amounts of data to be processed and/or huge solution spaces to be searched through. Various means may be adopted to preserve efficiency and obtain scalability of the systems aiming at mimicking superb human capabilities. Scalability may be understood as an ability of a system to continue to function when the sheer size of the problem in question or its complexity changes, usually grows up. In this sense scalability may mean that the system can be upgraded to process "larger" problems by, e.g., implementing it on a more powerful platform, and this upgrade can be carried out easily and transparently. On the other hand, scalability may be obtained by endowing the system with the capability to reduce the dimension of the problem in an "intelligent" way so as to avoid a degradation of the system performance. Both ways may be attributed to the human being who can involve more or less resources of its intellectual capacity to solve the problem in question as well as can reduce the problem, omit some relatively less important factors, etc. to scale down the problem to a tractable size and complexity. In terms of the computational approaches this may be emulated using the techniques of feature selection, on-line processing, generalization, interpolation and approximation, parallelization, connectionism, compression, simplification etc. All these techniques are usually combined with a proper representation of uncertainty which is characteristic of real-life practical problems, and the processing of which is another outstanding capability of a human brain. Computational intelligence/intellect related techniques employ a whole array of uncertainty models, starting from those based on the traditional probability theory to those involving fuzzy logic and rough sets theory.

Professors Boris Igelnik and Jacek Zurada, the editors of the current volume and world-wide known experts in the field, have to be congratulated, first, for coming up with the idea of this book, and then for perfectly implementing that novel idea. The papers collected deal with all issues mentioned above and treat them both from a theoretical and practical perspective. The contributors come from both academia and industry what makes the coverage of the area complete and exciting. The volume will surely be a valuable source of information for scholars and researchers, graduate and postgraduate students as well as practitioners. This volume is also a follow-up of an earlier volume edited by Professor Igelnik, a continuation expected by the entire research community.

Sławomir Zadrożny
Warszawa, Poland

Slawomir Zadrozny *is Deputy Director for Research, Systems Research Institute, Polish Academy of Sciences, Warsaw, Poland. His current research interests are in the areas of fuzziness in database management systems, fuzziness in information retrieval, intelligent decision support systems, fuzzy and possibilistic approaches to knowledge representation, and robotics.*

xiv

Preface

The methods of computational modeling and simulation of intellect have been developing in various fields, such as *digital signal processing and navigation* (Arasaratram & Haykin, 2009; Haykin, 2002; 2006; 2007; 2009; Swanson, 2002; Richaczek & Hershkowitz, 2000; Farrell & Barth, 1999; Grewal et al., 2007; Farrell, 2007; 1976), *image processing* (Batchelor & Whelen, 1997; Pratt, 2007; Jain, 1989), *robotics* (Bekey, 2005; Bekey et al., 2008; Haykonen, 2007; Thrun et al., 2005; Arkin, 1998; Nolfi & Floreano, 2000; Krans, 2001; Siegwart & Noarbakhsh, 2004), *control* (Hunt et al., 1995; Simon, 2008; Astrom, 2008), *systems biology* (Alon, 2007; Boogerd, 2007; Priami, 2009; Wilkinson, 2009), *molecular computing* (Adamatzky, 2001; Sienco et al., 2003), *nano-technologies* (Storrs Hall, 2005), *cognitive neuroscience and cognitive modeling* (Anderson, 2007; Feng, 2004; O'Reilly & Munakata, 2000; Davis, 2005; Polk & Seifert, 2002; Thelen & Smith, 1998; McLeod, Planket, & Rolls, 1998; Perlovsky & Kozma, 2007), *cognitive informatics* (Wang, 2009), *computational neuroscience* (Trappenberg, 2002; Lutton, 2002), *general artificial intelligence* (Goertzel & Pannacin, 2007), *knowledge-based neurocomputing* (Cloete & Zurada, 2000), knowledge based neurocomputing (Kolman & Margaliot, 2009), *multiagent systems* (Gorodetsky et al., 2007; Khosla & Dillon, 1997), *semiotics* (Gudvin & Queros, 2007), *neural-symbolic learning systems* (Garses et al., 2002), *social networks* (Bruggerman, 2008), *bioinformatics* (Zhang & Rajapakse, 2009), *data mining* (Han & Kamber, 2006; Witten & Frank, 2005), *computational intelligence* (Reisch & Timme, 2001; Schwefel, Wegener, & Weinert, 2003), *neural networks* (Haykin, 1994; Kasabov, 1996; Perlovsky, 2001), etc.

There appeared several books on what we call below "concepts," for example, Freeman (2000), Kitamura (2001), and Minsky (1986), and edited books, attempting to treat the topic of computational modeling and simulation of intellect (CMSI) on the broad basis of CMSI application to the spectrum of fields. The examples of such books are Zurada et al. (1994) and Igelnik (2011a).

The topic of CMSI is of great importance for information and management science and technology, both currently and in future. This book can be considered as a sequel to Igelnik (2011a) with a special stress on the methods of computational efficiency and scalability, utilized by CMSI in various fields of application. We hope that a posteriori effect of this publication will result in a discovery of similar features in different applications demonstrated in the book, fusion of them, and building in the discovered structure of the methods of computational efficiency and scalability in the general structure of the CMSI.

Researchers, instructors, designers of information and management systems, users of these systems, and graduate students will acquire the fundamental knowledge needed to be at the forefront of the research and to use it in the applications.

With progress in science and technology, humans experience increasing difficulties in computationally efficient and scalable processing huge amounts of high-dimensional data, extracting information from it, and eventually finding a meaning in the structured data. While computers definitely play a positive role in obtaining large databases, their current ability to computationally efficient and scalable make sense of the data is at best questionable. On the other hand, humans and their forerunners had millions years of experience (multiplied by billions of individuals) in information and technology exchange, and have developed an astonishingly efficient capability of extracting meaning from data. Facing tremendous difficulties in using computers for solving this task, the designers of information and management systems have started thinking: how do we do it? The complete answer to this question is still unknown, but attempts to make it using diverse computationally efficient and scalable methods and approaches have been emerging in many areas of science and technology. Therefore, it is important and useful to summarize this variety of methods and approaches and to target their fusion, computational efficiency, and scalability.

We came to the idea of this book while reviewing some of existing approaches to this discipline, which were actually based on a combination of the genetic, environmental, and social foundations in the different proportions. It is impossible to expect that there exists a unique approach best suited for the solution of the problem of modeling and simulation of intellect, just due to its giant complexity. Therefore, it is essential to fuse the knowledge contained in different approaches. The proportion of different foundations in an approach is also of great importance. We prefer to shift current attention more to environmental and social foundations than to its genetic base, and we have the long-term goal to implement the learning of intellect by a dynamic combination of the exchange data and knowledge first among humans, next among humans and computers, and next among the computers. This process of learning is supposed to evolve in time with the increasing role of interactions among computers. In our opinion, in the current, early period of development of the discipline, making a preference for social and environmental bases of intellect may save time in obtaining some practical results, while the methods of molecular and systems biology will be moving to a deeper understanding of the genetic foundations of the intellect. As was mentioned above, no general approach or idea (including our own) can be a panacea in the attempts to find a method for computational modeling and simulation of intellect.

ORGANIZATION OF THE BOOK

The book is divided into three main sections: Efficient and Scalable Methods in Machine Learning, Data Mining, and Medicine (Chapters 1-4); Efficient and Scalable Methods in Image Processing, Robotics, Control, Computer Networks Defense, and Combinatorial Optimization (Chapters 5-10; and Concepts (Chapters 11-14).

A brief description of each of the chapters follows below.

Chapter 1, entitled "Up-To-Date Feature Selection Methods For Scalable And Efficient Machine Learning," reviews modern feature selection methods, utilized for preprocessing the data from very large databases, by reducing input dimension and finding the minimal number of inputs that allows a following machine learning algorithm work with least degradation of its performance.

A number of examples of application of those feature selection algorithms to real world databases are given.

Chapter 2, entitled "Online Machine Learning," discusses online machine learning general framework and methods of its utilization in current application areas.

Chapter 3, entitled "Uncertainty in Concept Hierarchies for Generalization in Data Mining," focuses on providing the foundations for defining imprecise hierarchies and the generalization process with crisp and rough data and hierarchies. Scaling and efficiency issues here involve the problems of creation of appropriate concept hierarchies and the scaling of the generalization process to deal with large databases.

Chapter 4, entitled "Efficiency and Scalability Methods in Cancer Detection Problems," presents two new feature selection methods used by in cancer detection problems. First method focuses on the introduction of a new algorithm for selecting features with high stability, while the second method is into a specific class of projective classifiers and is based on compressive sensing (CS). The efficiency of the methods is demonstrated on cancer detection in Chest Xray (CXR) and mammography images.

Chapter 5, entitled "The Kolmogorov Spline Network for Authentication Data Embedding in Images," presents a novel approach for the embedding of authentication data (black and white logo, translucent or opaque image) in images. This approach offers similar functionalities than watermarking approaches, but relies on a totally different theory: the mark is not embedded in the 2D image space, but it is rather applied to an equivalent univariate representation of the transformed image. The author's contribution lies in proposing a robust embedding of authentication data (represented by a watermark) into an image using the 1D space of univariate functions based on the Kolmogorov superposition theorem and its numerical implementation by the Kolmogorov's spline network suggested in Igelnik and Parikh, (2003). Using a key, the watermark can be removed to restore the original image.

Chapter 6, entitled "Real-Time Fuzzy Logic-Based Hybrid Robot Path-Planning Strategies for a Dynamic Environment," examines the problem of real-time autonomous robot navigation, exhibiting target pursuit and obstacle avoidance behaviors in a dynamic environment. Three complete real-time systems are described addressing the navigation problem, using a highly reconfigurable architecture that allows for the different component algorithms to engage or disengage. A thorough investigation of the efficiency of the individual and combined component algorithms is provided. A fuzzy system design approach that takes advantage of symmetry in the input space is shown. All algorithms are demonstrated by employing them in a simulation of a real-world system: the robot soccer game.

Chapter 7, entitled "Evolutionary Optimization of Artificial Neural Networks for Prosthetic Knee Control," discusses closed-loop control development and simulation results for a semi-active above-knee prosthesis. The authors develop closed-loop control utilizing artificial neural networks (ANNs), which are trained with biogeography-based optimization (BBO), a recently developed evolutionary algorithm. This chapter contributes to the field of evolutionary algorithms by demonstrating that BBO is successful at finding optimal solutions to real-world, nonlinear, time varying control problems. It also shows that ANNs are able to mitigate some of the effects of noise and disturbances, and that they can provide better robustness and safer operation with less risk of stumbles and falls. The chapter demonstrates that ANNs are able to improve average performance over open-loop control by up to 8%, and that they show the greatest improvement in performance when there is high risk of stumbles.

Chapter 8, entitled "Techniques to Model and Derive a Cyber-Attacker's Intelligence," explores intrusion detection systems (IDSs) which are the traditional tool for cyber-attack detection, and attack graphs which are a formalism used to model cyber-attacks. The time required to detect an attack can be reduced by classifying the attacker's knowledge about the system to determine the traces or signatures for the IDS to look for in the audit logs. The adversary's knowledge of the system can then be used to identify their most likely next steps from the attack graph. A computationally efficient technique to compute the likelihood and impact of each step of an attack is presented. The chapter concludes with a discussion describing the next steps for implementation of these processes in specialized hardware to achieve real-time attack detection.

Chapter 9, is entitled "A Scalable Approach to Network Traffic Classification for Computer Network Defense Using Parallel Neural Network Classifier Architectures."

Chapter 10, entitled "Biogeography-Based Optimization (BBO) for Large Scale Combinatorial Problems," addresses the solution of combinatorial problems based on BBO combined with five techniques: (1) nearest neighbor algorithm (NNA), (2) crossover methods designed for traveling salesman problems (TSPs), (3) local optimization methods, (4) greedy methods, and (5) density-based spatial clustering of applications with noise (DBSCAN). This chapter also provides a discussion about the advantages and disadvantages for each of these five techniques when used with BBO, and describes the construction of a combinatorial solver based on BBO. A framework for large scale combinatorial problems based on hybrid BBO is proposed. Based on four benchmark problems, the experimental results demonstrate the quality and efficiency of this framework. On average, the suggested algorithm reduces costs by over 69% for a 2152-city TSP compared to other methods: genetic algorithm (GA), ant colony optimization (ACO), nearest neighbor algorithm (NNA), and simulated annealing (SA). Convergence time for this algorithm is only 28.56 sec on a 1.73-GHz quad core PC with 6 GB of RAM . The algorithm also demonstrates good results for small and medium sized problems such as ulysses16 (16-city TSP, where the best performance was obtained), st70 (70-city TSP, where the second best performance was obtained), and rat575 (575-city TSP, where also the second best performance was obtained).

Chapter 11, entitled "Kolmogorov Superpositions: A New Computational Algorithm," considers Kolmogorov's superpositions, which enable the representation of every real-valued continuous function f defined on the Euclidean n-cube in the form:

$$f(x_1,...,x_n) = \sum_{p=0}^{2n} g^q \circ h^q(x_1,...,x_n)$$

with continuous functions g^q that compute f, and fixed continuous functions:

$$h^q = \sum_{p=1}^{n} \psi^q(x_p)$$

dependent only on n. The functions h^q specify space-filling curves that determine characteristics that are not suitable for efficient computational algorithms. Reversing the process, the author specifies suitable space-filling curves that enable new functions h^q that give a computational algorithm better adaptable to applications. Detailed numerical constructions are worked out for the case $n = 2$.

Chapter 12, entitled "Evaluating Scalability of Neural Configurations in Combined Classifier and Attention Models," discusses the origins of some of the scalability issues and suggests the types of models that may address these limitations. The chapter describes the steps towards modeling both recognition and a form attention called biased competition while maintaining scalability. It explores models that are both static and dynamic during recognition.

Chapter 13, entitled "Numerical Version of the Non-Uniform Method for Finding Point Estimates of Uncertain Scaling Constants," focuses on the analysis of scaling constants when constructing a utility function over multi-dimensional prizes. Due to fuzzy rationality, those constants are elicited in an interval form. It is assumed that the decision maker has provided additional information describing the uncertainty of the scaling constants' values within their uncertainty interval. The non-uniform method is presented to find point estimates of the interval scaling constants and to test their unit sum. An analytical solution of the procedure to construct the distribution of the interval scaling constants is provided, along with its numerical realization. A numerical procedure to estimate p_{value} of the statistical test is also presented. The method allows making an uncertainty description of constants through different types of probability distributions and fuzzy sets.

Chapter 14, entitled "Widely Linear Estimation with Geometric Algebra," reviews the widely linear estimation for complex numbers, quaternions, and geometric algebras (or Clifford algebras) and their application examples. It was proved effective mathematically to add x^{*}, the complex conjugate number of x, as an explanatory variable in estimation of complex-valued data in 1995. Thereafter, the technique has been extended to higher-dimensional algebras. The widely linear estimation improves the accuracy and the efficiency of estimation, then expands the scalability of the estimation framework, and is applicable and useful for many fields including neural computing with high-dimensional parameters.

REFERENCES

Adamatzky, A. (2001). *Computing in nonlinear media and automata collectives.* Bristol, UK: Institute of Physics Publishing. doi:10.1887/075030751X.

Agrawal, R., Imielinski, T., & Swami, A. (1993). Mining association rules between sets of items in large databases. In *Proceedings of the 1993 ACM-SIGMOD International Conference on Management of Data* (pp. 207-216). New York, NY: ACM Press.

Alon, U. (2007). *An introduction to systems biology: Design principles of biological circuits.* London, UK: Chapman & Hall/CRC.

Anderson, J. R. (2007). *How can the human mind occur in the physical universe?* New York, NY: Oxford University Press. doi:10.1093/acprof:oso/9780195324259.001.0001.

Arasaratram, I., & Haykin, S. (2009). Cubature Kalman filters. *IEEE Transactions on Automatic Control, 54*(6).

Arkin, R. C. (1998). *Behavior-based robotics.* Cambridge, MA: The MIT Press.

Astrom, K. J., & Wittenmark, B. (2008). *Adaptive control* (2nd ed.). Mineola, NY: Dover Publications, Inc..

Batchelor, B. G., & Whelan, P. F. (1997). *Intelligent vision systems for industry.* New York, NY: Springer. doi:10.1007/978-1-4471-0431-5.

Beaubouef, T., Buckles, B., & Petry, F. (2007). An attribute-oriented approach for knowledge discovery in rough relational databases. In *Proc. of FLAIRS- 20* (pp. 507-09), Key West Fl.

Bekey, G. A. (2005). *Autonomous robots: From biological inspiration to implementation and control.* Cambridge, MA: The MIT Press.

Bekey, G. A. et al. (2008). *Robotics: State of the art and future challenges.* Hackensack, NJ: World Scientific Publishing.

Boogerd, F. C. et al. (Eds.). (2007). *Systems biology. Philosophical foundations*. Amsterdam, Netherlands: Elsevier.

Bruggerman, J. (2008). *Social networks. An introduction*. London: Routledge.

Cloete, I., & Zurada, J. M. (Eds.). (2000). *Knowledge-based neurocomputing*. Cambridge, MA: The MIT Press.

Davis, D. N. (Ed.). (2005). *Visions of mind. Architectures for cognition and affect*. Hershey, PA: Information Science Publishing.

Farrell, J. A., & Barth, M. (1999). *The global positioning system and inertial navigation*. New York, NY: McGraw-Hill.

Farrell, J. L. (2007). *GNSS aided navigation & tracking. Inertially augmented or autonomous*. Baltimore, MD: American Literary Press.

Farrell, J. L. (1976). *Integrated aircraft navigation*. New York, NY: Academic Press, Inc..

Feng, J. (Ed.). (2004). *Computational neuroscience: A comprehensive approach*. Boca Raton, FL: Chapman & Hall/CRC.

Freeman, W. J. (2000). *How brains make up their minds*. New York, NY: Columbia University Press.

Garcez, A. S. A., Broada, K. B., & Gabbay, D. M. (2002). *Neural-symbolic learning systems. Foundations and applications*. London, UK: Springer. doi:10.1007/978-1-4471-0211-3.

Goertzel, B., & Pennacin, C. (Eds.). (2007). *Artificial general intelligence*. Berlin, Germany: Springer-Ferlag. doi:10.1007/978-3-540-68677-4.

Gorodetsky, V. et al. (Eds.). (2007). *Autonomous intelligent systems: Agents and data mining*. Berlin, Germany: Springer-Verlag. doi:10.1007/978-3-540-72839-9.

Grewal, M. S., Weill, L. R., & Andrews, A. P. (2007). *Global positioning systems, inertial navigation, and integration* (2nd ed.). Hoboken, NJ: John Wiley & Sons. doi:10.1002/0470099720.

Gudvin, R., & Queiroz, J. (Eds.). (2007). *Semiotics and intelligent systems development*. Hershey, PA: Idea Group Publishing.

Guyon, I., Weston, J., Barnhill, S., & Vapnik, V. (2002). Gene selection for cancer classification using support vector machines. *Journal of Machine Learning, 46*(1-3), 389–422. doi:10.1023/A:1012487302797.

Guyon, I., Gunn, S., Nikravesh, M., & Zadeh, L. (2006). *Feature extraction. Foundations and applications* (*Vol. 207*). Berlin, Germany: Springer-Verlag. doi:10.1007/978-3-540-35488-8.

Haikonen, P. O. (2007). *Robot brains*. Hoboken, NJ: John Wiley & Sons, Inc. doi:10.1002/9780470517871.

Han, J., & Kamber, M. (2006). *Data mining: Concepts and techniques* (2nd ed.). San Diego, CA: Academic Press.

Haykin, S. (1994). *Neural networks: A comprehensive foundation*. Upper Saddle River, NJ: Prentice Hall.

Haykin, S. (2009). *Neural networks and learning machines* (3rd ed.). Upper Saddle River, NJ: Pearson Education Inc..

Haykin, S. (2002). *Adaptive filter theory* (4th ed.). Upper Saddle River, NJ: Prentice Hall.

Haykin, S. (2006). Cognitive dynamic systems. *Proceedings of the IEEE, 94*(11). doi:10.1109/ JPROC.2006.886014.

Haykin, S. et al. (Eds.). (2007). *New directions in statistical processing: From systems to brain.* Cambridge, MA: The MIT Press.

Hunt, K. J., Irwin, G. R., & Warwick, K. (Eds.). (1995). *Neural network engineering in dynamic control systems.* New York, NY: Springer. doi:10.1007/978-1-4471-3066-6.

Igelnik, B., & Parikh, N. (2003). Kolmogorov's spline network. *IEEE Transactions on Neural Networks, 14*(4), 725–733. doi:10.1109/TNN.2003.813830 PMID:18238055.

Igelnik, B. (Ed.). (2011a). *Computational modeling and simulation of intellect: Current state and future perspectives.* Hershey, PA: IGI Global. doi:10.4018/978-1-60960-551-3.

Igelnik, B. (2011b). Feature selection and ranking. In Igelnik, B. (Ed.), *Computational modeling and simulation of intellect* (pp. 361–383). doi:10.4018/978-1-60960-551-3.ch015.

Jain, A. K. (1989). *Fundamentals of digital image processing.* Englewood Cliffs, NJ: Prentice-Hall.

Kasabov, N. K. (1996). *Foundations of neural networks, fuzzy systems, and knowledge engineering.* Cambridge, MA: MIT Press.

Khosla, R., & Dillon, T. (1997). *Engineering intelligent hybrid multi-agent systems.* Norwell, MA: Kluwer Academic Publishers. doi:10.1007/978-1-4615-6223-8.

Kitamura, T. (Ed.). (2001). *What should be computed to understand and model brain function?: From robotics, soft computing, biology and neuroscience to cognitive philosophy.* Singapore: World Scientific. doi:10.1142/4607.

Kolman, E., & Margaliot, M. (2009). *Knowledge-based neurocomputing: A fuzzy logic approach.* Berlin, Germany: Springer-Verlag. doi:10.1007/978-3-540-88077-6.

Kraus, S. (2001). *Strategic negotiation in multiagent environments.* Cambridge, MA: The MIT Press.

Lytton, W. W. (2002). *From computer to brain. Foundations of computational neuroscience.* New York, NY: Springer-Verlag.

McLeod, P., Planket, P. K., & Rolls, E. T. (1998). *Introduction to connectionist modeling of cognitive processes.* Oxford, UK: Oxford University Press.

Minsky, M. (1986). *Society of minds.* New York, NY: Simon and Schuster.

Nolfi, S., & Floreano, D. (2000). *Evolutionary robotics: The biology, intelligence and technology of self-organizing machines.* Cambridge, MA: The MIT Press.

O'Reilly, R. C., & Munakata, Y. (2000). *Computational explorations in cognitive neuroscience*. Cambridge, MA: The MIT Press.

Pawlak, Z. (1984). Rough sets. *International Journal of Man-Machine Studies, 21*, 127–134. doi:10.1016/S0020-7373(84)80062-0.

Pawlak, Z. (1991). *Rough sets: Theoretical aspects of reasoning about data*. Norwell, MA: Kluwer Academic Publishers.

Perlovsky, L. I. (2001). *Neural networks and intellect. Using model-based concepts*. Oxford: Oxford University Press.

Perlovsky, L. I., & Kozma, R. (Eds.). (2007). *Neurodynamics of cognition and consciousness*. Heidelberg, Germany: Springer-Verlag. doi:10.1007/978-3-540-73267-9.

Polk, T. A., & Seifert, C. M. (2002). *Cognitive modeling*. Cambridge, MA: The MIT Press.

Pratt, W. K. (2007). *Digital image processing* (4th ed.). Hoboken, NJ: John Wiley & Sons, Inc. doi:10.1002/0470097434.

Priami, C. (2009). Algorithmic systems biology. *Communications of the ACM, 52*(5), 80–88. doi:10.1145/1506409.1506427.

Reusch, B., & Timme, K.-H. (Eds.). (2001). *Computational intelligence in theory and practice*. Heidelberg, Germany: Phisica-Verlag. doi:10.1007/978-3-7908-1831-4.

Rihaczek, A. W., & Hershkowitz, S. J. (2000). *Theory and practice of radar target identification. Norwood House*. Artech House.

Russell, S. J., & Norvig, P. (2003). *Artificial intelligence. A modern approach* (2nd ed.). Upper Saddle River, NJ: Pearson Education Inc..

Schwefel, H.-P., Wegener, I., & Weinert, K. (2003). *Advances in computational intelligence. theory and practice*. Berlin, Germany: Springer.

Siegwart, R., & Nourbakhsh, I. R. (2004). *Introduction to autonomous mobile robots*. Cambridge, MA: The MIT Press.

Sienco, T., Adamatzky, A., Rambidi, N., & Conrad, M. (Eds.). (2003). *Molecular computing*. Cambridge, MA: The MIT Press.

Simon, D. (2006). *Optimal state estimation. Kalman, H_∞, and nonlinear approaches*. Hoboken, NJ: Wiley& Sons. doi:10.1002/0470045345.

Sprecher, D. A. (1996). A numerical implementation of Kolmogorov's superpositions. *Neural Networks, 9*(5), 765–772. doi:10.1016/0893-6080(95)00081-X PMID:12662561.

Sprecher, D. A. (1997). A numerical implementation of Kolmogorov's superpositions II. *Neural Networks, 10*(3), 447–457. doi:10.1016/S0893-6080(96)00073-1.

Storrs Hall, J. (2005). *Nanofuture*. Amherst, NY: Prometheus Books.

Swanson, D. C. (2002). *Signal processing for intelligent sensing systems*. New York, NY: Marcel Dekker.

Thelen, E., & Smith, L. B. (1998). *A dynamic systems approach to the development of cognition and action*. Cambridge, MA: MIT Press.

Thrun, S., Burgard, W., & Fox, D. (2005). *Probabilistic robotics*. Cambridge, MA: The MIT Press.

Trappenberg, T. P. (2002). *Fundamentals of computational neuroscience*. Oxford: Oxford University Press.

Wang, Y. (Ed.). (2009). *Novel approaches in cognitive informatics and natural intelligence*.

Hershey, PA: IGI Global.

Wilkinson, D. J. (2006). *Stochastic modelling in systems biology*. Boca Raton, FL: Chapman & Hall/CRC.

Witten, I. H., & Frank, E. (2005). *Data mining. Practical machine learning tools and techniques* (2nd ed.). Amsterdam, Netherlands: Elsevier Inc..

Zang, Y.-Q., & Rajapakse, J. C. (Eds.). (2009). *Machine learning in bioinformatics*. Hoboken, NJ: J. Wiley & Sons, Inc..

Zurada, J. M., Marks, R. J. II, & Robinson, C. J. (Eds.). (1994). *Computational intelligence. Imitating life*. New York, NY: IEEE Press.

Section 1
Efficient and Scalable Methods in Machine Learning, Data Mining, and Medicine

Chapter 1
Up-to-Date Feature Selection Methods for Scalable and Efficient Machine Learning

Amparo Alonso-Betanzos
University of A Coruña, Spain

Diego Fernández-Francos
University of A Coruña, Spain

Verónica Bolón-Canedo
University of A Coruña, Spain

Iago Porto-Díaz
University of A Coruña, Spain

Noelia Sánchez-Maroño
University of A Coruña, Spain

ABSTRACT

With the advent of high dimensionality, machine learning researchers are now interested not only in accuracy, but also in scalability of algorithms. When dealing with large databases, pre-processing techniques are required to reduce input dimensionality and machine learning can take advantage of feature selection, which consists of selecting the relevant features and discarding irrelevant ones with a minimum degradation in performance. In this chapter, we will review the most up-to-date feature selection methods, focusing on their scalability properties. Moreover, we will show how these learning methods are enhanced when applied to large scale datasets and, finally, some examples of the application of feature selection in real world databases will be shown.

INTRODUCTION

In recent years, the dimensionality of datasets, as can be seen in (Zhao & Liu, 2012), has increased steadily. As new applications appear, a dataset with a dimensionality above 10,000 is common in applications such as, for example, medical images, text retrieval or genetic data, most of which are now measured in petabytes (PB, 2^{50} bytes). A database is considered high dimensional when (a) the number of samples is very high, (b) the number of features is very high, or (c) the number of samples and features is very high. Learning methods become particularly difficult when dealing with datasets with around 1,000,000 data (samples x features being data).

DOI: 10.4018/978-1-4666-3942-3.ch001

When data dimensionality is high, many of the features can be redundant or irrelevant, and when high dimensionality is based upon the number of features and not only on the sample size, can even be a more complex problem, more so if the data sample is small. As a typical example, DNA microarray data could contain more than 30,000 features with a sample size of usually less than 100. With datasets of this type, most techniques can become unreliable.

Theoretically, it seems logical that having a higher amount of information could lead to better results. However, this is not always the case due to the so-called curse of dimensionality (Bellman, 1957).This phenomenon occurs when dimensionality increases and the time required by the machine learning algorithm to train the data increases exponentially. High dimensionality constitutes a new challenge for data mining, because the performance of learning algorithms can degenerate due to over fitting. Also, learned models decrease their interpretability as they become more complex and consequently the speed and efficiency of the algorithms declines in accordance with size.

In order to deal with these problems, dimensionality reduction techniques are usually applied, so that the set of features needed for describing the problem can be reduced. Moreover, most of the times, the performance of the models can be improved, together with data and model understanding, as well as reducing the need for data storage (Guyon, Gunn, Nikravesh, & Zadeh, 2006). Dimensionality reduction techniques can be broadly classified into feature construction and feature selection methods. Feature construction techniques attempt to generate a set of useful features than can be used to represent the raw data of a problem. A pre-processing transformation could be considered which may alter the space dimensionality of the problem by enlarging or reducing it. The data set generated by feature extraction is represented by a newly generated set of features, different than the original. On the other hand, feature selection is the process of detecting the relevant features and discarding the irrelevant ones in order to obtain a subset of features that correctly describes the given problem with a minimum degradation of performance. In this case, dimensionality reduction is always achieved, and the set of features is a subset of the original set. As feature selection maintains the original features, it is especially interesting when they are needed for interpreting the model obtained. Feature selection techniques can be applied to both the two main areas of machine learning: classification and regression, although the former is the more common, the reason being that the typical classification problem has several variables whilst the common regression problem usually has just one.

Feature selection methods can be divided into two models: individual evaluation and subset evaluation (Yu & Liu, 2004). The former is also known as feature ranking and evaluates individual features by assigning them weights in a ranking according to their degree of relevance, whilst the latter produces candidate feature subsets based on a certain search strategy. Not all the ranker methods provide a weight of the features, so rankers can also be divided into score methods, i.e. those methods assigning a relevance value to each feature, and "pure rankers" that only return a list of ordered features and the difference in relevance of a feature and the next (or previous) one in the list is unknown.

Aside from this classification, three major approaches (see Figure 1) can be distinguished based upon the relationship between the feature selection algorithm and the inductive learning method used to infer a model (Guyon, Gunn, Nikravesh, & Zadeh, 2006):

- **Filters:** Which rely on the general characteristics of the data and perform the feature selection process as a pre-processing step,

Figure 1. Feature selection techniques

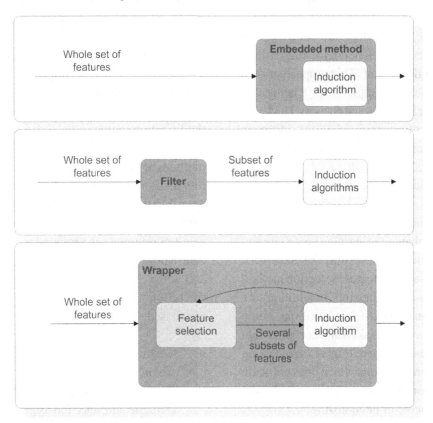

independently of the induction algorithm. This model is advantageous for its low computational cost and good generalisation ability.

- **Wrappers:** Which involve a learning algorithm as a black box and consist of using its prediction performance to assess the relative usefulness of subsets of variables. In other words, the feature selection algorithm uses the learning algorithm as a subroutine with the computational burden that comes from calling the learning algorithm to evaluate each subset of features. However, this interaction with the classifier tends to give better performance results than filters.

- **Embedded Methods:** Which perform feature selection when training the classifier and are usually specific to given learning

machines. Therefore, the search for an optimal subset of features is built into the classifier construction and can be seen as a search in the combined space of feature subsets and hypotheses. This approach is able to capture feature dependencies at a lower computational cost than wrappers.

With such a vast body of feature selection methods available, most researchers agree that "the best method" simply does not exist and their efforts are focused on finding a good method for a specific problem setting. In that sense, different methods have been developed to deal with large scale datasets where the importance of feature selection is beyond doubt, since it is essential to minimise training time and allocated memory while maintaining accuracy. Nevertheless, it is important to bear in mind that most feature selection methods use the performance of the learned model as part of the selection process. In fact, from the three categories shown above (filters, wrappers and embedded), only filters are algorithm-independent. This property makes filters computationally simple and fast, being able to handle extremely large-scale datasets. However, most filters are univariate, i.e. they consider each feature independently of other features, a drawback that can be overcome by multivariate techniques which usually demand more computational resources. Therefore, although feature selection methods may be helpful in reducing the dimension of a problem to enhance the learning procedure and obtain better performance results, the election of an efficient and scalable feature selection method is not an easy-to-solve question. In addition to a good selection among existing algorithms, some considerations have to be taken into account when applied to extremely large datasets to avoid using a feature selection technique which does not scale properly and, consequently, obtaining a model which is not capable of generalising.

This chapter is intended to provide some guidelines to help the reader choose a feature selection method when dealing with extremely high-dimensional data. In this scenario, sometimes a small degradation in the quality of learning is permitted at the expense of better generalisation ability, therefore the most up-to-date feature selection methods will be reviewed, focusing not also on effectiveness but also on their scalability properties. Machine learning algorithms can take advantage of feature selection when dealing with large-scale databases and so some examples of the enhancement accomplished will be presented. Finally, the reader can find some real applications where feature selection has proven to be effective.

FEATURE SELECTION METHODS

An important advantage of feature selection is to reduce the dimension of a problem to enhance the learning procedure and obtain better performance

results. When the dimensionality increases, the time required by the machine learning algorithm to train the data increases exponentially, so in order to increase the performance of machine learning algorithms, it is important to decrease the dimension of datasets and, for that reason, a large set of feature selection methods are available in the literature that have been extensively applied. However, explaining in detail all the available methods is beyond the scope of this chapter, and this section briefly intrSoduces the most popular ones. Firstly, a non-exhaustive list of well-known filters is illustrated in Table 1. For each filter, the original reference is provided, some basic characteristics are presented in the previous section and some data mining tools where these filters can be found already implemented are mentioned /discussed. These tools are:

- Weka, http://www.cs.waikato.ac.nz/ml/ weka/ (Witten & E., 2005),
- Feature Selection at Arizona State University (http://featureselection.asu.edu/) and
- Java-ML (http://java-ml.sourceforge.net/). Weka is also implemented in Java, so Java-ML has methods that allow one to run Weka algorithms.

The idea of the wrapper approach is to select a feature subset using a learning algorithm as part of the evaluation function. Instead of using subset sufficiency, entropy or another explicitly defined evaluation function, a kind of "black box" function is used to guide the search. The evaluation function for each candidate feature subset returns an estimate of the quality of the model that is induced by the learning algorithm. This can be rather time consuming, since, for each candidate feature subset evaluated during the search, the target learning algorithm is usually applied several times (e.g. in the case of 10-fold cross validation being used to estimate model quality).

One of the first studies of the wrapper approach was conducted by Kohavi and John (1997). Besides introducing the notion of strong and weak

Table 1. Some well-known filter methods in the relevant literature. The Tools column indicates software tools where these algorithms are implemented. A stands for Feature Selection at Arizona State University, J for Java-ML, and W for Weka.

	Uni /Multivariate	Score/Ranker/Subset	Tools	References
F-score (Fisher score)	Univariate	Score	A	Duda, Hart, & Stork, 2001
$\chi 2$	Univariate	Score	W, A	Wilson & Hilferty, 1931
Information gain	Univariate	Score	W, A, J	Quinlan, 1986
Consistency	Multivariate	Subset	W	Dash & Liu, 2003
RELIEF	Univariate	Score	W, A, J	Kira & Rendell, 1992
CFS	Multivariate	Subset	W, A	Hall, 1999
FCBF (SU)	Univariate	Ranker	A, J	Yu & Liu, 2003
INTERACT	Multivariate	Subset	W	Zhao & Liu, 2007
mRMR	Multivariate	Ranker	A	Peng, Long, & Ding, 2005

feature relevance, these authors showed the results achieved by different induction algorithms (ID3, C4.5, and naïve-Bayes) in several search methods (best first, hill-climbing, etc.). There are some software tools that include wrappers, for example, Weka provides a method that allows us to select between basic search strategies (Sequential Forward/Backward Search, hill climbing, etc.) and different learning algorithms (C4.5, naïve-Bayes, etc.), leading to different wrapper methods.

In contrast to filter and wrapper approaches, embedded methods do not separate the learning from the feature selection part. Embedded methods include algorithms, which optimise a regularised risk function J with respect to two sets of parameters: the parameters of the learning machine and the parameters indicating which features are selected. Guyon, Weston, Barnhill, and Vapnik (2002) introduce one of the most popular embedded methods: SVM-RFE (Recursive Feature Elimination for Support Vector Machines). This method performs feature selection by iteratively training an SVM classifier with the current set of features and removing the least important feature indicated by the SVM. This algorithm is available at Weka and Java-ML. Other embedded methods are Grafting, a gradient descent approach to feature selection in a regularised risk framework described by Perkins, Lacker, and Theiler (2003),

LASSO (Least Absolute Shrinkage and Selection Operator), that has been designed to enforce feature selection during the training of a linear model (Tibshirani, 1996) or Random Forest (RF), a classifier that combines many single decision trees (Breiman, 2001) available at Java-ML tool.

As regards the computational cost, it can be noticed in Table 1 that most proposed filter techniques are univariate. This means that each feature is considered separately, thereby ignoring feature dependencies, which may lead to worse classification performance when compared to other types of feature selection techniques. However, they have the advantage of being scalable, i.e., if we consider m samples and n features, the complexity of these methods is usually nm. In order to overcome the problem of ignoring feature dependencies, a number of multivariate filter techniques were introduced, aiming to incorporate feature dependencies to some degree, but at the cost of reducing their scalability. This depends on the search strategy used to form the subset of features. The complexity of embedded methods varies. For example, the complexity of RFE-SVM is $\max(n,m)m^2$, while on the other hand, RF complexity depends more on the number of samples than on the number of features, i.e. $t\sqrt{nm}\,\log(m)$, where t is the number of trees used in the construction of the forest (Guyon, Gunn, Nikravesh,

& Zadeh, 2006). Finally, wrappers complexity clearly depends on both the search strategy and the induction algorithm used. Considering the search strategy and bearing in mind that the number of features should be $r(r < n)$, exhaustive evaluation of features subsets involves $\binom{n}{r}$ combinations for a fixed number r, and 2^n combinations, if r must also be optimised. Therefore, an exhaustive search is unviable when leading with large data sets and different strategies have to be applied. Sequential algorithms add or remove features sequentially (quadratic complexity, n^2), but have a tendency to become trapped in local minima:

- **SF(F)S:** Sequential (Floating) Forward Search,
- **S(F)BS:** Sequential (Floating) Backward Search,
- **LRS:** Plus-L minus-R selection,
- **BDS:** Bidirectional search.

SFS starts with an empty set of features and adds features one by one, while SBS begins with a full set and removes features one by one. Features are added or removed on the basis of improvements in the evaluation function. SFS is less computationally demanding than SBS and performs best when the optimal subset is small, however its main disadvantage is that it is unable to remove features that become obsolete after the addition of other features. LRS is a generalisation of SFS and SBS; if (L> R), LRS starts from the empty set and repeatedly adds L features and removes R features, on the contrary, if L<R, LRS starts from the full set and repeatedly removes R features followed by L additions. Its main limitation is the lack of a theory to help predict the optimal values of L and R. BDS is a parallel implementation of SFS and SBS. Sequential floating selection (SFFS and SFBS) are an extension to LRS with flexible backtracking capabilities. Rather than fixing the

values of L and R, these floating methods allow those values to be determined from the data, and therefore the dimensionality of the subset during the search can be thought to be "floating" up and down.

Randomised algorithms incorporate randomness into their search procedure to escape local minima. It is worthwhile mentioning:

- Random generation plus sequential selection.
- Simulated annealing.
- Genetic algorithms.

The first is an attempt to introduce randomness into SFS and SBS in order to escape local minima. Simulated annealing is a stochastic optimisation method that derives its name from the annealing process used to re-crystallise metals (Kirpatrick, Gelatt, & Vecchi, 1983). Genetic algorithms (Holland, 1975) are an optimisation technique inspired by evolution, starting with an initial random population of solutions, evolving new populations by mating (crossover) pairs of solutions and mutating solutions according to their fitness (objective function). Random strategies have generally low complexity, but it is difficult to estimate some parameters (for example, degree of mutation or crossover).

In order to construct more efficient wrappers, considerable effort has been made in selecting the appropriate search strategy. Aha and Bankert (1995) used a wrapper approach in instance-based learning and proposed a new search strategy that performs beam search using a kind of backward elimination; that is, instead of starting with an empty feature subset, the search randomly selects a fixed number of feature subsets and starts with the best among them. Caruana and Freitag (1994) developed a wrapper feature subset selection method for decision tree induction, proposing bidirectional hill-climbing for the feature space (as this is more effective than either forward or backward selection). Genetic algorithms have been broadly adopted to perform the search for the best subset of features in a wrapper way (Liu & Motoda, 1998; Huang, Cai, & Xu, 2007).

The complexity of learning algorithms falls beyond the scope of this chapter because there are many algorithms in literature and it would be hard to highlight only two or three on which to focus one's attention. Besides, some algorithms have different variations that drastically change their computational demands, for example, SVM with a linear kernel could be affordable as part of a wrapper but it becomes too costly when using a non-linear one. It is also important to remember that, in many cases, FS is applied to existing problems, some of them with previous performance results. Therefore, if a wrapper model is previously applied to reduce the dimensionality of such a problem, it would be fair to employ the learning algorithm used in previous studies in order to obtain comparable results.

Therefore, as can be seen, there is a broad range of methods in the literature and so to make a correct choice, a user not only needs to know the domain well, but also is expected to understand technical details of available algorithms. Moreover, trying to overcome different problems such as scalability or robustness, new feature selection methods constantly appear using different strategies:

1. Combining several feature selection methods, which could be done by using algorithms from the same approach, such as the work presented by Zhang, Ding, and Li (2008) that combines ReliefF and mRMR, or coordinating algorithms from two different approaches, usually filter and wrapper methods with the aim to improve the classification performance of the features selected (Peng, Wu, & Jiang, 2010; El Akadi, Amine, El Ouardighi, & Aboutajdine, 2010)
2. Combining feature selection approaches with other techniques, such as feature extraction (Vainer, Kraus, Kamimka, & Slovin, 2010);
3. Reinterpreting existing algorithms (Sun, Todorovic, & Goodison, 2008)
4. Creating new methods to deal with still unresolved situations (Chidlovskii & Lecerf, 2008)
5. Using an ensemble of feature selection techniques to ensure better behaviour (Saeys, Abeel, & Peer, 2008).

Enhancement of Learning Methods by Using Feature Selection

A standard argument in favour of feature selection is that it is needed to "overcome the curse of dimensionality." In cases whereby the data matrix is skinny (many more features than training examples), feature selection may seem to be a requirement to avoid the unfavourable case whereby the number of free parameters of the model greatly exceeds the number of training examples, a case known to yield poor "generalisation." However, it is important to bear in mind, as explained in Guyon (2008), that today's state-of-the-art machine learning algorithms (which have harnessed the problem of over fitting using powerful "regularisation" techniques) do not require feature selection as a pre-processing step to perform well. These include regularised kernel methods (such as Support Vector Machines (SVM), kernel ridge or logistic regression and Gaussian processes) and ensemble methods (such as boosting and bagging). So, improving performance prediction may, after all, not be the main charter of feature selection. Rather, we may seek, for various other reasons, to limit the number of features used, without significantly degrading performance. These reasons can be:

•   Data understanding, gaining knowledge about the process and perhaps helping to visualize it.
•   Limiting storage requirements and perhaps helping in reducing future costs.
•   Simplicity, possibility of using simpler models and gaining speed.

Therefore, a user may be interested in applying feature selection for other reasons rather than reducing the dimensionality. This is the case in several applications, such as, for example, intrusion detection, classification of sleep apnea or microarray classification (Porto-Díaz, Bolón-Canedo, Alonso-Betanzos, & Fontenla-Romero, 2011; Álvarez-Estévez, Sánchez-Maroño, Alonso-Betanzos, & Moret-Bonillo, 2011; Bolón-Canedo, Sánchez-Maroño, & Alonso-Betanzos, 2010B; Peng, Wu, & Jiang, 2010; El Akadi, Amine, El Ouardighi, & Aboutajdine, 2010), in which not only we do need to obtain good performance of the methods, but also it is important to select which attributes are specifically related to an attack type, a sleep apnea or a cancer type, respectively.

Very large datasets (around 1,000,000 data) hinder the learning task of machine learning algorithms. A database is considered as having a high dimensionality when: (a) the number of samples is very high; (b) the number of features is very high; and (c) the number of samples and features is very high. Therefore, feature selection plays a crucial role in all the three situations described above since reducing the number of features reduces the size of the matrix to compute. In the next subsections, the enhancement of learning performance will be presented in three different situations. Moreover, new approaches such as incremental feature selection and distributed feature selection are included at the end of this section.

High Number of Samples

It may sound strange to apply feature selection techniques when the database has a high number of samples, but not features. However, feature selection has proven to be effective in this domain, since it aims to reduce the processing time as well as improve the performance of the machine learning algorithm. One of the benchmarks in this scenario is the intrusion detection database called KDD (Knowledge Discovery and Data Mining Tools Conference) Cup 99, used for the KDD Cup 99 Competition. This is a hard dataset for the sake of classification due to its large size (494021 samples). Among its 41 input features, some are irrelevant, correlated, or even constant, and this suggests the use of feature selection techniques. The work described in Bolón-Canedo, Sánchez-Maroño, and Alonso-Betanzos (2010A) showed that the dataset had very unbalanced continuous features and for which a possible solution could be to discretise numeric data. They proposed a method based on the combination of discretisation, filtering and classification algorithms that improved the performance results of the classifiers but using a reduced set of features. Results showed that the combination of the PKID (Proportional k-Interval Discretisation) discretizer, the Consistency-based filter and the C4.5 classifier, improves the classification accuracy achieved by the winner of the competition from 93.30% to 94.86%, using a mere 15% of the features. In Amiri, Rezaei Yousefi, Lucas, Shakery, and Yazdani (2011), it was also demonstrated that feature selection algorithms could greatly improve the classification accuracy over this dataset. Specifically, they proposed modified mutual information feature selection algorithms (MMIFS), which turned out to be the most effective among the methods tested in detecting some of the attack types present in the KDD Cup 99 database.

High Number of Features

One of the trending topics for feature selection researchers is DNA microarray data classification. In this domain, features represent gene expression coefficients corresponding to the abundance of mRNA (messenger Ribonucleic Acid) in a sample, for a given number of patients. The number of samples is usually small (less than 100 patients) but the number of features ranges from 6,000 to 60,000. Having a much higher number of features than samples causes difficulties for most machine learning methods, since they cannot generalise adequately, causing poor performance. To deal with this problem, feature selection plays a crucial role, especially because most genes measured in a DNA microarray experiment are irrelevant or redundant with each other, which degrades the performance of the machine learning algorithms. The work described in Bolón-Canedo, Sánchez-Maroño, and Alonso-Betanzos (2010B) applied the proposed method of combining discretisation, filtering, and classification, which had been tested with intrusion detection data over 10 different microarray datasets, showing that the performance of the classifiers was improved with a drastic reduction in the number of genes required (using in the order of dozens of genes instead of thousands). Fan & Fan (2008) evaluated over three microarray datasets their proposed method called FAIR (Feature Annealed Independent Rules). This method consists of selecting the statistically most significant features according to the component-wise two-sample t-statistics between two classes, and applying independence classifiers to those selected features. They demonstrated that for the independence classification rule, classification using all the features can be as poor as random guessing, so it is important to select a subset of important features.

The outburst of this kind of extreme high-dimensionality has brought about an explosion in the number of proposed feature selection algorithms, making the task of choosing which one is the best difficult. Most researchers try to find an appropriate method for a specific problem setting, as until now, an optimal method for any situation has not existed. The authors Hua, Tembe, and Dougherty (2009) presented a comparison of some basic feature selection methods in scenarios involving thousands of features, studying different kinds of relations among the features, as well as different proportions of useful and irrelevant features in the data. Although the results showed that none of the methods performed best across all scenarios, some general trends related to size and relations among features have been extracted. One of the approaches which tries to overcome the problem of not having a so-called

"best method" is the use of an ensemble of feature selection techniques to ensure better behaviour. The ensemble idea for feature selection consists of creating a set of different feature selectors, each providing their output and afterwards aggregating the results of the single models, usually by weighted voting. Saeys, Abeel and Peer (2008) chose two filters and two embedded methods for creating an ensemble version of each technique, tested over six microarray datasets. By comparing the results of ensemble feature selection to a classifier using the full feature set, it was shown that in most cases performance was increased, with the great advantage of using only 1% of the features. Bolón-Canedo, Sánchez-Maroño, and Alonso-Betanzos (2011) introduced a different concept of ensemble, where five different filters were chosen. Each filter selects a subset of features and this subset is used for training a classifier. There will be as many classification outputs as filters and subsequently the final prediction is derived by simple voting. This ensemble was tested over 10 microarray datasets. The proposed ensemble improved the results achieved by the classifier with the whole set of features and, on average, has demonstrated it performs better than the single filters.

Feature selection has also proven effective when it comes to clustering. In Chen, Ye, Xu, and Huang (2012), a new method to weight subspace in feature groups and individual features for clustering high-dimensional data was proposed. Experiments on feature selection were conducted over the Multiple Features dataset, which contains 649 features divided into six feature groups. The proposed algorithm determined that the fourth group was a noise feature group and further experiments confirmed this fact, since all the clustering algorithms improved their results.

As mentioned above, when dealing with problems of high dimensionality data, but with small sample size, the data mining methods can become unreliable. To try to overcome this issue, the sample size needs to be increased, which is either impossible or extremely expensive in several real applications. Another possibility which has been very recently explored is the use of additional information sources. That is the case, for example, of the microarray data, in which various knowledge sources, such as Gene Ontology, or NCI Gene-Cancer databases are available. The problem that needs to be solved is that most feature selection methods are designed for working only with a single data source and so new algorithms need to be developed. These algorithms, called multi-source feature selection methods, should be able to integrate different types of knowledge from different sources in the process of selecting features. One major challenge therefore will consist of addressing the heterogeneity in different types of knowledge sources, also taking into account that relations between those can be very different in different domains. In Spectral feature selection for data mining (Zhao & Liu, 2012), the authors describe such a multisource FS (Feature Selection) method in the field of genetic analysis based on microarray data. First, the different types of knowledge available are categorised, so as to identify the common characteristics of the knowledge that belong to the same category. Therefore knowledge is separated into two types: knowledge about features and knowledge about samples. The knowledge can have heterogeneous representation and nature, and some types of knowledge might fall into more than one of the categories. Then, two different algorithms are presented by the authors, one based on the use of similarity about samples as the common representation, while the other obtains multiple lists that rank features differently using the different types of knowledge. A probabilistic model for rank aggregation is then/ subsequently used.

High Number of Samples and Features

Feature selection becomes indispensable when dealing with a high number of samples and features, since with such this amount of data,

in many cases learning algorithms are not able to process the whole training set due to time or memory restrictions. The work described in Bolón-Canedo, Peteiro-Barral, Alonso-Betanzos, Guijarro-Berdiñas, and Sánchez-Maroño (2011) applied the CFS filter (Consistency-based Feature Selection) over four high dimensionality problems to check the influence of feature selection on the scalability of several training algorithms for ANNs (Artificial Neural Networks). Results showed that applying feature selection not only improved previous results with the whole set of features, but also allowed certain algorithms to be able to train on some datasets in cases where it was previously impossible due to the special / particular complexity. Guo, Damper, Gunn & Nelson (2008) proposed a framework of feature selection using mutual information for image classification. A greedy optimisation strategy was introduced to reduce the search space for the maximisation of mutual information and results on the AVIRIS high-dimensional dataset showed that the proposed method outperformed or was competitive with state-of-the-art methods.

Distributed Feature Selection

Moreover, most existing feature selection techniques are designed for traditional centralised computing environments and cannot readily utilise advanced distributed computing frameworks, such as MPI (Gropp, Luskand, & Skjellum, 1999), Microsoft´s Dryad (Isard, Budiu, Yu, Birrell, & Fetterly, 2007) or Google´s MapReduce (Dean & Ghemawat, 2010), to enhance their efficiency and scalability. There are few attempts in literature of using these, such as the one in Singh, Kubica, Larsen, and Sorokina (2009) and Kubica, Singh, and Sorokina (2012), in which the authors developed a wrapper method that employs forward feature selection and logistic regression, where in every step, new features are added to an existing model. In order to make it feasible, the evaluation of a single feature is sped up by a heuristic

SFO (Single Feature Optimization) that provides approximate models on the effect of adding new features to the model. The method starts up with an empty set of features, and then it selects features that improve performance iteratively until that improvement stops. At that moment, the features that have not been included are discarded. For evaluating new features, the authors consider three techniques: Full forward feature selection, Single feature optimisation (Singh, Kubica, Larsen, & Sorokina, 2009) and Grafting (Perkins, Lacker, & Theiler, 2003). All three methods provide fast greedy approaches to the problem of FS, but scale poorly with the number of features, becoming computationally expensive as the size of the data grows. For this reason, they are parallelised using the MapReduce framework, distributing the cost over many machines, and being able to scale to much larger feature sets. In the experiments carried out over several UCI datasets, the algorithm achieves a speedup of over 15 on a 20-node cluster.

Another approach to scaling up wrappers is the one described in Garcia, Hall, Goldgof, and Kramer (2006). In this paper, a feature selection algorithm based on support vector machine training time, (that can be run on all available processors in parallel), is proposed. Their feature selection method can be divided into two stages. The first stage consists of randomly generating a number of feature sets of fixed size, then a 10 fold cross validation using only the features found in these sets is carried out in order to determine their suitability to classify the data. The sets of features are then sorted by a given criteria, for example the training time or the number of support vectors generated, and the best of these randomly generated sets are selected for the second stage of the algorithm. In the latter, a new set made up of the union of the features found in the selected sets is created. At this point, the classifier is trained using the newly created feature sets, and then it is tested against a previously unseen test set to see how well it performs. The random feature sets created are completely independent from one another and all of them are evaluated during the same step in the algorithm. For this reason, every single random set created can be evaluated in parallel and thus the time it takes for this feature selection method to finish its task is greatly reduced. This feature selection approach is advantageous if new features need to be selected during data acquisition.

In another work (López, Torres, Batista, Pérez, & Moreno-Vega, 2006), an evolutionary algorithm parallelising the evaluation, combination and improvement of the solution population is presented. The work to be done is distributed for different subsets of the population. One disadvantage of these approaches is that although the work is distributed over several machines, the full model still needs to be relearned for each feature, with the subsequent costs. However, with heuristics such as the SFO described above, the computation is effectively partitioned first over the samples and then over the candidate features. This allows scaling both large number of samples and features. Backward elimination techniques could also be used for the wrapper approach, starting with a full feature set and removing iteratively the least important features. However, these techniques are also affected by high computational costs when models are fully relearned.

As described in previous sections, filter approaches select features independently of the underlying models, and thus some of these could also be implemented using the MapReduce framework. For example, Fleuret (2004) describes a filter method using conditional mutual information that selects the feature, maximising the minimum mutual information with the response variable conditioned on each of the features that are already selected by the model. Obviously, this method could also be implemented using the SFO philosophy. Other authors (Souza, Matwin, & Japkowicz, 2006) have attempted parallelisation, based on the master-slave design pattern, over a hybrid feature selection algorithm. Embedded approaches, such as LASSO, rely on the learning algorithm itself for feature selection, and so both the parallelisation and scalability are determined by the algorithm employed. Figure 2 shows two general approaches of distributed feature selection, where each node may assume or not the learning task, as shown. Along this section several alternatives exist, combining these two general ideas.

Finally, another interesting recent work regarding this matter is the Spectral Feature Selection Framework (Zhao & Liu, 2012). This is a new feature selection technique that evaluates the relevance of the features by measuring their capability of preserving sample similarity, that is,

Figure 2. Two different approaches of distributed feature selection. Each node in subfigure a) executes feature selection and learning task. On the other hand, in subfigure b), each node applies only the feature selection process, and later a general set of features is selected and subsequently the learning process is run. Tasks of Integration in subfigure a) and Integration and Learning in subfigure b) may be accomplished at any node or a specific one.

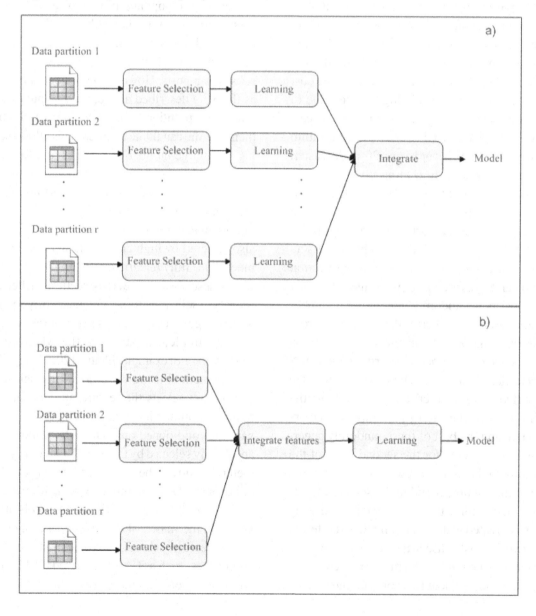

identifying features that associate similar values with the samples that are of the same affiliation. Besides this, the method can also handle redundant features. Among other advantages of the framework, one of the most interesting is that it permits the study as a whole of supervised, semi-supervised and unsupervised feature selection. The framework can manage large-scale data by applying the distributed parallel computing techniques mentioned above, specifically MPI and MapReduce frameworks.

Recently, a novel feature selection method denoted "dependency-aware feature ranking" has been introduced in Somol, Grim, and Pudil (2011). They attempt to generalise the idea of individually best ranking by evaluating the quality of each feature repeatedly in the context of randomly chosen feature subsets. This simple idea has been shown to be very suitable for high and very-high dimensional feature selection problems where it can considerably over-perform the commonly used individual feature ranking approaches due to its favourable mix of properties: the ability to reveal contextual information, reasonable speed, and generalisation ability. This method, has been tested using different datasets (the largest with more than 90M data), some of them (madelon and gisette) used in NISP 2003 feature selection challenge and now available through UCI Repository.

Incremental Feature Selection

As has been described along this chapter, feature selection is a research field that is increasingly important, relevant and difficult to manage as extremely high-dimensional datasets become the standard in real-world machine learning tasks. One way of dealing with these large scale datasets is working incrementally, and in this way, scalability can easily become a problem, even for simple approaches (Kubica, Singh, & Sorokina, 2012). In a distributed feature selection scenario, different subsets of features are obtained at each node of the parallelisation procedure or, similarly, if a learning

process has been executed, different models are derived. Consequently, these subsets or models have to be integrated in a unique subset or model. Usually this task is developed in a central node; however another alternative would be to follow an incremental procedure, where feature selection is made in a first node (with or without learning) and later on the rest of the nodes. Consequently, features are added /removed or the learned model fits the new data. Figure 3 illustrates this procedure. Authors of this chapter have not found many papers concerning incremental feature selection in the relevant literature. It is worth mentioning the work of Zhang, Ruan, and Tan (2011). Katakis, Tsoumakas, and Vlahavas (2006) described/ elaborated/spoke of the idea of a dynamic feature space. They state that the features that are selected (based on an initial collection of training documents) are subsequently considered by the learner during the operation of the system. However, these features may vary over time and, what is more, in some applications, an initial training set and consequently the feature space is unavailable. Therefore we need to use flexible algorithms and feature selection techniques which can execute in a dynamic feature space that would be empty in the beginning and add features when new information arrives (documents in their text categorisation application). Katakis, Tsoumakas, and Vlahavas (2006) applied incremental feature selection combined with what they called a feature based learning algorithm to deal with online learning in high-dimensional data streams. This framework is applied to a special case of concept drift inherent to textual data streams, which is the appearance of new predictive words over time. Perkins and Theiler (2003) present another approach where the set of features is not static and it is called Online Feature Selection (OFS). OFS assumes that, for several reasons, is not desirable to wait until all features have arrived before learning begins; therefore we have to derive a mapping function f from the inputs to the outputs that is as "good as possible" using a subset of just the features seen so far. These authors describe a promising alternative method, based on a stage-wise gradient descent technique which they call grafting that provides an approach to OFS which combines the speed of filters with the accuracy of wrappers. However, they do not test its effectiveness over high dimension datasets. In a recent work (Wu, Yu, Wang, & Ding, 2010), the authors present a promising alternative method, Online Streaming Feature Selection (OSFS), to select online highly relevant and non-redundant features. The authors also propose a faster Fast-OSFS algorithm to further improve selection efficiency. Their experimental results show that those algorithms achieve more compactness and better accuracy than existing streaming feature selection algorithms (such as Grafting) on various datasets. However, the largest dataset tested is made up of 14,374 samples and 216 features, therefore, it is not considered an extremely large dataset.

APPLICATIONS

Feature selection is currently being applied to problems of very different areas. In this section, some emblematic and representative fields of

application have been chosen. For each of them, a detailed description is provided and several up-to-date contributions are referenced.

Microarray Analysis

DNA microarrays are used to measure the expression levels of tens of thousands of genes at a time, as can be seen in Figure 4. Since the dimensionality of the problem is very high (each gene is a feature), manual observation is not feasible. Moreover, the sample sizes are usually small, which poses a great challenge for the machine learning methods that have been systematically applied over the last years. However, because of the features of these data sets, feature selection methods have proven valuable.

Microarray data sets began to be implemented by the end of the nineties. Soon feature selection was considered a de facto standard in this field. Further work was carried out at the beginning of the 2000s / 21st century, following two main paradigms: univariate and multivariate feature selection (Saeys, Inza, & Larrañaga, 2007).

- The univariate paradigm comprises efficient and scalable filter techniques and

Figure 3. General schema of incremental feature selection

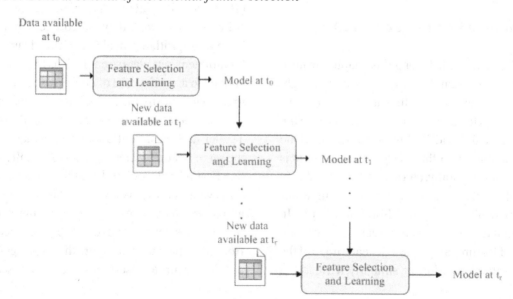

Figure 4. General process of acquiring gene expression data from DNA microarray

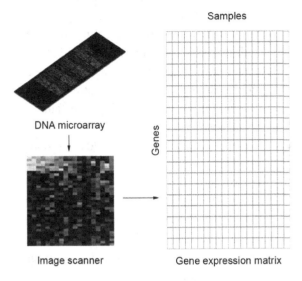

has dominated the field during the 2000s (Dudoit, Fridlyand, & Speed, 2002; Li, Zhang, & Ogihara, 2004; Lee, Lee, Park, & Song, 2005; Statnikov, Aliferis, Tsamardinos, Hardin, & Levy, 2005). The main reasons for its success are the simplicity of the approach, the lower computation time required and the ease of understanding the outputs.

- The multivariate paradigm methods are less scalable than univariate techniques, although they also model feature dependencies.
  - Multivariate filter methods (Ding & Peng, 2003; Yeung & Bumgarner, 2003; Wang, 2005; Gevaert, 2006).
  - Wrapper and embedded methods (Blanco, 2004; Jirapech-Umpai & Aitken, 2005; Inza, 2004; Ruiz, 2006).

Subsequently, researchers have proposed techniques that add complexity to the earlier attempts.

- Van den Ham, Moerland, Reinders, and Vergaegh (2009) analyse the sensitivity of microarray feature selection and classification when exposed to noise.

- The use of boosting techniques is covered by Guile and Wenjia (2008), who propose a method for feature ranking called LogitBoostNR.
- Zhang and Ren (2010) propose two algorithms based on energy and maximum eigenvalue.
- Meyer, Schretter and Bontempi (2008) introduce a new information-theoretic measure, the Double Input Symmetrical Relevance (DISR), which is based on a measure of variable complementarity.

Machinery Fault Diagnosis

Nowadays, the operation of complex industrial machinery requires advanced fault detection and diagnosis methods to improve reliability, safety and economy. Due to this, many new methods of machinery fault detection and diagnosis have been proposed in recent years. These methods extract features from measured signals and use process and signal models to determine possible faults. This last task can be performed by many different pattern classification techniques. However, as previously stated, these techniques suffer from the curse of dimensionality (Zhang, Li, Scarf, & Ball, 2011) when applied to high-dimensional data. Considering the fact that experimentation is sometimes performed on test rigs, (which are smaller than the machines used in production), scalability is a desirable feature in this problem. Therefore, it is interesting for fault diagnosis systems to include a selection of the informative variables for the classification task to increase the efficiency and reduce their computational cost. Data sets of machinery fault diagnosis are usually characterised as having a large number of features and samples, and, moreover, they have an unbalanced distribution of samples, because most of them represent the case of not having faults.

To that end, filter methods and distance evaluation techniques have been a common choice, due to their simplicity and their low computational cost.

- Verron, Tiplica, and Kobi (2008) present a procedure to diagnose the faults of a system in steady state conditions based on discriminant analysis. The procedure includes, like the previous step, a feature selection algorithm based on the mutual information between variables.
- He, Liu, Li, and Tao (2010) propose an intelligent gear fault detection method based on the relevance vector machine. As part of the process, feature selection based on Fisher criterion is made to select the optimal set of input features.
- Younus and Yang (2012) employ a feature selection tool based on Mahalanobis distance and the Relief algorithm to select the salient features obtained from infrared thermography in order to enhance the classification accuracy between different machine conditions.
- Lei, He, and Zi (2009) introduce a new method for intelligent fault diagnosis of rotating machinery. Wavelet packet transform and empirical mode decomposition techniques are used to extract fault characteristic information from vibration signals. Subsequently, the distance evaluation technique is utilised to calculate evaluation factors of the feature set, and accordingly, select the most sensitive features.

More complex techniques, such as wrappers, embedded or hybrid methods have also been used in this field:

- Hajnayeb, Ghasemloonia, Khadem, and Moradi (2011) optimise a system to diagnose gearbox faults by eliminating unimportant features using the utility additive (UTA) method.
- Casimir, Boutleux, Clerc, and Yahoui (2006) propose a sequential backward search (SBS) algorithm along with a k-nearest neighbour classifier to select the optimal set of features for fault diagnosis of induction motors.
- Sugumaran, Muralidharan, and Ramachandran (2007) and Sugumaran and Ramachandran (2011) present the use of decision trees for selecting an optimal subset of features, in order to diagnose faults in roller bearings.
- Zhang, Li, Scarf, and Ball (2011) propose a hybrid model which combines multiple feature selection models to discover the most relevant features for effective fault diagnosis. Among the models, eight filters are used to pre-rank the candidate features and two wrappers are utilised to minimise the number of features.
- Li, Zhang, Tian, Mi, Liu, and Ren (2011) propose a novel feature extraction and selection scheme for hybrid fault diagnosis of the gearbox. A two stage feature selection process combining filter and wrapper techniques based on mutual information and non-dominated sorting genetic algorithms II (NSGA-II) was presented to obtain a more compact feature subset for accurate classification among the classes of gearbox vibration data.

Face Recognition

Recognition of a human face is a complex visual pattern recognition problem. In the last two decades, face recognition has become one of the most active research fields due to its numerous commercial and legal applications including video surveillance, biometric identification, and face indexing in multimedia contents. Another reason is that technical issues related with face recognition are representative of object recognition in general. An important issue in object recognition is the question of which features of an object are the most informative for recognition purpose.

High information redundancy present in object images results in inefficiencies when these images are used directly for recognition, identification, and classification. Therefore a common objective in face recognition is to find an optimal way of representing image information whilst removing the redundancies contained in pixel images of faces. Another important issue in face recognition is that it contains a large number of features with a reduced number of samples.

In order to address these problems, a number of feature selection algorithms for face recognition have been recently suggested. In particular, methods based on evolutionary computation techniques have proven successful. Among them, the following methods are noteworthy:

- A novel PSO-based (particle swarm optimisation) feature selection algorithm is proposed by Ramadan and Abdel-Kader (2009). This algorithm is applied to coefficients extracted by two feature extraction techniques to find the optimal feature subset. The performance of this algorithm is compared to the performance of a GA-based feature selection algorithm and was found to yield comparable recognition results with a lower number of selected features.

- Amine, Elakadi, Rziza, and Aboutajdine (2009) present an efficient framework for face recognition based on GA-SVM for frequency feature selection. This method outperforms several other methods based on mutual information criteria.

- Mazumdar, Mitra, and Mitra (2010) apply the evolutionary-rough feature selection algorithm to the face recognition problem. Rough set theory is used to generate reducts, which represent the minimal sets of features capable of discerning between all objects, in a multiobjective framework.

- Kanan and Faez (2008) introduce a new improved feature selection algorithm based on ant colony optimisation (ACO). This

method is evaluated in a face recognition system and the results indicate that the proposed ACO-based feature selection method performs consistently superior to the GA-based and other ACO-based feature selection methods with less feature components.

Filter methods have also been extensively used in face recognition systems, as for example:

- Yang, Zhang, Yong, and Yang (2005) use a method based on the physical meaning of the generalised Fisher Criterion, to choose the most discriminative features for recognition. The experiments show that this method achieves its maximal recognition rate of 96.4% using only 25 features, and it needs less CPU time compared to other methods.

- Lu, Cohen, Zhou, and Tian (2007) propose a novel method, named Principal Feature Analysis (PFA), for dimensionality reduction by choosing a subset of the original features that contains most of the essential information, using the same idea as Principal Component Analysis (PCA) based methods.

- Matos, Batista, and Poel (2008) present a face recognition method based on Discrete Cosine Transform (DCT) coefficient's selection. Three different coefficient selection criterions were analysed: the first one is the average of the coefficients' amplitudes; the second one is based on counting the occurrence of each coefficient, (which are stored in a set of lists containing the most significant coefficients) and finally, the third criterion is based on the average position of the coefficients in a list of coefficients ordered by amplitude. The proposed method achieves high recognition accuracy (99.0% with a mere 50 coefficients).

- A new colour face recognition method which uses sequential floating forward search (SFFS) in order to obtain a set of optimal colour components for the recognition purpose is introduced in (Lee, Choi, Plataniotis, & Ro, 2010).

Text Classification

The problem of text classification consists of using a learning method to assign documents to a series of predefined categories or labels. This problem is of interest in Internet applications such as spam email, shopping and auction websites, etc. and has therefore received considerable attention. The problem is formalised from considering unique words that occur in documents as the feature space. This means that the number of potential features often exceeds the number of training documents by more than an order of magnitude. By selecting a fraction of the vocabulary, the learning algorithm requires less computation, storage and/or bandwidth. These features allow scalability in problems involving large numbers of classifiers or cases. Moreover, the number of categories or labels in real problems is often in the order of tens of thousands, which requires that the methods used scale accordingly.

In order to reduce the number of features, a processing stage prior to the feature selection stage is usually performed. Rare words are eliminated (for instance, words occurring once or twice.). Word forms such as plurals and verb conjugations are merged into the same term. And, lastly, common words such as 'in' or 'the' are also removed, as they do not help the classification process. After this stage, the proper feature selection phase comes. Several ways exist of representing the feature values. The simplest one is using a Boolean value to indicate if the word shows up in the document or not. More complex ways include the count of the number of occurrences of the word in the document or the frequency of occurrence.

Examples of up-to-date contributions are:

- Forman (2003) proposes a new feature selection metric, called, Bi-Normal Separation (BNS), which proves a useful heuristic for increased scalability when used with wrapper techniques. He also carries out a comparison between twelve feature selection methods over a data set of 229 texts and analyses the results using different performance metrics, suitable for different situations.
- Hyunsoo, Howland, and Park (2005) adopt several novel feature selection methods for clustered data. They obtain the same accuracy as in the original space with a dramatic dimension reduction.
- Dasgupta, Drineas, and Harb (2007) propose an unsupervised feature selection strategy which theoretically guarantees the generalisation power of the resultant classification function with respect to the classification function obtained when maintaining all the features.
- Forman (2008) reviews a series of filters applied to binary, multiclass, and hierarchical text classification problems, placing special focus on scalability.
- Chen, Huang, Tian, and Qu (2009) analyse the influence of feature selection over the Naive Bayes classifier, which is highly sensitive to feature selection. They perform feature selection using two new feature evaluation metrics and conclude that their own metrics work better than others.

Automatic Image Annotation

The process of automatic image annotation consists of automatically assigning metadata (i.e. keywords) to a digital image. A typical application of this subject is the organisation and location of images from a database. The problem can be formalised as a problem of multiclass classification with a very large number of classes (the number of keywords that can be used in the annotations) and where an image object can belong to multiple classes simultaneously. Since the number of classes is so large, scalability is a very desirable feature. Moreover, the number of features is usually small (images are segmented and each feature represents a property of the segment: colour, shape, texture and so on).

Examples of up-to-date contributions are:

- Jianjiang, Tianzhong, and Zhang (2008) present a wrapper based on a genetic algorithm to choose between MPEG-7 feature descriptors.
- Little and Ruger (2009) propose a method that evaluates subsets of features using a non-parametric density estimation algorithm.
- Wang and Khan (2006) and Setia and Burkhardt (2006) propose weighted feature selection algorithms to help the clustering algorithms deal with the large number of dimensions of data and scale well to a large number of keywords.
- Gao, Fan, Xue, and Jain (2006) and Jin and Yang (2011) propose a solution, based on hierarchical feature selection algorithms, to two different problems: automatic feature extraction and image classifier training and feature subset selection. The former is addressed by means of a multi-resolution grid-based framework. The latter, by means of a boosting algorithm to scale up SVMs in high-dimensional feature spaces.

In summary, it is clear that most machine learning methods obtain better results in reduced space than in the space of all the variables. So, as expected, in order to improve the accuracy and reduce the computational cost of any pattern recognition method, a feature selection task is necessary.

CONCLUSION AND FUTURE RESEARCH DIRECTIONS

With the advent of datasets of an extremely high dimensionality, machine learning researchers must focus their efforts not only on accuracy but also on the scalability of the algorithms. In scenarios with a large number of inputs, feature selection plays a crucial role by reducing the dimensionality of the problem and turning an impractical learning algorithm into a practical one. Therefore, the scalability of a feature selection algorithm now becomes extremely important. Some existing algorithms were designed for handling data with a small size. Their efficiency may be significantly downgraded, if not totally inapplicable, when the data size grows (Zhao & Liu, 2012). This chapter has reviewed the most up-to-date feature selection methods, focusing on their scalability properties, paving the way to their application on datasets containing a huge number of samples and features. Several feature selection methods were presented, showing their adequacy on different scenarios by achieving an enhancement in the performance of the learning algorithms applied afterwards.

Although there are a great number of feature selection methods available in the related literature, there is no optimal method applicable to all situations. Therefore, new feature selection methods constantly emerge. Recent areas of research of feature selection (which attract the attention of researchers in machine learning) are distributed, incremental and online feature selection. The former because distribution is a usual technique to deal with extremely large datasets, but also because many current data sets are distributed in origin. To this end feature selection methods must deal with how to indicate the relevance of several features that have been obtained at different partitions of data which can be very unbalanced or biased. On the other hand, incremental feature selection does not consider the whole set of data from the beginning. It starts with an initial subset of data and new information is later added. This new data may modify the set of features selected. Similarly, in online (streaming) feature selection, features are added one by one. Therefore, it evaluates each new feature by training a new model containing that feature and so requires learning a linear number of models each time a new feature is added. The computational cost can quickly grow when adding many new features iteratively. Even those techniques that use relatively computationally inexpensive tests of a feature's value, such as mutual information, require at least linear time in the number of features being evaluated. As an example, classifying websites and learning user's profiles of websites can imply datasets on the size of Gigabytes per day, and even using only very basic features, we can end up with thousands of potential features that can be used for the model.

REFERENCES

Aha, D., & Bankert, R. L. (1995). A comparative evaluation of sequential feature selection algorithms. In Proceedings of the Fifth International Workshop on Artificial Intelligence and Statistics (pp. 1-7). Springer-Verlag.

Álvarez-Estévez, D., Sánchez-Maroño, D., Alonso-Betanzos, A., & Moret-Bonillo, V. (2011). Reducing dimensionality in a database of sleep EEG arousals. *Expert Systems with Applications*, *38*(6), 7746–7754. doi:10.1016/j.eswa.2010.12.134.

Amine, A., Elakadi, A., Rziza, M., & Aboutajdine, D. (2009). GA-SVM and mutual information based frequency feature selection for face recognition. Journal of Computer Science.

Amiri, F., Rezaei Yousefi, M., Lucas, C., Shakery, A., & Yazdani, N. (2011). Mutual information-based feature selection for intrusion detection systems. *Journal of Network and Computer Applications*, 1184–1199. doi:10.1016/j.jnca.2011.01.002.

Bellman, R. (1957). *Dynamic programming*. Princeton, NJ: Princeton University Press.

Blanco, R. (2004). Gene selection for cancer classification using wrapper approaches. *International Journal of Pattern Recognition and Artificial Intelligence*, *18*, 1373–1390. doi:10.1142/S0218001404003800.

Bolón-Canedo, V., Peteiro-Barral, D., Alonso-Betanzos, A., Guijarro-Berdiñas, B., & Sánchez-Maroño, N. (2011). Scalability analysis of ANN training algorithms with feature selection. Lecture Notes in Artificial Intelligence, 84-93.

Bolón-Canedo, V., Sánchez-Maroño, N., & Alonso-Betanzos, A. (2010a). Feature selection and classification in multiple class datasets. An application to KDD cup 99 dataset. *Expert Systems with Applications*, 5947–5957.

Bolón-Canedo, V., Sánchez-Maroño, N., & Alonso-Betanzos, A. (2010b). On the effectiveness of discretization on gene selection of microarray data. International Joint Conference on Neural Networks, (pp. 3167-3174). ACM/IEEE.

Bolón-Canedo, V., Sánchez-Maroño, N., & Alonso-Betanzos, A. (2011). An ensemble of filters and classifiers for microarray data classification. *Pattern Recognition*, *45*, 531–539. doi:10.1016/j.patcog.2011.06.006.

Breiman, L. (2001). Random forests. *Machine Learning*, *45*(1), 5–32. doi:10.1023/A:1010933404324.

Caruana, R., & Freitag, D. (1994). Greedy attribute selection. In Proceedings of the Eleventh International Conference on Machine Learning (pp. 28-36). Burlington, MA: Morgan Kaufmann Publishers.

Casimir, R., Boutleux, E., Clerc, G., & Yahoui, A. (2006). The use of features selection and nearest neighbors rule for faults diagnostic in induction motors. *Engineering Applications of Artificial Intelligence*, 169–177. doi:10.1016/j.engappai.2005.07.004.

Chen, J., Huang, H., Tian, S., & Qu, Y. (2009). Feature selection for text classification with Naïve Bayes. *Expert Systems with Applications*, 5432–5435. doi:10.1016/j.eswa.2008.06.054.

Chen, X., Ye, Y., Xu, X., & Huang, J. (2012). A feature group weighting method for subspace clustering of high-dimensional data. *Pattern Recognition, 45*, 434–446. doi:10.1016/j.patcog.2011.06.004.

Chidlovskii, B., & Lecerf, L. (2008). *Scalable feature selection for multi-class problems. Machine Learning and Knowledge Discovery in Databases, (5211)* (pp. 227–240). New York, NY: Springer. doi:10.1007/978-3-540-87479-9_33.

Dasgupta, A., Drineas, P., & Harb, B. (2007). Feature selection methods for text classification. Proceedings of the 13th ACM SIGKDD International Conference on Knowledge Discovery and Data Mining, (pp. 230-239).

Dash, M., & Liu, H. (2003). Consistency-based search in feature selection. *Artificial Intelligence*, 155–176. doi:10.1016/S0004-3702(03)00079-1.

Dean, J., & Ghemawat, S. (2010). System and method for efficient large-scale data processing.

Ding, C., & Peng, H. (2003). Minimum redundancy feature selection from microarray gene expression data. Proceedings of the IEEE Conference on Computational Systems Bioinformatics, (pp. 523-528).

Duda, R., Hart, P., & Stork, D. (2001). *Pattern Classification* (2nd ed.). Hoboken, NJ: John Wiley & Sons.

Dudoit, S., Fridlyand, J., & Speed, T. (2002). Comparison of discrimination methods for the classification of tumors using gene expression data. *Journal of the American Statistical Association, 97*(457), 77–87. doi:10.1198/016214502753479248.

El Akadi, A., Amine, A., El Ouardighi, A., & Aboutajdine, D. (2010). A two-stage gene selection scheme utilizing mRMR filter and GA wrapper. *Knowledge and Information Systems, 26*(3), 487–500. doi:10.1007/s10115-010-0288-x.

Fan, J., & Fan, Y. (2008). High dimensional classification using features annealed independence rules. *Annals of Statistics, 36*(6), 2605–2637. doi:10.1214/07-AOS504 PMID:19169416.

Fleuret, F. (2004). Fast binary feature selection with conditional mutual information. *Journal of Machine Learning Research, 5*, 1531–1555.

Forman, G. (2003). An extensive empirical study of feature selection metrics for text classification. *Journal of Machine Learning Research, 3*, 1289–1305.

Forman, G. (2008). Feature selection for text classification. In Liu, H., & Motoda, H. (Eds.), *Computational methods of feature selection.* London, UK: Chapman & Hall.

Gao, Y., Fan, J., Xue, X., & Jain, R. (2006). Automatic image annotation by incorporating feature hierarchy and boosting to scale up SVM classifiers. Proceedings of the 14th annual ACM international conference on multimedia, (pp. 901-910).

Garcia, D., Hall, L., Goldgof, D., & Kramer, K. (2006). A parallel feature selection algorithm from random subsets. In Proceedings of the 17th European Conference on Machine Learning.

Gevaert, O. (2006). Predicting the prognosis of breast cancer by integrating clinical and microarray data with bayesian networks. *Bioinformatics (Oxford, England), 22*, 184–190. doi:10.1093/bioinformatics/btl230 PMID:16873470.

Gropp, W., Luskand, E., & Skjellum, A. (1999). *Using MPI: Portable Parallel Programming with the Message-Passing Interface.* Cambridge, MA: MIT Press.

Guile, G., & Wenjia, W. (2008). Boosting for feature selection for microarray data analysis. IEEE International Joint Conference on Neural Networks IJCNN 2008, (pp. 2559-2563).

Guo, B., Damper, R., Gunn, S., & Nelson, J. (2008). A fast separability-based feature-selection method for high-dimensional remotely sensed image classification. *Pattern Recognition, 41,* 1653–1662. doi:10.1016/j.patcog.2007.11.007.

Guyon, I. (2008). Practical feature selection: From correlation to causality. In Fogelman-Soulie, F., Perrotta, D., Piskorski, J., & Steinberger, R. (Eds.), *Mining Massive Data Sets for Security.*

Guyon, I., Gunn, S., Nikravesh, M., & Zadeh, L. (2006). *Feature extraction. Foundations and applications (Vol. 207).* Berlin, Germany: Springer-Verlag. doi:10.1007/978-3-540-35488-8.

Guyon, I., Weston, J., Barnhill, S., & Vapnik, V. (2002). Gene selection for cancer classification using support vector machines. *Journal of Machine Learning, 46*(1-3), 389–422. doi:10.1023/A:1012487302797.

Hajnayeb, A., Ghasemloonia, A., Khadem, S., & Moradi, M. (2011). Application and comparison of an ANN-based feature selection method and the genetic algorithm in gearbox fault diagnosis. *Expert Systems with Applications,* 10205–10209. doi:10.1016/j.eswa.2011.02.065.

Hall, M. (1999). Correlation-based feature selection for machine learning. (Doctoral Dissertation). The University of Waikato, New Zealand.

He, C., Liu, C., Li, Y., & Tao, J. (2010). Intelligent gear fault detection based on relevance vector machine with variance radial basis function kernel. IEEE/ASME International Conference on Advanced Intelligent Mechatronics (AIM), (pp. 785-789).

Holland, J. (1975). *Adaptation in natural and artificial systems.* Ann Arbor, MI: The University of Michigan Press.

Hua, J., Tembe, W., & Dougherty, E. (2009). Performance of feature-selection methods in the classification of high-dimension data. *Pattern Recognition, 42*(3), 409–424. doi:10.1016/j.patcog.2008.08.001.

Huang, J., Cai, Y., & Xu, X. (2007). A hybrid genetic algorithm for feature selection wrapper based on mutual information. *Pattern Recognition Letters, 28*(13), 1825–1844. doi:10.1016/j.patrec.2007.05.011.

Hyunsoo, K., Howland, P., & Park, H. (2005). Dimension reduction in text classification with support vector machines. *Journal of Machine Learning Research, 6,* 37–53.

Inza, I. (2004). Filter versus wrapper gene selection approaches in DNA microarray domains. *Artificial Intelligence in Medicine, 31,* 91–103. doi:10.1016/j.artmed.2004.01.007 PMID:15219288.

Isard, M., Budiu, M., Yu, Y., Birrell, A., & Fetterly, D. (2007). Dryad: Distributed data-parallel programs from sequential building blocks. *ACM SIGOPS Operating Systems Review, 41*(3), 59–72. doi:10.1145/1272998.1273005.

Jianjiang, L., Tianzhong, Z., & Zhang, Y. (2008). Feature selection based on genetic algorithm for image annotation. *Knowledge-Based Systems, 21,* 887–891. doi:10.1016/j.knosys.2008.03.051.

Jin, C., & Yang, C. (2011). Integrating hierarchical feature selection and classifier training for multi-label image annotation. Proceedings of the 34th International ACM SIGIR Conference on Research and Development in Information Retrieval.

Jirapech-Umpai, T., & Aitken, S. (2005). Feature selection and classification for microarray data analysis. Evolutionary methods for identifying predictive genes. *Bioinformatics (Oxford, England), 6*(148).

Kanan, H., & Faez, K. (2008). An improved feature selection method based on ant colony optimization (ACO) evaluated on face recognition system. *Applied Mathematics and Computation,* 716–725. doi:10.1016/j.amc.2008.05.115.

Katakis, I., Tsoumakas, G., & Vlahavas, I. (2006). Dynamic feature space and incremental feature selection for the classification of textual data streams. ECML PKDD Workshop on Knowledge Discovery from Data Streams, (pp. 107-116).

Kira, K., & Rendell, L. A. (1992). A practical approach to feature selection. Proceedings of the 9th International Conference on Machine Learning, (pp. 249-256). Burlington, MA: Morgan Kaufmann Publishers Inc.

Kirpatrick, S., Gelatt, C., & Vecchi, M. (1983). Optimization by simulation annealing. *Science, 220,* 671–680. doi:10.1126/science.220.4598.671 PMID:17813860.

Kohavi, R., & John, G. (1997). Wrappers for feature subset selection. *Artificial Intelligence, 97*(1-2), 273–324. doi:10.1016/S0004-3702(97)00043-X.

Kubica, J., Singh, S., & Sorokina, D. (2012). Parallel large-scale feature selection. In Bekkerman, R., Bilenko, M., & Langford, J. (Eds.), *Scaling Up Machine Learning: Parallel and Distributed Approaches.* Cambridge, MA: Cambridge University Press.

Lee, J., Lee, J., Park, M., & Song, S. (2005). An extensive comparison of recent classification tools applied to microarray data. *Computational Statistics & Data Analysis, 48*(4), 869–885. doi:10.1016/j.csda.2004.03.017.

Lee, S., Choi, J., Plataniotis, K., & Ro, Y. (2010). Color component feature selection in feature-level fusion based color face recognition. IEEE International Conference on Fuzzy Systems (FUZZ), (pp. 1-6).

Lei, Y., He, Z., & Zi, Y. (2009). Application of an intelligent classification method to mechanical fault diagnosis. *Expert Systems with Applications,* 9941–9948. doi:10.1016/j.eswa.2009.01.065.

Li, B., Zhang, P., Tian, H., Mi, S., Liu, D., & Ren, G. (2011). A new feature extraction and selection scheme for hybrid fault diagnosis of gearbox. *Expert Systems with Applications,* 10000–10009. doi:10.1016/j.eswa.2011.02.008.

Li, T., Zhang, C., & Ogihara, M. (2004). A comparative study of feature selection and multiclass classification methods for tissue classification based on gene expression. *Bioinformatics (Oxford, England), 20*(15), 2429–2437. doi:10.1093/bioinformatics/bth267 PMID:15087314.

Little, S., & Ruger, S. (2009). Conservation of effort in feature selection for image annotation. IEEE Workshop on Multimedia Signals Processing, (pp. 5-7).

Liu, H., & Motoda, H. (1998). *Feature extraction, construction and selection: A data mining perspective.* New York, NY: Springer. doi:10.1007/978-1-4615-5725-8.

López, F., Torres, M., Batista, B., Pérez, J., & Moreno-Vega, M. (2006). Solving feature subset selection problem by a parallel scatter search. *European Journal of Operational Research, 169*(2), 477–489. doi:10.1016/j.ejor.2004.08.010.

Lu, Y., Cohen, I., Zhou, X., & Tian, Q. (2007). Feature selection using principal feature analysis. Proceedings of the 15th international conference on Multimedia, (pp. 301-304). New York, NY: ACM.

Matos, F., Batista, L., & Poel, J. (2008). Face recognition using DCT coefficients selection. Proceedings of the 2008 ACM symposium on Applied computing, (pp. 1753-1757).

Mazumdar, D., Mitra, S., & Mitra, S. (2010). *Evolutionary-rough feature selection for face recognition. Transactions on rough sets XII* (pp. 117–142). New York, NY: Springer. doi:10.1007/978-3-642-14467-7_7.

Meyer, P., Schretter, C., & Bontempi, G. (2008). Information-theoretic feature selection in micro-array data using variable complementarity. *IEEE Journal of Selected Topics in Signal Processing*, 2(3), 261–274. doi:10.1109/JSTSP.2008.923858.

Peng, H., Long, F., & Ding, C. (2005). Feature selection based on mutual information: Criteria of max-dependency, max-relevance, and min-redundancy. *IEEE Transactions on Pattern Analysis and Machine Intelligence*, 27(8), 1226–1238. doi:10.1109/TPAMI.2005.159 PMID:16119262.

Peng, Y., Wu, Z., & Jiang, J. (2010). A novel feature selection approach for biomedical data classification. *Journal of Biomedical Informatics*, 43(1), 15–23. doi:10.1016/j.jbi.2009.07.008 PMID:19647098.

Perkins, S., Lacker, K., & Theiler, J. (2003). Grafting: Fast, incremental feature selection by gradient descent in function space. *Journal of Machine Learning Research*, 3, 1333–1356.

Perkins, S., & Theiler, J. (2003). Online feature selection using grafting. Proceedings of the Twentieth International Conference on Machine Learning (ICML) (pp. 592-599). Washington, DC: ACM Press.

Porto-Díaz, I., Bolón-Canedo, V., Alonso-Betanzos, A., & Fontenla-Romero, O. (2011). A study of performance on microarray datasets for a classifier based on information theoretic learning. *Neural Networks*, 24(8), 888–896. PMID:21703822.

Quinlan, J. R. (1986). Induction of decision trees. *Machine Learning*, 1(1), 81–106. doi:10.1007/BF00116251.

Ramadan, R., & Abdel-Kader, R. (2009). Face recognition using particle swarm optimization-based selected features. International Journal of Signal Processing, Image Processing and Pattern Recognition, 51-65.

Ruiz, R. (2006). Incremental wrapper-based gene selection from microarray data for cancer classification. *Pattern Recognition*, 39, 2383–2392. doi:10.1016/j.patcog.2005.11.001.

Saeys, Y., Abeel, T., & Peer, Y. (2008). Robust feature selection using ensemble feature selection techniques. European conference on Machine Learning and Knowledge Discovery in Databases-Part II, (pp. 313-325).

Saeys, Y., Inza, I., & Larrañaga, P. (2007). A review of feature selection techniques in bioinformatics. *Bioinformatics (Oxford, England)*, 23(19), 2507–2517. doi:10.1093/bioinformatics/btm344 PMID:17720704.

Setia, L., & Burkhardt, H. (2006). Feature selection for automatic image annotation. *Lecture Notes in Computer Science*, 4174, 294–303. doi:10.1007/11861898_30.

Singh, S., Kubica, J., Larsen, S., & Sorokina, D. (2009). *Parallel large scale feature selection for logistic regression* (pp. 1172–1183). SIAM.

Somol, P., Grim, J., & Pudil, P. (2011). Fast dependency-aware feature selection in very-high-dimensional pattern recognition. IEEE International Conference on System, Man and Cybernetics (SMC), (pp. 502-509).

Souza, J., Matwin, S., & Japkowicz, N. (2006). Parallelizing feature selection. *Journal of Algorithmica*, 45(3), 433–456. doi:10.1007/s00453-006-1220-3.

Statnikov, A., Aliferis, C., Tsamardinos, I., Hardin, D., & Levy, S. (2005). A comprehensive evaluation of multicategory classification methods for microarray gene expression cancer diagnosis. *Bioinformatics (Oxford, England)*, *21*(5), 631–643. doi:10.1093/bioinformatics/bti033 PMID:15374862.

Sugumaran, V., Muralidharan, V., & Ramachandran, K. (2007). Feature selection using decision tree and classification through proximal support vector machine for fault diagnostics of roller bearing. *Mechanical Systems and Signal Processing*, 930–942. doi:10.1016/j.ymssp.2006.05.004.

Sugumaran, V., & Ramachandran, K. (2011). Fault diagnosis of roller bearing using fuzzy classifier and histogram features with focus on automatic rule learning. *Expert Systems with Applications*, 4901–4907. doi:10.1016/j.eswa.2010.09.089.

Sun, Y., Todorovic, S., & Goodison, S. (2008). A feature selection algorithm capable of handling extremely large data dimensionality. SIAM International Conference on Data Mining, (pp. 530-540).

Tibshirani, R. (1996). Regression shrinkage and selection via the lasso. *Journal of the Royal Statistical Society. Series B. Methodological*, *58*(1), 267–288.

Vainer, I., Kraus, S., Kamimka, G., & Slovin, H. (2010). Obtaining scalable and accurate classification in large-scale spatio-temporal domains. *Knowledge and Information Systems*.

Van den Ham, H., Moerland, R., Reinders, M., & Vergaegh, W. (2009). A sensitivity analysis of microarray feature selection and classification under measurement noise. IEE International Workshop on Genomic Signal Processing and Statistics GENSIPS 2009, (pp. 1-4).

Verron, S., Tiplica, T., & Kobi, A. (2008). Fault detection and identification with a new feature selection based on mutual information. *Journal of Process Control*, 479–490. doi:10.1016/j.jprocont.2007.08.003.

Wang, L., & Khan, L. (2006). Automatic image annotation and retrieval using weighted feature selection. *Multimedia Tools and Applications*, *29*(1), 55–71. doi:10.1007/s11042-006-7813-7.

Wang, Y. (2005). Gene selection from microarray data for cancer classification. A machine learning approach. *Computational Biology and Chemistry*, *29*, 37–46. doi:10.1016/j.compbiolchem.2004.11.001 PMID:15680584.

Wilson, E., & Hilferty, M. (1931). The distribution of chi-squared. Proceedings of the National Academy of Sciences, (pp. 684-688). Washington.

Witten, I., & E., F. (2005). Data mining: Practical machine learning tools and techniques (2nd ed.). San Francisco, CA: Morgan Kaufmann.

Wu, X., Yu, K., Wang, H., & Ding, W. (2010). Online streaming feature selection. Proceedings of the 27th International Conference on Machine Learning, ICML.

Yang, J., Zhang, D., Yong, X., & Yang, J. (2005). Two-dimensional discriminant transform for face recognition. *Pattern Recognition*, 1125–1129. doi:10.1016/j.patcog.2004.11.019.

Yeung, K., & Bumgarner, R. (2003). Multiclass classification of microarray data with repeated measurements: Application to cancer. *Genome Biology*, *4*(R83). PMID:14659020.

Younus, A., & Yang, B. (2012). Intelligent fault diagnosis of rotating machinery using infrared thermal image. *Expert Systems with Applications*, 2082–2091. doi:10.1016/j.eswa.2011.08.004.

Yu, L., & Liu, H. (2003). Feature selection for high-dimensional data: A fast correlation-based filter solution. Proceedings of The Twentieth International Conference on Machine Learning, (pp. 856-863).

Yu, L., & Liu, H. (2004). Efficient feature selection via analysis of relevance and redundancy. *Journal of Machine Learning Research*, 5, 1205–1224.

Zhang, C., Ruan, J., & Tan, Y. (2011). An incremental feature subset selection algorithm base on boolean matrix in decision system. Journal of Convergence Information Technology, 16-23.

Zhang, K., Li, Y., Scarf, P., & Ball, A. (2011). Feature selection for high-dimensional machinery fault diagnosis data using multiple models and Radial Basis Function networks. *Neurocomputing*, 2941–2952. doi:10.1016/j.neucom.2011.03.043.

Zhang, Y., Ding, C., & Li, T. (2008). Gene selection algorithm by combining ReliefF and mRMR. *BMC Genomics*, 9(Suppl 2), S27. doi:10.1186/1471-2164-9-S2-S27 PMID:18831793.

Zhang, Y., & Ren, L. (2010). Two feature selections for analysis of microarray data. IEEE Fifth International Conference on Bio-Inspired Computing: Theories and Applications BIC-TA 2010, (pp. 1259-1262).

Zhao, Z., & Liu, H. (2007). Searching for interacting features. Proceedings of International Joint Conference on Artificial Intelligence, (pp. 1157-1161).

Zhao, Z., & Liu, H. (2012). *Spectral feature selection for data mining*. Boca Ratón, FL: CRC Press, Taylor & Francis Group.

KEY TERMS AND DEFINITIONS

Dimensionality Reduction: The process of reducing the number of features under consideration. The process can be classified in terms of feature selection and feature extraction.

Distributed Feature Selection: Distributed feature selection utilises advanced distributed computing to enhance the efficiency and scalability with respect to centralised environments.

Embedded Method: A feature selection method that performs the selection in the process of training of the classifier and is usually specific to given learning machines. Therefore, the search for an optimal subset of features is built into the classifier construction, and can be seen as a search in the combined space of feature subsets and hypotheses.

Feature Selection: A dimensionality reduction method that consists of selecting a subset of relevant features from a complete set while ignoring the remaining features.

Filter Method: A feature selection method that relies on the general characteristics of the training data to select and discard features. Different measures can be employed: distance between classes, entropy, etc.

Hybrid Method: A hybrid model combines multiple feature selection methods, which may be of different types.

Incremental Feature Selection: Incremental feature selection starts with an initial subset of data and new information is added afterwards. This new data may modify the set of features selected.

Wrapper Method: A feature selection method that uses a learning algorithm as a "black box" to score subsets of features according to their predictive value.

Chapter 2
Online Machine Learning

Óscar Fontenla-Romero
University of A Coruña, Spain

David Martinez-Rego
University of A Coruña, Spain

Bertha Guijarro-Berdiñas
University of A Coruña, Spain

Beatriz Pérez-Sánchez
University of A Coruña, Spain

Diego Peteiro-Barral
University of A Coruña, Spain

ABSTRACT

Machine Learning (ML) addresses the problem of adjusting those mathematical models which can accurately predict a characteristic of interest from a given phenomenon. They achieve this by extracting information from regularities contained in a data set. From its beginnings two visions have always coexisted in ML: batch and online learning. The former assumes full access to all data samples in order to adjust the model whilst the latter overcomes this limiting assumption thus expanding the applicability of ML. In this chapter, we review the general framework and methods of online learning since its inception are reviewed and its applicability in current application areas is explored.

INTRODUCTION

Since the pioneer works in Machine Learning (ML), two visions of tackling the problem of automatic learning have coexisted: batch and online learning. Batch learning paradigm assumes directly or indirectly the following restrictions:

- The whole training data set can be accessed in order to adjust the model. Each time the learning process needs access to the complete data set, access is immediate and complete.

- There are no time restrictions. This means that we have enough time to wait until the model is completely adjusted.
- The process underlying the data generation process does not change. Once the model is adjusted, no further updates are necessary to obtain accurate results.

We discover that if we assume all these restrictions, ML's applicability narrows significantly. Many significant applications of learning methods during the last 50 years would have been impossible to solve without the relaxation of these restrictions. The following are some examples:

DOI: 10.4018/978-1-4666-3942-3.ch002

- **Environments where Data Arrives Continuously:** In this kind of application, data arrives continuously and an up-to-date model is necessary every time, otherwise the learning process would be redundant. In this case, the access to the whole data can be neither complete (the volume of data grows continuously) nor immediate (one must await its arrival). In fact, it can be argued that the concept of training data set vanishes as it can be assumed that we never have access to it since it is never complete.

- **Massive ML Applications:** When the amount of data available makes its centralization impossible (the access cannot be complete) or impractical (due to time restrictions) two approaches can be taken: parallelize the training process while maintaining the batch formulation (see for example the formulation of ML algorithms in terms of Map-Reduce paradigm (Diel & Cauwenberghs, 2003) or follow a different formulation able to optimize the model using reduced data subsets.

- **The Process Underlying the Data Generation Changes:** In this case, the initial training set loses its validity as time passes due to changes of conditions in the aimed task. Thus, a mechanism to update a given model in order to adapt to new conditions is necessary.

There is not a clear agreement on the meaning of the term online learning. Some authors use it only for the first of the aforementioned environments, but in other sources the term can also be found referring to the last two environments. The source of controversy possibly stems from the fact that the philosophy of the solutions given to the three environments is similar. In this chapter, it will be assumed that the term online learning applies to any of the aforesaid situations.

Maybe one of the most paradigmatic practical successes of online learning algorithms is echo cancellation in telephone communication.

Since the advent of telephony, echoes have been a problem in communication networks. In particular, echoes can be generated electrically due to impedance mismatches at the hybrids of a Public Switched Telephone Network (PSTN), where the subscriber two-wire lines are connected to four-wire lines. The most important factor in echoes is called end-to-end delay, which is also known as latency. Latency is the time between the generation of the sound at one end of the call and its reception at the other end. Round trip delay, which is the time taken to reflect an echo, is approximately twice the end-to-end delay. Echoes become annoying when the round trip delay exceeds 30 milliseconds. Such an echo is typically heard as a hollow sound and echoes must be loud enough to be heard. When round trip delay exceeds 30 milliseconds and echo strength exceeds 30 dB, echoes become steadily more disruptive. The solution to this problem consists of finding a filter able to remove the echo signals from the audible ones in the two ends. When Bernard Widrow was a student, Finite Impulse Response (FIR) filter learning algorithms could not give an effective solution to this problem due to the need to build an accurate filter taking into account hard time restrictions (the filter is useful only during a conversation), the huge continuous source of data (voice signal) during a reduced time window and the fact that the echo signal generation process can change. Adaptation to these changes is needed. These restrictions made batch FIR filter learning algorithms ineffective for this purpose. In the 1960's, Bernard Widrow demonstrated that an optimal FIR filter could be found by applying continuously the following formula continuously to the weights of a linear filter:

$$\boldsymbol{w}_t = \boldsymbol{w}_{t-1} + \alpha(d_t - y_t)\boldsymbol{x}_t \qquad (1.1)$$

being $\boldsymbol{w}$ the weight vector, $\boldsymbol{x}$ the new input pattern, d the desired output of the filter, y the actual output of the filter, α the learning rate, and t and $t-1$ the current and previous time steps, respectively . This Equation (1.1), (which has inspired successive developments), meant that integration of the first modern echo cancellers in telephone communication was possible and it inspired developments which make our mobile phones, hands-free devices, etc. work properly in our everyday life.

Since the first developments, online learning methods have found their application in adaptive control (Astrom & Wittenmark, 1994), adaptive filtering (Kalman, 1960; Sayed, 2003; Haykin, 2002), communications (Claasen & Mecklenbraeuker, 1985), machine learning (Crammer, Dekel, Keshet, Shalev-Shwartz, & Singer, 2006), pattern recognition (Kivinen, Smola, & Williamson, 2004) and neural networks (Shiotani, Fukuda, & Shibata, 1995), etc. Nowadays, online learning is in vogue also in other fields of application which are very different from its original ones. The increasing size of modern data sets can be considered one of the fundamental drivers of this trend. Consider, for example, the case of a company which wants to analyze the access logs to its Web site in order to develop a model able to personalize contents to its users, suggest products on an e-commerce site and elicit its users' profiles, among other uses. It may even be interested in less commercial automatic systems such as one capable of detecting anomalous or malicious accesses to its site. Modern websites can generate from dozens to hundreds of gigabytes of data each day. Under these circumstances, it cannot be assumed that the time window of available data in order to adjust a model spans more than some days or weeks. Even in the case of this window being greater, the usefulness of a static learned model only lasts a reduced amount of time due to fast changes of trends. In this situation, batch learning is not applicable and the sole remaining option is learning based on each new data sample as it arrives and subsequently discarding it.

From a mathematical point of view, an online algorithm solves the restrictions of the afore-mentioned environments using the following principle: it minimizes a given cost function by updating certain model parameters by selecting data samples one (or a small set) at a time. Basically, these learning algorithms share a common update formulation:

$$\hat{\boldsymbol{\theta}}_t = \hat{\boldsymbol{\theta}}_{t-1} + \Delta\boldsymbol{\theta}(\boldsymbol{x}_t) \qquad (1.2)$$

where $\hat{\boldsymbol{\theta}}_t$ is the current updated parameter vector, $\hat{\boldsymbol{\theta}}_{t-1}$ is the parameter vector obtained from a previous computing step, and $\Delta\boldsymbol{\theta}(\boldsymbol{x}_t)$ is an adjustment or update term. This underlying learning methodology is shared by many online learning algorithms in literature which can be found under a variety of terms such as online learning, adaptive (filter) learning, sequential learning, incremental learning and stochastic learning.

The early formulation of online algorithms can be traced back to recursive least squares (RLS) by Plackett in 1950 (Plackett, 1950), *Perceptron* by Rosenblatt in 1958 (Rosenblatt, 1958), and *least mean square (LMS, also referred to as Adaline)* by Widrow and Hoff in 1960 (Widrow & Hoff, 1960). As we indicated previously, these algorithms have inspired numerous subsequent developments and extensions.

Recent developments of online learning algorithms have been focused towards: adaptive or robust performance (Haykin, 2002; Liang, Huang, Saratchandran, & Sundararajan, 2006; Kwong & Johnston, 1992; Nagumo & Noda, 1967; Albert & Gardner, 1967; Bitmead & Anderson, 1980; Ozeki & Umeda, 1984; Mayyas & Aboulnasr, 1997; Walach & Widrow, 1984; Sayed, 2003), margin maximization since the introduction of support vector machines (Crammer, Dekel, Keshet, Shalev-Shwartz, & Singer, 2006; Dredze, Crammer, & Pereira, 2008; Li & Long, 2002; Cauwenberghs & Poggio, 2001; Bordes, Bottou, & Gallinari, 2009) and kernel methodology, which has been used to overcome problems in linearly non separable classification problems and nonlinear regression problems (Kivinen, Smola, & Williamson, 2004; Liu, Pokharel, & Principe, 2008; Liu & Príncipe, 2008; Li & Long, 2002; Cauwenberghs & Poggio, 2001; Bordes, Bottou, & Gallinari, 2009; Cortes & Vapnik, 1995; Aizerman, Braverman, & Rozonoer, 1964; Gentile, 2001; Ishibashi, Hatano, & Takeda, 2008; Engel, Mannor, & Meir, 2004; Liu, Park, Wang, & Principe, 2009; Sayed, 2003).

Many algorithms have been proposed over the last 60 years, but online learning still lacks a unified learning theory and our understanding of its properties is not as complete as in the batch paradigm. Thus, we expect that current research to provide better methods in the near future and a more complete understanding of online learning process. In addition, modern kernelized algorithms incur in high computational complexity for large data sets since the size of the model keeps growing as the number of input samples increases. Current research is tackling this issue and, in the near future, we hope for solutions to this problem.

In this chapter, online learning approaches for regression, classification and clustering problems will be reviewed from the early 1960s approaches to the current trend developments. At the end of the chapter, four large application areas of the following types of algorithm will be presented: finance and economics, industrial technology, medical and Web. We hope that knowledge of these algorithms will improve reader's capabilities of tackling modern ML problems and widen their vision of the solutions that ML brings to the industry.

ONLINE REGRESSION ALGORITHMS

The goal of regression is to model one or more continuous desired variables d given the values of some other variables x with the aim of predicting future values of d. Thus, from the online machine learning point of view, the goal is to find a mapping $f(x; \theta)$ from the input space into the output space so that, if we denote the learning sample received on round t by $x_t \in \mathbb{R}^n$, $f(x_t; \theta)$ approximates d_t with little or no error, θ being the parameters of the model to be learned. In this section, we present some of the most important *online* algorithms for regression tasks, in which the data points x_t are considered one at a time and the model parameters θ are updated after each such presentation.

Linear Models

Although linear models have substantial limitations in many real-world applications they have suitable analytical properties and form the foundation for more complex methods that will be discussed in the next section.

Least-Mean-Square (LMS) Algorithm

The Least-Mean-Square (LMS) algorithm (Widrow & Hoff, 1960) is an adaptive algorithm which uses a stochastic gradient-based method of steepest descent. The LMS algorithm uses the estimates of the instantaneous gradient vector from the available data. LMS incorporates an iterative procedure that makes successive corrections to the weight vector in the direction of the negative of the gradient vector which eventually leads to the minimum mean square error. Compared to other algorithms LMS algorithm is relatively simple; it requires neither correlation function calculation nor matrix inversions.

For each iteration t of the algorithm the LMS requires the following steps:

The output of the system, y_t, is calculated using the equation:

$$y_t = \mathbf{w}_t^T \mathbf{x}_t$$

For the sake of simplicity, we have considered the case of a single output variable however this can be generalized for any number of outputs.

The value of the error estimation is calculated using:

$$e_t = d_t - y_t$$

The weights of the model are updated for the next iteration by equation:

$$\mathbf{w}_{t+1} = \mathbf{w}_t + \mu e_t \mathbf{x}_t \qquad (1.3)$$

where μ is the learning rate parameter. The value of this parameter needs to be carefully chosen to ensure that the algorithm converges.

The LMS algorithm is one of most commonly used adaptive algorithms due to its simplicity and reasonable performance. Since it is an iterative algorithm, it can be used in a highly time-varying signal environment. It also has a stable and robust performance when compared to different signal conditions. However, it may not have a fast convergence speed compared to other sophisticated algorithms such as the Recursive Least Square (RLS). It converges with slow speeds when the environment yields a correlation matrix possessing a large eigenvalue spread. Another of the main disadvantages of the LMS algorithm is the fact it has a fixed step size parameter for every iteration. This requires understanding the statistics of the input signal prior to commencing the adaptive filtering operation.

There are several variants of the LMS algorithm that deal with the shortcomings of its basic form. The Normalized LMS (NLMS) is an extension of the LMS which bypasses this issue by selecting a different step size value for each iteration of the algorithm. This step size is proportional to the inverse of the total expected energy of the instantaneous values of the coefficients of the input vector, i.e. the step size is determined by $\mu_t = 1/\left(\mathbf{x}_t^T \mathbf{x}_t\right)$. It improves the convergence speed in a non-static environment. In another version, the LMS-Newton, the weight update equation includes whitening in order to achieve a single mode of convergence (Widrow & Steams, 1985).

Recursive Least-Squares (RLS) algorithm

There is a popular alternative to the LMS called the Recursive Least-Squares (RLS) method. This model typically presents faster convergence, especially for highly correlated input signals, and smaller error than the LMS method, but at a cost of more computational effort per iteration. The complexity of the RLS method is $O(K^2)$, being K the number of parameters of the model, but for the much simpler LMS algorithm the complexity is $O(K)$. In contrast to the LMS, the RLS adaptive algorithm minimizes the total squared error between the desired signal and the output from the unknown system. LMS algorithm considers only the current error value in each step of the learning process but in the RLS method, the error considered is the global error from the beginning to the current data point. Therefore, the RLS has infinite memory as all error data is given the same consideration in the total error. In cases where the error value might come from a spurious input data point, the use of a forgetting factor (λ) allows the RLS algorithm to reduce the value of older error data by multiplying the old data by an exponential weighting factor.

In each iteration of the algorithm the parameters are updated using the following recursive equations:

$$\mathbf{P}_{t+1} = \frac{1}{\lambda}\left(\mathbf{P}_t - \frac{\mathbf{P}_t \mathbf{x}_{t+1} \mathbf{x}_{t+1}^T \mathbf{P}_t}{\lambda + \mathbf{x}_{t+1}^T \mathbf{P}_t \mathbf{x}_{t+1}}\right)$$

$$\mathbf{w}_{t+1} = \mathbf{w}_t + \mathbf{P}_{t+1}\mathbf{x}_{t+1}\left(d_{t+1} - \mathbf{x}_{t+1}^T \mathbf{w}_t\right)$$

where $\lambda \in (0, 1]$ is a forgetting factor.

For the initial step of the algorithm $w_0 = 0$ and $P_0 = \delta I$, while $\delta \gg 1$. The performance of the RLS algorithm in terms of the convergence rate, tracking, misadjustment, and stability depends on the forgetting factor. If the forgetting factor is very close to one, the algorithm achieves low misadjustment and good stability, but its tracking capabilities are reduced. A smaller value of the forgetting factor improves the tracking ability but increases the misadjustment, and it could affect the stability of the algorithm.

In summary, the main advantages of this method are:

- Guaranteed convergence to optimal w and results are exactly the same as for normal least squares update (batch update) after every data point was added once, but no matrix inversion is necessary.
- No learning rate is required.

- Forgetting factor λ permits forgetting data in the event of changing target functions.

However, the RLS algorithm could suffer from numerical instability problems under finite word-length conditions due to ill-conditioning.

Figure 1 contains an example of the convergence speed of the RLS, compared with the LMS, for the identification of a plant in a control system. As can be seen the RLS presents a faster convergence.

Nonlinear Models

Although linear methods are easy to understand and implement, the linearity assumption does not hold in many real-world problems. Consequently, online nonlinear methods are mandatory in some real-time applications in order to obtain acceptable results.

Figure 1. Comparative of RLS's and LMS's learning curves

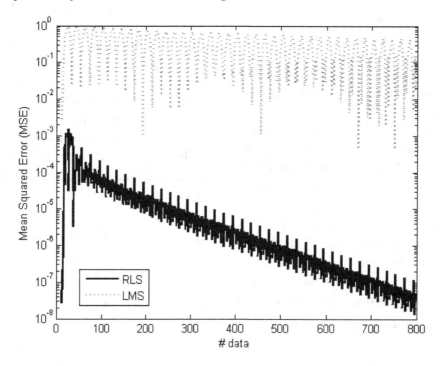

Kernel Least Mean Square (KLMS)

Recently, there has been an interest in the machine learning community to train kernel regressors, one sample at a time. Kernel methods are a relatively new class of learning algorithms utilizing Mercer kernels in order to produce nonlinear versions of conventional linear supervised and unsupervised models. The basic idea behind kernel methods is that a kernel function, which is applied to pairs of input vectors, can be interpreted as an inner product in a high-dimensional feature space (Hilbert space), thus allowing inner products in this space to be computed without making direct reference to feature vectors. This idea, which is commonly known as the "kernel trick," has been used extensively in recent years, most notably in classification and regression problems.

The basic idea behind of kernel algorithms is to transform the data x_t from the input space to a high dimensional feature space of vectors $\Phi(x_t)$, where the inner products can be computed using a positive definite kernel function, $K(x_i, x_j) = \Phi(x_i)^T \Phi(x_j)$, satisfying Mercer's conditions (Vapnik, 1995). This simple concept allows us to obtain nonlinear versions of any linear algorithm, expressed in terms of inner products, without actually knowing the exact mapping. Applying this for the case of the LMS, the linear model given by Equation (1.3) can be employed in the kernel feature space (Liu, Pokharel, & Principe, 2008). Is θ is the weight vector in this space so that the output is $y_t = \theta_t^T \Phi(x_t)$ where θ_t is θ at iteration t, then the stochastic instantaneous estimate of the gradient vector of the cost function in this new space yields to:

$$\theta_{t+1} = \theta_t + \mu e_t \Phi(x_n) \quad (1.4)$$

As in the previous case, μ is the step-size parameter that controls the convergence, speed, and misadjustment of the algorithm. The main differ-

ence here is that θ in Equation (1.4) is in a possibly infinite dimensional feature space and it would be practically impossible to update for θ directly. As an alternative, Equation (1.4) will be used to relate each θ_t to its initialization θ_0. This would easily give

$$\theta_t = \theta_0 + \mu \sum_{i=0}^{t-1} e_i \Phi(x_i)$$

For convenience $\theta_0 = 0$ and consequently $e_0 = d_0$. Thus, the final expression for θ_t becomes:

$$\theta_t = \mu \sum_{i=0}^{t-1} e_i \Phi(x_i) \quad (1.5)$$

At this time the kernel trick can be exploited. Given θ_t from Equation (1.5) and the transformed input $\Phi(x_t)$ the output at t is calculated by

$$y_t = \theta_t^T \Phi(x_t) = \mu \sum_{i=0}^{t-1} e_i \Phi^T(x_i) \Phi(x_t)$$

$$= \mu \sum_{i=0}^{t-1} e_i K(x_i, x_t)$$

Therefore, the output of the model in the t-th iteration can be calculated using the previous equation. Given the kernel, KLMS has a unique solution because it solves a quadratic problem in feature space. A common choice of the kernel is the multidimensional Gaussian kernel, which has a single parameter (bandwidth), although other functions can be employed. Notice also that the weights of the model are never explicitly used in the algorithm, so the order of the system is not controllable by the user.

In this algorithm, as the current output is determined exclusively by previous inputs and all the previous errors, it can be computed in the input space. Each new input sample results in an output and thus a corresponding error, which is never modified further and it is incorporated in the estimate of the next output. This recursive computation makes Kernel LMS especially useful for online nonlinear signal processing, but the complexity of the algorithm increases linearly as new error samples are used.

Kernel Recursive Least-Squares (KRLS)

As in the previous case, the kernel trick can be used for extending the RLS to a nonlinear scenario. Kernel methods present an alternative to parametric learning approaches. Solutions attained by these methods are nonparametric in nature and are typically of the form

$$f(\boldsymbol{x}) = \sum_{i=1}^{t} \alpha_i K(\boldsymbol{x}_i, \boldsymbol{x}) \qquad (1.6)$$

where $\boldsymbol{x}_i$ are the training data points, K is the kernel function and α_i are the adjustable parameters. Given that the number of parameters (α_i) in kernel solutions equals the size of the training data set, some form of sparsity must be introduced. Sparse solutions for kernel algorithms are desirable for two main reasons. First, instead of storing information belonging to the whole history of training instances, sparsity permits the solution to be stored in memory in a compact form. Second, sparsity is related to generalization ability, and is considered a desirable property in learning algorithms. The ability of a kernel machine to correctly generalize from its learned experience to new data can be shown to improve as the number of its free parameters decreases (providing the training error does not increase). Then, the sparsification may be used as a regularization instrument.

In some learning methods such as Support Vector Regression and Regularization Networks, sparsity is achieved by *elimination*. This means that at the beginning, these algorithms consider all training samples as potential contributing members of the expansion in Equation (1.6) and subsequently, when the optimization problem is solved, they eliminate those samples whose coefficients (α_i) vanish. An alternative methodology is to achieve sparsity by *construction*. In that case, the algorithm starts with an empty representation, in which all coefficients vanish, and gradually adds samples according to certain criteria. Constructive sparsification is normally used offline, in which case, the algorithm is free to choose any one of the training samples at each step of the construction process. Due to the intractability of finding the best subset of samples, these algorithms usually resort to employing various greedy selection strategies. In such strategies, at each step, the sample selected is the one that maximizes the amount of increase (or decrease) that its addition induces in some fitness criterion.

In the Kernel Recursive Least-Squares (KRLS) method proposed in (Engel, Mannor, & Meir, 2004) they use a form of online constructive sparsification that sequentially admits into the kernel representation only those samples that cannot be approximately represented by linear combinations of previously admitted samples. The proposed algorithm assumes that at step n, after having observed $n-1$ training samples, it has collected a dictionary D_{n-1}, consisting of a subset of the training samples that, by construction, are linearly independent feature vectors. Thus, when a new sample is presented, tests are conducted to see whether it is approximately linearly dependent on the dictionary vectors. If not, it is added to the dictionary. Consequently, all training samples up to step t can be approximated as linear combinations of the vectors in D_n.

More recently the Extended KRLS method (EX-KRLS) has been proposed as an alternative (Liu, Park, Wang, & Principe, 2009). Compared with the KRLS algorithm, EX-KRLS is a step closer to kernel Kalman filters and its main motivation is to improve the tracking performance of the original KRLS.

Support Vector Regression (SVR)

Support vector regression (SVR) fits a continuous-valued function to data in a manner which shares many of the advantages of support vector machine (SVM) classification. Several approximate online training algorithms have been proposed for SVMs (Syed, Liu, & Sung, 1999; Herbster, 2001; Kivinen, Smola, & Williamson, 2002; Ralaivola & d'Alche-Buc, 2001). However, most algorithms for SVR require that training samples be delivered in a single batch. In this chapter we will focus our attention on an accurate online support vector regression (AOSVR) algorithm (Ma, Theiler, & Perkins, 2003; Martin, 2002) that follows the approach of Cauwenberghs and Poggio (2001) for incremental SVM regression.

Given a training set

$$T = \left\{ (\boldsymbol{x}_i, d_i), \ i = 1, \ ..., l \right\}$$

where $\boldsymbol{x}_i \in R^N$ and $d_i \in R$ the following linear regression function is constructed on a feature space F,

$$f(\boldsymbol{x}) = \boldsymbol{w}^T \Phi(\boldsymbol{x}) + b$$

where $\boldsymbol{w}$ is a vector in F, and $\Phi(\boldsymbol{x})$ maps the input x to a vector in F. The $\boldsymbol{w}$ and b in the previous equation are obtained by solving an optimization problem:

$$\min \ \frac{1}{2} \boldsymbol{w}^T \boldsymbol{w} + C \sum_{i=1}^{l} (\xi_i + \xi_i^*)$$

$$s.t. \quad d_i - (\boldsymbol{w}^T \Phi(\boldsymbol{x}) + b) \leq \varepsilon + \xi_i \qquad (1.7)$$
$$(\boldsymbol{w}^T \Phi(\boldsymbol{x}) + b) - d_i \leq \varepsilon + \xi_i^*$$
$$\xi_i, \xi_i^* \geq 0, \quad i = 1,...,l$$

The optimization criterion penalizes data points whose d-values differ from $f(\boldsymbol{x})$ by more than ε. The slack variables, ξ and ξ^*, determine the size of this excess deviation for positive and negative deviations, respectively. Figure 2(a) depicts the situation graphically.

Using Lagrange multipliers the primal formulation in Equation (1.7) can be transformed to the following dual optimization problem:

$$\min \ D = \frac{1}{2} \sum_{i=1}^{l} \sum_{j=1}^{l} Q_{ij} (\alpha_i - \alpha_i^*)(\alpha_i - \alpha_i^*)$$

$$+ \varepsilon \sum_{i=1}^{l} (\alpha_i + \alpha_i^*) - d_i \sum_{i=1}^{l} (\alpha_i - \alpha_i^*)$$

$$s.t \quad 0 \leq \alpha_i, \alpha_i^* \leq C \qquad i = 1,...,l$$

$$\sum_{i=1}^{l} (\alpha_i - \alpha_i^*) = 0$$

where

$$Q_{ij} = \Phi\left(\boldsymbol{x}_i\right)^T \Phi\left(\boldsymbol{x}_j\right) = K\left(\boldsymbol{x}_i, \boldsymbol{x}_j\right)$$

is a kernel function and α_i and α_i^* are the Lagrange multipliers. According to the Karush-Kuhn-Tucker (KKT) conditions, at most one of α_i and α_i^* will be nonzero, and both nonnegative. Thus, a coefficient difference $\theta_i = \alpha_i - \alpha_i^*$ can be defined and it can be used to define three subsets into which the samples, in training set T, are classified (see Figure 2(b)):

- **Set E:** Error support vectors.
  $E = \{i / | q_i | = C\}$
- **Set M:** Margin support vectors.
  $M = \{i / 0 < | q_i | < C\}$
- **Set R:** Remaining samples.
  $R = \{i / | q_i | = 0\}$

The incremental algorithm proposed simultaneously in (Ma, Theiler & Perkins, 2003) and (Martin, 2002) updates the trained SVR function

Figure 2. (a) The ε-insensitive loss function and the role of the slack variables, and (b) decomposition of training set T following KKT conditions into three sets: margin support vectors M, error support vectors E and remaining vectors R

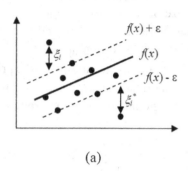

(a)

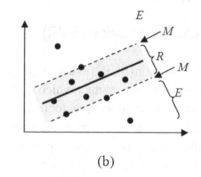

(b)

whenever a new sample x_t is added to the training set T. The basic idea is to change the coefficient θ_t corresponding to the new sample x_t, and then the function that defines the margin, in a finite number of discrete steps until it meets the KKT conditions, while ensuring that the existing samples in T continue to satisfy the KKT conditions at each step.

Online Passive-Aggressive Algorithms

This family of algorithms is closely related to Support Vector Machine methods. Its name, passive-aggressive, tries to reflect the idea that learning only takes place when certain circumstances occur (aggressive phase) whilst, in other cases, the model to be adapted remains the same even when new learning data arrives (passive phase).

Specifically, let $(x_t, d_t) \in \mathbb{R}^N \times \mathbb{R}$ be the learning sample received on time t, x_t being the inputs and d_t being the desired output. In a regression problem, our goal is to find a mapping f from the input space $\mathbb{R}^n$ into $\mathbb{R}$ based on a weight vector w, thus f takes the form $f(x) = w \cdot x$. Using f, for every x_t we can obtain a prediction $y_t = f(x_t)$. Based on this value, the instantaneous loss can be calculated as the discrepancy between d_t and y_t, and the goal is to minimize the cumulative loss. With this aim, an ε-insensitive loss is defined as

$$l_\varepsilon(w;(x,d)) = \begin{cases} 0 & |d - w \cdot x| \le \varepsilon \\ |d - w \cdot x| - \varepsilon & otherwise \end{cases}$$

where ε is a pre-established insensitivity parameter. Vector w_t used for prediction on round t is updated after receiving a new sample x_{t+1}. In (Crammer, Dekel, Keshet, Shalev-Shwartz, & Singer, 2006), the authors derive an updating scheme based on an optimization problem directly related to the one employed by Support Vector Machines (Vapnik, 1995). This updated scheme will be passive when the associated ε-insensitive loss is 0, and thus $w_{t+1} = w_t$ or, otherwise, it will be aggressive and force w_{t+1} to be the projection of w_t onto the set:

$$C = \left\{ w : |w \cdot x_t - d_t| \le \varepsilon \right\}$$

of all weight vectors that attain a loss of (near) zero. For a regression problem, this set is an ε-hyperslab. In this case, the updating equation attempts to keep w_{t+1} as close to w_t as possible so as to retain the information previously learned, while forcing w_{t+1} to achieve a zero loss on the most recent example. Then

$$w_{t+1} = w_t + \tau_t v_t$$

where, in the simplest approach:

$$\mathbf{v}_t = \text{sign}(d_t\text{-y}_t)\mathbf{x}_t$$

i.e. minus the gradient of the discrepancy, and:

$$\tau_t = l_\varepsilon(\mathbf{w}_t;(\mathbf{x}_t,d_t))/\|\mathbf{v}_t\|$$

As can be observed, the weight vector $\mathbf{w}_t$ is a linear combination of the instances, thus enabling the employment of Mercer kernels for a nonlinear transformation of the inputs (Vapnik, 1995).

In (Crammer, Dekel, Keshet, Shalev-Shwartz, & Singer, 2006) a single algorithmic framework is proposed that allows us to solve not only regression, but also uniclass and classification problems, as will be explained later. Moreover, this unified framework is completed by giving the loss bounds for both the realizable case and the non-realizable case.

Online Sequential Extreme Learning Machine (OS-ELM)

The Online Sequential Extreme Learning Machine (OS-ELM), proposed by Liang et al. (Liang, Huang, Saratchandran, & Sundararajan, 2006), is an online learning algorithm for single hidden layer feedforward networks. One of the novelties of this work is that a unified framework scheme is proposed that allows the network to have different types of hidden nodes. Specifically, they can be either additive neurons (i.e., neurons with sigmoid, threshold, etc. as activation functions) or radial basis function (RBF) neurons.

OS-ELM consists of two phases, as described below:

1. **Initialization Phase:** In this phase, firstly, random values are assigned to some of the parameters θ of the network. In the case of additive hidden nodes this vector θ of parameters corresponds to the input weights

connecting the input to hidden nodes and the biases. Similarly, in the case of RBF hidden nodes the centers and widths are randomly generated. Then, using a small portion S of the initial training data, with at least as many samples as hidden nodes, H_0 is calculated as the hidden layer output matrix of the network in which the i-th row is the output vector of the hidden layer with respect to the i-th sample $(x_i, d_i) \in S$, i.e.

$$\mathbf{H}_0 = \begin{bmatrix} G(,_1,x_1)\ldots & G(,_K,x_1) \\ \ldots & \ldots \\ G(,_1,x_I)\ldots & G(,_K,x_I) \end{bmatrix}_{I\times K}$$

I being the number of samples in S and K being the number of hidden nodes. Using H_0 the desired output of the network can be written as

$$\mathbf{H}_0\mathbf{W}_0 = \mathbf{D}$$

where $\mathbf{W}_0$ is the matrix of weights for the output layer. As the hidden node parameters θ need not be tuned during training and may simply be assigned with random values, the above equation becomes a linear system and then the weights $\mathbf{W}_0$ of the output layer are analytically estimated by least-squares as:

$$\mathbf{W}_0 = \mathbf{H}_0^T\mathbf{D}$$

where $\mathbf{H}_0^T$ is the Moore–Penrose generalized inverse of $\mathbf{H}_0$.

2. **Sequential Learning Phase:** In this phase, a new set $\mathbf{S}_t$ of observations is presented to the network and their parameters are updated. First, $\mathbf{H}_t$ is calculated as explained above. Afterwards, the new vector of output weights $\mathbf{W}_t$ is calculated as a function of $\mathbf{W}_{t-1}$, $\mathbf{H}_{t-1}$

and $\mathbf{D}_t$. In this step, a recursive algorithm for updating the least-squares solution is employed, which is similar to the recursive least-squares algorithm. As $\boldsymbol{S}_{t-1}$ is not used, every set of training samples can be discarded as soon as the learning procedure for that particular set is completed.

The performance comparison of OS-ELM with other popular sequential learning algorithms such as stochastic back propagation (LeCun, Bottou, Orr, & Müller, 1998), sequential minimal RBF neural network (Liang, Huang, Saratchandran, & Sundararajan, 2006) or GAP-RBF (Huang, Saratchandran, & Sundararajan, 2005) determine that OS-ELM is faster and produces better generalization performance. Moreover, it presents some other additional advantages:

1. Unlike other sequential learning algorithms which have many control parameters to be tuned, OS-ELM only requires the number of hidden nodes to be specified.
2. The algorithm can learn data one-by-one or by batches (a block of data) with fixed or varying batches size.
3. It can work with both additive or RBF hidden nodes

ONLINE CLASSIFICATION ALGORITHMS

The goal of a classification task is to find a mapping $f(x; \theta)$ from the input space into an output space defined by a set of labels, e.g. {-1; +1}. Thus, in contrast to a regression task, the output of $f(x; \theta)$ is not a continuous, but a discrete value. This special characteristic makes some of the algorithms previously explained not suitable or directly applicable for classification. In what follows, some of the most popular and promising algorithms for online classification learning will be described.

Models Based on Margin Maximization

Support Vector Machines (SVMs) are widely used tools for classification and regression problems based on margin maximization (Vapnik, 1995). The basis formulation of SVMs employed a fixed data set to construct a linear combination of simple functions depending on the data. However, in many application domains, the number of variables and/or samples may vary over time. In such situations, adaptive solutions that efficiently work in changing environments are of great interest.

Background

To fix notation, let

$$T = \left\{ \left(\boldsymbol{x}_i, d_i \right), \; i \; = \; 1, \; ..., l \right\}$$

be a data set, and consider the classification task given by T where each instance

$$\boldsymbol{x}_i = \left(\boldsymbol{x}_i^1, \boldsymbol{x}_i^2, ..., \boldsymbol{x}_i^N \right) \in \mathbb{R}^N$$

and $d_i \in \left\{ -1, +1 \right\}$. In (Vapnik, 1995), Vapnik described SVMs as follows: the input vectors are mapped onto an (usually high-dimensional) inner product space through some non-linear mapping ϕ, which has been previously chosen. In this feature space, an optimal separating hyperplane can be constructed. The mapping can be implicit if a kernel function $k(u, v)$ is used, since the inner product defining hyperplane can be evaluated as:

$$\left\langle \phi(u), \phi(v) \right\rangle = k(u, v)$$

for every two vectors $u, v \in \mathbb{R}^N$.

In the SVM framework, the hyperplane with maximal normalized margin for the examples of every class is an optimal hyperplane (see Figure

3). The normalized margin references to the minimum distance to the hyperplane.

In the event that the data set is not linearly separable (neither in the input space nor in the feature space), some tolerance to noise is introduced in the model. Using Lagrange theory, the maximal margin hyperplane for a binary classification problem given by a data set T is a linear combination of simple functions depending on the data

$$f(\boldsymbol{x}) = b + \sum_{i=1}^{L} d_i \alpha_i K(\boldsymbol{x}_i, \boldsymbol{x}) \qquad (1.8)$$

where $K(u, v)$ is a kernel function and the coefficients vector $(\alpha_i)_{i=1}^{L}$ is the solution of a constrained optimization problem in the dual space (Vapnik, 1995; Cauwenberghs & Poggio, 2001).

$$\underset{(\alpha,b)}{Minimize}\, W = \frac{1}{2} \sum_{i,j=1}^{L} d_i \alpha_i y_j \alpha_j K(\boldsymbol{x}_i, \boldsymbol{x}_j)$$
$$+ b \sum_{i=1}^{L} d_i \alpha_i - \sum_{i=1}^{L} \alpha_i \qquad (1.9)$$

s. t. $\;0 \leq \alpha_i \leq C, i = 1,...,L \qquad (1.10)$

where C is the regularization parameter which allows us to control the trade-off between the margin and training errors. The expression (1.9) does not correspond with the standard formulation, since dual and primal variables are presented at the same time. However, this fact allows us to deal with the bias term in a similar way to the rest of the variables (Romero, Barrio, & Belanche, 2007).

The classification of an example is correct, solely providing that its functional margin $d_i f(\boldsymbol{x}_i)$

Figure 3. SVM uses the hyperplane maximizing the margin as a classification function (example in 2-D space).

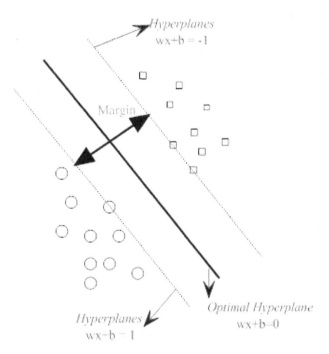

with respect to f is positive. The Karush-Kuhn-Tucker (KKT) conditions uniquely define the solution $\{\alpha, b\}$ of (1.9)

$$g_i = \frac{\partial W}{\partial \alpha_i} = d_i f(\boldsymbol{x}_i) - 1; \begin{cases} > 0 \text{ if } \alpha_i = 0 \\ = 0 \text{ if } 0 \le \alpha_i \le C \\ > 0 \text{ if } \alpha_i = 0 \end{cases}$$

$$\text{(1.11)}$$

$$h = \frac{\partial W}{\partial \alpha_i} = \sum_{i=1}^{L} d_i \alpha_i = 0 \qquad \text{(1.12)}$$

In principle, all developed approximations to train SVMs could be considered as incremental learning algorithms, as only a small part of the samples is used for optimization in each step. However, these approaches are not useful for true incremental learning, as none of the samples are discarded during training and therefore will have to be reconsidered in each working set selection step. Due to this fact, no improvement in terms of space and time consumption can be expected here. However, several incremental learning techniques for SVMs have been developed (Cauwenberghs & Poggio, 2001; Tax & Laskov, 2003; Martin, 2002; Syed & Sung, 1999).

Derivation of the Basis incremental SVM Algorithm

(Cauwenberghs & Poggio, 2001) presented an incremental algorithm for online training SVMs for classification problems. The main building block of the incremental SVM is a procedure for adding one example to an existing optimal solution. When a new point $\boldsymbol{x}_c$ is incorporated, its weight α_c is set to a zero value. If this assignment is not an optimal solution, the weights of other samples must be updated in order to obtain an optimal solution for the enlarged data set. Note that before an addition of a new example $\boldsymbol{x}_c$ the KKT conditions are satisfied for all previous examples. The goal of the weight update in the incremental SVM algorithm is to find a weight assignment so that the KKT conditions are also satisfied for the enlarged data set. This is done in a sequence of analytically computable steps. The whole procedure is reversible, thus allowing decremental learning.

Following Cauwenberghs and Poggio (2001) and Diel and Cauwenberghs (2003), the training examples can be partitioned into three different categories as illustrated in Figure 4 (Pontil & Verri, 1997): set of margin support vector strict-

Figure 4. Categorization of training samples in terms of the distance to the margin (g_i)

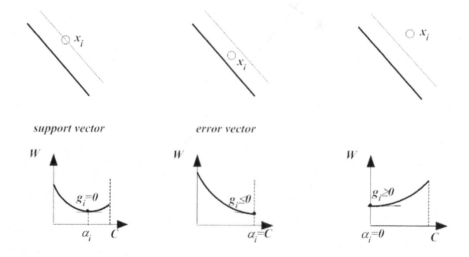

ly on the margin $\left(d_i f(\boldsymbol{x}_i) = 1, g_i = 0\right)$, set of error support vectors exceeding the margin $\left(g_i < 0\right)$ and the remaining set of reserve vectors exceeding the margin $\left(g_i > 0\right)$

Incremental Procedure

Let $l \to l+1$, when adding point (candidat margin or error vector) to D then $D^{l+1} = D^l \cup \{c\}$ and the new solution $\left\{\alpha_i^{l+1}, b^{l+1}\right\}, i = 1, ..., l+1$ is expressed in terms of a) the present solution $\left\{\alpha_i^l, b^l\right\}$, b) the present Jacobian inverse R, and c) the candidate $\boldsymbol{x}_c, y_c$ as

1. Initialize α_c to zero
2. If $g_c > 0$, terminate (c is not a margin or error vector)
3. If $g_c \le 0$, apply the largest possible increment α_c so that one of the following conditions occurs:
    a. $g_c = 0$: Add c to margin set S, update R accordingly and terminate
    b. $\alpha_c = 0$: Add c to error set E and terminate
    c. Elements of D^l migrate across S, E and R : Update membership of elements and, if S changes, update R accordingly and repeat as necessary.

The process continues until the gradient of the current example becomes zero or its weights reach C value. Over time the vectors corresponding to previously seen training data may modify their status, but the incorporation of new training data c to the previous solution converges in a finite number of steps.

Decremental Learning

The previous procedure can be reversed for the removal of an example: its weight is forced to zero while updating weights of the remaining

examples so that the solution obtained with $\alpha_c = 0$ is optimal for the reduced data set. Therefore, let $l \to l-1$, when removing point c (margin or error vector) from D then $D^{\setminus c} = D \setminus \{c\}$ and the solution $\left\{\alpha_i^{\setminus c}, b^{\setminus c}\right\}$, is expressed in terms of a) $\left\{\alpha_i, b\right\}$, and b) the removed point x_c, y_c. The solution yields $g_c^{\setminus c}$, which determines whether leaving c out of the training set generates a classification error $\left(g_c^{\setminus c} \le -1\right)$. Starting from the full l – point solution:

1. If c is not a margin or error vector: Terminate, "correct" (c is already left out, and correctly classified)
2. If c is a margin or error vector with $g_c \le 1$: Terminate, "incorrect" (by default as a training error)
3. If c is a margin or error with $g_c \ge -1$, apply the largest possible decrement α_c so that one of the following conditions occurs:
    a. $g_c < -1$: Terminate, "incorrect"
    b. $\alpha_c = 0$: Terminate, "correct"
    c. Elements of D^l migrate across S, E and R : Update membership of elements and, if S changes, update R accordingly and repeat as necessary.

Both procedures (incremental and decremental learning) can be directly extended to a broader class of kernel learning machines with convex quadratic cost functional under linear constraints, including Support Vector regression.

Incremental and decremental learning algorithms offer on the one hand a simple and computationally efficient scheme for online SVM training and on the other hand an exact leave-out-one evaluation of the generalization performance on the training data. The major shortcoming of the exact incremental learning is its memory requirement, since the set of support vectors must be retained in memory throughout the entire learning process. Due to this limitation, the algorithm is unlikely to be scalable beyond tens of thousands of examples; however, for data sizes within this limit it offers an advantage of immediate availability of the exact solution (crucial, for example, in learning of dynamic environments) and reversibility.

Online Passive-Aggressive Algorithm for Classification

As mentioned, Online Passive-Aggressive (Crammer, Dekel, Keshet, Shalev-Shwartz, & Singer, 2006) is a family of algorithms which propose solutions to three types of problems: regression, classification, and one-class classification. Moreover, the authors propose a unified framework that allows us to adapt the mechanism explained in the section Online Passive-Aggressive Algorithms for regression problems to classification problems by applying very simple changes. In the classification problem, the goal is to find a mapping from the instance space:

$$(\mathbf{x}_t, d_t) \in \mathbb{R}^N \times \{-1; \ +1\}$$

into the set of labels, $\{-1; +1\}$ and thus, for every $\mathbf{x}_t$, a prediction

$$y_t = sign(f(\mathbf{w}_t \mathbf{x}_t))$$

will be obtained. Subsequently, only the ε-insensitive loss and the discrepancy function need to be redefined as

$$l_\varepsilon(\mathbf{w}; (\mathbf{x}, d)) = \begin{cases} 0 & d(\mathbf{w} \cdot \mathbf{x}) \geq \varepsilon \\ \varepsilon - d(\mathbf{w} \cdot \mathbf{x}) & otherwise \end{cases}$$

and

$$\mathbf{v}_t = d_t \mathbf{x}_t$$

respectively.

ONLINE UNSUPERVISED LEARNING

Unsupervised learning studies how systems can learn to represent particular input patterns in a way that reflects the statistical structure of the overall collection of input patterns. In contrast with supervised learning, there are no explicit target outputs or environmental evaluations associated with each input (Dayan, 1999) Approaches to unsupervised learning include clustering and dimensionality reduction. We will focus here only on clustering algorithms.

Classical Clustering Methods

Data clustering is the unsupervised classification of patterns into groups (clusters). The goal is to develop an automatic algorithm that will discover the natural groups in a set of unlabeled data. Clustering algorithms (Jain, Murty, & Flynn, 1999; Jain, 2010) can be generally categorized into two groups: partitional and hierarchical. Partitional clustering algorithms attempts to simultaneously break down data into a set of disjoint clusters. Typically the criterion function involves minimizing dissimilarity in the data within each cluster whilst maximizing the dissimilarity of different clusters. Compared to partitional algorithms, hierarchical clustering algorithms impose a hierarchical structure of data. Consequently, hierarchical algorithms are more versatile than partitional algorithms, at the expense of time and space. Complexities of hierarchical algorithms (Arabic, Hubert, & De Soete, 1996) are typically higher than those of the partitional algorithms.

The following notation is used throughout this section. Let

$$T = \{\boldsymbol{x}_i, i = 1...l\}$$

be the set of l N-dimensional patterns to be clustered into a set of K clusters:

$$C = \left\{ c_k, k = 1...K \right\}$$

Let $\boldsymbol{\mu}_k$ be the center of cluster c_k. A basis to cluster algorithms is the measure of distance (similarity or dissimilarity) between two patterns. This function is required to satisfy the following conditions: positive definiteness, symmetry and triangle inequality (Bronshtein, Semendiaev, & Hirsch, 2007). The most popular function is the Euclidean distance,

$$d(\boldsymbol{x}_i, \boldsymbol{x}_j) = \sqrt{\sum_{n=1}^{N} (\boldsymbol{x}_i^n - \boldsymbol{x}_j^n)^2}$$

Alternatively, some other typical measures are Minkowski distance, City-block distance, Mahalanobis distance, or cosine similarity (Xu & Wunsch, 2005).

Partitional Algorithms

Partitional clustering algorithms split the data into K partitions, where each partition represents a cluster (see Figure 5). The partition is done based on certain objective functions. The most frequently used criterion function in partitional clustering techniques is minimizing the squared error criterion. The squared error between $\boldsymbol{\mu}_k$ (mean of cluster c_k) and the patters in cluster c_k is computed as

$$\varepsilon(T, c_k) = \sum_{\boldsymbol{x}_i \in c_k} \| \boldsymbol{x}_i - \boldsymbol{\mu}_k \|^2$$

The k-means (MacQueen, 1967) is the simplest algorithm employing a squared error criterion. Even though k-means was first proposed over 50 years ago, it is still one of the most widely used algorithms for clustering. A K-means algorithm finds a partition so that the squared error between the mean of a cluster and the patterns in the cluster is minimized, i.e.

$$\varepsilon(T, C) = \sum_{k=1}^{K} \sum_{\boldsymbol{x}_i \in c_k} \| \boldsymbol{x}_i - \boldsymbol{\mu}_k \|^2$$

A high level description of k-means is given below (Dubes & Jain, 1998),

Figure 5. Example of partitional clustering

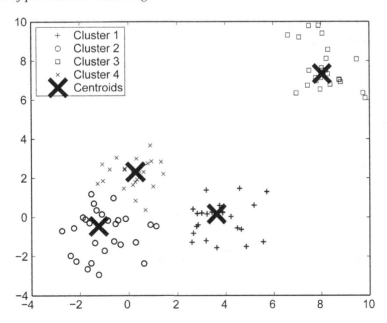

1. Select an initial partition with K clusters. Use K randomly-chosen patterns or K randomly-chosen points in the input space.
2. Generate a new partition by assigning each pattern to its closest cluster center.
3. Re-compute the cluster centers using the current cluster memberships.
4. Repeat steps 2 and 3 until a convergence criterion is met. Typical criteria are: minimal reassignment of patters to clusters or minimal decrease in squared error.

The most critical choice of the parameters of k-means is the number of clusters K. A number of heuristics are available (Milligan & Cooper, 1985; Gordon, 1999; Tibshirani, Walther, & Hastie, 2001) whereas no well-founded mathematical criterion exists. A major problem with k-means is that it is very sensitive to the selection of the initial partition and may converge to local minimum if the initial partition is not chosen in an appropriate way (Jain, 2010).

Hierarchical Clustering Algorithms

Hierarchical clustering algorithms organize data into a hierarchical structure. The result is usually depicted by a dendrogram (see Figure 6).

A dendrogram is a binary tree representing the nested grouping of patterns (or clusters) at which grouping changes. The height of the dendrogram represents the distance between each pair of patterns (or clusters). The dendrogram can be broken at different levels to produce different numbers of clusters of the data.

Hierarchical algorithms find clusters either in agglomerative (bottom-up) or divisive (top-down) mode (Jain, Murty, & Flynn, 1999). Agglomerative clustering starts with each pattern in its own cluster and merges the most similar pair of clusters successively to form a hierarchy. Divisive clustering proceeds in the opposite way. It starts with all patterns in one cluster and successively divides each cluster into smaller clusters. An outline of a hierarchical agglomerative clustering algorithm is as follows,

1. Compute the distance matrix containing all pair-wise distances between patterns.
2. Find the closest pair of clusters using the distance matrix and merge these two clusters into one.
3. Update the distance matrix considering this merger.
4. Repeat steps 2 and 3 until all patterns are in one cluster.

Figure 6. Example of a dendrogram in hierarchical clustering

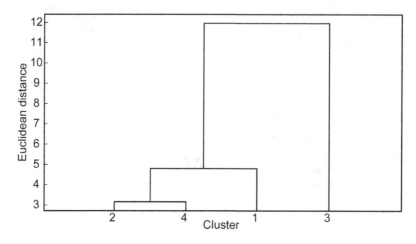

Based on the way the proximity matrix is updated in step 3, a variety of agglomerative algorithms can be implemented. Hierarchical divisive algorithms start with a single cluster which contains all patterns and keep splitting the clusters to obtain a partition of singleton clusters. For a cluster with M patterns, there are $2^{M-1} - 1$ possible divisions, which are very expensive in computation (Everitt, Landau, & Leese, 2001). Therefore, divisive clustering is not commonly used in practice. Most hierarchical clustering algorithms are derived from the single-link (Sokal, 1973) and complete-link (King, 1967) algorithms. These two algorithms differ in the way they measure the similarity between a pair of clusters. In the single-link method, the distance between two clusters is the minimum of all pair-wise distances between patterns drawn from the two clusters (one pattern from the first cluster, the other from the second). In the complete-link algorithm, the distance in between is the maximum. In either case, two clusters are merged based on the minimum distance criterion.

Online Clustering Methods

Literature in the field of clustering does not contain numerous implementation of clustering algorithms designed to work with online data. However, the advent of high dimensionality data has promoted the development of incremental clustering algorithms. These algorithms are designed to operate in a single pass over data, which opens the way for online data analysis. Incremental clustering assumes that it is possible to learn patterns one at a time and assign them to new or existing clusters. The fundamental steps of an incremental clustering algorithm are as follows,

1. Assign the first pattern to a cluster.
2. Assign the next pattern to an existing cluster or to a new cluster based on a pertinent criterion, e.g. the distance between the new pattern and the existing clusters.
3. Repeat step 2 until all data is clustered.

Incremental algorithms are non-iterative so it is not necessary to store previous data. Data are processed and learned and then discarded. Consequently, order-independence is the keystone of incremental clustering algorithms. An algorithm is order-independent if it generates the same result for any order in which data is presented (Jain, Murty, & Flynn, 1999). Most clustering algorithms are order-dependent but they implement mechanisms to reduce its impact.

There are several incremental (online) clustering algorithms,

- COBWEB (Fisher, 1987) is an incremental system for hierarchical conceptual clustering that organizes data so as to maximize inference ability. Conceptual clustering is a task defined in (Michalski, 1980) in which a system accepts a set of object descriptions and produces a classification scheme over the observations. COBWEB uses a heuristic measure to guide the search whilst incrementally incorporating objects into a classification tree and performs one of several operators at each level. These operators include creating a new cluster, combining two clusters into a single cluster, and dividing a cluster into several clusters.
- C2ICM (Cover-coefficient-based incremental clustering methodology) (Can, 1993) is an incremental clustering algorithm for dynamic information processing of document databases. It starts with a bunch of documents which are clustered with the C3M (Cover-coefficient-based clustering methodology) (Can & Ozkarahan, 1990). After this, clusters are updated due to newcomers (additions) and obsolete documents (deletions).
- Beringer and Hüllermeier (2006) proposed an efficient online version of the classical k-means algorithm for clustering data streams. A data stream can roughly be defined as a transient, continuously increasing sequence of time-stamped data. The

algorithm is based on an efficient method for computing the (approximate) pair-wise Euclidean distances between data streams in an incremental way. An important additional feature that distinguishes this algorithm from standard k-means is an incremental adaptation of the number of clusters k (note that the clustering structure can change over time).

- Barbakh and Fyfe (2008) introduced a family of algorithms that solve the problem of sensitivity to initial conditions in *k*-means (weighted *k*-means and inverse weighted *k*-means algorithms). Then, they extended the previous clustering algorithms and allowed them to learn in online mode by using them with an underlying latent space which enables topology preserving mappings to be developed.
- Katakis, Tsoumakas, and Vlahavas (2008) proposed an incremental clustering algorithm for the classification of concept-drifting data streams. Concept drift is a phenomenon related to the dynamic nature of data streams in which the distribution of data changes over time. The algorithm implements a probabilistic representation for data stream classification and uses incremental clustering to adapt the model to concept drift.
- Finally, SAFN (Self-adaptative feed-forward neural network) (Li, Yao, & Liu, 2011) is an online clustering algorithm which is able to learn from non-stationary data. It is based on a kernel-induced similarity measure and consists of five main stages: creation, adaptation, mergence, split and elimination.

Some other algorithms have been proposed for online unsupervised clustering, but they are mostly based on those presented in this section.

APPLICATION AREAS

In this section, we present four large application areas in which online learning is being applied to solve diverse problems.

Finance and Economics

In the fields of finance and economics, online machine learning methods have more benefits than batch learning. One could consider a major bank that needs to predict the probability of a client defaulting. Large data sets including returns of investment and defaults are generated every day and accurate up-to-date models are needed in order to process an increasing demand of transaction analysis (Friedman, Huang, & Sandow, 2004; Galindo & Tamayo, 2000; Khandani, Kim, & Lo, 2010; Crooka, Edelman, & Thomas, 2007). However, the most paradigmatic application of online machine learning to finance is probably stock market prediction. Since the advent of the stock market, there has been an increasing need of monitoring, understanding, and predicting the behavior of prices. Since the 1980's, automatic computerized methods, including both statistical and machine learning models, and human traders have been working together side by side. Automated trading has been a point of controversy in the market since the crash of 1987. In these types of programs, human decision-making is taken out of the equation and buy and sell orders are generated automatically, based on the levels of benchmark indexes or specific stocks. Some have speculated that the severe downturn in stock prices which hit a peak on October 19th (known as Black Monday) was caused by the combined effect of these automated systems. Since that moment, fully automated trading systems have been regarded with more scepticism, but the fact is that they still control a high number of investments each day and this automated processing needs to process a huge amount of information per minute and give a response on time. In this situation, online machine learning methods are a very profitable niche and so have been studied and mushroomed (although, naturally, major success has yet to be documented) (Huang, Wei, Nakamori, & Wang, 2004; Zemke, 2002; Yeh, Huang, & Lee, 2011; Allen, Powell, & Singh, 2012).

Industrial Technology

Another remarkable area in which online learning methods are indispensable tools for the application of Machine Leaning algorithms is Industrial Technology. In modern industry, the demands for low cost, high reliability, and human safety are greatly increasing. Thus, effective maintenance strategies to increase profitability and competitiveness play an important role. Condition Based-Maintenance (CBM) is a decision-making strategy based on real-time diagnosis of approaching failures and prognosis of future equipment health. In this context, online machine condition prognostics are useful for condition based maintenance in order to prevent unexpected machine breakdowns (Jardine, Lin, & Banjevic, 2006; Wu, Wang, & Lee, 2010; Qu & Zuo, 2012). Furthermore, with the emergence of more challenging environments for robotics, the design of robots is becoming more complex and their missions often involve unexpected interactions with the environment. To deal with these difficulties, the robots must be able to learn a model of their kinematics and dynamics under changing conditions. In these circumstances the use of online learning algorithms is becoming mandatory (Nguyen-Tuong & Peters, 2011; Sigaud, Salaün, & Padois, 2011). Moreover, applications for online learning control schemes are of great interest, such as adaptive neural controllers for helicopters performing highly nonlinear maneuvers. The controller compensates the nonlinearities in the system and uncertainties in the modeling of the dynamics to provide the desired performance (Suresh & Sundararajan,

2012). Finally, other methods are being developed for video-based face recognition which makes no assumptions about the pose, expressions or prior localization of facial landmarks. Learning is performed online while the subject is imaged and gives near real time feedback on the learning status (Mian, 2011).

Medical

Modern medical and healthcare settings generate a wide variety of data. These extensive records include important information such as patient conditions, diagnostic tests, treatments, etc. Online learning techniques can employ these databases in order to provide improvements in different tasks such as diagnosis, prognosis, etc. Among others we can find several important applications in the medical field such as for example: recurrence of hepatocellular carcinoma after curative resection (Iizuka et al., 2008), discrimination of tumor versus normal colon tissues (Alon, Barkai, Notterman, Gish, Ybarra, Mack, & Levine, 1999), classification of patients with glaucoma by tracking stable and progressive cases over time (Lazarescu, Turpin, & Venktest, 2002), brain state classification from functional magnetic resonance brain images (Taylor, Xu, Lee, & Ramadge, 2011) or classification of human activity (sit, stand, cycle, walk, run) and estimation of walk-run speed information of interest to several biomedical applications, from health monitoring to physical medicine and rehabilitation (Mannini & Sabatini, 2011).

Web

The Web contains a massive amount of data with valuable information for companies. For example, logs registering accessing patterns of users in a Web server. Analyzing this data may reveal interesting patterns and knowledge. The large size of the data and its inherent online behavior means that online machine learning methods are increasingly being used in the Web for automatic analysis. Such knowledge extracted from data is eminently being used in recommendation systems. In general terms, there are three main approaches to recommendations: personalized, whereby items are recommended based on the past activity of the user; collaborative, whereby goods are recommended based on the past activity of similar users; or item, whereby things are recommended based on the item itself. Additionally, there are methods that combine the three approaches. Most algorithms find a set of users which overlap with a given user in particular fields, e.g. purchases or rates. The algorithm aggregates items from the set of similar users and recommends those items for the given user. Two popular recommendation algorithms are collaborative filtering (Herlocker, Konstan, Terveen, & Riedl, 2004; Su & Khoshgoftaar, 2009) and clustering (Shepitsen, Gemmell, Mobasher, & Burke, 2008; Gong, 2010). Recommendation algorithms are best known for their use on e-commerce (e.g. Amazon.com) (Linden, Smith, & York, 2003), but nowadays are being applied in many other fields such as music or news (e.g. Last.fm or Google news) (Das, Datar, Garg, & Rajaram, 2007), among others.

CONCLUSION

Online machine learning has re-emerged during the last decade thanks to the increasing necessity of processing huge amounts of data both in the academic field and in industry. This chapter emphasizes the fact that online machine learning is not a new paradigm and has coexisted with batch learning since the early days of ML development. More recent techniques in this field stem from classical methods used traditionally in control and communications and thus the roadmap from the primitive methods to modern approaches has been revised. Learning theory in its online counterpart is not as developed as in the case of batch learning. In addition, batch learning techniques still outperform online methods for many purposes.

Therefore one expects both paradigms to coexist in the near future. Despite this being the case, there is a tangible trend in favor of online paradigms due to their capacity of dealing with modern hard storage and time requirements.

REFERENCES

Aizerman, M. A., Braverman, E. A., & Rozonoer, L. (1964). Theoretical foundations of the potential function method in pattern recognition learning. *Automation and Remote Control, 25*, 821–837.

Albert, A. E., & Gardner, L. A. (1967). *Stochastic approximation and nonlinear regression. MIT Press Research Monograph, 42*. Cambridge, MA: MIT Press.

Allen, D. E., Powell, R. J., & Singh, A. K. (2012). Machine learning and short positions in stock trading strategies. *Handbook of Short Selling*, pp. 467-478.

Alon, A., Barkai, D., Notterman, A., Gish, K., Ybarra, S., Mack, D., & Levine, A. J. (1999). Broad patterns of gene expression revealed by clustering analysis of tumor and normal colon tissues probed by oligonucleotide arrays. In *Proceedings of the Proc. Natl. Acad. Sci.* (pp. 6745–6750). PNAS.

Arabic, P., Hubert, L. J., & De Soete, G. (1996). *Complexity theory: An introduction for practitioners of classification* (pp. 199–233). Clustering and Classification.

Astrom, K., & Wittenmark, J. B. (1994). *Adaptive Control.* Boston, MA: Addison-Wesley.

Barbakh, W., & Fyfe, C. (2008). Online clustering algorithms. *International Journal of Neural Systems, 18*(3), 185–194. doi:10.1142/S0129065708001518

Beringer, J., & Hüllermeier, E. (2006). Online clustering of parallel data streams. *Data & Knowledge Engineering, 58*(2), 180–204. doi:10.1016/j.datak.2005.05.009

Bitmead, R., & Anderson, B. (1980). Lyapunov techniques for the exponential stability of linear difference equations with random coefficients. *IEEE Transactions on Automatic Control, 25*(4), 782–787. doi:10.1109/TAC.1980.1102427

Bordes, A., Bottou, L., & Gallinari, P. (2009). SGD-QN: Careful quasi-Newton stochastic gradient descent. *Journal of Machine Learning Research, 10*, 1737–1754.

Bronshtein, I. N., Semendiaev, K. A., & Hirsch, K. A. (2007). *Handbook of mathematics*. New York, NY: Springer.

Can, F. (1993). Incremental clustering for dynamic information processing. [TOIS]. *ACM Transactions on Information Systems, 11*(2), 43–164. doi:10.1145/130226.134466

Can, F., & Ozkarahan, E. A. (1990). Concepts and effectiveness of the covercoefficient-based clustering methodology for text databases. [TODS]. *ACM Transactions on Database Systems, 15*(4), 483–517. doi:10.1145/99935.99938

Cauwenberghs, G., & Poggio, T. (2001). Advances in neural information processing systems: *Vol. 13. Incremental and decremental support vector machine learning* (pp. 409–123). Cambridge, MA: MIT Press.

Claasen, T., & Mecklenbraeuker, W. (1985). Adaptive techniques for signal processing in communications. *IEEE Communications Magazine, 23*, 8–19. doi:10.1109/MCOM.1985.1092451

Cortes, C., & Vapnik, V. (1995). Support-vector networks. *Machine Learning, 20*, 273–297. doi:10.1007/BF00994018

Crammer, K., Dekel, O., Keshet, J., Shalev-Shwartz, S., & Singer, Y. (2006). Online passive-aggressive algorithms. *Journal of Machine Learning Research, 7*, 551–585.

Crooka, J. N., Edelman, D. B., & Thomas, L. C. (2007). Recent developments in consumer credit risk assessment. *European Journal of Operational Research*, 1447–1465. doi:10.1016/j.ejor.2006.09.100

Das, A. S., Datar, M., Garg, A., & Rajaram, S. (2007). Google news personalization: Scalable online collaborative filtering. In *Proceedings of the 16th international conference on World Wide Web* (pp. 271-280). ACM.

Dayan, P. (1999). Unsupervised learning. In Wilson, R. A., & Keil, F. (Eds.), *The MIT Encyclopedia of the Cognitive*. Cambridge, MA: MIT Press.

Dean, J., & Ghemawat, S. (2008). MapReduce: Simplified data processing on large clusters. *Communications of the ACM, 51*(1), 107–113. doi:10.1145/1327452.1327492

Diel, C., & Cauwenberghs, G. (2003). SVM incremental learning, adaptation and optimization. In *Proceedings of the International Joint Conference on Neural Networks (IJCNN)* (vol. 4, pp. 2685—2690). ACM/IEEE.

Dredze, M., Crammer, K., & Pereira, F. (2008). Confidence-weighted linear classification. In *ICML, ACM International Conference Proceeding Series* (vol. 307, pp. 264–271).

Dubes, A. K., & Jain, R. C. (1998). *Algorithms for clustering data*. New York, NY: Prentice-Hall.

Engel, Y., Mannor, S., & Meir, R. (2004). The kernel recursive least-squares algorithm. *IEEE Transactions on Signal Processing, 52*(8), 2275–2285. doi:10.1109/TSP.2004.830985

Everitt, B. S., Landau, S., & Leese, M. (2001). *Cluster analysis*. London, UK: Arnold.

Fisher, D. (1987). Knowledge acquisition via incremental conceptual clustering. *Machine Learning, 2*(2), 139–172. doi:10.1007/BF00114265

Friedman, C. A., Huang, J., & Sandow, S. (2004). A financial approach to machine learning with applications to credit risk. In *Proceedings of IMA Workshop of Financial Modeling*. New York, NY: Springer.

Galindo, J., & Tamayo, P. (2000). Credit risk assessment using statistical and machine learning: Basic methodology and risk modeling applications. *Journal of Comparative Economics, 15*(2).

Gentile, C. (2001). A new approximate maximal margin classification algorithm. *Journal of Machine Learning Research, 2*, 213–242.

Gong, S. (2010). *An efficient collaborative recommendation algorithm based on item clustering* (pp. 381–387). Advances in Wireless Networks and Information Systems. doi:10.1007/978-3-642-14350-2_48

Gordon, A. (1999). *Classification*. Boca Raton, FL: Chapman & Hall, CRC.

Haykin, S. (2002). *Adaptive Filter Theory* (4th ed.). New York, NY: Prentice Hall.

Herbster, M. (2001). Learning additive models online with fast evaluating kernels. In *Proceedings of the 14th Annual Conference on Computational Learning Theory* (pp. 444–460). New York, NY: Springer.

Herlocker, J. L., Konstan, J. A., Terveen, L. G., & Riedl, J. T. (2004). Evaluating collaborative filtering recommender systems. *ACM Transactions on Information Systems, 22*(1), 5–53. doi:10.1145/963770.963772

Huang, G.-B., Saratchandran, P., & Sundararajan, N. (2005). A generalized growing and pruning RBF (GGAP-RBF) neural network for function approximation. *IEEE Transactions on Neural Networks, 16*(1), 57–67. doi:10.1109/TNN.2004.836241

Huang, W., Nakamori, Y., & Wang, S. Y. (2004). Forecasting stock market movement direction with support vector machine. *Computers & Operations Research*. doi:10.1016/j.cor.2004.03.016

Iizuka, N., Oka, M., Yamada-Okabe, H., Nishida, M., Maeda, Y., & Mori, N. (2003). Oligonucleotide microarray for prediction of early intrahepatic recurrence of hepatocellular carcinoma after curative resection. *Lancet, 9361*(361), 923–929. doi:10.1016/S0140-6736(03)12775-4

Ishibashi, K., Hatano, K., & Takeda, M. (2008). Online learning of approximate maximum p-norm margin classifiers with biases. In *Proceedings of the 21st Annual Conference on Learning Theory* (vol. 1599, pp. 154–161).

Jain, A. K. (2010). Data clustering: 50 years beyond k-means. *Pattern Recognition Letters, 31*(8), 651–666. doi:10.1016/j.patrec.2009.09.011

Jain, A. K., Murty, M. N., & Flynn, P. J. (1999). Data clustering: A review. *ACM Computing Surveys, 31*(3), 264–323. doi:10.1145/331499.331504

Jardine, A. K. S., Lin, D., & Banjevic, D. (2006). A review on machinery diagnostics and prognostics implementing condition-based maintenance. *Mechanical Systems and Signal Processing, 20*, 1483–1510. doi:10.1016/j.ymssp.2005.09.012

Kalman, R. E. (1960). A new approach to linear filtering and prediction problems. *Transactions of the ASME-Journal of Basic Engineering, Series D, 82*, 35–45.

Katakis, I., Tsoumakas, G., & Vlahavas, I. (2008). *Incremental clustering for the classification of concept-drifting data streams*. Retrieved from http://www.researchgate.net/publication/228980443_Incremental_Clustering_for_the_Classification_of_Concept-Drifting_Data_Streams?ev=prf_pub

Khandani, A. E., Kim, A. J., & Lo, A. W. (2010). Consumer credit-risk models via machine-learning algorithms. *Journal of Banking & Finance, 34*, 2767–2787. doi:10.1016/j.jbankfin.2010.06.001

King, B. (1967). Step-wise clustering procedures. *Journal of the American Statistical Association*, 86–101. doi:10.1080/01621459.1967.10482890

Kivinen, J., Smola, A. J., & Williamson, R. C. (2002). Advances in neural information processing systems: *Vol. 14. Online learning with kernels* (pp. 785–792). Cambridge, MA: MIT Press.

Kivinen, J., Smola, A. J., & Williamson, R. C. (2004). Online learning with kernels. *IEEE Transactions on Signal Processing, 52*(8), 2165–2176. doi:10.1109/TSP.2004.830991

Kwong, R. H., & Johnston, E. W. (1992). A variable step size LMS algorithm. *IEEE Transactions on Signal Processing, 40*(7), 1633–1642. doi:10.1109/78.143435

Lazarescu, M., Turpin, A., & Venktest, S. (2002). An application of machine learning techniques for the classification of glaucomatous progression. In *Proceedings of the Joint IAPR International Workshop on Structural, Syntactic, and Statistical Pattern Recognition* (pp. 243–251).

LeCun, Y., Bottou, L., Orr, G. B., & Müller, K.-R. (1998). Efficient backprop. In Orr, G., & Muller, K. (Eds.), *Neural networks: Tricks of the trade* (pp. 9–50). New York, NY: Springer. doi:10.1007/3-540-49430-8_2

Li, K., Yao, F., & Liu, R. (2011). An online clustering algorithm. In *Eighth International Conference on Fuzzy Systems and Knowledge Discovery (FSKD)* (vol. 2, pp. 1104–1108).

Li, Y., & Long, P. M. (2002). The relaxed online maximum margin algorithm. *Machine Learning, 46*(1-3), 361–387. doi:10.1023/A:1012435301888

Liang, N.-Y., Huang, G.-B., Saratchandran, P., & Sundararajan, N. (2006). A fast and accurate online sequential learning algorithm for feedforward networks. *IEEE Transactions on Neural Networks, 17*, 1411–1423. doi:10.1109/TNN.2006.880583

Linden, G., Smith, B., & York, J. (2003). Amazon.com recommendations: Item-to-item collaborative filtering. *IEEE Internet Computing*, 76–80. doi:10.1109/MIC.2003.1167344

Liu, W., Park, I., Wang, Y., & Principe, J. C. (2009). Extended kernel recursive least squares algorithm. *IEEE Transactions on Signal Processing, 57*(10), 3801–3814. doi:10.1109/TSP.2009.2022007

Liu, W., Pokharel, P., & Principe, J. C. (2008). The kernel least-mean-square algorithm. *IEEE Transactions on Signal Processing, 56*(2), 543–554. doi:10.1109/TSP.2007.907881

Liu, W., & Príncipe, J. C. (2008). Kernel affine projection algorithms. *EURASIP Journal on Advances in Signal Processing, 56*(2), 12.

Ma, J., Theiler, K., & Perkins, S. (2003). Accurate on-line support vector regression. *Neural Computation, 15*, 2683–2703. doi:10.1162/089976603322385117

MacQueen, J. (1967). Some methods for classification and analysis of multivariate observation. In *Proceedings of the Fifth Berkeley Symposium on Mathematical Statistics and Probability* (vol. 1, pp. 281-297). Berkeley, CA: University of California Press.

Mannini, A., & Sabatini, A. M. (2011). On-line classification of human activity estimation of walk-run speed from acceleration data using support vector machines. In *Proccedings of IEEE Egineering in Medicine & Biology Society* (pp. 3302–3305). New York, NY: ACM. doi:10.1109/IEMBS.2011.6090896

Martin, M. (2002). *On-line support vector machines for function approximation. Technical Report*. Catalonia, Spain: Universitat Politècnica de Catalunya, Departament de Llengatges i Sistemes Informàtics.

Martin, M. (2002). On-line support vector machine regression. In *Proceedings of the 13th European Conference on Machine Learning (ECML'02)* (In Lecture Notes in Artificial Intelligence 2430, pp. 282-294). Berlin, Germany: Springer-Verlag.

Mayyas, K., & Aboulnasr, T. (1997). Leaky LMS algorithm: MSE analysis for Gaussian data. *IEEE Transactions on Signal Processing, 45*(4), 927–934. doi:10.1109/78.564181

Mian, A. (2011). Online learning from local features for video-based face recognition. *Pattern Recognition, 44*(5), 1068–1075. doi:10.1016/j.patcog.2010.12.001

Michalski, R. (1980). Knowledge acquisition through conceptual clustering: A theoretical framework and an algorithm for partitioning data into conjunctive concepts. *Journal of Policy Analysis and Information Systems, 4*(3), 219–244.

Milligan, G. W., & Cooper, M. C. (1985). An examination of procedures for determining the number of clusters in a data set. *Psychometrika, 50*(2), 159–179. doi:10.1007/BF02294245

Nagumo, J. I., & Noda, A. (1967). A learning method for system identification. *IEEE Transactions on Automatic Control, 12*(3), 282–287. doi:10.1109/TAC.1967.1098599

Nguyen-Tuong, D., & Peters, J. (2011). Incremental online sparsification for model learning in real-time robot control. *Neurocomputing, 74*(11), 1859–1867. doi:10.1016/j.neucom.2010.06.033

Ozeki, K., & Umeda, T. (1984). An adaptive filtering algorithm using an orthogonal projection to an affine subspace and its properties. *Electronics and Communications in Japan, 67-A*(5), 19–27.

Plackett, R. (1950). Some theorems in least squares. *Biometrika, 37*(1/2), 149–157. doi:10.2307/2332158

Pontil, M., & Verri, A. (1997). Properties of support vector machines. *Neural Computation, 10*, 955–974. doi:10.1162/089976698300017575

Qu, J., & Zuo, M. J. (2012). An LSSVR-based algorithm for online system condition prognostics. *Expert Systems with Applications, 39*(5), 6089–6102. doi:10.1016/j.eswa.2011.12.002

Ralaivola, L., & d'Alche-Buc, F. (2001). Incremental support vector machine learning: A local approach. In *International Conference on Artificial Neural Networks (ICANN 2001)* (pp. 322–330). Berlin, Germany: Springer-Verlag.

Romero, E., Barrio, I., & Belanche, L. (2007). Incremental and decremental learning linear support vector machines. In *International Conference on Artificial Neural Networks (ICANN 2007)* (Part I, LNCS 4668, pp. 209-218). Berlin, Germany: Springer.

Rosenblatt, F. (1958). The perceptron: A probabilistic model for information storage and organization in the brain. *Psychological Review, 65*(6), 386–408. doi:10.1037/h0042519

Sayed, A. H. (2003). *Fundamentals of Adaptive Filtering*. Hoboken, NJ: Wiley–IEEE Press.

Shepitsen, A., Gemmell, J., Mobasher, B., & Burke, R. (2008). Personalized recommendation in social tagging systems using hierarchical clustering. In *Proceedings of the ACM conference on Recommender systems* (pp. 259-266). New York, NY: ACM.

Shiotani, S., Fukuda, T., & Shibata, T. (1995). A neural network architecture for incremental learning. *Neurocomputing, 9*(2), 111–130. doi:10.1016/0925-2312(94)00061-V

Sigaud, O., Salaün, C., & Padois, V. (2011). On-line regression algorithms for learning mechanical models of robots: A survey. *Robotics and Autonomous Systems*, *59*(12), 1115–1129. doi:10.1016/j.robot.2011.07.006

Sokal, P. S. (1973). *Numerical taxonomy*. San Francisco, CA: Freeman WH and Co.

Su, X., & Khoshgoftaar, T. M. (2009). A survey of collaborative filtering techniques. *Advances in Artificial Intelligence*. doi:10.1155/2009/421425

Suresh, S., & Sundararajan, N. (2012). An online learning neural controller for helicopters performing highly nonlinear maneuvers. *Applied Soft Computing*, *12*(1), 360–371. doi:10.1016/j.asoc.2011.08.036

Syed, N. A., Liu, H., & Sung, K. K. (1999). Incremental learning with support vector machines. In *Proceedings of the Workshop on Support Vector Machines at the International Joint Conference on Artificial Intelligence—IJCAI-99*. Burlington, MA: Morgan Kaufmann.

Tax, D. M. J., & Laskov, P. (2003). Online SVM learning: From classification to data description and back. In C. Molina, T. Adali, J. Larsen, M. Van Hulle, S. Douglas, and J. Rouat (Eds.), *Proceedings of IEEE 13th Workshop on Neural Networks for Signal Processing (NNSP'03)*, pp. 499–508. IEEE.

Taylor, Y., Xu, H., Lee, R., & Ramadge, P. J. (2011). Online kernel SVM for real-time fMRI brain state prediction. In *Proceedings of the International Conference on Acoustics, Speech and Signal Processing*, 2040–2043. ACM/IEEE.

Tibshirani, R., Walther, G., & Hastie, T. (2001). Estimating the number of clusters in a data set via the gap statistic. *Journal of the Royal Statistical Society. Series B, Statistical Methodology*, *63*(2), 411–423. doi:10.1111/1467-9868.00293

Vapnik, V. (1995). *The nature of statistical learning theory*. New York, NY: Springer.

Walach, E., & Widrow, B. (1984). The least mean fourth (LMF) adaptive algorithm and its family. *IEEE Transactions on Information Theory*, *40*(2), 275–283. doi:10.1109/TIT.1984.1056886

Widrow, B., & Hoff, M. E. (1960). Adaptive switching circuits. In *Proceedings of IRE WESCON Convention* (vol. 4, pp. 96–104). Los Angeles, CA: Institute of Radio Engineers.

Widrow, B., & Steams, S. D. (1985). *Adaptive signal processing*. Englewood Cliffs, NJ: Prentice-Hall.

Wu, F., Wang, T., & Lee, J. (2010). An online adaptive condition-based maintenance method for mechanical systems. *Mechanical Systems and Signal Processing*, *24*(8), 2985–2995. doi:10.1016/j.ymssp.2010.04.003

Xu, R., & Wunsch, D. (2005). Survey of clustering algorithms. *IEEE Transactions on Neural Networks*, *16*(3), 645–678. doi:10.1109/TNN.2005.845141

Yeh, C. Y., Huang, C. W., & Lee, S. J. (2011). A multiple-kernel support vector regression approach for stock market price forecasting. *Expert Systems with Applications*, *38*(3), 2177–2186. doi:10.1016/j.eswa.2010.08.004

Yingwei, L., Sundararajan, N., & Saratchandran, P. (1998). Performance evaluation of a sequential minimal radial basis function (RBF) neural network learning algorithm. *IEEE Transactions on Neural Networks*, *9*(2), 308–318. doi:10.1109/72.661125

Zemke, S. (2002). On developing a financial prediction system: Pitfalls and possibilities. In *Proceedings of DMLL Worshop at ICML 2002*. ICML.

KEY TERMS AND DEFINITIONS

Convergence Speed: Rate of an algorithm to achieve the goal parameters that solves a specific problem. Typical convergences speeds are: linear convergence, quadratic convergence, etc.

Cumulative Loss: Value of the loss function calculated for a set of inputs, usually, the set of samples of the training set already processed by the model.

Forgetting Factor: Parameter of a learning algorithm that provides bias toward more recent data thus placing less emphasis on older data and helping the estimator react more quickly to parameter changes in the system. This parameter leads to a compromise between the tracking capabilities of the algorithm and its misadjustment and stability.

Generalization Error: Function that indicates the capacity of a machine learning model to infer a rule based only on a few examples.

Instantaneous Loss: Value of the loss function for just one new input instance.

Kernel Function: It is a symmetric function K: $X \times X \to R$ so that for all $\mathbf{x}_i$ and $\mathbf{x}_j$ in X, $K(\mathbf{x}_i, \mathbf{x}_j)$ $= \langle \varphi(\mathbf{x}_i), \varphi(\mathbf{x}_j) \rangle$ where φ is a non-linear mapping from the input space X into the Hilbert space F provided with the inner product $\langle .,. \rangle$.

Loss Function: Function that measures the error of a learnt model as a function of the difference between the expected output and the real output obtained for a given instance. During learning, parameter estimation is done in order to minimize this function.

Machine Learning (ML) Model: Mathematical model able to predict a particular characteristic of interest based on external stimuli.

Maximal Margin Hyperplane: Separating hyperplane with the largest margin. Machine learning theory says that this hyperplane minimizes the error bound.

Online Learning: Process of adjusting a ML model in such a manner that it is able to do so under restricted time and storage conditions.

Squared Error: It is a common loss function defined by $E = \frac{1}{2} \sum_{n=1}^{N} (y_n - d_n)$ where y_n is the real output of the model, d_n the desired output and N the number of samples in the input data set.

Chapter 3
Uncertainty in Concept Hierarchies for Generalization in Data Mining

Theresa Beaubouef
Southeastern Louisiana University, USA

Frederick E. Petry
Stennis Space Center, USA

ABSTRACT

Attribute oriented induction is an approach used in data mining to provide summaries of data in a database by the process of generalization that can be used for knowledge discovery in the form of rules or patterns. This is accomplished through the use of a concept hierarchy. When uncertainty is involved in the development and use of the concept hierarchy, the theory behind the uncertainty models in use must first be established. This chapter focuses on providing the foundations for defining imprecise hierarchies and the generalization process with crisp and rough data and hierarchies. Scaling and efficiency issues here involve the problems of creation of appropriate concept hierarchies and the scaling of the generalization process to deal with large databases.

INTRODUCTION

The world abounds in data, and as technology advances, opportunities for collecting, storing, and using this data increases. The magnitude of such data, as well as its typical lack of organization, however, can prove to be daunting without some means of automatically generating useful information from it. The process of data mining has developed into a useful tool for discovering interesting patterns and relationships in data, and these techniques have benefited information systems and users in a wide variety of fields.

One of the more widely known uses of data mining is for marketing purposes. Often the goal is to predict customer behavior (Chopra, Bhanbri, & Krishan, 2011) or to target selected groups for advertising purposes. Managers can use information from data mining to determine strategies for maximizing results without investing in strategies determined to have lower impact on the bottom line.

DOI: 10.4018/978-1-4666-3942-3.ch003

In the healthcare industry, data mining can help patients obtain better and less expensive healthcare while providing better information for both healthcare providers and patients (Koh & Tan, 2005; Rafalsky, 2002). It can be used to evaluate treatment practices, help with customer relation management, and detect fraud and insurance abuses. Data mining in healthcare can also alert providers and authorities about possible epidemics and bioterrorism threats (Piazza, 2002).

Data mining is also well established in a variety of scientific and engineering applications (Grossman, Kamath, Kegelmeyer, & Kumar, 2001). In spatial databases and geographic information systems, data contains positional information that often allows for the discovery of patterns involving spatial relationships (Miller & Han, 2001; Kopersky & Han, 1995). It has been used in numerous ways including the study of demographics (Malerba, 2002).

With new technologies, Web usage, social media, and smart devices come additional opportunities for data mining applications. Radio frequency identification (RFID), for example, can generate huge volumes of data and there is a great need for data mining techniques to assist with tracking, business processes, and organization (Kim, Kim, Jung, Kang, &Noh, 2009). Use of data mining for Web use has also been developed (Pohle & Spiliopoulou, 2002).

In data mining applications it is often the case that data or concepts can be generalized in an effort to discover useful patterns or rules in the data. This generalization must be done in some systematic and meaningful way. One approach is through the use of attributed oriented induction which provides summaries of data in a database by generalization. Generalization is achieved by using a concept hierarchy. Specific attribute values in a database tuple are replaced by more general values higher in the hierarchy. The resulting tuples may then be merged, ultimately producing a reduced number of tuples that represent a summarization of the data. This is related to, but more general than the roll-up operation on a data cube. This provides data summarization, a process of grouping of data, enabling transformation of similar item sets, stored originally in a database at the low (primitive) level, into more abstract conceptual representations. When either the data or the generalization process incorporates uncertainty, however, there can be many ways to determine how data is generalized.

Existing data mining techniques often do not incorporate some type of uncertainty management, and with the advancement of state of the art systems for modeling real world applications, this is an important issue. As systems become larger and more complex, the importance of elegant mathematical foundations will help to ensure robustness and scalability. This chapter focuses on capturing the uncertainty possible in concept hierarchies by use of fuzzy set and rough set approaches. In order to understand how uncertainty generalization and data mining can take place in databases, it is necessary to first establish the foundation by defining such imprecise hierarchies and the way generalization is to be accomplished with crisp and imprecise data and hierarchies. This chapter provides these foundations and the applications in generalization data mining. Scaling and efficiency issues here involve the problem of creation of appropriate concept hierarchies and the scaling of the generalization process to deal with large databases.

BACKGROUND

Data Mining

Data mining or knowledge discovery generally refers to a variety of techniques that have developed in the fields of databases, machine learning, and pattern recognition (Tan, Steinbach, & Kumar, 2005). The intent is to uncover useful patterns and associations from large databases.

The initial steps of data mining are concerned with preparation of data, including data cleaning intended to resolve errors and missing data and integration of data from multiple heterogeneous sources. Next are the steps needed to prepare for actual data mining. These include the selection of the specific data relevant to the task and the transformation of this data into a format required by the data mining approach. These steps are sometimes considered to be those in the development of a data warehouse, i.e., an organized format of data available for various data mining tools.

There is a wide variety of specific knowledge discovery algorithms that have been developed (Han & Kamber, 2006). These discover patterns that can then be evaluated on some interest based measure used to prune the huge number of available patterns. Finally as true for any decision aid system, an effective user interface with visualization/alternative representations must be developed for the presentation of the discovered knowledge.

Specific data mining algorithms can be considered as belonging to two categories - descriptive and predictive data mining. In the descriptive category are class description, association rules, and classification. Class description can either provide a characterization or generalization of the data or comparisons between data classes to provide class discriminations. Data generalization is a process of grouping of data, enabling transformation of similar item sets, stored originally in a database at the low (primitive) level, into more abstract conceptual representations. This process is a fundamental element of attribute-oriented induction (Cai, Cercone, & Han, 1991), a descriptive database mining technique, allowing compression of the original data set into a generalized relation, which provides concise and summative information about the massive set of task-relevant data.

Association rules correspond to correlations among the data items (Han & Kamber, 2006). They are often expressed in rule form showing attribute-value conditions that commonly occur at the same time in some set of data. An association rule of the form X →Y can be interpreted as meaning that the tuples in the database that satisfy the condition X are also "likely" to satisfy Y, so that the "likely" implies that this is not a func-

tional dependency in the formal database sense. Note specifically that association rules express the dependency between a particular combination of the related attributes values while a functional dependency applies in the case of *all* combinations. Finally, a classification approach analyzes the training data (data whose class membership is known) and constructs a model for each class based on the features in the data.

Predictive analysis is also a very developed area of data mining. Prediction techniques are used to predict possible missing data values or distributions of values of some attributes in a set of objects. First, one must find the set of attributes relevant to the attribute of interest and then predict a distribution of values based on the set of data similar to the selected objects. There are a large variety of techniques used, including regression analysis, correlation analysis, genetic algorithms and neural networks to mention a few.

Uncertainty Background

Rough Sets

Rough set theory, introduced by Pawlak (1984) and discussed in greater detail in (Grzymala-Busse, 1991; Komorowski, Pawlak, & Polkowski, 1999; Pawlak, 1991), is a technique for dealing with uncertainty and for identifying cause-effect relationships in databases as a form of database learning (Slowenski, 1992). It has also been used for improved information retrieval (Srinivasan, 1991) and for uncertainty management in relational databases (Beaubouef & Petry, 1994; Beaubouef, Petry, & Buckles, 1995). Rough sets involve the following:

- U is the universe, which cannot be empty: R is the indiscernibility relation, or equivalence relation.
- A = (U,R), an ordered pair, is called an approximation space,
- $[x]_R$ denotes the equivalence class of R containing x, for any element x of U

- Elementary sets in A are the equivalence classes of R, and a definable set in A is any finite union of elementary sets in A.

Therefore, for any given approximation space defined on some universe U and having an equivalence relation R imposed upon it, U is partitioned into equivalence classes called elementary sets which may be used to define other sets in A. Given that $X \subseteq U$, X can be defined in terms of the definable sets in A by the following:

- The *lower approximation of X in A* is the set $\underline{R}X = \{x \in U \mid [x]_R \subseteq X\}$, and
- The *upper approximation of X in A* is the set $\overline{R}X = \{x \in U \mid [x]_R \cap X \neq \varnothing\}$.

A rough set, then, is an approximation of a crisp set that results in a lower and an upper approximation. The lower set contains only the objects that are *certain* members while the upper set contains all objects that are *possible* members. $\underline{R}X \subseteq \overline{R}X$, and $\overline{R}X - \underline{R}X$ is called the boundary, or uncertain, region of the upper approximation. .

In Figure 1 the universe U is partitioned into equivalence classes denoted by the squares. Those elements in the lower approximation of X, $\underline{R}X$ (the R-positive region) are denoted with the letter

P and elements in the R-negative region ($NEG_R(X) = U - \overline{R}X$) by the letter N. All other classes belong to the boundary region of the upper approximation.

Fuzzy Sets

Fuzzy set theory is an approach in which the elements of a set belong to the set to varying degrees known as membership degrees (Nguyen & Walker, 2005). Conventionally we can specify a set C by its characteristic function, $Char_C(x)$. If U is the universal set from which values of C are taken, then we can represent C as

$$C = \{ x \mid x \in U \text{ and } Char_C(x) = 1 \}$$

This is the representation for a crisp or non-fuzzy set. For an ordinary set C the range of $Char_C(x)$ are just the two values: { 0, 1 }. However for a fuzzy set A we have a range of the entire interval [0,1].

That is, for a fuzzy set the characteristic function takes on all values between 0 and 1, and not just the discrete values of 0 or 1 representing the binary choice for membership in a conventional crisp set. For a fuzzy set the characteristic function is often called the membership function and denoted $\mu_A(x)$. Figure 2 provides an example of

Figure 1. Example of a rough set X

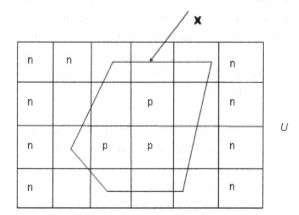

Figure 2. Membership function for the linguistic term "deep"

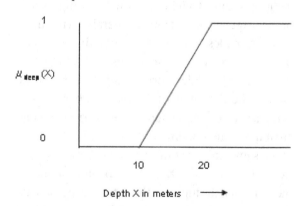

a membership function for a linguistic term representing the depth in a particular area in which "deep" is any depth greater than 20 meters, but between 10 and 20 meters it is "deep" to some degree.

One fuzzy set concept used in modeling uncertainty in databases is the similarity relation, S(x, y), denoted also as xSy (Buckles & Petry 1982). For a given domain D this is a mapping of every pair of values in the particular domain onto the unit interval [0, 1], which reflects the level of similarity between them. A similarity relation is reflexive and symmetric as a traditional identity relation. However, special forms of transitivity are used. So a similarity relation has the following three properties for x, y, z $\in$ D (Zadeh, 1970):

1. **Reflexive:** $s_D(x, x) = 1$
2. **Symmetric:** $s_D(x, y) = s_D(y, x)$
3. **Transitive:** $s_D(x, z) \geq Max_y (Min [s_D(x, y), s_D(y, z)])$

So we can see that there are different aspects of uncertainty dealt with in fuzzy set compared to rough set representations. The major rough set concepts of interest are the use of an indiscernibility relation to partition domains into equivalence classes and the concept of lower and upper approximation regions to allow the distinction between certain and possible, or partial, inclusion in a rough set. The indiscernibility relation allows us to group items based on some definition of 'equivalence' as it relates to the application domain.

A complementary approach to rough set uncertainty management is fuzzy set theory. Instead of the "yes-maybe-no" approach to belonging to a set, a more gradual membership value approach is used. An object belongs to a fuzzy set to some degree. This contrasts with the more discrete representation of uncertainty from indiscernibility relations or rough set theory.

Concept Hierarchies and Generalization

Generalization is a broad concept that has been used in several contexts. One is the idea of data summarization, a process of grouping data, enabling transformation of similar item sets, stored originally in a database at the low (primitive) level, into more abstract conceptual representations. Summarization of data is typically performed with utilization of concept hierarchies ((Cai, Cercone, & Han, 1991; Han, 1995), which in ordinary databases are considered to be a part of background knowledge. One approach is the use of linguistically quantified propositions to summarize the content of a database, by providing a general characterization of the analyzed data (Yager, 1991; Kacprzyk, 1999). There have also been several approaches to the use of fuzzy hierarchies for data generalization (Lee & Kim, 1997; Raschia & Mouaddib, 2002; Petry & Zhao, 2009). In a previous research effort (Yager & Petry, 2006), one author developed an approach to data summarization that involves aspects of generalization and compression using concept hierarchies and ontologies.

Now consider an example of data generalization letting D= {Oakland, San Jose, …., Sacramento} be a set of cities. However for a particular application, this data may be at too low a level, i.e. too specific.

Figure 3 illustrates part of a concept hierarchy H_1 for an attribute Location, describing US cities based on the geographical location. This concept hierarchy represents some of the domain background knowledge we have a priori.

By ascending the hierarchy, for the attribute Location in the set D, the values San_Francisco, Santa_Cruz, Oakland, and San_Jose are generalized to the higher level category Bay_Area, while the value Sacramento is generalized to Sacramento_Metropolitan_Area. Thus $R_1 = G(D, H_1)$

Figure 3. Example concept hierarchy H₁ for cities in california

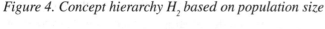

= {Bay_Area, Sacramento_Metropolitan_Area}, where G represents the generalization operation.

Depending on a semantic context, there may be a different hierarchy for the data being generalized. This may represent another application for the data or another context that is desired to be related to the original one. For the domain of cities we have discussed, another context might be the classification of the city based on population compared to the geographical context of Figure 3. This is illustrated by H₂ below in Figure 4.

The problem of how to provide appropriate concept hierarchies such as shown above represents one of the main scalability and efficiency issues for the attribute oriented generalization process. One way this can be approached is through the use of lexicons and thesauri to generalize a set data terms. This will usually lead to partially ordered sets or general graphs representing the relationships found from the thesauri. For example some of this can be obtained from using WordNet (2012), which is an online large lexical database of English words grouped into sets of cognitive synonyms. After the general structures are derived, tree substructures can be extracted. Useful hierarchies may then be selected by various heuristics or by some human intervention.

Concept Hierarchies Theory

We begin by providing the context for a concept hierarchy associated with an attribute. Let A be an attribute variable and let D(A) be the domain of possible data values of A. A concept hierarchy

Figure 4. Concept hierarchy H₂ based on population size

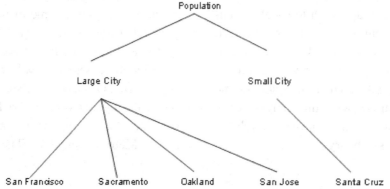

consists of a number of levels each of which is a partitioning of the space D(A). Furthermore, this partitioning becomes coarser and coarser as we go up the hierarchy. The lowest possible level of a hierarchy consists of a partitioning by the individual elements of D(A) and the highest level possible is the whole domain D(A). For the purposes of discussing concept hierarchies for generalization, since we ascend the hierarchy from the bottom or leaf nodes, we will index the hierarchy levels with lowest level denoted as 1.

Formally, under our assumptions, each level of a crisp concept hierarchy H as opposed to a fuzzy hierarchy, is an equivalence relationship. Thus at level k of the concept hierarchy we have a relationship $RL_k: D(A) \times D(A) \rightarrow \{0, 1\}$ that is $(x, y, z \in D(A))$:

1. **Reflexive:** $RL_k(x, x) = 1$,
2. **Symmetric:** $RL_k(x, y) = RL_k(y, x)$ and
3. **Transitive:** If $RL_k(x, y) = RL_k(y, z) = 1$ then $RL_k(x, z) = 1$.

The semantics of this relationship is that $RL_k(x, y) = 1$ indicates these two elements, x and y, are essentially the same.

As is well known such an equivalence relationship partitions the space D(A) into n_k disjoint subsets of D(A). These subsets are denoted by E_{kli}, the ith equivalence class for the partition of level k. So for x, y $\in E_{kli}$ we have $RL_k(x, y) = 1$.

The increased coarseness of partitioning as we ascend the concept hierarchy is reflected in the requirement that if k > j then for all pairs x and y we have $RL_k(x, y) \geq RL_j(x, y)$. Essentially this requires that if x and y are in the same class for level j of the hierarchy, they are in the same class in any higher-level k. This implies that if k > j then for any equivalence class E_{jlh} at level j there exists an equivalence class $E_{kl\,i}$ at level k such that $E_{jlh} \subseteq E_{kli}$

As we have discussed above, the indexing of the levels begins with the lowest level denoted 1. At this lowest level we have $RL_1(x, y) = 0$ iff x $\neq$ y, which means that any distinct data value is in its own class. If the highest level of the hierarchy, k=m, consists simply of one concept describing the whole domain D(A), then RL_m is such that $RL_m(x, y) = 1$ for all x and y.

So at each level k, the concept hierarchy is a partition of the set of possible data values D(A) into n_k categories (equivalence classes):

$$E_{kl1}, E_{kl2}, ..., E_{klnk}$$

If we have m levels then the concept hierarchy is a collection of m partitions of the space D(A). In particular the concept hierarchy consists of

Partition 1: E_{1li} for i = 1 to n_1
Partition 2: E_{2li} for i = 1 to n_2
Partition m: E_{mli} for i = 1 to n_m

We should note that while formally each category E_{kli} corresponds to a subset of the data space D(A), typically the category has an associated name C_{kli} which essentially describes the elements in E_{kli}. In general we make no distinction between these two uses of E_{kli}, as a subset of D(A) and as a denotation of the subset. However, when actually generalizing data for a given attribute in a tuple, we use the representative name, C_{kli}, in the generalized tuple.

GENERALIZATION DATA MINING

The basis of a generalization data mining approach rests on three aspects (Han & Kamber, 2006): (1) the set of data relevant to a given data mining task, (2) the expected form of knowledge to be discovered and (3) the background knowledge, which usually supports the whole process of knowledge acquisition. Generalization of data is typically performed with utilization of concept hierarchies, which in ordinary databases are considered to be a part of background knowledge, and are indispensable for the process. We assume that for selected attributes, A_i, in the database, one or more concept hierarchies, H_k, are available to provide generalization for the attribute values. Consider an attribute specifying the cities of California. These cities can be related by various semantics such as population, politics, geography, etc, such as in Figures 3 and 4.

The idea of using concept hierarchies for attribute-oriented induction in data mining has been investigated by several research groups (Cai, Cercone, & Han, 1991; Han, 1994; Carter & Hamilton, 1998; Hilderman, Hamilton, & Cercone, 1999). Generalization of database objects is performed on an attribute-by-attribute basis, applying a separate concept hierarchy for each of the generalized attributes included in the relation of task-relevant data.

The basic steps / guidelines for attribute-oriented generalization in relational database are summarized below (Cai, Cercone, & Han, 1991):

1.   An initial query Q to the database DB provides the starting generalization relation

$R_G (A_1, \ldots A_n)$ which contains the set of data that is relevant to the user's generalization interest.

$$Q(DB) \Rightarrow R_G$$

2.   Let $D(A_i)$ be the domain set of the attribute A_i in the database DB and $D_G(A_i)$ be the corresponding set of distinct values in R_G. Note $| D(A_i) |$ is the cardinality of $D(A_i)$. After the query Q, we will have $|D_G(A_i)| \leq | D(A_i) |$. Now if there is a large set of distinct values for an attribute A_i in R_G but there is no higher level concept in any H_k provided for the attribute, it should be removed in the generalization process. That is if

$$| D_G (A_i) | \geq N_{Large} (A_i)$$

and generalization is not possible for A_i then

$R'_G (A_1, \ldots A_{i-1}, A_{i+1} \ldots A_n) \leftarrow R_G (A_1, \ldots A_{i-1}, A_i, A_{i+1} \ldots A_n)$

When all such attributes have been deleted we can show the relation re-indexed for convenience as

$R'_G (A_1, \ldots A_m)$ where $m = n - \#$ of deleted attributes

For this step we could assume in general that there is a supplied threshold $N_{Large} (A_i)$ of distinct values for each attribute A_i. Such a threshold could be expressed as a fuzzy bound to represent the linguistic term "Large".

3.   Assume a hierarchy H_k is now available that generalizes the values, $D_G(A_i)$, for some attribute A_i. If there exists a higher-level concept in the concept tree for a specific attribute value of a tuple t_r, the substitution of the value by its higher-level concept generalizes the tuple. Minimal generalization should be enforced by ascending the tree one level at a time.

For example assume some subset $S = \{x_1, x_2, x_3\}$, $S \subseteq D_G(A_i)$, of values generalizes to the concept z_p in H_k (see Figure 5).

Figure 5. Portion of a concept hierarchy H_k for attribute A_i

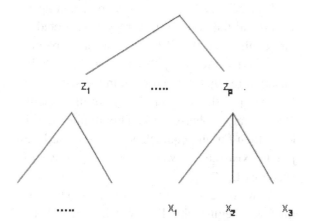

Then, since the value, v_{ri} of A_i, is x_2 we have

$$t_r (v_{r1}, \ldots v_{ri} = z_p, v_{r(i+1)}, \ldots) \leftarrow t_r (v_{r1}, \ldots v_{ri} = x_2, v_{r(i+1)}, \ldots)$$

4. As the tuples of the relation R_G are generalized as in step 3 above some may become similar or equal and so should not be maintained as "duplicates" in R'_G. Let $S(t_r, t_s)$ be the similarity of the two tuples. If two generalized tuples have become similar enough they are merged, and an attribute, A_{Count}, is added to keep track of how many tuples have been merged to form the current generalized tuple. So if

$$S(t_r, t_s) = 1, \text{ then}$$

$$t_r (v_{r1}, \ldots v_{ri}, \ldots) = t_s (v_{s1}, \ldots v_{si}, \ldots)$$

and we have the merger of these tuples

$$t' (v_1 = v_{r1} = v_{s1}, \ldots v_i = v_{ri} = v_{si} \ldots v_{Count} = 2)$$

The value of the count of a tuple should be carried to its generalized tuple and the counts should be accumulated when merging identical tuples in generalization.

For databases that utilize representations of uncertainty such as fuzzy (Petry, 1996) and rough databases (Beaubouef, Buckles, Petry, 1995), determination of the similarity of tuples is more complex than with exact matching as above. In such cases we may have $S(t_r, t_s) < 1$. However this does not imply that these tuples should not be merged. For these databases we could have a similarity threshold T_S and if

$$S(t_r, t_s) > T_S$$

then the two tuples should be merged. The form of the resultant merged tuple would depend on the database representation.

5. The generalization process is controlled by providing thresholds that specify how far the attribute induction process should proceed. For example if the number of distinct values of an attribute in the given relation is larger than the attribute generalization threshold value, further generalization on this attribute should be performed. Also if the number of tuples in a generalized relation is larger than the tuple generalization threshold value, the generalization should continue. An alternative approach in (Yager & Petry, 2006) presents the idea that the usefulness of a summarization is largely based on the purpose for which the user will employ the information provided in the summary. If the categories used in a summary are at a level too high in the concept hierarchy they may be too broad (imprecise) for the user's purpose. Such a criterion can be formulated by considering the similarity of the user's objectives and the concepts at a particular level in the hierarchy.

The user can examine and utilize the results of the generalized data in number of ways. One technique is to represent the conditions for a class of the data by extracting characteristic rules from generalized data. Each tuple relevant to the class represents a disjunct of a rule where the count attribute is used to formulate condition strength. Characteristic rules will present the conditions characterizing the particular class of interest.

GENERALIZATION IN TERMS OF PARTITIONS

We will find it useful to describe attribute generalization in terms of the preceding hierarchy concepts notation. We will focus on simple one attribute relation $R(A_1)$ to begin our discussion where $D(A_1)$ is the domain of values for A_1. Assume at level k in a concept hierarchy we have

E_{kl1} , E_{kl2} , …..

For the relation $R(A_1)$ the specific database data is $D(A_1)' \subseteq D(A_1)$ in general. Corresponding to this subset of data we have E'_{kli}

$$E'_{kli} \subseteq E_{kli}$$

Some E'_{kli} may be empty, i.e., none of the specific data values in R generalize to the concept C_{kli} .

In our simplified case of a single attribute relation E'_{kli} corresponds to those tuples that are merged. So the merged tuple is

$$t' (C_{kli}, |E'_{kli}|)$$

where the cardinality of E'_{kli} is the count, the number of tuples merged into t'. The number of tuples in the single attribute relation R after generalization to a level k is

$$N = \sum_{i\,=\,1,..n_k} \{1 \text{ if } E'_{k|i} \neq \varnothing;\ 0 \text{ otherwise } \}$$

For a relation with more than one attribute – say 2 attributes – $R(A_1, A_2)$ then when we generalize on A_1 as above it is possible that not all tuples can be merged. That is we may have two generalized tuples in which the values of A_2 are different, even after generalization, such as

$$t'(C_{kli}, C_{klp}) \neq t'(C_{kli}, C_{klq})$$

which cannot be merged since $C_{klp} \neq C_{klq}$. If R' is the relation after merging then we see that N is a lower bound on the size (number of tuples) of R'

$$|R'| \geq N$$

We have represented generalization of crisp data using crisp hierarchies. Next we must consider the cases where we have fuzzy data or/and fuzzy hierarchies.

Attribute generalization should not be mistaken for simple record summarization. The appropriate attribute-oriented generalization allows extraction of knowledge on a specific abstraction level but without omitting even rare attribute values. It might occur that such atypical values, despite being initially (at low level of the generalization hierarchy) infrequent, can sum up to quite impressive cardinalities when generalized to a sufficiently high abstraction level, which can then strongly influence sometimes the suspected proportions among the original data.

Relative to efficiency and scalability, the two of the earliest introduced attribute generalization algorithms are O(n log n) (Cai, Cercone, & Han, 1991) and O(np) (Han, 1994) where n is the number of input tuples and p the number of tuples in the generalized relation. Both of these require O(n) space that, for large input, causes memory problems. Enhanced approaches were developed by Carter and Hamilton (1998). One called Generalize DataBase Relation was a fast, space efficient, on-line algorithm that takes the same input and produces the same output as the earlier approaches, but executes in O(*n*) time. Another algorithm is also incremental and allows fast re-generalization of previous results without rereading any input data.

GENERALIZATION WITH UNCERTAIN HIERARCHIES

Generalization with Fuzzy Hierarchies

Fuzzy hierarchies enable the expression of partial ISA relationships with membership values as fraction numbers between two incident concept nodes (Lee & Kim, 1997). For fuzzy hierarchies, a concept is regarded as a partial specification of its upper concept with the corresponding membership degree μ in the [0, 1] interval. If μ = 1, there is a complete specification as in crisp concept hierarchies.

Next we need to describe a fuzzy hierarchy as was done for a crisp concept hierarchy in terms of partitions. For a fuzzy hierarchy at each level k we have a defining fuzzy relationship

$$Z_k : X \times X \rightarrow [0, 1]$$

Such a fuzzy relationship naturally leads to fuzzy equivalence classes (Ciric, Ignjatovic, & Bogdanovi, 2007) of concepts at each level k of the corresponding hierarchy. However, the sets of these fuzzy equivalence classes are fuzzy sets and as a consequence do not form a formal set partitioning of a domain as for crisp equivalence classes (Ovchinnikov, 1991). So rather than a partitioning of the domain X, we have a set decomposition. At each level this is D_{kl1}, D_{kl2}, .. where in general

$$D_{kli} \cap D_{klj} \neq \varnothing$$

This implies that there may not be a unique concept at level k to which a value at level k-1 generalizes. Graphically we can illustrate this in Figure 6.

So D_{kli} corresponding to C_{kli} is the set $\{...p,q,r,...\}$ and D_{klj} representing C_{klj} is $\{...r,s,t...\}$. An overlapping value such as r has a degree of membership $\mu_{kli}(r)$ in D_{kli} and $\mu_{klj}(r)$ in D_{klj} as determined by Z_k.

From Figure 6 we see that for the single attribute relation as previously described a tuple $t(A_1 = r)$ will generalize to two tuples, given that we do not want to allow non-first normal form tuples with a set of values for an attribute. Note that in general there may be cases in which a given tuple generalizes to more than two tuples. This depends on the number of concepts a lower-level concept is related to in a particular fuzzy hierarchy. In the case of Figure 6 we would generalize t to

$$t'_1 (A_1 = C_{kli}), t'_2 (A_1 = C_{klj})$$

However, a tuple with an attribute partially belonging to the generalized tuple is not identical to the one with an attribute which is a complete specification to the generalized tuple when we count the contributions. If n of these also correspond to other concepts then these n are being "double counted" (in general multiply counted). This distorts the count accumulated during generalization. Tuples are counted each time they generalize in fuzzy hierarchy regardless of the membership degrees in the hierarchy. So we additionally introduce a new attribute, A_{HCount}, to resolve this problem where its value is based on the membership degree of generalized attribute. This count can then be used to produce the value of the strength S in extracted rules.

Figure 6. Fuzzy hierarchy

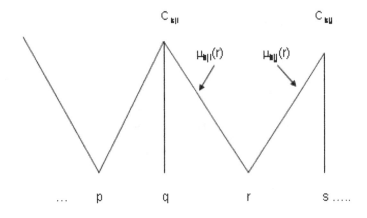

Suppose generalization is performed on a relation with the data: (San_Francisco, San_Jose, Santa Cruz, Sacramento), using the fuzzy concept hierarchy illustrated in Figure 7. After one step of a generalization, we have

$$E'_{211} = \{ \text{San\_Francisco, San\_Jose, Santa Cruz, Sacramento} \}$$

and for the corresponding generalized tuple with A1 = Bay Area

$$A_{HCount} (\text{Bay Area}) = \Sigma (1.0, 0.5, 0.9, 0.3) = 2.7$$

Note this contrasts with the ordinary count of 4 based on the four merged tuples. Similarly we obtain a generalized tuple corresponding to Sacramento_Metropolitan_Area with both counts equal to one; so the original tuple corresponding to Sacramento has been counted in both generalized tuples.

Generalization of Rough Data with Crisp Hierarchies

In the previous section a hierarchy was derived for a particular partitioning on a particular universe. However, in attribute oriented induction, we do not necessarily have all members of the domain represented, nor are we concerned with all possible combinations of relationships of roughness.

What we are interested in is how the rough data fit into our concept hierarchy for generalization concepts of interest to us.

In this section, we focus on the generalization process as applied to attribute-oriented induction in a rough database. Recall that tuples of a rough relation may be in non-first normal form, and each rough relation is made up of tuples that are part of the lower approximation region and also those of the boundary region of the upper approximation. These denote "certain" and "possible" information, respectively. For the simplest case, let us consider a relation schema $R(A_1)$, where R has one attribute, A_1, the domain of A_1 is U = {A, B, C, D, E, F, G}, and the equivalence relation representing the indiscernibility is {[A, B], [C, D], [E, F, G]}. For our tuples, there are several possibilities: (A), which is equal to (B), (C) = (D), and (E) = (F) = (G). We might also have because of the non-first normal form requirement, tuples of the form ({A, C}) or ({A, D, F}), for example, and any of these tuples may belong to either the lower or upper approximation region of the rough relation. In this case of one attribute, we generalize to higher level concepts and the tuple remains in the upper or lower approximation region of the generalized concept, adding one to the count for it. A count is maintained for certain information, and a separate count for possible information, at each level in the concept hierarchy.

Figure 7. Example for fuzzy concept hierarchies

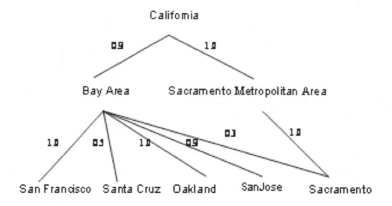

Consider a particular example for color of animals. Let U = {white, tan, yellow, light-gray, brown, black, red-brown, beige, dark-brown, ebony}. A hierarchy as shown in Figure 8 might exist.

For the example, to follow this particular hierarchy, tuples could be single values, or values that are very similar. We could have a tuple (yellow) that would generalize to Light-browns, then to Light-colored, then to Any Color. It would remain in its original approximation region and it would add one to the count on its way up for that approximation region. We might also have tuples of the form ({yellow, beige}), but not of the form ({yellow, black}) since that cannot be generalized based on this concept hierarchy. For crisp hierarchy of rough data both certain and possible rules are generated. More complicated hierarchies could be defined based on more than one attribute. We next investigate rough hierarchies.

Generalization of Crisp Data with Rough Hierarchy

In a rough hierarchy we allow generalization to occur in multiple ways, which leads additionally to "possible" generalizations rather than all "certain" ones. For example, assume our domain included another color, *dark-Tan*, which could generalize to both *Light-Browns* and *Browns*. It would then be an element of the upper approximation region for each of the generalized tuples. The count is

evenly divided amongst the two since this case should not be as strong as one that generalizes to exactly one concept. Here the count for each of the two generalizations would be .5. For the general case, a tuple *t* that generalizes to n higher level concepts (n>1) becomes an upper approximation or uncertain tuple having count 1/n.

Rough Generalization of Rough Data in Rough Hierarchy

Here we combine the uncertainty from the database itself (generalization of rough data with crisp hierarchies) with the uncertainty introduced in the rough hierarchy. There are four cases to consider:

1. Rough tuple is certain and generalizes to one concept.
2. Rough tuple is uncertain and generalizes to one concept.
3. Rough tuple is certain and generalizes to n concepts.
4. Rough tuple is uncertain and generalizes to n concepts.

For cases 1 and 2, we simply generalize the tuple and add one to its count. It remains in the same approximation region to which it originally belonged (certain or uncertain). For case 3 we generalize the tuple, but this time it becomes part of the uncertain region of each of the n concepts to which it generalizes and its count is computed as 1/n. Case 4 is done similarly.

Example Implementation of Generalization with Fuzzy Hierarchies

A prototype example was implemented in C++ to illustrate data generalization with fuzzy concept hierarchies (Petry & Zhao, 2009). A representative data set of employee evaluation records of a typical firm was used, Company_Evaluations, with the schema:

Figure 8. Hierarchy for generalization of attribute 'color' of animals

- **Company_Evaluations:** ID, Age, Position, Degree, Major, Years of Employment, Evaluation.

The intention of the generalization was to show how to provide a human resources department with common characteristics of employees having better evaluations, which could focus a company's recruiting/retention process Table 1 shows a representative selection of 220 employee tuples that were used in the examples.

Data generalization was carried out using fuzzy hierarchies using the tuples of better performing employees, i.e. Evaluation >0.70 Figures 9 and 10 show the fuzzy hierarchies used for the attributes *Major* and *Years_Of_Employment*.

With the attribute generalization threshold set to 3, by performing attribute removal and multi-attribute generalization on *Major* and *Years_Of_ Employment*, the generalized relation is shown in Table 2

As previously discussed, HCount is used to reflect the partial contributions of the fuzzy hierarchy to the generalized tuples. One conclusion that might be drawn is that more recent hires, especially in the technology areas, evaluated well. So the human resources department might consider responding by focusing more on the retention of such higher performing employees.

FUTURE RESEARCH DIRECTIONS

Other data mining techniques can also make use of imprecise concept hierarchies. In particular the process to extract association rules will use some sort of a hierarchy (Agrawal, Imielinski, & Swami, 1993) and could benefit by consideration of fuzzy and rough hierarchies. Fuzzy association rules also have been considered by a number of researchers (Bosc & Pivert, 2001; Lee, 2001). Both attribute generalization and association rule extraction have been investigated for the domain of spatial data (Koperski & Han, 1995; Petry, 2011) and further research on the naturally occurring uncertainty of spatial data hierarchies is worthwhile. Additionally, all of these approaches could benefit from extensions of data mining approaches with other uncertainty approaches such as fuzzy rough sets (Nanda & Majumdar, 1992) and Type-2 fuzzy sets (Mendel, 2007).

CONCLUSION

Data mining has proven to be an important tool in this age of massive data collection, Internet applications, and smart device technology. It allows for the discovery of interesting patterns and rules that can provide information for managerial analysis and decision making as well as providing insight into new ideas. Concept hierarchies play

Table 1. Company Evaluations

ID	Age	Position	Degree	Major	Years Employed	Evaluation
0007	36	Engineer	Undergraduate	Electrical Engineering	8	0.91
0016	38	R&D	Doctorate	Computer Science	21	0.71
0019	27	Secretary	Undergraduate	Political Science	4	0.25
0020	53	Technician	Community College	Mechanical Engineering	15	0.77
0021	32	Engineer	Non Univ College	Math	6	0.40
0029	31	Marketing	Undergraduate	Music	6	0.83
0033	35	Engineer	Undergrad Plus	Physics	5	0.71

Table 2. Generalized relation by ascending fuzzy hierarchies on attributes Major and Years Of_Employment

Major	Years of Employment	Count	HCount
Non_Technology	Mature	26	12.3
Non_Technology	Recent	70	40.4
Technology	Mature	87	42.1
Technology	Recent	259	125.2

Figure 9. A fuzzy concept hierarchy tree for attribute major

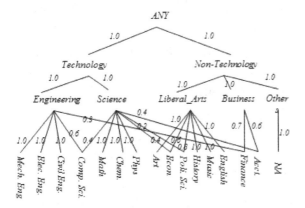

an important role in attribute oriented induction for data mining. These techniques can also be applied to the more real-world databases that incorporate uncertainty management such as those based on fuzzy and rough set techniques. This paper investigated the theory behind fuzzy and rough sets and their use in the establishment of concept hierarchies.

A formalism for concept hierarchies and their use in the detailed attribute generalization algorithm was described. Several examples and discussions of these approaches were also provided. The use of these formalisms as a way to integrate uncertainty management as part of the data mining process allows for improved results in applications in a wide variety of areas such as business and marketing, scientific modeling and geographic information systems, health care, and homeland security to name a few.

ACKNOWLEDGMENT

We would like to thank the Naval Research Laboratory's Base Program, Program Element No. 0602435N for sponsoring this research.

Figure 10. A fuzzy concept hierarchy tree for attribute Years_Of_Employment

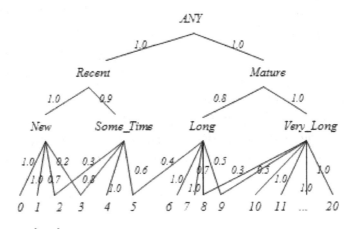

REFERENCES

Agrawal, R., Imielinski, T., & Swami, A. (1993). Mining association rules between sets of items in large databases. In *Proceedings of the 1993 ACM-SIGMOD International Conference on Management of Data* (pp. 207-216). New York, NY: ACM Press.

Beaubouef, T., & Petry, F. (1994). Rough querying of crisp data in relational databases. In *Third Int. Workshop on Rough Sets and Soft Computing (RSSC'94)* (pp. 34-41).Higher School of Economics.

Beaubouef, T., Petry, F., & Buckles, B. (1995). Extension of the relational database and its algebra with rough set techniques. *Computational Intelligence, 11*, 233–245. doi:10.1111/j.1467-8640.1995.tb00030.x

Bosc, P., & Pivert, O. (2001). On some fuzzy extensions of association rules. In *Proceedingsof IFSA-NAFIPS 2001* (pp. 1104–1109). Piscataway, NJ: IEEE Press. doi:10.1109/NAFIPS.2001.944759

Buckles, B., & Petry, F. (1982). A fuzzy representation for relational data bases. *International Journal of Fuzzy Sets and Systems, 7*, 213–226. doi:10.1016/0165-0114(82)90052-5

Cai, Y., Cercone, N., & Han, J. (1991). Attribute-oriented induction in relational databases. In Piatetsky-Shapiro, G., & Frawley, J. (Eds.), *Knowledge discovery in databases* (pp. 213–228). Boston, MA: MIT Press.

Carter, C., & Hamilton, H. (1998). Efficient attribute-oriented generalization for knowledge discovery from large databases. *IEEE Transactions on Knowledge and Data Engineering, 10*, 193–208. doi:10.1109/69.683752

Chopra, B., Bhambri, V., & Krishan, B. (2005). Implementation of data mining techniques for strategic CRM issues. *International Journal of Computer Technology and Applications, 2*(4), 879–883.

Ciric, M., Ignjatovic, J., & Bogdanovi, S. (2007). Fuzzy equivalence relations and their equivalence classes. *International Journal of Fuzzy Sets and Systems, 158*(12), 1295–1313. doi:10.1016/j.fss.2007.01.010

Grossman, R., Kamath, C., Kegelmeyer, P., & Kumar, V. (2001). *Data mining for scientific and engineering applications*. Boston, MA: Kluwer Publishers. doi:10.1007/978-1-4615-1733-7

Grzymala-Busse, J. (1991). *Managing uncertainty in expert systems*. Boston, MA: Kluwer Academic Publishers. doi:10.1007/978-1-4615-3982-7

Han, J. (1994). Towards efficient induction mechanisms in database systems. *Theoretical Computer Science, 133*, 361–385. doi:10.1016/0304-3975(94)90194-5

Han, J., & Kamber, M. (2006). *Data mining: Concepts and techniques* (2nd ed.). San Diego, CA: Academic Press.

Hilderman, R., Hamilton, H., & Cercone, N. (1999). Data mining in large databases using domain generalization graphs. *Journal of Intelligent Information Systems, 13*(3), 195–234. doi:10.1023/A:1008769516670

Kacprzyk, J. (1999). Fuzzy logic for linguistic summarization of databases. In *Proc. 8th Int'l Conf. on Fuzzy Systems* (pp. 813-818). IEEE.

Kim, Y., Kim, U., Jung, M., Kang, W., & Noh, Y. (2009). Mining association rules for RFID data with concept hierarchy. In *Proceedings of the 11th international conference on Advanced Communication Technology* (Vol. 2, pp. 1002-1006). Piscataway, NJ: IEEE Press.

Koh, H., & Tan, G. (2005). Data mining applications in healthcare. *Journal of Healthcare Information Management, 19*(2), 64–72.

Komorowski, J., Pawlak, Z., & Polkowski, L. (1999). Rough sets: A tutorial. In Pal, S., & Skowron, A. (Eds.), *Rough fuzzy hybridization: A new trend in decision-making* (pp. 3–98). Singapore: Springer-Verlag.

Koperski, K., & Han, J. (1995). Discovery of spatial association rules in geographic information databases. In *Proceedings of 4th International Symposium on Large Spatial Databases* (pp. 47-66). Berlin, Germany: Springer-Verlag.

Lee, D., & Kim, M. (1997). Database summarization using fuzzy ISA hierarchies. *IEEE Transactions on Systems, Man, and Cybernetics - part B, 27*(1), 68–78. doi:10.1109/3477.552186

Lee, K. (2001). Mining generalized fuzzy quantitative association rules with fuzzy generalization hierarchies. In *Proceedings of IFSA-NAFIPS 2001* (pp. 2977-2982). Piscataway NJ: IEEE Press.

Malerba, D., Lisi, F., Appice, A., & Sblendorio, F. (2002). Mining spatial association rules in census data: A relational approach. *Research in Official Statistics, 5*(1), 19–44.

Mendel, J. (2007). Type-2 fuzzy sets and systems: An overview. *IEEE Comp. Intell Mag., 2*(10), 20–29.

Miller, H., & Han, J. (2001). Geographic data mining and knowledge discovery: An overview. In Miller, H. J., & Han, J. (Eds.), *Geographic data mining and knowledge discovery* (pp. 3–32). London, UK: Taylor and Francis. doi:10.4324/9780203468029_chapter_1

Nanda, S., & Majumdar, S. (1992). Fuzzy rough sets. *Fuzzy Sets and Systems, 45*, 157–160. doi:10.1016/0165-0114(92)90114-J

Nguyen, H., & Walker, E. (2005). *A first course in fuzzy logic* (3rd ed.). Boca Raton, FL: CRC press.

Ovchinnikov, S. (1991). Similarity relations, fuzzy partitions and fuzzy orderings. *International Journal of Fuzzy Sets and Systems, 40*, 107–126. doi:10.1016/0165-0114(91)90048-U

Pawlak, Z. (1984). Rough sets. *International Journal of Man-Machine Studies, 21*, 127–134. doi:10.1016/S0020-7373(84)80062-0

Pawlak, Z. (1991). *Rough sets: Theoretical aspects of reasoning about data.* Norwell, MA: Kluwer Academic Publishers.

Petry, F. (1996). *Fuzzy databases: Principles and application.* Norwell, MA: Kluwer Academic Publishers. doi:10.1007/978-1-4613-1319-9

Petry, F. (2011). Data discovery approaches for vague spatial data. In Igelnik, B. (Ed.), *Computational modeling and simulation of intellect* (pp. 342–360). Hershey, PA: IGI Global. doi:10.4018/978-1-60960-551-3.ch014

Petry, F., & Yager, R. (2008). Evidence resolution using concept hierarchies. *IEEE Transactions on Fuzzy Systems, 16*(2), 299–308. doi:10.1109/TFUZZ.2007.895966

Petry, F., & Zhao, L. (2009). Data mining by attribute generalization with fuzzy hierarchies in fuzzy databases. *Fuzzy Sets and Systems, 160*(15), 2206–2223. doi:10.1016/j.fss.2009.02.014

Piazza, P. (2002). Health alerts to fight bioterror. *Security Management, 46*(5), 40.

Pohle, C., & Spiliopoulou, M. (2002). Building and exploiting ad hoc concept hierarchies for Web log analysis. In *Proceedings of the 4th International Conference on Data Warehousing and Knowledge Discovery* (pp. 83-93). London, UK: Springer-Verlag.

Rafalski, E. (2002). Using data mining and data repository methods to identify marketing opportunities in healthcare. *Journal of Consumer Marketing, 19*(7), 607–613. doi:10.1108/07363760210451429

Raschia, R., & Mouaddib, N. (2002). SAINTETIQ: A fuzzy set-based approach to database summarization. *Fuzzy Sets and Systems*, *129*, 37–162. doi:10.1016/S0165-0114(01)00197-X

Slowinski, R. (1992). A generalization of the indiscernibility relation for rough sets analysis of quantitative information. *Rivista di Matematica per le Scienze Economiche e Sociali*, *15*(1), 65–78. doi:10.1007/BF02086527

Srinivasan, P. (1991). The importance of rough approximations for information retrieval. *International Journal of Man-Machine Studies*, *34*, 657–671. doi:10.1016/0020-7373(91)90017-2

Tan, P., Steinbach, M., & Kumar, V. (2005). *Introduction to data mining*. Boston, MA: Addison Wesley.

WordNet. (2012). Website. Retrieved from wordnet.princeton.edu

Yager, R. (1991). On linguistic summaries of data. In Piatesky-Shapiro, G., & Frawley, J. (Eds.), *Knowledge Discovery in Databases* (pp. 347–363). Boston, MA: MIT Press.

Yager, R., & Petry, F. (2006). A multicriteria approach to data summarization using concept ontologies. *IEEE Transactions on Fuzzy Systems*, *14*(6), 767–780. doi:10.1109/TFUZZ.2006.879954

Zadeh, L. (1970). Similarity relations and fuzzy orderings. *Information Sciences*, *3*, 177–200. doi:10.1016/S0020-0255(71)80005-1

ADDITIONAL READING

Angryk, R., Ladner, R., & Petry, F. (2005). Generalization data mining in fuzzy object-oriented databases. In Ma, Z. (Ed.), *Fuzzy object-oriented databases: Modeling and applications* (pp. 85–112). Hershey, PA: Idea Group Press.

Angryk, R., & Petry, F. (2003). Consistent fuzzy concept hierarchies for attribute generalization. In *Proceedings IASTED International Conference on Information and Knowledge Sharing* (pp. 158-193). Anaheim, CA: ACTA Press.

Angryk, R., & Petry, F. (2007). Attribute-oriented generalization in proximity and similarity-based relational database systems. *International Journal of Intelligent Systems*, *22*, 763–779. doi:10.1002/int.20227

Au, W., & Chan, K. (2003). Mining fuzzy association rules in a bank-account database. *IEEE Transactions on Fuzzy Systems*, *11*, 238–248. doi:10.1109/TFUZZ.2003.809901

Beaubouef, T., Buckles, B., & Petry, F. (2007). An attribute-oriented approach for knowledge discovery in rough relational databases. In *Proc. of FLAIRS- 20* (pp. 507-09). Association for the Advancement for Artificial Intelligence.

Chen, G., Wei, Q., & Kerre, E. (2000). Fuzzy data mining: Discovery of fuzzy generalized association rules. In Bordogna, G., & Pasi, G. (Eds.), *Recent issues on fuzzy databases* (pp. 45–66). Heidelberg, Germany: Physica-Verlag. doi:10.1007/978-3-7908-1845-1_3

Cubero, J., Medina, J., Pons, O., & Vila, M. (1999). Data summarization in relational databases through fuzzy dependencies. *Information Sciences*, *121*, 233–270. doi:10.1016/S0020-0255(99)00104-8

Delgado, M., Marin, N., Sanchez, D., & Vila, M. (2003). Fuzzy association rules: General model and applications. *IEEE Transactions on Fuzzy Systems*, *11*, 214–225. doi:10.1109/TFUZZ.2003.809896

Dubois, D., & Prade, H. (2000). Fuzzy sets in data summaries - outline of a new approach. In *Proc. 8th Int'l Conf. on Information Processing and Management of Uncertainty in Knowledge-Based Systems* (pp. 1035-1040). Berlin, Germany: Springer.

Elmasri, R., & Navathe, S. (2010). *Fundamentals of database systems* (6th ed.). Boston, MA: Addison Wesley.

Feng, I., & Dillon, T. (2003). Using fuzzy linguistic representations to provide explanatory semantics for data warehouses. *IEEE Transactions on Knowledge and Data Engineering, 15*, 86–102. doi:10.1109/TKDE.2003.1161584

George, R., Srikanth, R., Petry, F., & Buckles, B. (1996). Uncertainty management issues in the object-oriented data model. *IEEE Transactions on Fuzzy Systems, 4*, 179–192. doi:10.1109/91.493911

Gyenesei, A. (2001). A fuzzy approach for mining quantitative association rules. *Acta Cybernetica, 15*, 305–320.

Han, J. (1995). Mining knowledge at multiple concept levels. In *Proc. 4ᵗʰ International Conf. on Information and Knowledge Management* (pp. 19-24). New York, NY: ACM Press.

Han, J., Cai, Y., & Cercone, N. (1992). Knowledge discovery in databases: An attribute-oriented approach. In *Proceedings of 18ᵗʰ VLDB Conf.* (pp. 547-559).

Han, J., Koperski, K., & Stefanovic, N. (1997). GeoMiner: A system prototype for spatial data mining. In *Proceedings of the 1997 ACM-SIGMOD International Conference on Management of Data* (pp. 553-556). New York, NY: ACM Press.

Hirota, K., & Pedrycz, W. (1999). Fuzzy computing for data mining. *Proceedings of the IEEE, 87*, 1575–1599. doi:10.1109/5.784240

Hong, T., Lin, K. K., & Wang, S. (2003). Fuzzy data mining for interesting generalized association rules. *Fuzzy Sets and Systems, 138*, 255–269. doi:10.1016/S0165-0114(02)00272-5

Kuok, C., Fu, A., & Wong, H. (1998). Mining fuzzy association rules in databases. *SIGMOD Record, 27*, 41–46. doi:10.1145/273244.273257

Laurent, A. (2003). A new approach for the generation of fuzzy summaries based on fuzzy multidimensional databases. *Intelligent Data Analysis, 7*, 155–177.

Lipschutz, S. (1998). *Set theory and related topics.* New York, NY: McGraw-Hill.

Pawlak, Z. (1985). Rough sets and fuzzy sets. *Fuzzy Sets and Systems, 17*, 99–102. doi:10.1016/S0165-0114(85)80029-4

Polkowski, L. (2002). *Rough Sets.* Heidelberg, Germany: Physica Verlag.

Prade, H., & Testemale, C. (1984). Generalizing database relational algebra for the treatment of incomplete/uncertain information and vague queries. *Information Sciences, 34*, 115–143. doi:10.1016/0020-0255(84)90020-3

Shu, J., Tsang, E., & Yeung, D. (2001). Query fuzzy association rules in relational databases. [Piscataway, NJ: IEEE Press.]. *Proceedings of IFSA-NAFIPS, 2001*, 2989–2993.

Ughetto, I., Voglozin, W., & Mouaddib, N. (2008). Database querying with personalized vocabulary using data summaries. *International Journal of Fuzzy Sets and Systems, 159*, 2030–2046. doi:10.1016/j.fss.2008.02.015

Voglozin, W., Raschia, G., Ughetto, L., & Mouaddib, N. (2006). Querying a summary of a database. *International Journal of Intelligent Systems, 26*(1), 59–73.

Yen, J., & Langari, R. (1999). *Fuzzy logic: Intelligence, control and information.* Upper Saddle River, NJ: Prentice Hall.

Zhang, W. (1999). Mining fuzzy quantitative association rules. In *Proceedings of IEEE Int. Conference on Tools with Artificial Intelligence* (pp. 99-102). Piscataway, NJ: IEEE Press.

KEY TERMS AND DEFINITIONS

Association Rule: A rule that capture the idea of certain data items commonly occurring together.

Attribute–Oriented Induction: A process that summarizes large amounts of data by generalization using a concept hierarchy.

Concept Hierarchy: A tree structure in which the concepts or terms are related successively to parents in the tree that represent broader concepts covering several lower level concepts.

Data Mining: The process of applying a variety of algorithms to discover useful patterns and relationships from data.

Fuzzy Set: In ordinary crisp sets an element x either belongs to a given set or not (membership of x is either 0 or1). However for a fuzzy set an element x can have a degree of membership in set ranging from 0 to 1, i.e. in the interval [0, 1].

Generalization: The process of replacing more specific terms or concepts by more general or broader concepts.

Geographic Information System: A software system that provides a wide variety of tools to manipulate spatial data.

Rough Sets: A theory for the management of uncertainty based on an approximation space (indiscernibility) and approximation regions (lower and upper) that define complete and partial inclusion in the set.

Spatial Data: Geographic data that can be represented by points, lines, or areas.

Chapter 4
Efficiency and Scalability Methods in Cancer Detection Problems

Inna Stainvas
General Motors - Research & Development, Israel

Alexandra Manevitch
Siemens Computer Aided Diagnosis Ltd., Israel

ABSTRACT

Computer aided detection (CAD) system for cancer detection from X-ray images is highly requested by radiologists. For CAD systems to be successful, a large amount of data has to be collected. This poses new challenges for developing learning algorithms that are efficient and scalable to large dataset sizes. One way to achieve this efficiency is by using good feature selection.

INTRODUCTION

CAD system for cancer detection in mammography and chest X-ray (CXR) is a viable and efficient source of assistance to radiologists. The CAD systems are based on statistical modeling of cancer using data from collected X-ray images. These images are extremely heterogeneous due to substantial differences in the human population and in image acquisition conditions. For cancer detection modeling, large datasets representing this variability are required. Recently, this has

become possible due to an exceptional increase in computing power, storage capacity and networking technologies.

Today medical datasets are growing rapidly. This poses new challenges for developing learning algorithms that are both efficient and scalable to dataset size. There are two main approaches to address the challenge: by intelligently manipulating large amounts of data[1] and by reducing its dimensionality. Data manipulation is non-trivial for medical data. Firstly, this is due to the cost of data labeling by medical experts. Secondly, the medical data is imbalanced, i.e. the number of pathological cases is always insufficient. Thus, the

DOI: 10.4018/978-1-4666-3942-3.ch004

second approach emerges as an important one in medical applications. It is preferable to describe data succinctly, rather than manipulate it.

This chapter presents two new feature selection methods proposed by us. Feature selection is usually done in two steps referred to as filters and wrappers (Dash, 1997). In the filter stage the best features are selected based on some heuristic goodness measure such as mutual information (MI), Fisher discriminative measure, etc. This stage is unseen by the specific classifier and does not optimize the same goal as the classifier. Tuning to the classifier is done later in the wrapper stage. In this step, the best number of features or filter stage parameters optimizing the classifier is found. Whereas this two stage approach is good for reducing data dimensionality, it does not guarantee the optimality of a selected feature set for a given classifier.

Although many different feature goodness measures have been proposed, the stability of feature selection is an issue that has not been commonly addressed (Loscalzo, Yu, & Ding, 2009). Similar to Loscalzo et al. (2009), we separate features into clusters. But unlike this work, we utilize feature space clustering to provide diversity in feature selection. This is because features of different clusters are dissimilar and, as such, are independent of each other.

After separating the features into the clusters, we take the best features of a certain number from each cluster. Our selection is based on a new goodness measure which is a combination of feature's discriminative and stability powers. The balance between discrimination and stability is controlled by a regularization parameter. The final stability of feature selection is defined by us as stability of the classification results on the unseen data. The efficacy of the method is demonstrated on real data for cancer detection in CXR images.

Our second feature selection method is designed for a specific type of classifiers and is based on compressive sensing (CS). This method allows us to find features that are wired into a classifier's architecture instead of blindly selecting features on the basis of external heuristics and to train classifiers robustly. This method enables the training of classifiers in very high dimensional spaces and with a large amount data.

We adapted the compressive sensing approaches to find salient features required for classification. Similar to Davenport (2007), we constrain ourselves to a specific class of projective classifiers. These obtained features are wired into the classifiers' structure. Our feature selection is driven by the classification task, rather than by data reconstruction. Moreover, we avoid the usual two step feature selection procedure. Our method efficiently reduces the computational burden and is computationally "light-weight."

More specifically, we first randomly project the data into a lower dimensional space. Secondly, the classifier's weights are learned in this space. Lastly, the classifier's weights are reconstructed in the original feature space under the l_1 norm constraint that allows us to find a small subset of computed features. After feature selection is completed, the classifier is rebuilt once again. The efficiency of our technique is demonstrated with specially constructed synthetic data and with the medical application of finding cancer in mammography images.

Our feature selection methods not only alleviate computational burdens in model learning, but also lead to robust classifiers. In addition, our feature selection leads to interpretable models that are understandable by domain experts. Moreover, there is an extra gain in computational efficiency by extracting a small number of features from the X-ray images during a dataset creation.

BACKGROUND

In CAD, the goal is to detect malignant regions (lesions) in the images.

Though cancer detection problems from X-ray images have many commonalities, they also have many differences. The lesion detection in CXR images is difficult as other structures, such as bones and the heart overlap with lung tissues. In contrast with lung cancer detection from a single X-ray image, mammographic breast cancer detection is based on four images of the same person taken at the same time. These four images represent left and right breasts acquired from two viewing angles (Paredes, 2007).

Most of the CAD systems consist of the following three steps: (1) candidate generation, (2) feature extraction and (3) classification. In the first step, suspicious regions (lesion candidates) are found as blob-like structures for example, based on gradient field analysis (Valades, 2011). While this step detects most of the anomalies, the number of false positives is extremely high.

In the second step, features describing each lesion candidate are extracted. The features usually consist from two groups: a relatively small set of specific features and a huge number of standard texture features (Haralick, 1973; Wei, 1997). The specific features are elaborately designed to reflect the nature of the lesions, such as spiculation features, for example (Sampat, 2006). The texture features are usually the non-linear derivatives of the outputs of the bank of different types of filters or outputs of wavelet transforms. The number of specific features is in the hundreds and the number of texture-like may be in the thousands.

In the third step, the suspicious candidates should be classified as either malignant or not by reducing the number of false positives without decreasing the sensitivity. Problems of this type yield binary classifiers, where the goal is to discriminate data between two classes referred to as positive (pathologic) and negative. In the medical domain, the multiple instance learning concept (MIL) (Maron, 1998) is conventionally used to build the classifiers. According to this concept, the data is considered to be aggregated into the so called "bags" that can be positive or negative. The candidates that are close to the radiologist mark

are considered as belonging to a positive bag; all the other candidates are considered as negative. The classifier is considered to be successful, if at least one of the candidates from the positive bag is classified as malignant and all the negative candidates are classified as non-malignant. We use logistic regression binary classifiers with the MIL concept for cancer detection. Below we give a short review of this classifier.

Logistic Regression Classifier

The classifier optimization criterion is obtained as the maximum likelihood (ML) estimator of the weight vector $w \in R^n$ from the observed data D. The data D is considered to be aggregated into so called bags

$$\mathbf{x}_\mu, \mu = 1 \ldots S_M$$

that can be positive or negative. The bag-μ is considered to be negative if all its instances

$$x_\mu^s, s = 1 \ldots S_\mu$$

are negative; and positive if at least one its instance is positive. The final optimization criterion is expressed as

$$w^* = arg \max{}_w [log(p(D / w))]$$

where the log-likelihood of the data is defined as:

$$
\begin{aligned}
F(w; D) &= \log p(D \mid w) \\
&= \sum_{\mu=1}^{M} (y_\mu \log p_\mu + (1 - y_\mu) \log(1 - p_\mu))
\end{aligned}
\tag{1}
$$

$$p_\mu = p(y_\mu = 1 \mid \mathbf{x}_\mu) = 1 - \prod_{s=1}^{S_\mu} (1 - \sigma(w^t x_\mu^s)) \tag{2}$$

$$\sigma(z) = \frac{1}{1 + e^{-z}}$$

The final classification in our classifier is given by:

$$y = \begin{cases} 1, if\, w^t x > T_\theta \\ 0, if\, w^t x \le T_\theta \end{cases} \quad (3)$$

The T_θ parameter determines the operating point of the classifier and is set outside the training process by building the receiver operating characteristic (ROC) curve as T_θ is swept from $-\infty$ to ∞ (Fawcett, 2006). The ROC curve plots the sensitivity (fraction of true positives) versus specificity (fraction of false positives) for a binary classifier system. ROC analysis establishes a right trade-off in making diagnostic decision.

STABLE FEATURE SELECTION

As was explained earlier, in order for classifiers to be robust and efficient, the number of features has to be reduced. Usually the choice of good features is based on their discriminative power without taking into account their stability. In this section, we describe an algorithm that takes both these criteria into account.

The feature selection algorithm proposed by us consists of the following steps:

1. Divide features into groups $G_s, s = 1, 2, \ldots S$ using any reasonable clustering method. The number of clusters S is defined automatically.

2. Weigh each group G_s in order to redistribute the desired number of features N_d between the groups, so that

$$N_d = \sum_{s=1}^{S} N_s .$$

3. Score features inside each group G_s based on a criterion that is a combination of their discriminative and stability powers.
4. Select the best N_s features inside each group G_s according to their score.

The initial condition for the feature selection algorithm is the number of desired features to use. This number is usually dictated by computational limitations and we do not discuss this issue here.

Feature Clustering

Our main motivation in using feature clustering is to select diverse features as data in different clusters are expected to be dissimilar. In general any clustering algorithm can be used with features being perceived as n-dimensional vectors, where n is the number of data samples. As the number of data samples grows the feature vector lies in a higher dimensional space and clustering becomes a more difficult problem; this happens despite the intuition that with more data such a separation would be more feasible and robust. The simple trick to resolve the paradox is to constrain ourselves to clustering methods which are based on similarity measures.

We used the spectral clustering toolbox (Agarwal, 2002) for a normalized cut algorithm and its version with Nystrom approximation (Shi, 2000; Fowlkes, 2001) for clustering. The edge similarity weights of the Laplacian graph are defined as the absolute value of the correlation coefficient between the feature nodes. Before calculating the correlation coefficient, the features are shifted and scaled to have a zero-mean value and unit standard deviation. In other words, features are invariant to shift, scaling, and change of orientation.

The number of clusters is calculated automatically by considering all the possible data partitions with a different number of clusters running up to a predefined maximal number S_{max} and evaluating the quality of each partition. The clustering quality Q_M per partition with the number of clusters M is defined as the average worst pair-wise separability

$$Q_M = \frac{1}{M} \sum_{i=1}^{M} ncut(C_i, C_{i^*})$$

The cluster C_{i^*} is the worst separable cluster (the farthest cluster) from the cluster C_i and the separability *ncut* is measured as:

$$ncut(C_i, C_j) = cut(C_i, C_j)$$

$$(\frac{1}{asso(C_i, C_i \sqcup C_j)} + \frac{1}{asso(C_j, C_i \sqcup C_j)})$$

$$C_{i^*} = \arg \max_C ncut(C_i, C)$$

The standard notations as in (Shi, 2000) are accepted by us:

$$cut(A, B) = \sum_{u \in A, v \in B} w(u, v)$$

and

$$asso(A, V) = \sum_{u \in A, t \in V} w(u, t)$$

where V are all the nodes in the graph. The *asso* measures the total connection from nodes in A to all nodes in the graph and $w(u, v)$ is the similarity weight between two nodes u and v.

A small value means that the separation is good on average, so that the number of clusters M^* is defined as the one minimizing Q_M:

$$M^* = \arg \max_M Q_M.$$

Feature Scoring

A feature's quality inside the group is based on the hybrid criterion that balances between the feature's discriminative power S^{disc} and stability S^{stab} to data resampling. The balance between discrimination and stability is controlled by a regularization parameter $\lambda \in [0, 1]$:

$$S(\lambda) = \lambda S^{disc} + (1 - \lambda)S^{stab} \qquad (4)$$

The discriminative score S^{disc} is calculated as a standard Fisher discriminative score; while the stability is calculated with a type of bootstrap experiment. The data is randomly sampled several times into two disjoint halves and Fisher discriminative measures inside the positive and negative classes $S_k^{+,disc}, S_k^{-,disc}$ for each sampling $k = 1, \dots K$ are calculated. The larger is one of these measures, the less stable the feature is, as the samples inside the class should be non-separable. It is natural to define an instability measure as the average of the worst instability, i.e.

$$S^{instab} = \sum_{k=1}^{K} \max(S_k^{+,disc}, S_k^{-,disc})$$

we defined stability as the negative value of:

$$S^{stab} = -S^{instab}$$

The Kolmogorov-Smirnov test may be an alternative to this stability measure.

Feature Capacity Inside the Groups

The single input parameter to our algorithm is the number of desired features N_d. We redistribute this number of features between the groups based on their capacities as:

$$N_s = \max(1, round(N_d w_s))$$

The features weighing per group:

$$s = 1, \ldots, N_c$$

is defined as

$$w_s = (C_s)^d / \sum_{k=1}^{N_c} (C_k)^d$$

where C_s is a cluster capacity (a number of features in the cluster). This reweighing strategy reflects our belief that the number of desired features per group grows with the group's capacity. In general as d decreases towards 0, the dependency between a desired number of features in a cluster and its capacity weakens. In other words, the parameter d controls the degree of our belief in such a dependency. We found that a degree equal to $d = 0.3$ led to good results in many of our experiments.

It is possible that, weighing based on the intrinsic dimensionality of the group measured by using principal component analysis (PCA) or measuring the average discrimination power of the group (or some type of a fusion criterion) would be a better strategy. We did not focus on this aspect in this research.

Comparison with Consensus Group Selection Algorithm

In order to compare consensus group selection and our algorithm, the number of features inside the groups G_s has to be preset in advance. This leads to a simplification of algorithm described in Section 2. We propose the following scenario that allows switching and comparing between consensus group selection and our simplified algorithm:

1. Cluster features into groups $G_s, s = 1, 2, \ldots S$. The number of clusters S is defined manually by the user. In contrast with our previous proposal in Section 2.1, it is an input parameter of the algorithm.
2. Select the same predefined number of best features according to one of two strategies a-b:
   a. Select features based on the regularized score $S(\lambda)$.
   b. Select the closest features to the feature group center, which is defined as a mean of the feature vectors in the group. The closest features are selected using the nearest neighbors algorithm[2].

Strategy a is based on our proposal and strategy b is a core idea of the consensus group selection algorithm. Note that in contrast to our strategy a, the strategy b is based on the reconstruction criterion, while the final goal is a feature selection suitable for discrimination. In the next section 3.2, we compare these two strategies and evaluate the influence of the number of clusters on the final results.

EVALUATION OF THE STABLE FEATURE SELECTION

As described earlier in Section 1, we use the logistic regression with the MIL concept in the final step of the CAD system design. This classifier is built a multiple number of times with differently selected features. The analysis of the classifiers' performance trained with different features enables us the comparison of different features selection strategies (Section 3.2). The CXR CAD data is used to evaluate the performance of our feature selection algorithm.

CXR CAD Data Description

The data used in CXR CAD consists of two subsets: training and testing. The numbers of overall images at our disposal are 546 and 344 in the training and testing data sets, respectively. Among the overall images, the number of malignant images having at least one ground truth (GT) mark is equal to 69 and 47 in the training and testing data sets, respectively. The numbers of malignant nodules are 100 and 57 nodules in training and testing data sets, and the numbers of suspicious regions are 25,111 and 15,868 in the training and testing data sets, respectively.

The suspicious candidates are described by a feature vector of dimensionality 1,143. In summary, we deal with a high dimensional and imbalanced classification problem.

Comparison with Consensus Group Selection Algorithm

First, we present the results of the simplified version of our algorithm as described in Section 2.4. In our experiments the number of clusters was increased from 30 to 120 with step 30. We select the single best feature from each of the group based on both strategies a-b. The feature clustering and classifier training is performed using the training data only; then, the sensitivity results are presented for both training and testing data. The classifiers are trained on two subsets of features selected by strategies a-b. The sensitivity is calculated at the operating point equal to $FP = 0.5$ false positive candidates per image. This FP point is set based on the classifier performance on the training data. The low false positive rate is the vital system requirement. Higher FP values are not acceptable by radiologists who tend to become tired inspecting large numbers of CAD marks and, as a result, become more susceptible to making mistakes. The second requirement is a high sensitivity both on lesions and images[3].

Sensitivities of the classifiers trained with features selected by strategy A and with different regularization λ parameters are shown as curves in the top subplots per each N_c. The sensitivities for the consensus group feature selection strategy B are shown as the horizontal lines. The curves and lines marked by a black color stand for image sensitivity and by a gray color for nodule sensitivity (lesion sensitivity). The results on the training data are marked by bold style and on the testing data by the dashed one. For each group of experiments per N_c, the low subplots show the absolute difference in sensitivities on testing and training data sets. The color convention in the low subplots is the same as for the top subplots.

The sensitivity of the classifiers for $FP = 0.5$ and for a different number of clusters and the two feature selection strategies a-b are presented in Figure 1. The sensitivity results for strategy a are shown by regularization-like curves. These curves show sensitivity as a function of regularization λ parameters in our feature selection criterion. The sensitivities for the consensus group feature selection strategy b are shown by the horizontal lines.

It is easily seen, that for most of the regularization parameters independent of the number of clusters, our strategy a outperforms the consensus group selection strategy. It leads to better sensitivity results both on the training and testing data sets; as well, the difference between sensitivities on testing and training data is smaller for most of the λ parameters. It is interesting to note (Figure 1) that there exist λ values leading to classifiers that are superior to the classifier trained on features selected by strategy a and with $\lambda = 1.0$. At the same time, there exist λ values that lead to classifiers that are more stable than the classifier corresponding to $\lambda = 0$. In the interval $\lambda \in [0 \ 0.2]$ the sensitivity has two maximal local peaks for different numbers of clusters. For the larger number of clusters the sensitivity exhibits a smoother behavior. The best optimal λ parameter is different for different numbers of clusters.

Figure 1. Sensitivity curves for $FP = 0.5$ and different number of clusters. We consider 4 groups of experiments with a different number of clusters equal to: $N_c = 30, 60, 90, 120$

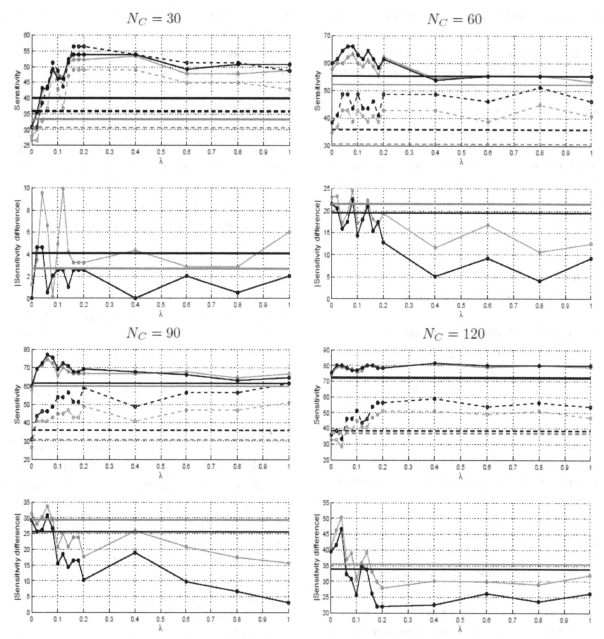

We do not concentrate on the optimal λ parameter selection in this research, but it is easily seen that $\lambda^* = 0.2$ is a good option. A regularization parameter $\lambda = 0.2$ is a good suboptimal parameter; the optimal parameter depends on the number of clusters for different number of clusters.[4] The ROC curves for classifiers trained on features selected by strategy a and $\lambda = 0.2$ and consensus feature selection strategy b for different number of clusters are shown in Figure 2. It is easily seen that our

Figure 2. ROCs for strategy B and strategy B with the suboptimal $\lambda = 0.2$. The sensitivity of the classifier for strategy A is marked by dark grays and strategy B by light grays. The light gray stand for GT (lesion) sensitivity (top subplots) and the dark gray for the image sensitivity (bottom subplots). The results on the training data are marked by bold style and on the testing data by the dashed one. It is easily seen that our strategy is superior to consensus group selection even when used with suboptimal parameters.

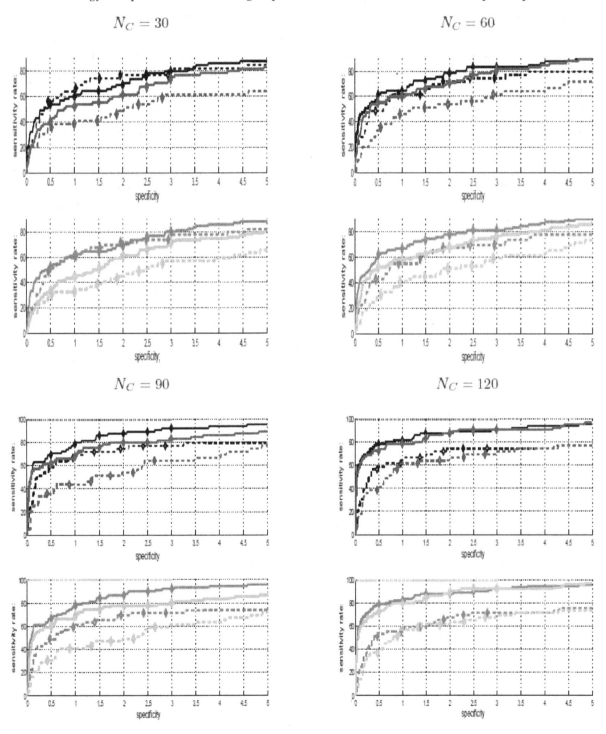

strategy is superior to consensus group selection even when used with suboptimal parameters.

In summary, feature selection based on a soft combination between the stability criterion that we introduced and discriminative power of the features (strategy a) leads to better and more stable results than strategy b, where the feature group is represented by its center. An improvement in sensitivity is obvious and predictable as representation of the feature group by its center is based on the reconstruction criterion, while the final goal is discrimination.

Strategy A with Automatic Number of Clusters

In the previous section, it was shown that the simplified version of our algorithm (strategy **A**) outperforms the consensus group selection algorithm (strategy b). In this section, we compare the full version of our algorithm with the automatic selection of the number of clusters, and its simplified version, strategy a with the suboptimal $\lambda = 0.2$.

In our experiments below, we select $N_d = 60$ features. This choice is based on multiple experiments and our vast experience in cancer detection problems. Our analysis shows that a considerably larger number of features does not improve classification results whilst slows down the application run time. The number of clusters extracted automatically by the full version of the algorithm is equal to 12. The sensitivity curves for $FP = 0.5$ and different values of the regularization parameter λ are shown in Figure 3a. There are two concurrent suboptimal λ values leading to large sensitivity values in this case: $\lambda = 0.2$ and $\lambda = 0.6$

Figure 3. Top subplot: The sensitivity curves for a full version of our algorithm for different values of the regularization parameter λ. The curves and lines marked in black stand for image sensitivity and the gray ones for nodule (lesion sensitivity) sensitivity. The results on the training data are marked by the bold style and on the testing data by the dashed one. (a) Bottom subplot: absolute difference in sensitivity for different values of the regularization parameters λ. (b) Comparison for classifier with features based on automatic number of clusters and $\lambda = 0.6$ and classifier build with number of clusters equal to 60, one feature per cluster and $\lambda = 0.2$. The dark grays stand for classifiers with automatic numbers of clusters and light grays for algorithms with manual number of clusters. The false positive rate is equal to $FP = 0.5$ in our consideration.

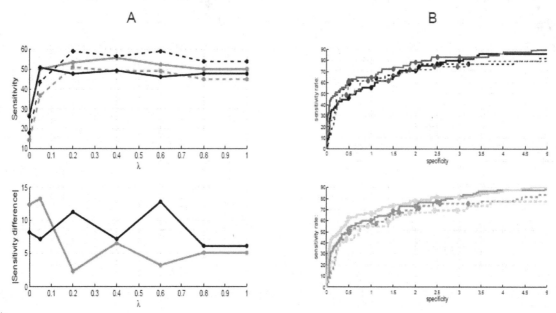

We select the full version of our algorithm with $\lambda = 0.6$ to compare to the simplified version strategy **A** ($\lambda = 0.2$). The superimposed ROC curves for these two cases are presented in Figure 3b. There is no a significant difference in sensitivity results between those two cases; the ROCs curves intertwine for different specificity values (*FP* values). However, with the full version of the algorithm, there is no need to train multiple classifiers corresponding to feature selection with different number of clusters. In summary, the main advantage of the full version of our algorithm over its simplified version is selecting the number of clusters automatically.

COMPRESSIVE SENSING BASED FEATURE SELECTION

Compressive sensing (CS) theory states that a sparse signal of length n can be recovered from a smaller set of linear projections via ℓ_1 minimization (Donoho, 2006). The same framework was later on used to perform classification directly on the compressive measurements (Davenport, 2007). This method works by first projecting the input into a lower dimensional space using a random ortho-projector matrix

$$\Phi \in R^{m \times n}, \Phi \Phi^t = I_{m \times m},$$

$x_p = \Phi x$ and then by training the ML classifier directly in the obtained space of $x^p \in R^m$.

This becomes possible due to the Theorem 3.1 of (Baraniuk, 2006) according to which under some mild conditions on the k-dimensional Riemaninan submanifold M, the distances between any pair of points $x, z \in M$ with a high probability decreases by a factor $f = \sqrt{m/n}$ after projecting; namely,

$$(1 - \epsilon)f \leq \frac{\| \Phi x - \Phi z \|}{\| x - z \|} \leq (1 + \epsilon)f \qquad (5)$$

where ϵ can be taken as small as desired. Since the inner product is expressed as:

$$2x^t z = \| x \|^2 + \| z \|^2 - \| x - z \|^2,$$

and due to Equation (5), the inner product $x^t z$ with a high probability can be approximated by:

$$x^t z \approx f^* (\Phi x)^t \Phi z, \quad f^* = 1/f^2 \qquad (6)$$

Based on this approximation (Equation (6)) and noticing that the optimization function F of the logistic regression Equation (1)-(2) depends on the inner product between the weight vector and input vectors $w^t x_\mu^s$, the original optimization problem can be approximated by a similar optimization problem in the lower dimensional space with the projected data D_p:

$$w_p^* = arg \max_{w_p} F(w_p^t; D_p),$$

$$w_p = f^* \Phi w, w_p \in R^m,$$
$$x_{\mu,p}^s = \Phi x_\mu^s, \ (x_{\mu,p}^s \in R^m) \qquad (7)$$

In other words, the same logistic regression classifier with the MIL concept is an approximation of the original problem in a high dimensional space.

If we had followed the same strategy as in (Davenport, 2007), we would have terminated the CS application at this point and have been satisfied by the constructed classifier in the low-dimensional projection space. However, since we are interested in feature selection and in computing a small number of original features, the weight vector w has to be reconstructed in the original high-dimensional space under the constraint that most of the components of the w-vector are zero valued. This constraint is equivalent to a small ℓ_0 norm of the weight vector w.

In other words, we are seeking w that satisfies the projection constraints of Equation (7) and has a small ℓ_0 norm:

$$\min_{w \in R^n} \| w \|_{\ell_0} : w_p = f^* \Phi w$$

The ℓ_0-problem is combinatorial and generally NP-hard and is usually relaxed by the ℓ_1-problem (Yin, 2008):

$$\min_{w \in R^n} \| w \|_{\ell_1} : w_p = f^* \Phi w .$$

The above problem is the standard CS optimization problem:

$$w^* = arg \min(\| w \|_1 + \nu \| \Phi w - w_p / f^* \|_M), \tag{8}$$

where the M-norm:

$$\| z \|_M = \sqrt{z^t M z}$$

$$M \in R^{m \times m}$$

is a positive definite matrix and ν is a trade-off between the weight reconstruction and a small ℓ_1 norm. We use the fixed-point continuation (FPC) method (Hale, 2007) and the software developed by the authors. The found w vector is sparse and its non-zero components correspond to the selected features.

In summary, the CS feature selection for logistic MIL classifier works by first randomly ortho-projecting data into the lower dimensional space and training the same type of the classifier in this space. Lastly, the classifier's weights are reconstructed in the original feature space under the l_1 norm con-

straint (solving CS problem Equation (8)) that allows us to find a small subset of computed features. After feature selection is completed, the classifier is rebuilt again.

The proposed feature selection method is applicable for any binary classifier with the optimization function being dependent on the inner product between weight vector and data.

We refer to this type of classifiers as projective classifiers.

EVALUATION OF CS FEATURE SELECTION

The efficiency of the proposed feature selection method is demonstrated on two data sets (i) a specially constructed synthetic data and (ii) medical application of finding cancer in mammography images. The data and evaluation results for the synthetic data are presented in Sections 5.1-5.2 and for cancer detection is Sections 5.3.

Synthetic Data

We tested the proposed technique on the specially constructed synthetic data, so that features required for classification are known in advance. The features are generated independently in each dimension of $x \in R^n$. The first k-components of x are generated to be discriminative and the remaining to be irrelevant for classification. We generate the irrelevant components as a random Gaussian noise:

$$x_j \sim N(0, \sigma_n), j = k + 1, \ldots n .$$

The discriminative components are created in two steps. In the first step, each discriminative feature

$$x_j, j = 1, 2, \ldots k$$

is generated as a mixture of two Gaussian distributions $N(0, \sigma_j^1)$ and $N(\mu_j, \sigma_j^2)$ with the controlled priors π and $1 - \pi$ on the positive and negative classes. The larger the μ_j and smaller σ_j^1, σ_j^2, the better is the discriminative power of the feature.

In the second stage, each discriminative feature is normalized to lie with a high probability in the range [0, 1] and then is mapped by the monotonically increasing transform T (this breaks the normality of the feature distribution inside the classes):

$$T(x_j, f_j) = x_j - \frac{\cos(x_j f_j)}{f_j}, \quad f_j > 1 \tag{9}$$

The derivative of this transform:

$$T'_{x_j} = 1 + \sin(x_j f_j) \tag{10}$$

lies in the [0 2] range. The frequency f_j in Equation (9) is taken as a ratio between 1 and a random number sampled from a uniform distribution in the open interval $(0, 1)$. This transform locally stretches or shrinks the data dependent on T' being more or less than 1, respectively.

Figure 4. Synthetic Data: (a). Two independent discriminative components of the data, each component is a mixture of Gaussians. (b). Two independent discriminative components after transformations $T_j, j = 1, 2$. (c-d). The derivatives of transformation T'_j for two discriminative directions. The high frequency f_j leads to wobbling of the data density and splitting one cluster into several ones.

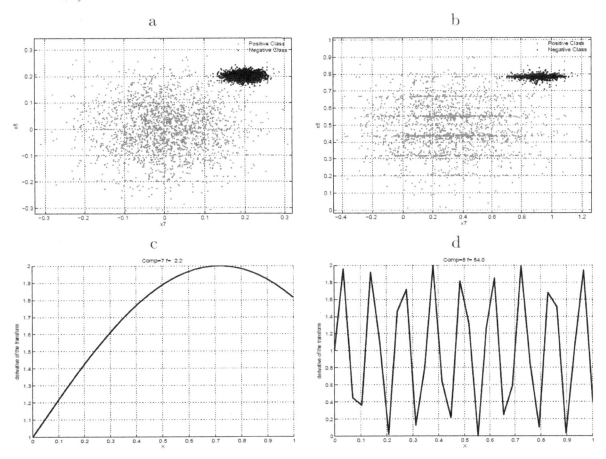

Since the transform is monotonically increasing; it always preserves the feature order, so that if one cluster is on the left side from another one, this relation holds after transformation T as well.

However, it allows splitting clusters into sub-clusters for large f_j values. In order to eliminate the scaling effect in data creation, a simple shift and normalization is performed so that all features are of zero-mean and unit variance.

Results on Synthetic Data

We generate data as described in the previous section with overall $n = 200$ features among which $k = 20$ are discriminative. The number of samples taken is $M = 4000$ and the data is split in half to create training and test data sets. The prior on the positive and negative data is assumed to be the same $\pi = 1/2$ and the center of the negative data:

$$\mu_j = 0.05, j = 1, \ldots, k;$$

The variance of the positive data is selected as

$$\sigma_j^1 = 0.1, j = 1, \ldots, k$$

and

$$\sigma_j^2 = 0.05z, j = 1, \ldots, k$$

and z is a uniform distribution on the $[0, 1]$ interval. The irrelevant components have a variance $\sigma_n = 0.01$. The Fisher discriminative score of each of the features before and after transformation T is shown in Figure 5a. It is clearly seen that the sinusoidal transformation T changes the Fisher score values.

We project data to a random space of dimensionality

$$m = 100(m = \rho k, \rho = 5)$$

and run our classifier $K = 30$ times. The ortho-projector matrix Φ is created by first generating a random matrix A with the elements being samples of the standard normal distribution $N(0, 1)$ and then performing a QR factorization. We use the $qr.m$ routine of MATLAB to perform

Figure 5. Fisher Score (Synthetic Data). (a) The Fisher discriminative score of the 20 discriminative directions and some 20 irrelevant. The black line shows the score before the transformation T and the gray line after the transformation. (b) The Fisher discriminative score in the randomly projected space of dimensionality $m = 100$.

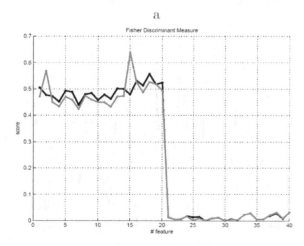

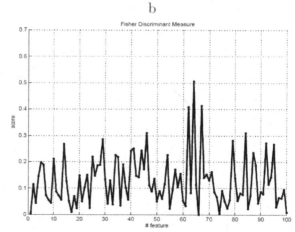

Figure 6. CS features (Synthetic Data). A_1. *Restored original weights represented as images. The columns correspond to classifiers and the rows to weight vector components (features).* A_2. *Frequency of the feature selection by* $K = 30$ *-classifiers. It is clearly seen that the first 20 features (that are discriminative by construction and marked by light gray) are selected with a very high probability. The method selects 9 features from 20 discriminative and 8 features from 180 irrelevant.* B_1. *The Fisher score after mixing the discriminative variables.* B_2. *The frequency of selecting the features by the CS method for mixed discriminative variables. The method selects 5-features from 20 discriminative and 4-features from 180 irrelevant ones.*

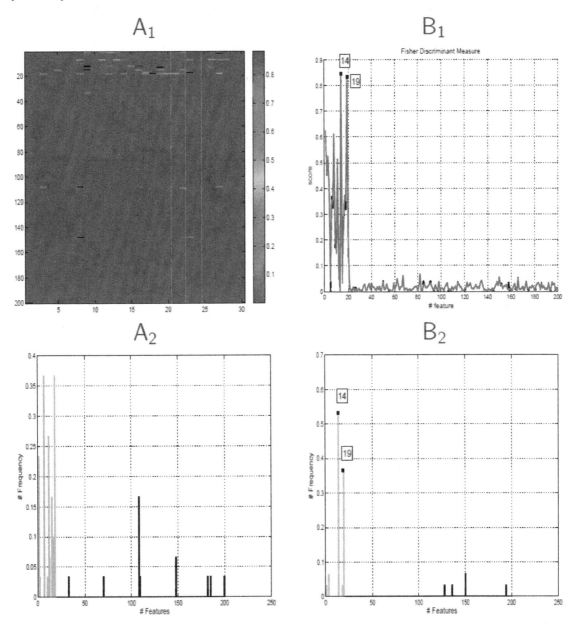

the QR factorization of the matrix A. The Fisher discriminative score in the projected space is shown in Figure 5b. Comparing figures (a-b), one can conclude that the random projective features have lower discriminative power than the original discriminative features.

The CS features restored using CS optimization for each run of the classifier is presented in Figure 6. The features that were selected at least once by one of the classifiers are considered by us as CS features. As can be easily seen the first 20 features (generated as discriminative) are selected with a very high frequency (see Figure 6, A_2).

The classification results of the two ensembles of classifiers trained (and validated) in the projective space of dimensionality $m = 100$ and in the space of CS selected features are shown in Figure 7 by blue and red color respectively. The classi-

Figure 7. Classification Results (Synthetic Data). Classification results for the two ensembles of classifiers trained and validated in the randomly projected space (black line) and with the original CS selected features (gray line).

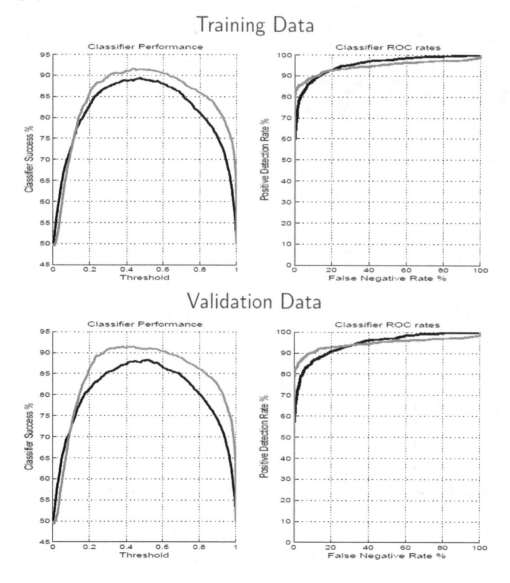

fication performance (classification success in percent) as a function of the threshold T_θ (see Equation (3)) is shown in Figure 7 (left subgraphs); the ROCs are shown on the right graphs. It is clearly seen that in the area of interest (small false negative rate) the classifier built in the space of CS features leads to a better classification result (higher ROC-curve).

The data simulated by us is not likely to be representative of the real data as all the features are independent. In order for the experiment to mimic reality, an additional mixing transformation of the discriminative features was performed as

$$P[x_1, x_2, \ldots, x_k]^t$$

where $P \in R^{k \times k}$ is a random matrix with the elements being independently sampled from $N(0, 1)$. After the mixing transform, the data is scaled once again so that all features are of zero-mean and unit variance.

The CS results of this additional experiment are presented in Figure 6: B_1 - B_2. As can be easily seen the frequency of selecting the discriminative features by classifiers (Figure 6 B_1) is correlated with the calculated Fisher scores (Figure

6 B_2). The classification results of the ensembles of the classifiers in this case are very similar to the previous results shown in Figure 7 and are not presented here due to lack of space.

In order to emphasize the difference between the standard CS feature selection based on a reconstruction and the one proposed by us that is based on classification, the standard CS was performed in the original space; i.e. the projected data (instead of the classifier weights) were reconstructed in the original space with ℓ_1 regularization. The frequency of the feature selection in this case is shown in Figure 8. It is clearly seen that discriminative features are not the important ones from the reconstruction point of view. This is a manifestation of the well-known fact that although recognition (classification) and reconstruction tasks are related, they require different data encoding (O'Toole, 1993) (e.g., in the context of principal component analysis).

Mammography

The number of images at our disposal is 2012 in training and 1498 in validation. The numbers of malignant images in the training and validation

Figure 8. Standard CS. Frequency of the features selected by reconstructing the projected data with the ℓ_1- regularization. The experiment for the data with the discriminative features being mixed. Gray and black colors correspond to discriminative and irrelevant features, respectively.

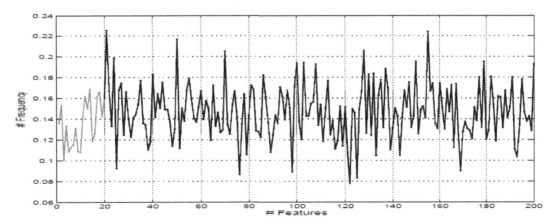

data are 808 and 590, respectively. The number of specific features is 150 and the number of texture-like is 1000. Our task is to find a small subset of texture-like features that are good for classification. The specific features are hidden from us in the feature pre-selection step; however, it is known to us that a logistic regression classifier with the MIL concept is used for classification.

We use the proposed CS feature selection to find a small subset of texture features assuming intrinsic data dimensionality of $k = 60$. This choice is based on multiple experiments and our vast experience in cancer detection problems. Our analysis shows that a larger number of features does not improve results and additionally slows down the application run time. Similar to Section

5.2, we project the data onto a random space of dimensionality

$$m = \rho k = 300, \ (\rho = 5)$$

and run the classifier $K = 20$ times. The classification ROC results for the 68 CS features[5] selected by our method is shown in Figure 9a. For comparison Figure 9b presents classification results with 68 features selected using the slightly improved version of the minimum-redundancy maximum-relevancy (MIR) feature selection method (Peng, 2005). Comparing Figure 9 (a-b), we see that though the two methods are comparable, the CS feature selection leads to slightly better results (has higher ROC curves). The region of interest in the ROC curves in our application

Figure 9. Classification (ROC) Results (Lesion Detection).} a. CS feature selection; b. MIR feature selection; Classification (ROC) results for the ensemble of 20 classifiers trained and validated in the randomly projected space (black line) and with the original CS selected features (gray line). The x-axes stands for a number of FOP per image and y-the sensitivity.

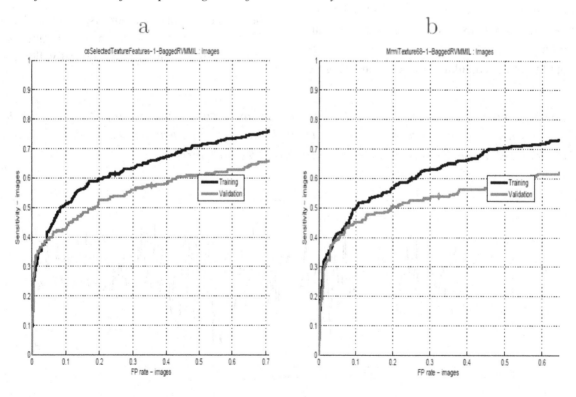

lies in the interval [0.2 0.3] false positive candidates per image.

CONCLUSION

In this chapter, we presented two new feature selection methods. The first method focuses on introducing new stable feature selection, while the second method is prewired into a specific class of projective classifiers and is based on a compressive sensing (CS). The efficacy of the methods is demonstrated on cancer detection in chest X-ray and mammographic images.

Our first algorithm for stable feature selection (Sections 2-3) is based on feature space clustering and a hybrid criterion, which is a linear combination of the discriminative power of features and their stability. The stability is measured in a type of bootstrap resampling experiments. The balance between discrimination and stability is controlled by a regularization parameter. We have shown that our method is superior to consensus group clustering that does not use the sample labels in the feature selection procedure.

The stable feature selection method presents a framework that can be easily modified by using other clustering algorithms, other strategies for feature redistribution between clusters, and usage of other criteria for stability measurement. Similar, to regularization methods used in classification, it requires the selection of the optimal regularization parameter and of running multiple experiments. However, it is more preferable in practice since learning is faster with smaller number of features and feature clustering is fast.

Our second method for feature selection is designed for the specific class of projective binary classifiers. The obtained features from are wired to the classifier structure and classification task from the start and not to data reconstruction (representation). This feature selection method is based on the compressive sensing (CS) approach. The method is tested on two data sets: specially generated synthetic data and real medical image data for lesion detection in mammography images. The feasibility of the method is demonstrated on the synthetic data, by showing that CS features coincide with the generated discriminative features. The CS feature selection is shown to outperform the modern MIR feature selection for the real problem of lesion detection.

REFERENCES

Agarwal, S. (2002). *Spectral clustering toolbox*. Retrieved from http://homes.cs.washington.edu/~sagarwal/code.html

Baraniuk, R., & Wakin, M. (2006). Random projections of smooth manifolds. *Foundations of Computational Mathematics*.

Dash, M., & Liu, A. (1997). Feature selection for classification. *Intelligent Data Analysis*, *1*(3), 1–12.

Davenport, M., Duarte, M., Wakin, M., Laska, J., Takhar, D., Kelly, K., & Baraniuk, R. (2007). The smashed filter for compressive classification and target recognition. In *Proceedings of SPIE (Vol. 6498)*. SPIE. doi:10.1117/12.714460

Donoho, D. (2006). Compressed sensing. *IEEE Transactions on Information Theory*, *52*(4), 1289–1306. doi:10.1109/TIT.2006.871582

Fawcett, T. (2006). An introduction to ROC analysis. *Pattern Recognition Letters*, *27*, 861–874. doi:10.1016/j.patrec.2005.10.010

Fowlkes, C., Belongie, S., & Malik, J. (2001). Efficient spatiotemporal grouping using the Nystrom method. In *Proc. IEEE Conf. Comput. Vision and Pattern Recognition* (pp. 231-238). IEEE.

Hale, E., Yin, W., & Zhang, Y. (2007). *A fixed-point continuation method for `1-regularized minimization with applications to compressed sensing*. CAAM Technical Report TR07-07. Rice University.

Haralick, R., Shanmugan, K., & Its'hak, D. (1973). Textural Features for Image Classification. *IEEE Transactions on Systems, Man, and Cybernetics*, SMC-3(6), 610–621. doi:10.1109/TSMC.1973.4309314

Loscalzo, S., Yu, L., & Ding, C. (2009). Consensus group stable feature selection. In *KDD '09: Proceedings of the 15th ACM SIGKDD international conference on Knowledge discovery and data mining* (pp. 567-576). ACM.

Maron, O., & Lozano-Perez, T. (1998). A framework for multiple instance learning. *Neural Information Processing Systems, 10.*

O'Toole, A., Valentin, D., & Abdi, H. (1993). A low dimensional representation of faces in the higher dimensions of the space. *Journal of the Optical Society of America, series A, 10,* 405–411. doi:10.1364/JOSAA.10.000405

Paredes, E. S. (2007). *Atlas of mammography* (3rd ed.). Alphen aan den Rijn, The Netherlands: Wolters Kluwer (Health).

Peng, H., Long, F., & Ding, C. (2005). Feature selection based on mutual information: Criteria of max-dependency, max-relevance, and min-redundancy. *Pattern Analysis and Machine Intelligence*, 27(8), 1226–1238. doi:10.1109/TPAMI.2005.159

Peteiro-Barral, D., Guijarro-Berdinas, B., & Perez-Sanchez, B. (2011). Dealing with "very large" datasets. An overview of a promising research line: Distributed learning. In *Proceedings of the 3rd International Conference on Agents and Artificial Intelligence* (Vol. 1, pp. 476-481). New York, NY: Springer.

Sampat, M. P., Bovik, A. C., Markey, M. K., Whitman, G. J., & Stephens, T. W. (2006). Toroidal gaussian filters for detection and extraction of properties of spiculated masses. *IEEE International Conference on Acoustics, Speech, and Signal Processing* (pp. 610-621). IEEE.

Shi, J., & Malik, J. (2000). Normalized cuts and image segmentation. *IEEE Transactions on Pattern Analysis Intelligence, 22*(8).

Valades, G. P. (2011). *Patent 7925065B2.* Washington, DC: US Patent Office.

Wei, D., Chan, H., Petrick, N., Sahiner, B., Helvie, M., Adler, D., & Goodsitt, M. (1997). False-positive reduction technique for detection of masses on digital mammograms: Global and local multiresolution texture analysis. *Medical Physics, 24*(6), 903–914. doi:10.1118/1.598011

Yin, W., & Zhang, Y. (2008). Extracting salient features from less data via L1-minimization. *SIAG/OPT Views-and-News, A Forum for the SIAM Activity Group on Optimization, 19,* 11-19.

ENDNOTES

[1] For example, using incremental or batch learning (Peteiro-Barral. D., 2011)

[2] In our experiments, two distance measures L_1 and L_2 have been tried. We have not observed a big difference in qualitative behavior when selecting between two these distances. The results reported by us are given for L_2 distance.

[3] When measuring image sensitivity, it is sufficient to detect at least one malignant nodule in the image. In other words, finding of at least one real nodule by CAD is considered as a success.

[4] Regularization parameter $\lambda = 0.2$ is a good suboptimal parameter; the optimal parameter depends on the number of clusters for different number of clusters.

[5] Note that the final number of CS features is equal 68, while the intrinsic dimensionality was set to 60. This is due to CS method reconstruction stage. The final CS components are the ones that survive after thersholding procedure, where threshold is set automatically (Hale, 2007).

Section 2
Efficient and Scalable Methods in Image Processing, Robotics, Control, Computer Networks Defense, Human Identification, and Combinatorial Optimization

Chapter 5
The Kolmogorov Spline Network for Authentication Data Embedding in Images

Pierre-Emmanuel Leni
University of Franche-Comte, France

Yohan D. Fougerolle
University of Burgundy, France

Frédéric Truchetet
University of Burgundy, France

ABSTRACT

In 1900, Hilbert declared that high order polynomial equations could not be solved by sums and compositions of continuous functions of less than three variables. This statement was proven wrong by the superposition theorem, demonstrated by Arnol'd and Kolmogorov in 1957, which allows for writing all multivariate functions as sums and compositions of univariate functions. Amongst recent computable forms of the theorem, Igelnik and Parikh's approach, known as the Kolmogorov Spline Network (KSN), offers several alternatives for the univariate functions as well as their construction. A novel approach is presented for the embedding of authentication data (black and white logo, translucent or opaque image) in images. This approach offers similar functionalities than watermarking approaches, but relies on a totally different theory: the mark is not embedded in the 2D image space, but it is rather applied to an equivalent univariate representation of the transformed image. Using the progressive transmission scheme previously proposed (Leni, 2011), the pixels are re-arranged without any neighborhood consideration. Taking advantage of this naturally encrypted representation, it is proposed to embed the watermark in these univariate functions. The watermarked image can be accessed at any intermediate resolution, and fully recovered (by removing the embedded mark) without loss using a secret key. Moreover, the key can be different for every resolution, and both the watermark and the image can be globally restored in case of data losses during the transmission. These contributions lie in proposing a robust embedding of authentication data (represented by a watermark) into an image using the 1D space of univariate functions based on the Kolmogorov superposition theorem. Lastly, using a key, the watermark can be removed to restore the original image.

DOI: 10.4018/978-1-4666-3942-3.ch005

INTRODUCTION

Igelnik and Parikh's approach, known as Kolmogorov Spline Network (KSN), approximates the univariate functions as well as offers flexibility on several parameters of the algorithm (*i.e.*, univariate function constructions, number of layers, tile size, and etc.).

In the KSN, a multivariate function f is approximated by

$$f(\boldsymbol{x}) = f(x_1, \cdots, x_n)$$
$$\approx \sum_{q=1}^{N} a_q g_q \left(\sum_{i=1}^{n} \lambda_i \psi_{q,i}(x_i) \right) \qquad (1)$$
$$= \sum_{q=1}^{N} a_q g_q (\xi_q(\boldsymbol{x})).$$

In this formulation, the number of layers N ($N \geq 2n + 1$) is variable. Similarly to the number of neurones constituting the hidden layer of a feed-forward neural network, increasing N improves the accuracy and an optimal value corresponding to the decomposed function has to be determined. A function $\psi_{q,i}$ is associated for each layer q along each dimension i. The functions $\xi_q(\boldsymbol{x})$ are mapping functions from $[0,1]^d$ to $\mathbb{R}$ (similar to hash functions), and are used to evaluate the argument of the outer functions g_q according to the coordinates $\boldsymbol{x}$.

The algorithm for the creation of a KSN is divided into two parts: a construction step, in which the univariate functions are interpolated by cubic splines, and a second stage, in which the spline parameters and the weights of the layers a_n are optimized to ensure the convergence of the approximation to the function f. To construct the functions g_q and $\psi_{q,i}$, a tilage over the space $[0,1]^d$ is generated. By definition, the tiles are disjoint; therefore, in order to cover the entire space, several tilage layers are created. The inner and outer univariate functions are associated with each tilage layer, and the superposition of these layers constitutes what is called a network. One network contains several various parameters, such as the spline parameters and the layer weights that are further optimized to improve the reconstruction accuracy. Consequently, using Igelnik and Parikh's approximation scheme, images can be represented as a superposition of layers, *i.e.*, a superposition of images with a fixed (and low) resolution.

For progressive transmission (Leni, 2011), we modified the generation of the tilage and the construction of the univariate functions to obtain one tilage density per layer, and progressively construct the outer functions. Thus, for every layer, an image representing the original image at a lower resolution can be computed. The univariate functions can be transmitted one after the others to progressively reconstruct the original image. The approach is fully scalable: the resolution and the number of intermediate reconstructions can be adjusted by the user. Each function adds new data to the previously transmitted functions, which limits the quantity of data transmitted at each step. In other words, the original image can be progressively reconstructed up to its original resolution, without error. Only a limited quantity of data is required to increase the resolution between intermediate reconstructions.

The work presented in this chapter is built upon this approach and aims at exploring the potential of KSN for progressive transmission with authentication and data protection. The key idea is to take advantage of the decomposition property when using KSN: the random sweeping of the image. Using a mapping of the functions $\xi_q(\boldsymbol{x})$ over $[0,1]$, it is possible to recover the ordering of the pixel obtained through the inner functions. In other words, the random values generated during the construction of the inner functions provide a random re-ordering of the pixels (as detailed in section III-A). Therefore, the pixel information contained in the outer functions does not contain any localization information, and requires the inner function to be properly reordered and to reconstruct the original image.

Taking advantage of the natural encryption of the data contained in the outer functions and the information separation provided by the modified KSN, we propose to embed authentication information into images. More precisely, the marked image is reconstructed as in the original progressive transmission approach. Furthermore, the pixels covered by the mark are mixed into the outer functions. Using the corresponding inner functions, the data in the external function related to the pixels covered by the watermark can be reordered to remove the mark and restore the original image. Thus, the flexibility and resilience towards packet loss inherited from the progressive transmission are preserved, while offering the ability to add authentication information to the transmitted image. Furthermore, the inner functions can be different for any intermediate resolutions, leading to different keys for the recovery of the image at different resolutions.

One should note that the KSN can decompose any multivariate functions with a dimension greater than 2. Thus, we illustrate the watermark embedding into grey level images (bivariate functions). However, the approach can be extended to other multidimensional data, such as videos or 3D meshes with texture information.

BACKGROUND

Reversible Visible Watermarking and Image Authentication

Our approach is close to reversible watermarking. Nevertheless, both methods cannot be directly compared. In our approach, all the transformations are performed in the univariate function space (1D) instead of the image space. Therefore, to remain relevant, potential attacks have to be considered from the point of view of univariate functions, rather than in the classical image space.

Image watermarking has been a growing concern over many years (Perez, 2006; Hartung, 1999). The goal of image watermarking is to embed given information into an image, either to prove its ownership or its genuineness. The watermark is visible or hidden whether it alters visibly or not the original image.

In the case of hidden watermarking, the mark can be robust or fragile. A robust watermark allows the claiming of ownership by attempting at resisting as much as possible image compression and transformations. On the other hand, a fragile watermark allows the determining of whether the image has been tampered or not. Its role is to prove if an image has been modified after watermarking.

Aside from the publications dealing with invisible watermarking, some authors have dealt with the problem of proposing removable visible watermarking schemes (Feng, 2006): an image with a visible watermark is widely distributed, and some specific users are provided the ability to recover the original image by removing the watermark. Two other approaches have been proposed in (Hu, 2006a) and (Yang, 2008), consisting in embedding data in the Discreet Wavelet Transform or Discreet Cosine Transform (respectively) of the image. These approaches are not reversible, because the original image cannot be restored without loss in any case. In those propositions, the embedded visible watermark is blurred, the watermark covers the whole image and its transparency level cannot be directly controlled by the user.

On the other side, several authors have proposed reversible visible watermarking approaches for semi-transparent or binary watermarks, where the original image can be perfectly recovered. Some data are hidden in the image, allowing a perfect recovery of the area covered by the watermark. Therefore, the user has limited (or nonexistent) control over the size of the watermark: the quantity of data that can be embedded to recover the image without watermark is limited by the resolution of the image. In addition, these data add some noise and decrease the overall quality of the watermarked image.

Using pixel value mapping and pixel position shifting, Yip et al. (2006) have proposed lossless visible watermarking approaches. In Tsai (2010), the authors present an approach for a secure reversible binary watermarking, combining an almost inverse function and the embedding of a restoration packet to ensure perfect reconstruction of the original image.

Nevertheless, both approaches require the original watermark to recover the original image together with the watermarked image, which is often unknown at decoding time. To overcome this drawback, Yang et al. (2009) have presented a contrast-sensitive approach, which optimally adjusts the visibility of the watermark and embeds the recovery data in the image according to the human visual system. The goal is to minimize the distortion outside of the watermarked area (caused by the integration of recovery data), at the cost of user control over the watermark transparency and visibility.

Hu et al. (2006b) have proposed an approach inspired by lossless invisible techniques for watermarking, allowing the user to control the size and transparency level, but only for binary watermarks and with a limited embedding capacity. For the color translucent to the opaque monochrome watermarks (of arbitrary size), Liu et al. (2010) propose a reversible visible watermarking. Nevertheless, the proposed approach is only compatible with RGB bitmaps.

The existing techniques for reversible image watermarking alter the image or one of its representation (wavelets) to add the watermarking information, and also the recovery information for some reversible approaches. Therefore, the mark characteristics (resolution, number of components, …) are limited, since the bandwidth that can be dedicated to the watermark and recovery information is limited.

The 1D decomposition of the images offers several advantages: any image can be used as an authentication mark. Moreover, in a heterogeneous display environment, the rights can be managed per resolution: the key to recover the original image can be independent for every resolution.

THE KOLMOGOROV SPLINE NETWORK FOR SECURED PROGRESSIVE TRANSMISSION

The Kolmogorov Spline Network has been introduced and presented by Igelnik and Parikh (2003).

The first step is the construction of the inner functions using the definition of a disjoint tilage over the definition space $[0,1]^d$ of the multivariate function f. For a given tilage layer n, the inner functions ψ_{ni} are generated, one per dimension, and are independent from the function f. The functions ψ_{ni} are step functions, with randomly generated step heights, to ensure that the function is increasing. To ensure the continuity of the inner functions ψ_{ni}, their values are interpolated by cubic splines. The convex combination of the inner functions ψ_{ni} with real values λ_i corresponds to the functions $\xi_n(x)$, and is the argument of the outer functions g_n. The second step is the construction of the outer functions, using the *a priori* known values of the multivariate function f at the centres of the hypercubes of the disjoint tilage. By construction, one couple of inner and outer functions is associated with each tilage layer.

For progressive transmission, the key idea is the construction of disjoint tilages at different resolutions with the corresponding outer functions, such that any outer function at a given resolution can be built from the outer functions at lower resolutions. Therefore, we modify the generation of the tilage and the construction of both the inner and outer functions using different tilage densities, one for every layer, in order to progressively reconstruct the final univariate functions.

The first step is the generation of the highest density tilage, *i.e.* one tile per pixel, and its related outer function. Intermediate layers, corresponding to lower resolutions, are then generated using larger tiles, such that the outer functions obtained are sub-samples of the initial outer function generated for the image at the highest resolution. To build the sub-samples of the initial outer functions, the inner functions associated to the intermediate layers have to be constructed using the values of the plateaus generated for the inner functions coupled to the highest density tilage. This realizes the sub-sampling of the inner functions and ensures that the real value referring to a position of the 2D space is the same for all layers. Then, transmitting the outer functions associated to each intermediate layer allows for the progressive reconstruction of the original outer function linked to the full resolution image. With each intermediate outer function, partial reconstruction of the image can be computed, progressively increasing the resolution of the reconstructed image.

Figure 1 presents an overview of such a modified network.

The third and last step is the embedding of authentication data. By taking advantage of the decomposition property (no neighborhood properties), we embed the watermark information into the univariate functions, while leaving the ability to remove the watermark and restore the original

Figure 1. Overview of a 5-tilage layer network modified for progressive transmission. The outer function is progressively reconstructed by adding points from the previously constructed outer functions, and the inner functions are adjusted for the increasing number of tiles by adding the corresponding steps.

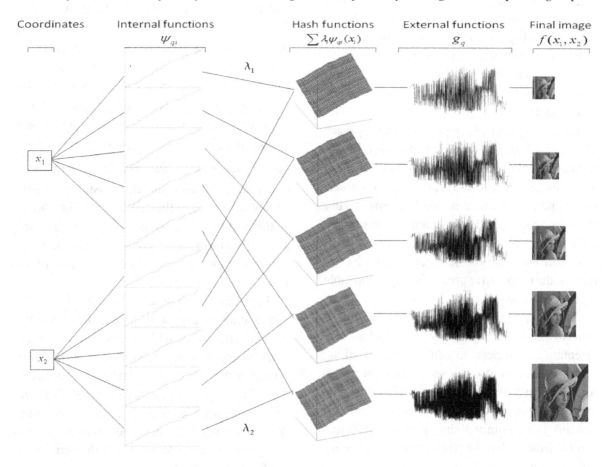

image providing a key. Additionally, this authentication can support heterogeneous display environments, since the key can be different for any sub-resolution of the image.

Technically, the watermarked image is decomposed and the data allowing for the pixels to recompose covered by the watermark are encrypted into the univariate functions. This can later be decoded if an authentication check is passed.

The combination of the image and the watermark implies that additional data have to be transmitted, but the user can fully control the watermark transparency and size.

The definition of the tilage takes into account the layer number n. The tilage is obtained by the Cartesian product of the intervals $I_n(j)$, defined as follows:

$$\forall n \in [[1, N]], j \geq -1, I_n(j)$$
$$= \left[(N+1) j\delta_n, (N+1) j\delta_n + N\delta_n \right]. \quad (2)$$

One can note that δ from the original algorithm has been replaced by δ_n, which means that the distance between tiles changes for each layer. Specifically,

$$\forall n_1, n_2 \in [[1, N]], n_1 < n_2 \Rightarrow \delta_{n_1} > \delta_{n_2}, \quad (3)$$

i.e., starting from large tiles, the tilage densities will increase with the number of layers, ending with a tilage covering each pixel of the image. Figure 2 shows the superposition of the generated layers.

Construction of the Inner Function ψ_{ni}

For every interval $I_n(j)$, the inner functions ψ_{ni} have constant values y_{nij}, called plateaus. The intervals I are disjoint, so are the plateaus. To construct a continuous inner function, sampling points are computed using existing values of plateaus y_{nij} and random values between two consecutive plateaus.

According to the tillage construction, the length of the plateaus y_{nij} will decrease as n increases. The plateaus y_{nij} will be used in the next section, since they constitute the secret and public keys, allowing to reconstruct the image with and without the mark. The inner functions associated to the latest layer N are first constructed using a tilage in which for one tile corresponds to one pixel. The inner functions associated to the intermediate layers ($n < N$) are generated by sub-sampling the inner functions of the layer N as follows: to each interval $I_n(j)$, associate a real number y_{nij} that will be the image of the interval $I_n(j)$ by the function ψ_{ni}. From the layer N, find the index j', such that the center of the interval $I_n(j)$ belongs to the interval $I_N(j')$, which can be written as

$$(N+1) j\delta_n + \frac{\delta_n}{2} \in I_N(j'), \quad (4)$$

and also implies $y_{nij} = y_{Nij'}$.

Figure 2. Superposition of disjoint tilages with size variation according to layer number

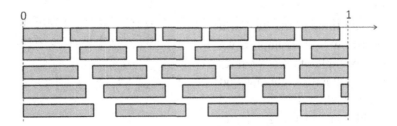

Then, ψ is sampled along regularly spaced points. These sampling points are then interpolated by a cubic spline to obtain a continuous and increasing function. One algorithm of cubic spline interpolation can be found in Moon (2001). The choice of a cubic spline is to ensure the convergence of the algorithm, as demonstrated in Igelnik (2003).

Once the functions ψ_{ni} are constructed, the argument of outer function g_n, *i.e.* the value of the function ξ_n, can be evaluated. On hypercubes $H_{nj_1,\cdots,nj_d}$, the function ξ_n has constant values

$$p_{nj_1,\cdots,nj_d} = \sum_{i=1}^{d} \lambda_i y_{nij_i}$$

Every random number y_{nij_i} generated verifies that the generated values $p_{nj_1,\cdots,nj_d}$ are all different:

$$\forall i \in [[1,d]]$$

$$\forall n \in [[1,N]]$$

$$\forall j \in \mathbb{Z}, \quad j \geq -1$$

The real numbers λ_i must be chosen linearly independent, strictly positive, and such that $\sum_{i=1}^{d} \lambda_i \leq 1$. The coordinate vector of the centre of the hypercube $H_{nj_1,\cdots,nj_d}$ is denoted $C_{nj_1,\cdots,nj_d}$.

Sprecher and Draghici (2002) have demonstrated that space-filling curves can be defined using the functions ξ_n. The linear combination of the inner functions associates a unique real value with every couple from $[0,1]^d$. Sorting these values defines a unique path through the tiles of a layer, which corresponds to a sweeping curve. Figure 3 illustrates an example of such a curve: the pixels are swept without any neighbourhood property conservation, which is used to embed the data for the reversible watermarking scheme.

Figure 3. Example of a sweeping curve obtained from Igelnik's approximation scheme with $\lambda_1 = 0.55$ and $\lambda_2 = 0.4$

Construction of the Outer Functions g_n

One outer function g_n is defined per tilage layer of index n. First, a set of points is computed: the abscissas of each point are the images of the associated function ξ_n, *i.e.*, real values $p_{nj_1,\cdots,nj_d}$ that uniquely identify a hypercube $H_{nj_1,\cdots,nj_d}$ from the tilage layer. The ordinates of each point are the images of the multivariate function *f* for the centres of the hypercubes $C_{nj_1,\cdots,nj_d}$. Then, to obtain a continuous function, these points are connected with nine-degree splines and straight lines to define a continuous function g_n. Specifically, each function g_n is constructed as follows:

- For every real number $t = p_{nj_1,\cdots,nj_d}$, $g_n(t)$ is equal to the N*th* of the value of the function *f* at the centre of the hypercube

$$H_{nj_1,\cdots,nj_d} : g_n\left(p_{nj_1,\cdots,nj_d}\right) = f\left(C_{nj_1,\cdots,nj_d}\right),$$

denoted as points

$$A_k = \left(t, g_n\left(t\right)\right), k \in \mathbb{N}$$

- The definition interval of function g_n is extended to all $t \in [0,1]$ as follows:
  - Two points B_k and $B_k^{'}$ are randomly placed in A_k neighbourhoods, such that $t_{B_k} < t_{A_k} < t_{B_k^{'}}$. The placement of points B_k and $B_k^{'}$ in the neighbourhood of A_k must preserve the order of points:

$$\cdots, B_{k-1}^{'}, B_k, A_k, B_k^{'}, B_{k+1}, \cdots;$$

i.e., the distance between B_k and A_k or A_k and $B_k^{'}$ must be smaller than half of the length between two consecutive points A_k and A_{k+1}.

  - Points $B_k^{'}$ and B_{k+1} are connected with a line of slope r.
  - Points A_k and $B_k^{'}$ are connected with a nine degree spline, noted s, such that:

$$s\left(t_{A_k}\right) = g_n\left(t_{A_k}\right),$$

$$s\left(t_{B_k^{'}}\right) = r,$$

$$s^{(2)}\left(t_{B_k^{'}}\right) = s^{(3)}\left(t_{B_k^{'}}\right) = s^{(4)}\left(t_{B_k^{'}}\right) = 0.$$

Points B_k and A_k are connected with a similar nine-degree spline. The connection conditions at points A_k of both nine degree splines yield the remaining conditions.

The extension of the definition for every $t \in [0, 1]$ does not require more data to be transmitted: it can be fully reconstructed using only the values of f at the centres of the hypercubes. Moreover, it may be proved useful for future works aiming at extending the current scheme to detect tampering attempts (cf. Future perspective directions section for details).

The Reversible Watermarking Scheme

Using the KSN, the pixels contained in the outer functions cannot be reordered without the inner functions ψ_{ni} that define the sweeping curve. Therefore, the encryption constituted by the steps of these functions is used for watermarking.

The watermarked image W and the area C of the image covered by the watermark (can be translucent) are converted into univariate functions using our modified KSN. We introduce the following notations:

$$\forall n \in [[1, \mathrm{N}]], \psi_{W,n1}, \psi_{W,n2}, \xi_{W,n}$$
$$= \lambda_1 \psi_{W,n1} + \lambda_2 \psi_{W,n2},$$

and $g_{W,n}$ designates the inner and outer functions obtained from the decomposition of the watermarked image.

$$\forall j \in \{\mathbb{N} \cup \{-1\}\}, y_{W,n1j}$$

refers to the plateaus of the function $\psi_{W,n1}$ and $y_{W,n2j}$ to $\psi_{W,n2}$, respectively.

We introduce similar notations with index C to refer to the decomposition of the image area covered by the watermark.

The steps of the functions $\xi_{C,n}$ decomposing the sub-image C must be different from all existing steps of the functions $\xi_{W,n}$ used to decompose the image W, to ensure that all the points of the sets S obtained for both C and W are distinct. Finally, the outer functions $g_{C,n}$ and $g_{W,n}$ corresponding to the same layer are merged together:

$$\forall n \in [[1, \mathrm{N}]], g_n = g_{C,n} \cup g_{W,n}$$

One can note that

$$Card(g_n) = Card(g_{C,n}) + Card(g_{W,n}),$$

Since the points of both sets $g_{C,n}$ and $g_{W,n}$ are disjoint. Therefore, the transmitted data g_n corresponds to a higher resolution image than the original one. For example, the decomposition of a 256×256 image with a 64×64 watermark corresponds to an amount of data equivalent to decomposition of a 264×264 image. This overhead is the cost of the flexibility over the watermark transparency and size. It is to be noted that all the data are uncompressed, which leaves space for later improvements to reduce this overhead cost. Moreover, the watermarked image does not suffer from noise effect and is perfectly reconstructed.

Algorithm 1: Encoding

From the watermarked image (the users embed the desired watermark on the image by themselves, using pixel substitution for example) and the original image, the algorithm extracts the area covered by the watermark and decomposes this sub-image into univariate functions that are merged with the univariate functions obtained

from the decomposition of the watermarked image. The algorithm returns the public key allowing to decode the watermarked image, and the secret keys (one per resolution) allowing to restore the area covered by the watermark.

- **Input:** Image W with the embedded watermark and original image I.
- **Output:** Univariate functions g_n,
  - **Public Key:** $\{y_{W,N1j}, y_{W,N2j}\}$
  - **Secret Keys:** $\{y_{C,n1j}, y_{C,n2j}\}$
- **Steps:**
  - Crop the original image I according to the watermark position in W to define a sub-image C corresponding to the area covered by the watermark.
  - Set the number N of intermediate resolutions.
  - Decompose W into inner functions $\psi_{W,n1}, \psi_{W,n2}$ and outer functions $g_{W,n}$. The plateaus:

$$\{y_{W,N1j}, y_{W,N2j}\}$$

of the inner functions of the last layer correspond to the key used to decompose the watermarked image.

Figure 4. Merging of two outer functions $g_{C,n}$ and $g_{W,n}$

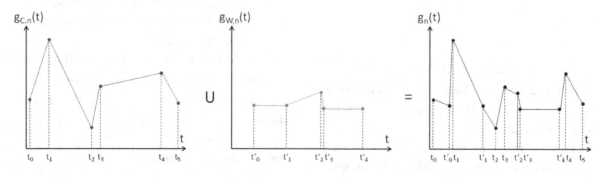

○ Decompose C into inner functions $\psi_{C,n1}, \psi_{C,n2}$ and outer functions $g_{C,n}$. the plateaus

$$\forall n \in \ [[1, \mathrm{N}]], \{y_{C,n1j}, y_{C,n2j}\}$$

have to be distinct from the steps

$$\{y_{W,N1j}, y_{W,N2j}\}$$

The plateaus

$$\{y_{C,n1j}, y_{C,n2j}\}$$

of the inner functions correspond to the key used to decomposed the area C, and consequently, allow to restore the original image without watermark.

○ Compute the union of the outer function corresponding to the same layer:

$$\forall n \in \ [[1, \mathrm{N}]], g_n = g_{C,n} \cup g_{W,n}$$

Algorithm 2: Decoding

Using the public key, the watermarked image is reconstructed. Additionally, if some secret keys are provided, the original image (without mark) can be restored.

One can note that no knowledge about the watermark is required to remove it.

- **Input:** Univariate functions g_n, the public key $\{y_{W,N1j}, y_{W,N2j}\}$, and optionally, secret keys $\{y_{C,n1j}, y_{C,n2j}\}$.
- **Output:** Image W with the embedded watermark and/or original image I.
- **Steps:**
  ○ Compute ξ_n using $\{y_{W,N1j}, y_{W,N2j}\}$

○ Read the values in g_n corresponding to the hypercubes identified in ξ_n.
○ Reconstruct the image, with a resolution of one pixel per hypercube.
- If a secret key $\{y_{C,n1j}, y_{C,n2j}\}$ is provided:
  ○ Compute $\xi_{C,n}$ using $\{y_{C,n1j}, y_{C,n2j}\}$
  ○ Read the values in g_n corresponding to the hypercubes identified in $\xi_{C,n}$.
  ○ Reconstruct The Area C, With A Resolution Of One Pixel Per Hypercube, And Replace The Watermark Area By C

Figure 5 presents the watermarking scheme and illustrates the combination of the outer functions.

During the image reconstruction, the watermarked image is decoded using the steps of the inner functions $\psi_{W,ni}$. The pixels of the sub-image C representing the area of W covered by the watermark can be identified in the outer function g_n. However, they cannot be reordered as long as the steps:

$$\{y_{C,n1j}, y_{C,n2j}\}$$

are not provided: these steps are the encryption key and must be known to remove the watermark. Therefore, for a watermark included in a bounding box of size $l \times h$, the size of the key (the number of steps of $\psi_{C,Ni}$) is $l + h$ real values: roughly $(l + h) \times 8$ bytes without compression.

APPLICATION

Figure 6 presents a progressive reconstruction of Lena, with and without the key allowing to remove the translucent watermark. The key is different for every resolution. The final image is perfectly reconstructed: the mean square error is null. Figure 7 illustrates the optional removal of an opaque watermark over the Peppers

Figure 5. Overview of watermarking with progressive transmission using a 3-layer network. The water-marked image and the area covered by the watermark are decomposed into univariate functions. The outer functions are merged, for every layer.

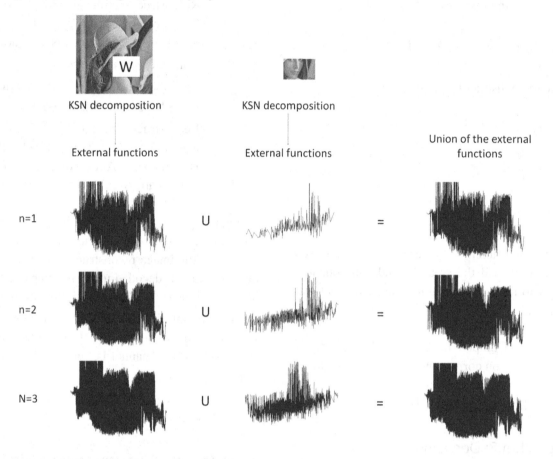

image. The main advantage is that users can reconstruct the original image without water-mark at only one resolution, at the cost of re-dundancy of the pixels covered by the water-mark. All the pixels covered by the watermark (area C) must be transmitted, since the inter-mediate keys cannot be obtained by sub-sam-pling the key of the full resolution image.

From the same watermarked image and de-composed file, Figure 8 (a)(b)(c) show the recon-structions in which the two first keys are wrong and the last one is correct; whereas Figure 8 (d)(e)(f) show the opposite situation: the two first keys are correct, and the last one is not.

These figures illustrate that a key is not shared between the different resolutions: knowing the keys at lower resolutions (d,e) does not give in-formation about the key for the final reconstruc-tion (f). Similarly, even if the lower-resolution watermarks (a,b) cannot be decoded, the final image can be reconstructed without artifact (c) if the correct key is provided.

Furthermore, when the key is not correct, the values are extracted from random positions in the outer functions g_n, which is equivalent to using random gray pixels to cover the watermark.

To estimate the distortion between the original and the reconstructed images, we use the Peak Signal to Noise Ratio (PSNR), defined as follows:

Figure 6. Progressive reconstruction of the watermarked Lena (left column) and of the recovered Lena after the watermark removal (right column). The final reconstruction without watermark is the exact reconstruction of the original image.

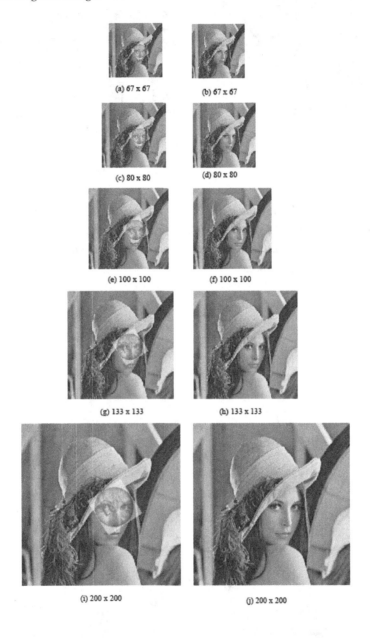

$$PSNR = 20 \log_{10} \left(\frac{255}{\sqrt{MSE}} \right)$$

$$MSE = \frac{1}{r^2} \sum_{i=0}^{r-1} \sum_{j=0}^{r-1} \left[O(i,j) - R(i,j) \right]^2$$

where MSE is the mean squared error:

between the original image O and reconstructed one R of resolution $r \times r$ pixels.

Figure 7. Final reconstruction of Peppers with an opaque watermark (a), and after watermark removal (b).

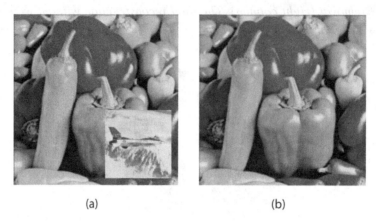

(a) (b)

Figure 8. (a)(b) A watermarked Lena is decoded at two intermediate resolutions with an incorrect key, and finally with a correct key (c). (d)(e) Decoding of a watermarked Lena with a correct key at the first two intermediate resolutions, and then with an incorrect key for final reconstruction (f). The key is distinct for all the resolutions of the image.

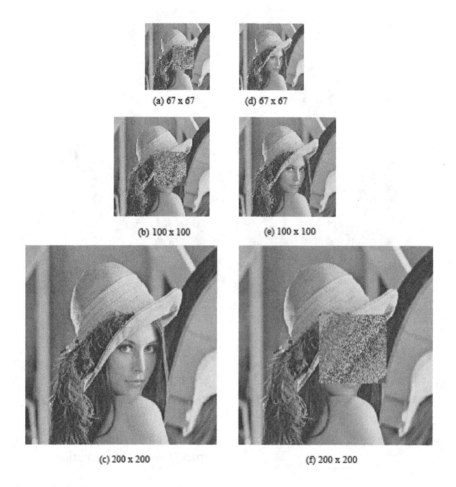

(a) 67 x 67 (d) 67 x 67

(b) 100 x 100 (e) 100 x 100

(c) 200 x 200 (f) 200 x 200

Figure 9. PSNR of a watermarked image using valid and invalid keys. The attempts at removing the watermark using invalid keys lead to reconstructions with an almost constant PSNR.

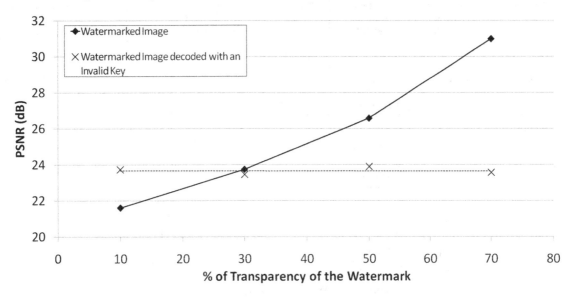

Figure 10. (a) Watermarked Mandrill after packet losses. (b) Restoration of (a) with a median filter. (c) Unlocked watermarked Mandrill after packet loss. (d) Restoration of (c) with a median filter. Both the watermark and the original image are degraded in a similar manner and can be globally restored.

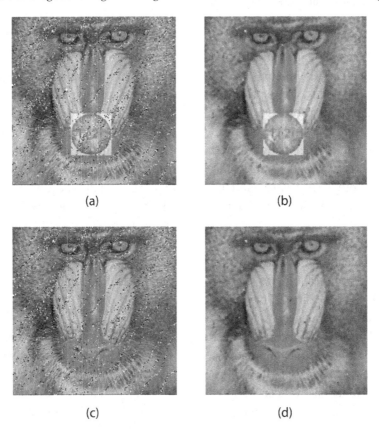

(a) (b)

(c) (d)

Table 1. Comparison of reversible visible watermarking techniques, updated from (Liu, 2010).

Methods	Legitimate recovery (PSNR)	Illegitimate recovery (PSNR)	Watermark size	Binary transparent watermark	Binary opaque watermark	Color translucent watermark
Hu (2006b)	43-44 dB	37-39dB	Unlimited	Yes	-	-
Tsai (Tsai2007)	Lossless	Not reported	Limited	Yes	-	-
Yip (Yip2006)	Lossless	Not reported	Unlimited	Yes	Yes	-
Liu (Liu2010)	Lossless	12-14dB	Unlimited	Yes	Yes	Yes
Proposed	Lossless	~23dB (depending on watermark size)	Unlimited	Yes	Yes	Yes (theoretically)

Figure 9 presents the PSNR of a 200×200 image watermarked with a 50×50 logo using different transparency levels, and the corresponding decoding attempts with an invalid key. We can observe that the reconstructed image with an invalid key has an almost constant PSNR, the watermark being replaced by a "noisy" pattern (as shown in Figure 8(f) for example), which does not depend on the transparency of the watermark.

We simulate a transmission with packet losses and a restoration with a median filter, as in (Leni, 2011). The univariate functions are divided into packets of 100 points, with a probability of 10% for a packet to be lost. During the simulation, 46 packets are lost. Figure 10(b) and (d) show that the image can be globally restored using a median filter, as well as the watermark. We can also note that both the watermark and the original image are degraded with a similar importance ((a)(c)).

Table 1 summarizes the comparison between our method and other recently published reversible visible watermarking approaches. We used a 64×64 watermark over a 256×256 image, preserving the ratio of $1 / 16$ between watermark and image they used (128×128 watermark over 512×512 images). Although our approach is fundamentally different because of the decomposition into univariate functions, we can see that its functionalities are similar to other classical approaches, with better results, or improved flexibility.

Moreover, since a function of any dimension can theoretically be decomposed using the KSN, we can support embedding of binary, gray level and color watermarks on binary, gray level and color images.

FUTURE RESEARCH DIRECTIONS

Several promising perspectives can be pointed out. As a consequence of the original (and non conventional) representation into univariate functions, most of attacks cannot be directly considered since they almost all belong to 2D attacks: the resilience to standard attacks has to be fully explored but extends beyond the scope of this paper which focuses on the novelty and the feasibility of the method. Nevertheless, some behaviours of the algorithm for various attack patterns can be predicted.

Classical attacks can be separated into four families (Le, 2010):

- Simple attacks aim at modifying the whole image to damage the watermark. For example, in our approach, cropping the image to remove the watermark will result in a white noise image when decoding. The resolution of the image will no longer correspond to the inner functions. This will lead to incorrect re-arrangement of values from the outer functions, thus the pixels will be random gray values. Another attack could be the addition of noise either to the univariate functions or the image, which will have the same consequences as packet-losses. The error will be spread equally on the watermark and the image.

- Detection-disabling attacks consist in breaking the correlation between hidden data and the watermarked image. Shifting or permuting data in the outer functions leads to effects similar to random values generation during the construction. It will give same results than those presented for noise addition. Therefore, similarly to packet-losses, the watermark and the image will equally be distorted.

- Concerning ambiguity attacks, the detector is confused by embedded fake watermarks. If the same public keys are used to decompose the image with another watermark, then the previous data will be overwritten. When embedding a fake watermark of same size and same position, the problem is to determine, during decoding, if the embedded watermark is genuine or not. One possible solution would be to store more values of the outer functions than required to reconstruct the images, to check if the functions are continuous. Indeed, when overwriting the outer functions with a new watermarked image, it will not be possible to determine if the remaining data are for restoration or for continuity check. During reconstruction, it is thus possible to check if the additional points are coherent with the outer functions to determine if the watermarked image is the original one.

- Removal attacks attempt at detecting and discarding hidden information. After the reconstruction using the public keys, the outer function can be analyzed to extract the unused data. Nevertheless, these data are not the watermark data, but the restoration ones. Therefore, if removed, only the ability to recover the original image is compromised.

These are only prospective examples of the potential of our approach to resist to traditional attacks, and new attacks and appropriate modifications can probably be developed. Therefore, a complete study has to be dedicated to the resilience of our scheme.

Another natural perspective concerns the extension to higher dimensions, *e.g.* colour images or video. The Superposition theorem states that any multivariate functions can be decomposed into univariate functions, and our watermarking approach remains unchanged for any number of dimensions, so it should be possible to extend it for such applications.

Eventually, this representation might be considered for compression. The advantages of representing the images by univariate functions have been illustrated, but the potential compression that could be applied to these functions remains unexplored.

CONCLUSION

We have presented a modification of the KSN algorithm for progressive transmission to embed a visible (either translucent or not) reversible watermark. The key idea is to represent the image and the authentication data by sets of univariate functions using the KSN. Once the image and the mark are converted, their pixels are re-arranged within this representation. Then, the only way to reconstruct the image or remove the watermark is to know how the arrangement has been performed, which constitutes the encryption keys. By default, the image is reconstructed with the watermark. If the user provides a correct key, the pixels covered by the watermark can be decoded to retrieve the original image without loss; otherwise, the restored image portions are random noise.

We have illustrated our approach on natural images and highlighted several advantages: the watermark is degraded similarly to the image in case of packet losses during transmission, and its global aspect can be restored, as well as the original image. In other words, the watermark cannot be removed by transmission errors, and will have a reconstruction quality similar to the image one. Another advantage lies in the ability to have different keys for any intermediate resolutions. In an environment with heterogeneous display resolutions, the rights of users with different devices can be managed separately. Furthermore, the size and transparency of the watermark can be controlled, and the watermarked image does not suffer from noise due to the embedding of additional data.

REFERENCES

Feng, J. B., Lin, I. C., Tsai, C. S., & Chu, Y. P. (2006). Reversible watermarking: Current status and key issues. *International Journal of Network Security*, 2(3), 161–171.

Hartung, F., & Kutter, M. (1999). Multimedia watermarking techniques. *Proceedings of the IEEE*, 87(7), 1079–1107. doi:10.1109/5.771066

Hecht-Nielsen, R. (1987). Kolmogorov's mapping neural network existence theorem. In *Proceedings of the IEEE International Conference on Neural Networks III* (pp. 11-13). IEEE.

Hu, Y., & Jeon, B. (2006b). Reversible visible watermarking and lossless recovery of original images. *IEEE Transactions on Circuits and Systems for Video Technology*, 16(11), 1423–1429. doi:10.1109/TCSVT.2006.884011

Hu, Y., Kwong, S., & Huang, J. (2006a). An algorithm for removable visible watermarking. *IEEE Transactions on Circuits and Systems for Video Technology*, 16(1), 129–133. doi:10.1109/TCSVT.2005.858742

Igelnik, B. (2009). Kolmogorov's spline complex network and adaptative dynamic modeling of data. In *complex-valued neural networks: Utilizing high dimensional parameters* (pp. 56-78). Hershey, PA: IGI Global.

Igelnik, B., Pao, Y.-H., & LeClair, S. R. (1999). The ensemble approach to neural-network learning and generalization. *IEEE Transactions on Neural Networks*, 10(1), 19–30. doi:10.1109/72.737490

Igelnik, B., & Parikh, N. (2003). Kolmogorov's spline network. *IEEE Transactions on Neural Networks*, 14(4), 725–733. doi:10.1109/TNN.2003.813830

Igelnik, B., Tabib-Azar, M., & LeClair, S. R. (2001). A net with complex weights. *IEEE Transactions on Neural Networks*, 12(2), 236–249. doi:10.1109/72.914521

Le, T. H. N., Nguyen, K. H., & Le, H. B. (2010). Literature survey on image watermarking tools, watermark attacks and benchmarking tools. *Second International Conferences on Advances in Multimedia (MMEDIA)* (pp. 67-73). IEEE.

Leni, P.-E., Fougerolle, Y. D., & Truchetet, F. (2009). Kolmogorov superposition theorem and wavelet decomposition for image compression. *Lecture Notes in Computer Science*, 5807, 43–53. doi:10.1007/978-3-642-04697-1_5

Leni, P.-E., Fougerolle, Y. D., & Truchetet, F. (2011). The Kolmogorov spline network for image processing. In Igelnik, B. (Ed.), *Computational Modeling and Simulation of Intellect: Current State and Future Perspectives* (pp. 25–51). Hershey, PA: IGI Global. doi:10.4018/978-1-60960-551-3.ch002

Liu, T. Y., & Tsai, W. H. (2010). Generic lossless visible watermarking - A new approach. *IEEE Transactions on Image Processing, 19*(5), 1224–1235. doi:10.1109/TIP.2010.2040757

Moon, B. S. (2001). An explicit solution for the cubic spline interpolation for functions of a single variable. *Applied Mathematics and Computation, 117,* 251–255. doi:10.1016/S0096-3003(99)00178-2

Perez-Freire, L., Comesana, P., Troncoso-Pastoriza, J. R., & Perez-Gonzalez, F. (2006). Watermarking security: A survey. *Lecture Notes in Computer Science, 4300,* 41–73. doi:10.1007/11926214_2

Sadeghi, A. R. (2008). *The marriage of cryptography and watermarking - beneficial and challenging for secure watermarking and detection* (pp. 2–18). Digital Watermarking. doi:10.1007/978-3-540-92238-4_2

Singh, J., Garg, P., & De, A. N. (2009). Watermarking of unified multimedia data types, audio and image. *Annual IEEE India Conference (INDICON)* (pp. 1-4). IEEE.

Sprecher, D. A., & Draghici, S. (2002). Space-filling curves and Kolmogorov superposition-based neural networks. *Neural Networks, 15*(1), 57–67. doi:10.1016/S0893-6080(01)00107-1

Tsai, H. M., & Chang, L. W. (2007). A high secure reversible visible watermarking scheme. In *IEEE International Conference on Multimedia and Expo* (pp. 2106-2109). ISBN 1424410169

Tsai, H. M., & Chang, L. W. (2010). Secure reversible visible image watermarking with authentication. *Signal Processing Image Communication, 25*(1), 10–17. doi:10.1016/j.image.2009.11.002

Yang, Y., Sun, X., Yang, H., & Li, C. T. (2008). Removable visible image watermarking algorithm in the discrete cosine transform domain. *Journal of Electronic Imaging, 17*(3), 033008. doi:10.1117/1.2952843

Yang, Y., Sun, X., Yang, H., Li, C. T., & Xiao, R. (2009). A contrast-sensitive reversible visible image watermarking technique. *IEEE Transactions on Circuits and Systems for Video Technology, 19*(5), 656–667. doi:10.1109/TCSVT.2009.2017401

Yip, S. K., Au, O., Ho, C. W., & Wong, H. M. (2006). Lossless visible watermarking. *IEEE International Conference on Multimedia and Expo* (pp. 853-856). IEEE.

ADDITIONAL READING

Bodyanskiy, Y., Kolodyazhniy, V., & Otto, P. (2005). Neuro-fuzzy Kolmogorov's network for time series prediction and pattern classification. *Lecture Notes in Computer Science, 3698,* 191–202. doi:10.1007/11551263_16

Brattka, V. (2004). *Du 13-ième problème de Hibert à la théorie des réseaux de neurones: Aspects constructifs du théorème de superposition de Kolmogorov*. Paris, France: Editions Belin.

Braun, J., & Griebel, M. (2007). On a constructive proof of Kolmogorov's superposition theorem. *Constructive Approximation, 30*(3), 653–675. doi:10.1007/s00365-009-9054-2

Cheng, H., & Li, X. (1996). On the application of image decomposition to image compression and encryption. In *Proceedings of Communications and Multimedia Security II, IFIP TC6/TC11 Second Joint Working Conference on Communications and Multimedia Security, 96,* 116-128. IEEE.

Coppejans, M. (2003). On Kolmogorov's representation of functions of several variables by functions of one variable. *Journal of Econometrics, 123,* 1–31. doi:10.1016/j.jeconom.2003.10.026

Girosi, F., & Poggio, T. (1989). Representation properties of networks: Kolmogorov's theorem is irrelevant. *Neural Computation, 1*(4), 465–469. doi:10.1162/neco.1989.1.4.465

Ismailov, V. E. (2008). On the representation by linear superpositions. *Journal of Approximation Theory, 151*(2), 113–125. doi:10.1016/j.jat.2007.09.003

Kolodyazhniy, V., & Bodyanskiy, Y. (2004). Fuzzy Kolmogorov's network. *Lecture Notes in Computer Science*, 764–771. doi:10.1007/978-3-540-30133-2_100

Köppen, M. (2002). On the training of a Kolmogorov Network. *Lecture Notes in Computer Science, 2415*, 140–145. doi:10.1007/3-540-46084-5_77

Köppen, M., & Yoshida, K. (2005). Universal representation of image functions by the Sprecher construction. *Soft Computing as Transdisciplinary Science and Technology, 29*, 202–210. doi:10.1007/3-540-32391-0_28

Kurkova, V. (1991). Kolmogorov's theorem is relevant. *Neural Computation, 3*, 617–622. doi:10.1162/neco.1991.3.4.617

Kurkova, V. (1992). Kolmogorov's theorem and multilayer neural networks. *Neural Networks, 5*, 501–506. doi:10.1016/0893-6080(92)90012-8

Lagunas, M. A., Pérez-Neira, A., Najar, M., & Pagés, A. (1993). The Kolmogorov signal processor. *Lecture Notes in Computer Science, 686*, 494–512. doi:10.1007/3-540-56798-4_194

Lamarque, C. H., & Robert, F. (1996). Image analysis using space-filling curves and 1D wavelet bases. *Pattern Recognition, 29*(8), 1309–1322. doi:10.1016/0031-3203(95)00157-3

Leni, P.-E., Fougerolle, Y. D., & Truchetet, F. (2008). Kolmogorov superposition theorem and its application to multivariate function decompositions and image representation. In *Proceedings of IEEE conference on Signal-Image Technology & Internet-Based System* (344-351). Washington, DC: IEEE.

Liu, Y., Wang, Y., Zhang, B. F., & Wu, G. F. (2004). Ensemble algorithm of neural networks and its application. In *Proceedings of 2004 International Conference on Machine Learning and Cybernetics* (vol. 6).

Nakamura, M., Mines, R., & Kreinovich, V. (1993). Guaranteed intervals for Kolmogorov's theorem (and their possible relation to neural networks). *Interval Computations, 3*, 183–199.

Nees, M. (1993). Approximation versions of Kolmogorov's superposition theorem, proved constructively. *Journal of Computational and Applied Mathematics, 54*, 239–250. doi:10.1016/0377-0427(94)90179-1

Ozturk, I., & Sogukpinar, I. (2004). Analysis and comparison of image encryption algorithms. [International Conference on Information Technology.]. *Proceedings of ICIT, 2004*, 38–42.

Pednault, E. (2006). Transform regression and the Kolmogorov superposition theorem. In *Proceedings of the Sixth SIAM International Conference on Data Mining* (35-46). Society for Industrial Mathematics.

Sprecher, D. A. (1965). On the structure of continuous functions of several variables. *Transactions of the American Mathematical Society, 115*(3), 340–355. doi:10.1090/S0002-9947-1965-0210852-X

Sprecher, D. A. (1996). A numerical implementation of Kolmogorov's superpositions. *Neural Networks, 9*(5), 765–772. doi:10.1016/0893-6080(95)00081-X

Sprecher, D. A. (1997). A numerical implementation of Kolmogorov's superpositions II. *Neural Networks, 10*(3), 447–457. doi:10.1016/S0893-6080(96)00073-1

Vecci, L., Piazza, F., & Uncini, A. (1998). Learning and approximation capabilities of adaptive spline activation function neural networks. *Neural Networks, 11*, 259–270. doi:10.1016/S0893-6080(97)00118-4

Chapter 6

Real-Time Fuzzy Logic-Based Hybrid Robot Path-Planning Strategies for a Dynamic Environment

Napoleon H. Reyes
Massey University, New Zealand

Teo Susnjak
Massey University, New Zealand

Andre L.C. Barczak
Massey University, New Zealand

Peter Sinčák
Technical University of Košice, Slovakia

Ján Vaščák
Technical University of Košice, Slovakia

ABSTRACT

This chapter sets out to explore the intricacies behind developing a hybrid system for real-time autonomous robot navigation, with target pursuit and obstacle avoidance behaviour, in a dynamic environment. Three complete systems are described, namely, a cascade of four fuzzy systems, a hybrid fuzzy A* system, and a hybrid fuzzy A* with a Voronoi diagram. A highly reconfigurable integration architecture is presented, allowing for the harmonious interplay between the different component algorithms, with the option of engaging or disengaging from the system. The utilization of both global and local information about the environment is examined, as well as an additional optimal global path-planning layer. Moreover, how a fuzzy system design approach could take advantage of the presence of symmetry in the input space, cutting down the number of rules and membership functions, without sacrificing control precision is illustrated. The efficiency of all the algorithms is demonstrated by employing them in a simulation of a real-world system: the robot soccer game. Results indicate that the hybrid system can generate smooth, near-shortest paths, as well as near-shortest-safest paths, when all component algorithms are activated. A systematic approach to calibrating the system is also provided.

DOI: 10.4018/978-1-4666-3942-3.ch006

INTRODUCTION

The unrelenting demands of real-world systems for computing speed, high-precision, and adaptability have always pushed intelligent systems to their limits. Within the confines of the problem of robot navigation in a dynamic and competitive environment many design issues arise (Kim, 2012). Firstly, real-time execution must be accomplished. A system that employs computer vision for perceiving the environment (Chang & Chen, 2005; Chang & Chen, 2000; Reyes & Dadios, 2004) will have to respond approximately every 33-50msec., depending on the frame rate of the camera and object tracking algorithms. Secondly, optimal path-planning might be required. A deterministic algorithm with a guarantee of optimality (Garrido, Moreno, Blanco, & Jurewicz, 2011) would usually require a global map of the environment to succeed. Otherwise, this map will have to be built on the fly, requiring substantial memory space and running time. On the other hand, if optimal path planning is not a must, reactionary algorithms (Jayasiri, Mann, & Gosine, 2011) can respond quickly with smooth navigation, without the need for a global map. Their performance, however, is easily curtailed when barricades form a U-shape, and gets them trapped. Last but not least, system calibration is also another major issue. Considering the number of parameters that can be fiddled with, and the number of possible permutations involved, a conglomeration of algorithms tied up together can be burdensome to fine-tune, in order to produce the desired robot behaviour. A calibration map is later presented in one of the subsections of this chapter to demonstrate how this daunting calibration task can be alleviated.

The chapter starts-off with an overview of the problem of real-time robot navigation with target pursuit and obstacle avoidance in a dynamic and competitive environment. Three suitable algorithm solutions are presented in detail, namely the cascade of fuzzy systems, the hybrid fuzzy A* algorithm operating on a fixed grid (Gerdelan & Reyes, 2006b; Gerdelan & Reyes, 2006a;

Gerdelan & Reyes, 2009) and the hybrid fuzzy A* utilizing a Voronoi diagram. Each algorithm is discussed with accompanying insights on how it is adapted to the problem domain, followed by a characterisation of its performance and limitations, via a simulation system, in the context of the robot soccer game. In contrast to traditional fuzzy system designs, this chapter presents a solution that capitalizes on the presence of symmetry inherent to the problem, and cuts down the number of fuzzy rules significantly without sacrificing precision and smooth navigation.

The algorithms are discussed in increasing order of complexity. The discussions eventually lead to the fusion of the algorithms into one powerful hybrid fuzzy A* system. An extension of the hybrid system, utilising a Voronoi diagram for increased path safety in hostile environments is also presented. Lastly, essential calibration techniques are provided and this is accompanied by experimental results.

BACKGROUND

Path planning algorithms in the context of robot soccer need to deal with two important problems, among many others: target pursuit and obstacle avoidance. In this context, the environment is well-known (e.g., the limits of the field), and any changes in the inputs are also well constrained. The targets can be the ball, or the goal, or a point within the field where the robot has to be strategically positioned. Changes are updated by the camera on top of the field, and a relatively simple computer vision algorithm keeps track of the positions (including angles) of the ball and the robots. The challenge is to find an optimal (or at least near-optimal one that does not get the robot stuck in corners and partial enclosures) path to arrive as fast as possible on the target coordinates, while avoiding other robots. The scope of this chapter is confined to near-optimal, path-planning and reactionary algorithms that utilize some local or global information about the space of traversal.

Kim, Kim, Kim, Kim, and Vadakkepat (1998) proposed several reactionary solutions to path planning. A very successful algorithm is the Potential Field algorithm. In this method, the robot can move in proportion to forces resulting from a target (attractive force) or an obstacle (repulsive force). Although the algorithm is simple to implement and can run in real-time, there are limitations, such as the size of obstacles. In extreme cases, the final point cannot be guaranteed. Kim, Kim, Kim, Kim, and Vadakkepat (1998) explored the potential field approach in an evolutionary way (Evolutionary Artificial Potential Field) and proposed real-time algorithms for robot soccer. Simulation results were reported to be very consistent with the needs, although in practice a combination with other methods is used. Other remarkable works in path-planning include Park, Kim, Ahn, and Jeon (2006), Park, Stonier, Kim, Ahn, and Jeon (2007), Kim and Kim (n.d.), Kim, Kim, Choi, and Park (2009), Lee and Kim (2009), Lee, Na, and Kim (2010), Lee, Kim, and Myung, (2011), and Zaheer and Kim (2011).

Fuzzy Cognitive Maps, a member of decision-making algorithms resembling the structure of Neural Networks have also been applied to the area of control and robotics in the last decade (Golmohammadi, Azadeh, & Gharehgozli, 2006; Vašák & Madarasz, 2010). It was shown in Vašák & Madarasz (2010) that under some limiting conditions, FCMs can be trained using supervised learning, allowing them to be adapted for solving navigation problems. FCMs also fall under the category of reactionary algorithms, without the need for global information about the space of traversal. Therefore, FCMs would perform better if it is used in conjunction with an optimal path-planning algorithm, like A* (Hart, Nilsson, & Raphael, 1968).

Bruce (2006) has surveyed several solutions to problems in the robot soccer context. He also proposed solutions considering some of the important issues when dealing with cooperative robots. He proposed a Waypoint cache to allow for the re-use of previous waypoints to plan for the next path move. He also surveyed collision detection algorithms. One of the interesting observations is that most of the research done in the area of collision detection focused on simulations or graphics, where it is important to find all possible pairs of objects that can collide. This approach usually leads to computationally expensive algorithms, usually not very useful in this context. He applied an algorithm based on RRT (Rapidly Exploring Random Tree), which allowed for a better performance. However, RRTs are usually not sufficient to resolve the path alone.

In the robot soccer game, having the ability to do optimal path-planning is certainly a big advantage, but not all algorithms possess that capability. Reactionary algorithms, such as the one described in Jayasiri, Mann, and Gosine (2011) and Calisi (2009), can respond quickly with smooth navigation, without the need for a global map. However, their performance gets easily curtailed when barricades form a U-shape, entrapping them.

Yetisenler and Ozkurt (2006) and Behring, Bracho, Castro, and Moreno (2000) used a Cellular Automata-based approach to find the path. Although the algorithm can be made to work in real time, it is not clear how it would cope-up with a reasonable number of dynamic obstacles, as the empirical results do not show detailed scenarios.

Genetic Algorithms (GA) do not guarantee returning an optimal solution and are not generally amenable to solving real-time problems. On the other hand, there is a GA-based system reported in the literature that works in real-time for robot soccer navigation (e.g. Linquan, Zhongwen, Zhonghua, & Weixian, 2008).

CASCADE OF FUZZY SYSTEMS

Algorithm Description

Target pursuit and obstacle avoidance robot behaviour are implemented using a cascade of four fuzzy systems that are automatically triggered based on the prevailing environment conditions.

These are reactionary systems that deliver fast and smooth control response without requiring a complete mapping of the entire exploratory space. They are executed every few milliseconds (approx. 33 msec.) depending on the rate of updates of the sensors (e.g. camera) and environment processors (e.g. image processing and object tracking algorithms). Each of these fuzzy systems feed on only two types of inputs: angle and distance values, as illustrated in Figure 1. For target pursuit, the inputs are the angle of the target relative to the robot's heading angle, and the distance of the target from the robot. Similarly, obstacle avoidance feeds on the angle of the nearest obstacle, relative to the robot's heading angle, and the distance of the nearest obstacle from the robot.

In contrast to traditional fuzzy system designs, the approach taken by the fuzzy systems described in this chapter takes advantage of the presence of symmetry in the input space. Traditional fuzzy system designs typically use an odd number of fuzzy sets (Figures 2a & 3a), taking into account the negative, positive and central regions in the input space. Smooth control response is typically produced by defining roughly about 5 to 7 fuzzy sets per input parameter (Figure 3a), allowing for

a refined set of control rules. Moreover, a sample rule using the traditional approach would explicitly indicate the direction of turning of the robot, apart from the magnitude of turning.

Sample Traditional Fuzzy Rule for Target Pursuit (Steering angle):

Sample Rule 1: If Distance from Target is NEAR and Angle from Target is NEGATIVELY LARGE Then Turn the robot Sharply to the LEFT.

In this system, only half of the angle space is actually used to define the fuzzy sets for the input angle. From Figures 2b & 3c, it can be seen that only three fuzzy sets are defined, namely SMALL, MEDIUM and LARGE. In effect, there are no fuzzy sets defined for negative angles. As a consequence, the outputs of the fuzzy rules are generic. They no longer indicate the direction of turning of the robot, as the fuzzy sets do not indicate whether the target is on the left or right-hand side of the robot. A sample rule used by the system is as follows:

Sample Fuzzy Rule for Target Pursuit Taking Advantage of Symmetry:

Figure 1. Angle and distance calculations

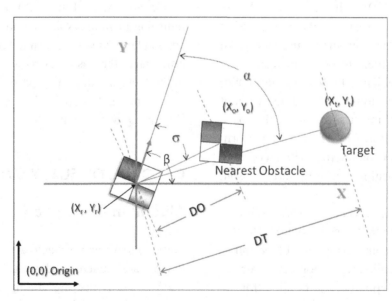

Figure 2. a) Traditional fuzzy logic system design. b) Symmetry-based fuzzy logic system design. Legend: NL-Negatively Large, NM-Negatively Medium, NS-Negatively Small, ZE-Zero, PS-Positively Small, PM-Positively Medium and PL-Positively Large).

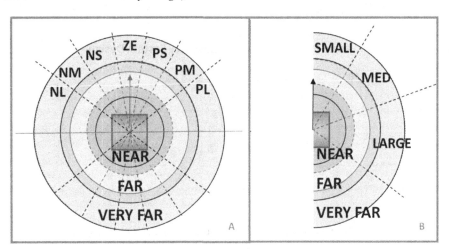

Sample Rule 2: If (Distance from Target is NEAR) and (Angle from target is LARGE) Then Turn the robot Sharply.

Since the fuzzy rule does not indicate any specific direction, but merely the magnitude of turning, the same rule can be used regardless of whether the target is on the left, or right, provided that the magnitude of the angle meets the fuzzy set parameters. The only requirement is to keep track of the relative position of the target (left-hand side or right-hand side), with respect to the robot's heading angle. In order to calculate the precise angle of turning, the final output of the fuzzy system is negated whenever the target is on the right-hand side; that is, to turn the robot clockwise, to pursue the target. On the other hand, if the target is on the left-hand side, the final (positive) output of the fuzzy system is used as it is, in order to turn the robot counter-clockwise towards the target. It is worth-noting that by taking advantage of the presence of symmetry in the input space, and negating the fuzzy system's output whenever deemed necessary, the system described here (using only three fuzzy sets) is equivalent to using six fuzzy sets covering the left and right regions of the input space.

The approach described here significantly reduces the number of required fuzzy sets; thereby, reducing also the number of required fuzzy rules, allowing the algorithm to execute much faster without compromising the accuracy of control. The complete algorithmic description of the cascade of fuzzy systems for target pursuit and obstacle avoidance can be found in Algorithm 1. We describe target pursuit first, and then we describe the details of the obstacle avoidance system next, and show how it is integrated with target pursuit.

Target Pursuit

A combination of two fuzzy systems is employed to implement the complete target pursuit behavior. One of the fuzzy systems (fuzzy system 1, Algorithm 1) handles the steering angle calculation, while another handles the speed adjustment calculations (fuzzy system 2, Algorithm 1). Both fuzzy systems feed exactly on the same set of inputs.

The complete definition of the fuzzy associative memory matrix (FAMM) for adjusting the steering angle for target pursuit is shown in Table 1, defining only 9 rules for a 3x3 FAMM, but taking advantage of symmetry in the input space. This is comparable to a traditional fuzzy

Figure 3. Membership functions for the angle and distance. (a) Angle membership functions for the traditional fuzzy system design (b) Distance membership functions for the traditional fuzzy system design (c) Angle membership functions for the symmetry-based fuzzy system design (d) Distance membership functions for the symmetry-based fuzzy system design

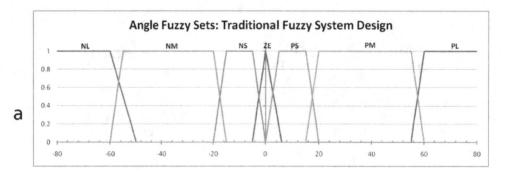

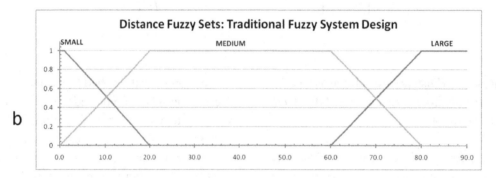

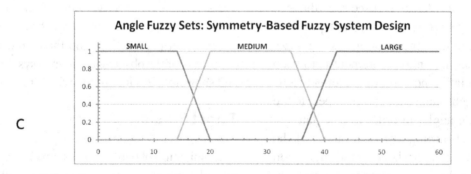

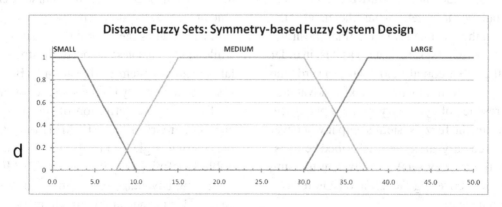

Table 1. Fuzzy Associative Memory Matrix for Target Pursuit, Steering Angle

	Near	Far	Very far
Small	Mild Turn	Mild Turn	Zero Turn
Medium	Med Turn	Mild Turn	Mild Turn
Large	Sharp Turn	Med Turn	Med Turn

Table 2. Fuzzy Associative Memory Matrix for Target Pursuit, Speed Adjustment

	Near	Far	Very far
Small	Med Speed	Fast Speed	Very Fast
Medium	Slow Speed	Med Speed	Fast Speed
Large	Very Slow	Slow Speed	Slow Speed

system design that uses a 7x3 FAMM, requiring 21 rules to solve the same problem.

Lines 1 to 7 of Algorithm 1 describes the calculation steps for executing target pursuit. The target pursuit behaviour is only activated when the target is far enough to be sought; that is, if the distance from the target (DT) is greater than some pre-defined constant K1. K1 specifies how close enough the robot needs to be to hit the target.

As described previously, the fuzzy system 1 considers only the magnitude of the input parameters. To be precise, it feeds on the absolute value of the input angle from the target (α) and the distance from the target (DT). Furthermore, the fuzzy system returns only the magnitude of the steering angle adjustment (θ, line *2*, Algorithm 1). The direction of the final steering angle adjustment relies on another variable (TP) that specifies the position of the target, relative to the robot's heading angle (lines *3,4,5*, Algorithm 1). The negation operation is performed based on the value of variable TP.

Fuzzy system 2 is responsible for adjusting the speed of the robot while pursuing a target. It feeds on exactly the same inputs used by fuzzy system 1 and also uses the same fuzzy sets for angle and distance. The only difference is that the outputs of the rules reflect the absolute speed of the robot. Its complete FAMM is defined in Table 2 and a sample rule is given below.

Sample Fuzzy Rule for Adjusting the Speed for Target Pursuit:

Sample Rule 2: If the Angle from the target is Large and the Distance is Near Then move the robot Very Slowly.

The rationale behind the given speed adjustment rule is that the robot should move very cautiously when the target is already close by, so as not to overshoot it.

Obstacle Avoidance

Similar to the architecture of the fuzzy systems for target pursuit, a combination of two fuzzy systems is employed to implement the complete obstacle avoidance behavior. Fuzzy system 3 (Algorithm 1) handles the steering angle calculation, while another system handles the speed adjustment calculations (fuzzy system 4, Algorithm 1). Both fuzzy systems feed exactly on the same set of inputs.

The complete definition of the fuzzy associative memory matrix (FAMM) for adjusting the steering angle for target pursuit is shown in Table 3, defining a generic set of rules that takes advantage of symmetry in the input space.

Lines *8* to *15* of Algorithm 1 describes the calculation steps for executing the obstacle avoidance behaviour. Obstacle avoidance overrides the calculated angle for pursuit (θ) and pursuit speed (RS) whenever the nearest obstacle is getting too close to the robot, and if it is located on the same

Table 3. Fuzzy Associative Memory Matrix for Obstacle Avoidance, Steering Angle

	Near	Far	Very far
Small	Very Sharp	Sharp Turn	Med Turn
Medium	Sharp Turn	Med Turn	Mild Turn
Large	Med Turn	Mild Turn	Zero Turn

side as the target, as indicated by variables OP and TP (line *8*, Algorithm 1). K2 specifies the safe distance tolerance.

Similar to fuzzy system 1 and 2, fuzzy system 3 considers only the magnitude of the input parameters. To be precise, it feeds on the absolute value of the input angle from the nearest obstacle, relative to the robot's heading angle (σ) and the distance from the nearest obstacle (DO). For clarity, these parameters are illustrated in Figure1.

As compared to target pursuit rules, the fuzzy rules for obstacle avoidance work in the opposite fashion.

Referring to Sample Rule 3, the robot is instructed to turn very sharply away from the obstacle to avoid collision, as the obstacle is close by and the angle is small.

Sample Fuzzy Rule for Adjusting the Steering Angle for Obstacle Avoidance:

Sample Rule 3: If (Angle from the nearest Obstacle is SMALL and the Distance from the nearest Obstacle is NEAR) Then turn the robot Very Sharply.

Furthermore, the fuzzy system returns only the magnitude of the steering angle adjustment (θ, line *9*, Algorithm 1). The direction of the final steering angle adjustment relies on another variable (OP) that specifies the position of the nearest obstacle, relative to the robot's heading angle (lines *10*, *11 & 12*, Algorithm 1). The negation operation is performed based on the value of variable OP.

Lastly, fuzzy system 4 is responsible for adjusting the speed of the robot to avoid an obstacle safely (line *13 & 14*, Algorithm 1). It feeds on exactly the same inputs used by fuzzy system 3 and also uses the same fuzzy sets for angle and distance. The only difference is that the outputs of the rules reflect the absolute speed of the robot. Its complete FAMM is defined in Table 4 and a sample rule is given below.

Table 4. Fuzzy Associative Memory Matrix for Obstacle Avoidance, Speed Adjustment

	Near	**Far**	**Very far**
Small	Very Slow	Slow Speed	Fast Fast
Medium	Slow Speed	Fast Speed	Very Fast
Large	Fast Speed	Very Fast	Top Speed

Sample Fuzzy Rule for Adjusting the Speed for Obstacle Avoidance:

Sample Rule 4: If the Angle from the obstacle is Large and the Distance is Near Then move the robot Very Fast.

The rationale behind the given speed adjustment rule is that even if the obstacle is near, the robot is still at liberty to speed up, as it is not moving towards the obstacle (large angle). Therefore the robot is instructed to move very fast. A sample run of Algorithm 1 can be found in Figure 4.

Utilizing the Outputs of the Cascade of Fuzzy Systems in a Simulation System and in the Real Micro-Soccer Robots

As can be seen from Algorithm 1, the cascade of fuzzy systems for target pursuit and obstacle avoidance is only invoked when the target is deemed far enough to be pursued (line *1*, Algorithm 1). The final results of the combined fuzzy systems calculations represent the target steering angle adjustment (θ) and the absolute speed of the robot (RS). The steering angle adjustment (θ) is then algebraically added to the current angle of the robot (β) (line *16*, Algorithm 1). Angle β represents the absolute angle of the robot, while RS represents the absolute speed of the robot. Both can be readily used by the simulation system for plotting the robot on screen straight away.

Figure 4. Cascade of fuzzy systems with target pursuit and obstacle avoidance behaviour

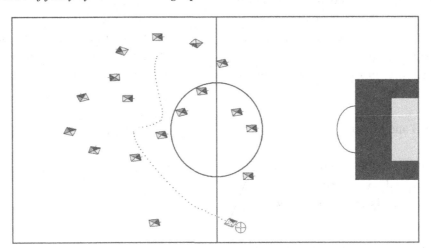

On the other hand, for controlling the real micro-soccer robots, the calculated steering angle adjustment (θ) needs to be transformed into left and right wheel velocities that will produce the same angle (θ) of turning the robot. Moreover, the absolute speed (RS) will have to be mapped into its equivalent left and right wheel velocities that will drive the robot at speed RS. A typical conversion approach in the literature would suggest employing physics equations that calculate for the pivot point of the turn, the radius of the turn, and so on, and so forth. In this chapter we present a way of alleviating this conversion problem. The robot turning action is generally produced by introducing a wheel velocity difference between the left and right wheels, proportional to the calculated steering angle adjustment (θ). This is carried out by empirically deriving a mapping function between the effective robot turning angle, and the combination of left and right wheel motor control units. This approach therefore avoids the rigors of physics equations altogether, while still producing smooth control.

To illustrate our approach, let us consider one concrete motor control instruction mapping example. Given that the cascade of fuzzy systems returned a desired robot speed RS of 5 cm./sec., and that the calculated target steering angle adjustment

θ is 30 degrees, the left and right wheel motor control instructions can be calculated as follows:

Assumptions:

- Motors attached to the wheels can be spun within a range of [0, 255] motor control units.

- It takes the vision system to capture a frame and track all the objects in the scene at T_{vision} seconds, within the range [0.033 sec., 0.050 sec.].

- A steering angle adjustment of $\theta = 30$ degrees, to be achieved in T_{vision} sec. is equivalent to having a motor control instruction difference of (30 degrees. * $K_{angularVelocity}$ control units/degrees) = 6 control units, between the left and right motors; where $K_{angularVelocity}$ represents an angular velocity coefficient, set to a constant value of 1/5 control units/degrees, and is empirically derived.

- A speed of RS = 5 cm./sec. can be effected by setting $Motor_{left}$ = 35 control units, and $Motor_{right}$ = 35 control units; that is, (5 cm./sec. * $K_{velocity}$ (control units * sec.)/cm.) = 35 control units. We have an empirically derived constant, $K_{velocity}$ = 7 (control units * sec.)/cm.

Subsequently, the motor control instruction set that will drive the robot to turn 30 degrees at a speed of 5 cm./sec. can be calculated directly by adding/subtracting (6 control units / 2) = 3 control units, from each of the wheels' motor control instructions.

$$\text{Motor}_{left} = 35 + 3 \text{ and } \text{Motor}_{right} = 35 - 3$$

The application of the addition/subtraction operation will depend on whether target pursuit or obstacle avoidance is engaged, and whether the location of the target or obstacle is on the left or right-hand side of the robot's heading angle.

It is worth-noting that the set of motor control instructions do not guarantee getting the robot to the target steering angle (e.g. due to wheel slippage, for instance). Nevertheless, since the control system quickly recalculates a new set of motor control instructions, for every captured frame, for only a fraction of a second (T_{vision} sec.), any deficit/overshoot is quickly compensated for accordingly, resulting in a smooth navigation.

Algorithm 1. Cascade of fuzzy systems for target pursuit and obstacle avoidance

```
Inputs:
        angle to target              α  //absolute value of the input angle
        angle to nearest obstacle    σ // absolute value of the input angle
        target position              TP (RIGHT or LEFT)
        distance to target           DT
        distance to nearest obstacle DO
        distance coefficients     K1 , K2
        obstacle position            OP (RIGHT or LEFT)
        angle of the robot        β
        speed of the robot        RS
        fuzzy angle                  θ //angle increment/decrement

        4 structures with fuzzy information:
            pursuit steering    PA
            pursuit speed       PS
            avoidance steering angle  AA
            avoidance speed     AS
        Temporary variables:
        Temporary robot speed        FS

Outputs:    robot's angle    β
            robot's speed    RS

1    if (DT > K1 )then
            //Fuzzy system 1
2        θ = Fuzzy(α , DT , PA)
3        if ( TP = RIGHT) then                  ⎫
4            θ = -θ                             ⎪
5        endif                                  ⎬  Target Pursuit
            //Fuzzy system 2                    ⎪
6        FS = Fuzzy(α , DT , PS)                ⎪
7        RS = FS                                ⎭
8        if ( DO < K2 && OP == TP) then        ⎫
            //Fuzzy system 3                    ⎪
9            θ = Fuzzy(σ , DO , AA)  //conditionally overrides θ  ⎪
10           if ( OP == LEFT ) then             ⎪
11               θ = -θ                         ⎬  Obstacle Avoidance
12           endif                              ⎪
            //Fuzzy system 4                    ⎪
13           FS  = Fuzzy(σ , DO , AS)           ⎪
14           RS = FS      //conditionally overrides RS  ⎪
15       endif                                  ⎭
16       β = β + θ
17    endif
18    return RS, β
```

SAMPLE EMPIRICAL RESULT: THE HYBRID FUZZY A* ALGORITHM USING A FIXED GRID

The cascade of fuzzy systems described in the previous section is a fast reactionary algorithm that is not capable of optimal path-planning. It is actually susceptible to getting trapped in a tight U-shaped obstacles formation, especially when the robot, obstacle and target align with each other. This is not much of a concern for the robot soccer game, as the obstacles are usually moving, but for static obstacles forming an enclosure, as in a maze, the problem will become more evident.

Interestingly, an optimal and deterministic path-planning algorithm can be fused with the cascade of fuzzy systems to solve this problem. We take a fast and popular search algorithm called A* (Hart, 1968) for this purpose. The A* algorithm guarantees finding an optimal path, provided that the heuristic used is admissible. By applying the dynamic programming optimality principle, A*'s performance is enhanced further by limiting its search down to the number of states in the graph, rather than to the number of non-looping paths. This is accomplished by employing the A* algorithm with the strict expanded list, and using a consistent heuristic (Lozano-Pérez & Kaelbling, 2005). This enhancement to A* is employed in the experiments.

We describe a highly modular and flexible hybrid fuzzy A* architecture in Algorithm 2. The A* algorithm is used as an optimal path-planning layer that generates the waypoints (comprising the shortest path) leading towards the target. In turn, these waypoints serve as a rough guide to the cascade of fuzzy systems, preventing the robot from getting trapped in enclosures, while calculating a near-optimal smooth path towards the target.

As indicated in line 1 of Algorithm 2, the A* algorithm feeds on the x and y coordinates of all objects in the exploratory space (i.e. x_t, y_t, x_r, y_r, SO), to calculate the optimal path. However, A* could only calculate the optimal path on a grid

world representation of the space. Therefore, prior to calculating the path itself, the space of traversal is first discretized by generating its grid world representation (using a fixed cell size = robot's width) and marking all cells occupied by the obstacles, target and the robot itself. From the grid world, A* uses the cell occupied by the robot as the starting state, and it also uses the cell occupied by the target as the goal state. In addition, all cells occupied by the obstacles are blocked so that they will never be considered as part of the shortest path. Once the shortest path is determined based on the grid world (Figure 5a), A* passes the coordinates of the next waypoint to the cascade of fuzzy systems, leading the robot towards the target (Figure 5b). It is worth-noting that the fuzzy systems no longer refer to the final target destination, not unless it is the next waypoint. In order to produce a smooth path, the fuzzy systems do not force the robot to pass through the waypoints at all. As can be seen from line *3* of Algorithm 2, the robot will only be pursuing a waypoint up to some distance threshold value (K1). When the robot gets

Figure 5. Hybrid Fuzzy A(using a fixed grid) for near-optimal path-planning (shortest path)*

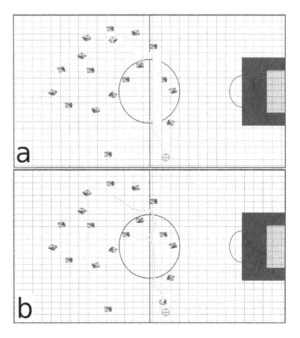

Algorithm 2. Cascade of Fuzzy Systems with A* (Hybrid Fuzzy A*)

```
Inputs:
        coordinates of the target      x_t, y_t
        coordinates of the robot       x_r, y_r
        coordinates of the next way point    x_W, y_W
        set of coordinates of all obstacles   SO={(x_o1, y_o1), (x_o2, y_o2),...(x_oN, y_oN)}
        angle to next way point        γ
        angle to nearest obstacle      σ
        next way point position        WP (RIGHT or LEFT) //to the left or to the right, relative to the robot's heading angle

        distance to next way point     DW
        distance to nearest obstacle        DO
        distance coefficients          K1 , K2
        obstacle position              OP(RIGHT or LEFT)
        angle of the robot             β
        fuzzy angle                       θ  //angle increment/decrement

        4 structures with fuzzy information:
                pursuit steering     PA
                pursuit speed        PS
                avoidance steering angle  AA
                avoidance speed      AS
        Temporary variables:
        Temporary robot speed        FS

Outputs:    robot's angle          β
            robot's speed          RS

            Intermediary output:
            //a set of coordinates of waypoints towards the target
            path = {(x1_w, y1_w),(x2_w, y2_w),(x3_w, y3_w),...,(xM_w, yM_w)}

1       path = ComputePathA*(x_t, y_t, x_r, y_r, SO) //compute shortest path from robot to target
2       (x_W, y_W, γ, DW) = GetNextWayPoint(path) //get next way point using the path
3       if (DW > K1 )then
                //Fuzzy system 1
4               θ = Fuzzy(γ , DW , PA)
5               if ( WP = RIGHT) then
6                    θ = -θ
7               endif                                    } Target Pursuit
                //Fuzzy system 2
8               FS = Fuzzy(γ , DW , PS)
9               RS = FS
10              if ( DO < K2 && OP == WP) then
                        //Fuzzy system 3
11                      θ = Fuzzy(σ , DO , AA) //conditionally overrides θ
12                      if( OP == LEFT) then
13                           θ = -θ
14                      endif
                        //Fuzzy system 4                     } Obstacle Avoidance
15                      FS = Fuzzy(σ , DO , AS)
16                      RS = FS //conditionally overrides RS
17              endif
18              β = β + θ
19      endif
20      return RS, β
```

too close to the waypoint, the current waypoint is dropped and the next waypoint is retrieved from the A*. Apart from extracting waypoints from the path-planning algorithm A*, the operations of the cascade of fuzzy systems in Algorithm 2 is similar to the one described in Algorithm 1.

SAMPLE EMPIRICAL RESULT: THE HYBRID FUZZY A* UTILISING THE VORONOI DIAGRAM: NEAR-OPTIMAL PATH PLANNING (SHORTEST SAFEST PATH)

In robot soccer, a typical problem suffered by path determination algorithms is that the environment is very dynamic. Although it is possible to carry out predictive algorithms for the ball and know where the other robots of the same team are going to move, the same is not true for the robots of the opponent team. This problem will eventually cause collisions. If collision avoidance is a priority (safety first), one can use a Voronoi diagram to set a path that is the furthest away from any other opponent, and take this path as an initial guess that will be used by the fuzzy system. However, as soon as the Voronoi diagram is computed, the obstacles (opponent robots) may have moved already. The computation needs to be very fast, so it can be recomputed for every single frame.

Voronoi diagrams have been used for path optimisation for a long time. For example, Vachhani, Mahindrakar, and Sridharan (2011) and Garrido, Moreno, Blanco, and Jurewicz (2011) are two recently published works that rely on the computation of Voronoi diagrams for the determination of the path. There are variations on how to compute these diagrams, depending on the nature of the problem. For the scope of this chapter, we can use the obstacles themselves as input points to generate the Voronoi diagram, which will result in edges and vertices. Every point in the edge is equidistant to two of the obstacles, so it can be used as a safe path. Considering the diagram as a

graph, the shortest path becomes trivial. However, there are a few challenges for the scope of the robot soccer that requires heuristic modifications. If the two obstacles are really close to each other, then collisions may still occur, even if a path exists between them. The system requires a minimum distance between obstacles (larger than the robot's width), in such a way that edges that are equidistant to obstacles that are too close can be deleted from the graph. There may be edges that are not fully connected (open edges). These can also be deleted, as any path going through them would collide with the walls of the robot soccer field.

Voronoi diagrams can be computed in $O(N \log N)$ time. In this system, Fortune's algorithm is used (Fortune, 1992), returning a set of points that determine the edges of the diagram. At a certain point in time, the Voronoi diagram V will be represented by a set of M edges $\{(x1_{e1}, y1_{e1}, x2_{e1}, y2_{e1}), (x1_{e2}, y1_{e2}, x2_{e2}, y2_{e2}), ..., (x1_{eM}, y1_{eM}, x2_{eM}, y2_{eM})\}$.

The implementation can be made fast enough considering that there are around 21 obstacles (considering robots from the opponent team, as well as its own team). First, the diagram is generated (Figure 6a), the edges that have the problems described above deleted, and then the minimum path is computed (Figure 6b). However, we are left with a final problem: how to choose the starting and finishing points. The robot and its target were not used in the generation of the diagram. Instead, the vertex closest to the robot is used as the starting point in the graph, and the one closest to the target is used as the finishing point for the determination of the shortest path (Figure 6c).

The actual robot's path is not going to be determined only by the Voronoi diagram. The Fuzzy system can override the angle and velocity of the robot, making it a smoother path, very close to the Voronoi edges that happen to be part of the shortest path (see Figure 6).

Finally, there are many scenarios where the diagram may not be the sensible option for the minimum path. In a situation where the target is

Figure 6. Hybrid Fuzzy A*(using a Voronoi diagram) for finding the shortest safest path

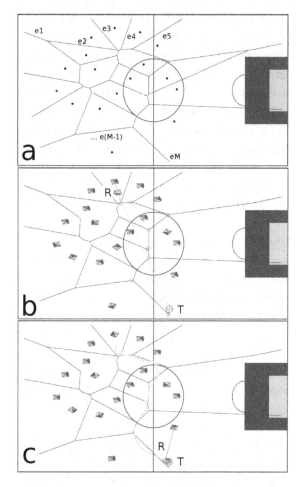

robot and its target passes outside the convex hull. In that case, the path should be the segment and the Voronoi diagram is discarded in the current frame (see Figure 7).

- The edges of the Voronoi that represent paths between two obstacles that are closer than the minimum distance set for the system are discarded

- The open edges of the Voronoi diagram are discarded

- The vertices of the Voronoi diagram that are the closest to the robot and the target (Euclidian distance) are chosen as the initial and final points respectively

- Once the minimum path is computed, this can still be overruled by the fuzzy system. The diagram and its shortest path are recomputed for every frame, until the fuzzy system is in action for the same image frame.

The entire algorithm is described in pseudo-code form, in Algorithm 3.

Figure 7. Deciding on when to utilise the Voronoi diagram for path-planning

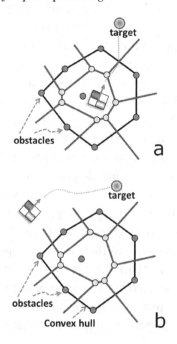

in a corner alone, and all the other obstacles are at other parts of the field, it would be better to go straight to the target and not use the diagram. Geometrically this situation happens when the straight line between the robot and its target passes outside the convex hull defined by the obstacle points. This scenario can be determined soon after the computation of the Voronoi diagram.

Summing up, the following heuristic rules had to be added to the algorithm in order to achieve the safest/shortest path:

- The convex hull of the obstacle points define the region where the robot should pass through, except if the segment between the

Algorithm 3. Hybrid Fuzzy A* with the Voronoi Diagram

Inputs:

coordinates of the target x_t, y_t

coordinates of the robot x_r, y_r

coordinates of the next way point x_W, y_W

set of coordinates of all obstacles $SO = \{(x_{O1}, y_{O1}), (x_{O2}, y_{O2}),...(x_{ON}, y_{ON})\}$

angle to next way point γ

angle to nearest obstacle σ

next way point position   WP (RIGHT or LEFT) //to the left or to the right, relative to the robot's heading angle

distance to next way point   DW

distance to nearest obstacle   DO

distance coefficients   K1 , K2

obstacle position   OP (RIGHT or LEFT)

angle of the robot β

fuzzy angle θ //angle increment/decrement

Voronoi diagram $V = \{(x1_{e1}, y1_{e1}, x2_{e1}, y2_{e1}), (x1_{e2}, y1_{e2}, x2_{e2}, y2_{e2}), ..., (x1_{eM}, y1_{eM}, x2_{eM}, y2_{eM})\}$ //a set of edges

4 structures with fuzzy information:

pursuit steering   PA

pursuit speed   PS

avoidance steering angle   AA

avoidance speed   AS

Temporary variables:

Temporary robot speed   FS

Outputs: robot's angle β

     robot's speed   RS

     Intermediary output:

     path = $\{(x1_w, y1_w),(x2_w, y2_w),(x3_w, y3_w),... ,(xM_w, yM_w)\}$ //a set of coordinates of waypoints towards the target

```
1      V=GenerateVoronoiDiagram(SO)
2      path = ComputePathA*(V, xt, yt, xr, yr) //now the path is over the vertices of V
3      (xw, yw, γ, DW) = GetNextWayPoint(path) //get next way point using the path
4      if (DW > K1 ) then
              //Fuzzy system 1
5          θ = Fuzzy( γ , DW , PA)
6          if ( WP = RIGHT) then
7              θ = -θ
8          endif
              //Fuzzy system 2
9          FS = Fuzzy( γ , DW , PS)
10         RS = FS
11         if ( DO < K2 && OP == WP) then
                  //Fuzzy system 3
12             θ = Fuzzy(σ , DO , AA)     //conditionally overrides θ
13             if ( OP == LEFT ) then
14                 θ = -θ
15             endif
                  //Fuzzy system 4
16             FS  = Fuzzy(σ , DO , AS)
17             RS = FS //conditionally overrides RS
18         endif
19         β = β + θ
20     endif
21     return RS, β
```

Target Pursuit (lines 5–10)

Obstacle Avoidance (lines 11–19)

Sample Empirical Result

Empirical Results

Many scenarios were simulated to observe whether the Voronoi diagram was being used correctly, as well as the minimum path was also a safe path. Figure 8 shows a complete example. In Figure 8a,

a robot R needs to arrive at target T. Note that the diagram changes continuously. During the course of traversal, new waypoints are generated, and then fed to the fuzzy system (see Figure 8b-8i). Also, the robot does not need to pass through exactly all vertices, taking slight deviations as the Fuzzy system overrides the detailed path for a certain frame.

Figure 8. Hybrid Fuzzy A*(using the Voronoi diagram) operating in a dynamic environment (moving obstacles)

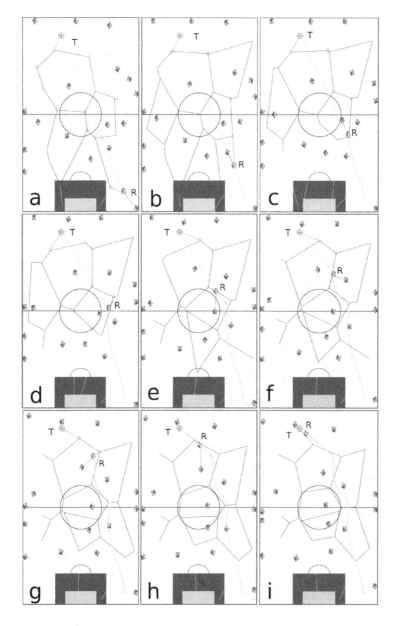

There are some theoretical scenarios that can cause the algorithm to fail to find a path using the Voronoi diagram. A typical case is where all the obstacles would be located at the exactly the same coordinates on X axis, or on the same coordinates on the Y axis. The resulting Voronoi diagram is composed of parallel lines, i.e., all the edges are open and should be discarded. In such cases, the Fuzzy system takes over for the duration of the scenario, and collisions should still be avoided.

The system is safer when compared to the pure Fuzzy, but it still suffer from being a reactive system i.e., when the path on the diagram is chosen, the obstacles have already moved. Although one could incorporate predictive algorithms based on the path that each obstacle is following, one has to remember that the path may be unpredictable. The path of the obstacle of the opponent team can change according to rules are unknown, so they can turn suddenly and try to follow of block the robot.

SYSTEM CALIBRATION

The cascade of four fuzzy systems was designed to work hand in hand for varying cases of target pursuit and obstacle avoidance, and therefore requires a systematic approach to fine-tuning them. In this section, we introduce a fine-tuning methodology that uses a calibration map to perform a thorough test on the control response of the integrated fuzzy systems. The algorithmic steps for target pursuit calibration are described in Algorithm 4, while the calibration steps for target pursuit with obstacle avoidance are described in detail in Algorithm 5. It is worth-noting that Algorithm 4 needs to be executed first to calibrate the target pursuit behavior. Afterwards, the fuzzy systems for obstacle avoidance are fine-tuned together with the calibrated target pursuit systems. This section provides some useful insights and analysis that shed some light on the algorithms.

Target Pursuit Calibration

The target pursuit behavior is implemented using a fusion of two fuzzy systems that is executed for every single frame, as described in Algorithm 1. Fuzzy system 1 (using PA) calculates the steering angle adjustment, while fuzzy system 2 (using PS) calculates the speed adjustment. These two systems are meant to work in tandem, and therefore fine-tuned together with the aid of a calibration map. Initially, the calibration map assigns a random position for one stationary object in the space of traversal (line *1*, Algorithm 4). Secondly, an army of robots is generated to occupy the entire soccer field (line *2*, Algorithm 4). These robots are initialized with the same heading angle (e.g. 45 degrees), and the same initial speed (e.g. speed = 0), and they are distributed across the field so that the entire soccer field is covered, excluding the position of the target with some allowance space around it (lines *3, 4 &5*, Algorithm 4). Next, using the fuzzy system structures PA and PS, the army of robots are made to pursue the given target for a number of trials. For each step, the calibration map presents a graphical view of how the robots would behave at different distances and angles from the target. The combined fuzzy systems are expected to produce smooth control response, and therefore the change in steering angles should be gradual. In addition, the colour intensity of each of the robots reflects the calculated robot speed coming from fuzzy system 2. Darker colours indicate faster pursuit speed.

During the calibration process, the movements of all the robots are carefully observed. The change in steering should be gradually pointing towards the target, as the robot traverses the field. In addition, the speed adjustments should be smooth. This will be reflected by the colour gradient of the robots. The calibration map readily provides an immediate feedback to the fuzzy designer. Faulty fuzzy rules could easily be pin-pointed as the map shows the robot's behavior for different distances from the target and different angles. If the system is not producing the desired behavior, the fuzzy rules and/or the shape of membership functions in PA and PS are altered to produce smoother motion for the robots. The calibration process is restarted from step 1.

Figure 9 depicts the sequence of robot motion exhibiting the target pursuit behavior. The frames were captured at different time sequences (i.e. time sequence 1 to 21), in order to demonstrate how the robots are pursuing the target. The target is labeled with an 'X' mark, and it is the darkest object in the field. It can be observed that the colours of the robots intensify as their angle from the target

gradually decreases. This is indicative of their increasing speed. On the other hand, the robots with pale colours are moving relatively slowly, as they cautiously orient themselves gradually towards the target.

Target Pursuit with Obstacle Avoidance Calibration

It is adamant that the target pursuit calibration (Algorithm 4) for fuzzy systems 1 & 2 be accomplished first before proceeding with the calibration of the obstacle avoidance systems (fuzzy systems 3 & 4).

Figure 9. Target Pursuit Calibration (time sequence: 1, 2, 3, 4, 5, 9, 14, 21)

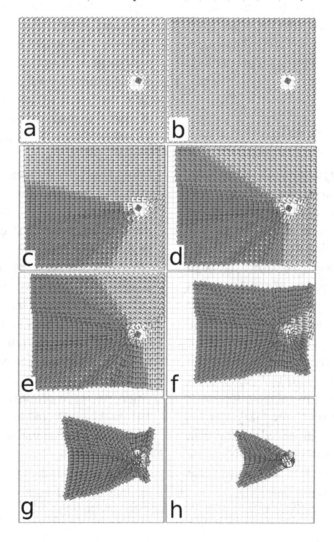

Algorithm 4. Target Pursuit Calibration

```
Inputs:
        robots' angle to target    α₁, α₂ₛ, ..., αₙ
        target position            TP₁, TP₂, ...,TPₙ    (RIGHT or LEFT) //relative to the robot's heading angle
        robots'distance to target  DT₁ , DT₂ , ..., DTₙ
        distance coefficient       K1
        angle of the robots        β₁, β₂, ..., βₙ

        4 structures with fuzzy information:
                pursuit steering    PA
                pursuit speed       PS

        Temporary variables:
        calculated robot speed  FS
        calculated fuzzy angle  θ //angle increment/decrement


Outputs:        robots' angle    β₁, β₂, ..., βₙ  //set of angles of robots
                robots' speed    s₁, s₂, ..., sₙ

1       t = CreateTarget(xₜ, yₜ) //place one stationary target in an arbitrary position on the soccer field
2       Robots = CreateRobots(N) //create an army of robots
3       for each r in Robots
4           r = initialize(xᵣ, yᵣ, sᵣ, βᵣ)
5       endloop
        //use the same fuzzy system structures (i.e. PA, PS) for controlling all the robots
6       for 1 to numOfTrials
7               for each r in Robots
8                   if (DTᵣ > K1 ) then
                        //Fuzzy system 1
9                       θ = Fuzzy(αᵣ, DTᵣ , PA)
10                      if ( TPᵣ = RIGHT) then
11                          θ = -θ
12                      endif
13                      βᵣ = βᵣ + θ
                        //Fuzzy system 2
14                      FS = Fuzzy(αᵣ , DTᵣ , PS) //calculate absolute robot speed
15                      sᵣ = FS
16                      r = move(sᵣ, βᵣ)
17                  endif
18              endloop //for each loop
19      endloop //end of trials loop
```

As can be viewed from Algorithm 5, fuzzy systems 1 & 2 are both engaged while fuzzy systems 3 & 4 are being calibrated (lines *13* to *17*, Algorithm 5). The same general guidelines suggested for Algorithm 4 apply here. The challenge is on determining how to strike a balance between pursuing the target and avoiding obstacles. Smooth transition between pursuit and avoidance behaviour is desired and safety of the robots is always kept as a priority.

Figure 10 depicts the sequence of robot motion exhibiting the integration of target pursuit and obstacle avoidance behaviour. The obstacles are the four static round objects placed at arbitrary positions across the field. Similar to Figure 9, the target is the object marked with an 'X' label. From the progression of robot movements, it can be observed that the robots close to the obstacles appear pale in colour. This is indicative of their cautious behavior; that is, they are slowing down first to steer away from the obstacle. On the other hand, robots that are positioned away from any of the obstacles and pointing towards the target appear darker in colour as they accelerate towards the target. Lastly, it is important to note that the cascade of fuzzy systems will have some limitations. Robots that are directly in front of an obstacle that aligns with the target will get stuck in their positions. This is common to most reactionary algorithms. This problem is addressed appropriately by utilizing the A* algorithm to guide the cascade of fuzzy systems (Algorithms 2 & 3).

Lastly, in order to determine the effects of tweaking the fuzzy system parameters during the calibration process, we present a way of quantify-

Figure 10. Integrated Target Pursuit and Obstacle Avoidance Calibration: (time sequence: 1, 4, 6, 10, 15, 22, 53, 77)

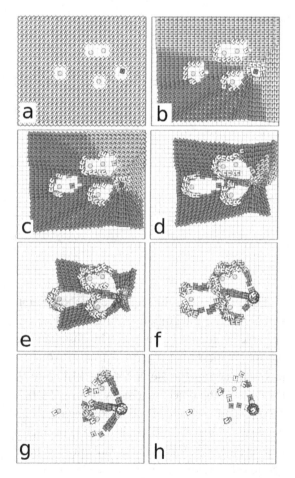

ing the performance of the integrated target pursuit and obstacle avoidance fuzzy logic-based navigation systems. From the calibration map (Figure 11a), each of the robots are monitored in terms of their travel time to reach the target, and their accumulated number of collisions. These values serve as the performance measures of the system, and are plotted on a 3-D graph to aid overall system analysis.

As an example, Figure 11 shows a performance comparison between an uncalibrated system (Figure 11b, 11d), and a calibrated system (Figure 11c, 11e). The initial state of the calibration map is shown in Figure 11a, comprising of 660 robots, 3 obstacles and 1 target. Figure 11b and Figure 11c depict the X-Y-Travel time graphs, while Figure 11d and Figure 11e depict the X-Y-Accumulated number of collisions graphs. The peaks in the graph pinpoint which among the robots ran the slowest, and which one of them accumulated the most number of collisions. Since all the robots are running the same navigation algorithm but with different start positions and start angles relative to the obstacles and the target, the peaks in the graph provide some useful cues as to which fuzzy rule or membership function could be tweaked next for improvement. As indicated earlier in Section 4, note however, that there's a limit to the best attainable performance of a pure reactionary system - the pure fuzzy logic system (without the aid of the A* path-planner). It is only expected that the robot may exhibit some oscillatory behaviour and may get trapped in enclosures, especially when the target and obstacle align with each other. Nevertheless, these problems are addressed by the hybrid system architectures discussed in Sections 4 & 5.

CONCLUSION

This chapter presents a reconfigurable hybrid architecture comprising of a cascade of four fuzzy systems, the A* search algorithm using the strict

Algorithm 5. Integrated Target Pursuit and Obstacle Avoidance Calibration

Inputs:

coordinates of the target $\{(x_t, y_t)\}$

coordinates of the robots $\{(x_{r1}, y_{r1}), (x_{r2}, y_{r2}), ..., (x_{rN}, y_{rN})\}$

coordinates of the obstacles $\{(x_{b1}, y_{b1}), (x_{b2}, y_{b2}), ..., (x_{bM}, y_{bM})\}$

robots' angle to target $\alpha_1, \alpha_{2s}, ..., \alpha_N$

robots' angle to nearest obstacle $\sigma_1, \sigma_2, ..., \sigma_N$

target position $TP_1, TP_2, ...TP_N$ (RIGHT or LEFT) //relative to the robot's heading angle

robots' distance to target $DT_1, DT_2, ..., DT_N$

robots' distance to nearest obstacle $DO_1, DO_2, ..., DO_N$

distance coefficients K1, K2

obstacle position $OP_1, OP_2, ..., OP_N$ (RIGHT or LEFT) //relative to the robot's heading angle

angle of the robots $\beta_1, \beta_2, ..., \beta_N$

4 structures with fuzzy information:

pursuit steering PA

pursuit speed PS

avoidance steering angle AA

avoidance speed AS

Temporary variables:

calculated robot speed FS

calculated fuzzy angle θ //angle increment/decrement

Outputs: robots' angle $\beta_1, \beta_2, ..., \beta_N$ //set of angles of robots

robots' speed $s_1, s_2, ..., s_N$ //set of robot speed values

```
1    t = CreateTarget(xt, yt) //place one stationary target in an arbitrary position on the soccer field
2    Obstacles = CreateObstacles(M) //create M static obstacles at random positions on the soccer field
3    Robots = CreateRobots(N) //create N robots
4    for each b in Obstacles
5        b = initialize(xb, yb)
6    endloop
7    for each r in Robots
8        r = initialize(xr, yr, sr, βr) //avoid any of the obstacles and target positions
9    endloop

     //use the same fuzzy system structures (i.e. PA, PS, AA, AS) for controlling all the robots
10   for 1 to numOfTrials
11       for each r in Robots
12           if (DTr > K1 ) then
                 //Fuzzy system 1
13               θ = Fuzzy(αr , DTr , PA)
14               if ( TPr = RIGHT) then
15                   θ = -θ
16               endif
                 //Fuzzy system 2
17               FS = Fuzzy(αr , DTr , PS)  //calculate absolute robot speed

18               if ( DOr < K2 && OPr == TPr ) then
                     //Fuzzy system 3
19                   θ = Fuzzy(σr , DOr , AA)  //conditionally overrides θ
20                   if ( OPr == LEFT ) then
21                       θ = -θ
22                   endif
                     //Fuzzy system 4
23                   FS = Fuzzy(σr , DOr , AS)
24                   RS = FS        //conditionally overrides RS
25               endif
26               sr = FS
27               βr = βr + θ
28               r = move(sr, βr) //move robot
29           endif
30       endloop //for each loop
31   endloop //end of trials loop
```

Target Pursuit (lines 12–17)

Obstacle Avoidance (lines 18–27)

expanded list, for optimal path-planning and a Voronoi diagram generator that aids in calculating the near-shortest-safest path. The system works in real-time, providing near-optimal path-planning with target pursuit and obstacle avoidance behaviour. The hybrid architecture implements a modular approach, allowing parts of the system to be engaged or disengaged as the robot traverses

Figure 11. Sample navigation performance results, before and after the calibration of the integrated target pursuit and obstacle avoidance fuzzy systems. a) initial state of the calibration map - start positions of 660 robots, 3 obstacles and 1 target (T). b) X-Y-Travel time graph for the uncalibrated system. c) X-Y-Travel time graph for the calibrated system. d) X-Y-Accumulated number of collisions graph for the uncalibrated system. e) X-Y-Accumulated number of collisions graph for the calibrated system.

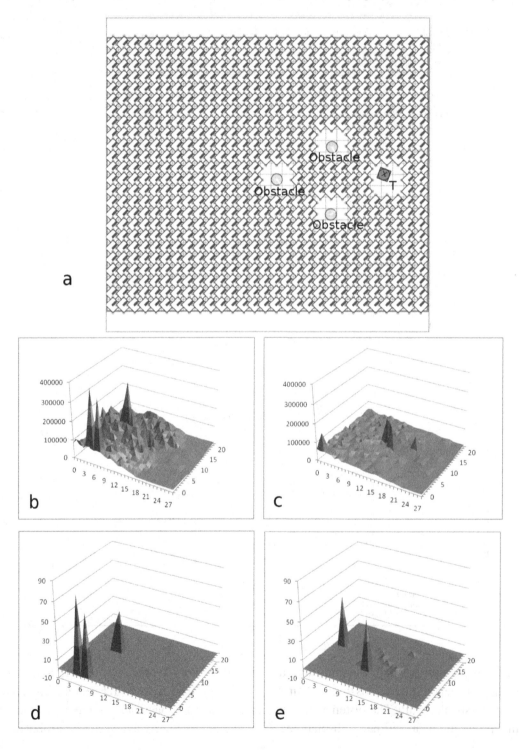

a dynamic environment. Three different complete autonomous navigation algorithms can be formed out of the hybrid system, as discussed throughout the chapter.

In general, the algorithms can be categorized as reactionary, with or without using an optimal path-planning component. Moreover, both global and local information about the environment can be utilized by the different modules. With the A* component, the hybrid system is able to return a smooth, near-shortest path, while escaping from local minima (or any entrapment scenarios). Lastly, with the combination of the Voronoi diagram component, the system is able to return a smooth, near-shortest-safest path.

FUTURE RESEARCH DIRECTIONS

One of the extensions of this work will include a through testing of a complete system with two teams of the real MiroSot robots (Kim, 2012). Performance measurements will be recorded to characterize the algorithms more efficiently, e.g. time to reach the target, and number of collisions. Further, these measurements lend themselves amenable to be used collectively as a fitness function to optimisation algorithms (e.g. Genetic Algorithms), so that system calibration can be fully automated.

Also, a predictive system can be incorporated to the current cascade of fuzzy systems to deal with the position of the ball in a real scenario, in the robot soccer hardware platform. In situations where the ball has to be followed, the current system sufficed to get good results in our simulations. However, there are scenarios where it is desirable that the robot moves quickly to a position where the ball is going to be in the future (a few seconds or milliseconds ahead).

Finally, specific high-level game strategies can be incorporated into the system, using the cascades described here as the core module for implementing other complex robot behaviour.

REFERENCES

Behring, C., Bracho, M., Castro, M., & Moreno, J. A. (2000). An algorithm for robot path planning with cellular automata. In S. Bandini and T. Worsch (Eds.), *Fourth international conference on cellular automata for research and industry: Theoretical and practical issues on cellular automata* (pp. 11-19). London, UK: Springer-Verlag.

Bruce, J. R. (2006). *Real-time motion planning and safe navigation in dynamic multi-robot environments*. (Unpublished doctoral dissertation). Carnegie Mellon University.

Calisi, D. (2009). *Mobile robots and vehicles motion systems: A unifying framework*. (Unpublished doctoral dissertation). Sapienza Universita di Roma.

Chang, Y.-C., & Chen, B.-S. (2000). Robust tracking designs for both holonomic and nonholonomic constrained mechanical systems. *Fuzzy Systems*, *8*(1), 46–66. doi:10.1109/91.824768

Chang, Y.-C., & Chen, B.-S. (2005). Intelligent robust tracking controls for holonomic and nonholonomic mechanical systems using only position measurements. *IEEE Transactions on Fuzzy Systems*, *13*(4), 491–507. doi:10.1109/TFUZZ.2004.840125

Chen, H., Sun, D., Yang, J., & Chen, J. (2010). Localization for multirobot formations in indoor environment. *IEEE/ASME Transactions on Mechatronics*, *15*(4), 561–574. doi:10.1109/TMECH.2009.2030584

Fortune, S. (1992). Voronoi diagrams and Delaunay triangulations. In Du, D., & Hwang, F. K. (Eds.), *Euclidean geometry and computers* (pp. 193–233). Singapore: World Scientific Publishing Co. doi:10.1142/9789814355858_0006

Garrido, S., Moreno, L., Blanco, D., & Jurewicz, P. (2011). Path planning for mobile robot navigation using voronoi diagram and fast marching. *International Journal of Robotics and Automation*, 2, 154–176.

Gerdelan, A., & Reyes, N. (2006a, February). A novel hybrid fuzzy a star robot navigation system for target pursuit and obstacle avoidance. In *1st Korean-New Zealand joint workshop on advance of computational intelligence methods and applications* (pp. 75-79). Auckland, New Zealand: Auckland University of Technology.

Gerdelan, A., & Reyes, N. (2006b). Synthesizing adaptive navigational robot behaviour using a hybrid fuzzy a star approach. In B. Reusch (Ed.), *9th Dortmund fuzzy days: Computational intelligence, theory and applications* (pp. 699-710). Berlin, Germany: Springer-Verlag.

Gerdelan, A., & Reyes, N. (2009). Towards a generalised hybrid path-planning and motion control system with auto-calibration for animated characters in 3D environments. In M. Köppen, N. Kasabov, & G. Coghill (Eds.), *15th International Conference on Neural Information Processing: Advances in neuro-information processing* (Vol. 5506, pp. 1079-1086). New York, NY: Springer.

Golmohammadi, S. K., Azadeh, A., & Gharehgozli, A. (2006). Action selection in robots based on learning fuzzy cognitive map. In *Proceedings of IEEE International Conference on Industrial Informatics*, (pp. 731-736). IEEE.

Hart, P., Nilsson, N., & Raphael, B. (1968). A formal basis for the heuristic determination of minimum cost paths. *IEEE Transactions of Systems Science and Cybernetics*, 4(2), 100–107. doi:10.1109/TSSC.1968.300136

Hong, S.-W., Shin, S.-W., & Ahn, D.-S. (2001). Formation control based on artificial intelligence for multi-agent coordination. In *International Symposium on Industrial Electronics* (vol.1, pp. 429 -434). IEEE.

Jayasiri, A., Mann, G., & Gosine, R. (2011). Behavior coordination of mobile robotics using supervisory control of fuzzy discrete event systems. *IEEE Transactions on Systems, Man, and Cybernetics. Part B*, 41(5), 1224–1238.

Kim, J.-H. (2012). *Federation of International Robot-soccer Association*. Korea Advanced Institute of Science and Technology (KAIST). Retrieved May 25, 2012, from http://www.fira.net/

Kim, J.-H., Kim, K.-C., Kim, D.-H., Kim, Y.-J., & Vadakkepat, P. (1998). Path planning and role selection mechanism for soccer robots. In *IEEE International Conference on Robotics and Automation* (Vol. 4, pp. 3216-3221). IEEE.

Kim, J.-H., Kim, Y.-H., Choi, S.-H., & Park, I.-W. (2009). Evolutionary multiobjective optimization in robot soccer system for education. *IEEE Computational Intelligence Magazine*, 2, 31–41.

Kim, Y.-H., & Kim, J.-H. (2009) Multiobjective quantum-inspired evolutionary algorithm for fuzzy path planning of mobile robot. In *Proceedings of the Eleventh Congress on Evolutionary Computation* (pp. 1185-1192). IEEE.

Lee, D.-H., & Kim, J.-H. (2009). Motivation and context-based multi-robot architecture for dynamic task, role and behavior selections. In *Fira 2009* (pp. 161–170). New York, NY: Springer. doi:10.1007/978-3-642-03983-6_20

Lee, D.-H., Na, K.-I., & Kim, J.-H. (2010). Task and role selection strategy for multi-robot cooperation in robot soccer. In *Fira roboworld congress* (pp. 170–177). New York, NY: Springer. doi:10.1007/978-3-642-15810-0_22

Lee, S.-M., Kim, J.-H., & Myung, H. (2011). Design of interval type-2 fuzzy logic controllers for flocking algorithm. In *IEEE international conference on fuzzy systems* (pp. 2594–2599). IEEE.

Linquan, Y., Zhongwen, L., Zhonghua, T., & Weixian, L. (2008). Path planning algorithm for mobile robot obstacle avoidance adopting belzier curve based on genetic algorithm. In *IEEE Conference on Decision and Control* (pp. 3286-3289). IEEE.

Lozano-Pérez, T., & Kaelbling, L. (2005). *Massachusetts Institute of Technology Open CourseWare: Artificial intelligence*. Retrieved May 25, 2012, from http://ocw.mit.edu/courses/electrical-engineering-and-computer-science/6-034-artificial-intelligence-spring-2005/

Park, J.-H., Kim, J.-H., Ahn, B.-H., & Jeon, M.-G. (2006). A selection scheme for excluding defective rules of evolutionary fuzzy path planning. In *Pacific Rim International Conference in Artificial Intelligence* (pp. 747-756). New York, NY: Springer.

Park, J.-H., Stonier, D., Kim, J.-H., Ahn, B.-H., & Jeon, M.-G. (2007). Recombinant rule selection in evolutionary algorithm for fuzzy path planner of robot soccer. In *Proceedings of the 29th annual German Conference on Artificial Intelligence: KI'06* (pp. 317-330). Berlin, Germany: Springer-Verlag.

Reyes, N., & Dadios, E. (2004). Dynamic colour object recognition. *Journal of Advanced Computational Intelligence, 8*, 29–38.

Stoian, V., & Ivanescu, M. (2008). In Zemliak, A. (Ed.), *Frontiers in robotics, automation and control* (pp. 111–132). New York, NY: Intechopen.

Vachhani, L., Mahindrakar, A., & Sridharan, K. (2011). Mobile robot navigation through a hardware-efficient implementation for control-law-based construction of generalized voronoi diagram. *IEEE/ASME Transactions on Mechatronics, 16*(6), 1083–1095. doi:10.1109/TMECH.2010.2076825

Vašák, J., & Madarasz, L. (2010). Adaptation of fuzzy cognitive maps - a comparison study. *Acta Polytechnica Hungarica, 7*(3), 109–122.

Yetisenler, C., & Ozkurt, A. (2006). Multiple robot path planning for robot soccer. In *Proceedings of the 14th Turkish Conference on Artificial Intelligence and Neural Networks* (pp. 11–23). New York, NY: Springer.

ADDITIONAL READING

Braunl, T. (2008). *Embedded robotics* (3rd ed.). Berlin, Germany: Springer-Verlag. doi:10.1007/978-3-540-70534-5

Browning, B., Wyeth, G., & Tews, A. (1999). A navigation system for robot soccer. In *Australian Conference on Robotics and Automation, it acra '99*. IEEE.

Cai, C., Yang, C., Zhu, Q., & Liang, Y. (2007). Collision avoidance in multi-robot systems. In *Proceedings of the 2007 International Conference on Mechatronics and Automation* (pp. 2795-2800). IEEE.

Hong, Y.-D., & Kim, J.-H. (2012). An evolutionary optimized footstep planner for the navigation of humanoid robots. *International Journal of Humanoid Robotics, 9*, 1–18. doi:10.1142/S0219843612500053

Jones, M. T. (2005). *Ai application programming* (2nd ed.). Newton Center, MA: Charles River Media.

Jung, M.-J., Kim, H.-S., Shim, H.-S., & Kim, J.-H. (1999). Fuzzy rule extraction for shooting action controller of soccer robot. In *Proceedings of the 1999 IEEE International Fuzzy Systems Conference* (Vol. 1, pp. 556 -561).

Kyriakopoulos, K., & Sardis, G. (1993). An integrated collision prediction and avoidance scheme for mobile robots in non-stationary environments. *Automatica, 29,* 309–322. doi:10.1016/0005-1098(93)90125-D

Llorca, D., Milanes, V., Alonso, I., Gavilan, M., Daza, I., Perez, J., & Sotelo, M. (2011). Autonomous pedestrian collision avoidance using a fuzzy steering controller. *IEEE Transactions on Intelligent Transportation Systems, 12*(2), 390–401. doi:10.1109/TITS.2010.2091272

Maeda, Y. (1990a). Collision avoidance control among moving obstacles for a mobile robot on the fuzzy reasoning. *Journal of the Robotics Society of Japan, 6*(6), 50–54.

Maeda, Y. (1990b). Fuzzy obstacle avoidance method for a mobile robot based on the degree of danger. In *Proceedings of the North American Fuzzy Information Processing Society Workshop (nafips'90)* (Vol. 1, pp. 169-172).

Maeda, Y. (1996). Evolutionary algorithm for behavior learning of multi-agent robots. In *Proceedings of 4th International Fuzzy Systems and Intelligent Control Conference (ifsicc'96)* (pp. 360-367). IEEE.

Maeda, Y. (1997). Behavior learning and group evolution for autonomous multi-agent robot. In *Proc. of 6th IEEE International Conference on Fuzzy Systems (fuzz-IEEE'97)* (Vol. 3, pp. 1355-1360). IEEE.

Maeda, Y. (1998). Simulation for behavior learning of multi-agent robot. *Journal of Intelligent and Fuzzy Systems, 6,* 53–64.

Maeda, Y. (1999). Behavior-decision fuzzy algorithm for autonomous mobile robot. In Kasabov, N. (Ed.), *Future directions for intelligent systems and information sciences -the future of speech and image technologies, brain computers, www, and bioinformatics* (pp. 75–101). Berlin, Germany: Springer-Verlag.

Maeda, Y., & Li, Q. (2005). Parallel genetic algorithm with adaptive genetic parameters tuned by fuzzy reasoning. *International Journal of Innovative Computing, Information, & Control, 1*(1), 95–107.

Maeda, Y., Tanabe, M., Yuta, M., & Takagi, T. (1992). Hierarchical control for autonomous mobile robots with behavior-decision fuzzy algorithm. In *Proceedings of IEEE International Conference on Robotics and Automation* (pp. 117-122). IEEE.

Maeda, Y., & Yamanaka, T. (1991). Fuzzy obstacle avoidance control with the strategy map obtained by operation learning. In *Proceedings of Joint Hungarian-Japanese Symposium on Fuzzy Systems and Applications* (pp. 110-113). ACM/IEEE.

Nishi, T., & Takagi, T. (2001). A proposal of collision avoidance algorithm for driving support system. In *Proceedings of the 27th Annual Conference of the IEEE Industrial Electronics Society* (Vol. 1, pp. 80 -83). IEEE.

Obayashi, M., Kuremoto, T., & Kobayashi, K. (2008). A self-organized fuzzy-neuro reinforcement learning system for continuous state space for autonomous robots. In *Proceedings of the 2008 International Conference on Computational Intelligence for Modelling Control Automation* (pp. 551 -556). IEEE.

Patnaik, S. (2007). *Robot cognition and navigation.* Berlin, Germany: Springer-Verlag.

Pozna, C., Troester, F., Precup, R.-E., Tar, J. K., & Preitl, S. (2009). On the design of an obstacle avoiding trajectory: Method and simulation. *Mathematics and Computers in Simulation, 79*(7), 2211–2226. doi:10.1016/j.matcom.2008.12.015

Ross, T. (2004). *Fuzzy logic with engineering applications.* Hoboken, NJ: John Wiley & Sons, Inc.

Syose, T., Maeda, Y., & Takahashi, Y. (2012). Skill acquisition and rule extraction method of expert's operation. In *2012 IEEE International Conference on Fuzzy Systems (fuzz-IEEE)* (pp. 1 -6). IEEE.

Takagi, T., & Sugeno, M. (1985). Fuzzy identification of systems and its applications to modeling and control. *IEEE Transactions on Systems, Man, and Cybernetics, SMC-15*, 116–132. doi:10.1109/TSMC.1985.6313399

Takahashi, Y., Nonoshita, H., Nakamura, T., & Maeda, Y. (2010). Behavioral development of ball kicking motion of a two-wheeled inverted pendulum mobile robot. In *Proceedings of WCCI 2010 IEEE World Congress on Computational Intelligence* (pp. 1-6). IEEE.

Tanabe, M., Maeda, Y., Yuta, M., & Takagi, T. (1991). Path planning method for mobile robot using fuzzy inference under vague information of environment. In *Proceedings of International Fuzzy Engineering Symposium* (pp. 758-769). New York: Springer.

Tikk, D., Johanyák, Z. C., Kovács, S., & Wong, K. W. (2011). Fuzzy rule interpolation and extrapolation techniques: Criteria and evaluation guidelines. *Journal of Advanced Computational Intelligence and Intelligent Informatics, 15*(3), 254–263.

Wang, M., & Liu, J. N. (2008). Fuzzy logic-based real-time robot navigation in unknown environment with dead ends. *Robotics and Autonomous Systems, 56*, 625–643. doi:10.1016/j.robot.2007.10.002

Winston, P. H. (1993). *Artifcial intelligence.* Boston, MA: Addison-Wesley.

Yager, R. R., & Zadeh, L. (Eds.). (1994). *Fuzzy sets, neural networks, and soft computing.* New York City, NY: Van Nostrand Reinhold.

KEY TERMS AND DEFINITIONS

A* (A star): A fast optimal search algorithm that guarantees finding the shortest path.

Collision Avoidance: A decision problem related to path planning, with the additional constraint that collisions cannot occur.

Fuzzy Systems: Decision systems based on Fuzzy logic.

Holonomic Robots: Robots that have the same number of degrees of freedom as controllable degrees of freedom.

Hybrid Systems: Flexible algorithms that combine multiple techniques.

Path Planning: A decision problem to find the near-optimal path for a robot to carry out a task.

Robot Simulation: Processes and software that allows for the simulation of scenarios in robotics.

Robot Soccer (MiroSot): A standardized league of cubic robots that play soccer with a golf ball.

Target Pursuit: A decision problem related to path planning, where the target can move randomly.

Voronoi Diagrams: A data structure containing edges and vertices that constrains spatial properties in relation to certain given points.

Chapter 7
Evolutionary Optimization of Artificial Neural Networks for Prosthetic Knee Control

George Thomas
Cleveland State University, USA

Steve Szatmary
Cleveland State University, USA

Timothy Wilmot
Cleveland State University, USA

Dan Simon
Cleveland State University, USA

William Smith
Cleveland Clinic, USA

ABSTRACT

This chapter discusses closed-loop control development and simulation results for a semi-active above-knee prosthesis. This closed-loop control is a delta control that is added to previously developed open-loop control. The control signal consists of two hydraulic valve settings. These valves control a rotary actuator that provides torque to the prosthetic knee. Closed-loop control using artificial neural networks (ANNs) are developed, which is an intelligent control method. The ANNs are trained with biogeography-based optimization (BBO), which is a recently developed evolutionary algorithm. This research contributes to the field of evolutionary algorithms by demonstrating that BBO is successful at finding optimal solutions to real-world, nonlinear, time varying control problems. The research contributes to the field of prosthetics by showing that it is possible to find effective closed-loop control signals for a newly proposed semi-active hydraulic knee prosthesis. The research also contributes to the field of ANNs; it shows that they are able to mitigate some of the effects of noise and disturbances that will be common in normal operation of a prosthesis and that they can provide better robustness and safer operation with less risk of stumbles and falls. It is demonstrated that ANNs are able to improve average performance over open-loop control by up to 8% and that they show the greatest improvement in performance when there is high risk of stumbles.

DOI: 10.4018/978-1-4666-3942-3.ch007

INTRODUCTION

We propose using artificial neural networks (ANNs) for closed-loop control of a newly designed hydraulic prosthetic knee for above knee amputees. The prosthesis harvests energy and provides controlled release of energy during the gait cycle with a spring loaded high pressure hydraulic chamber, a low pressure hydraulic chamber, and a rotary actuator. An onboard microprocessor controls the pressure in the hydraulic accumulators via two valves. We have found that solving the control problem by analytical means is not feasible, but that ANNs can provide control after evolutionary training with biogeography-based optimization (BBO). This demonstrates the effectiveness of ANNs for nonlinear model-independent control in real-world biomedical problems, and the effectiveness of BBO for finding solutions to difficult optimization problems.

Prostheses have long been known to produce degenerative side effects such as arthritis and spinal pain because of the unnatural and high torques that a user's hip produces to compensate for the inadequacy of his prosthesis (Kulkarni, Gaine, Buckley, Rankine, & Adams, 2005; Gailey, Allen, Castles, Kucharik, & Roeder, 2008; Modan et al., 1998). This provides motivation to develop semi-active prostheses that store and release energy in order to reduce the need for these abnormal torques (Seymour et al., 2007). Further, semi-active prostheses use less power than their fully active counterparts at the cost of limiting the power available for use by the prosthesis at any given moment (Kim & Oh, 2001). For these reasons, semi-active prostheses seek to find a balance between efficiency and efficacy. However, because the reactive energy that a semi-active knee prosthesis can produce is limited by the energy that it can harvest from the user, its performance cannot perfectly match a biological knee (Seymour

et al., 2007). Thus, our goal is to produce a controller that tracks able-bodied human gait parameters as closely as possible.

Because of the degenerative effects associated with unnatural hip torques, we place a high priority not only on the appearance of normal gait through tracking reference angles and coordinates, but also on the hip torques that the amputee has to produce to use the prosthesis. We use these criteria for the performance evaluation of our prosthetic controller.

In previous work, we developed open-loop prosthetic control via biogeography-based optimization (BBO), which is a recently developed evolutionary algorithm (EA) (Wilmot et al., 2013). We have found that although the open-loop control produced by BBO is locally optimal, it is sensitive to noise and to the initial conditions of each gait cycle. We observed instability in the open-loop control when noise and disturbances were injected into simulations of our prosthetic system. This fact helped motivate us to develop closed-loop control to compensate for the sensitivity of the open-loop control.

Our closed-loop control approach focuses on using an ANN to add a delta control to the open-loop control to compensate for disturbances and measurement noise. We use BBO to train the network to input error signals, and to output delta controls that compensate for disturbances and noise. As with open-loop control, BBO optimizes the parameters of the closed-loop controller.

BACKGROUND

Microprocessor control has been used successfully in several different commercial prostheses. Most notably, the Otto Bock C-Leg has become the benchmark for microprocessor controlled prosthetic knees. The performance of the C-Leg depends on the controls embedded in its microcontroller. Otto Bock's leg reacts well to a variety of situations and has proven to decrease detrimental side effects compared to conventional prostheses (Seymour et al., 2007; Seroussi, Gitter, Czerniecki, & Weaver, 1996). Microprocessor control has proven to be the best option for a high performance prosthesis through a series of performance evaluation tests comparing the C-leg to non-microprocessor controlled prostheses (Seymour et al., 2007; Seroussi, Gitter, Czerniecki, & Weaver, 1996). However, even the most modern and technically sophisticated knee prostheses still do not fully restore normal gait and do not prevent all detrimental side effects (Seroussi, Gitter, Czerniecki, & Weaver, 1996; Johansson, Sherrill, Riley, Bonato, & Herr, 2005; Chin et al., 2006; Bellmann, Schmalz, Blumentritt, 2010; Segal et al., 2006).

Artificial neural networks are often used for pattern recognition and to model complicated nonlinear relationships between inputs and outputs (Jang, Sun, & Mizutani, 1997). Their structure is inspired by biological neurons and they have been used in bioengineering applications like prosthetic control (Nayak, Jain, & Ting, 2001). The network contains weighted connections between the artificial neurons that determine how the inputs propagate through the network. These networks can learn behaviors by adjusting these weights. If trained heuristically for closed-loop control, they do not need to have any information about the controlled dynamic system in order to learn; that is, the controlled dynamic system can be viewed as a black box, and the network does not need any model information. An EA such as BBO can find the optimal weight vectors for the ANN to maximize performance for a given number of training data sets. ANNs can also generalize and are able to handle a large number of input cases not in the training data and still make correct control decisions. These factors make them ideal for prosthetic control.

ANNs have been used for prosthesis control by processing myoelectric signals as inputs. Cerebellar model arithmetic computer (CMAC) is an effort for neural network control of cybernetic limb prostheses (Bergantz & Barad, 1988). It is a perceptron-like ANN that mimics the cerebellum in complex motor tasks. CMAC is used for control of the elbow prosthesis and takes the myoelectric signals and feedback to form the input vector to the network. What is particularly interesting about CMAC is why it is used: "Because of the dynamics of prosthetic limb control, a Perceptron-like network which '… generalizes only over a small neighborhood of input-space [sensory input vectors], and which has good dichotomizing properties for [trajectory] points well separated …' would serve as a suitable limb controller" (Albus, 1975) ANNs have also been used to control a hand prosthesis with myoelectric inputs (Elsley, 1990). The ANN is trained to mimic the behavior of the prosthetic hand by comparing the hand model to the prosthetic hand movements. Then the hand model motions are compared to the biological hand and the errors are propagated back to the controller ANN and used as the target signals for the controller training.

No above-knee prosthesis exists that can truly provide "natural walking," and even the acclaimed C-leg is unable to accomplish this task (Kalanovic, Popovic, & Skaug, 2000). Researchers believe that control of a powered above knee prosthetic using ANNs might enable more natural walking (Kalanovic, Popovic, & Skaug, 2000). This approach uses a feedback error learning network that is used to identify inverse dynamics of the prosthetic joint movements with simple sinusoidal inputs. The inverse of the system can then be used to determine what inputs should be used for a given set of outputs. ANNs are a good choice of control technique for systems like the prosthetic knee where inverse dynamics are very hard to solve.

ARTIFICIAL NEURAL NETWORK CLOSED-LOOP CONTROL

Optimal open-loop control, optimal initial conditions, and an optimal spring constant for our hydraulic prosthesis were simultaneously found by BBO search techniques (Wilmot et al., 2013). The control is locally optimal, and therefore we do not attempt to improve on this control through the use of closed-loop control. Instead, we try to mitigate the effects of noise and disturbances. In (Wilmot et al., 2013) it was demonstrated that varying initial conditions had by far the largest impact on the open-loop control performance, and without closed-loop control the prosthesis would be dangerous to the user.

We have developed rotary actuator equations to determine the knee torque, M_k, and fluid flows through the high and low pressure valves, v_1 and v_2, as a function of the normalized high and low pressure valve controls, u_1 and u_2, the high pressure accumulator volume, s, and the knee angle velocity $\dot{\varphi}_k$. In particular, holding s and $\dot{\varphi}_k$ constant, one can view the knee torque as a function of the valve controls only. Thus, in order to produce the knee torques necessary for gait, we need a control algorithm to produce the necessary valve controls.

A simple closed-loop control algorithm is proportional-integral-derivative (PID) control. The PID controller output as a function of time, *u(t)* is given by

$$u(t) = K_p e(t) + K_i \int_0^t e(v)dv + K_d \frac{d}{dt} e(t)$$

(1)

where K_p, K_i, and K_d are the proportional, integral, and derivative controller gains, and *e(t)* is the error in the process that we wish to control as a function of time. In order to use a PID controller in our case, we would need the inverse of the rotary actuator equations, or a lookup table that gives a unique ordered pair of normal-

ized high and low pressure valve controls for a given knee torque value. We show in Wilmot et al. (2013) that such an inverse does not exist, because, for a given s, $\dot{\varphi}_k$, and M_k, there is not a unique solution in $[u_1, u_2]$. However, even if an inverse existed or we determine a workaround to this issue, we will still have problems trying to apply a PID determined knee torque. To determine the best torque to provide, PID tries to minimize the torque error signal. The best torque to correct for a particular error at one time step might deplete the energy of the hydraulic actuator too soon in the gait, causing the prosthesis to collapse or causing the angle tracking to deteriorate significantly later in the gait cycle. The research in (Wilmot, 2011) shows that the PID controller is not an effective form of control.

We need a controller that can intelligently manipulate the hydraulic valves to provide torques for different situations in gait; this controller should produce optimal angle tracking. Artificial neural networks are capable of providing the solution to the closed-loop control problem. Through training they can learn behaviors and generalize to handle a large number of similar cases. ANNs are attractive because of universal approximation theorems (Jang, Sun, & Mizutani, 1997) and because they mimic the way that humans control natural knees. ANNs are also attractive because they do not need to explicitly incorporate any information about the system.

We show that closed-loop ANN control is capable of mitigating the worst effects of varying initial conditions at the beginning of a gait cycle, and that ANN control reduces the effects of other kinds of noise and disturbances on angle tracking. When operating under noisy conditions, the ANN controller does better on average than pure open-loop control and significantly reduces high and dangerous errors that could cause stumbles and falls. In order to discuss the development of our ANN control, we first discuss the prosthetic system that we wish to control.

Figure 1. The human gait cycle. The stance phase of the shaded leg begins when the heel first makes contact with the ground, and ends when the foot leaves the ground. The swing phase of the shaded leg begins when the foot leaves the ground, and ends when the heel first strikes the ground. The stance phase comprises about the first 60% of the stride, and the swing phase comprises about the last 40%. This figure is adapted from (Delusio, 2011).

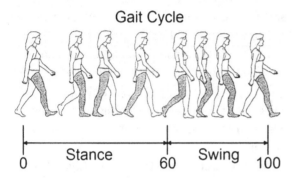

Problem Formulation

The problem formulation for prosthetic knee control begins with the derivation of the governing dynamic equations. There are two distinct phases of the human gait cycle that are represented by two different dynamic system models. The stance phase of a leg is defined as the period of time when the foot is in contact with the ground. It begins when the heel first makes contact with the ground, and ends when the foot lifts up off the ground. Swing phase follows stance phase, and is defined as the period of time when the foot is not in contact with the ground. During stance phase, the dynamic system that describes the behavior of the leg can be represented as an inverted double pendulum. During swing phase, the dynamic system that describes the behavior of the leg can be represented as a regular double pendulum. Figure 1 shows the stance and swing phase of the human gait during one stride.

The dynamic equations are given in (Wilmot et al., 2013). The equations are unwieldy and so we do not list them in detail here. The general form of the dynamic equations is given as:

- **Stance Phase Hip Angle Dynamics:**

$$\ddot{\varphi}_1 = f_1(M_k, M_h, F_{yh}, F_{xh}, \varphi_1, \varphi_k, \dot{\varphi}_1, \dot{\varphi}_k) \qquad (2)$$

- **Stance Phase Knee Angle Dynamics:**

$$\ddot{\varphi}_k = f_2(M_k, M_h, F_{yh}, F_{xh}, \varphi_1, \varphi_k, \dot{\varphi}_1, \dot{\varphi}_k) \qquad (3)$$

- **Swing Phase Knee Angle Dynamics:**

$$\ddot{\varphi}_k = f_3(M_k, \ddot{y}_h, \ddot{x}_h, \varphi_1, \varphi_k, \ddot{\varphi}_1) \qquad (4)$$

Note that during swing phase, the thigh angle ϕ_1 is entirely controlled by the user, and so we do not have a dynamic equation for $\ddot{\varphi}_1$ during swing phase. M_h, F_{xh} and F_{yh} are moments and forces applied at the hip by the user. M_k is the moment applied by the prosthesis at the knee. Table 1 shows the definitions of the variables in Equations 1–3. Figure 2 shows the diagram of the limb along with the definition of the angles and forces.

Next we discuss the modeling of the rotary hydraulic actuator. The actuator provides a mechanism for controlled storage and release of energy during the gait cycle. This storage and release enables the hydraulic actuator to deliver

Table 1. Dynamic equation variables

ϕ_1	Thigh angle	F_{yh}	Hip force y-coordinate
ϕ_k	Knee angle	H_{xh}	Hip force x-coordinate
M_h	Hip moment (torque)	y_h	Hip position y-coordinate
M_k	Knee moment (torque)	x_h	Hip position x-coordinate

Figure 2. The prosthetic limb diagram

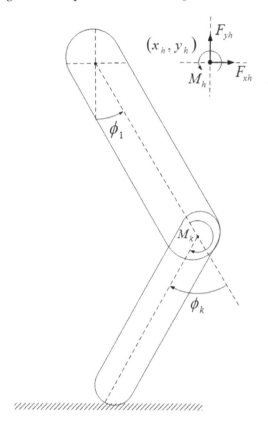

torque and damping to the knee without external power; the only power required by the knee is for opening and closing hydraulic valves. This significantly reduces the amount of power needed for operation when compared to a fully active, powered knee. Figure 3 shows the hydraulic rotary actuator.

Table 2 shows the rotary actuator parameter definitions. The equations that describe the rotary actuator are given as:

$$u_1^2 C_1^2 (ks - M_k G - B_1 v_1) - v_1 |v_1| = 0 \qquad (5)$$

$$u_2^2 C_2^2 (ks - M_k G - B_2 v_2) - v_2 |v_2| = 0 \qquad (6)$$

$$\dot{\varphi}_k - G(v_1 + v_2) = 0 \qquad (7)$$

$$\dot{s} + v_1 = 0 \qquad (8)$$

We collected reference data from an able-bodied human subject in our gait lab. Cameras in the lab track thigh and knee angles, and a force plate collects ground contact data while the subject walks at a normal but slow pace. The test subject has a mass of 78 kilograms and a height of 1.83 meters. Gait lab software also calculates the hip and knee torques that the able-bodied human generates during his slow walk. We use the able-bodied knee and thigh angles as reference trajectories for our prosthetic controller. The able-bodied hip torque is also of particular interest. We want an amputee to be able to walk with hip torque that is close to the reference trajectory to minimize the degenerative side effects due to long-term use of the prosthesis.

Operation of the prosthesis during stance phase exerts forces and torques on the hip. The user needs to compensate for the forces and torques that the prosthesis exerts on the hip. We model the user's compensation with a simple proportional feedback controller that adds hip torque to the reference hip torque based on the thigh angle tracking error that occurs during prosthetic operation. The equation is shown as:

$$M_h = M_{href} + P_f (\varphi_{1ref} - \varphi_1) \qquad (9)$$

where $P_f = 100$

P_f was obtained by manual tuning to provide good thigh angle tracking while maintaining hip torques that were still reasonably close to reference values. Note that Equation (8) models the user control of his hip torque, but the user does not consciously implement this control. The user subconsciously implements this control to exert a hip torque that allows him to approximately track a natural thigh angle trajectory. There may be times when the user is actually unable to apply the torque of Equation (9). In this case the prosthetic knee control should attempt to compensate for the user's lack of control. Although we do not investigate this issue in this chapter, we recognize its importance and leave it for future work.

Figure 3. Rotary hydraulic actuator. The high pressure accumulator (HPA) is loaded with a spring. The low pressure accumulator (LPA) is loaded with a bladder to maintain constant pressure. The solid shaded part of the rotary device is the stator, and the dashed-filled part is the rotor. The four dot-filled parts are the hydraulic chambers. Control is provided by two valves that enable fluid flow into and out of the high and low pressure accumulators, and u_1 and u_2 are the control signals. The high pressure accumulator is spring loaded and this spring provides the energy storage and release capabilities.

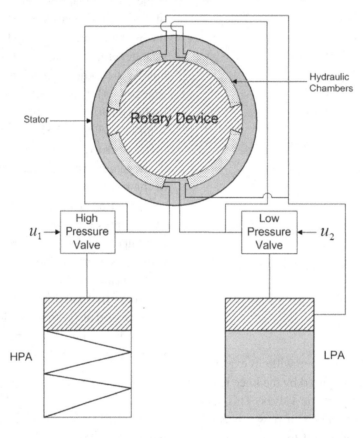

Table 2. Rotary equation parameters. The valve controls are normalized between 0 (fully closed) and 1 (fully open).

B_1	Constant viscous drag through valve 1	P_0	Pressure in the low pressure accumulator
B_2	Constant viscous drag through valve 2	S	High pressure fluid volume
C_1	Maximum cross-sectional area of valve 1	u_1	Valve 1 control normalized to [0, 1]
C_2	Maximum cross-sectional area of valve 2	u_2	Valve 2 control normalized to [0, 1]
G	Moment-pressure proportional constant	v_1	Upward fluid flow through valve 1
k	High pressure accumulator spring elasticity	v_2	Upward fluid flow through valve 2

During swing phase we assume that the thigh angle and its derivatives are supplied by the user, and are exactly equal to the gait data values. We make this assumption because during swing phase, the operation of the prosthesis will have little impact on the hip torque. Because of this assumption, during swing phase we only want to track the knee angle.

ANN Structure

Our ANN structure has several data inputs and one bias input. Adding a bias input to the network allows for improved performance (Jang, Sun, &

Mizutani, 1997). The ANN passes the inputs through one hidden layer, and an output layer. The ANN has two outputs (Δu_1 and Δu_2). We want the ANN to gather information about the tracking error of the system and generate a delta control that performs a corrective action. We used sigmoidal activation functions at the hidden layer and output layer. The sigmoidal function maps outputs to values between zero and one. The sigmoidal function is given in the following equation.

$$f(x) = (1 + e^{-x})^{-1} \qquad (10)$$

We changed the bias input in our ANN from the standard value of 1 to 0.001. This is because when we have zero or very small tracking errors, we want our ANN output to be close to zero. We can adjust the weights of the ANN to produce certain behaviors for certain inputs (this is called training the ANN). The typical training mechanism is called back propagation. For the classic implementation of this method, we need to know the desired output for a given input so that we can use the partial derivative of the error with respect to the weights and propagate the error backwards through the weights. Then we can use gradient descent to minimize the error for a particular training input. We do not know what

the desired output should be for a particular input, which makes back propagation difficult to use. In this case, approaches such as inverse model control may be used, where back propagation is first used to train an ANN as a system model, and then used to train another ANN to control that model, but back propagation may not be able to find a globally optimal set of weights (Jang, Sun, & Mizutani, 1997). We instead use BBO to train the weights. BBO evolves an ANN by considering a candidate ANN as an individual in an evolving population. BBO, like other EAs, is a global optimization algorithm. BBO evaluates the fitness of an individual in the population (that is, a set of ANN weights) by using the ANN for closed-loop control and evaluating the cost function. BBO then finds the ANN that minimizes the cost function.

Figure 4 shows how the ANN takes information about the system state and generates a delta control to add to the open-loop control. This provides corrective actions for tracking errors.

ANN Parameters

We want to investigate the inputs and hidden neuron structure that give optimal performance. This optimal performance consists of not only effectively reducing the error of the training data, but

Figure 4. A block diagram showing how the delta controls from the neural network are added to the original open-loop controls. Note that the error in thigh angle, ϕ_p is only used as a closed-loop control input during stance phase.

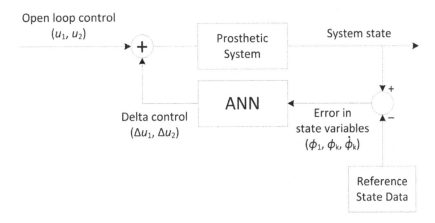

also having robustness to handle situations other than the training data. Also, we want the network to converge on this solution in a reasonable amount of training time. This section discusses some of the tests that we ran in order to answer questions about what ANN parameters to use.

To test the effectiveness of adding hidden neurons to the network, we run a series of simulations. Each simulation is a BBO training session that has a population size of 50, a generation limit of 50, and allowed weight ranges between ±0.5. Starting with four hidden neurons, we increase the number by two until the final control cost stabilizes. This is a very rudimentary approach because every time neurons are added, the search space grows significantly, yet we are using the same amount of computational time to search in different sized search spaces. A network with four hidden neurons is simply a subset of a network with six hidden neurons. We know that compared to a four neuron network, a better or equal solution exists with the six neuron network. Further, the network is trained only for stance phase in this section.

However, we are also interested in how long it takes to find a good solution and in keeping the network as simple as possible. When we add more hidden neurons, we increase the search space. This increase in possible solutions is a benefit because it means that it is more likely that a better solution exists than with a smaller search space. However, this also means that it will take much longer to search this space and the number of poor solutions will increase. It may be infeasible to find the optimum of a very large search space, thus it can be more efficient to search a subset of that space to find good, but potentially suboptimal solutions. Also, when an ANN grows in size it tends to lose the ability to generalize and it starts to memorize a solution that is specific to the training data rather than a solution that will work generally for a large number of situations (Jang, Sun, & Mizutani, 1997). The bottom line is that adding neurons adds complexity to our system

and it is desirable to find the simplest solution. Figure 5 shows the results of the test.

By the time we reached 10 hidden neurons, the cost of the stance phase ANN control converged. This indicates that 10 neurons is a point of diminishing returns; if we add more than 10 neurons, we will gain little in performance. Thus, we conclude that 10 neurons provide a good compromise between an ANN that has a high possibility of containing a good solution and an ANN that is not too complex. This number of hidden neurons seems to agree with current research. In Dosen and Popovic (2008), an ANN is used to map electromyography inputs to joint angles and torques. The ANN that they use has one hidden layer, ten hidden neurons, and one output. This is a similar ANN structure to the one that we are using.

Another question is what the proper range of weights is for the network. Increasing the range increases the likelihood of a better solution, but also increases the search space and the time it may require to find a good solution. To help answer this question we can look at the optimal ANN weights that BBO obtains for our system. If the weights are mostly tending towards the limits of the search space, then we need to increase the limits of the search space. If the weights are mostly far from the limits, then we need to reduce the limits of the

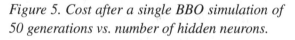

Figure 5. Cost after a single BBO simulation of 50 generations vs. number of hidden neurons.

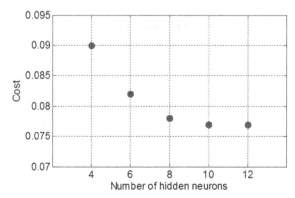

search space. Figure 6 shows a typical example of the optimal ANN weights obtained by BBO. This particular run is with only angle errors for the inputs, and eight hidden neurons.

We can see that the ANN weights lie in a wide range of values and do not, in general, tend towards the upper or lower bound. This indicates that a good ANN solution can be found with weight ranges of ±0.5.

ANN Tests

We devised several tests to determine the effectiveness of using ANNs for closed-loop control. We saw in Wilmot et al. (2013) that BBO is able to find a control that is locally optimal; therefore we do not try to improve the open-loop control through adding closed-loop control. Instead, we add different disturbances and noise to the system and attempt to mitigate their detrimental effects with closed-loop control.

Noise and Disturbance

We add several different disturbances and noises into the system to see how the output is affected. We model all of the noise and disturbances as normally distributed random numbers. It is pos-

sible that more realistic noise models could be utilized. For instance, we could simulate real physical phenomena such as the prosthetic foot slipping or sticking to the ground, or forces from gusts of wind, however, more complicated noise models are outside of the scope of this chapter, especially because we do not yet have a foot model. We defer these additional noise models for future work. We can select different profiles of random noise by selecting a particular seed value for our random number generator. This way we can repeat random noise profiles for training purposes and use a particular seed value (and hence a particular noise profile) to objectively compare the performance of the closed-loop control to the open-loop control.

The first disturbance that we add to the system is random noise to the control signal. Some noise is to be expected with any control signal in a real system. We model the control system noise by adding a random number to the control signal at each time the control is input to the system. This means that the random noise will be added to the control signal every time the differential equation solver in our MATLAB system simulation calls the routine that calculates the system state. The random noise is normally distributed, as is all of

Figure 6. Stem plot of typical ANN weights for eight hidden neurons.

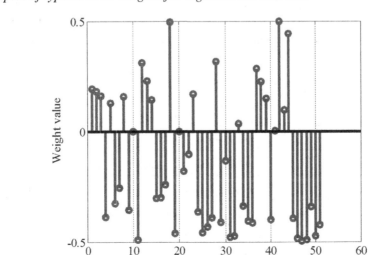

the noise, with a standard deviation of 0.01. Recall that the controls are normalized to the range [0, 1].

We also add disturbance to the hip feedback proportionality constant P_f used to correct thigh angle errors during the stance phase of the gait (see Equation 8). This simulates the fact that the user will not react exactly as we have assumed when deriving the open-loop control. We simulate the user's possible differences from the open-loop assumption by adding a random number to the feedback proportionality constant. The random number has a standard deviation of 60. We add upper and lower bounds on the proportionality constant to ensure that it is still reasonable. The upper bound is 200, which is twice the nominal value of 100 but still well within human capability. The lower bound is 30 which is much less than the nominal value. We band limit this random disturbance to 30 radians/second by passing white noise through a low pass filter. We use band limited noise because we know that the user can only change his walking control strategy at relatively low frequencies.

We also know that the user will not control the thigh angle exactly like we have simulated it. When calculating open-loop control we assume that the thigh angle is exactly equal to the reference thigh angle calculated from one human subject in the gait lab. We know that even the reference angle will have a nonzero standard deviation among healthy non-amputees. An amputee's thigh angle during swing phase will also be affected by the addition of the prosthesis as it will add unnatural torques that are different from the torques that a healthy knee might exert on the subject. Therefore we add noise to the swing phase thigh angle that is input into the ANN. The noise has a standard deviation of 0.1 radians. We band limit the noise frequency to 30 radians/second.

Another set of parameters we add noise to are the optimal initial conditions found by BBO during open-loop optimization. These initial conditions are in no way guaranteed to be exactly the same as in the simulation. We add a random variable to each of the initial condition parameters to simulate reality. The random numbers we add to the initial conditions have a standard deviation of 10% of the optimal value. We have seen in (Wilmot et al., 2013) that the open-loop control is very sensitive to the initial conditions.

Finally, we add noise to the measured values that the feedback controller uses to calculate the closed-loop control. All measurements will have some noise. We can deal with this noise to an extent by adding filters. The standard deviation of the measurement noise is 0.01 radians. We show all the different noise parameters in Table 3.

ANN Training

Initially, we thought that one ANN for the entire gait cycle would be good enough. It would keep things simple and hopefully provide the robustness we are looking for. However, the resulting ANN did not perform well. We concluded that the closed-loop controller should consist of two

Table 3. Noise parameters for ANN training and testing.

	Standard Deviation	Frequency
Control Signal	0.01 (control signal between 0 and 1)	Infinite
Hip Feedback Proportionality Constant	60 Newton*Meters / Radian	30 Rad/Sec
Swing Phase Thigh Angle	0.1 Radians	30 Rad/Sec
Initial Conditions (φ_1, $\dot{\varphi}_1$, φ_k, $\dot{\varphi}_k$, s)	10% of BBO Open-loop Value	Not Applicable
Measurements (φ_1, φ_k, $\dot{\varphi}_k$)	0.01 Radians	Infinite

different ANNs. One ANN is trained for stance phase and one ANN is trained for swing phase. This makes sense because stance phase and swing phase are two entirely different dynamic systems (see Equations 1–3). A single ANN trained for the whole gait cycle would not be able to make the correct control decisions for both systems. Instead it would make decisions that are compromising for both stance and swing phase in an attempt to decrease the average cost.

The inputs we use for training the ANNs are based on the experimental ANN. The inputs for stance phase are knee angle error, thigh angle error, knee angle velocity error, and the small bias input. Swing phase will not use the thigh angle error because we assume that the operation of the prosthesis has negligible effects on the thigh angle during swing phase. Therefore the ANN inputs for swing phase are knee angle error, knee angle velocity error, and the small bias input.

First we train the stance phase ANN. Then we can train the swing phase ANN by running the stance phase ANN simulation and using the final conditions of the stance phase as the initial conditions of the swing phase. We can use any number of the different types of noise to impose on the open-loop control and then train the ANN with BBO to minimize the cost of imposing the noise. In order to ensure that the ANN will be able to handle many different noise cases, we run the simulation a number of times for each candidate ANN in the BBO population. Each time we use a different seed value for the random number generator, and thus different noise profiles for each type of disturbance. After the candidate ANN has been evaluated the specified number of times, we can assign a cost to the ANN that is some function of the separate simulations. This way the ANN is trained to give good performance on average for a large number of noise cases.

Training two separate ANNs poses some difficulties. We have to decide what cost function will provide the best overall tracking, not just the best tracking during stance or swing phase. When training a stance phase ANN we need to make sure that the network will not only attempt to minimize angle tracking error, but also the final conditions of stance phase must be favorable initial conditions for swing phase. We tried many different cost functions for stance phase to find the best way to combine these two criteria. One approach was to use the open-loop BBO optimal trajectory as the reference angle data for error calculation and cost calculation. We could use a cost function that utilized a weighted cost of the angle tracking data and weighted endpoint cost to help ensure that swing phase will start with favorable initial conditions.

We experimented with many different weights for the different objectives with some success, however we settled on a different technique for ensuring good angle tracking as well as good final conditions. To train the stance phase ANN we evaluated the cost of the ANN by evaluating the cost of the whole gait cycle using the reference data from the gait lab to calculate errors and costs. We use closed-loop control for stance phase and open-loop control for swing phase. This way we avoid trying to determine what the best weights should be for the endpoint values. If closed-loop control provides good initial conditions for swing phase, then the open-loop BBO-generated control will give good swing phase tracking. The cost function we used for stance phase is

$$J_{st} = \int_{t=0}^{T} \begin{bmatrix} w_1 \left(\varphi_1(t) - \varphi_{1ref}(t) \right)^2 \\ + w_2 \left(\varphi_k(t) - \varphi_{kref}(t) \right)^2 \\ + w_3 U \left(\varphi_k(t) \right) \varphi_k(t) \end{bmatrix} dt \qquad (11)$$

where T is the gait cycle time period, and $U(\cdot)$ is the unit step function. With this cost function we choose the weights to be $w_1 = w_2 = 1$, and $w_3 = 2$.

The swing phase ANN cost function is the same as the stance phase cost function except that it is only integrated over swing phase operation. We are only concerned with single strides at this time and we are not researching the effects of the swing phase final conditions. The swing phase cost function is

$$J_{st} = \int_{t=T_{st}}^{T} \begin{bmatrix} w_1 \left(\varphi_1(t) - \varphi_{1ref}(t) \right)^2 \\ + w_2 \left(\varphi_k(t) - \varphi_{kref}(t) \right)^2 \\ + w_3 U \left(\varphi_k(t) \right) \varphi_k(t) \end{bmatrix} dt \qquad (12)$$

where T_{st} is the time at the end of stance phase (which is also the time at the start of swing phase). With this cost function we choose the weights to be $w_1 = 0$ $w_2 = 1$, and $w_3 = 2$. Remember that we do not need to assign a cost to the thigh angle in swing phase operation, which is why $w_1 = 0$.

These cost functions assign a cost to the candidate ANN for a particular noise profile. We train the ANN with more than one noise profile so we have an array of costs ($J = J_{st}$ or J_{sw} depending on which ANN we are training) that will be used to determine the final cost. To obtain the final cost of the stance or swing phase ANN we use the following calculation:

$$J_{ANN} = \max(J) + w \times \text{average}(J) \qquad (13)$$

where the maximum and average are taken over multiple ANN simulations, where each simulation uses a different noise profile. The motivation for this overall cost function is twofold. First we are interested in ensuring safe operation of the prosthesis. This means we want consistent results that are not wildly affected by the noise. We especially want to reduce high costs that might cause the user to stumble or have especially detrimental side effects with prolonged use. Second, we want better overall performance over open-loop control when dealing with noise. The weight $w = 0.5$, which has shown to give an effective balance between minimizing the worst-case and average cost.

ANN Results

To show that ANN closed-loop control makes our open-loop control more robust, we train the ANN under noisy initial conditions. This noise has the most dramatic effect on the open-loop control (Wilmot et al., 2013). We train each ANN (stance phase and swing phase) with 10 different noise profiles. Then we evaluate the performance of the ANN on 20 different noise profiles (test cases). This shows how well the ANN is able to perform on the training noise profiles as well as how it is able to generalize over noise profiles that it has not trained with. It is important that the ANN is able to generalize over a large set of operating conditions, as the differences in gait between any two people can be dramatic. Further, even for a given person, system parameters can change; for instance, if the user wears heavy boots instead of their usual shoes, the system dynamics will change. In order to evaluate the ANN's ability to generalize its error correcting capabilities, we add control signal noise and user feedback noise to the varying initial conditions and run these same 20 noise profiles. For a final experiment, we added initial conditions noise, control signal noise, user feedback noise, and measurement noise to the 20 test cases.

The costs from these three combinations of noise are shown in Table 4. From these results, we see that the ANN is able to generalize well in

Table 4. Open-loop BBO vs. closed-loop ANN control average cost.

Noise Type	BBO Cost	ANN Cost	% Difference
Initial Conditions	0.066671	0.061187	8.23
Initial Conditions, Feedback, Control Signal	0.070077	0.064058	8.59
Initial Conditions, Feedback, Control Signal, Measurement	0.070077	0.063881	8.84

spite of various sources of noise. As more noise conditions are included in the simulation, the ANN becomes more effective at reducing the effects of the noise.

Figure 7 shows the cost for BBO open-loop control and ANN closed-loop control for 20 different noise profiles with all of the sources of noise. The first 10 noise profiles are the profiles that the ANN was trained with and the next 10 are profiles the ANN was not trained for.

Next we discuss the ankle position of the prosthetic leg. We are especially interested in the ankle y-coordinate of the prosthesis when evaluating a closed-loop controller's performance. Stumble prevention is the most important task of our closed-loop controller, and stubbing the toe of the prosthesis during the swing phase of operation is a likely way to cause a stumble. We show the minimum and mean swing phase ankle y-coordinates for open-loop BBO and closed-loop ANN control with the 20 test cases in Figure 8. The reference ankle coordinate is also shown for comparison. We do not show stance phase ankle coordinates because ankle position is mostly independent of the prosthetic system during stance phase. Figure 8 shows that the ANN closed-loop controller is less likely to cause a stumble by the prosthesis stubbing its toe. We come to this con-

clusion because the foot has a greater chance of striking the ground prematurely if the ankle is close to the ground. For most of swing phase, the ankle y-coordinate of the ANN control is slightly higher and thus further from the ground than the open-loop control. Also notice that the standard deviation of the ANN control ankle y-coordinate is generally smaller than the open-loop control ankle y-coordinate. It is important that the final conditions for swing phase be consistent, because they are also the initial conditions for stance phase of the next stride. The ANN control significantly decreases the standard deviation of the ankle y-coordinate at the end of swing phase. Another factor determining whether the foot will hit the ground accidentally is what type of foot will be implemented in the prosthetic and its dimensions. All we can say at this point is that the ANN controller is less likely to cause these sorts of accidents. The higher value of the ankle y-coordinate during swing phase will give the user more confidence in the prosthesis.

We conclude from these simulations that ANNs are capable of providing robustness against variable initial conditions, feedback uncertainties, control signal noise, and measurement noise. Conditions that cause high costs have consistently lower costs when we implement the ANN

Figure 7. Cost vs. noise profile index for both BBO open-loop control and ANN closed-loop control with initial conditions noise, control signal noise, user feedback noise, and measurement noise. The first 10 noise profiles are training cases, and the last 10 are test cases.

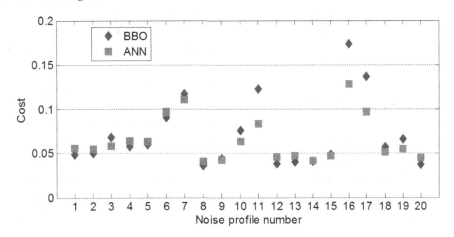

Figure 8. Comparison between swing phase ankle y-coordinates produced by BBO open-loop control (left) and ANN closed-loop control (right) for 20 noise profiles. The ankle y-coordinate trajectory from the reference data is plotted, along with the simulation that results in the smallest y-coordinate, and the mean y-coordinate with vertical bars corresponding to ±1 standard deviation.

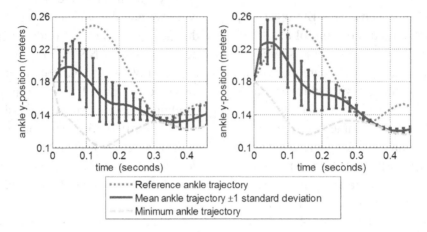

closed-loop control compared to open-loop control. Also, closed-loop control provides a better cost on average than open-loop control alone. High costs are dangerous and could lead to stumbles and falls. It is of great value that the closed-loop ANN control is able to reduce these high costs and avoid potential falls. The ANN closed-loop control is also able to produce more consistent results despite the noise. This consistency is helpful to the user for training, optimum performance, and health reasons. We can reasonably assume that with a larger set of training patterns, a larger population size, and more generations of BBO training, we could further improve the performance of the ANN closed-loop control. With a modification of the cost function used we can also modify exactly what type of performance the ANN will provide.

FUTURE RESEARCH DIRECTIONS

Future work includes improvements in the mechanical design of the prosthetic knee, and embedded system implementation of the valve controls. Further, our dynamic models currently do not include a foot; a foot must be incorporated into

our model so that it will more accurately represent a real prosthesis. Modifications to our current neural network model, such as adding multiple hidden layers or recurrence to the network should be evaluated. Recurrent neural networks feature feedback paths and exhibit dynamic behavior. These networks can capture the same performance as classic, feedforward ANN using fewer connections; however, they are more likely to be unstable (Mandic & Chambers, 2002). There are also many other issues that need to be addressed by a prosthetic implementation, such as sensor selection (Williamson & Andrews, 2001) and gait phase recognition (McDonald, Smith, Brower, Ceberio, & Sarkodie-Gyan, 2007; Gu, Ding, Wang, & Wu, 2010; Pappas, Popovic, Keller, Dietz, & Morari, 2001; Zhang, Pu, Chen, & Fleischer, 2010). Also, a commercial prosthesis needs to function correctly in various operating modes, such as running, going up and down stairs, standing up, and sitting down. A commercial prosthesis also needs to implement user intent recognition (Varol, Sup, & Goldfarb, 2010; Zahedi, Sykes, Lang, & Cullington, 2005), and stumble detection and recovery (Zahedi, Sykes, Lang, & Cullington, 2005), and it needs to have a reliable and long-lasting power source (Dellon & Matsuoka, 2007). The results that we present in this chapter thus form only one component of a large, multifaceted, multidisciplinary research effort.

CONCLUSION

We have shown the potential of ANNs for closed-loop control. Specifically, our approach uses ANNs for closed-loop delta controls that are added to optimal open-loop control. Our ANN control has been shown to be effective at reducing the effects of noisy measurements and controls, as well as disturbances in the user interaction with the prosthesis. We have seen that the BBO open-loop control is sensitive to initial conditions. We have shown that ANNs can reduce the negative effects of varying initial conditions, potentially avoiding stumbles and falls. We have also shown that the ANN is able to be trained with the initial conditions variations and can generalize the desired effect to other types of noise and disturbances. Small measurement noise has little effect on the ANN performance. We show that ANNs can improve average performance by up to 8% compared to open-loop control. ANNs have demonstrated that they can be used effectively as a closed-loop controller for prosthetic knees.

ACKNOWLEDGMENT

This work was supported by the Cleveland State University (CSU) Provost's Office, and by the National Science Foundation under Grant No. 0826124. The Cleveland Clinic acknowledges the contribution of the State of Ohio, Department of Development and Third Frontier Commission, which provided funding in support of Rapid Rehabilitation and Return to Function for Amputee Soldiers project. We also acknowledge the system modeling and simulation work of Antonie van den Bogert (Cleveland Clinic and Orchard Kinetics), Sergey Samorezov (Cleveland Clinic), and Richard Rarick (CSU), which provided the foundation for this work.

REFERENCES

Albus, J. (1975). A new approach to manipulator control: The Cerebellar model articulation controller. *Transactions of the American Society of Mechanical Engineers. Journal of Dynamic Systems, Measurement, and Control, 97,* 220–227. doi:10.1115/1.3426922

Bellmann, M., Schmalz, T., & Blumentritt, S. (2010). Comparative biomechanical analysis of current microprocessor-controlled prosthetic knee joints. *Archives of Physical Medicine and Rehabilitation, 91,* 644–652. doi:10.1016/j.apmr.2009.12.014

Bergantz, D., & Barad, H. (1988). Neural network control of cybernetic limb prostheses. *IEEE International Conference on Engineering in Medicine and Biology Society* (Vol. 3, pp. 1486–1487). IEEE.

Chin, T., Machida, K., Sawamura, S., Shiba, R., Oyabu, H., & Nagakura, Y. (2006). Comparison of different microprocessor controlled knee joints on the energy consumption during walking in trans-femoral amputees: Intelligent knee prosthesis (IP) versus C-leg. *Prosthetics and Orthotics International, 30,* 73–80. doi:10.1080/03093640500533414

Dellon, B., & Matsuoka, Y. (2007). Prosthetics, exoskeletons, and rehabilitation. *IEEE Robotics & Automation Magazine, 14,* 30–34. doi:10.1109/MRA.2007.339622

Deluzio, K. (2011, May). *Gait analysis.* Retrieved from http://me.queensu.ca/people/deluzio/GaitAnalysis.php

Dosen, S., & Popovic, D. (2008). Accelerometers and force sensing resistors for optimal control of walking of a hemiplegic. *IEEE Transactions on Bio-Medical Engineering, 55*, 1973–1984. doi:10.1109/TBME.2008.919715

Elsley, R. (1990, June). Adaptive control of prosthetic limbs using neural networks. *International Joint Conference on Neural Networks* (Vol. 2, pp. 771–776). IEEE.

Gailey, R., Allen, K., Castles, J., Kucharik, J., & Roeder, M. (2008). Review of secondary physical conditions associated with lower limb amputation and long-term prosthesis use. *Journal of Rehabilitation Research and Development, 45*, 15–29. doi:10.1682/JRRD.2006.11.0147

Gu, J., Ding, X., Wang, S., & Wu, Y. (2010). Action and gait recognition from recovered 3-D human joints. *IEEE Transactions on Systems, Man, and Cybernetics. Part B, Cybernetics, 40*, 1021–1033. doi:10.1109/TSMCB.2010.2043526

Jang, J., Sun, C., & Mizutani, E. (1997). *Neuro-fuzzy and soft computing: A computational approach to learning and machine intelligence.* Upper Saddle River, NJ: Prentice Hall. doi:10.1109/TAC.1997.633847

Johansson, J., Sherrill, D., Riley, P., Bonato, P., & Herr, H. (2005). A clinical comparison of variable-damping and mechanically passive prosthetic knee devices. *American Journal of Physical Medicine & Rehabilitation, 84*, 563–575. doi:10.1097/01.phm.0000174665.74933.0b

Kalanovic, V., Popovic, D., & Skaug, N. (2000). Feedback error learning neural network for trans-femoral prosthesis. *IEEE Transactions on Rehabilitation Engineering, 8*, 71–80. doi:10.1109/86.830951

Kim, J., & Oh, J. (2001). Development of an above knee prosthesis using MR damper and leg simulator. In *Proceedings of the 2001 IEEE International Conference on Robotics & Automation* (pp. 3686–3691). IEEE.

Kulkarni, J., Gaine, W., Buckley, J., Rankine, J., & Adams, J. (2005). Chronic low back pain in traumatic lower limb amputees. *Clinical Rehabilitation, 19*, 81–86. doi:10.1191/0269215505cr819oa

Mandic, D., & Chambers, J. (2002). *Recurrent neural networks for prediction: Learning algorithms, architectures and stability.* Hoboken, NJ: John Wiley and Sons.

McDonald, C., Smith, D., Brower, R., Ceberio, M., & Sarkodie-Gyan, T. (2007, June). Determination of human gait phase using fuzzy inference. In *IEEE International Conference on Rehabilitation Robotics,* (pp. 661–665). IEEE.

Modan, M., Peles, E., Halkin, H., Nitzan, H., Azaria, M., & Gitel, S. (1998). Increased cardiovascular disease mortality rates in traumatic lower limb amputees. *The American Journal of Cardiology, 82*, 1242–1247. doi:10.1016/S0002-9149(98)00601-8

Nayak, R., Jain, L., & Ting, B. (2001). Artificial neural networks in biomedical engineering: A review. *Proceedings of the 1st Asian-Pacific Congress on Computational Mechanics* (pp. 887–892). Amsterdam, The Netherlands: Elsevier Science Limited.

Pappas, I., Popovic, M., Keller, T., Dietz, V., & Morari, M. (2001). A reliable gait phase detection system. *IEEE Transactions on Neural Systems and Rehabilitation Engineering, 9*, 113–125. doi:10.1109/7333.928571

Segal, A., Orendurff, M., Klute, G., McDowell, M., Pecoraro, J., Shofer, J., & Czerniecki, J. (2006). Kinematic and kinetic comparisons of transfemoral amputee gait using C-Leg and Mauch SNS prosthetic knees. *Journal of Rehabilitation Research and Development*, *43*, 857–870. doi:10.1682/JRRD.2005.09.0147

Seroussi, R., Gitter, A., Czerniecki, J., & Weaver, K. (1996). Mechanical work adaptations of above-knee amputee ambulation. *Archives of Physical Medicine and Rehabilitation*, *77*, 1209–1214. doi:10.1016/S0003-9993(96)90151-3

Seymour, R., Engbretson, B., Kott, K., Ordway, N., Brooks, G., & Crannell, J. (2007). Comparison between the C-leg microprocessor-controlled prosthetic knee and non-microprocessor control prosthetic knees: a preliminary study of energy expenditure, obstacle course performance, and quality of life survey. *Prosthetics and Orthotics International*, *31*, 51–61. doi:10.1080/03093640600982255

Varol, H., Sup, F., & Goldfarb, M. (2010). Multiclass real-time intent recognition of a powered lower limb prosthesis. *IEEE Transactions on Bio-Medical Engineering*, *57*, 542–551. doi:10.1109/TBME.2009.2034734

Williamson, R., & Andrews, B. (2001). Detecting absolute human knee angle and angular velocity using accelerometers and rate gyroscopes. *Medical & Biological Engineering & Computing*, *39*, 294–302. doi:10.1007/BF02345283

Wilmot, T. (2011, August). *Intelligent controls for a semi-active hydraulic prosthetic knee*. (Master's Thesis). Cleveland State University. Retrieved from http://www.csuohio.edu/engineering/ece/research/ thesis.html

Wilmot, T., Rarick, R., Bogert, A., Szatmary, S., Samorezov, S., Smith, W., & Simon, D. (2013). *Biogeography based optimization for hydraulic prosthetic knee control*. (Submitted for publication). Retrieved from http://embeddedlab.csuohio.edu/BBO

Zahedi, S., Sykes, A., Lang, S., & Cullington, I. (2005). Adaptive prosthesis – a new concept in prosthetic knee control. *Robotica*, *23*, 337–244. doi:10.1017/S0263574704001365

Zhang, J., Pu, J., Chen, C., & Fleischer, R. (2010). Low-resolution gait recognition. *IEEE Transactions on Systems, Man, and Cybernetics. Part B, Cybernetics*, *40*, 986–996. doi:10.1109/TSMCB.2010.2042166

ADDITIONAL READING

Abo-Hammou, Z. S., Yusuf, M., Mirza, N. M., Mirza, S. M., Arif, M., & Khurshid, J. (2004). Numerical solution of second-order, two-point boundary value problems using continuous genetic algorithms. *International Journal for Numerical Methods in Engineering*, *6*, 1219–1242. doi:10.1002/nme.1108

Bitzer, S. (2006, May). Learning EMG control of a robotic hand: Towards active prostheses. In *IEEE International Conference on Robotics and Automation* (pp. 2819 – 2823). IEEE.

Chan, A. D. C. (2005). Continuous myoelectric control for powered prostheses using hidden Markov models. *IEEE Transactions on Bio-Medical Engineering*, *52*(1), 121–124. doi:10.1109/TBME.2004.836492

Crispin, Y. (2006). An evolutionary approach to nonlinear discrete-time optimal control with terminal constraints. In Braz, J., Vieira, A., & Encarnacao, B. (Eds.), *Informatics in Control, Automation and Robotics I* (pp. 89–97). New York, NY: Springer. doi:10.1007/1-4020-4543-3_10

Dejnabadi, H., Jolles, B., & Aminian, K. (2005). A new approach to accurate measurement of uniaxial joint angles based on a combination of accelerometers and gyroscopes. *IEEE Transactions on Bio-Medical Engineering, 52*, 1478–1484. doi:10.1109/TBME.2005.851475

Heyuan, B., Dahu, W., Zhiguo, H., & Jiaolong, Z. (2010). A prosthetic hand system based on neural network theory. In *International Conference on Bioinformatics and Biomedical Technology* (pp. 332-334). IEEE.

Inohira, E., Uoi, T., & Yokoi, H. (2008). Generalization capability of neural networks for generation of coordinated motion of a hybrid prosthesis with a healthy arm. *International Journal of Innovative Computing, Information, & Control, 4*(2), 471–484.

Kalanovic, V., Popovic, D., & Skaug, N. (2000). Feedback error learning neural network for above-knee prosthesis. *IEEE Transactions on Neural Systems and Rehabilitation Engineering, 8*, 71–80. doi:10.1109/86.830951

Lee, S., Fink, W., von Allmen, P., Petropoulos, A., Russell, R., & Terrile, R. (2005). Evolutionary computing for low-thrust navigation. *American Institute of Aeronautics and Astronautics Space Conference* (pp. 1–7). AIAA.

Leonard, L., Sirkett, D. M., Langdon, I. J., Mullineux, G., Tilley, D. G., & Keogh, P. S. ... Miles, A.W. (2002). Engineering a new wrist joint replacement prosthesis—a multidisciplinary approach. In *Proceedings of the Institution of Mechanical Engineers, Part B (Journal of Engineering Manufacture), 216*(9), 1297-1302.

Liu, S., Wang, Y., & Huang, J. (2006). Advances in neural networks. *Third International Symposium on Neural Networks* (pp.792-798). New York, NY: Springer.

Martinez-Villalpando, E. C., & Herr, H. (2009). Agonist-antagonist active knee prosthesis: A preliminary study in level-ground walking. *Journal of Rehabilitation Research and Development, 46*(3), 361–374. doi:10.1682/JRRD.2008.09.0131

Pandy, M., Anderson, F., & Hull, D. (1992). A parameter optimization approach for the optimal control of large-scale musculoskeletal systems. *Transactions of the American Society of Mechanical Engineers, 114*, 450–460.

Popovic, D. B. (2008, June). Advanced methods for control of neural prostheses. *IET Irish Signals and Systems Conference* (pp. 252). IEEE.

Popovic, D. B., & Popovic, M. B. (2006). Design of a control for a neural prosthesis for walking: Use of artificial neural networks. In *8th Seminar on Neural Network Applications in Electrical Engineering* (p.8). IEEE.

Popovic, D. B., & Popovic, M. B. (2008). External control of movements and artificial neural networks. *9th Symposium on Neural Network Applications in Electrical Engineering* (pp. 115-119). IEEE.

Rahatabad, F. N., Nekoui, M. A., Golpaygani, M. R. H., Fallah, A., & Narbat, M. K. (2007). Towards cybernetic hand: A neural network method for hand prosthesis control. *Mediterranean Conference on Control & Automation* (pp. 1-4). IEEE.

Rai, J. K., Tewari, R. P., & Chandra, D. (2009). Hybrid control strategy for robotic leg prosthesis using artificial gait synthesis. *International Journal of Biomechatronics and Biomedical Robotics, 1*(1), 44–50. doi:10.1504/IJBBR.2009.030059

Reed, R. D., Sanders, J. E., & Marks, R. J. (1995). Neural network aided prosthetic alignment. *IEEE International Conference on Systems, Man, and Cybernetics, Intelligent Systems for the 21st Century* (pp. 505-508). IEEE.

Scharer, C. (1993). Trainable command recognition for a microprocessor-controlled prosthetic arm. *Journal of Microcomputer Applications*, *16*(3), 287–292. doi:10.1006/jmca.1993.1029

Simon, D. (2008). Biogeography-based optimization. *IEEE Transactions on Evolutionary Computation*, *12*, 702–713. doi:10.1109/TEVC.2008.919004

Song, L., Wang, X., Gong, S., Shi, Z., & Chen, L. (2002). Design of active artificial knee joint. *7th Asian-Pacific Conference on Medical and Biological Engineering* (pp. 155-158). New York, NY: Springer.

Torresen, J. (2002). A scalable approach to evolvable hardware. *Genetic Programming and Evolvable Machines*, *3*(3), 259–282. doi:10.1023/A:1020163325179

Yang, Z., Fang, J., & Qi, Z. (2005). Flight midcourse guidance control based on genetic algorithm. *Conference on Genetic and Evolutionary Computation* (pp. 1501–1506). ACM.

Yu, H., Xu, Z., Qian, X., Zhao, Z., & Shen, L. (2009). Inverse dynamic compound control for intelligent artificial leg based on PD-CMAC. *WSEAS Transactions on Computers*, *8*(9), 1554–1563.

Zecca, M., Micera, S., Carrozza, M. C., & Dario, P. (2002). Control of multifunctional prosthetic hands by processing the electromyographic signal. *Critical Reviews in Biomedical Engineering*, *30*, 459–485. doi:10.1615/CritRevBiomedEng.v30.i456.80

KEY TERMS AND DEFINITIONS

Active Knee Prosthesis: A prosthetic knee joint that is actuated with a motor powered from an external source.

Artificial Neural Network (ANN): A nonlinear mapping that propagates a vector of inputs through one or more layers of artificial neurons to generate a vector of outputs. The neurons have weighted connections and the output of each neuron is often a sigmoidal function of the inputs fed into it.

Biogeography-Based Optimization (BBO): An evolutionary algorithm inspired by the models of biogeography, where candidate solutions are modeled as habitats, and solution variables are modeled as habitat features. BBO migrates the habitat features among habitats based on differences between the cost values of the habitats, which are known as habitat suitability indices.

Evolutionary Algorithm (EA): A class of optimization algorithms, inspired by evolutionary processes in nature, in which candidate problem solutions are improved in parallel. Solution costs are computed at each iteration of the EA, and modifications to the variables of each solution are made based on these costs.

Passive Knee Prosthesis: A prosthetic knee that uses uncontrolled hydraulic or spring-based damping.

Semi-active Knee Prosthesis: A prosthetic knee joint that is actuated using energy that is stored and released and controlled electronically.

Stance Phase: The portion of a gait cycle where the foot is firmly on the ground. Stance phase begins with heel-strike and ends with toe-off.

Swing Phase: The portion of a gait cycle where the leg swings and the foot does not make contact with the ground. The swing phase begins with toe-off and ends with heel-strike.

Chapter 8
Techniques to Model and Derive a Cyber–Attacker's Intelligence

Peter J. Hawrylak
The University of Tulsa, USA

Michael Haney
The University of Tulsa, USA

Chris Hartney
The University of Tulsa, USA

Jonathan Hamm
The University of Tulsa, USA

John Hale
The University of Tulsa, USA

ABSTRACT

Identifying the level of intelligence of a cyber-attacker is critical to detecting cyber-attacks and determining the next targets or steps of the adversary. This chapter explores intrusion detection systems (IDSs) which are the traditional tool for cyber-attack detection, and attack graphs which are a formalism used to model cyber-attacks. The time required to detect an attack can be reduced by classifying the attacker's knowledge about the system to determine the traces or signatures for the IDS to look for in the audit logs. The adversary's knowledge of the system can then be used to identify their most likely next steps from the attack graph. A computationally efficient technique to compute the likelihood and impact of each step of an attack is presented. The chapter concludes with a discussion describing the next steps for implementation of these processes in specialized hardware to achieve real-time attack detection.

INTRODUCTION

Cyber-attackers are a grave threat to the security of the United States and to other nations. As the critical infrastructure systems are becoming increasingly interconnected through connections to the Internet it is possible for a cyber-attack originating anywhere in the world to cause significant damage within the United States. Monitoring of critical networks is a standard tool in the defenders arsenal, but when an attack is detected the defender could benefit from knowing the level of intelligence of the cyber-attacker. Intrusion detection systems (IDSs) provide this monitoring capability. Armed with better information about the cyber-attacker's intelligence and what the cyber-attacker knows about the system under attack, the defenders can identify and deploy their defenses in the most optimal fashion to protect the system and minimize negative impact to users.

DOI: 10.4018/978-1-4666-3942-3.ch008

Attack graphs are one metric to model cyber-attacks and their consequences. They provide the sequence of events necessary to reach a particular goal (e.g. gaining access to a database with credit card information). The defender can use attack graphs to determine the set of possible next moves the cyber-attacker may take. However, without being able to infer the cyber-attacker's intelligence their ability to correctly determine the attacker's most likely next moves is greatly impaired.

Reconnaissance of a network or system is an important early, if not first, step in an attack. It is to the attacker's benefit to discover as much information as possible about a network or system before launching their attack. This allows the attacker to determine the best course of action to achieve their goals. However, too much reconnaissance increases the risk that the attacker will be identified before they can achieve their goals or even launch their attack. This is especially true in the Smart Grid (next generation electric grid) which will utilize network connections and the Internet to connect grid components together (Farhangi, 2010). In the Smart Grid the types of devices, the IT (information technology) network architecture, and the power system architecture are the important pieces of information that the attacker needs to construct an attack (NIST, 2010).

This chapter will explore techniques to incorporate estimates of an adversary's knowledge of the system to improve intrusion detection systems (IDSs) and attack graphs. First, the use of IDSs to detect attacks and the challenges associated with them are described. Next, a brief background and description of attack graphs are presented. The use of vulnerability databases, such as the National Vulnerability Database (National Vulnerability Database, 2012), to generate attack graphs is described. Then, a variation of attack graphs, termed an attack dependency graphs is described. An analysis technique using the attack dependency graph to infer an adversary's future actions based on their past behavior is presented.

Attack graphs and IDSs can be combined to improve (reduce time) attack detection. A methodology to construct attack signatures or traces for the IDS using attack graphs is presented. This process is computationally intensive and ideas for future research directions for development of specialized hardware are presented.

Intrusion Detection: Detecting the Attack

Defenders of modern enterprise networks are increasingly challenged to quickly and accurately identify intrusion attempts and successful exploitation of vulnerabilities on their networks. The volume of alerts and monitoring data generated is the main reason preventing real-time monitoring of networks. Traditional software based systems mine logs of network traffic looking for suspicious patterns. The reaction is often delayed allowing the adversary valuable time to carry-out the next step in their attack. In doing so, a number of technological approaches may be adopted to prevent and/or detect those intrusion attempts, and historically these approaches have been fraught with the problem of false positives. False positives are the alerts raised by IDSs for analysts to investigate which have been triggered for various benign reasons. False positives must be minimized without reducing the detection of malicious events. Often, the signature that matches network traffic and generates these alerts is written in such a way that it matches other normal network traffic patterns. For example, an alert that refers to a directory traversal attack on a web server, which is serving HTML pages with relative links that contain a link to a parent or adjacent directory. In the normal course of accessing the web server, alerts may be generated. Much has been written in the past decade to discuss this problem and how to build a better IDS (Ning & Xu, 2003; Ning, Cui, Reeves, & Xu, 2004; Zhou, Heckman, Reynolds, Carlson, & Bishop, 2007; Chivers,

Clark, Nobles, Shaikh, & Chen, 2010), and yet enterprise network defenders are continuing to struggle to manage the volumes of data related to security events recorded every day.

False positives in signature-based intrusion detection systems occur for several reasons. The first relates to how a particular signature is written and designed. Often these signatures must be written in a way that is general enough to catch variations in an attacker's possible exploit attempt. This leads signature authors to make general assumptions about the traffic pattern, which may match normal traffic on a given network. As an IDS analyst reviews these alerts, decisions must be made to tailor these signatures, or tune them by adding more specific criteria. Other false positives come from attackers themselves attempting to flood a network with bogus attack traffic in order to deliberately overwhelm the IDS system and analysts. This could be part of an attempt for by the attacker to hide or erase evidence of their real attack.

The efforts of attackers to hide their attacks include obfuscation and other techniques to try to produce a "false negative" (not trigger an alert when one should be triggered). Alternatively, it may be that these actual attacks will be hidden in a stream of attack patterns known or thought to trigger copious alerts on the analyst's dashboard. Additionally, tactics may include low-and-slow intrusions which are designed to delay attack steps long enough to overflow any queues that the IDS is keeping track of, either for time or number of alerts (Chivers, Clark, Nobles, Shaikh, & Chen, 2010). For networked systems, such overflow attacks can be very effective and easily made to blend in with false positive (background noise) alerts.

Thus, IDS analysts and network defenders need to be able to focus in on key and actual attacks on their network, so that a response can be made which isolates the attacker, determines where else on the network the attacker may have been, and where else she/he may be going (or have already gone). Correlation of attacks should provide visibility into intrusions by showing sequential exploits that progress through a network. By assuming that an attacker coming from outside the network must chronologically scan systems, find vulnerabilities, exploit the vulnerability and then "island hop" on this system to another system, analysts should be able to follow an attack in the myriad of IDS alerts if sequential attacks can be correlated and highlighted.

There are many techniques that have been developed to properly correlate different low-level alerts into multi-stage attack events. Some are based on probabilities, and others are based on similarities between alerts (same source IP, same destination port, same window of time, etc.). Some of the most promising work has been in the area of correlating alerts with attack graphs, as shown in (Ahmadinejad, Jalili, & Abadi, 2011; Chu, Ingols, Lippmann, Webster, & Boyer, 2010; Liao, Striegel, & Chawla, 2010).

Attack Graphs: Modeling the Attack

Attack graphs are used to visualize how an attack can occur (Hawrylak, Louthan, Daily, Hale, & Papa, 2011). They model the system under investigation as a state space. Each state represents a particular level of security or condition (state) of the system. Edges in the attack graph represent actions that can be taken to alter the security level or state of the system. Typically, edges represent security vulnerabilities, which an attacker can exploit to undermine a system. Edges can be weighted with quantities such as probability of success or a cost associated with a successful exploit. Attack graphs were introduced by Philips and Swiler in 1998 (Philips & Swiler, 1998). Attack trees (Schneier, 1999) and privilege graphs (Dacier, Deswarte, & Kaâniche, 1996) are similar to attack graphs and can also be used to illustrate attacks.

Attack graphs are generated by matching vulnerabilities to a system of architecture. Figure 1 illustrates this process for generating attack

Figure 1. Attack graph generation

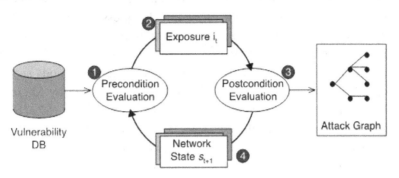

graphs. Preconditions that are required for each vulnerability are enumerated (step 1 in Figure 1). These preconditions can be obtained from vulnerability databases. If a system component has the set of preconditions then the vulnerability associated with those preconditions is present and could be exploited by an attacker (step 2 in Figure 1). The system is altered as a result of the exploit and these alterations are described in the postconditions (steps 3 and 4 in Figure 1). This process produces a sequence or chain of events leading to a successful attack on the system. The collection of all such sequences is the attack graph for a particular system.

The procedure illustrated in Figure 1 can be used to automatically generate attack graphs. Formal languages to describe attack graphs, such as the one developed by Templeton and Levitt (Templeton & Levitt, 2001), need to be used in this process. Attack graphs can be integrated into system defense tools, such as intrusion detection systems (Tidwell, Larson, Fitch, & Hale, 2001; Noel & Jajodia, 2004), for reachability anaylsis (Lippmann & Ingols, 2005; Ingols, Chu, Lippmann, Webster, & Boyer, 2009), or for model checking (Ritchey & Ammann, 2000) to determine which goals an attacker can achieve.

The collection of all possible chains quickly leads to attack graphs that are unweildy and methods for improving scalability (Ingols, Lippmann, & Piwowarski, 2006; Ammann, Wijesekera, & Kaushik, 2002) are an active area of research.

Analysis of attack graphs can yield security recommendations that can be used to improve system security (Clark, Tyree, Dawkins, & Hale, 2007; Wang, Noel, & Jajodia, 2006; Clark, Tyree, Dawkins, & Hale, 2004; Ammann, Wijesekera, & Kaushik, 2002). These analysis methods are primarily static analysis, but great benefits are possible if the analysis could be conducted in real-time. Such real-time analysis would provide the information necessary for systems to intelligently react and adapt to attacks.

National Vulnerability Database

Enumerating all possible preconditions necessary for a vulnerability to be exploited is a critical step in the attack graph generation process illustrated in Figure 1. The National Vulnerability Database (NVD) is an online search engine (National Vulnerability Database, 2012) containing known vulnerabilities for various software packages and can be used to provide the necessary precondition information needed in step 1 in Figure 1. The precondition information can be gathered from the NVD and converted into an XML (eXtensible Markup Language) representation. The network model can also be converted into XML and then the two XML descriptions compared to determine where vulnerabilities are present in the system under investigation. The network model is a model of the network connections in the system from which, the network state is determined. Often it contains information about each device, such as the operating system, connected to the network. The XML representation of the network must include information about both the network and the devices (e.g. computers, routers, etc.) connected to that network. While, XML is not the only method of encoding such information, it is convenient. However, other encoding techniques could be applied instead of XML. The network model can be obtained from an nmap capture, which provides detailed information such open ports, running applications, and the running operating system on a given node. In addition, the version number is usually obtainable for both applications and operating systems. The version number is crucial for vulnerabilities since an exploit often depends on a specific software release. National Vulnerability Database provides a description of a known vulnerability, and keywords can be mined from this description and compared with the XML network model, this is step 2 in Figure 1. If the mined keywords match a node's description within the XML model, that node can be considered vulnerable.

Intelligence Derived from Attack Graphs

Attack graphs are a tool that can be used to give more information about an attacker's actions on a target network. Attack graphs connect an attacker's actions with the resulting outcomes of those actions. By using exploits in junction with other exploits, the attacker can gain access and privileges that would have been unobtainable with just a single exploit. Attack graphs can be used to see how vulnerabilities chain together to give a more complete view of the security of a given system (Lippmann, Ingols, & Scott, 2006).

While attack graphs already give system context to an attacker's actions, additional information can be incorporated to give the user an even better sense of security for their system. The addition of a security risk metric on top of an attack graph can give the end user more information with which

to make their security decisions. Being able to quickly assess the risk of different nodes in an attack graph lets the user focus their defense assets to mitigate and manage the remaining risk on their system. Methods such as DREAD and STRIDE, developed by Microsoft, can be used to help quantify these risks (Howard & Leblanc, 2003). STRIDE is a threat detection method where software developers analyze code modules for threats relating to (1) Spoofing, (2) Tampering, (3) Repudiation, (4) Information disclosure, (5) Denial of service, and (6) Elevation of privilege (Hernan, Lambert, Ostwald, & Shostack, 2006). Threats that are identified from STRIDE are then analyzed and addressed. This method can be applied to individual code modules and to larger systems made up of sub-systems and code modules. Understanding how secure components fit together is important because vulnerabilities may be present in these connections. The DREAD method provides a way to quantize risk based on five factors: (1) Damage potential, (2) Reproducibility, (3) Exploitability, (4) Affected users, and (5) Discoverability (Meier, Mackman, Dunner, Vasireddy, Escamilla, & Murukan, 2003). Vulnerabilities are rated on these five factors and these ratings are combined to compute an overall risk factor. The DREAD method can be used to rank vulnerabilities in terms of severity and can be used to quantify the impact of a vulnerability. Such a ranking can be used to prioritize more severe vulnerabilities to be addressed.

The metric information given in this chapter will pertain to a metric over a specific type of attack graph, termed an attack dependency graph. An attack dependency graph splits the vulnerability into its three distinct base parts: precondition(s), exploit, and postcondition(s). The attack dependency graph is limited to only start with conditions that match the system profile; therefore, only those exploits that apply to our system are shown. This is useful because it helps reduce the number of exploits that the IDS must monitor. One can see how the postconditions from one exploit can be used as a precondition for another exploit. This gives information and context about how vulnerabilities chain together and clearly shows the postconditions for exploits that an attacker might use.

Attack Dependency Graph Metric

Attack dependency graphs are very modular by design. This metric takes advantage of the modular nature of attack dependency graphs by splitting the concept of risk onto the atomic parts of a vulnerability: its conditions and its exploits. The metric takes into consideration the impact that conditions can have on a system and the likelihood that an attacker can perform a given exploit. The metric presented in this chapter models risk as a function of likelihood and impact (Hartney, 2012).

$$Risk = Likelihood * Impact \qquad (1)$$

In this way, the metric modularizes the concept of risk across the vulnerability. The metric also makes use of the fact that attack dependency graphs are chains that rely upon each other. Hence, risk is propagated forward and backward in the attack dependency graph. Metric values are propagated through the chains in a way that each node's concept of risk depends on its parents or children. The calculation of absolute likelihood and impact is thus reduced to basic probability theory using intersection (AND) and union (OR) type operations.

The system uses an "absolute" likelihood that represents the likelihood of a given exploit without considering any sort of vulnerability chaining. The absolute likelihood represents the likelihood that a particular exploit will occur based only on that exploit and not on any past history. After the system has absolute likelihoods for each exploit, a cumulative likelihood for each exploit is calculated from likelihoods of the exploits that precede it (Noel, Jajodia, Wang, & Singhal, 2010). Likelihood values can be assigned or estimated using

a probability distribution function. Monte Carlo methods are one means to generate this probability distribution function that allows the analyst to quantify the sensitivity of absolute likelihood on the attacker obtaining their goal (Noel, Jajodia, Wang, & Singhal, 2010) by reaching a leaf node in the attack dependency graph. The analysis method presented in this chapter considers impact in a similar way.

There are values for "absolute" impact, which represent the impact of a given condition without considering any sort of chaining (previous impacts). A cumulative impact is calculated by looking at all of the conditions that follow it (can be generated as a result of the exploit). The difference between impact and likelihood is that likelihood relies on the likelihood of what comes before it, because every exploit relies on previous exploits/conditions to be able to be performed. Conversely, impact relies on the impact of exploits and conditions from what may occur in the future, because the condition could now possibly allow more dangerous conditions, which should be considered when thinking about impact (Wang, Islam, Long, Singhal, & Jajodia, 2008). This chaining and propagation is demonstrated below.

- **Definitions:** Let $L(x)$ represent the cumulative likelihood of a node x. Let $l(x)$ represent the absolute likelihood of a node x.

For any exploit e that relies on parent conditions $c1$ and $c2$ (logical AND operation), the cumulative likelihood, $L(e)$, is given by:

$$L(e) = l(e) * L(c1) * L(c2) \qquad (2)$$

For a condition c that can be satisfied by either $e1$ or $e2$ (union operation), the cumulative likelihood, $L(c)$, is given by:

$$L(c) = l(c)*[(L(e1) + L(e2) - L(e1)*L(e2)] \qquad (3)$$

- **Definitions:** Let $I(x)$ represent the cumulative impact of a node x. Let $i(x)$ represent the absolute impact of a node x.

For any exploit e that gives children conditions $c1$ and $c2$, the cumulative impact, $I(e)$, is given by:

$$I(e) = i(e) * I(c1) * I(c2) \qquad (4)$$

For a condition c that can be used in either $e1$ or $e2$, the cumulative impact, $I(c)$, is given by:

$$I(c) = i(c) * [(I(e1) + I(e2) - I(e1)*I(e2)] \qquad (5)$$

In the described metric, every node has a value for cumulative impact and cumulative likelihood. If these two scores are combined, the result is a risk score for every node. The calculated risk scores can be used in a number of different ways to help inform the user as to how best to secure their system. An example of the output of a system is illustrated in Figure 2 for a scenario where a student hacks into a grading system to change

Figure 2. Attack dependency example based on the grade changer attack graph (greyer is more severe)

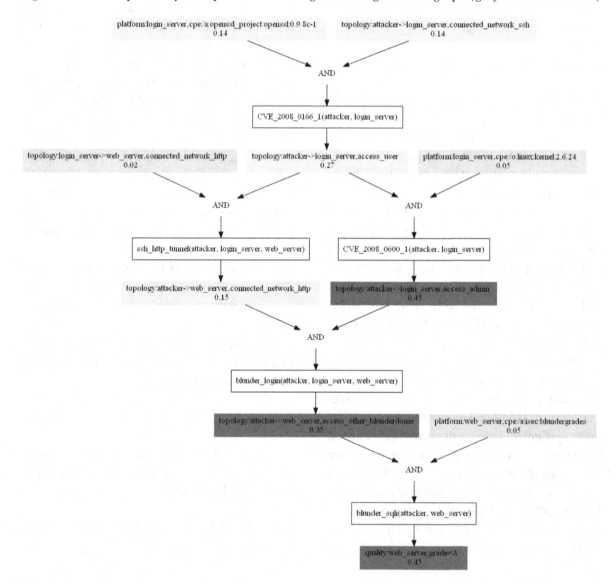

their grade to an 'A'. The impact for each of the nodes is illustrated in Figure 2 where the darker grey represents a more severe (larger) impact.

Runtime Analysis of the Proposed Risk Metric

One of the key benefits of the proposed risk metric is the simplicity of calculating and updating the absolute risk quantities. Recall that the cumulative likelihood depends on events (exploits) preceding the node in question, and that the cumulative impact depends on the actions that can be caused (happen after) the exploit in question. Pseudocode for an algorithm to compute cumulative impact is presented below.

- Let x represent the current node.
- Let i_x the absolute impact of node x.
- Let I_x the absolute impact of node x.
- Let y_i represent a child of node x.

- Let V represent the number of nodes in the system.
- Let E represent the number of edges in the system.
- Let L represent the set of leaf nodes (nodes with no children).

One algorithm to compute the absolute risk values is described below.

The runtime of the first while loop is O(V). The second while loop can be implemented as a modified breadth-first search starting with the leaf nodes and working its way to the root (top). The runtime of this modified breadth-first-search is O(V+E). Thus, the overall runtime of the is O(V+E), which is a polynomial runtime and is computationally efficient. Using this algorithm impact can be propagated efficiently. The polynomial runtime ensures that the algorithm will scale well with the size of the graph (number of nodes and edges).

Algorithm 1.

```
Set L to the empty set
WHILE(Unprocessed nodes) DO
        Select a node x
        IF(x has no children) THEN
                Set I  = i
                   x     x
        Add x to the set L
END IF
Mark x as processed
END WHILE
WHILE(Unprocessed nodes) DO
        Select a node x from set L
        IF(All of x's children, y , have cumulative impacts assigned) THEN
                                 i
                Calculate I  based on Equations (4) and (5)
                           x
                Add x to set L
                Mark x as processed
        END IF
END WHILE
```

Efficient dynamic impact updates are possible by recomputing cumulative impact for the entire graph. Alternative implementations that limit the update to only the effective parts may be more efficient. The difference in runtime between the two update methods (updating the entire graph or just the affected parts) is the effort required to identify those nodes where cumulative impact changes (needs to be updated) and those where the cumulative impact is unchanged. Depending on how many nodes must be traversed (checked) to obtain this information, it may be quicker to simply recompute cumulative impact for the entire graph.

Likelihood can be computed using the process described by Wang et al. (Wang, L., Islam, T., Long, T., Singhal, & Jajodia, 2008) where an absolute likelihood is applied to each exploit and cumulative likelihood computed using Equations 2 and 3. Cumulative likelihood is computed based on the likelihood of prior exploits. This is a top-down process, starting from the root of the tree and working toward the leaves. A breadth-first-search is used starting at the root because the absolute likelihood values are assigned a priori and Equations 2 and 3 are based on the absolute likelihood values. The breadth-first-search has a runtime of O(V+E), where V is the number of vertices (nodes) and E is the number of edges (exploits). This method for computing cumulative likelihood has a polynomial runtime and is thus efficient.

Other Attack Graph Analysis Methods

A number of other attack graph analysis methods have been proposed. Wang, Singhal, and Jajodia (2007) have proposed a framework for a security metric based on five principles: (1) all values used in the metric should be specified and based on concrete definitions, (2) the metric should capture and make use of all relevant information, (3) decisions which cannot be decided through rules require user input to evaluate, (4) assets (hosts) are viewed as a set of vulnerabilities, and (5) the

output of the metric should be meaningful and useful. Item (2) could be problematic because the set of input parameters is very large and they suggest that cost, amount of damage caused by the exploit, and difficulty of executing the exploit be used as the three metrics for this item, with cost being used to rank exploits in terms of severity (Wang, Singhal, & Jajodia, 2007).

Attack surfaces think of vulnerabilities in terms of a surface, which a system presents to the attacker (Manadhata & Wing, 2011). The surface captures the entry points through which the system can be attacked and the area of the surface quantifies the level of vulnerability the system in question contains: smaller areas indicate a less vulnerable system. Impact is described in terms of the damage potential-effect ratio, which relates the impact of a particular exploit to the effort the attacker must expend to execute that exploit (Manadhata & Wing, 2011).

Model checking has been used to generate attack graphs (Sheyner, Haines, Jha, Lippmann, & Wing, 2002). The use of model checking enables the analyst to search the graph to identify the minimum set of exploits that can be removed to prevent the attacker from reaching their goal (Sheyner, Haines, Jha, Lippmann, & Wing, 2002). This is analogous to the minimum cut set problem from graph theory. Data on difficulty and cost to prevent each exploit must be identified a priori. Model checking enables the use of formal mathematical and theorem proving methods to prove security properties of systems. Another generation method has been developed using the programming language Prolog (Mao & Zhang, 2007) that could be incorporated into formal mathematical and theorem proving tools.

Metrics looking at the qualities required for an attacker are useful in quantizing the level of attacker that a system is resistant to. One method identifies the weakest attacker capable of compromising a system based on the attack graph (Pamula, Jajodia, Ammann, & Swarup, 2006). This method uses the initial conditions required for each attack to find the minimal set of initial conditions needed to carry out the attack (Pamula, Jajodia, Ammann, & Swarup, 2006). Weakness can be ranked based on the raw number of initial conditions, or on a weighted sum of initial conditions where the weight quantifies the difficulty in obtaining the condition (Pamula, Jajodia, Ammann, & Swarup, 2006).

Privilege graphs (Dacier, Deswarte, & Kaâniche, 1996) are another graph structure that can be used to represent security properties. In a privilege graph, nodes represent a set of privileges within a system and edges represent vulnerabilities. Ortalo et al. (Ortalo, Deswarte, & Kaâniche, 1999) developed a method to apply the Markov property to privilege graphs and use this to extract the mean effort to security failure (METF). The METF provides insight into how much time and effort is required by an attacker to compromise a given system.

Prediction and Intelligence

Prediction of an attacker's next move is an achievable goal using attack graphs. Attack graphs natively contain information about how vulnerabilities chain together. If the system can detect and predict where an attack might be in an attack graph, it is then possible to look at the next states available to the attacker. If the system contains information from the metric previously mentioned, it is possible to list which attack states are the most likely or impactful. Ranking these potential next steps in order of probability allows the analyst to alter the system to defeat the adversary. For example, the analyst may temporarily disconnect a part of the network or reroute that traffic through a different router to prevent the adversary from using those assets in the next stage of their attack. Alternatively, the system can be altered to allow the analyst to collect additional information or evidence about the adversary. Such information can be useful in analyzing the intrusion and used in court if charges are filed.

The basis of this prediction requires strong monitoring tools to identify attacker actions. Without knowledge of what the attacker is doing or the exploits they have already preformed, it is difficult to determine the next possible steps with any certainty.

Strong monitoring tools can give additional information used to help predict the attacker's actions, outside of attack graphs and attack graph metrics. It is also possible to determine some characteristics about the attacker (Wang, Liu, & Jajodia, 2006). If the system knows what exploits an attacker has executed already, it is likely the attacker would be able to perform that exploit again at a different exposure. The system could also increase the likelihood of similar or related exploits based on an attacker's previous actions. If historical data tells us that exploits A, B, and C are usually done together to provide a goal to the attacker and our system determines it has seen exploit A and B performed, the likelihood of C could be increased. In another example, if the attacker performed a computationally intense attack, it is relatively safe to assume that the attacker has significant resources supporting themselves. This would warrant a more severe response. The way an attacker moves through a network can help inform the defender to the type of attacker they might be dealing with (Ramsbrok, Berthier, & Cikuer, 2007).

After attempting to identify the attacker type, the intelligence can be reworked back into the original security metric to aid in future predictions. If the system believes an attacker might be a specific attacker type, the potential goals and next actions can be reconsidered. With some additional work by the user, the metric can be adapted to fit this new information. For example, if the system thinks the attacker is an insider, the metric can increase the likelihood value of potential exploits that an insider would be more likely to perform, such as accessing internal information, rather than exploits that might be less likely, like connecting to the system remotely.

Network Simulation

Computer networks are often simulated using discrete event simulators. Simulation provides a powerful tool to analyze network performance and system properties (Hawrylak, Cain, & Mickle, 2009). OMNeT++ (Varga & Hornig, 2008; Varga, 2001) is a discrete event simulator specifically designed to for network simulations and can be used to test artificial user-defined traffic or recreate captured network traffic. This allows the analyst to analyze known attacks and normal network traffic to improve the rule set of the IDS. The impact and feasibility of theoretical attacks derived from attack graphs and attack dependency graphs can be explored. The network traffic can be captured using a number of programs and pcap is one such program to store the captured traffic that is supported by OMNeT++. A pcap file contains traffic as seen from the local host over a period of time; therefore, many assumptions must be made in order to generate an OMNeT++ simulation. A primary example would be the network's topological information. In order to partially reconstruct the network's topology, the sniffer must have been run when the host captured the appropriate traffic. The accuracy of a reconstructed topology is heavily dependent on chance, in that the capture must have occurred when the appropriate traffic was present on the network. For example, it is easy to obtain the hardware address of directly linked nodes, but matching the hardware address with a protocol address would rely on ARP (Address Resolution Protocol) captures. ARP captures can also be used to gather a list of known nodes in the local network. While their exact topology is uncertain, they can easily be separated from external IP addresses. Some indirectly linked nodes can be appended to the directly linked nodes that forwarded their traffic. Although this is only an approximation of their topology, it is still more accurate than randomly linking local nodes. Other possible methods of determining a node's distance

is examining a packet's time to live in its IP header, or if the capture happened to contain a timestamp ICMP (Internet Control Message Protocol) packet. The first method is somewhat unreliable because a packet's initial time-to-live (TTL) is variable. However, it might be possible to compare TTL's in the local network and determine if there exists a uniform initial TTL. Packets with smaller TTL's could be considered more distant.

Attack Graphs Leveraged to Help Intrusion Detection and Incident Response

The primary goal of an IDS analyst is to be able to quickly and accurately identify real attacks hidden in a large number of false positive alerts. In order to do so, one assumes that attacks progress in a basically forward-moving chronological way, and that most of these events will trigger some alert (or multiple alerts), and that if the attack is successful, the state of the attacked system will have changed in some measurable way. Therefore, if an analyst can string together a series of alerts that form an attack path through the network and/or focus on the alerts that change a system's state in a negative way, these are likely to point to an incident and an intruder (or malicious software working autonomously). This should ultimately also reduce or eliminate false positives by measuring the system's state change following an alert.

Generally, the problem with current IDS efforts is a focus entirely on network traffic and a lack of a clear correlation of alerts detected and system state change. In most cases, false positives can be reduced significantly if IDS signature rules are tailored to a network's actual systems and known state. As we will examine, the use of attack graphs can greatly assist in intrusion detection efforts, that IDSs can help generate attack graphs and provide more accurate attack scenarios, and finally that the efforts needed to generate usable attack graphs are many of the same necessary for tuning an IDS: system inventory, known vulnerabilities, known good configurations, and other properties of system state.

The focus of much of the IDS research in the last 10 years has been on methods to correlate IDS alerts together into a string of stages of an attack (Ning, Cui, & Reeves, 2002; Ning & Xu, 2003; Noel, Robertson, & Jajodia, 2004; Wang, Liu, & Jajodia, 2006; Zhou, Heckman, Reynolds, Carlson, & Bishop, 2007; Tedesco & Aickelin, 2008). This may include pairing an alert regarding a ping sweep of the network from a particular IP with an alert regarding a port scan of one active host in that port range. This alert may be followed by a TCP connection to a listening port on that machine. This connection may or may not trigger an alert depending on the tuning of the IDS alerts. For example, if the connection is to port 22 and is encrypted, and this system is known to listen on port 22 with sshd and accept connections normally, any signature matching this activity may have already been removed from the IDS signature set.

The next thing that may happen if this is an actual attack is that the system state will change in some way. A user may be added or given elevated privileges, a .rhosts file may be updated, or an sshd session may be started on a port other than 22. A more sophisticated attacker may also next try to connect out from this system, perhaps to download additional hacker tools, a rootkit, or some additional scanning and sniffing tools to use from this system. This may occur as an ssh connection out of the network, or as an SSL connection to a web server where the tool package is waiting to be downloaded. Again, if this is normal activity such as a user browsing to web servers with SSL encryption, the IDS signatures may not see this. But undoubtedly, the system's state will change in some way. Tools will be installed, users will be added, user privileges elevated, cron jobs and scheduled tasks will set up to maintain persistent connections, etc. The next activity that the IDS may see is an alert regarding this system appearing to attack others on the internal network. Based on the

earlier alerts, and the new alerts coming from the source, which was previously the target, analysts may guess that this machine was compromised.

But how might an IDS system correlate these alerts to notify an analyst with what some (Ning, Cui, & Reeves, 2002) call a "hyper alert"? Some IDS correlation engines associate alerts based on similarities in their properties (Ning, Cui, Reeves, & Xu, 2004) (e.g. the same source IP, destination port, etc.). Much research (Ning, Cui, Reeves, & Xu, 2004; Zhou, Heckman, Reynolds, Carlson, & Bishop, 2007; Frigault, Wang, Anoop, & Jajodia, 2008) focuses on the use of mathematical models to detect anomalies in network traffic and IDS alerts to determine unauthorized behavior. Other correlation engines are based on a probabilistic model (Valdes & Skinner, 2001). However, it should be clear to see that the use of attack graphs can greatly assist the process of correlating separate and seemingly unconnected alerts. Individual attacks may not be linked together, but the attack graph will show this linkage. This linkage information can be used to design new signatures and correlate previously unrelated alerts to a larger attack. If attack scenarios can be predicted, alerts should trigger in a sequential order, which matches a known attack path in a network's attack graph. Attack graphs can be used to assist the IDS correlation engine, and can provide valuable insight to an analyst, which can help with additional monitoring and investigation of incidents. The attack graph provides the order or sequence of alerts that will be generated for a given attack. This sequence can be mined for in data logs to identify evidence of an attack.

Large static attack graphs of a network may by themselves be unwieldy and difficult to leverage for valuable information in real-time. Most analysts prefer to visually monitor their network and assets for attacks and use this visual display to make decisions on how best to react. However, if IDS alerts which signify a particular attack attempt, actual exploit, or system change can be mapped on the attack graphs, an analyst would be able to "zoom in" or magnify the attack graph to focus on a particular portion of the attack scenario. By zooming in, the analyst is able to focus on the details of the current stage of the attack and make decisions how to best respond. For example, the analyst may wish to see what resources are connected to the affected asset to decide if they should simply disconnect that asset from the larger system. Alternatively, the analyst may use the fine-grained information to determine the attackers probable next steps. This may be accomplished with ad hoc queries of the attack graph, specifying particular conditions as contained in the IDS alert, and determining which portions of the network and systems may be affected as well. The display system can then compute a polygon around the affected area and "zoom in" to show that area in greater detail. The "zoom in" feature can be implemented as part of the graphical user interface (GUI) used by the analyst to monitor their system.

One implementation of the "zoom-in" feature is to use a breadth-first-search starting with the node(s) representing the identified portion of the attack. Such a search would execute for n levels from the starting nodes where the n level is defined as the node (vertex) n edges away from the starting nodes. Depending on the complexity of the interactions of the system (number of edges) the value of n will typically between 2 and 4. The runtime of this algorithm will increase with n (and the number of edges) and it is important to be able to provide the "zoom in" capability quickly. Again, the runtime of this algorithm would be $O(V+E)$ which is polynomial and scales well.

Another potential application is the ability to generate dynamic attack graphs with limited datasets based on a changed system state or increased knowledge about an attacker's knowledge or capabilities at a given stage in the attack. The likelihood and impact equations described previously can be quickly and efficiently computed as those parameters change dynamically. These updates require only basic multiplication, addition, and subtraction, combined with the modified breadth-first-search. The mathematical operations have a constant runtime and the modified breadth-first-search has a polynomial runtime. This may be automated in a way to give an analyst clues about other possible attack steps, which will be discussed next. By generating dynamic attack graphs based on the alerts at a given time, state changes can be accounted for more realistically, and the time to generate the graphs should be reduced to a fraction given a limited and focused data set of known states and next steps. In this case, the attack graph is generated or grows as the attack progresses. This is in contrast to building the entire attack graph at once in order to evaluate security properties of a system. The analyst would most likely prefer to have the attack graph grow with the attack so they can focus their attention only on the possible next steps of the attacker rather than weed out the attacker's next steps from the larger but complete attack graph. Conversely, the designer needs to work with the entire attack graph to define the security requirements for the system and to evaluate security properties of the system.

For use in correlation of IDS alerts, one approach (Ning, Cui, Reeves, & Xu, 2004) is based on the ordering of alerts and linking them to both pre-conditions and postconditions of the attack at that stage. That is, what are the prerequisites for that attack to have been successful, and what are the consequences of the attack at that stage. These can be tracked in the attack graph in a way that allows even out-of-sequence alerts to be correlated if they lie along the same attack path in the graph.

In addition, an analyst or correlation engine may hypothesize about state changes or other attacks for which no alert was received (Tedesco & Aickelin, 2008). If two alerts are separated by one (or more) intermediate steps, based on the attack graphs, one can assume this step in the attack has been successfully carried out. This may help in correlating alerts and reducing false positives. But it may also provide feedback for the attack graph that not all scenarios are accurately reflected. That is, some other intermediate step may exist that is not accounted for, and for which there may be no IDS alert, or another alert may not have been properly correlated. In either case, the alignment of IDS alerts along an attack graph provides the analyst an area to focus his/her investigation of the incident.

In the event of an intrusion in which an analyst is able to investigate an attack through the use of an attack graph, it may also be possible to determine other attack scenarios that are related, or which may be triggered by other state changes in the network and systems. This may provide valuable insight to an investigator to determine if an attack may not be contained to the systems on which alerts were received. Other systems with similar states may have also been compromised, or they may yet be targets of the attacker, and actions can be taken to secure, monitor, or investigate these other systems.

In order to support these efforts, analysts need the ability to manipulate the data available to them in unique ways. Reporting needs to be available through ad hoc data transformations and queries (i.e. replacing hostnames in system logs with IP addresses, to query against network-based alerts). This can lead to the ability to play out "what if" scenarios and look for other possible intrusion paths taken by an attacker.

It should also be noted that much of the information gathering, which is necessary to support tuning an IDS, is also valuable to analysts in constructing an accurate and complete attack graph of the network. This information includes the number, type, and category of all the systems and application on the network, as well as their reachability. This information may be gathered in asset inventory systems, by scanning the network, possibly on a continuous basis, and by checking individual systems and the details of their current state (e.g., patch level, vulnerability to a given exploit, and connectivity to other systems). Technologies considered for producing that information include network monitoring with the capability to listen and learn a network's nodes, or from vulnerability scanning technologies that connect to a system and scan it, or policy compliance technologies that authenticate to a system and query it for information about its state.

All of these benefits are provided by efforts to correlate intrusion detection system alerts with attack graphs. Attack graphs provide valuable information to IDS analysts regarding other possible attack stages or targets. The IDS provides valuable attack scenario information to the attack graph analyst. Ultimately, both of these characteristics will lead to a reduction in false positive alerts and an ability to quickly and accurately identify attacks on the network.

Future research should include leveraging attack graphs to produce a means of focusing additional ad hoc security measures, such as "turning up" logging and monitoring for systems, network segments, or traffic types. Also, focus should be given to leveraging technologies beyond network intrusion detection and monitoring and correlate alerts to system state changes via host-based system logs, log aggregation tools, and analytical methods applied to these. Currently correlation engines generally struggle to match alerts based on source and destination IP information (with some given payload to inspect) with an alert regarding a user, a hostname, and a process name or ID. Data normalization is a key concern for correlating alerts in unrelated formats. Attack graphs again provide a means to track both network-based events (in attacks) and system-based events (in state conditions) to allow for correlation.

Solutions and Recommendations

IDSs require traces or patterns of attacks to function effectively. Attack graphs can generate these traces through walks from a starting state to a particular goal state. Signature based IDS technology uses a library of such traces to determine if traffic is benign or malicious. Unfortunately, signature based methods are always behind the attacker because an attack must be first identified or discovered in a research laboratory before a signature can be developed. Attack graphs can be traversed in real-time or on demand as conditions warrant. For example, when the IDS detects traffic that is suspicious it can walk the appropriate attack graphs using the current network state as the starting point. This information provides the possible next steps of the attacker and can be used to identify traces of events to further the attack.

The IDS must be able to scan and react to traffic in real-time. For a traditional computer network, such as a 1Gbps (gigabits per second) network, real-time requires the IDS to support high throughput to handle the network traffic. Such throughput requires dedicated hardware components such as an FPGA (field programmable gate array) or an ASIC (application specific integrated circuit). Typically, the FPGA solution is preferred because it can be economically updated through reprogramming. Such real-time detection enables the analyst to respond to the attack immediately. Using the attack graph, they can determine the potential next steps of the attacker and take precautions against those steps. This may include disconnecting part of a network temporarily to prevent the attack from progressing.

Attack graphs map all possible attacks against a system and this produces information overload. This is a similar situation as the IDS analyst faces in identifying alerts generated by malicious traffic verses those generated by normal traffic. Applying a probability or likelihood to the attack graph enables the analyst to rank potential attack vectors in order of severity. Metrics such as the likelihood metric described in this chapter are potential options for this ranking. The likelihood metric described in this chapter is computationally efficient, consisting of multiplication and addition, and is computed based only on present and past results.

FUTURE RESEARCH DIRECTIONS

Efficient generation of attack graphs is a major issue. Attack graphs scale poorly, quickly becoming very large for realistic systems. Matching vulnerabilities to a system state accounts for the bulk of the processing time in the generation process (Louthan, 2011). Parallelism is one option to address this problem, and requires specialized hardware. FPGAs are one solution because they are economical and reprogrammable (simplifying the update and patch process). Development of a specialized processing unit to perform the matching search would greatly reduce the time required to generate attack graphs. This will enable research in the area of attack graph analysis. Ultimately, these analysis routines will need to be converted into specialized hardware to provide the needed response time and throughput.

There are many ways to carry out an attack and each method has a corresponding attack graph. This duplication could be as simple as the order in which a sequence of vulnerabilities are exploited. Here the underlying attack is the same in each case, just in a different sequence. Research into methods to condense attack graphs without losing valuable information and accuracy are required. Methods such as topological entities described by Hawrylak et al. (Hawrylak, Cain, & Mickle, 2007) are one potential solution that may be able to be ported to the attack graph domain.

IDSs are powerful tools in detecting attacks. Traditionally, these tools are not real-time due to the need to sift through large data logs. This problem is essentially a string-matching problem where the IDS searches for an attack signature. Attack signatures can be derived from attack graphs. Specialized hardware solutions provide significant speedup by parallelizing this process. Development of such solutions, most likely FPGA based, are required to reduce the identification time.

CONCLUSION

Attack graphs provide a means to model attacks against a system, typically a computer or network. These tools are widely used by security analysts to study vulnerabilities and attacks against computer systems. However, the modeling feature of the attack graph provides a standardized means to identify the potential next steps of the adversary. Armed with such information the defender can alter the system to counter the attack. In a typical attack, there will be numerous possible next steps in the attack and these must be reduced to a manageable set. Analysis techniques such as the likelihood metric described in this chapter are needed to identify the most likely next steps in an attack. Research into the development of methods to relate previous movement through the attack graph to determine the level of knowledge of the attacker is needed to better rank the potential next steps. The impact metric described in this chapter can be applied to determine the impact on the system of each step in the attack. This metric can be leveraged to quantify the impact in terms of intelligence the attacker gains about the system at each step in the attack dependency graph. This impact can be used as part of the analysis to identify the most probable set of adversary next steps.

ACKNOWLEDGMENT

This material is based on research sponsored by DARPA under agreement number FA8750-09-1-0208. The U.S. Government is authorized to reproduce and distribute reprints for Governmental purposes notwithstanding any copyright notation thereon. The views and conclusions contained herein are those of the authors and should not be interpreted as necessarily representing the official policies or endorsements, either expressed or implied, or DARPA or the U.S. Government.

REFERENCES

Ahmadinejad, S. H., Jalili, S., & Abadi, M. (2011). A hybrid model for correlating alerts of known and unknown attack scenarios and updating attack graphs. *Computer Networks*, 55(9), 2221–2240. doi:10.1016/j.comnet.2011.03.005

Ammann, P., Wijesekera, D., & Kaushik, S. (2002). Scalable, graph-based network vulnerability analysis. In *Proceedings of the 9th ACM conference on computer and communications security* (pp. 217-224). New York, NY: ACM.

Chivers, H., Clark, J., Nobles, P., Shaikh, S., & Chen, H. (2010). Knowing who to watch: Identifying attackers whose actions are hidden within false alarms and background noise. *Information Systems Frontiers*, 1–18.

Chu, M., Ingols, K., Lippmann, R., Webster, S., & Boyer, S. (2010). Visualizing attack graphs, reachability, and trust relationships with NAVIGATOR. In *Proceedings of the Seventh International Symposium on Visualization for Cyber Security (VizSec '10)* (pp. 22-33). New York, NY: ACM.

Clark, K., Tyree, J., Dawkins, J., & Hale, J. (2004). Quantitative and qualitative analytical techniques for network security assessment. *IEEE Workshop on Information Assurance and Security* (pp. 321-328). West Point, NY: IEEE.

Clark, K., Tyree, S., Dawkins, J., & Hale, J. (2007). Guiding threat analysis with threat source models. *Information Assurance and Security Workshop* (pp. 321-328). IEEE.

Dacier, M., Deswarte, Y., & Kaâniche, M. (1996). Quantitative assessment of operational security: Models and tools. *LAAS Research Report 96493*.

Farhangi, H. (2010). The path of the smart grid. *IEEE Power and Energy Magazine*, 8, 18–28. doi:10.1109/MPE.2009.934876

Frigault, M., Wang, L., Anoop, S., & Jajodia, S. (2008). Measuring network security using dynamic bayesian network. In *Proceedings of the 4th ACM workshop on Quality of protection (QoP '08)* (pp. 23-30). New York, NY: ACM.

Hartney, C. J. (2012, July). Security risk metrics: An attack graph-centric approach. (Unpublished Master's thesis). The University of Tulsa.

Hawrylak, P. J., Cain, J. T., & Mickle, M. H. (2007). Analytic modeling methodology for analysis of energy consumption for ISO 18000-7 RFID networks. *International Journal of Radio Frequency Identification Technology and Applications*, *1*(4), 371–400. doi:10.1504/IJRFITA.2007.017748

Hawrylak, P. J., Cain, J. T., & Mickle, M. H. (2009). Analysis methods for sensor networks. In Misra, S., Woungang, I., & Misra, S. C. (Eds.), *Guide to wireless sensor networks* (pp. 635–658). New York, NY: Springer. doi:10.1007/978-1-84882-218-4_25

Hawrylak, P. J., Louthan, G., Daily, J., Hale, J., & Papa, M. (2011). Attack graphs and scenario driven wireless computer network defense. In Onwubiko, C., & Owens, T. (Eds.), *Situational awareness in computer network defense: Principles, methods and applications* (pp. 284–301). Hershey, PA: IGI Global.

Hernan, S., Lambert, S., Ostwald, T., & Shostack, A. (2006, November). Uncover security design flaws using the STRIDE approach. *MSDN Magazine*.

Howard, M., & Leblanc, D. (2003). *Writing secure*. Redmond, WA: Microsoft Press.

Ingols, K., Chu, M., Lippmann, R., Webster, S., & Boyer, S. (2009). Modeling modern network at-tacks and countermeasures using attack graphs. *Computer Security Applications Conference* (pp. 117-126). IEEE.

Ingols, K., Lippmann, R., & Piwowarski, K. (2006). Practical attack graph generation for network defense. In *Proceedings of the 22nd Annual Computer Security Applications Conference* (pp. 121-130). Washington, DC: IEEE Computer Society.

Liao, Q., Striegel, A., & Chawla, N. (2010). Visualizing graph dynamics and similarity for enterprise network security and management. In *Proceedings of the Seventh International Symposium on Visualization for Cyber Security (VizSec '10)* (pp. 34-45). New York, NY: ACM.

Lippmann, R., & Ingols, K. (2005). *An annotated review of past papers on attack graphs*. Lexington, MA: Massachusetts Institute of Technology, Lincoln Laboratory.

Lippmann, R., Ingols, K., & Scott, C. (2006). Validating and restoring defense in depth using attack graphs. *Military Communications Conference (MILCOM)* (pp. 1-10). IEEE.

Louthan, G. (2011, November). *Hybrid attack graphs for modeling cyber physical systems security*. (Unpublished Master's thesis). The University of Tulsa.

Manadhata, P. K., & Wing, J. M. (2011). An attack surface metric. *IEEE Transactions on Software Engineering*, *37*(3), 371–386. doi:10.1109/TSE.2010.60

Mao, H.-D., & Zhang, W.-M. (2007). An approach for network security analysis using logic exploitation graph. In *7th IEEE International Conference on Computer and Information Technology* (pp. 761-766). IEEE.

Meier, J. D., Mackman, A., Dunner, M., Vasireddy, S., Escamilla, R., & Murukan, A. (2003, June). *Improving Web application security: Threats and countermeasures roadmap*. Redmond, WA: Microsoft Press.

National Vulnerability Database. (2012). Website. Retrieved Aug. 22, 2012, from http://nvd.nist.gov/

Ning, P., Cui, Y., & Reeves, D. S. (2002). Constructing attack scenarios through correlation of intrusion alerts. In V. Atluri (Ed.), *Proceedings of the 9th ACM conference on Computer and communications security (CCS '02)* (pp. 245-254). New York, NY: ACM.

Ning, P., Cui, Y., Reeves, D. S., & Xu, D. (2004). Techniques and tools for analyzing intrusion alerts. *ACM Transactions on Information and System Security*, 7(2), 274–318. doi:10.1145/996943.996947

Ning, P., & Xu, D. (2003). Learning attack strategies from intrusion alerts. In *Proceedings of the 10th ACM conference on Computer and communications security (CCS '03)* (pp. 200-209). New York, NY: ACM.

NIST. (2010, August). *Guidelines for Smart Grid Cyber Security* (NISTIR 7628). National Institute of Standards.

Noel, S., & Jajodia, S. (2004). Managing attack graph complexity through visual hierarchical aggregation. In *Proceedings of the 2004 ACM workshop on visualization and data mining for computer security (VizSEC/DMSEC '04)* (pp. 109-118). New York, NY: ACM.Noel, S., Robertson, E., & Jajodia, S. (2004). Correlating intrusion events and building attack scenarios through attack graph distances. *20th Annual Computer Security Applications Conference* (pp. 350-359). IEEE.

Noel, S., Jajodia, S., Wang, L., & Singhal, A. (2010). Measuring security risk of networks using attack graphs. *International Journal of Next-Generation Computing*, 1(1), 135–147.

Ortalo, R., Deswarte, Y., & Kaâniche, M. (1999). Experimenting with quantitative evaluation tools for monitoring operational security. *IEEE Transactions on Software Engineering*, 25(5), 633–650. doi:10.1109/32.815323

Pamula, J., Jajodia, S., Ammann, P., & Swarup, V. (2006). A weakest-adversary security metric for network configuration security analysis. In *Proceedings of the 2nd ACM workshop on Quality of protection (QoP '06)* (pp. 31-38). New York, NY: ACM.

Philips, C., & Swiler, L. (1998). A graph-based system for network-vulnerability analysis. In *Proceedings of the 1998 Workshop on New Security Paradigms* (pp. 71-79). New York, NY: ACM.

Ramsbrok, D., Berthier, R., & Cikuer, M. (2007). Profiling attacker behavior following SSH compromises. *Dependable Systems and Networks, 2007. DSN'07. 37th Annual IEEE/IFIP International Conference*, (pp. 199-124). IEEE.

Ritchey, R., & Ammann, P. (2000). Using model checking to analyze network vulnerabilities. In *Proceedings of the 2000 IEEE Symposium on Research on Security and Privacy* (pp. 156-165). Washington, DC: IEEE Computer Society.

Saha, D. (2008). Extending logical attack graphs for efficient vulnerability analysis. In *Proceedings of the 15th ACM conference on Computer and communications security (CCS '08)* (pp. 63-74). New York, NY: ACM.

Schneier, B. (1999, December). Attack trees: Modeling security threats. *Dr. Dobb's Journal*, 21-29.

Sheyner, O., Haines, J., Jha, S., Lippmann, R., & Wing, J. M. (2002). Automated generation and analysis of attack graphs. In *Proceedings of the 2002 IEEE Symposium on Security and Privacy* (pp. 273-284). IEEE.

Tedesco, G., & Aickelin, U. (2008). Real-time alert correlation with type graphs. *Lecture Notes in Computer Science*, 5352, 173–187. doi:10.1007/978-3-540-89862-7_16

Templeton, S., & Levitt, K. (2001). A requires/provides model for computer attacks. In *Proceedings of the 2000 workshop on new security paradigms* (pp. 31-38). New York, NY: ACM.

Tidwell, T., Larson, R., Fitch, K., & Hale, J. (2001). Modeling Internet attacks. In *Proceedings of the 2001 IEEE workshop on information assurance and security* (Vol. 59). IEEE.

Valdes, A., & Skinner, K. (2001). Probablistic alert correlation. In *Recent advances in intrusion detection, lecture notes in computer science* (pp. 54–68). Heidelberg, Germany: Springer-Valdeg. doi:10.1007/3-540-45474-8_4

Varga, A. (2001). The OMNeT++ discrete event simulation system. In *Proceedings of the European Simulation Multiconference*. IEEE.

Varga, A., & Hornig, R. (2008). An overview of the OMNeT++ simulation environment. In *Proceedings of the 1st International Conference on Simulation Tools and Techniques for Communications, Networks and Systems* (pp. 1-10). ACM.

Wang, L., Islam, T., Long, T., Singhal, A., & Jajodia, S. (2008). An attack graph-based probabilistic security metric. In *Data and Applications Security XXII* (pp. 283–296). New York, NY: Springer. doi:10.1007/978-3-540-70567-3_22

Wang, L., Liu, A., & Jajodia, S. (2006). Using attack graphs for correlating, hypothesizing, and predicting intrusion alerts. *Computer Communications*, *29*(15), 2917–2933. doi:10.1016/j.comcom.2006.04.001

Wang, L., Noel, S., & Jajodia, S. (2006). Minimum-cost network hardening using attack graphs. *Computer Communications*, *29*(18), 3812–3824. doi:10.1016/j.comcom.2006.06.018

Wang, L., Singhal, A., & Jajodia, S. (2007). Toward measuring network security using attack graphs. In *Proceedings of the 2007 ACM workshop on Quality of protection (QoP '07)* (pp. 49-54). New York, NY: ACM.

Wang, L., Yao, C., Singhal, A., & Jajodia, S. (2008). Implementing interactive analysis of attack graphs using relational databases. *Journal of Computer Security*, *16*(4), 419–437.

Zhou, J., Heckman, M., Reynolds, B., Carlson, A., & Bishop, M. (2007). Modeling network intrusion detection alerts for correlation. *ACM Transactions on Information and System Security*, *10*(1). doi:10.1145/1210263.1210267

KEY TERMS AND DEFINITIONS

Attack Dependency Graph: A graph structure that documents security vulnerabilities based on exploits, pre-conditions, and post-conditions. These graphs are limited to the pre-conditions that exist for the system is question.

Attack Graph: A graphical representation of the various steps an adversary can take to achieve their goal of compromising a system.

Multi-Stage Attacks: An attack where the primary goal is achieved using a series of smaller attacks. Often these smaller attacks are not noticed by the defender. Attack graphs provide a means to identify which of the smaller attacks is of particular concern.

National Vulnerability Database (NVD): An online resource that documents and ranks security vulnerabilities.

Nmap: Nmap stands for Network Mapper and is used (often by IT system administrators) to identify machines on their network for security and inventory purposes.

OMNeT++: A discrete event simulation package that specializes in modeling computer networks.

Pcap: Pcap stands for Packet Capture and is a recording of traffic (packets) on a computer network.

Chapter 9
A Scalable Approach to Network Traffic Classification for Computer Network Defense using Parallel Neural Network Classifier Architectures

Bereket M. Hambebo
Florida Institute of Technology, USA

Marco Carvalho
Florida Institute of Technology, USA

Fredric M. Ham
Florida Institute of Technology, USA

ABSTRACT

The ability to recognize network traffics plays an important role in securing modern computer network infrastructures. In this chapter, we propose a machine learning approach that is based on statistical features of communication flow between two end-points. The statistical features are then used to develop and test a Parallel Neural Network Classifier Architecture (PNNCA), which is trained to recognize specific HTTP session patterns in a controlled environment, and then used to classify general traffic. The classifier's performance and scalability measures have been compared with other neural network based approaches. The classifier's correct classification rate (CCR) is calculated to be 96%.

INTRODUCTION

Online traffic classification is an important capability for modern computer network defense infrastructures. The ability to recognize, at runtime, specific network traffic as belonging to a particular

application or activity allows automated defense systems and analysis to better access risk and better contextualize other observed events, or alarms in the system. In the majority of cases, automated monitoring systems for computer defense rely on well-defined traffic features and signatures to track and identify specific communications and application activity. Such signatures may include,

DOI: 10.4018/978-1-4666-3942-3.ch009

for example, the source or destination network ports in use, or specific sequences of network commands and keywords.

While conventional methods for traffic classification in cyber defense are still useful as a first indicator, more advanced attacks are likely to disguise their activities, avoiding easily identifiable features that can be detected by an automated system. An advanced adversary may rely, for example, on end-point redirection through non-standard port numbers, or on encrypted tunnels to an internal machine in the victim's network to hide well-known payload signatures. The simple techniques may greatly impair the capacity of standard monitoring tools to properly classify the traffic.

The problem is especially relevant in the context of critical infrastructure protection systems, where port numbers, protocols and basic traffic signatures are very specific and well defined. In such contexts, there is a natural tendency to look for these known features and fail to recognize that they can be, sometimes easily, manipulated by a sophisticated adversary.

In order to mitigate this problem, an alternative approach to traffic classification may take into account second order statistical properties of the communications. For example, statistical properties of communication flow between end-points may be a good indicator or the context, or specific applications involved. In most cases, even if using non-standard port numbers or encrypted payloads, there are required steps and timings in the protocol that have to be respected to ensure a successful transaction. In general, this is especially true for the critical infrastructure protection setting, where protocol timing is often critical in networked control systems. If such statistical patterns of communications can be efficiently learned and used for online classification, they could provide a powerful support capability for advance network defense systems and security analysis.

In the context of the work, traffic classification consists of the ability to identify a type, or a class of network traffic between applications, based only on its network properties, that is, without any pre-conceived knowledge about the source and destination applications, or their host operating systems. The underlying assumption is that network traffic can be observed at any point between source and destination and an assessment about its class can be made based on its properties.

The specific classes of interest are application dependent and will drive the required set of features, and often the proposed classification strategy. For example, previous research efforts have sought to classify the end-point applications (e.g. email, web-browsers, etc.) based on their network traffic, while others, have focused on the identification of specific protocols and its variants, or on the detection of traffic anomalies for intrusion detection and network defense.

To illustrate our approach, we focus on the specific problem of classifying TCP/IP session patterns between source and destination. The goal is to create a tool that recognizes specific HTTP session patterns so they can be compared with known, or expected profiles for given services or applications. The motivation for this work comes from a cyber security application for supervisory control and data acquisition (SCADA) systems.

One intuitive approach to enable access to SCADA systems is through the deployment of protected web services and web interfaces (Zecevic, 1998). This capability enables and greatly facilitates remote access to the systems, but it also tends to create an opportunity for cyber attacks and compromises.

We propose that a general traffic classifier that can be trained to recognize access to these specific web servers and services, independent of the source, destination and network delays will help protect these networks by identifying unexpected and unauthorized sessions that could be traced to compromised proxies, or fake interface sites used for capturing passwords or other use information.

For that purpose, our approach is focused on the classification of specific web-sessions, using a pretraining parallel neural network classifier (Ham & Kostanic, 2001). Our classification features are based on statistical metrics of the traffic, rather than native features of the network connection and flows such as IP addresses or port numbers, etc. The goal is to build a classifier that can be trained to recognize a session in a controlled environment, which, then, can be used to classify general traffic. To illustrate our approach, our preliminary results were based on the session analysis of well-known websites, chosen as surrogates to specific SCADA interface systems and web-services.

The proposed approach was previously introduced by the authors in 2011 (Mathewos et al., 2011). In this article, we focus on the scalability and performance aspects of the approach; comparing the proposed PNNCA strategy with alternative NN based approaches, and other classifiers. Our results and technical discussion illustrate that PNNCAs are not only more scalable, but also more effective for practical applications, as they allow the independent training of specialized cells that can be then shared and combined to constructed parallel classifiers.

RELATED WORK

Online traffic classification is certainly not new. Some of the earlier efforts refer back to (Paxson, 1994) who proposed an empirically derived model for TCP/IP Internet traffic.

Previous researchers have developed and discussed different techniques for the classification of internet traffic. We can broadly group these techniques into two: exact matching and statistics based approach. Both techniques have been used to classify traffics according to their application.

Exact Matching

An exact matching technique classifies traffic based on certain fixed parameters which should match the requirements set by a classifier. These include but not limited to, port numbers, protocols, etc. Two methods that demonstrate the use of exact matching are port based classification methods and payload based classification methods.

Port-Based Classification Methods

Classification of traffic and their applications based on port numbers is one of the most common techniques that has used in the past (Karagiannis et al., 2005). This method uses only that part of the packet header which contains the port number. A packet header analysis is applied to associate a particular port number with a given application (Moore et al., 2001; Logg & Cottrel, 2003); for example, port number 80 is for hypertext transfer protocol (HTTP), and port number 21 for file transfer protocol (FTP). Port number based classification is prone to incorrect classifications due to the fact that specific ports can carry traffics of different applications, i.e., the same port may be shared by different applications (Auld & Moore, 2007). For example, port number 80, corresponding to the hypertext transfer protocol (HTTP), transports web traffics as well as virtual local area network (VLAN) traffics through HTTP.

There are a number of traffic applications that make use of other protocols to mask their identity in order to pass through firewalls without being recognized. For example, different applications channeled through HTTP include p2p, chat and VLAN as stated above. This tunneling of many applications in one protocol makes it even more difficult to rely on port based classifications. In addition, since many applications use dynamic port allocation methods to bypass a firewall and secured networks, the port based classification is inadequate (Auld & Moore, 2007; Roughan et al., 2004; Karagiannis et al., 2005).

Payload-Based Classification Methods

Payload based IP classification is another widely used method for examining network traffic. This technique avoids the reliance on port numbers. Sen et al. (2004) presented a payload based classification of P2p traffic by studying the signatures of the traffic at the application level.

Combining the aforementioned techniques of classifications, Moore and Papagiannaki (2005) developed an improved classifier for traffic applications. First, the algorithm developed checks whether a well-known port is used to relay the flow. It will check to determine whether or not the packet contains a known signature if there is no well known port number. If a signature is not found, then the packet is examined to see if it contains any well-known protocols.

The payload based method avoids the dependence of classification by port numbers only. However, it comes with a shortcoming, complexity. When dealing with large number of traffic flows, the rigorous examinations will take more time and add complexity. In addition, signature inspection may not work with encrypted traffics as well as propriety protocols. By examining payloads, payload based classification methods also add to privacy concerns.

Statistics-Based Approach

The other technique widely used for traffic classifications is traffic characteristics based or statistics based classifications. Recent studies have used statistical properties of network traffics instead of port numbers to avoid or overcome the inefficiency of port-based classifications (Moore & Zuev, 2005a; Crotti et al., 2004). Here, statistical features of packet trace data are used for classification purpose.

(Auld & Moore, 2007) used predefined statistical features of traffic flows to classify Internet traffic according to the network application they use. The applications of traffics are listed in the Table 1.

A set of discriminators is chosen to classify flows, and the set of the discriminators used include statistical features obtained from

Table 1. Network traffic applications

Traffic Application Classes
WWW (e.g. www)
DATABASE (e.g. postgres, ingres)
MAIL (e.g. smtp, imap)
SERVICES (e.g. dns, ntp)
BULK (e.g. ftp)
P2P (e.g. bittorrent, gnutella)
MULTIMEDIA (e.g. media player)
ATTACK (e.g. worms, viruses)

packet size information of a flow, inter-arrival times between packets, and duration of a flow. Auld and Moore proposed a machine learning approach for the classification of traffics according to their application types. They were able to achieve classification without further pre-known source and destination IP addresses or port numbers by using Bayesian neural networks (Auld & Moore, 2007). This technique offers classification without the use of the actual content of the packets. In other words, this method doesn't require payload information for classification; instead, it uses the commonly available information obtained from the packet headers themselves.

Moore and Zuev (2005a) proposed the use of Bayesian Analysis techniques to categorize Internet traffic flows. The method proposed in (Moore & Zuev, 2005a) is used to classify traffics according to their application. Karagiannis et al. (2005) proposed the classification of traffic based on host behavior, and Crotti et al. (2007) proposed the classification of traffic based solely on statistical properties of the flows. Crotti et al. (2007) have shown that information obtained from packet inter-arrival time, size of the IP packets and their order can exclusively be used to categorize traffics. These properties or features are independent of a particular network configuration; especially IP addresses which, even on the same site, can change over time.

CLASSIFICATION

In our work, we propose a Neural Network based classifier. The hypothesis is that for an appropriate set of features, the classifier can be trained in a controlled environment and can be used on general deployments with reasonable accuracy.

Proposed Approach

The proposed classifier uses a Parallel Neural Network Classifier Architecture (PNNCA). A PNNCA is made up of blocks of classifiers that work parallel (Ham et al., 2008). This approach was previously introduced by the authors in 2011 (Mathewos et al., 2011). In this work, we focus on the scalability and performance aspects of the approach, comparing the proposed PNNCA strategy with alternative machine learning based approaches namely support vector machines (SVMs) and single Radial Basis Function Neural Networks. Our results presented in section 5 and technical discussion illustrate that PNNCAs are not only more scalable and have higher performance, but also more effective for practical applications, as they allow the independent training of specialized cells that can be then shared and combined to constructed parallel classifiers.

PNNCA consists of parallel blocks of neural classifiers working together. Each block consists of Radial Basis Function Neural Networks (RBF NNs) for classification. The Number of blocks in the PNNCA corresponds to the number of classes of the classifier. For example, if a classifier is developed to classify inputs as only x or y, then the PNNCA for that classifier would consist of two blocks.

Each block of the PNNCA is trained to independently classify whether the element under test as part of its own category or not – effectively determining if the element "belongs" to it or not. Also, the weights of each block are set during the training phase of the network. The PNNCA makes use of a negative reinforcement learning technique. While it learns to determine if a session of internet traffic belongs to a particular class, it also learns to reject sets that do not belong to that particular class. Figure 1 shows a typical parallel neural network classifier architecture (PNNCA).

There are, however, several other methods that can be used for online classification. For our purposes, PNNCA provides a higher level of accuracy with no significant increase in performance costs (regarding training samples and time) in comparison with other methods. To illustrate the relative performance of PNNCA we will introduce

Figure 1. A Parallel Neural Network Classifier Architecture (PNNCA)

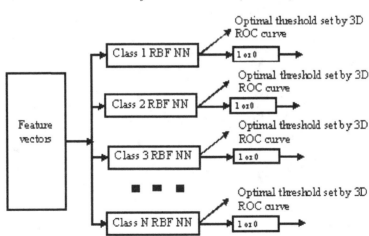

two alternative classification methods that will be used in this work, for a comparison of accuracy and performance.

The alternative methods suggested and used in this work only to provide a comparison between the accuracy and performance of the proposed PNNCA for these tasks, for different sizes of training sets.

Radial Basis Function (RBF) Neural Networks

Radial Basis Function neural networks are widely used for prediction and classification purposes. RBF neural networks use a curve-fitting approach to neural network design problems (Ham & Kostanic, 2001). These neural networks are capable of performing a nonlinear mapping between input and output vector spaces and are known for their fast learning algorithm and simple network architecture. Figure 2 shows the architecture of a Radial Basis Function neural network.

As can be seen from the above figure, the RBF neural network consists of the following three layers: the input layer, the hidden layer, and the output layer. Each input is passed to the hidden layer by the input nodes. After the hidden layer

receives the input, it performs a nonlinear transformation of the input. The Euclidean distance between the center and the input is calculated for each neuron. The number of neurons is determined by the training process. The output is then calculated as

$$y_i = \sum_{k=1}^{N} w_{ik} \phi_k \left(x, c_k \right) \, , \quad i = 1, 2, \ldots, m \qquad (1)$$

where, x is an input vector, N is the number of neurons in the hidden layer, w_{ik} are weights in the output layer, c_k are the RBF centers in the output vector and m represents the number of output units. ϕ_k is a Gaussian radial basis function given as

$$\phi = e^{\left(-\frac{(x-c)^2}{\sigma^2} \right)} \qquad (2)$$

The spread parameter σ, which controls the width of the RBF, is a very important parameter and directly influences the accuracy of the classifier.

Here, the purpose of the classifier is to train a neural network that classifies sessions according to their statistical properties, so that when it is

Figure 2. Radial Basis Function (RBF) Neural Network

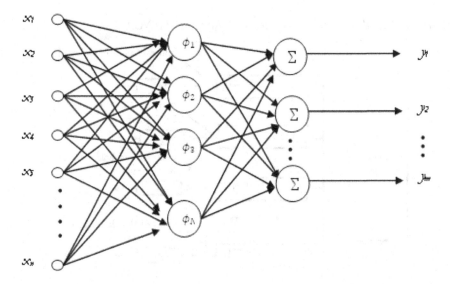

introduced with a new session, it should be able to group it correctly with a reasonable accuracy (i.e. even if the source or destination IP address is masked or a proxy server is used).

Support Vector Machines (SVM)

Another method of classification worth studying is the Support Vector Machine (SVM). SVM classifiers are mainly used for two-class classifications. The basic idea behind SVMs is that input vectors are non-linearly mapped into a higher dimensional feature space (Cortes & Vapnik, 1995). This method's performance is based on the notion that decision boundaries are defined by decision planes.

Consider a data set $\left\{\left(x_i, y_i\right)\right\}_i^M$, where x_i is the ith input vector and y_i is the target output associated with x_i. Also, assume y_i is a label that can be represented by +1 or - 1. For linear classification, in order for a hyperplane

$$w^T \mathbf{x} + b = 0 \qquad (3)$$

to divide the two classes, it must satisfy the following conditions:

$$
\begin{aligned}
w^T x_i + b \geq 0 \quad &for\, y_i = +1 \\
w^T x_i + b < 0 \quad &for\, y_i = -1
\end{aligned}
\qquad (4)
$$

where w is an adjustable weight vector that maps the training data to the output, and is a bias. An illustration of the use of hyperplane for linear classification is shown in Figure 3.

As can be seen from the above figure, an optimal plane separates the two classes, which are represented by circles and squares. The boundary between the two separated regions is called the decision boundary of the classifier. The points that are lying on the two planes, $w^T x_i + b \geq 1$

Figure 3. A two-dimensional example of SVM

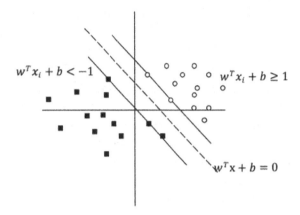

and $w^T x_i + < 1$, are called support vectors. The main aim of support vector machines is to find an optimal hyperplane that maximizes the decision boundary.

For linearly separable input patterns, linear SVM classification could be appropriate. However, if the input patterns are not linearly separable, it is very difficult to form a hyperplane that separates the patterns linearly. Therefore, it is important to map the patterns to a higher dimensional space where the data can be separated linearly (Cover, 1965). The separating hyperplane after the mapping becomes a linear function in the transformed space but nonlinear in the original space.

Consider a mapping function $\Phi(\cdot)$ that transforms the input vector $\mathbf{x}$ to a higher dimensional vector space. The hyperplane is then given by

$$w \cdot \Phi\left(\mathbf{x}\right) + b = 0 \qquad (5)$$

A kernel function $k(\mathbf{x}, \mathbf{x_i})$ allows us to construct a hyperplane in the new multidimensional space and is given by

$$k\left(\mathbf{x}, \mathbf{x_i}\right) = \Phi\left(\mathbf{x}\right)^T \Phi\left(\mathbf{x_i}\right) \qquad (6)$$

The kernel function can be a polynomial function, radial-basis function network, or a two-layer perceptrons.

Since SVM classifiers are used for two class classifications, and the classes of web traffic sessions under consideration in this study are six classes, a parallel SVM classifier of six modules has been developed and compared to the Parallel RBF NN. Each module, similar to the case of the Parallel RBF NN, consists of a two class SVM classifiers and outputs binary results. The performance comparison between the PNNCA and the SVM for traffic classification is presented in section 5

Thresholding and Receiver Operating Characteristic Curves

The classifier developed is a binary classifier (i.e. its final output is a '0' or a '1'). Each block of the parallel neural network has a binary output. If the output of a block is '0', then it means that the input does not belong to that class. Similarly, if the output of a block is '1', then the input belongs to that class.

The optimal thresholds at each blocks of the classifier are determined using the Receiver Operating Characteristic (ROC) curve. A 2D ROC curve is a plot representing the true positive (TP) rate, or sensitivity, versus the false positive (FP) rate, or specificity (Fawcett, 2006). A true positive occurs when the outcome is correctly classified as positive, while a false positive occurs when the outcome is incorrectly classified as a positive when it is, in fact, negative. Figure 4 shows an example of a 2D ROC curve.

The optimum threshold is the minimum Euclidean distance between the point (0,1) and the curve. This minimum distance minimizes false positives while maximizing true positives.

The 3D ROC curve, an extension of the 2D ROC curve, adds an additional dimension, corresponding to misclassifications. In this work a 3D ROC curve (Ham et al., 2007) is used for setting the threshold. The third dimension accounts for misclassifications that may occur between blocks of the parallel neural classifier. Each block of the parallel neural network classifier has a threshold set by the ROC curve. So here, the ideal point on the ROC curve would be

Figure 4. An example of a 2D ROC curve

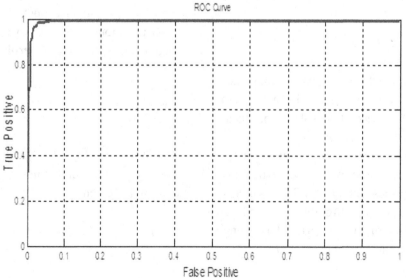

(0, 1, 0) corresponding to FP, TP, and Misclassification. A typical 3D ROC curve is shown in Figure 5.

Performance Evaluation

The performance of a classifier is measured from the results obtained by testing the classifier using a set of test data. A Confusion matrix provides the important information needed to evaluate the performance of a classifier. It contains information about actual and predicted classifications done by a classifier. Table 2 shows the confusion matrix for a two class classifier:

The elements in the matrix are defined as:

- w: Number of correct predictions that an event is positive
- x: Number of correct predictions that an event is negative
- y: Number of incorrect predictions that an instance is negative
- z: Number of correct predictions that an instance is positive

True positive, (i.e., proportion of positive cases that are correctly classified) is calculated as

Table 2. Confusion matrix for a two class classifier

		Predicted	
		Positive	Negative
Actual	Positive	w	x
	Negative	y	z

$$TP = \frac{w}{w+x} \tag{7}$$

False Positive, (i.e., proportion of negative cases that are incorrectly classified) is calculated as

$$FP = \frac{y}{y+z} \tag{8}$$

The two performance measures used in this study are the accuracy (ACC) and the Correct Classification Rate (CCR) (Ham et al., 2008). They are given by the following equations:

$$ACC = \frac{No.\,of\,Correct\,Classifications}{No.\,of\,Total\,Predictions} \tag{9}$$

$$CCR = \frac{No.\,of\,Correct\,Classifications - No.\,of\,Multiple\,classifications}{No.\,of\,Total\,Predictions} \tag{10}$$

Figure 5. An example of a 3D ROC Curve

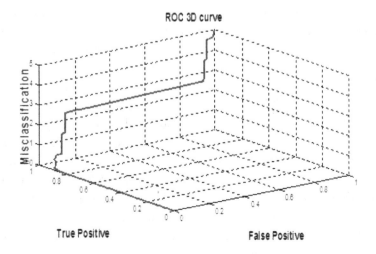

EXPERIMENTAL EVALUATION

Data Set

We have used data collected at the Information Processing laboratory, at the Florida Institute of Technology. The data used for training the classifier contains only forward packet flows to websites. To ensure the robustness of the classifier, the data was captured multiple times in one week at different times in a day. As discussed earlier, specific web-sessions can be classified using a trained parallel neural network classifier. For this purpose, well-known websites were chosen in this research to demonstrate the proposed approach. The websites under observation are listed in the following table:

Packets captured using capturing tools consist of more than 20 fields of which we use only 5 of them; time, source IP address, destination IP address, protocol and frame length or packet size. All flows from same destination and source IP addresses are grouped together. Flows with protocols different from TCP and HTTP were filtered out as we are only concerned with web traffic. After arranging the data according to their source and destination IPs, statistical features can be computed from the corresponding time and packets size information of the packets.

Our first goal was to identify patterns that can be seen in flows of web traffic data. (Crovella & Bestavros, 1997) have shown that self-similarity properties exist in Web traffics. Self-similarity

Table 3. Websites used

Web service	Designated as:
www.google.com	Class 1
www.yahoo.com	Class 2
www.fit.edu	Class 3
www.cnn.com	Class 4
www.bbc.com	Class 5
www.bing.com	Class 6

is the property of Web traffic patterns to remain unchanged regardless of time. Since we are looking at temporal patterns, our search for a pattern was focused on observing how a session behaves through time. Packet sizes of different sessions for a specific website exhibit patterns.

Feature Selection

Feature selection plays an important role in any classification problem. Before classification it is important that we know the characteristics of flows. The classification is carried out based on a feature vector. The attributes contain important information regarding the data they represent.

For web traffic classification, features are computed for each bursty packet (Park et al., 2006). When a user's request to a website is acknowledged, a burst of packets will be sent to the website's server. Bursty packets are consecutive packets grouped together representing a session.

Burst Characteristics

The inter-arrival time information can be used to determine burst characteristics (Park et al., 2006). Packets are grouped together as bursts if their inter arrival time is greater than a certain predefined threshold. The predefined threshold is set in such a way that it separates one set of flow or a session from the next. For example, if a user accesses a webpage three times, then the threshold should be able to separate the packets in three bursts.

Each session is described by a set of features. Previous studies have used a number of features to describe network traffic and classify them (Sun et al., 2010; Zander et al., 2005). The features are used to discriminate individual web traffic flows. Moore and Zuev (2005b) described sets of discriminators for use in traffic classification. They use 248 features to define a traffic sample. Other researchers have used a smaller number of features because of the redundancy in the 248 available features. Sun et al. (2010) used 22 statistical features to represent traffic; we have reduced that number to 17, shown in Table 4, because only forward traffic flows are considered in this study. 8 statistical features related to inter-arrival time and 8 related to packet size information were computer as traffic features. The number of forward packets is the other feature. Inter-arrival time is the time difference between consecutive packet flows in a complete HTTP request, and it is represented by the expression:

$$time_{int-arr} = time_i - time_{i-1} \ i= 1,2,3, \dots n, \qquad (11)$$

where n is the number of flows in a session

Figure 6. shows the set of normalized feature vectors for one session of the class www.google.com. Feature vectors are fed to a neural network for classification.

Table 4. Features used

Category	Features
inter-arrival time information	mean, variance, median, 1st and 3rd quartile, inter-quartile range, maximum, minimum
packet size information	mean, variance, median, 1st and 3rd quartile, inter-quartile range, maximum, minimum
packet count information	total no. of forward packet flows

After the feature vectors are extracted from the raw data, the data is separated into two parts: a training data set and a testing set. The training set is the data used during the learning process of the classifier under development, while the testing set is the data that is used to assess the efficiency of the trained classifier. Classes and the number of sessions associated with their training and testing data are shown in Table 5. Out of a total number of 7309 numbers of sessions, 4874 were used for training and 2435 were used for testing purposes.

RESULTS AND DISCUSSIONS

The classifier used is A Parallel RBF Neural Network. As discussed in chapter 3 the Parallel Neural Network Classifier Architecture (PNNCA) is trained to categorize traffic flows belonging to one of the six classes. Each of these six classes corresponds to a known website chosen for evaluating the developed classifier under development. Each block, corresponding to one of the six classes, has its own classifier. A negative reinforcement approach is applied here. That is, when training one block by introducing samples from a specific class to say that it belongs to that class, sessions from

Figure 6. Normalized feature vectors for Class 1

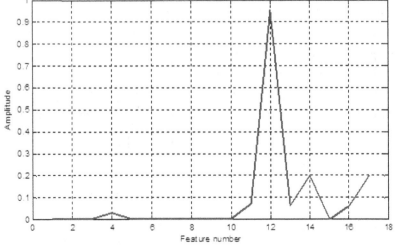

Table 5. Training and testing data used

	# of Training sessions	# of Testing sessions
Class 1	892	346
Class 2	696	445
Class 3	660	329
Class 4	848	423
Class 5	903	450
Class 6	875	436

the rest of the five classes are also introduced to tell the block that they do not belong to the class.

Results

Once trained, each module of the classifier should be able to classify sessions of traffic belonging to the websites associated with that website. For example, if a session belonging to Class 1 is passed through module 1, then the module would categorize the session, with high degree accuracy, as traffic from 'www.google.com' (Class 1).

The output of each block of the classifier is binary; '1' if the signal belongs to the class of that block or a '0' if it doesn't. A 3D receiver operating characteristics (3D ROC) curve has been used to set the minimum threshold values for each class. In a previous paper by the authors of this chapter (Mathewos et al., 2011), 2D curves were used. However, the use of 3D ROC curves in this work has significantly improved the overall performance of the classifier.

Table 6 gives the final threshold values obtained for each class from the 3D ROC curves.

The classification results obtained upon testing the 6-class classifier are presented in the following confusion matrix (Kohavi & Provost, 1998), Table 7. The diagonal elements in the matrix represent correct classifications, while the non-diagonal elements represent misclassifications.

As shown in Table 7, Classes 1 to 6 represent sessions from the following website: www.google.com, www.yahoo.com, www.fit.edu, www.cnn.com, www.bbc.com, and www.bing.com, respectively.

The Correct Classification Rate (CCR) and the Accuracy (ACC) measure the efficiency of the web-sessions classifier which was developed in this research. The CCR is more conservative

Table 6. threshold values for the classifier

Class	1	2	3	4	5	6
Threshold	0.2623	0.3210	0.3926	0.4700	0.4733	0.4570

Table 7. confusion matrix for the classifier developed

		Predicted						
		Class 1	Class 2	Class 3	Class 4	Class 5	Class 6	Unclassified
Actual	Class 1	437	0	0	0	0	4	5
	Class 2	0	335	1	0	0	1	15
	Class 3	0	2	321	0	0	10	5
	Class 4	13	0	0	411	1	0	0
	Class 5	2	0	0	2	447	0	0
	Class 6	0	4	13	0	0	425	9

because it takes into account the misclassifications between the blocks of the parallel neural networks in addition to the correct classifications.

The CCR and ACC were calculated as discussed in section 3. For training data with a total of 4874 sessions, as shown in Table 8, a CCR of approximately 96% and ACC of 97.5% were achieved in this project. Statistics of the performance measure is described by the confidence interval (CI), and is given as

$$CI = \left(\hat{p} - z_{a/2} \sqrt{\frac{\hat{p}(1-\hat{p})}{m}}, \; \hat{p} + z_{a/2} \sqrt{\frac{\hat{p}(1-\hat{p})}{m}} \right)$$

$$(12)$$

where $\hat{p}$ is the performance measure, m is the number of sessions used for testing and z is the standard normal distribution critical value. A 95% CI is used, that means it is expected that 95% if the intervals include the performance measure, or CCR.

The table below shows the total PNNCA classifier CCR, and ACC with a 95% confidence interval.

Comparison with Other Algorithms

To further investigate and evaluate the performance of the Parallel RBF NN classifier, its performance is with two different classifiers. They are the Single RBF NN, and Parallel Support Vector Machines (PSVM). With similar experimental settings, simulations were carried out for each of the three classifiers stated. Figure 7 shows per-

Table 8. PNNCA classification results

	Performance in %	95% CI(min,max)
CCR	96.67	(0.9596, 0.9739)
ACC	97.57	(0.9697, 0.9819)

formance plots for the three types of classifiers used. It shows the performance as measured by CCR (%) of the Parallel RBF NN classifier with the PSVM, and single RBFNN.

The following table summarizes for each type of classifier, the performance (CCR) with a fixed testing sample and the training time it takes with varying number of training sessions.

Further Evaluation

Once trained, the PNNCA should be able to classify sessions to the same website (in this example), even if initiated by clients located in different networks. For that purpose, the trained PNNCA was used to classify traffic collected from several different networks. The data set collected contains other web traffics in addition to the 6 trained traffics is also used. It is different from the data set used previously because it also contains other traffics. The proposed classifier is expected to perform well on traffic generated from other networks, with different conditions. The goal was to evaluate the system against datasets that would be under the influence of different network conditions, including bandwidth, utilization and capacity. In all cases, the CCR was above 85%. Table 10 shows an example of a confusion matrix from one of the remote networks, just to illustrate the classification error in each case.

CONCLUSION AND FUTURE WORK

In this work a machine learning technique to classify internet traffics has been implemented. A supervised learning algorithm, Parallel Neural Network Classifier Architecture, was developed and employed to classify web-based HTTP sessions. In order to provide an evaluation of the technique, client HTTP sessions from a set

Figure 7. Performance comparison of RBF PNNCA, PSVM, and Single RBF NN

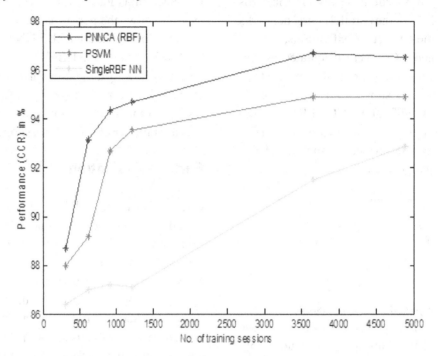

Table 9. Results comparison

#of Training sessions	PNNCA (RBF)		Single RBFNN		PSVM	
	CCR(%)	Time(sec)	CCR(%)	Time(sec)	CCR(%)	Time(sec)
307	88.70	0.69	86.42	0.02	88	0.31
611	93.14	1.18	87	0.19	89.16	0.72
916	94.33	2.26	87.2	0.8	92.7	2.1
1219	94.7	3.405	87.1	2.3	93.53	3.3
3655	96.67	26.7	91.5	18.7	94.9	27.2
4874	96.5	46.65	92.86	112.3	94.9	37.5

Table 10. Confusion Matrix for a test dataset collected from a different network

		Predicted						
		Class 1	Class 2	Class 3	Class 4	Class 5	Class 6	Unclassified
Actual	Class 1	724	2	32	0	0	0	29
	Class 2	0	801	1	0	0	53	17
	Class 3	0	0	497	18	0	1	22
	Class 4	0	1	5	907	7	15	31
	Class 5	2	2	0	0	452	4	22
	Class 6	0	0	2	0	32	493	25
	Others	3	1	1	5	1	2	218

of well-known websites have been used. This was motivated by the possibility of identifying SCADA-related traffic (to web-proxies and web-interfaces).

The method is based on statistics of traffics obtained from packet header information. It has been shown in previous studies that statistical features represent traffics distinctively and from the pool of features presented in [14], only packet size and interarrival time related features were used to train and test the neural network developed in this study.

A high CCR and accuracy has been achieved without access to packet loads or any complex network traffic processing. The implementation of the RBF Parallel Neural Network Classifier Architecture (PNNCA) has shown that it effectively identifies sessions with up to 96% correct classification rate.

This study also evaluated two more classification algorithms, namely support vector machines and single radial basis function neural networks. The results of the comparison showed that the PNNCA is an effective machine learning technique for web traffic classifications.

A supervised learning algorithm was used for the purpose of classifying web-traffics in this work, which shows statistical features of traffics can be applied for machine learning based internet classifications. This work can be extended to unsupervised learning methods so that when traffics are introduced with an unknown set of HTTP sessions it would form and categorize a group for the new traffics. A further assessment of the developed algorithm can also be done with the introduction of non-static websites.

REFERENCES

Auld, T., & Moore, A. W. (2007). Bayesian neural networks for Internet traffic classification. *IEEE Transactions on Neural Networks, 18*(1), 223–239. doi:10.1109/TNN.2006.883010

Cortes, C., & Vapnik, V. (1995). Support vector networks. *Machine Learning, 20*, 273–297. doi:10.1007/BF00994018

Cover, T. M. (1965). Geometrical and statistical properties of systems of linear inequalities with applications in pattern recognition. *IEEE Transactions on Electronic Computers, 14*, 326–334. doi:10.1109/PGEC.1965.264137

Crotti, M., Dusi, M., Gringoli, F., & Salgarelli, L. (2007). Traffic classification through simple statistical fingerprinting. *ACM IGCOMM CCR, 37*(1).

Crovella, M. E., & Bestavros, A. (1997). Self-similarity in World Wide Web traffic: Evidence and possible causes. *IEEE/ACM Transactions on Networking, 5*, 835–846. doi:10.1109/90.650143

Fawcett, T. (2006). An introduction to ROC analysis. *Pattern Recognition Letters, 27*, 861–874. doi:10.1016/j.patrec.2005.10.010

Ham, F. M., & Acharyya, R. (2007). A universal neural network-based infrasound event classifier. In Chen, C. H. (Ed.), *Signal and image processing for remote sensing*. New York, NY: Taylor & Francis Group. doi:10.1201/9781420066678.ch3

Ham, F. M., & Kostanic, I. (2001). *Principles of neurocomputing for science and engineering*. New York, NY: McGraw-Hill Higher Education.

Ham, F. M., Rekab, K., Acharyya, R., & Lee, Y. C. (2008). Infrasound signal classification using parallel RBF neural networks. *International Journal of Signal and Imaging Systems Engineering, 1*(¾), pp. 155-167.

Karagiannis, T., Papagiannaki, K., & Faloutsos, M. (2005, August). BLINC: Multilevel traffic classification in the dark. In *SIGCOMM'05: Proceedings of the 2005 Conference on Applications, Technologies, Architectures and Protocols for Computer Communications* (pp. 229-240). Philadelphia, PA.

Kohavi, R., & Provost, F. (1998). 'Glossary of Terms', special issue on applications of machine learning and the knowledge discovery process. *Machine Learning, 30*, 271–274. doi:10.1023/A:1017181826899

Logg, C., & Cottrell, L. (2003, October). Characterization of the traffic between SLAC and the internet. Retrieved from http://www.slac.stanford.edu/comp/net/slacnetflow/html

Mathewos, B., Carvalho, M., & Ham, F. M. (2011, October). Network traffic classification using a parallel neural network classifier architecture. In *CSIIRW '11: Proceedings of the 7th Annual Workshop on Cyber Security and Information Intelligence Research.* New York, NY.

Moore, A., & Papagiannaki, K. (2005, April). Toward the accurate identification of network applications. In *Proc. Passive and Active Measurement Workshop.* Boston, MA.

Moore, A. W., & Zuev, D. (2005a). Internet traffic classification using Bayesian analysis techniques. *SIGMETRICS Performance Evaluation Review, 33*, 50–60. doi:10.1145/1071690.1064220

Moore, A. W., & Zuev, D. (2005b). *Discriminators for use in flow based classification. Technical report.* Cambridge: Intel Research.

Moore, D., Keys, K., Koga, R., Lagache, E., & Claffy, K. C. (2001, December). The CoralReef software suite as a tool for system and network administrators. In *LISA'01: Proceedings of the 15th USENIX Conference on Systems Administration* (pp. 133- 144). San Diego, CA.

Park, J., Tyan, H. R., & Kuo, C. (2006). Internet traffic classification for scalable QoS provision. In *2006 IEEE International Conference on Multimedia and Expo* (pp. 1221-1224). Toronto, Ontario, Canada.

Paxson, V. (1994, August). Empirically derived analytic models of wide-area TCP connections. *IEEE/ACM Transactions on Networking, 2*, 316–336. doi:10.1109/90.330413

Roughan, M., Sen, S., Spatscheck, O., & Duffield, N. (2004). Class-of-service mapping for QoS: A statistical signature-based approach to IP traffic classification. In *Internet Measurement Conference.* ACM.

Sen, S., Spatscheck, O., & Wang, D. (2004, May). Accurate, scalable in network identification of P2P traffic using application signatures. In *WWW 2004,* New York, NY.

Sun, R., Yang, B., Peng, L., Chen, Z., Zhang, L., & Jing, S. (2010). Traffic classification using probabilistic neural networks. *International Conference on Natural Computation* (Vol. 4, pp. 1914-1919).

Zander, S., Nguyen, T.T.T., & Armitage, G. (2005, March/April). Self-learning IP traffic classification based on statistical flow characteristics. *Passive & Active Measurement Workshop (PAM) 2005,* Boston, USA.

Zecevic, G. (1998). Web based interface to scada system. In *Power System Technology. Proceedings. POWERCON '98. 1998 International Conference* (Vol. 2, pp. 1218–1221).

KEY TERMS AND DEFINITIONS

3D ROC Curves: Three dimensional receiver operating characteristic curves.

CCR: Correct classification rates.

Packet Capturing: Capturing of data packets passing through a network.

Parallel Neural Network Classifier Architecture (PNNCA): Blocks of parallel neural networks used to for classification.

RBF Neural Networks: Neural networks that use radial basis functions as activation functions.

Web Traffic Classification: Classification of web traffics.

Chapter 10
Biogeography–Based Optimization for Large Scale Combinatorial Problems

Dawei Du
Cleveland State University, USA

Dan Simon
Cleveland State University, USA

ABSTRACT

Biogeography-based optimization (BBO) is a recently-developed heuristic algorithm that has shown impressive performance and efficiency over many standard benchmarks. The application of BBO is still limited because it was only developed four years ago. The objective of this chapter is to expand the application of BBO to large scale combinatorial problems. This chapter addresses the solution of combinatorial problems based on BBO combined with five techniques: (1) nearest neighbor algorithm (NNA), (2) crossover methods designed for traveling salesman problems (TSPs), (3) local optimization methods, (4) greedy methods, and (5) density-based spatial clustering of applications with noise (DBSCAN). This chapter also provides a discussion about the advantages and disadvantages for each of these five techniques when used with BBO, and describes the construction of a combinatorial solver based on BBO. In the end, a framework is proposed for large scale combinatorial problems based on hybrid BBO. Based on four benchmark problems, the experimental results demonstrate the quality and efficiency of our framework. On average, the algorithm reduces costs by over 69% for a 2152-city TSP compared to other methods: genetic algorithm (GA), ant colony optimization (ACO), nearest neighbor algorithm (NNA), and simulated annealing (SA). Convergence time for the algorithm is only 28.56 sec on a 1.73-GHz quad core PC with 6 GB of RAM . The algorithm also demonstrated good results for small and medium sized problems such as ulysses16 (16-city TSP, where we obtained the best performance), st70 (70-city TSP, where the second best performance was obtained), and rat575 (575-city TSP, where the second best performance was obtained).

DOI: 10.4018/978-1-4666-3942-3.ch010

INTRODUCTION

Heuristic algorithms are well known for their robustness and easy application. With the sustainable development of modern computer hardware, the long computation time is no longer a critical bottleneck for heuristic algorithms. In contrast, researchers benefit from using heuristic algorithms because it is not necessary to have a good understanding of the problem's structure. This is extremely helpful for industries which may have very complex systems.

Biogeography-based optimization (BBO) was first introduced in 2008 (Simon) making it a relatively young algorithm compared to others. But the performance of BBO on benchmark problems is better than many classical algorithms which have had many years of development. In BBO, the population is analogous to an archipelago, and each island in this archipelago is a possible solution to the optimization problem. From here on we refer to candidate solutions as *solutions* or *individuals*. The implementation of the algorithm is based on the following four terms - habitat suitability index (HSI), suitability index variable (SIV), immigration rate, and emigration rate. The HSI represents the goodness of the island, where a high HSI means that the solution represented by the island has relatively good performance on the optimization problem, and a low HSI means

poor performance. Each SIV represents a solution feature (that is, an independent variable of an optimization solution) in an island. The immigration rate and emigration rate are important solution characteristics for migration, and are the features of BBO that distinguish it from other evolutionary algorithms. A high performing island has a high emigration rate and low immigration rate. Conversely, a low performing island has a low emigration rate and high immigration rate. The emigration rate indicates how likely a solution is to share its features with other solutions. The immigration rate indicates how likely a solution is to accept features from other solutions. For BBO, the method to create the next generation is to share the individuals' information with other individuals in the population. In BBO, this information sharing is called immigration and emigration, which involves updating the population by migrations between islands. The basic procedure of BBO is as follows in Box 1.

Combinatorial problems are confirmed as NP-hard problems, and their huge search space determines their incompatibility with traditional mathematic methods. This makes them a perfect benchmark for heuristic algorithms. For the demonstration and simulation purposes of this chapter, the traveling salesman problem (TSP) will be used. Assume there exists a 100-city TSP. The total number of candidate solutions are $100! = $

Box 1.

```
For each solution Hi in the population
    For each SIV in the solution
            Select solution Hi for immigration with probability proportional to immigration rate
                If Hi is selected for immigration
                    Select Hj for emigration with probability proportional to emigration rate
                        Randomly select an SIV α from Hj
                        Replace a random SIV β in Hi with SIV α
        end
    end
end
```

9.3326×10^{157}. Therefore new methods must be developed for TSPs without using exhaustive search methods.

The reason we abandon exhaustive search is its high computational expense. But even with heuristic algorithms, the TSP is still very time consuming, and computational expense is still the top concern. Two general directions are proposed to increase the efficiency of BBO to decrease its computation time.

First is the modification of BBO algorithm. Four types of techniques are added to BBO: nearest neighbor algorithm, crossovers designed for TSPs, local optimization methods, and greedy methods. The idea is to search for the best combination of techniques to create a hybrid BBO in order to achieve the best balance between its computation time and performance.

The second direction modifies the problems by proposing a new framework for combinatorial problems. We will generate a framework based on a clustering algorithm, nearest neighbor algorithm, and parallel computing. The goal here is the same as in the previous goal, which is to achieve the best balance between computation time and performance for combinatorial problems.

The organization of this chapter is as follows. In the second section, we introduce the background of combinatorial problems and heuristic algorithms. In the third section, we propose all the modifications for BBO. The fourth section talk about increasing the efficiency of modified BBO for large scale problems. In the fifth section, we simulate all the proposed techniques to test the performance of the modified BBOs. Finally the results and topics covered are summarized and ideas for future efforts are presented.

BACKGROUND

Combinatorial problems are not new to heuristic algorithms. As a matter of fact, they are considered as standard benchmarks for heuristic algorithms. For example, TSP, a famous combinatorial problem, is an ancient problem whose origins have been lost in the mists of history. But we know that the TSP was first formulated as a mathematical problem by Karl Menger in 1930 (Mitchell, 1998). There are three major reasons that the TSP has become a standard benchmark for heuristic algorithms. First, the TSP is an easily stated problem and it is similar to many practical problems such as sensor selection (Boilot, 2003), the mailman problem (Desrochers, 1990), robotic path planning (Lozovyy, 2011), and many others. Second, the TSP can easily be modified to become a multi-objective problem (Jaszkiewicz, 2002) and solving multi-objective problems is a practical challenge in many areas of engineering and industry. Third, the optimal TSP solution is extremely hard to find using analytical methods. Even using numerical methods, it is still quite a challenge.

Because of the reasons above, many TSPs are formed to challenge the performance of existing heuristic algorithms, and many new heuristic algorithms are specially formed to conquer TSPs. Almost all the famous algorithms have already been tested with TSP benchmarks. For example, the genetic algorithm (GA) is the most famous and widely used heuristic algorithm. P. W. Poon (1995) invented cycle crossover for GAs which allows GAs to solve the TSP. Ant colony optimization is another widely used heuristic algorithm which has also been tested and confirmed as a good TSP solver by M. Dorigo (1997). Simulated annealing, another well known heuristic algorithm, also uses the TSP as a benchmark for its performance test in (Aarts, 1989).

But among all the algorithms, which one is the most powerful algorithm in this area is always a question. But there is no conclusive answer because of the diversity of TSPs. No one can achieve full domination in this area. However, in a general sense one might still outperform the other. As mentioned in the introduction, the performance of BBO has been tested in (Simon, 2008). In that paper, the performance of BBO was tested against seven popular evolutionary algorithms on 14 benchmarks. Based on the simulation results, BBO outperformed most of the algorithms. This gives us the confidence to apply it to combinatorial problems.

In (Mo, 2010), BBO has already been applied to TSPs. The new algorithm is called biogeography migration algorithm for traveling salesman problem (TSPBMA) which is a specially modified version of BBO for combinatorial problems. BBO is tested on four TSP benchmark problems against five popular algorithms: ant colony optimization (ACO), genetic algorithm (GA), immune algorithm (IA), fish swarm (FS), and particle swarm optimization (PSO). Based on the simulation results in Table 1, BBO provides promising results. This gives us reason to continue the development of BBO for combinatorial problems.

In 2011, M. Ergezer and D. Simon published a paper regarding BBO application to combinatorial problems (Ergezer, 2011). BBO with Circular Opposition (BBO/CO) was introduced as a modified version of BBO which can achieve promising results. Two techniques are implemented to create BBO/CO: CW, which is clockwise circular opposition; and combinatorial BBO migration, which is also called the simple version of inver-over crossover that will be detailed in the following sections. The performance of BBO/CO compared with original BBO was tested based on 16 benchmarks which are shown in Table 2. Based on the performance comparison, it indicates that appropriate modifications of BBO can have a positive impact.

Although BBO has already been modified for combinatorial problems, the modifications have been relatively simple. For example, in Mo (2010), only the migration component has been modified. Cycle crossover is used to replace the original migration method in order to process combinatorial problems. In Ergezer (2011), the migration component becomes inver-over crossover combined with circular opposition, which is the only changed compared to the original BBO. But the modification should not be restricted to just one component. In this chapter, modification of migration is just a small part of our work. In order to achieve the best solution, we modify all three major components of BBO: population initialization, migration, and mutation, and we explore their modifications with multiple methods. Also, we propose a technique to significantly increase the efficiency of BBO for combinatorial problems.

Table 1. TSP cost values achieved by various evolutionary algorithms (Mo, 2010). The best performance for each benchmark is shown in bold font.

	TSPBMA	**ACO**	**GA**	**IA**	**FS**	**PSO**
Oliver30 Problem	**420**	**420**	425	442	430	520
Eil50 Problem	425	**424**	428	464	451	554
Eil75 Problem	**535**	**535**	545	583	572	684
KroA100 Problem	**21282**	**21282**	21761	22435	22067	66635

Table 2. Mean of the best solutions obtained by BBO and BBO/CO on TSP benchmarks (Ergezer, 2011)

Benchmark	BBO	BBO/CO
att532	1,154,304	**1,140,103**
berlin52	9,795	9,811
bier127	302,056	**298,700**
ch130	20,552	**20,304**
d18512	58,521,418	**58,369,040**
kroA150	109,793	**108,651**
kroA200	169,256	**165,191**
kroC100	57,509	57,799
lin105	42,005	**41,661**
lin318	375,896	**374,011**
p654	1,440,864	**1,422,779**
rat575	83,835	**82,699**
rl11849	85,134,513	**84,926,068**
st70	1,162	**1,147**
usa13509	2,105,421,221	**2,098,340,568**
vm1084	7,208,117	**7,142,633**

BBO SOLUTION FOR COMBINATORIAL PROBLEMS

As mentioned in the introduction, the huge search space and search time is the main reason to abandon exhaustive search and turn to more intelligent heuristic algorithms. But even with heuristic algorithms, their mechanisms mean they are still more time consuming than other algorithms. So our top task is to increase the efficiency of the algorithm to achieve the best balance between computation time and performance. Because of the shortcomings of heuristic algorithms, many modifications have been invented for the purpose of performance improvement. Today, hybrid algorithms have become a trend in heuristic algorithms. In the rest of this section, we introduce four different types of techniques that will help in creating hybrid BBOs.

Population Initialization of BBO

Population initialization is usually the first step for all heuristic algorithms. But for most of the problems to which we apply heuristic algorithms, we do not have a good understanding of the effect of each independent variable. That means we do not know how to create a good population based on our expertise, so we randomly create it. It is no doubt the simplest way for population initialization. Lacking expertise, it is also the most inefficient way to create a population. But random population initialization is not the only way for population initialization. For certain problems like the TSP, there exist certain ways of creating an initial population which can provide a great benefit to the algorithm.

For TSPs, the most commonly used technique is called nearest neighbor algorithm (NNA) (Cover & Hart, 1967). The detailed procedure is as follows.

1. Randomly select a city as the ending point of the trip, which is also the starting point.
2. Calculate the distance between the ending point city and the cities which are not included in the trip.
3. Based on the distances calculated in step 2, find the nearest city to the ending point city. Link them and name the most recently added city as the ending point city.
4. If all the cities are included in the trip, terminate; otherwise, go to step 2.

The procedure is fairly easy to operate, and clearly not time consuming even for a large scale problem. The most time consuming part is the calculation of Euclidean distances between cities. For a TSP with n cities, the total number of calculations of Euclidean distance is

$$\text{number of calculations} = \frac{n(n-1)}{2}$$

For a 1000-city problem, the total number of calculations is only 499,500 which is an acceptable number when considering the problem size.

Migration of BBO

Migration is the method to combine features or modify features based on parent individuals to create offspring. It is also the most important component in BBO. But as we know, combinatorial problems are coded differently compared to other types of problems. Each element in the individual contains no information, but the order of the elements in that individual is what contains information. Since the original BBO is coded for continuous problems rather than combinatorial problems, in order to migrate order information more efficiently and validly between individuals, we need new types of migrations. Three types of migration methods are discussed in this book chapter - matrix crossover, cycle crossover, and inver-over crossover.

Matrix Crossover

Matrix crossover is introduced by Fox and McMahon (1991). The advantage of matrix crossover is that the application is very straightforward, and easy to operate for any TSP. Based on this method, the offspring can inherit information from both parents, and also generate random information to create a child not identical to either parent. But the drawback is also obvious for matrix crossover. As we see from the name of the method, all ordering information is represented by matrices, which requires heavy calculations for transformation between the standard TSP array expression and the matrix expression. Matrix crossover is thus contrary to our goal of reducing the total computation time for BBO.

The detailed procedure of matrix crossover is as follows.

- First, for an n-city problem, we need to convert the ordering information of all individuals to an n by n matrix. Each row in the matrix expression provides the position information of a city in the trip. For example, the k-th row represents the position information of city k. Each column in each row represents a certain city. The number in each column represents the ordering relationship between the column city and row city. For example, if city g is before city k, the number in the g-th column in the k-th row is 1. In other words, if city g is after city k, the number in the g-th column in the k-th row is 0. Based on this method, we convert all the individuals in the population (that is, all candidate solutions) to the matrix expression.

- Second, based on the selection methods - for example, roulette wheel – we select individuals to perform migration. Once the parents are selected, we perform AND logic on two matrices and we obtain one child matrix.

- Third, we will find that the child matrix is incomplete; that is, it does not completely represent a TSP tour. In this next step, we randomly fill in necessary information to create a valid child.

- In the last step, we transform the child from matrix expression to sequential representation.

An example is provided in Figure 1 to illustrate how to apply matrix crossover.

Cycle Crossover

Cycle crossover has already been tested in Oliver (1987) and obtained superior performance against competitors. It also achieves satisfying results in Mo (2010). Cycle crossover is first introduced in

Figure 1. Example of matrix crossover with a 5-city TSP

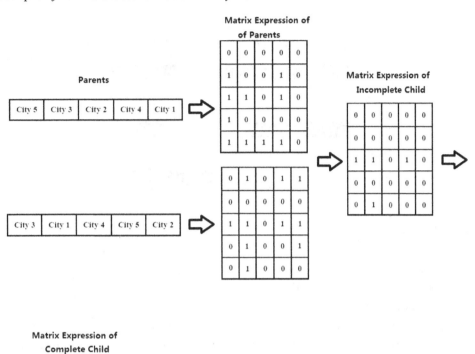

Oliver (1987). The application of cycle crossover is fairly easy. In contrast to matrix crossover, no expression transformation is needed, and it guarantees that every child generated is valid and complete. That is also the reason cycle crossover has been widely used for combinatorial problems.

The basic procedure of cycle crossover is as follows.

1. We randomly select a city as the starting point in parent 1, and record its position.
2. In parent 2, find the city at the position we recorded in parent 1 and then record this city. Go back to parent 1, search for the city we found in parent 2 and then record its position in parent 1.
3. Repeat step 2 until we obtain a closed cycle, which means we have returned to the starting city. Then we copy the cities from the closed cycle in parent 2, and the cities that are not in the closed cyle in parent 1, to obtain child 1. Similarly, we copy the cities from the closed cycle in parent 1, and the cities that are not in the closed cycle in parent 2, to obtain child 2.

We provide an example in Figure 2 to illustrate the application of cycle crossover.

Figure 2. Example of cycle crossover with a 9-city TSP

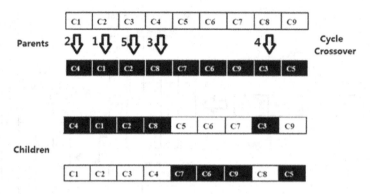

Inver-Over Crossover

The third migration method is called inver-over crossover. It was invented by G. Tao and Z. Michalewicz in 1998 (Tao, 1998). According to its experimental performance, it is a powerful tool for the TSP. Like cycle crossover, all the children generated by inver-over crossover are valid and complete. Inver-over crossover does not require any additional expression transformation.

The basic procedure of inver-over crossover is as follows.

1. Two parents are used to generate a child. Randomly select a city in parent 1 as the starting point, city s.
2. Find s in parent 2 and choose the city next to it as the ending point, city e. Then find this ending point city in parent 1.

3. Reverse the cities between $s+1$ (the city next to the starting point city) and e in parent 1. That is the child created by inver-over crossover.

An example is provided in Figure 3 to illustrate how to operate inver-over crossover.

Let's Talk about Local Optimization

Combinatorial problems have some special characteristics that are different from continuous or other discrete benchmarks. For example, candidate solutions for most benchmarks are composed of variables and each variable has its own domain. In that case, heuristic algorithms need to search each variable in each domain for the optimal solution. But combinatorial problems are different. In the TSP, for example, the coordinates of each

Figure 3. Example of inver-over crossover with a 5-city TSP

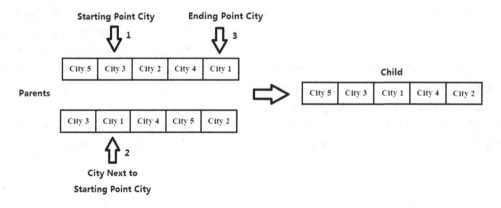

city are fixed. The task of heuristic algorithms is to rearrange the order of the cities for the optimal solution. In other words, each individual in the population has enough information to create an optimal solution.

Local search optimization is a kind of method that can find the optimal solutions by modifying the candidate solutions. Although the number of unique candidate TSP solutions is $n!$, there are only n cities in the TSP. All the necessary city indices to create an optimal solution are contained in every individual. Since the combination of techniques can be more powerful than techniques that are used on their own, in BBO we intend to use local search as a complement to migration. In the remainder of this section, we introduce three local optimization methods which have been successfully implemented in TSPs: 2-opt, 3-opt, and k-opt. These methods are applied after migration as a complement to our migration strategy.

2-opt is a simple but effective local research method invented by G. Croes in 1958 (Johnson, 1997). The operation of 2-opt is as follows:

1. Find a random individual in a sequence-based problem.
2. Break two links in this individual.
3. Connect the cities which only have one link connected, with the constraint that the resulting path includes all cities.

In Figure 4, we apply 2-opt to an 8-city TSP as an example.

3-opt is an updated technique based on 2-opt (Johnson, 1997). Instead of replacing two links in the individual as in 2-opt, the 3-opt technique breaks three links and then randomly reconnects the cities that have broken links. Even though 2-opt and 3-opt have good performance in sequence-based problems, their limitation is that the number of links to break and reconnect is predefined, and is difficult to adapt to the current situation.

In order to improve 2-opt and 3-opt, k-opt is introduced by Shen Lin in 1965 and is discussed in Johnson (1997). k-opt is a method for adaptively choosing the number of links to break and reconnect. According to experimental results, when the number of the replaced links increases, the performance of the k-opt increases too. But the computation burden also increases. So we need to find a balance between the expected performance and the computation burden. In heuristic algorithms, at the beginning of the generations, the population improvement speed is very fast. As the complement to migration, we do not need very intense k-opt. So the k value should be a small number. But as time progresses, the convergence speed of the algorithm slows down. In this situation, we need to increase the intensity of k-opt to increase the population improvement speed,

Figure 4. Example of 2-opt with an 8-city TSP

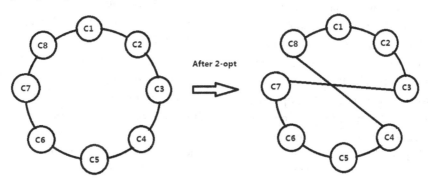

so we should use a bigger k value. Here we can conclude that k should increase as the generation count increases:

$$k = \frac{nc}{2m}$$

where n is the number of cities, m is the maximum generation number, c is the current generation number, and $\lfloor x \rfloor$ is the greatest integer that is less than or equal to x.

How About Being Greedy?

Greedy methods have a long history as an effective technique in heuristic algorithms, and many algorithms use them as a basic component. The definition of a greedy method is just as its name implies: always choose the immediate benefit, and refuse to take any losses (Gutin, 2002). But it may not be the best choice for all situations. For example, when playing chess, the players can plan 10 to 20 steps ahead and don't focus on instant benefits. But in some problems, like the TSP and the network routing problem, a greedy method can still be helpful as a complement to the optimization algorithm.

For BBO, we can use the greedy method in three places – migration, local optimization, and mutation. As we know, migration is a function for an individual to share and receive information with other individuals in order to generate offspring. Although individuals with better fitness have higher probabilities to share features, and individuals with worse fitness have higher probabilities to receive features, there is no guarantee the child will outperform its parents During mutation we introduce random information to the population. The performance of new individuals is unpredictable in this case. So should we keep an offspring with worse performance? The answer is different according to different situations. If the algorithm really needs fresh blood in the population, then even though the offspring has worse performance than either of the parents, we still keep it. But if we want to make sure the performance of the entire population improves, then we might want to apply a greedy method and abandon offspring with worse performance.

SOLUTION FOR LARGE SCALE PROBLEMS

Combinatorial problems arc not necessary large scale problems, but usually they are. As mentioned in Section 1, the number of combinations is 9.3326×10157 for a 100-city TSP, but a 100-city TSP is not even considered a large problem in the TSP family. The computational time is always the top concern for a large scale problem. It is also the top priority when we design an algorithm. In this section, a framework is designed for large scale problems, which will look for the best balance of computational expense and performance. In order to achieve our goal, two advanced techniques are introduced in the framework: problem decomposition and parallel computing.

Problem Decomposition

Problem decomposition is a classic method because of the lack of powerful computation methods and machines in the past. A common way to treat a large scale problem is to divide it into small pieces, then solve them individually. The combination of the solution of each small piece then becomes the solution to the original problem.

Based on today's technology, the processing ability of CPUs is incredible. But it still has limitations, and the calculation speed is still not sufficient for many problems like TSPs. That is the reason we turn to problem decomposition in order to reduce the time expense.

How can we decompose a TSP? Recall in the statistics area that when performing data analysis, we prefer applying clustering algorithms before the analysis. This is because when all the data inside a group is more similar to each other than to the data outside the group, it is easier to conduct an analysis to determine its characteristics.

Although there is no need to perform data analysis for combinatorial problems, clustering algorithms are still an inspiration and can be used directly in TSP decomposition. In 1996, density-based spatial clustering of applications with noise (DBSCAN) was proposed by Martin Ester *et al.* (Ester, 1996).

Here we need to define four terms: eps-neighbor, minPts, direct density-reachable, and density-reachable. We assume that the space under discussion is two dimensional.

- **EPS-Neighborhood:** Choose an arbitrary point; its eps-neighborhood is the area with radius eps whose center is the given point.
- **MinPts:** The minimum number of points in a cluster.
- **Direct Density-Reachable:** Two points are direct density-reachable if the distance between them is less than eps.
- **Density-Reachable:** Two points are density-reachable if there exists a sequence of points between them such that each adjacent pair in the sequence is direct density-reachable.

The concept of DBSCAN is as follows.

1. Start with an arbitrary point that has not been labeled.
2. Determine its eps-neighborhood. If it contains at least minPts points, then label these points as visited and go to step 3; otherwise, label this point as noise, then go to step 1.
3. Find all the density-reachable points of the arbitrary point chosen in step 1, then label

them as visited. A cluster is formed by these points. If all the point are labeled, then terminate; otherwise, go to step 1.

This results in clusters of points that are labeled as visited, and also isolated points that are labeled as noise. DBSCAN is a good fit for TSP. In many traveling salesman problems, the cities we plan to visit have certain patterns. In many TSPs, people intend to go to a major city at first and then explore the cities around it. After that, we head to another major city. We can treat each major city as the center of a cluster, and classify this major city along with its satellite cities as a cluster. This type of density based problem is a perfect match for DBSCAN.

Parallel Computing

Parallel computing has a long history, but for a long time it could not perform well due to the restrictions of hardware (Kumar, 1994). But with today's technology, CPUs with multiple cores are very common. However we cannot effectively use the power of most multi-cored CPUs, as most software operates based on one core. This is the reason we plan to introduce parallel computing to our framework, because it is an effective way to reduce our long computation time for TSPs. But still, parallel computing can only significantly benefit for large scale problems because of the parallel computing setup time and master to slave communication time. For smaller problems, the setup time and communication time may comprise a large portion of the simulation time.

As mentioned in Section 4.1, we can take advantage of problem decomposition for a large scale problem based on DBSCAN. Solving one large scale problem can be transferred into solving several smaller ones. This solution also raises another question: how should we process all of these small problems? That is why we introduce parallel computing. In our framework, all the decomposed problems are handled by parallel computing to achieve the maximum CPU usage. Combining all the ideas in this section and previous ones, we propose a framework designed for large scale TSPS, which is called BBO for TSP based on DBSCAN (BBO/DBTSP). The detailed scheme is shown in Figure 5.

Figure 5 describes a framework based on parallel computing for the TSP. In this framework, the large size problem is decomposed to n smaller sub-problems. The number n is determined by DBSCAN. In the following steps, each CPU core acts as a slave in parallel computing, and applies BBO to the assigned sub-problem independently. In order to balance the load of each slave, we equally partition the work each slave receives based on the size of each sub-problem. Once the BBO simulations are finished in all cores, we combine the outputs from each core using NNA to obtain the near-optimal result. In the end, we perform BBO, including the near-optimal result obtained in the previous step, to search for the globally optimal solution. One benefit of this structure is that there is no communication between cores during the parallel computing process, so

it significantly reduces the complexity of the process while still attaining 100% CPU usage. But problem decomposition and parallel computation both require time consuming overhead. Although we can benefit a lot from BBO/DBTSP when the problem size is large enough, the run time for small problems may be slower than non-decomposition-based algorithms.

Experimental Results

In this section, all the techniques mentioned in Section 3 and the framework we proposed in Section 4 are tested on four TSP benchmarks. All the benchmarks are selected from TSPlib (Reinelt, 1991) - ulysses16, st70, rat575, and u2152. Ulysses16 is a 16-city TSP; st70 is a 70-city TSP; rat575 is a 575-city TSP; and u2152 is a 2152-city TSP. In order to obtain a broad comparison between techniques, benchmark sizes vary from small to extra large problems. The definition of the size of a problem is calculated based on the following rule.

Assume the calculation of the distance between two cities only needs one instruction in a CPU.

Figure 5. Decomposition framework for large scale problems

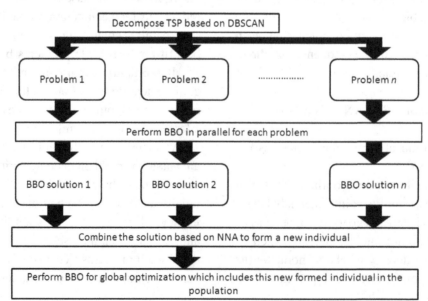

The operating frequency of a top line CPU (intel i7-2600, quad core) is 3.4 GHz per core. The total operating frequency is therefore 13.6 GHz.

For an n city problem, the total time T needed to calculate the distances of all possible trips is given as follows:

$$T = \frac{n(n!)}{1.36 \times 10^{10}} \sec$$

Based on the calculation time, TSPs are divided into four categorites:

1. **For Problems Less than 16 Cities (Small Problems):** $T \leq 2.46 \times 10^4$ sec. Brute force methods are suitable.
2. **For Problems between 17 to 50 (Normal Problems):** 2.46×10^4 sec $< T \leq 1.12 \times 10^{56}$ sec. In this case, for a 50 city problem, it will take 8.51×10^{49} years to find the solution based on a brute force method.
3. **For Problems between 50 to 100 (Large Problems):** 1.12×10^{56} sec $< T \leq 6.68 \times 10^{149}$ sec.
4. **For Problems Larger than 100 (Extra Large Problems):** $T > 6.68 \times 10^{149}$

In this book chapter, the aim is not only to find the best modification for BBO, it is also to compare BBO with other popular competitors. Five popular competitors are selected: GA (Poon, 1995), NNA (Cover & Hart, 1967), ant colony optimization (ACO) (Dorigo, 1997), simulated annealing (SA) (Aarts, 1989) and BBO/CO (Ergezer, 2011). In order to guarantee fairness, we set two termination criteria for each algorithm. The algorithm will terminate when either of them is met.

1. **Number of Evaluations of Cost Function:** 10,000
2. **CPU Time:** 300 sec

Also, since the performance of heuristic algorithms varies from one simulation to the next, a single comparison between algorithms may not reflect their true performances. To guarantee a fair comparison, Monte Carlo simulations are performed. We conduct each simulation 20 times, and take the average performance as the overall performance metric.

In order to compare the performance of techniques without affecting other factors, each modified BBO uses the following parameters.

Default BBO setup:

- **Population Size:** 100
- **Number of Elite Individuals per Generation:** 1
- **Population Initialization:** Random
- **Migration:** Cycle crossover
- **Local Optimization Method:** None
- **Greedy Method:** None

In the following sections, we study four major modifications - population initialization, different types of migration, local optimization methods, and greedy methods.

Initialization Methods

The first test is the performance of different population initialization methods. We designed six population initialization methods: no NNA; NNA for 1 individual, 5 individuals, 50 individuals, 75 individuals, and 100 individuals (the entire population). The simulation results are shown in Table 3.

On the basis of computation time, no NNA is the quickest. But the performance difference between no NNA and NNA is large, especially for larger scale problems. But when we apply NNA to the algorithm, the performance between different setups is very similar to each other. Based on the simulation results, the best setup of NNA is to perform 1 NNA, which means NNA only needs to be performed on one individual in the initial population.

Table 3. Performance of NNA initialization in BBO, averaged over 20 Monte Carlo simulations. The best results are shown in bold font in each row.

TSP		Best distance and CPU time per simulation (sec)					
		No NNA	1 NNA	5 NNA	50 NNA	75 NNA	100 NNA
ulysses16	Distance	75.68	74.72	**74.23**	74.65	74.66	74.62
	CPU Time	**3.11**	3.13	3.13	3.21	3.24	3.25
st70	Distance	1432	728	729	727	726	**725**
	CPU Time	**4.23**	4.55	4.56	4.61	4.62	4.65
rat575	Distance	128090	54487	54483	**54481**	54485	54482
	CPU Time	**19.23**	19.31	19.34	19.37	19.56	19.58
u2152	Distance	241745	74355	**74322**	74323	74333	74325
	CPU Time	**40.23**	41.92	42.35	42.58	42.62	42.66

Crossover Methods

The second test is the performance of different crossover methods in the migration of BBO. In this book chapter, three crossover methods were discussed: matrix crossover, cycle crossover and inver-over crossover. Their performances are shown in Table 4.

The simulation results show that both in performance and computation, inver-over crossover dominates the other methods. Also, the calculation speed of matrix crossover becomes very slow when the problem size increases, and therefore it is not a good method for large scale problems.

Local Optimization

Next is the evaluation of local optimization methods. Three methods were proposed in this book chapter: 2-opt, 3-opt, and k-opt. When using local optimization, we optimized each individual in the population at the end of each generation. The performances of different local optimization methods are shown in Table 5.

The setup with the best computation time is no local optimization. But with small increases of computation time, the improvement is significant when using local optimization, especially for large scale problems. For a small size problem,

Table 4. Performance of matrix crossover, cycle crossover and inver-over crossover, averaged over 20 Monte Carlo simulations. The best results are shown in bold font in each row.

TSP		Best distance and CPU time per simulation (sec)		
		Matrix	Cycle	Inver-Over
ulysses16	Distance	74.22	75.68	**74.21**
	CPU Time	**0.64**	3.11	0.97
st70	Distance	2725	1432	**820**
	CPU Time	2.22	4.23	**1.05**
rat575	Distance	102763	128090	**78765**
	CPU Time	300.00	19.23	**2.93**
u2152	Distance	434209	241745	**237372**
	CPU Time	300.00	40.23	**10.23**

Table 5. Performance of No-opt, 2-opt, 3-opt and k-opt, averaged over 20 Monte Carlo simulations. The best results are shown in bold font in each row.

TSP		Best distance and CPU time per simulation (sec)			
		No-opt	2-opt	3-opt	*k*-opt
ulysses16	Distance	75.68	74.67	**74.65**	80.59
	Time	**3.11**	3.18	3.23	3.57
st70	Distance	1432	**1180**	1695	1773
	CPU Time	**4.23**	5.67	6.72	7.55
rat575	Distance	128090	100069	97759	**94763**
	CPU Time	**19.23**	25.45	27.56	30.01
u2152	Distance	241745	240001	235987	**235876**
	CPU Time	**40.23**	54.34	58.31	153.99

2-opt and 3-opt outperform *k*-opt. But with large scale problems, *k*-opt is the best choice.

Greedy Methods

Next we test different greedy method setups. Three setups are introduced: no greedy method, half of the population uses a greedy method (the individuals that use greedy methods in this approach are randomly selected), and the entire population uses a greedy method. The greedy method is applied at three steps of the BBO al-gorithm each generation: first we apply it after migration, then we apply it after local optimization, and finally we apply it after mutation. The performances of different greedy method setups are shown in Table 6.

The simulation results reflect that the best strategy from the perspective of computational effort is not to apply a greedy method. Also, when the population is small, the performance is better without the use of a greedy method. But for large scale problems, Table 6 shows the advantage of greedy methods.

Table 6. Performance of different greedy method setups, averaged over 20 Monte Carlo simulations. The best results are shown in bold font in each row.

TSP		Best distance and CPU time per simulation (sec)		
		No Greedy	Half Greedy	All Greedy
ulysses16	Distance	**75.68**	79.41	88.51
	CPU Time	**3.11**	3.12	3.15
st70	Distance	**1432**	1770	2795
	CPU Time	**4.23**	4.62	4.73
rat575	Distance	128090	**10360**	10456
	CPU Time	**19.23**	19.35	19.47
u2152	Distance	241745	242356	**23632**
	CPU Time	**40.23**	42.44	43.12

BBO/DBTSP

Next we test the BBO/DBTSP framework shown in Figure 5, which is especially designed for large scale problems. Based on the previous simulation results, the best setup for large scale BBO is the following: 1 NNA for population initialization; inver-over crossover; *k*-opt for local optimization method; and all greedy for the greedy method setup. We use these options in BBO/DBTSP. Then we conduct simulations on the same four TSP benchmarks.

Here, we compare the results between BBO and GA (Kirk, 2007), NNA (Kirk, 2008), ACO (Wang, 2007), SA (Seshadri, 2006) and BBO/CO (Ergezer, 2011). The setups of these algorithms are as follows.

- **GA:** Population size is 100; Crossover is a combination of flip crossover, swap crossover and slide crossover; Crossover rate is 0.5; Mutation rate is 0.01.
- **NNA:** It is not a heuristic algorithm, so no tuning parameters are needed.
- **ACO:** Population size is 20 ants; Initial pheromone value is 10-6; Pheromone update constant is 20; Exploration constant is 1; Global pheromone decay rate is 0.9; Local pheromone is decay rate 0.1; Pheromone sensitivity is 1; Visibility sensitivity is 1.
- **SA:** Initial temperature is 2000; Maximum trails at a temperature are 10 times the population size.
- **Default BBO:** Population size is 100; Number of elite individuals per generation is 1; Population initialization is random initialization; Migration method is cycle crossover; No local optimization method; No greedy method.
- **BBO/CO:** Population size is 100; Number of elite individuals per generation is 1; Population initialization is random initial-

ization; Migration method is inver-over crossover combined with CW circular opposition; No local optimization method; No greedy method.
- **BBO/DBTSP:** Population size is 100; Number of elite individuals per generation is 1; Population initialization is 1 NNA; Migration method is inver-over crossover; Local optimization method is *k*-opt; Greedy method is all greedy. The CPU contains four cores (considered as four workers in the parallel computation).

Based on the simulation results in Table 7, in ulysses16, BBO/DBTSP achieved the best solution among all. Although the computation time is slightly longer than the others, it is still in the tolerable range. In st70, SA has the best performance. BBO/DBTSP has the second best which is close to the results from SA, and far better than others. In rat575, ACO is the best choice in the solution aspect, but it is very time consuming compared to the others. This can be a major drawback especially when dealing with large scale problems. BBO/DBTSP is still the second best algorithm, with similar results to ACO but far better computation time. With the largest benchmark u2152, BBO/DBTSP achieved the best performance and fastest convergence speed among all heuristic algorithms. According to these results, BBO/DBTSP has the best overall performance.

CONCLUSION AND FUTURE RESEARCH DIRECTIONS

In this book chapter, we introduced a BBO algorithm especially designed for combinatorial problems. We presented two fundamental improvements to BBO. First, we introduced additional search techniques to BBO to create hybrid BBO for better performance and convergence speed. Second, we created a framework designed

Table 7. Performance of GA, NNA, ACO, SA, default BBO and BBO/DBTSP, averaged over 20 Monte Carlo simulations. The best results are shown in bold font in each row.

TSP		Best distance and CPU time per simulation (sec)						
		GA	NNA	ACO	SA	Default BBO	BBO/CO	BBO /DBTSP
ulysses16	Distance	74.63	104.43	74.62	74.77	75.68	74.71	**74.21**
	CPU Time	3.41	**0.18**	0.38	1.01	3.11	1.12	5.12
st70	Distance	1509	3208	1359	**741**	1432	2042	802
	CPU Time	6.22	**0.19**	4.47	3.98	4.23	2.14	5.21
rat575	Distance	12493	12952	**68311**	12399	128090	97973	76321
	CPU Time	11.12	**0.24**	300.00	8.18	19.23	3.17	24.32
u2152	Distance	82205	82209	150341	709209	241745	240009	**77828**
	CPU Time	18.45	**0.67**	300.00	23.16	40.23	11.21	6.04

for large scale combinatorial problems based on a combination of clustering, parallel computing, and BBO.

In the first part of this chapter, we focused on four improvements to BBO: population initialization, migration, local optimization methods, and greedy methods. For population initialization, we introduced the nearest neighbor algorithm (NNA). With the increase of the problem size, we receive more benefit from NNA. Based on the simulation results, 1 NNA is a good complement to the original BBO. For migration, we used three crossover methods especially designed for TSP: matrix crossover, cycle crossover, and inver-over crossover. With the combination of BBO and these crossover methods, BBO gains the ability to provide solutions to TSPs. According to the performance results in Section 5, inver-over crossover achieves the best overall performance.

Local optimization methods are introduced into BBO to complement the global optimization. The advantage of BBO is that it is designed for global optimization, and it doesn't easily get stuck in locally optimal solutions. However, convergence speed is relatively slow. In contrast, local optimization methods are designed to modify a single individual to search for the local optimum. So we can benefit from local optimization and improve

the performance of the BBO. The simulation shows 2-opt and 3-opt give BBO better performance with small problems. k-opt achieves better performance with large problems.

The last BBO enhancement was greedy methods, which always accept changes with better performance, and never takes a step back. It is a common strategy for heuristic algorithms. When combined with BBO, the simulation results show greedy methods can increase performance when the problem size is relatively large.

In the second part, our focus was on large scale problems. A framework was introduced in Section 4. In this framework, we first decompose a large scale problem to smaller sub-problems based on DBSCAN. After successfully decomposing the problems, we apply the concept of parallel computing. Every sub-problem is solved individually with BBO in parallel. The BBO used here benefits from the previous studies by combining the techniques with the best performance - 1 NNA for population initialization; inver-over crossover; k-opt for local optimization; and all greedy for the greedy method setup. After obtaining the sub-problem solutions from the parallel BBO algorithms, we use NNA to group them and form an overall solution to the problem, which is also an individual in the overall BBO algorithm (each individual in the population in BBO is a candidate solution to the problem). The last step is to perform BBO for global optimization, and include this newly formed individual in the population. Based on comparisons with other algorithms, BBO/DBTSP has the best overall performance.

FUTURE DIRECTIONS

Combinatorial problems are good benchmarks for heuristic algorithms. Based on the work provided here, BBO has shown its potential in this field. For future work, we suggest four different directions. First, since information sharing techniques are the key component in evolution, we suggest continued study of new techniques to achieve better performance. Second, we note that operations in BBO such as population initialization, mutation, and elitism, affect the performance of the algorithm. We therefore suggest continued study of new techniques for these operations. Third, in order to further test the pontential of the scability of BBO/DBTSP, we suggest that it be tested on larger scale benchmarks like TSPs with over 10,000 cities. Fourth, we note that combinatorial problems represent many real world problems (for example, scheduling). We therefore suggest studying real-world applications of BBO and the TSP.

ACKNOWLEDGMENT

This work was supported by the National Science Foundation under Grant No. 0826124. Technical writing assistance was provided by Ron Davis from Cleveland State University.

REFERENCES

Aarts, E. (1989). Simulated annealing: An introduction. *Statistica Neerlandica*, *43*(1), 31–52. doi:10.1111/j.1467-9574.1989.tb01245.x

Boilot, P. (2003). Electronic noses inter-comparison, data fusion and sensor selection in discrimination of standard fruit solutions. *Sensors and Actuators. B, Chemical*, *88*(1), 80–88. doi:10.1016/S0925-4005(02)00313-1

Cover, T., & Hart, P. (1967). Nearest neighbor pattern classification. *IEEE Transactions on Information Theory*, *13*(1), 21–27. doi:10.1109/TIT.1967.1053964

Desrochers, M. (1990). A classification scheme for vehicle routing and scheduling problems. *European Journal of Operational Research*, *46*(3), 322–332. doi:10.1016/0377-2217(90)90007-X

Dorigo, M., & Gambardella, L. (1997). Ant colonies for the traveling salesman problem. *Bio Systems*, *43*(2), 73–81. doi:10.1016/S0303-2647(97)01708-5

Du, D., Simon, D., & Ergezer, M. (2009). Oppositional biogeography-based optimization. *IEEE Conference on Systems, Man, and Cybernetics* (pp. 1035-1040). San Antonio, TX.

Ergezer, M., & Simon, D. (2011). Oppositional biogeography-based optimization for combinatorial problems. *IEEE Congress On Evolutionary Computation* (pp.1496-1503). New Orleans, LA.

Ester, M. (1996). A density-based algorithm for discovering clusters in large spatial databases with noise. *2nd International Conference Knowledge Discovery and Data Mining* (pp. 226-231). Menlo Park, CA.

Fox, B., & McMahon, M. (1991). Genetic operators for sequencing problems. In Rawlin, G. (Ed.), *Foundations of genetic algorithms 1* (pp. 284–300). San Mateo, CA: Morgan Kaufmann.

Gutin, G., Yeo, A., & Zverovich, A. (2002). Traveling salesman should not be greedy: Domination analysis of greedy-type heuristics for the TSP. *Discrete Applied Mathematics*, *117*, 81–86. doi:10.1016/S0166-218X(01)00195-0

Jaszkicwicz, A. (2002). Genetic local search for multi-objective combinatorial optimization. *European Journal of Operational Research, 137*(1), 50–71. doi:10.1016/S0377-2217(01)00104-7

Johnson, D., & McGeoch, L. (1997). The traveling salesman problem: A case study in local optimization. In Aarts, E., & Lenstra, J. (Eds.), *Local search in combinatorial optimization* (pp. 215–310). New York, NY: John Wiley & Sons.

Kirk, J. (2007). *Traveling salesman problem - genetic algorithm.* Retrieved April 1, 2012, from: http://www.mathworks.com/matlabcentral/fileexchange/13680

Kirk, J. (2008). *Traveling salesman problem - nearest neighbor.* Retrieved April 1, 2012, from: http://www.mathworks.com/matlabcentral/fileexchange/21297

Kumar, V., Grama, A., Gupta, A., & Karypis, G. (1994). *Introduction to parallel computing.* Redwood City, CA: The Benjamin/Cummings Publishing Company.

Lozovyy, P., Thomas, G., & Simon, D. (2011). Biogeography-based optimization for robot controller tuning. In Igelnik, B. (Ed.), *Computational modeling and simulation of intellect: Current state and future perspectives* (pp. 162–181). Hershey, PA: IGI Global. doi:10.4018/978-1-60960-551-3.ch007

Mitchell, M. (1998). *An introduction to genetic algorithms.* Cambridge, MA: MIT Press.

Mo, H., & Xu, L. (2010). Biogeography migration algorithm for traveling salesman problem. In Tan, Y., Shi, Y., & Tan, K. (Eds.), *Advances in swarm intelligence* (pp. 405–414). Beijing, China: Springer. doi:10.1007/978-3-642-13495-1_50

Oliver, I., Smith, D., & Holland, J. (1987). A study of permutation crossover operators on the traveling salesman problem. *2nd International Conference on Genetic Algorithm and their application* (pp. 224-230).

Poon, P., & Carter, J. (1995). Genetic algorithm crossover operators for ordering applications. *Computers & Operations Research, 22*(1), 135–147. doi:10.1016/0305-0548(93)E0024-N

Reinelt, G. (1991). TSPLib - A traveling salesman problem library. *ORSA Journal on Computing, 3*, 376–384. doi:10.1287/ijoc.3.4.376

Seshadri, A. (2006). *Traveling salesman problem (TSP) using simulated annealing.* Retrieved April 1, 2012, from http://www.mathworks.com/matlabcentral/fileexchange/9612-traveling-salesman-problem-tsp-using-simulated-annealing

Simon, D. (2008). Biogeography-based optimization. *IEEE Transactions on Evolutionary Computation, 12*(6), 702–713. doi:10.1109/TEVC.2008.919004

Tao, G., & Michalewicz, Z. (1998). Inver-over operator for the TSP. *Parallel problem solving from nature V,* pp. 803–812.

Wang, H. (2007). *Solving symmetrical and symmetrical TSP base on ant colony algorithm.* Retrieved April 1, 2012, from http://www.mathworks.com/matlabcentral/fileexchange/14543

ADDITIONAL READING

Applegate, D., Bixby, R., Chvatal, V., & Cook, W. (2007). *The traveling salesman problem: A computational study.* Princeton, NJ: Princeton University Press.

Back, T. (1996). *Evolutionary algorithms in theory and practice*. Oxford, UK: Oxford University Press.

Beyer, H. (2001). *The theory of evolution strategies*. New York, NY: Springer. doi:10.1007/978-3-662-04378-3

Bhattacharya, A., & Chattopadhyay, P. (2010). Solution of economic power dispatch problems using oppositional biogeography-based optimization. *Electric Power Components and Systems*, *38*(10), 1139–1160. doi:10.1080/15325001003652934

Cook, W. (2011). *In pursuit of the traveling salesman: Mathematics at the limits of computation*. Princeton, NJ: Princeton University Press.

Darwin, C. (1859). *On the origin of species by means of natural selection, or the preservation of favoured races in the struggle for life*. New York, NY: D. Appleton. doi:10.5962/bhl.title.59991

Edelkamp, S., & Schroedl, S. (2011). *Heuristic search: Theory and applications*. San Jose, CA: Morgan Kaufmann.

Goel, L., Panchal, V., & Gupta, D. (2010). Embedding expert knowledge to hybrid bio-inspired techniques: An adaptive strategy towards focused land cover feature extraction. *International Journal of Computer Science & Information Security*, *8*(2), 244–253.

Gong, W., Cai, Z., Ling, C., & Li, H. (2010). A real-coded biogeography-based optimization with mutation. *Applied Mathematics and Computation*, *216*(9), 2749–2758. doi:10.1016/j.amc.2010.03.123

Hanski, I., & Gilpin, M. (1997). *Metapopulation biology*. New York, NY: Academic.

Johal, N., Singh, S., & Kundra, H. (2010). A hybrid FPAB/BBO algorithm for satellite image classification. *International Journal of Computers and Applications*, *6*(5), 31–36. doi:10.5120/1074-1403

Kumar, S., Bhalla, P., & Singh, A. (2009). Fuzzy rule base generation from numerical data using biogeography-based optimization. *Institution of Engineers Journal of Electronics and Telecomm Engineering*, *90*, 8–13.

Kundra, H., & Sood, M. (2010). Cross-country path finding using hybrid approach of PSO and BBO. *International Journal of Computers and Applications*, *7*(6), 15–19. doi:10.5120/1167-1370

Ma, H. (2010). An analysis of the equilibrium of migration models for biogeography-based optimization. *Information Sciences*, *180*(18), 3444–3464. doi:10.1016/j.ins.2010.05.035

MacArthur, R., & Wilson, E. (1967). *The theory of island biogeography*. Princeton, NJ: Princeton University Press.

Panchal, V., Singh, P., Kaur, N., & Kundra, H. (2009). Biogeography based satellite image classification. *International Journal of Computer Science and Information Security*, *6*(2), 269–274.

Rarick, R., Simon, D., Villaseca, F., & Vyakaranam, B. (2009). Biogeography-based optimization and the solution of the power flow problem. *IEEE Conference on Systems, Man, and Cybernetics* (pp. 1029-1034). San Antonio, TX: IEEE.

Rosenkrantz, D., Stearns, R., & Lewis, P. (1977). An analysis of several heuristics for the traveling salesman problem. *SIAM Journal on Computing*, *6*, 563–581. doi:10.1137/0206041

Roy, P., Ghoshal, S., & Thakur, S. (2010). Biogeography based optimization for multi-constraint optimal power flow with emission and non-smooth cost function. *Expert Systems with Applications*, *37*(12), 8221–8228. doi:10.1016/j.eswa.2010.05.064

Savsani, V., Rao, R., & Vakharia, D. (2009). Discrete optimisation of a gear train using biogeography based optimisation technique. *International Journal of Design Engineering*, *2*(2), 205–223. doi:10.1504/IJDE.2009.028652

Simon, D., Ergezer, M., Du, D., & Rarick, R. (2011). Markov models for biogeography-based optimization. *IEEE Transactions on Systems, Man, and Cybernetics. Part B, Cybernetics, 41*(1), 299–306. doi:10.1109/ TSMCB.2010.2051149

Singh, U., Singla, H., & Kamal, T. (2010). Design of Yagi-Uda antenna using biogeography based optimization. *IEEE Transactions on Antennas and Propagation, 58*(10), 3375–3379. doi:10.1109/ TAP.2010.2055778

Wang, K., Huang, L., Zhou, C., & Pang, W. (2003). Particle swarm optimization for traveling salesman problem. *IEEE International Conference on Machine Learning and Cybernetics* (pp. 1583 - 1585). IEEE.

Yao, X., Liu, Y., & Lin, G. (1999). Evolutionary programming made faster. *IEEE Transactions on Evolutionary Computation, 3*, 82–102. doi:10.1109/4235.771163

KEY TERMS AND DEFINITIONS

BBO: Biogeography-Based Optimization is an evolutionary algorithm designed by Dan Simon.

DBSCAN: A density-based algorithm for discovering clusters in large spatial databases with noise.

Greedy Method: It is a kind of methods which always choose the immediate benefit, and refuse to take any losses.

Migration: Component of BBO, a technique to share information between candidate solutions.

NNA: Nearest neighbor algorithm is designed to connect nearest cities to form a valid TSP solution.

Parallel Computing: A form of computation in which many calculations are carried out simultaneously.

TSP: Traveling Salesman Problem is a classic type of combinatorial problem in which the goal is to find a route which allows a traveler to visit a set of cities while covering the minimum distance.

Section 3
Concepts

Chapter 11
Kolmogorov Superpositions:
A New Computational Algorithm

David Sprecher
University of California at Santa Barbara, USA

ABSTRACT

Kolmogorov's superpositions enable the representation of every real-valued continuous function f defined on the Euclidean n-cube in the form $f(x_1,...,x_n) = \sum_{p=0}^{2n} g^q \circ h^q(x_1,...,x_n)$, *with continuous functions* g^q *that compute f, and fixed continuous functions* $h^q = \sum_{p=1}^{n} \psi^q(x_p)$ *dependent only on n. The functions* h^q *specify space-filling curves that determine characteristics that are not suitable for efficient computational algorithms. Reversing the process, we specify suitable space-filling curves that enable new functions* h^q *that give a computational algorithm better adaptable to applications. Detailed numerical constructions are worked out for the case n = 2.*

INTRODUCTION

This chapter concerns the computation of continuous functions of $n > 2$ variables with superpositions of continuous functions of $m < n$ variables. The function

$$f(x_1, x_2) = x_1 x_2$$

of two variables can offers a simple example of a representation with superpositions of functions of one variable:

$$f(x_1, x_2) = g_1 \circ (\psi_{1,1}(x_1) + \psi_{1,2}(x_2))$$
$$+ g_2 \circ \psi_{2,1}((x_1) + \psi_{2,1}(x_2)),$$

where

$$g_1(t_1) = \tfrac{1}{4} t_1^2,$$

$$g_2(t_2) = -\tfrac{1}{4} t_2^2,$$

$$\psi_{1,1}(x_1) = \psi_{2,1}(x_1) = x_1$$

and

DOI: 10.4018/978-1-4666-3942-3.ch011

$$\psi_{1,2}(x_2) = -\psi_{2,2}(x_2) = x_2,$$

i.e.,

$$x_1 x_2 = \tfrac{1}{4}(x_1 + x_2)^2 - \tfrac{1}{4}(x_1 - x_2)^2.$$

In general, we are interested in representations

$$f(x_1, ..., x_n) = \sum_{q=1}^{r} g^q \circ \psi^q(x_1, ..., x_n)$$

for some number r of summands, in which

$$\psi^q(x_1, ..., x_n)$$

are fixed continuous functions that are independent of

$$f(x_1, ..., x_n).$$

In their most general form, such superpositions belong to a class of problems conveniently described by means of a commuting diagram with metric spaces X, Y, and T, and a given mapping $f : X \rightarrow Y$ (Figure 1): The problem is to find continuous mappings $\Psi : X \rightarrow T$ and $g : T \rightarrow Y$ such that f can be replaced with the superposition $f = g \circ \Psi$, where Ψ is a fixed embedding of X into T, and when this representation is valid for a sufficiently large class of

Figure 1. Superpositions $f = g \circ h$ as a commuting diagram

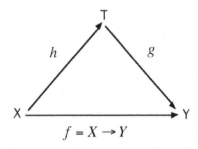

functions f. We are not going to pursue here this aspect of generality, and instead will adhere to the setting $X = E^n$, in which

$$E^n = E \times ... \times E$$

is the n-dimensional Euclidean unit cube, $E = [0, 1]$,

$$T = R^r = \{(t_1, ..., t_r)\}$$

is the r-dimensional Euclidean space, and $Y = R$.

What we are leading up to is the remarkable superpositions theorem of Kolmogorov, which states that all real-valued continuous functions defined on E^n can be represented with superpositions of continuous functions of one variable and addition (Kolmogorov, 1957). Its substance is as follows:

Theorem 1

Every real-valued continuous function f defined on the n-dimensional Euclidean cube has a representation with sums of monotonic increasing continuous functions ψ_p^q that are independent of f, and continuous functions g^q that compute it:

$$f(x_1, ..., x_n) = \sum_{q=0}^{2n} g^q \circ \sum_{p=1}^{n} \psi_p^q(x_p) \qquad (1)$$

The algorithm that this formula outlines:

$$(x_1, ..., x_n) \rightarrow \Sigma \psi_p^q(x_p) \rightarrow$$

$$\Sigma_q g^q \circ \Sigma_p \psi_p^q(x_p) = f(x_1, ..., x_n)$$

is based on a kernel of what might be called arbiter functions,

$$t^q = \Sigma_p \psi_p^q(x_p):$$

$$(x_1, ..., x_n) \to t^0, t^1, ..., t^{2n}$$

that transform the ordered n-tuples $(x_1, ..., x_n)$ into parameterized unordered $(2n+1)$-tuples $t^0, t^1, ..., t^{2n}$. For a given value of q, any sequence

$$t_1^q < t_2^q < t_3^q < ...$$

orders the corresponding sequence of points

$$(x_{1,1}, ..., x_{n,1}), (x_{1,2}, ..., x_{n,2}), (x_{1,3}, ..., x_{n,3}), ...$$

in the domains of $\Sigma_p \psi_p^q(x_p)$. These points determine, in turn, the *a priori* sampling sequence of functional values:

$$f(x_{1,1}, ..., x_{n,1}), f(x_{1,2}, ..., x_{n,2}),$$
$$f(x_{1,3}, ..., x_{n,3}), ...,$$

and this determines for each q the graph of

$$y^q = g^q(t^q).$$

For a given value $t^q = c$, the equation

$$\Sigma_p \psi_p^q(x_p) = c$$

has generally infinitely many solutions $(x_1, ..., x_n)$, but this does not affect the shape of the graph, which lies in the (t^q, y)-plane. In both parts of Equation 1, dimension manifests itself only through the commutative operation of addition, enabling its implementation through parallel computations. These, however, are inhibited by the characteristics of the sums $\Sigma_p \psi_p^q$, and these turn out to the computational Achilles heel of Kolmogorov's superpositions.

Kolmogorov's paper outlines a mathematical blueprint for the iterative construction of the functions ψ_p^q, and an inductive construction of the functions g^q, and these have served as a basis of the existing numerical algorithms of the superpositions. A number of streamlined and accessible constructions and proofs of Theorem 1 have since been published, the most elegant of the proofs being that of Lorentz (1962). The functions ψ_p^q that Kolmogorov devised are limits of iterations of ingenious devil staircase-type functions ψ_{pk}^q:

$$\lim_{k \to \infty} \psi_{pk}^q = \psi_p^q,$$

and even with numerical improvements, the sums $\Sigma_p \psi_{pk}^q$, which themselves are more complicated staircase functions, and the functions g^q depending on them, are not suited for efficient machine implementation, even though the functions ψ_p^q belong to class

$$Lipschitz(\tfrac{\ln 2}{\ln(2n+2)}):$$

$$\left| \psi_p^q(x_p) - \psi_p^q(x_p') \right|$$
$$\leq A \, | \, x_n - x_n' \, |^{\ln 2 / \ln(2n+2)}$$

for some constant A. Using a different algorithm than that of Kolmogorov, Fridman (1967) proved the theorem with functions ψ_p^q belonging to class *Lipschitz* (1), but the constructions he employed do not easily translate to an implementable algorithm. Efforts to date to sufficiently smooth the inner functions based on Kolmogorov's algorithm while retaining superposition representations of the form (1) have been unsuccessful for the most part.

This briefly outlines the context of this chapter and its goal: to investigate the nature of the alluded to computational difficulties, and to propose an alternative to the fixed functions $\Sigma_p \psi_p^q$ that would improve computational algorithms for the superpositions while retaining the following essential feature of Theorem 1: An arbitrary continuous function $f : E^n \to R$ can be completely specified with an ordered pair $f = (G, H)$, where H is a rule that associated with every point

$$(x_1, ..., x_n) \in E^n$$

an unordered set of parameters $(t^0, t^1, ..., t^{2n})$, and G computes f continuously with these parameters.

The genealogy of Kolmogorov's superpositions can be traced to interest in France and Germany towards the end of the 18th century in analogue mechanical devices for solving functional equations through graphical means with nomographic functions (Evesham, 1982), a technique involving suitable parameterizations. Interest in this area of mathematics peaked with the publication of d'Octagne's (1899) definitive treatise on the subject. For nomographic constructions, however, it is generally necessary that no more than two parameters be used at any given stage of the process. This limitation defined its own form of functional complexity, and it is functional complexity that is the immediate antecedent of the superposition formula. It represents the unexpected outcome, even for Kolmogorov himself, of his and Arnol'd's effort to resolve an assertion of David Hilbert in this general area, made in his address to the International Congress of Mathematics (Hilbert, 1900).

In general, the theory of functional complexity deals with the relative characteristics of functions, and one of its aims is to develop criteria for assigning numerical measures of complexity to given classes of functions. Hilbert's interest in functional complexity was focused on representability of continuous functions in terms of superpositions, using as a measure of comparison that two functions have the same complexity if they can be composed in a finite number of steps from functions belonging to the same class. Such measures would depend on the choices of superpositions and on the conditions imposed on the

classes of functions allowed for these superpositions: For example, these may be required to be of a certain form, or to satisfy algebraic or differentiability conditions (Buck, 1975). Smoothness conditions provide a useful measure of functional complexity, and it was Hilbert's notion that the number of variables of a function can also serve as a useful measure in the following sense: Consider a continuous function f of n variables, and a class S_m of continuous functions of $m \le n$ variables. If the function f can be represented as a finite superposition of functions of class S_m, and if m is the *least* natural number for which this is true, then we can use m as a measure of the functional complexity of the function f relative to the classes $S_m : f \in S_m$ but $f \notin S_k$ for all positive integers $k < m$. More interesting answers can be expected when the classes S_m have suitable restrictions, and imposing smoothness conditions is clearly the tenor of Hilbert's Problem 13. The representation of the function:

$$f(x_1, x_2) = x_1 x_2$$

served to illustrate this line of thought. This function can be said to have the same functional complexity as the function $g(t) = t$ when our measure is representability with continuous functions of one variable.

The class of nomographic functions,

$$g(a(x_1) + b(x_2)),$$

is basic in the application of graphical solutions to functional equations, and based on the use of such functions, Hilbert identified in Problem 13 a specific continuous function $f(x_1, x_2, x_3)$ (the roots of the general 7th degree polynomial equation) that he asserted cannot be obtained in a finite number of steps with continuous functions of only two variables, implying that there is a continuous function of three variables $f(x_1, x_2, x_3)$ whose complexity index is 3. Research by Hilbert and his contemporaries using generally algebraic techniques tended to confirm the substance of this assertion, to the extent that number of variables with suitable smoothness conditions did provide a complexity characterization. Kolmogorov and his then student Arnol'd returned to this problem with a fresh approach, using Menger's research on trees, especially his discovery of a universal tree (Menger, 1932). Building on an initial attempt by Kolmogorov (1956) based on Menger's work, Arnol'd (1957) refuted Hilbert's assertion, and Kolmogorov then discovered, through an analysis of their two papers, that he can go beyond the refutation of Hilbert's assertion and show that all continuous functions $f : E^n \to R$ of any finite number of variables have complexity index 1.

Although the number of variables turned out not to be a valid measure of complexity, a different approach tied to the number of variables did give an important insight to this line of reasoning: Vituskin considered the class $\chi = \frac{n}{p+\alpha}$ of continuous function of n variables having partial derivates of order $\leq p$, and whose p^{th} partial derivatives are Lipschitz continuous with index $0 < \alpha \leq 1$. He showed that not all functions of class $\chi = \frac{n}{p+\alpha}$ can be obtained with superpositions of class

$$\chi_o = \frac{n_o}{p_o + \alpha_o} < \chi = \frac{n}{p+\alpha}$$

when $p + \alpha \geq 1$ (Vituskin, 1954). This still stands as the most profound insight into dimension-related functional complexity, but these and other mathematical considerations along such lines do not relate directly to our limited and pragmatic focus of investigating computability. Yet one cannot dismiss the inevitable descent in smoothness of superposition classes in Vituskin's result: As the number of variables in the superpositions decreases from those of the target functions, so does their smoothness, and one should not rule

out the computational significance of these considerations in future targeted applications. Further elaboration on this line of reasoning can be found in Vituskin (1954), Lorentz (1966), Sprecher (1972) and elsewhere.

Kolmogorov's formula shows that the increase in dimension-related degrees of freedom does not increase the functional complexity of continuous functions, an interesting outcome in itself, by implying that the 'worst' continuous functions of one variable are as 'bad' as the 'worst' continuous functions of n variables. A word of caution should be inserted here: We are speaking of *continuity* when we really mean uniform continuity, a concept that is essential in deriving Kolmogorov's superpositions. The danger of confusion is minimal here since all domains of definition under consideration are compact. There are results, however, that pertain to continuous functions that are not necessarily uniformly continuous. Doss (1977) has obtained a result in this direction using a theorem of Ostrand (1965) that proves Kolmogorov's theorem for compact metric spaces of finite covering dimension. He showed that continuous functions defined on an open cube or an open ball or all of n-dimensional Euclidean space R^n can be represented with *4n* superpositions of a somewhat different form, except that the fixed functions are functions of n variables, not expressible in terms of continuous functions of fewer variables. This theorem therefore lacks the basic feature of Theorem 1.

An important distinction must be drawn between the operations of representation (exact computation) and approximation: as a rule, approximations do not preserve the format of the approximating functions in the limit, whereas Kolmogorov's superpositions do. Depending on the goal, the researcher must therefore decide on the choice of computational techniques. We illustrate this point with an example, again using the function

$$f(x_1, x_2) = x_1 x_2 :$$

it can be obtained as a uniform limit:

$$x_1 x_2 = \lim_{k \to \infty} exp\left[ln\left(x_1 + \tfrac{1}{k}\right) + ln\left(x_2 + \tfrac{1}{k}\right)\right],$$

$$(x_1, x_2) \in E^2 .$$

The approximating functions are of the form

$$g\left(a_k\left(x_1\right) + b_k\left(x_2\right)\right)$$

$$a_k = ln\left(x_1 + \tfrac{1}{k}\right),$$

$$b_k = ln\left(x_2 + \tfrac{1}{k}\right),$$

and $g = \exp c$, each strictly monotonic increasing, and the limit function f is strictly monotonic in each variable, except on the coordinate axes, yet it is not expressible in the form:

$$g\left(a\left(x_1\right) + b\left(x_2\right)\right).$$

The appeal of Equation 1 as a computational tool is natural because of its structural simplicity and its two-stage algorithm consisting of independent computation of fixed functions $t^q = \Sigma_p \psi_p^q$ followed by the computation $g^q(t^q)$ of a target function f. Continuity is an analogue concept, and Equation 1 was conceived and constructed in this context, and so it remains as a mathematical object; as a contemporary computational algorithm, however, considerations shift to the digital domain. This shift of Kolmogorov's superpositions was preceded by changes in their own representation, especially that of the fixed inner functions ψ_p^q. The first change in Equation 1 was made by Lorentz (1962), who observed that the $2n+1$ functions g^q that compute f could be replaced by a single function g, a consequence of an appropriate choice of

the ranges of the functions $\Sigma_p \psi_p^q$. Following this, the inner functions were replaced by translates of a single (monotonic increasing) continuous function ψ and rationally-independent constants λ_p (Sprecher, 1965):

$$h^q = \sum_{p=0}^{n} \lambda_p \psi(x_p + q a_n), \tag{2}$$

replacing Equation 1 with the formula

$$f(x_1, ..., x_n) = \sum_{q=0}^{2n} g \circ \sum_{p=0}^{n} \lambda_p \psi(x_p + q a_n) + b^q. \tag{3}$$

where a_n and b^q are certain constants. The constants λ_p are rationally independent if

$$c_0 \lambda_0 + c_1 \lambda_1 + ... + c_n \lambda_n \neq 0$$

for any set of positive rational numbers $c_0, c_1, ..., c_n$.

We mention in passing that the function ψ in (2), and the inner functions in Kolmogorov's original formulation, depend on n, but this dependence can be eliminated without basically altering their construction (Sprecher, 1972). A first attempt at numerical algorithms (Sprecher, 1996; 1997) enabled a level of implementation, but significant computational difficulties remained. A computational error in these papers, in the definition of the approximating functions ψ_k converging to ψ resulted in discontinuous functions. This error, regretfully propagated in Sprecher (1997; 2002), was corrected by Köppen (2002) and Braun (2009) with transparency of construction and great detail that aids in their computation; Köppen and Yoshida also made important progress toward significant applications (Köppen & Yoshida, 2005) as did Braun (2009) and Leni (2011); their papers, in addition, offer valuable analyses and insights.

The first to recognize the potential of Kolmogorov superpositions as a computational device was Robert Hecht-Nielsen, by interpreting Equation 3 as a feedforward neural network with a three-layer topology having an input layer, a middle, hidden layer corresponding to the fixed inner functions (2), and an output layer in which a target function f is computed (Hecht-Nielsen, 1987, 1990). The limitations that the pathology of the functions ψ_p^q, also shared by the single function ψ, and the non-smoothness that effects the computation of the functions h^q imposed on implementation, was already recognized by Hecht-Nielsen. The practical limitations of his neural network application were called into question (Girosi & Poggio, 1989), but in a very perceptive analysis of the anatomy of Kolmogorov's superpositions, Kurková (1991) showed the validity of Hecht-Nielsen's approach by introducing a modified algorithm to compute approximations. Other research, such as Nakamura, Mines, and Kreinovich (1993) establish procedures for achieving such approximations by superpositions with predetermined accuracy. A recent innovative computable algorithm with superposition was introduced by Igelnik and Parikh (2003), who applied splines to the functions ψ_p^q, yielding superior computability and results in applications, such as image compression, when compared to an application of the standard superposition model (Leni, Fougerolle & Truchetet, 2008). In this approach, however, the functions ψ_p^q are no longer monotonic, and the superposition format is not preserved in the limit. This is an instant of trading the method of representation with approximation; Braun (2009) also explored approximation models.

THE ANATOMY OF DIMENSION REDUCTION

As noted, the inherent pathology of nomographic functions gets in the way of efficient computations. A review of the literature since the 1970s shows numerous approaches and attempts of dealing with this pathology in implementing Kolmogorov's superpositions, and if we seek to use representation algorithms in an efficient computational way, the dimension-reducing algorithm of the fixed functions must be changed. Questions about characterizations of these functions from a mathematical perspective have been raised long before Hecht-Nielsen's linking of superposition with computer networks, but the answers sought then were different from those we are seeking now, in the context of computational algorithms. We start with a generalized phrasing of Kolmogorov's Theorem 1 (Sprecher, 1972):

Theorem 2

1. For a given integer $n \geq 2$, let $\{ S_{kr}^0, S_{kr}^1, ..., S_{kr}^{2n} \}$ be families of closed cubes with $\text{diameter}(S_{kr}^q) \to 0$ as $k \to \infty$ and such that

   a. $S_{kr}^q \cap S_{kt}^q = \varnothing$ when $r \neq t$ for each q and k;

   b. Every point of E^n belongs to at least $n+1$ cubes S_{kr}^q for each value of k.

2. Let $\Psi^q : E^n \to E$ be continuous functions with the property:

$$\Psi^q(S_{kr}^q) \cap \Psi^q(S_{kt}^q) = \varnothing$$

for all values of k when $r \neq t$.

Then every continuous function $f : E^n \to R$ has a representation

$$f(x_1, ..., x_n) = \sum_{q=0}^{2n} g^q \left[\Psi^q(x_1, ..., x_n) \right] \qquad (4)$$

with continuous functions g^q.

This phrasing is closer to Kolmogorov's original phrasing, and it includes conditions on the coverings that are not stated in the statement of Theorem 1. The continuous fixed functions

$\Psi^q(x_1,...,x_n)$ must satisfy condition (B), but no specific format is imposed on them, leaving their structure undetermined. This opens the formula to wider choices of inner functions, and this holds the key to constructing alternative algorithms. Recall that Equation 1 resulted from solving a mathematical problem that required reducing the number of variables, but from the point of view of modern computational algorithms, that goal in itself no longer holds center stage, especially in view of the high cost in using nomographic functions. The search for alternative algorithms now brings us to this basic question:

What is the underlying mechanism of dimension-reduction in Kolmogorov's formula, and how can it be achieved with functions other than the nomographic functions of Kolmogorov?

Before attempting to answer this question, we digress to look into an unstated property of the aggregate of the inner functions that is basic in validating Kolmogorov's superpositions. Returning to the inner functions

$$h^q = \Psi^q(x_1,...,x_n)$$

in any version of Kolmogorov's theorem, they each map continuously the unit cube E^n onto the interval E in a special way, by mapping almost all points of the cube one-one onto points of the range interval; i.e., they map all points one-one except for a set of (Lebesgue) measure zero. This fundamental feature of Kolmogorov's constructions merits further remarks:

Consider a function $\Psi = \Psi^q$. A *level set* of $\Psi(x_1,...,x_n)$ is the inverse image of a point t in its range:

$$\Psi^{-1}(t) = \left\{(x_1,...,x_n) \in E^n = \Psi(x_1,...,x_n) = t\right\}$$

Generally, the equation

$$\Psi(x_1,...,x_n) = t$$

has infinitely many solutions for a given value of t, and this implies that there are points

$$(x_1,...,x_n) \neq (x'_1,...,x'_n)$$

at which

$$\Psi(x_1,...,x_n) = \Psi(x'_1,...,x'_n),$$

implying that a single continuous function cannot separate all points of its domain: Invariably there will be points at which the function has the same image. This, of course, implies that also

$$g \circ \Psi(x_1,...,x_n) = g \circ \Psi(x'_1,...,x'_n)$$

at these points for any function g, but for any two such points there is a continuous function f such that

$$f(x_1,...,x_n) \neq f(x'_1,...,x'_n).$$

This implies in turn that to compute an arbitrary continuous function f with Kolmogorov-type superpositions with f-independent fixed functions, there must be functions Ψ^q among the functions

$$\Psi^0, \Psi^1, \Psi^2,..., \Psi^{2n}$$

for which

$$\Psi^q(x_1,...,x_n) \neq \Psi^q(x'_1,...,x'_n):$$

As a consequence of Lebesgue's covering theorem there must be $n+1$ values of q for which this is true. Kolmogorov's constructions satisfy this requirement, and he has shown that the property of mapping almost all points of E^n one-one into the points of E is sufficient to establish his superpositions. I note in passing that

$\Psi(\Psi^{-1})$ is always meaningful as the identity mapping of $\Psi(E^n) = E$ onto itself, but the mapping $\Psi^{-1}(\Psi)$ is not defined as a pointwise mapping of E^n into E^n.

The inevitable conclusion is that any iterative construction of superpositions that is based on coverings of the domain E^n with pairwise disjoint cubes of diminishing diameters is subject to Lebesgue's Covering Theorem, and must possess this point separating property. This property contributes to the pathology of the fixed inner functions and it is further exacerbated, as already noted for the case f two variables, by the order in which the images of the cubes are distributed by the functions Ψ^q on the line.

We are now in a position to look at the mechanism of the anatomy of dimension reduction underlying Kolmogorov's superpositions, and we return to Theorem 1. Kolmogorov's original formulation includes a construction of systems of cubes $\{ S_{kr}^q \}$ satisfying Property (B) above, and to analyze the mechanism whereby the inner functions

$$h^q(x_1, ..., x_n) = \Sigma_p \psi_p^q(x_p)$$

in Equation 1 enable the theorem, we assume that these functions and systems of cubes are given, and for fixed q and given k we examine the image intervals,

$$h^q(S_{kr}^q) = \left\{ t \in S_{kr}^q : \Psi(x_1, ..., x_n) = t \right\},$$

of a family of cubes $\{ S_{kr}^q \}$. A sequence of pairwise disjoint cubes

$$S_{kr_1}^q, S_{kr_2}^q, S_{kr_3}^q, ...$$

that cover the unit cube E^n except for narrow gaps between them, is mapped onto a sequence of pairwise disjoint intervals on the real line with a linear order dictated by the function h^q. This order can be simply computed by the lower left endpoint of the image intervals $h^q(S_{kr}^q)$, and we write symbolically

$$h^q(S_{kr_{k1}}^q) < h^q(S_{kr_{k2}}^q) < h^q(S_{kr_{k3}}^q) < ...$$

Each cube can be mapped continuously onto its main diagonal D_{kr}^q in a variety of ways, and these diagonals can be connected in the order of their images $h^q(S_{kr}^q)$ to form a continuous curve Γ_k^q with polygonal sections that lies in a closed cube containing E^n and that does not intersect itself; that is, it does not have loops. For $k = 1, 2, 3, ...$ these are approximating curves to a space-filling curve Γ^q:

$$\lim_{k \to \infty} \Gamma_k^q = \Gamma^q$$

(Sprecher, 2002). We short-circuit the mathematical arguments that underlay the definition and construction of space filling curves, and simply state:

Γ is a space-filling curve if it is the graph of a continuous image of an injective mapping

$$\Gamma : E \to E^n$$

(Sagan, 1994). It should be observed that continuous mappings

$$\Gamma : E \to E^n$$

and

$$\Psi : E^n \to E$$

are not inverses of each other. From a computational perspective, the mathematical theory behind space-filling curves as such plays no direct role in actual computations, especially since computations are limited to iterations only. Their existence as a limit is important, because they shape the superpositions, and the linear order of chains of cubes

$$S^q_{kr_1}, S^q_{kr_2}, S^q_{kr_3}, ...$$

that they determine through the approximating curves at every stage is of central importance. The function ψ can be computed with a simple iteration, but not so the sum (3): this computation involves combinatorial-type considerations and difficult algebraic number theory estimates. The imposed linear order on the sampling of functional values $g^q \circ \Sigma_p \psi^q_p$ is the Achilles heel of Kolmogorov's superpositions, as we already mentioned. The connection between this *a priori* ordering and space-filling curves is insightfully analyzed in (Braun, 2009) through the approximating curves: He points out that the limiting curve is outside the range of computational considerations, though its role in shaping computations is significant.

Like the discovery of black holes in astrophysics, the discovery of space-filling curves was the consequence of a theory that deals with something else: since they are a crucial backdrop to Kolmogorov's superpositions, we include some basic information about them. In the second half of the 19th century, as a result of working on the problem of uniqueness of Fourier (trigonometric) series, Georg Cantor was led to study infinite sets, compare and classify them in new ways. Cantor devised schemes for showing when elements of two infinite sets can be put in a one-one relationship, and he demonstrated that the unit interval E can be put in one-one relationship with the Cartesian product cube

$$E^n = E \times E \times ... \times E$$

for any n. This implies the existence of a one-one (bijective) relationship $E \leftrightarrow E^n$ between the points $t \in E$ and the points

$$(x_1, ..., x_n) \in E^n,$$

a somewhat startling and counter-intuitive result. That a bijective one-one mapping between the interval and a cube must necessarily be discontinuous was quickly proved by Netto (Sagan, 1994), and this led to the question: If the one-one condition of a bijective mapping $E \leftrightarrow E^n$ is replaced with the less stringent *injective* condition $E \rightarrow E^n$, that does not require a one-one relation, is there a continuous mapping $\Gamma : E \rightarrow E^n$ of the interval onto the cube? This was answered in the affirmative by Peano, who was first to produce such a curve in 1890, whose graphs are called space-filling curves. A considerable variety of space-filling curves have since been discovered, and Hilbert himself produced one of the more intuitive such curves (Sagan, 1994). A comprehensive treatment of space-filling curves can be found in Sagan's book.

A NEW ALGORITHM

Recall that, for given values q and k, the approximating curves Γ^q_k determine the linear order in which the images of cubes are arranged on the line:

$$h^q(S^q_{kr_{k1}}) < h^q(S^q_{kr_{k2}}) < h^q(S^q_{kr_{k3}}) < ...,$$

and as importantly, the order in which function values that compute a target function f are sampled:

$$g^q \circ h^q(S^q_{kr_{k1}}) < g^q \circ h^q(S^q_{kr_{k2}}) < g^q \circ h^q(S^q_{kr_{k3}}) < ... :$$

To change the graph

$$t^q = g^q \circ h^q(x_1, ..., x_n)$$

and improve computability, we must be able to determine this ordering. This means that alternative space-filling curves must be found, and this, in turn, would reverse the construction of the middle layer algorithm: first defining the order of the chains of cubes for each q and k, and then constructing functions that satisfy Condition (B). The proposed algorithm is described schematically in Figure 2.

This figure is read as follows:

- Existing Algorithm
  - A priori functions ψ^q are given
  - Image intervals $\psi^q(S_{kr_j}^q)$ of cubes $\{S_k^q\}$ are ordered by ψ^q
  - Linear order of cubes $S_{kr_j}^q$ follows
- New Algorithm
  - A priori linear order of cubes $S_{kr_j}^q$ is given
  - The cubes $S_{kr_j}^q$ determine image intervals $\psi^q(S_{kr_j}^q)$
  - Functions ψ^q are defined

Each algorithm now determines sampling of functional valued $f(S_{kr_j}^q)$ that give the output layer values:

$$g^q \circ \psi_p^q(S_{kr_j}^q)$$

To define and implement a new algorithm and a new function ψ in two variables, we construct in tandem a space-filling curve and a related function using polygonal curves Γ_k:

$$\Gamma_k \to \psi_k(x_1,...,x_n) \to \psi(x_1,...,x_n)$$

and simultaneously, $\Gamma_k \to \Gamma$. We do this here with a numerical construction of the first four approximating curves, and we then infer the kth polygonal approximating curve for arbitrary k with an iteration. To this end, let

$$d_{pk} = \sum_{r=1}^{k} \frac{i_{pr}}{10^r},$$

$$i_{p1} = 01,,2,...,10,$$

$$i_{pr} = 01,,2,...,9$$

for $r > 1$, and $p=1,2$, and consider systems of square tiles for values

$$q = 0,1,,2,3,4$$

and $k=1,2,3,...$:

$$S_k^q(d_{1k},d_{2k}) = \left[d_{1k} - \frac{q}{9 \cdot 10}, d_{1k} + \frac{8}{9 \cdot 10^k} - \frac{q}{9 \cdot 10}\right]$$
$$\times \left[d_{2k} - \frac{q}{9 \cdot 10}, d_{2k} + \frac{8}{9 \cdot 10^k} - \frac{q}{9 \cdot 10}\right]$$
(5)

(see Figure 3). Observe that each family of tiles is translated along a diagonal so that the family $\{S_k^{q+1}\}$ covers as much as possible the gaps of the

Figure 2. Schematic comparison of algorithms

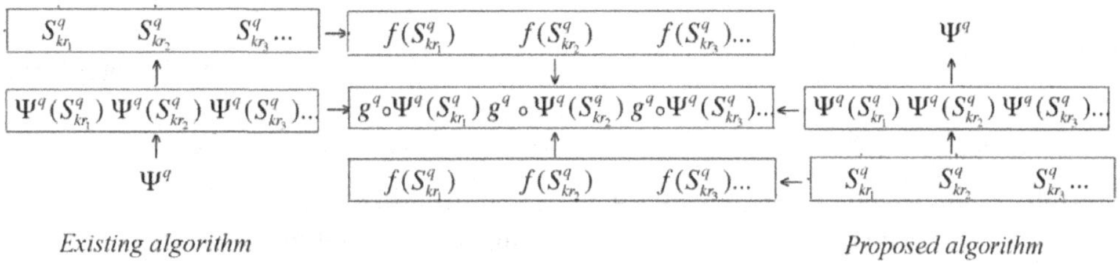

Existing algorithm   *Proposed algorithm*

Figure 3. Systems of tiles $S_k^q(d_{1k}, d_{2k})$

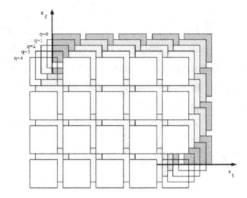

family $\{S_k^q\}$, and the range of the values is extended to include $i_{p1} = 10$ to ensure that each of the systems $\{S_k^q\}$ covers the unit square for each value of k and all values of q, except for gaps of width $\frac{1}{9 \cdot 10^k}$ separating them. The tiles have sides $\frac{8}{9 \cdot 10^k}$ and are pairwise disjoint:

$$S_k^q(d_{1k}, d_{2k}) \cap S_k^q(d'_{1k}, d'_{2k}) = \varnothing$$

when

$$|d_{1k} - d'_{1k}| + |d_{2k} - d'_{2k}| = 0;$$

They have the following nested property:

$$S_{k+1}^q(d_{1k+1}, d_{2k+1}) \subset S_k^q(d_{1k}, d_{2k})$$

when

$$i_{1,k+1}, i_{2,k+1} = 0, 1, 2, ..., 8;$$

$$S_{k+1}^q(d_{1k+1}, d_{2k+1}) \cap S_k^q(d_{1k}, d_{2k}) = \varnothing$$

when $i_{1,k+1} = 9$ or $i_{2,k+1} = 9$.

These specific systems of tiles have been used in Sprecher (2002) and elsewhere.

With these tiles, the superposition theorem can be paraphrased as follows for functions of two variables:

Theorem 3

Let

$$\psi : E^2 \to E$$

be a continuous function with the property

$$\psi(S_k^0(d_{1k}, d_{2k})) \cap \psi(S_k^0(d'_{1k}, d'_{2k})) = \varnothing$$

when

$$|d_{1k} - d'_{1k}| + |d_{2k} - d'_{2k}| = 0.$$

Then every continuous function

$$f : E^2 \to R$$

has a representation

$$f(x_1, x_2) = \sum_{q=0}^{4} g^q \circ \psi(x_1 + \tfrac{q}{9 \cdot 10}, x_2 + \tfrac{q}{9 \cdot 10}) \qquad (6)$$

with continuous functions g^q.

Any of the existing proofs of Kolmogorov's theorem can be readily adapted to prove this version of the theorem. It suffices to compute ψ for the value $q = 0$, setting for the purpose

$$S_k^0(d_{1,k}, d_{2,k}) = S_k(d_{1k}, d_{2k}),$$

and for this we follow the strategy outlined in Figure 2:

Constructing a space-filling curve to define the linear order each family of tiles

$$S_k(d_{1,r_{1,k}}, d_{2,r_{1,k}}), S_k(d_{1,r_{2,k}}, d_{2,r_{2,k}}), S_k(d_{1,r_{3,k}}, d_{2,r_{3,k}}), \ldots$$

for $k = 1, 2, 3, \ldots$ while preserving their nested properties;

Using the ordered tiles to define piecewise mappings

$$\psi_k(S_k(d_{1,r_{1,k}}, d_{2,r_{1,k}})) = I_{kr_1}$$
$$\psi_k(S_k(d_{1,r_{2,k}}, d_{2,r_{2,k}})) = I_{kr_2}$$
$$\psi_k(S_k(d_{1,r_{3,k}}, d_{2,r_{3,k}})) = I_{kr_3}$$

with pairwise disjoint intervals having the nested properties of the tiles $S_k(d_{1k}, d_{2k})$, and extended to continuous mappings converging to ψ.

We state at this point that not every ordering scheme of systems of tiles will lead to a convergent sequence of continuous function ψ_k, and return to this later in this chapter.

For the purpose of the numerical constructions to follow, we introduce the notation

$$S_k(d_{1,k}, d_{2,k}) = S_k(n_1, \ldots, n_k)$$

with numbers n_r to be specified below, and corresponding to the families of tiles we set
$e_k = \sum_{r=1}^{k} \dfrac{n_r}{110^r}$ and define the intervals

$$I_k(n_1, \ldots, n_k) = \left[e_k, e_k + \frac{80}{109 \cdot 110^k} \right] \tag{7}$$

They have length

$$\left| I_k(n_1, \ldots, n_k) \right| = \frac{80}{109 \cdot 110^k}$$

and are separated by gaps of length $\frac{29}{109 \cdot 110^k}$, and are pairwise disjoint; they have nested properties to match those of the tiles $S_k(n_1, \ldots, n_k)$:

$$I_{k+1}(n_1, \ldots, n_{k+1}) \subset I_k(n_1, \ldots, n_k)$$

when

$$n_{k+1} = 0, 1, \ldots, 80,$$

$$I_{k+1}(n_1, \ldots, n_{k+1}) \cap I_k(n_1, \ldots, n_k) = \varnothing$$

when $n_{k+1} > 80$.

The numbers used here are chosen to facilitate subsequent computations. The geometric approach that we shall follow will make the configuration of iterations more transparent as we implement the new algorithm.

An alternative to Kolmogorov's algorithm is started with the construction of a space-filling curve Γ, one choice of many, through approximating polygonal curves $\Gamma_k \to \Gamma$. This is done through iteratively ordering of sequences of tiles:

$$S_k(n_1, \ldots, n_k)$$

for $k = 1, 2, 3, \ldots$ that are also used to define approximating mappings

$$\psi_k(x_1, \ldots, x_n) \to \psi(x_1, \ldots, x_n)$$

These functions are going to be defined iteratively piecewise:

$$\psi_k(x_1, x_2) \in I_k(n_1 \ldots n_k)$$

when

$$(x_1, x_2) \in S_k(n_1 \ldots n_k),$$

and being defined on pairwise disjoint compact sets, they are readily extended in a variety of ways to a continuous function

$$\psi_k : U^2 \to V,$$

where

$$U^2 = [0, 1 + \tfrac{8}{9 \cdot 10}]^2$$

and

$$V = [0, 1 + \tfrac{1}{11} + \tfrac{8}{109 \cdot 11}],$$

without exceeding

$$\max_{(x_1, x_2) \in S_k(n_k)} | \psi_k(x_1, x_2)) | .$$

First Approximation

The piecewise function

$$\psi_1(x_1, x_2) \in I_1(n_1)$$

when

$$(x_1, x_2) \in S_1(n_1)$$

is defined for the sequence of tiles

$$S_1(n_1) = S_1\left(\frac{i_{1,1}}{10}, \frac{i_{1,2}}{10}\right),$$

$$n_1 = 0, 1, 2, ..., 120,$$

ordered by the following scheme in Box 1.

This order of tiles follows the switchback path shown in Box 3, where also an expanded representation of $S_1(n_1)$ is given. For example,

$$S_1(95) = S_1(\tfrac{i_{1,95}}{10}, \tfrac{i_{2,95}}{10}) = S_1(\tfrac{8}{10}, \tfrac{7}{10}),$$

and the corresponding interval is

$$I_1(95) = [\tfrac{95}{110}, \tfrac{95}{110}, + \tfrac{80}{109 \cdot 110}]$$

Accordingly, as shown in Box 2.

We recall that when mapping each tile $S_1(n_1)$ onto its main diagonal, these diagonals can be connected to form a continuous curve without loops within the area defined by the tiles to give the first approximation to a space-filling curve.

Intermediate Constructions

The scheme of identifying tiles:

$$S_k(d_{1,r_j}, d_{2,r_j})$$

with single numbers as in Box 3 is not practical for increasing k, and we resort to a technique of numbering tiles by groupings, ranging in size from 81 to 110 tiles each. For $k > 1$, we devise seven basic patterns, specified as Configurations $C_r^p(n_r)$, $p=1,2,...,7$ (see Box 4). These configu-

Box 1.

$$n_1 \leftrightarrow (i_{1,1}, i_{2,1}) \leftrightarrow \begin{cases} 11i_{1,1} + i_{2,1} & i_{1,1} = 0, 2, 4, ..., 10 \\ 11i_{1,1} - i_{2,1} + 10, & i_{1,1} = 1, 3, ..., 9 \end{cases} \quad i_{2,1} = 0, 1, 2, ..., 10,$$

giving

$$S_1(n_1) = S_1\left(\frac{i_{1,1}}{10}, \frac{i_{1,2}}{10}\right) \leftrightarrow \begin{cases} \left[\left[\dfrac{11i_{1,1} + i_{2,1}}{110}, \dfrac{11i_{1,1} + i_{2,1}}{110} + \dfrac{80}{109 \cdot 110}\right], & i_{1,1} = 0, 2, 4, ..., 10 \\ \left[\left[\dfrac{11i_{1,1} - i_{2,1} + 10}{110}, \dfrac{11i_{1,1} - i_{2,1} + 20}{110} + \dfrac{80}{109 \cdot 110}\right], & i_{1,1} = 1, 3, ..., 9 \end{cases} \quad , i_{2,1} = 0, 1, 2, ..., 10$$

Box 2.

$$
\psi_1\left(\frac{i_{1,1}}{10},\frac{i_{1,2}}{10}\right)=
\begin{cases}
\dfrac{11i_{1,1}+i_{2,1}}{110} & i_{1,1}=0,2,4,...,10 \\[2mm]
\dfrac{11i_{1,1}-i_{2,1}+10}{110}, & i_{1,1}=1,3,...,9
\end{cases}
\qquad i_{2,1}=0,1,2,...,10
$$

and

$$
\psi_1:S_1\left(\frac{i_{1,1}}{10},\frac{i_{1,2}}{10}\right)\rightarrow
\begin{cases}
\left[\dfrac{11i_{1,1}+i_{2,1}}{110},\dfrac{11i_{1,1}+i_{2,1}}{110}+\dfrac{80}{109\cdot110}\right], & i_{1,1}=0,2,4,...,10 \\[3mm]
\left[\dfrac{11i_{1,1}-i_{2,1}+10}{110},\dfrac{11i_{1,1}-i_{2,1}+20}{110}+\dfrac{80}{109\cdot110}\right], & i_{1,1}=1,3,...,9
\end{cases}
\quad ,i_{2,1}=0,1,2,...,10
$$

Box 3. Sequencing tiles $S_1(n_1)$ and the mapping $\psi_1:S_1(n_1)\rightarrow I_1(n_1)$

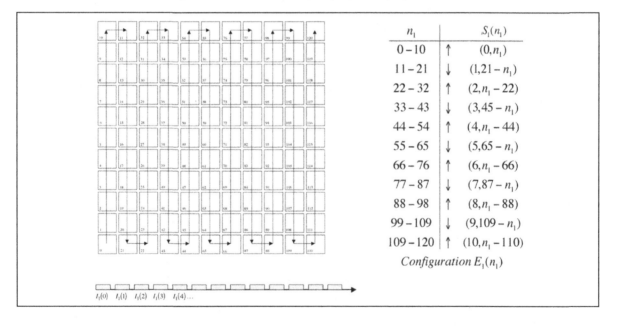

n_1		$S_1(n_1)$
$0-10$	↑	$(0,n_1)$
$11-21$	↓	$(1,21-n_1)$
$22-32$	↑	$(2,n_1-22)$
$33-43$	↓	$(3,45-n_1)$
$44-54$	↑	$(4,n_1-44)$
$55-65$	↓	$(5,65-n_1)$
$66-76$	↑	$(6,n_1-66)$
$77-87$	↓	$(7,87-n_1)$
$88-98$	↑	$(8,n_1-88)$
$99-109$	↓	$(9,109-n_1)$
$109-120$	↑	$(10,n_1-110)$

Configuration $E_1(n_1)$

$I_1(0)\quad I_1(1)\quad I_1(2)\quad I_1(3)\quad I_1(4)\dots$

rations will be used geometrically like pieces of a jigsaw puzzle to define numerical ordering of tiles: note that Configuration $C_r^1(n_r)$ is common to the other six configurations, and that their organization is invariant under changes of r. These will be used iteratively to device higher order sets of configurations for increasing k, as explained below.

Corresponding to these configurations, we define three configurations for the intervals (6) for values $k>1$ (Figure 4):

$$
D_k^1(n_1,...,n_k)=\{I_k(n_1,...,n_k):
$$
$$
n_k=0,1,...,80\}
$$

$$
D_k^2(n_1,...,n_k)
$$
$$
=\begin{cases}I_k(n_1,...,n_k): \\ n_k=0,1,...,80,83,96,89,...,107\end{cases}
$$

$$
D_k^3(n_1,...,n_k)=\{I_k(n_1,...,n_k):
$$
$$
n_k=0,1,...,80,81,82,83,...,109\}
$$

Box 4. Configurations $C_r^p(n_r)$ $p = 1, 2, ..., 7$

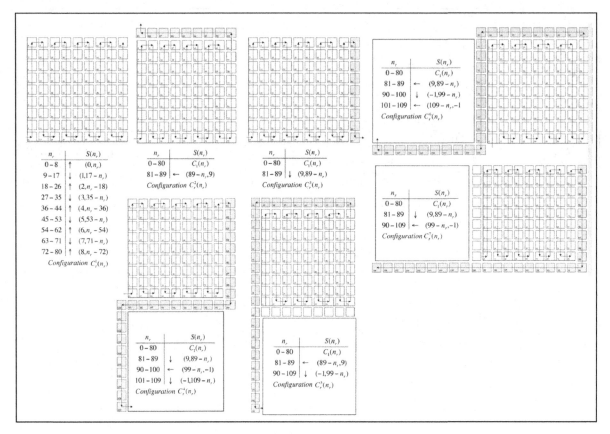

Figure 4. Configurations $D_r^p(n_r)$

$$D_r^2(n_r) = \{I_r(n_r) : n_r = 0, 1, ..., 80, 83, 86, 89, ..., 107\}$$

n_r: 0 1 2 ...... 79 80 83 86 89 107

$$D_r^1(n_r) = \{I_r(n_r) : n_r = 0, 1, ..., 80\}$$

$$D_r^1(n_r + 1)$$

$$D_r^3(n_r) = \{I_r(n_r) : n_r = 0, 1, ..., 80, 81\ 82\ ..., 109\}$$

n_r: 0 1 2 79 80 81 82 83 109

$$D_r^1(n_r + 1)$$

Second Approximation

The piecewise mapping,

$$\psi_2(x_1, x_2) \in I_2(n_1 n_2)$$

when

$$(x_1, x_2) \in S_2(n_1 n_2),$$

is defined in $E(n_1 n_2)$ with a direct application of the four Configurations $C_2^p(n_2)$, $p=1,2,3,4$:

$$\psi_2 : C_2^p(n_2) \rightarrow \begin{cases} D_2^1(n_2), \; p = 1 \\ D_2^2(n_2), \; p = 2,3 \\ D_2^3(n_2), \; p = 4 \end{cases}$$

(see Box 5). The sequence of tiles now also involves rows and columns in the gaps separating the tiles $S_1(n_1)$; the first two columns of $E(n_1 n_2)$ define the sequencing of tiles $S_2(n_1 n_2)$, and the third column defined the piecewise mapping. The pattern in which the four configurations fit to form the sequence is illustrated geometrically in the accompanying graphical illustration in Box 5.

Box 5. Sequencing tiles $S_2(n_1 n_2)$ and the mapping $\psi_2 : S_2(n_1 n_2) \rightarrow S_2(n_1 n_2)$

n_1		$S_2(n_1 n_2)$	$I_2(n_1 n_2)$
0 – 9	↑	$C_2^2(n_2)$	$D_2^2(n_2)$
10		$C_2^3(n_2)$	$D_2(n_2)$
11 – 20	↓	$C_2^4(n_2)$	$D_2^3(n_2)$
21		$C_2^3(n_2)$	$D_2(n_2)$
22 – 31	↑	$C_2^2(n_2)$	$D_2^2(n_2)$
32		$C_2^3(n_2)$	$D_2^2(n_2)$
33 – 42	↓	$C_2^4(n_2)$	$D_2^3(n_2)$
43		$C_2^3(n_2)$	$D_2^2(n_2)$
44 – 53	↑	$C_2^2(n_2)$	$D_2^2(n_2)$
54		$C_2^3(n_2)$	$D_2^2(n_2)$
55 – 64	↓	$C_2^4(n_2)$	$D_2^3(n_2)$
65		$C_2^3(n_2)$	$D_2^2(n_2)$
66 – 75	↑	$C_2^2(n_2)$	$D_2^2(n_2)$
76		$C_2^3(n_2)$	$D_2^2(n_2)$
77 – 86	↓	$C_2^4(n_2)$	$D_2^3(n_2)$
87		$C_2^3(n_2)$	$D_2^2(n_2)$
88 – 97	↑	$C_2^2(n_2)$	$D_2^2(n_2)$
98		$C_2^3(n_2)$	$D_2^2(n_2)$
99 – 108	↓	$C_2^4(n_2)$	$D_2^3(n_2)$
109		$C_2^3(n_2)$	$D_2^2(n_2)$
110 – 119	↑	$C_2^2(n_2)$	$D_2^2(n_2)$
120		$C_2^1(n_2)$	$D_2^1(n_2)$

Configuration $E_2(n_1, n_2)$

An examination of $E_2(n_1 n_2)$ shows that for the technique that uses configurations $C_2^p(n_2)$ as parts of a jigsaw puzzle, $n_1 \leftrightarrow (i_{1,1}, i_{2,1})$ has to be refined beyond the first approximation (as shown in Box 6).

For computational purposes, this representation obscures the rhythmic patterns of the constructions, and the compact representation $E_2(n_1 n_2)$ is preferable.

Third Approximation

The strategy of implementation for values $k > 2$ is summarized schematically in Figure 5. Following this blueprint, we begin by contracting and re-labeling the configurations from $k = 2$ to $k = 3$. Whereas the gaps separating the tiles $S_1(n_1)$ contain in the previous case only single rows and columns of tiles $S_2(n_1 n_2)$, now gaps contain in addition rows and columns of tiles $S_3(n_1 n_2 n_3)$. To account for this, the new set of configurations $C_3^p(n_2 n_3)$, $p = 1, \ldots, 7$, is required. The ordering algorithm is given in Box 7. Note that $C_3^1(n_2, n_3)$ gives the configuration of tiles $S_3(n_1 n_2 n_3)$ within a single tile $S_1(n_1)$, and configurations:

$$C_3^2(n_2, n_3), C_3^3(n_2, n_3), C_3^4(n_2, n_3)$$

are configurations of tiles $S_2(n_1 n_2)$ and $S_3(n_1 n_2 n_3)$ in the gaps separating tiles $S_1(n_1)$. Configuration $E(n_1 n_2 n_3)$ gives the sequencing of tiles $S_3(n_1 n_2 n_3)$ in the first two columns, and this is the basis for the third approximation of the space-filling curve and the piecewise mapping ψ_3 that follows. It may be worth noticing that configuration $C_{r+1}^1(n_{r+1})$ for $r > 1$ can be obtained from $E(n_1 \ldots n_r)$ by changing it to $E(n_2 \ldots n_{r+1})$ and

Box 6.

$$n_1 \leftrightarrow (i_{1,1}, i_{2,1}) \leftrightarrow \begin{cases} 11i_{1,1} + i_{2,1}, & i_{1,1} = 0, 2, 4 \ldots, 10, \quad i_{2,1} = 0, 1, 2, \ldots, 9 \\ 11i_{1,1} + i_{2,1}, & \begin{cases} i_{1,1} = 1, 3, 5 \ldots, 9, & i_{2,1} = 0 \\ i_{1,1} = 0, 2, 4 \ldots, 8 & i_{2,1} = 10 \end{cases} \\ 11i_{1,1} + i_{2,1}, & i_{1,1} = 1, 3, 5, \ldots, 9 \quad i_{2,1} = 0, 1, 2, \ldots, 9 \\ 11i_{1,1} + i_{2,1}, & i_{1,1} = 10 \quad i_{2,1} = 10 \end{cases}$$

where to each branch the appropriate configurations $C_2^p(n_2)$ must be worked in. In the case $C_2^2(n_2)$, for example, in constructing

$$\psi_2\left(\frac{i_{1,1}}{10} + \frac{i_{2,1}}{10^2}, \frac{i_{1,2}}{10} + \frac{i_{2,2}}{10^2}\right),$$

$$\begin{cases} \dfrac{9i_{1,2} + i_{2,2}}{110^2}, & i_{1,2} = 0, 2, 4, 6, 8, \\ \dfrac{9i_{1,2} + (8 - i_{2,2})}{110^2}, & i_{1,2} = 1, 3, 5, 7, \, i_{22} = 0, 1, 2 \ldots, 8 \\ \dfrac{9i_{1,2} + 3(9 - i_{2,2}) - 1}{110^2}, & i_{1,2} = 9, \end{cases}$$

follows every branch

$$11i_{1,1} + i_{2,1}, \quad i_{1,1} = 0, 2, 4 \ldots, 10,$$

$$i_{2,1} = 0, 1, 2, \ldots, 9$$

Figure 5. Strategy of implementation

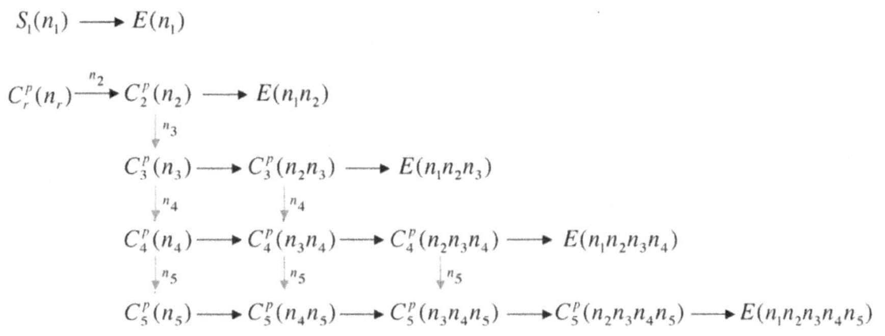

$$S_1(n_1) \longrightarrow E(n_1)$$

$$C_r^p(n_r) \xrightarrow{\;n_2\;} C_2^p(n_2) \longrightarrow E(n_1 n_2)$$

$$\downarrow{\scriptstyle n_3}$$

$$C_3^p(n_3) \longrightarrow C_3^p(n_2 n_3) \longrightarrow E(n_1 n_2 n_3)$$

$$\downarrow{\scriptstyle n_4} \qquad\qquad \downarrow{\scriptstyle n_4}$$

$$C_4^p(n_4) \longrightarrow C_4^p(n_3 n_4) \longrightarrow C_4^p(n_2 n_3 n_4) \longrightarrow E(n_1 n_2 n_3 n_4)$$

$$\downarrow{\scriptstyle n_5} \qquad\quad \downarrow{\scriptstyle n_5} \qquad\qquad \downarrow{\scriptstyle n_5}$$

$$C_5^p(n_5) \longrightarrow C_5^p(n_4 n_5) \longrightarrow C_5^p(n_3 n_4 n_5) \longrightarrow C_5^p(n_2 n_3 n_4 n_5) \longrightarrow E(n_1 n_2 n_3 n_4 n_5)$$

then formally adjusting rows and columns to accommodate the smaller 81-tile format of $C_{r+1}^1(n_{r+1})$ instead of the 121-tile format of $E(n_2...n_{r+1})$ (see Box 7).

Fourth Approximation

The routine of obtaining the numbering of tiles $S_4(n_1 n_2 n_3 n_4)$ needs no further explanation, except to note that an expanding tabulation that is built on the previous approximation is needed. Care must be exercised in lining up the image interval configurations with tile configurations (Box 8).

The Construction of ψ

From Box 8 we deduce the iterative step of obtaining

$$S_{k+1}(n_1...n_{k+1})$$

and

$$C_{k+1}^p(n_1,...,n_{k+1})$$

when

$$S_k(n_1...n_k)$$

and

$$C_k^p(n_1,...,n_k)$$

are given.

This is summarized schematically in Figure 6. The functions ψ_1, ψ_2, ψ_3, and ψ_4 are known from the constructions above, and we assume that ψ_k and the intervals $I_k(n_1...n_k)$ are given. Referring to $E(n_1...n_{k+1})$, that is computed from the computations of $E(n_1...n_k)$, we set

$$\psi_{k+1} : C_{k+1}^p(n_{k+1}) \to \begin{cases} D_{k+1}^1(n_{k+1}), \; p = 1 \\ D_{k+1}^2(n_{k+1}), \; p = 2,3 \\ D_{k+1}^3(n_{k+1}), \; p = 4 \end{cases}$$

The mappings ψ_{k+1} can be extended to continuous functions as above. To bring this construction to closure, we prove

Theorem 4

The functions $\psi_k(x_1, x_2)$ converge uniformly to a continuous function $\psi(x_1, x_2)$.

Proof

We begin with the observation that the domain of each function $\psi_k(x_1, x_2)$ is the compact square:

$$U^2 = [0, 1 + \tfrac{8}{9 \cdot 10}]^2$$

Box 7. Sequencing tiles $S_3(n_1 n_2 n_3)$ and the mapping $\psi_3 : S_3(n_1 n_2 n_3) \to I_3(n_1 n_2 n_3)$

n_2		$S_2(n_2 n_3)$	$I_3(n_2 n_3)$
$0-7$	↑	$C_3^2(n_3)$	$D_3^2(n_3)$
8		$C_3^3(n_3)$	$D_3^2(n_3)$
$9-16$	↓	$C_3^4(n_3)$	$D_3^3(n_3)$
17		$C_3^3(n_3)$	$D_3^2(n_3)$
$18-25$	↑	$C_3^2(n_3)$	$D_3^2(n_3)$
26		$C_3^3(n_3)$	$D_3^2(n_3)$
$27-34$	↓	$C_3^4(n_3)$	$D_3^3(n_3)$
35		$C_3^3(n_3)$	$D_3^2(n_3)$
$36-43$	↑	$C_3^2(n_3)$	$D_3^2(n_3)$
44		$C_3^3(n_3)$	$D_3^2(n_3)$
$45-52$	↓	$C_3^4(n_3)$	$D_3^3(n_3)$
53		$C_3^3(n_3)$	$D_3^2(n_3)$
$53-61$	↑	$C_3^2(n_3)$	$D_3^2(n_3)$
62		$C_3^3(n_3)$	$D_3^2(n_3)$
$63-70$	↓	$C_3^2(n_3)$	$D_3^3(n_3)$
71		$C_3^3(n_3)$	$D_3^2(n_3)$
$72-79$	↑	$C_3^2(n_3)$	$D_3^2(n_3)$

Configuration $C_3^1(n_2 n_3)$ and $D_3^1(n_2 n_3)$

n_2		$S_2(n_2 n_3)$	$I_3(n_2 n_3)$
$(0-79)$		$C_3^1(n_2 n_3)$	$D_3^1(n_2 n_3)$
80		$C_3^3(n_3)$	$D_3^2(n_3)$
$81-88$	←	$C_3^6(n_3)$	$D_3^3(n_3)$
89		$C_3^2(n_3)$	$D_3^2(n_3)$

Configurations $C_3^2(n_2 n_3)$ and $D_3^2(n_2 n_3)$

n_2		$S_2(n_2 n_3)$	$I_3(n_2 n_3)$
$(0-79)$		$C_3^1(n_2 n_3)$	$D_3^1(n_2 n_3)$
80		$C_3^3(n_3)$	$D_3^2(n_3)$
$81-88$	↓	$C_3^4(n_3)$	$D_3^3(n_3)$
89		$C_3^3(n_3)$	$D_3^2(n_3)$

Configuration $C_3^3(n_2 n_3)$ and $D_3^3(n_2 n_3)$

n_2		$S_2(n_2 n_3)$	$I_3(n_2 n_3)$
$(0-79)$		$C_3^1(n_2 n_3)$	$D_3^1(n_2 n_3)$
80		$C_3^3(n_3)$	$D_3^2(n_3)$
$81-89$	↓	$C_3^4(n_3)$	$D_3^3(n_3)$
90		$C_3^7(n_3)$	$D_3^3(n_3)$
$91-99$	←	$C_3^6(n_3)$	$D_3^3(n_3)$
100		$C_3^5(n_3)$	$D_3^3(n_3)$
$101-108$	↓	$C_3^4(n_3)$	$D_3^3(n_3)$
109		$C_3^3(n_3)$	$D_3^2(n_3)$

Configuration $C_3^4(n_2 n_3)$ and $D_3^4(n_2 n_3)$

n_1		$S_1(n_1 n_2 n_3)$	$I_2(n_1 n_2 n_3)$
$0-9$	↑	$C_3^2(n_2 n_3)$	$D_3^2(n_2 n_3)$
10		$C_3^3(n_2 n_3)$	$D_3^2(n_2 n_3)$
$11-20$	↓	$C_3^4(n_2 n_3)$	$D_3^3(n_2 n_3)$
21		$C_3^3(n_2 n_3)$	$D_3^2(n_1 n_2)$
$22-31$	↑	$C_3^2(n_2 n_3)$	$D_3^2(n_1 n_2)$
32		$C_3^3(n_2 n_3)$	$D_3^2(n_1 n_2)$
$33-42$	↓	$C_3^4(n_2 n_3)$	$D_3^3(n_2 n_3)$
43		$C_3^3(n_2 n_3)$	$D_3^2(n_1 n_2)$
$44-53$	↑	$C_3^2(n_2 n_3)$	$D_3^2(n_1 n_2)$
54		$C_3^3(n_2 n_3)$	$D_3^2(n_1 n_2)$
$55-64$	↓	$C_3^4(n_2 n_3)$	$D_3^3(n_2 n_3)$
65		$C_3^3(n_2 n_3)$	$D_3^2(n_1 n_2)$
$66-75$	↑	$C_3^2(n_2 n_3)$	$D_3^2(n_1 n_2)$
76		$C_3^3(n_2 n_3)$	$D_3^2(n_1 n_2)$
$77-86$	↓	$C_3^4(n_2 n_3)$	$D_3^3(n_2 n_3)$
87		$C_3^3(n_2 n_3)$	$D_3^2(n_1 n_2)$
$88-97$	↑	$C_3^2(n_2 n_3)$	$D_3^2(n_1 n_2)$
98		$C_3^3(n_2 n_3)$	$D_3^2(n_1 n_2)$
$99-108$	↓	$C_3^4(n_2 n_3)$	$D_3^3(n_2 n_3)$
109		$C_3^3(n_2 n_3)$	$D_3^2(n_1 n_2)$
$110-119$	↑	$C_3^2(n_2 n_3)$	$D_3^2(n_1 n_2)$
120		$C_3^1(n_2 n_3)$	$D_3^1(n_1 n_2)$

Configuration $E_3(n_1 n_2 n_3)$

From the definition of the intervals $I_k(n_1 \ldots n_k)$ we note that for each point:

$$(x_1, x_2) \in U^2 :$$

$$|\psi_{k+1}(x_1, x_2) - \psi_k(x_1, x_2)|$$

$$\leq \frac{109}{110^{k+1}} + \frac{80}{109 \cdot 110^{k+1}} < \frac{1}{110^k}$$

(Care must be taken in computing these differences in gaps, but careful reflection shows that the estimate can be maintained.) Hence,

$$\sum_{s=1}^{r} |\psi_{k+s}(x_1, x_2) - \psi_{k+s-1}(x_1, x_2)|$$

$$\leq \sum_{s=1}^{r} \frac{1}{110^{k+1-s}} < \frac{1}{109 \cdot 110^{k-1}}$$

and this proves the assertion of the theorem.

To satisfy Theorem 3 we set

$$\psi^q(x_1, x_2) = \psi(x_1 + \tfrac{q}{9 \cdot 10}, x_2 + \tfrac{q}{9 \cdot 10}) :$$

these functions, like Kolmogorov's functions

$$\psi_1^q(x_1) + \psi_2^q(x_2),$$

Box 8. Sequencing tiles $S_4(n_1n_2n_3n_4)$ and the mapping $\psi_4 : S_4(n_1n_2n_3n_4) \to I_4(n_1n_2n_3n_4)$

n_1	$S_4(n_3n_4)$	$I_4(n_3n_4)$
0–7 ↑	$C_4^2(n_4)$	$D_4^3(n_4)$
8	$C_4^3(n_4)$	$D_4^3(n_4)$
9–16 ↓	$C_4^4(n_4)$	$D_4^3(n_4)$
17	$C_4^3(n_4)$	$D_4^2(n_4)$
22–31 ↑	$C_4^2(n_4)$	$D_4^3(n_4)$
26	$C_4^3(n_4)$	$D_4^2(n_4)$
33–42 ↓	$C_4^4(n_4)$	$D_4^3(n_4)$
35	$C_4^3(n_4)$	$D_4^2(n_4)$
44–53 ↑	$C_4^2(n_4)$	$D_4^3(n_4)$
44	$C_4^3(n_4)$	$D_4^2(n_4)$
55–64 ↓	$C_4^4(n_4)$	$D_4^3(n_4)$
53	$C_4^3(n_4)$	$D_4^2(n_4)$
66–75 ↑	$C_4^2(n_4)$	$D_4^3(n_4)$
63	$C_4^3(n_4)$	$D_4^2(n_4)$
77–86 ↓	$C_4^4(n_4)$	$D_4^3(n_4)$
71	$C_4^3(n_4)$	$D_4^2(n_4)$
72–79 ↑	$C_4^2(n_4)$	$D_4^2(n_4)$

Configuration $C_4^1(n_3n_4)$ and $D_4^1(n_3n_4)$

n_1	$S_4(n_3n_4)$	$I_4(n_3n_4)$
(0–79)	$C_4^1(n_3n_4)$	$D_4^1(n_3n_4)$
80	$C_4^2(n_4)$	$D_4^4(n_4)$
81–88 ←	$C_4^6(n_4)$	$D_4^3(n_4)$
89	$C_4^2(n_4)$	$D_4^4(n_4)$

Configuration $C_4^2(n_3n_4)$ and $D_4^2(n_3n_4)$

n_1	$S_4(n_3n_4)$	$I_4(n_3n_4)$
(0–79)	$C_4^1(n_3n_4)$	$D_4^1(n_3n_4)$
80	$C_4^3(n_4)$	$D_4^2(n_4)$
81–88 ↓	$C_4^4(n_4)$	$D_4^3(n_4)$
89	$C_4^3(n_4)$	$D_4^2(n_4)$

Configuration $C_4^3(n_3n_4)$ and $D_4^1(n_3n_4)$

n_3	$S_4(n_3n_4)$	$I_4(n_3n_4)$
(0–79)	$C_4^1(n_3n_4)$	$D_4^1(n_3n_4)$
80	$C_4^3(n_4)$	$D_4^2(n_4)$
81–88 ↓	$C_4^4(n_4)$	$D_4^3(n_4)$
89	$C_4^7(n_4)$	$D_4^3(n_4)$
90–99 ←	$C_4^6(n_4)$	$D_4^3(n_4)$
100	$C_4^5(n_4)$	$D_4^3(n_4)$
101–108 ↓	$C_4^4(n_4)$	$D_4^3(n_4)$
109	$C_4^3(n_4)$	$D_4^2(n_4)$

Configuration $C_4^4(n_3n_4)$ and $D_4^1(n_3n_4)$

n_3	$S_4(n_3n_4)$	$I_4(n_3n_4)$
(0–79)	$C_4^1(n_3n_4)$	$D_4^1(n_3n_4)$
80	$C_4^2(n_4)$	$D_4^2(n_4)$
81–89 ←	$C_4^6(n_4)$	$D_4^3(n_4)$
90	$C_4^5(n_4)$	$D_4^3(n_4)$
91–108 ↓	$C_4^4(n_4)$	$D_4^3(n_4)$
109	$C_4^4(n_4)$	$D_4^2(n_4)$

Configuration $C_4^5(n_3n_4)$ and $D_4^5(n_3n_4)$

n_3	$S_4(n_3n_4)$	$I_4(n_3n_4)$
(0–79)	$C_4^1(n_3n_4)$	$D_4^1(n_3n_4)$
80	$C_4^2(n_4)$	$D_4^2(n_4)$
81–88 ←	$C_4^6(n_4)$	$D_4^3(n_4)$
89	$C_4^5(n_4)$	$D_4^3(n_4)$
90–99 ↓	$C_4^4(n_4)$	$D_4^3(n_4)$
100	$C_4^7(n_4)$	$D_4^3(n_4)$
101–108 ←	$C_4^6(n_4)$	$D_4^3(n_4)$
109	$C_4^5(n_4)$	$D_4^2(n_4)$

Configuration $C_4^6(n_3n_4)$ and $D_4^6(n_3n_4)$

n_1	$S_4(n_3n_4)$	$I_4(n_3n_4)$
(0–79)	$C_4^1(n_3n_4)$	$D_4^1(n_3n_4)$
80	$C_4^3(n_4)$	$D_4^2(n_4)$
81–89 ↓	$C_4^4(n_4)$	$D_4^3(n_4)$
90	$C_4^7(n_4)$	$D_4^3(n_4)$
91–108 ←	$C_4^6(n_4)$	$D_4^3(n_4)$
109	$C_4^2(n_4)$	$D_4^2(n_4)$

Configuration $C_4^7(n_3n_4)$ and $D_4^7(n_3n_4)$

n_2	$S_4(n_2n_3n_4)$	$I_4(n_2n_3n_4)$
0–7 ↑	$C_4^2(n_3n_4)$	$D_4^2(n_3n_4)$
8	$C_4^3(n_3n_4)$	$D_4^2(n_3n_4)$
9–16 ↓	$C_4^4(n_3n_4)$	$D_4^3(n_3n_4)$
17	$C_4^3(n_3n_4)$	$D_4^2(n_3n_4)$
22–31 ↑	$C_4^2(n_3n_4)$	$D_4^2(n_3n_4)$
26	$C_4^3(n_3n_4)$	$D_4^2(n_3n_4)$
33–42 ↓	$C_4^4(n_3n_4)$	$D_4^3(n_3n_4)$
35	$C_4^3(n_3n_4)$	$D_4^2(n_3n_4)$
44–53 ↑	$C_4^2(n_3n_4)$	$D_4^2(n_3n_4)$
44	$C_4^3(n_3n_4)$	$D_4^2(n_3n_4)$
55–64 ↓	$C_4^4(n_3n_4)$	$D_4^3(n_3n_4)$
53	$C_4^3(n_3n_4)$	$D_4^2(n_3n_4)$
66–75 ↑	$C_4^2(n_3n_4)$	$D_4^2(n_3n_4)$
63	$C_4^3(n_3n_4)$	$D_4^2(n_3n_4)$
77–86 ↓	$C_4^4(n_3n_4)$	$D_4^3(n_3n_4)$
71	$C_4^3(n_3n_4)$	$D_4^2(n_3n_4)$
72–79 ↑	$C_4^2(n_3n_4)$	$D_4^2(n_3n_4)$

Configuration $C_4^1(n_2n_3n_4)$ and $D_4^1(n_2n_3n_4)$

n_2	$S_4(n_2n_3n_4)$	$I_4(n_2n_3n_4)$
(0–79)	$C_4^1(n_2n_3n_4)$	$D_4^1(n_2n_3n_4)$
80	$C_4^2(n_3n_4)$	$D_4^2(n_3n_4)$
81–88 ←	$C_4^5(n_3n_4)$	$D_4^3(n_3n_4)$
89	$C_4^2(n_3n_4)$	$D_4^2(n_3n_4)$

Configuration $C_4^2(n_2n_3n_4)$ and $D_4^2(n_2n_3n_4)$

n_2	$S_4(n_2n_3n_4)$	$I_4(n_2n_3n_4)$
(0–79)	$C_4^1(n_2n_3n_4)$	$D_4^1(n_2n_3n_4)$
80	$C_4^3(n_3n_4)$	$D_4^2(n_3n_4)$
81–88 ↓	$C_4^4(n_3n_4)$	$D_4^3(n_3n_4)$
89	$C_4^3(n_3n_4)$	$D_4^2(n_3n_4)$

Configuration $C_4^3(n_2n_3n_4)$ and $D_4^3(n_2n_3n_4)$

n_2	$S_4(n_2n_3n_4)$	$I_4(n_2n_3n_4)$
(0–79)	$C_4^1(n_2n_3n_4)$	$D_4^1(n_2n_3n_4)$
80	$C_4^3(n_3n_4)$	$D_4^2(n_3n_4)$
81–89 ↓	$C_4^4(n_3n_4)$	$D_4^3(n_3n_4)$
90	$C_4^7(n_3n_4)$	$D_4^3(n_3n_4)$
91–99 ←	$C_4^6(n_3n_4)$	$D_4^3(n_3n_4)$
100	$C_4^5(n_3n_4)$	$D_4^3(n_3n_4)$
101–108 ↓	$C_4^4(n_3n_4)$	$D_4^3(n_3n_4)$
109	$C_4^3(n_3n_4)$	$D_4^2(n_3n_4)$

Configuration $C_4^4(n_2n_3n_4)$ and $D_4^1(n_2n_3n_4)$

n_1	$S_4(n_1n_2n_3n_4)$	$I_4(n_1n_2n_3n_4)$
0–9 ↑	$C_4^2(n_2n_3n_4)$	$D_4^2(n_2n_3n_4)$
10	$C_4^3(n_2n_3n_4)$	$D_4^2(n_2n_3n_4)$
11–20 ↓	$C_4^4(n_2n_3n_4)$	$D_4^3(n_2n_3n_4)$
21	$C_4^3(n_2n_3n_4)$	$D_4^2(n_2n_3n_4)$
22–31 ↑	$C_4^2(n_2n_3n_4)$	$D_4^2(n_2n_3n_4)$
32	$C_4^3(n_2n_3n_4)$	$D_4^2(n_2n_3n_4)$
33–42 ↓	$C_4^4(n_2n_3n_4)$	$D_4^3(n_2n_3n_4)$
43	$C_4^3(n_2n_3n_4)$	$D_4^2(n_2n_3n_4)$
44–53 ↑	$C_4^2(n_2n_3n_4)$	$D_4^2(n_2n_3n_4)$
54	$C_4^3(n_2n_3n_4)$	$D_4^2(n_2n_3n_4)$
55–64 ↓	$C_4^4(n_2n_3n_4)$	$D_4^3(n_2n_3n_4)$
65	$C_4^3(n_2n_3n_4)$	$D_4^2(n_2n_3n_4)$
66–75 ↑	$C_4^2(n_2n_3n_4)$	$D_4^2(n_2n_3n_4)$
76	$C_4^3(n_2n_3n_4)$	$D_4^2(n_2n_3n_4)$
77–86 ↓	$C_4^4(n_2n_3n_4)$	$D_4^3(n_2n_3n_4)$
87	$C_4^3(n_2n_3n_4)$	$D_4^2(n_2n_3n_4)$
88–97 ↑	$C_4^2(n_2n_3n_4)$	$D_4^2(n_2n_3n_4)$
98	$C_4^3(n_2n_3n_4)$	$D_4^2(n_2n_3n_4)$
99–108 ↓	$C_4^4(n_2n_3n_4)$	$D_4^3(n_2n_3n_4)$
109	$C_4^3(n_2n_3n_4)$	$D_4^2(n_2n_3n_4)$
110–119 ↑	$C_4^2(n_2n_3n_4)$	$D_4^2(n_2n_3n_4)$
120	$C_4^3(n_2n_3n_4)$	$D_4^4(n_2n_3n_4)$

Configuration $E_4(n_1n_2n_3n_4)$

are defined through systems of steps, a procedure imposed by the necessity to separate points, except that now they are easier to implement (see below).

The Space-Filling Curve

Every tile $S_r(n_1...n_r)$ can be mapped onto the diagonal joining the lower left to the upper right of its vertices, and these diagonals can be joined in the order of their sequence to form a polygonal curve Γ_r without loops. The diameters of the tiles $S_r(n_1...n_r)$ and the widths of the gaps separating them tend uniformly to zero, and roughly speaking, these curves constitute approximating curves to a space-filling curve Γ. The proof, which would require a good deal of mathematics alien to the analysis of superpositions, is omitted.

Figure 6. The iteration from k to k+1

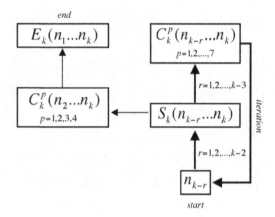

An intuitive geometric approach due to Hilbert is illustrated in Figure 7, where the interval V is mapped onto the square U^2 by mapping subsegments into a division of the square, as follows:

Consider the intervals

$$I_r = \left[\frac{n_r}{110^r}, \frac{n_r}{110^r} + \frac{80}{109 \cdot 110^r} \right]$$

and the gap-intervals

$$J_r = \left[\frac{n_r}{110^r} + \frac{80}{109 \cdot 110^r}, \frac{n_r+1}{110^r} \right]$$

Figure 7. Detail of a mapping $E \to E^2$

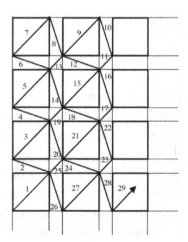

An interval I_r is mapped onto a tile $S_r(n_1...n_r)$ and the interval J_r is mapped proportionally onto the segments connecting the upper right vertex of square $S_r(n_1...n_r)$ to the lower left vertex of next square in the sequence, and each of these is mapped onto a rectangle or square in a gap, as indicated in Figure 7. With this method, the interval V is mapped onto the square U^2 at every step of the construction. Care must be taken, of course, to have appropriate proportions of the line segments so as to ensure that nested properties of the tiles and their image intervals are maintained.

We shall not elaborate on construction of the space-filling curve beyond these rudimentary remarks. A good discussion of this approach can be found in Sagan (1994, pp. 9–13).

The Computational Algorithm

From a computational perspective, the space-filling curve has more than a ghostly presence in the proposed algorithm, through the middle layer computations, and its direct role in shaping the approximating functions. This is made clear in Figure 8, where the algorithm for computing a target function f is described. The computation of f is by induction: Beginning with $k_0 = 0$ and $f_0 \equiv f$, it is assumed that an integer k_{r-1} and approximating function f_{r-1} are known, and select for $r > 1$ an integer $k_r > k_{r-1}$ such that

$$\max_{S^q_{k_r}} \left| f_{r-1}(x_1, x_2) - f_{r-1}(x_1{}', x_2{}') \right| < \frac{1}{3} \| f_{r-1} \| \quad (8)$$

where the fluctuation is measured over all tiles $S^q_{k_r}$. This condition is necessary to ensure convergence of the approximating functions to f. The algorithm now follows the steps in Figure 8 and Box 9.

The process repeats with the selection of a new integer, $k_{r+1} > k_r$, that satisfies condition

Figure 8. Computational algorithm

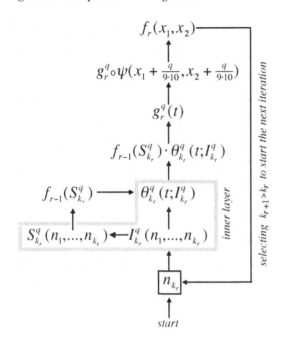

(7) for the function f_r and tiles $S_{k_{r+1}}^q$. Note that the sets:

$$S_{k_r}^q (d_{1k_r}^q, d_{2k_r}^q) \cap E^2$$

are contained in the domain of functions ψ_r^q. The detailed constructions and arguments in Köppen (2002) can be appropriately modified for this algorithm.

CONCLUSION

To make superpositions an effective computational tool, mappings

$$\Gamma : V \to U^2$$

and

$$\psi : U^2 \to V$$

were constructed in tandem; sketchy mathematical arguments have been used for the sake of a leaner presentation. The first of these mappings orders tiles on which a target function f is computed, and the second mapping defines the ranges of approximating functions. In the Kolmogorov superpositions, a mapping:

$$\Sigma_p \psi_p : U^2 \to V$$

determines the mapping:

$$\Gamma : V \to U^2,$$

and it determines the order of approximating functions and their ranges: The latter is thus an incidental consequence of the construction of $\Sigma_p \psi_p$, but one that determines sub rosa the character and computability of superpositions that were not conceived for computational purposes. In either model, however, the sequencing of tiles is the essential step, and this received the most attention in the two constructions.

This chapter offers one specific example of an alternative superpositions model; the first approximation of another example is given in Figure 10, but the possible choices are many. There is the possibility of selecting sequencing models to fit specific applications. Finally, we note that the constructions of this chapter can be extended to Euclidean spaces of arbitrary dimension n. From a conceptual and computational perspective, Euclidean spaces E^n have the same properties for any finite value of n, and therefore the constructions and proofs in Kolmogorov (1957) are stated for general n. Difficulties arise only in the implementation of superpositions when integers greater than 2 are used. These difficulties are purely technical, however, due to more elaborate computations. This remains true when applied to tracing approximating paths to space filling curves: A linear ordering of grid-points:

Box 9.

---

1. The first step computes the intervals:

$$I_{k_r}^q (n_1...n_{k_r}) = \left[\sum_{s=1}^{k_r} \frac{n_s}{110^s} - \frac{q}{109 \cdot 110}, \sum_{s=1}^{k_r} \frac{n_s}{110^s} + \frac{80}{109 \cdot 110^{k_r}} - \frac{q}{109 \cdot 110} \right]$$

2. The intervals then define the order the tiles:

$$S_{k_r}^q (n_1...n_{k_r}) = \left[\sum_{s=1}^{k_r} \frac{i_{n_s}}{10^s} - \frac{q}{9 \cdot 10}, \sum_{s=1}^{k_r} \frac{i_{n_s}}{10^s} + \frac{8}{9 \cdot 10^{k_r}} - \frac{q}{9 \cdot 10} \right]$$

This ordering of tiles determines the inner functions.

3. This step has two parallel computations: generic continuous functions

$$\theta_{k_r}^q \left(t; I_{k_r}^q \right) = \sigma \left[\left(t - \sum_{s=1}^{k_r} \frac{n_s}{110^s} + \frac{90}{109 \cdot 110^{k_r}} + 1 \right) 110^{k_r+1} - \frac{q}{109 \cdot 110} \right]$$

$$- \sigma \left[\left(t - \sum_{s=1}^{k_r} \frac{n_s}{110^s} - \frac{80}{109 \cdot 110^s} \right) 110^{k_r+1} - \frac{q}{109 \cdot 110} \right]$$

are constructed on the intervals $I_{k_r}^q$, where the function equals 1, and it vanishes outside a small neighborhood of $I_{k_r}^q$, and the already known function f_{r-1} is evaluates at arbitrary points of the tiles $S_{k_r}^q$ (Figure 9).

4. The piecewise product of the two functions of step (iii) gives functions whose sums

$$g_r^q(t) = \frac{1}{5} \sum_{I_{k_r}^q} f_{r-1} \left(S_{k_r}^q \right) \cdot \theta_{k_r}^q \left(t; I_{k_r}^q \right)$$

are continuous functions defined on the line.

5. The substitution $t = \psi(x_1 + \frac{q}{9 \cdot 10}, x_2 + \frac{q}{9 \cdot 10})$ into (iii) transforms these functions into functions

$$g_r^q \circ \psi(x_1 + \tfrac{q}{9 \cdot 10}, x_2 + \tfrac{q}{9 \cdot 10}) = \frac{1}{5} \sum_{I_{k_r}^q} f_{r-1} \left(S_{k_r}^q \right) \cdot \theta_{k_r}^q \left(\psi(x_1 + \tfrac{q}{9 \cdot 10}, x_2 + \tfrac{q}{9 \cdot 10}); I_{k_r}^q \right)$$

that are continuous on the square.

6. The final step computes the rth approximation to f:

$$f_r(x_1, x_2) = f(x_1, x_2) - \sum_{q=0}^{4} \sum_{s=1}^{r} g_r^q \circ \psi(x_1 + \tfrac{q}{9 \cdot 10}, x_2 + \tfrac{q}{9 \cdot 10})$$

and this completes this iteration cycle.

Figure 9. The function $\theta_{k_r}^q \left(t; I_{k_r}^q \right)$

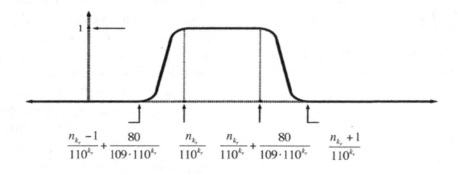

$$\frac{n_{k_r} - 1}{110^{k_r}} + \frac{80}{109 \cdot 110^{k_r}} \qquad \frac{n_{k_r}}{110^{k_r}} \qquad \frac{n_{k_r}}{110^{k_r}} + \frac{80}{109 \cdot 110^{k_r}} \qquad \frac{n_{k_r} + 1}{110^{k_r}}$$

Figure 10. The first iteration of an alternative scheme

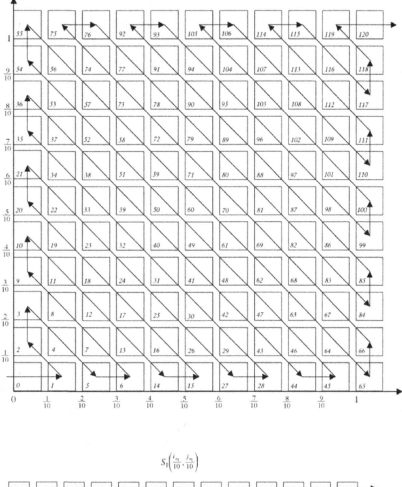

$(x_1, x_2, ..., x_n)$

$(x_1, x_2, x'_3 ..., x_n)$

when $n > 2$ is more complicated than the ordering of grid-points (x_1, x_2) for the simple reason that in cataloguing the points:

$(x_1, x_2, ..., x_n)$

according to their linear order in following the approximating curve, any one of the points:

$(x_1, x'_2, x_3 ..., x_n)$,

and so on when changing one coordinate could be the successor. Examples of three-dimensional space filling curves can be found in Sagan (1994).

The Achilles heel inherent in superpositions based on nomographic functions has been removed with the new algorithm, and with the choice of different orderings of grid-points its implementation can be better adapted to specific applications. In image compression, for example, this could enable different scanning techniques and groupings of pixels.

Can Theorem 3 be generalized to answer the following question raised by Hecht-Nielsen in the early 1990s: Are there representations of the form (6) when f is a real-valued continuous mapping $f : A \rightarrow R$ when $A \not\subset E^2$ is a compact domain? A similar question could be asked about a compact domain $A \not\subset E^n$ for arbitrary n. One approach might be to characterize the domains A through subsets of the families of the Lebesgue coverings used in Kolmogorov constructions.

REFERENCES

Arnol'd, V. I. (1957). On functions of three variables. *Transactions of the American Mathematical Society*, 2(28), 51–54.

Braun, J. (2009). *An application of Kolmogorov's superposition theorem to function reconstruction in higher dimensions*. (Unpublished Doctoral Dissertation). Rheinischen Friedrich-Wilhelms-Universiät, Bonn, Germany.

Braun, J., & Griebel, M. (2007). On a constructive proof of Kolmogorov's superposition theorem. *Constructive Approximation*.

Buck, R. C. (1975). Approximate functional complexity. *Bulletin of the American Mathematical Society*, 81(6). doi:10.1090/S0002-9904-1975-13938-3

Buck, R. C. (1979). Approximate complexity and functional representation. *Journal of Mathematical Analysis and Applications*, 70, 280–298. doi:10.1016/0022-247X(79)90091-X

d'Ocagne, M. (1899). *Traite de Nomographie*. Paris, France.

Doss, R. (1977). A superposition theorem for unbounded continuous functions. *Transactions of the American Mathematical Society*, 233, 197–203. doi:10.1090/S0002-9947-1977-0582781-1

Evesham, H. A. (1982). *Nomography*. Boston, MA: Docent Press.

Fridman, B. L. (1967). Improvement in the smoothness of functions in the Kolmogorov superposition theorem. *Soviet Mathematics Dokladi*, 8(6).

Girosi, F., & Poggio, T. (1989). Representation properties of networks: Kolmogorov's theorem is irrelevant. *Neural Computation*, 1, 465–469. doi:10.1162/neco.1989.1.4.465

Hecht-Nielsen, R. (1987). Kolmogorov's mapping neural network existence theorem. *Proceedings International Conference on Neural Networks, Iii* (pp. 11-13). IEEE.

Hecht-Nielsen, R. (1990). *Neurocomputing*. New York, NY: Eddison-Wesley Publishing Company.

Hilbert, D. (1900). *Mathematische probleme* (pp. 253–297). Gottingen: Nachrichten Akademi der Wissenschaften.

Igelnick, B., & Parikh, N. (2003). Kolmogorov's spline network. *IEEE Transactions on Neural Networks*, 14, 725–733. doi:10.1109/TNN.2003.813830

Kolmogorov, A. N. (1956). On the representation of continuous functions of several variables by superpositions of continuous functions of a smaller number of variables. *Transactions of the American Mathematical Society*, 2(17), 369–373.

Kolmogorov, A. N. (1957). On the representation of continuous functions of many variables by superposition of continuous functions of one variable and addition. *Transactions of the American Mathematical Society*, 2(28), 55–59.

Köppen, M. (2002). Lecture Notes in Computer Science: *Vol. 140. On the training of a Kolmogorov network*. Berlin, Germany: Springer-Verlag. doi:10.1007/3-540-46084-5_77

Köppen, M., & Yoshida, K. (2002). Universal representation of image functions by their Sprecher construction. *Soft Computing as Transdisciplinary Science and Technology*, 202-210.

Kurková, V. (1991). Kolmogorov's theorem is relevant. *Neural Computation, 3*, 617–622. doi:10.1162/neco.1991.3.4.617

Leni, P.-E. (2011). *Nouvelles méthods de traitement de signaux multidimensionnels par décomposition suivant le théorème de Superposition de Kolmogorov.* (Doctoral Dissertation). Université de Bourgogne, Le Creusot, France.

Leni, P.-E., & Fougerolle, Y. D., Truchetet, F. (2008). Kolmogorov superposition theorem and its application to multivariate function decomposition and image representation. *IEEE Conference on Signal-Image Technology & Interned-Based Systems*. Bali, Indonesia.

Lorentz, G. G. (1962). Metric entropy, widths, and superpositions of functions. *The American Mathematical Monthly, 69*(6), 469–485. doi:10.2307/2311185

Lorentz, G. G. (1966). *Approximation of functions.* New York, NY: Holt, Rinehart and Winston.

Menger, K. (1932). *Kurventheorie.* Berlin, Germany: Teubner Verlag.

Nakamura, M., Mines, R., & Kreinovich, V. (1993). Guaranteed intervals for Kolmogorov's theorem (and their possible relation to neural networks). *Interval Computations, 3*, 183–199.

Ostrand, P. A. (1965). Dimension of metric spaces and Hilbert's problem 13. *Bulletin of the American Mathematical Society, 71*(4), 619–622. doi:10.1090/S0002-9904-1965-11363-5

Sagan, H. (1994). *Space-filling curves.* New York, NY: Springer-Verlag. doi:10.1007/978-1-4612-0871-6

Sprecher, D. A. (1965). On the structure of continuous functions of several variables. *Transactions of the American Mathematical Society, 115*(3), 340–355. doi:10.1090/S0002-9947-1965-0210852-X

Sprecher, D. A. (1965). On the structure of representations of continuous functions of several variables as finite sums of continuous functions of one variable. *Proceedings of the American Mathematical Society, 17*(1), 98–105. doi:10.1090/S0002-9939-1966-0194565-5

Sprecher, D. A. (1965). On the structure of continuous functions of several variables. *Transactions of the American Mathematical Society, 15*(3), 340–355. doi:10.1090/S0002-9947-1965-0210852-X

Sprecher, D. A. (1972). A survey of solved and unsolved problems in superposition of functions. *Journal of Approximation Theory, 6*, 123–134. doi:10.1016/0021-9045(72)90069-X

Sprecher, D. A. (1993). A universal mapping for Kolmogorov's superposition theorem. *Neural Networks, 6*, 1089–1094. doi:10.1016/S0893-6080(09)80020-8

Sprecher, D. A. (1996). A numerical implementation of Kolmogorov's superpositions. *Neural Networks, 9*(5), 765–772. doi:10.1016/0893-6080(95)00081-X

Sprecher, D. A. (1997). A numerical implementation of Kolmogorov's superpositions II. *Neural Networks, 10*(3), 447–457. doi:10.1016/S0893-6080(96)00073-1

Sprecher, D. A. (2002). Space-filling curves and Kolmogorov superpositions-based neural networks. *Neural Networks, 15*, 57–67. doi:10.1016/S0893-6080(01)00107-1

Vituskin, A. G. (1954). On the 13th problem of Hilbert. *Doklady Akademii Nauk, 95*, 701–704.

Vituskin, A.G. (1977). On representation of functions by means of superpositions and related topics. *L'enseignement Mathématique, 2nd Series XXIII*(3-4), 255-320.

Chapter 12
Evaluating Scalability of Neural Configurations in Combined Classifier and Attention Models

Tsvi Achler
Los Alamos National Labs and IBM Research Almaden, USA

ABSTRACT

The brain's neuronal circuits that are responsible for recognition and attention are not completely understood. Several potential circuits have been proposed using different mechanisms. These models may vary in the number connection parameters, the meaning of each connection weight, the efficiency, and the ability to scale to larger networks. Explicit analysis of these issues is important because for example, certain models may require an implausible number of connections (greater than available in the brain) in order to process the amount of information the brain can process. Moreover certain classifiers may perform recognition, but may be difficult to efficiently integrate with attention models. In this chapter, some of the limitations and scalability issues are discussed and a class of models that may address them is suggested. The focus is on modeling both recognition and a form attention called biased competition. Models are also explored that are both static and dynamic during recognition.

INTRODUCTION

Recognition and attention are closely tied together and underlie most aspects of cognition. This chapter reviews models of a form of attention known as biased competition and classifiers. Both can be modeled by different neural configurations. We begin by introducing possible neural configurations for single-layer supervised classifiers. We show that different versions of these classifiers which perform identical classification can be implemented with two different configurations.

We ask which is more scalable. Is there a configuration that is more optimal to demonstrate biased competition along with recognition? We conclude that feedforward-feedback models of recognition and attention are more scalable and efficient.

BACKGROUND

Neural Network Configurations and Recognition Algorithms

Many types of neural network classifiers and attention models can be found in the literature. Fortunately most can be described using a stan-

DOI: 10.4018/978-1-4666-3942-3.ch012

dard notation. Thus before we review begin with a review of classifiers, let's define a standard notation. Let vector Y represent the activity of a set of labeled nodes that may be called output neurons or classes in different literatures and individually written as

$$Y=(Y_1, Y_2, Y_3, \ldots Y_H)^T.$$

They are considered supervised if the nodes can be labeled for example: Y_1 represents *"dog"*, Y_2 represents *"cat"*, and so on. Vector X represents sensory neurons or nodes that sample the environment and represent the input space to be recognized. These nodes represent input features and written as $X=(X_1, X_2, X_3, \ldots X_N)^T$. The input features can be sensors that detect edges, lines, frequencies, kernel features, and so on. Output neurons are tuned to specific patterns so let's expand the notation further. Assume neuron Y_1 is most-optimally tuned to an input pattern "A". We will label the neuron with this pattern and write it as neuron Y_A. We describe its optimal input pattern as X_A where pattern "A" is represented by the feature sensory nodes with values $X_A=(X_{1A}, X_{2A}, X_{3A}, \ldots X_{NA})^T$.

Next, lets distinguish between supervised and unsupervised methods and phases in recognition. Unsupervised algorithms learn patterns without label constraints on Y and may find efficient representations (e.g. Olshausen & Fields, 1996; Hyvärinen et al., 2009). Although the unsupervised methods perform essential roles in dimensionality reduction and efficient coding, recognition is ultimately a process of associating labels with patterns. Without labeled associations the brain cannot interact with the world, e.g.: find food, mates, and hazards. Thus we initially focus on single-layer supervised models here. Future work will include comparisons of methods that include hidden layers and mixtures of supervised and unsupervised methods.

To distinguish between supervised recognition models, let's define two phases in algorithm func-

tion: during recognition and learning. Recognition is when an algorithm finds values for outputs Y without modifying connection weights. Learning is when an algorithm modifies its connection weights (regardless of whether it calculates Y in the process). The most crucial aspect to understanding the difference between the models is the underlying neural configuration and when the model displays dynamics. Figure 1 compares basic neural connections between inputs and outputs.

It is important to keep in mind the distinction of phases in algorithm function otherwise these configurations can be confusing. For example even though feedforward methods are feedforward during recognition, to implement their learning algorithms such as backprop (Rumelhart & McClelland, 1986) or a delta rule (Rosenblatt, 1958), auto-associative feedforward-feedback connections and dynamics are required. Thus feedforward methods are feedforward during recognition but feedforward-feedback during learning. Conversely, methods that are feedforward-feedback during recognition may use simple feedforward configurations during learning (Achler, 2012). Now we are ready to evaluate recognition algorithms.

Feedforward Models of Recognition

Feedforward neural networks are the first generation of biologically motivated algorithms. They are considered feedforward because the direction of information flow during recognition is feedforward: one-way from inputs to the outputs. W represents a feedforward matrix of weights or parameters that associates inputs and outputs. WX calculates the output using the feedforward weights and inputs.

$$Y=WX \text{ or } Y=f(W,X) \tag{1}$$

Various feedforward networks can be found in the literature with different algorithm optimizations, for example: single-layer Perceptron

Figure 1. Comparison of Configurations. Using feedforward methods, information flows from inputs to output nodes (top). After feedforward processing lateral connections may connect between outputs or back to inputs of a different node (middle). Generative methods use Auto-Associative connections with symmetrical feedforward and feedback connections: each node projects back to its own inputs (bottom).

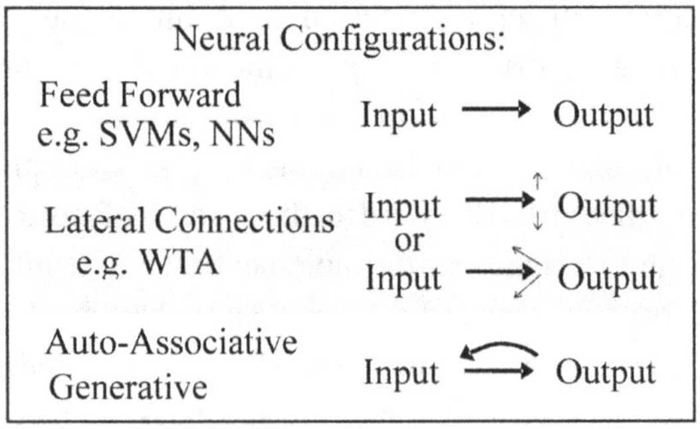

(Rosenblatt, 1958), multilayer Neural Networks with nonlinearities introduced into calculation of Y (Rumelhart & McClelland, 1986). Others include machine learning methods such as Support Vector Machines (SVM) with nonlinearities introduced into the inputs through the "kernel trick" (Vapnik, 1995). Yet other methods may use more-complex nonlinearities and ensembles (Igelnik et al., 2001). Although these algorithms vary in specifics such as nonlinearities determining the function f, they share the commonality in that recognition involves a feedforward transformation using W during recognition.

Some feedforward algorithms include lateral connections for competition between output nodes Y, during recognition. Lateral connections can be designated as one-vs-all, winner-take-all, all-vs-all e.g. (Rifkin & Klautau, 2004). One method Adaptive Resonance Theory (Carpenter & Grossberg, 1987) measures a goodness-of-fit after a strong winner-take-all competition. However such competition methods still rely on initially calculating Y node activities based on feedforward-trained weights W and do not iteratively modify the input layer activity as part of classification.

A variation of feedforward algorithms are recurrent networks. In most versions some of the inputs are outputs from a lower layer in the hierarchy and the network can be unfolded into a feedforward network. This allows the processing of time e.g. (Schmidhuber, 1992; Williams & Zipser, 1994; Boden, 2006). However, most do not modify the same inputs.

Feedforward-Feedback Models of Recognition

Networks based on feedforward-feedback structures are auto-associative networks and generative models. Generally, a Lyapanov function can be written and the networks converge to stable fixed-points. In auto-associative networks, the feedforward and feedback connections have the same weights. Subsequently when an output node is active it generates an input and such networks can be called generative. Such methods generate a prototype pattern.

Two early auto-associative networks that generate patterns are Anderson's "brain-state-in-a-box" and Hopfield networks (Anderson et al., 1977; Hopfield, 1982). When part of a learned input pattern is given, the network can complete the whole pattern through a dynamic process. However, these methods may be limited by capacity e.g. (McEliace, 1987). More recent models implement directed acyclic graphs within a restricted Bolzman machine: binary activation networks with input and output layers stacked in a hierarchy. Such methods can include a supervised label as an input which may be reconstructed (Hinton et al., 2006). However this is not a conventional supervised method like the feedforward neural networks of Rumelhart & McClelland (1986) or Rosenblatt (1958).

Certain generative methods also determine an error measure by comparing the generative reconstruction with the inputs. Many of these methods use the generative error signal for learning efficient representations e.g. (Olshausen & Field,

1996; Hyvernin, 2001). They may in addition use that error during recognition e.g. (Friston, 2009; Friston et al., 2011). However, these generative methods are unsupervised and outputs are unlabeled. Thus the unsupervised generative networks are commonly followed by a supervised feedforward classifier for recognition using labels e.g. (Zieler et al., 2010).

The supervised recognition method proposed here uses a supervised paradigm akin to the feedforward neural networks of Rumelhart & McClelland (1986) or Rosenblatt (1958) but functions like the generative methods that measure error. During testing it uses auto-associative feedforward-feedback connections and exhibits dynamics. During learning weights are obtained using a simple feedforward Hebbian-like average (Achler, 2012). We show that equivalent supervised recognition can be implemented using either (feedforward vs feedforward-feedback) methods during testing. However, learning and competition phenomena such as biased competition are more efficient and scalable using the feedforward-feedback method.

Mathematical Formulation of the Supervised Feedforward-Feedback Classifier

The linear perceptron of Equation 1 can be rewritten using an inverse or pseudoinverse:

$$W^{-1}\vec{Y} = \vec{X} \tag{2}$$

Lets define matrix M as the inverse or pseudoinverse of matrix W. The relation becomes:

$$M\vec{Y} - \vec{X} = 0 \tag{3}$$

Models founded on this equation can be referred to as generative models because they "generate" a reconstruction. The term MY is an internal prototype of pattern(s) constructed using learned information M, that best matches patterns present in X.

Information flows from Y to X using M and recognition is determined in the input or X domain. This flow of information describes top-down feedback, the opposite direction of feedforward. The fixed-points or solutions of Equations 3 and 1 are identical, so the same Y's match the feedforward and feedback equations. This duality suggests that analogous network connectivity can be described in both feedforward and feedback manners.

However, Equation 3 does not provide a way to project input information from the inputs to the outputs. To get around this, we use dynamic networks or equations that converge to Equation 3.

One method that can be used is based on Least Squares to minimize the energy function: $E=\|X - MY\|^2$. Taking the derivative relative to Y and solving the equation becomes:

$$\frac{d\vec{Y}}{dt} = M^T(M\vec{Y} - \vec{X}) \tag{4}$$

This equation can be iterated until steady state, dy/dt=0 resulting in the fixed point solution that is equivalent to Y=WX. Both feedforward and feedback connections of this method are determined by M. Together the feedforward and feedback weights emulate the feedforward weights

Table 1. Comparison of weights and dynamics between methods

Method	Recognition Connectivity	Dynamics	Weights
Feedforward	Feedforward	During Learning	W
Auto-Associative Generative	Feedforward-Feedback	During Testing	M
Feedforward with Lateral Inhibition	Feedforward with Lateral Inhibition	During Learning and During Testing (limited)	W + Lateral Weights

W of the feedforward method. MY transforms Y information into the X domain, thus a feedback process. M^T transforms X information into the Y domain, thus a feedforward process.

Another way to converge to equation 3 is to use Regulatory Feedback equations e.g. (Achler, 2011). The equation can be written as:

$$\frac{dY}{dt} = Y\left(\frac{1}{V} M^T \left(\frac{\vec{X}}{M\vec{Y}}\right) - 1\right)$$

where

$$V = \sum_{j=1}^{N} M_{ji} \qquad (5)$$

In alternative notation, this can be written as:

$$\frac{dY_i}{dt} = \frac{Y_i}{\left(\sum_{j=1}^{N} M_{ji}\right)} \sum_{k=1}^{N} M_{ki} \left(\frac{X_k}{\sum_{h=1}^{H} M_{kh}Y_h}\right) - Y_i$$

$$(6)$$

where M_{NxH} are the dimensions of M. Both generative-type models have the identical fixed points (Achler & Bettencourt, 2011).

We have established that Equation 1 can be solved during recognition by equations 4 or 5 using the pseudoinverse of feedforward weights: M. However, we have not established how this improves scalability and is advantageous.

IMPLICATIONS

Example of a Simple Recognition Problem

We compare supervised recognition methods using a simple example to show the weights in M are more intuitive, easier to learn, and are symbolic compared to W. We only need a simple intuitive

example here because we have already shown mathematically that they can both solve the same problems.

Suppose we want to discriminate between idealized drawings of a bicycle or unicycle using features of wheels horizontal lines and vertical lines. We can describe the expectation based of these features. The expectation matrix Exp is written below.

$$
Exp = \begin{array}{cccc}
X_1 & X_2 & X_3 & X_4 \\
2 & 1 & 1 & 2 \\
1 & 0 & 0 & 1
\end{array}
\begin{array}{l}
Y_1 \quad Bicycle \; = M1 \\
Y_2 \quad Unicycle
\end{array}
$$

$$(7)$$

Expectation matrix Exp indicates characteristic bicycles and unicycles based on features $X_1=$ circles (wheels), X_2: horizontal lines, X_3: handlebar features, X_4: seat features. Although binary values are given they can be any real number. For example if 50% of bicycles have seats then the entry can be 0.5.

Two wheels are expected in a bicycle. Horizontal frame and handlebar features are expected for a bicycle. One wheel is expected and no handlebar features are expected for a unicycle. A matrix such as this only requires the expectation of the features relative to the label to be written. This can be determined by a simple averaging function, calculating the co-occurrence of features with labels, or through Hebbian-like learning e.g. (Achler, 2012). It may also be determined by symbolic expressions and language.

Any supervised classifier trained based on the information above, and given X= [1,0,0,1] ^{T}, a unicycle, should respond with Y=[0,1]^T, indicating a unicycle label. X= [2,1,1,1]^T, bicycle, should generate Y=[1,0]^T.

Optimal Feedforward Weights are not Representative of Expectation

Even though supervised weights W may store input-label associations, it is not easy to incorporate expectations into W. To demonstrate, let's assume feedforward weights represent expectations and lets make W0 = Exp. Setting the input to represent a unicycle: $X_{test} = [1,0,0,1]^T$ and solving Y=W0 X_{test} we get Y=$[3,2]^T$. This is not the expected solution: Y=$[0,1]^T$. W should be trained using the expectation matrix as a training set.

Solving Recognition Using M

If M represents the fixed points one should be able to make M equal to the expectation matrix (M1=Exp), then insert M1 and X_{test} into either equations 4 or 5, and obtain the correct solution. When we do this and wait until the dynamics go to zero (dY/dt→0), the solution obtained for X_{test} = $[1,0,0,1]^T$ is Y=$[0,1]^T$. Unicycle is correctly recognized. The solution for X_{test}=$[2,1,1,1]^T$ is Y=$[1,0]^T$ representing bicycle. Both patterns are correctly recognized demonstrating recognition using the expectation matrix.

W and Solving Recognition Using W

To demonstrate the relation between M and W, let's go back to Equation 1 and calculate W1 from M1 using the pseudoinverse. This is analogous to using a feedforward learning algorithm such as the delta rule. Since these matrixes may not be square, the standard pseudoinverse method is used where $W=(M^TM)^{-1}M^T$. W represents the feedforward weights. The transpose W1 is shown.

$$W1 = \begin{matrix} 0.2 & 0.4 & -0.4 & -0.2 & Y1 & Bicycle \\ 0.2 & -0.6 & -0.6 & 0.8 & Y2 & Unicycle \end{matrix}$$
$$(8)$$

Compared to M1, W1 is more complex, has negative values, and the values do not clearly indicate fixed-points. To demonstrate that W1 represents correct feedforward weights, lets calculate Y=W1 X_{test}. Correct answers are obtained: Y=$[1,0]^T$ for X_{test}=$[2,1,1,1]^T$ and Y=$[0,1]^T$ for X_{test} = $[1,0,0,1]^T$. Correct recognition is obtained either a) with the feedforward-feedback method (e.g. equation 4) using expectation values from

matrix 7, or b) with the feedforward method (Equation 1) using W values from matrix 8. The disadvantage of the feedforward method is that W is more difficult to obtain and is sub-symbolic.

Symbolic Information

Suppose we want to ask do bicycles have wheels? How many? These are symbolic questions. Using M1 we can look up label for bicycle, Y_1, and feature for wheel, X_1, and read the value: 2. If we want to do the same thing for unicycle we can look up label for unicycle, Y_2, and feature for wheel, X_1, and read the value: 1. If we attempt this with W1 we do not retrieve symbolically useful information (0.2 and 0.2 respectively). W is sub-symbolic while M maintains symbolic access and represents recognition weights. This is possible because M represents fixed-point solutions.

We have shown that the feedforward-feedback method can be equivalent to the feedforward method but may be less complex. Analogously modeling phenomena like biased competition using a feedforward method can be more complex than modeling the same phenomena using a feedforward feedback method.

We now review the biased competition phenomena and feedforward methods used to model it.

Competition

The phenomena of biased competition is revealed by recording neurons that are selective to separate patterns within a common receptive field (Desimone & Duncan, 1995). Using single pattern presentations, neurons are sorted based on the specific patterns they prefer. For example, neurons responsive to pattern X_A are labeled Y_A. Neurons responsive to pattern X_B are labeled Y_B and so on.

This establishes a recognition baseline. Such selective neurons are known to be found especially in the infero-termporal region of the brain. When patterns associated with both neurons are presented at the same time (e.g. $X_{test} = X_B \cup X_A$), the interaction between the neurons is mutually suppressive compared to single pattern presentation. Both neurons selective to both patterns initially become activated but less vigorously. This phenomenon is labeled competition interference.

Then the animal is trained/instructed to focus on a single pattern (e.g. focus on X_A). Y_A neurons that respond preferably to the focused pattern show a higher baseline activation "bias" even without a pattern in the visual field. When two patterns are presented simultaneously ($X_{test} = X_B \cup X_A$), the neuron associated with the focused pattern shows an increased activation relative to the neurons associated with the non-focused pattern. This is called biased competition. These interactions can occur before eye movements or without "spatial attention" information. The balance of competition appears to be controlled through the bias.

In experiments (e.g. Chelazzi et al., 1993; Luck et al., 1997) patterns are presented using a delayed match-to-sample-task with expectation paradigm. A desired pattern is presented followed by a blank pause. Then, two patterns (one is the desired) are simultaneously presented in random locations. The monkey cannot use spatial locations to select the patterns because location is random. Recordings of neurons are categorized by which pattern is selected for attention and multiple neurons are averaged together.

When to patterns are presented (e.g. $X_{test} = X_B \cup X_A$), the biased neuron shows an increased activation relative to the neuron associated with unbiased pattern, see Figure 2. Furthermore, the unbiased neuron shows a decreased activation relative to a pre-biased, competition interference scenario.

The initial neuron responses after pattern presentation (0 - ~200ms) are hypothesized to be due to neural competitive interactions within recognition circuits that perform recognition and are the focus of this chapter. Subsequent visual response characteristics in these experiments (> 200ms) likely also incorporate spatial selection

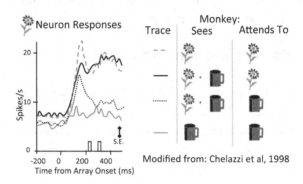

Figure 2. Biased Competition and Dynamics. Characteristic single neuron recordings in the infero-temporal cortex (IT) of the macaque brain. Bias of one neuron causes gain in that neuron and loss in the other.

processes e.g. (Tsotsos, 1990; Itti & Koch, 2001), which is beyond the focus of this chapter.

Biased competition also occurs in other cortical regions that have limited spatial resolution (e.g. sound) and using various patterns types appropriate to those regions (Treue & Martinez-Trujillo, 1999; Bichot et al., 2005).

Models of Competition

Models of biased competition that are based on feedforward and lateral weights between Y's are reviewed here. Then models that show both recognition and biased competition are discussed. The number of parameters required is evaluated. This is not a complete comparison of all possible models, but it is meant to show the difficulties of only using feedforward and lateral connections compared to a feedforward-feedback method.

The biased competition model of Reynolds & Desimone (1999) defines two connection weight sets: one set of weights is designated for a biased representation and another for an unbiased representation. It implies that weights between neurons are changed with biasing. It requires 5 parameters for every connected pair (inhibitory & excitatory set for each neuron and a rate constant). This model is descriptive, but does not implement the neural mechanisms to control these connection weights. Furthermore, the model focuses on the interaction between two neurons. Thus this model must be further expanded to multiple neurons and this model does not perform recognition.

Implementing of competition using lateral connections can have the advantage that connection weights between neurons do not change with biasing. A small increase in activation to the desired representation (a bias) can change the balance of competition. In this fashion, competition is controlled by activation. This is a more complete formalization of the necessary mechanisms for biased competition.

Thus in these models a single positive bias value (determined by attention preference) is applied to the networks to select the patterns.

$$Y_l = Y_l + bias \qquad (9)$$

The model of Spratling & Johnson (2004) implements biased competition with lateral connections and requires 12 parameters (excitatory feed forward & feedback from the two output neurons to the two inputs, and two inhibitory con-

nections to each input of the opposite neurons). Every output representation is connected to every other one. The variables and weights are specifically chosen for biased competition.

In the model of Usher & Niebur (1996) the patterns are composed of predetermined features that support letter representations. Their inhibitory assembly determines the degree of relatedness by connectivity (see Figure 3B). The relations are as follows: X_A is more similar to X_C than X_L. Thus, by connectivity the neuron of Y_A should be connected closer in the inhibitory assembly to neuron Y_C than to neuron Y_L. Subsequently if patterns are presented simultaneously, e.g. $X_{test} = X_A \cup X_C$ or $X_{test} = X_A \cup X_L$ then neurons Y_A & Y_C will mutually inhibit each other more than neurons Y_A & Y_L. In this way, the model emulates both biased competition and pattern similarity effects (Duncan & Humphreys, 1989). The inhibitory assembly determines how close representations are related. If two representations are connected next to another in the assembly then they will mutually inhibit each other more than if they were connected farther apart from each other. The relationship of relatedness determines both competition for classification and biased competi-

Figure 3. Review of mechanisms of biased competition models. A: Weights between neurons are changed during biasing (Reynolds & Desimone, 1999). B: Lateral competition through a population of inhibitory neurons (Usher & Niebur, 1996). C: Lateral inhibition of neighbors and neighbors' inputs (Spratling & Johnson, 2004). D: How related should the shapes be to each other? Direct connections require association weights between representations. Connections to all existing shapes need to be determined for each new shape.

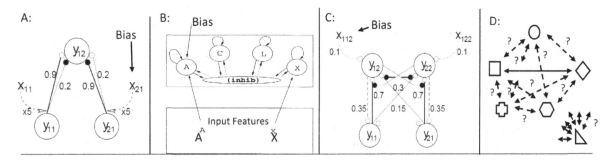

tion. These connections are also a form of lateral connections albeit more indirect. However, more than nine variables are chosen to assure stability of these assemblies, input-output weights and relatedness. The assemblies are evaluated using mean-field population coding.

Other versions of biased competition models partition both input and output nodes (Deco & Rolls, 2005; Deco & Zihl, 2001).

Limitations of lateral connections

Models using lateral connections may require a large number of variables and connections because potentially every representation may affect another. Thus, such models may be: 1) difficult to justify from the perspective of combinatorial plausibility and 2) it is difficult to obtain correct weights for both recognition and the biased competition phenomena.

Most of the reviewed models of biased competition used lateral connections (Spratling & Johnson, 2004; Usher & Niebur, 1996; Deco & Rolls, 2005; Deco & Zihl, 2001). Models using lateral connections become intractable as objects become numerous, because the number of connections between neurons increases combinatorially. For example, neurons representing square and diamond patterns may be encoded between assemblies implementing lateral competition (see Figure 3D). How would a parallelogram, triangle, circle or hexagon neuron relate to these assemblies? Each shape may have unique features while sharing some features with diamond or square. If the network is small this is not a problem. One pair of connection weights (or assembly relations) is sufficient for two shapes. However if three more shapes are added this requires 10 pairs of connections (5 shapes). Addition of another shape, circle, now adds 5 more pairs (15 total). As the 'shape-space' becomes more complex, the number of possible combinations and variables

increases (10,000 stored shapes require 10,000 new connections for one new shape). Requiring every combination (no matter how obscure) to have a predetermined connection weight (or assembly relation) is implausible, resulting in a combinatorial explosion.

The brain can recognize over thousands or millions unique patterns. The number of combinations grows exponentially as the number of possible outputs (n) increases. The number of combinations for two pattern combinations $k=2$ is given by:

$$\binom{n}{k} = \frac{n!}{k!(n-k)!}$$

If the brain contains 100,000 patterns, there are 5 billion connections representing combinations. The brain cannot train for each possible combination for the simple reason that there are not enough resources, such as neurons, let alone the time needed for such preparation. There are a prohibitive number of potential combinations in the brain, and every possible representation combination would have to be pre-determined. In addition, determining the 'correct' weight values is not trivial. This is why lateral connections are not ideally suited for biased competition. Moreover, winner-take-all networks (strong lateral connections) limit simultaneous neuron activation (processing only one neuron at a time). This would not allow biased competition. Furthermore, the weights of this biased competition model are also not designed for recognition. Finding the 'correct' weight values is not trivial. The weights that are optimal for recognition are not necessarily optimal for biased competition. Furthermore, if a new shape is added, all of the weights both new and previously existing may have to be re-determined (not just the new connections).

Modeling Biased Competition and Recognition

Here we discuss how to set up a biased competition experiment scenario using classifier patterns and notation. We use the pattern data set for training that was used in Achler, Vural & Amir (2009) and Achler (2011) because it is motivated by letter patterns and has a good distribution of variously similar patterns. However, we can produce similar results with randomly generated sets of patterns. The network is given 26 pattern → label associations for training $(X_A, X_B, \ldots X_Z) \rightarrow (Y_A, Y_B, \ldots Y_Z)$ respectively.

Testing is conducted by presenting patterns and pattern manipulations to the input layer X and evaluating the output layer Y responses. Thus if a single pattern e.g. $X_{test} = X_A$ is presented to the network, then it should recognize it, namely: neuron Y_A should go to 1 and the rest of the neurons Y go to 0. This is an example of multiclass classification (Achler Vural & Amir 2009; Achler 2011).

The expected behavior for biased competition is as follows. If two patterns are presented simultaneously e.g. $X_{test} = X_B \cup X_A$ then competition interference is observed: neurons Y_A and Y_B become active but less than what they would be if X_A and X_B were presented separately. If one pattern is biased e.g.: $Y_A = Y_A + bias$, then given $X_{test} = X_B \cup X_A$, Y_A becomes closer to 1 and its value increases more than just the bias value. Y_B becomes less active than that it would be without the bias. The unbiased neuron decreases in activation. A feedforward classifier would not be able to do this because it is feedforward. It can only affect the neuron that is biased.

Classifier and Competition

Here we briefly discuss pilot results using our recognition method. A more detailed paper is planned focusing on the combined model. The feedforward-feedback classifier displays the similar dynamics as revealed as experiments (Figure

Figure 4. (A,B): Biased Competition: Biased (preferred) neurons gain activity while unbiased neurons lose activity.

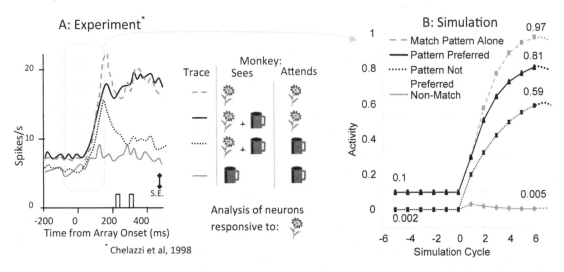

Averaged dynamics of *A*: in-vivo experiment; *B*: simulation (6 cycles after onset).
-- *Match Pattern Alone* –single pattern is presented. Response of associated neuron
___ *Non-Match Pattern Alone* – a single pattern is presented. Response of non-associated neurons
___ *Pattern Preferred* - two patterns presented. Focus is on the recorded neuron
.... *Pattern Not Preferred* - two patterns presented. Focus is on a different neuron
[onset of eye movement.

4, nodes and neurons averaged). The bias appears to increase both the final steady state activity and the rate steady state is reached. This represents both a "sharpening" and "facilitation" of activation (Grill-Spector et al., 2006).

The competition interference is manipulated with the application of a bias. The biased neuron is labeled pattern preferred and the non-biased neuron is labeled pattern not preferred. The dynamics of the first 6 cycles of the classifier is show in Figure 4B.

DISCUSSION AND CONCLUSION

The feedforward-feedback recognition model is similar to a single-layer supervised feedforward models. However, M is easier to learn and modify compared to W since it only requires the expectation of the features relative to the label to be stored. Expectation can be determined by a simple averaging function, co-occurrence, or symbolic-like association between features with labels. This does not require feedback dynamics or error propagation during learning. Thus M can be learned using simple Hebbian learning. Moreover, the feedforward-feedback classifier displays biased competition and dynamics as revealed in experiments (comparing Figure 4 A vs. B). This is significant because this model is a classifier and it does not include empirical variables for biased competition. Thus the inherent nature of the classifier (as opposed to specialized neuron parameters) appears to determine biased competition and dynamics. Subsequently when evaluating the amount of variables, this is by far the most efficient and scalable model.

We presented a novel classifier based on neural networks which uses dynamics during testing. Pilot simulations show how this classifies and inherently displays biased competition. We show this method can perform classification like feedforward methods, but is easier to modify. It also avoids scalability problems associated with lateral competition. These findings combined with experimental findings suggest that the brain performs recognition using feedforward-feedback mechanisms.

FUTURE RESEARCH DIRECTIONS

Future work will include further integration of control and recognition. One possibility is to use symbolic and generative properties of the network with bias control in order to produce "recognition reasoning". Other applications are towards computer vision and machine learning scenarios, combinations of supervised and unsupervised methods, and evaluation of other cognitive phenomena. Additional work in progress includes a more detailed comparison of different types of feedforward-feedback methods.

REFERENCES

Achler, T. (2011). Non-oscillatory dynamics to disambiguate pattern mixtures. In Rao, R., & Cecchi, G. A. (Eds.), *Relevance of the time domain to neural network models*. New York, NY: Springer.

Achler, T. (2012). *Towards bridging the gap between pattern recognition & symbolic representation within neural networks. Neural-Symbolic Learning & Reasoning*. AAAI.

Achler, T., & Bettencourt, L. (2011). *Evaluating the contribution of top-down feedback and post-learning reconstruction. Biologically Inspired Cognitive Architectures*. AAAI.

Achler, T., Vural, D., & Amir, E. (2009). Counting objects with biologically inspired regulatory-feedback networks. In *Proceedings of the 2009 IEEE International Joint Conference on Neural Networks*. ACM/IEEE.

Bichot, N. P., Rossi, A. F., & Desimone, R. (2005). Parallel and serial neural mechanisms for visual search in macaque area V4. *Science, 308*(5721), 529–534. doi:10.1126/science.1109676

Carpenter, G. A., & Grossberg, S. (1987). A massively parallel architecture for a self-organizing neural pattern-recognition machine. *Computer Vision Graphics and Image Processing*, *37*(1), 54–115. doi:10.1016/S0734-189X(87)80014-2

Chelazzi, L., Duncan, J., Miller, E. K., & Desimone, R. (1998). Responses of neurons in inferior temporal cortex during memory-guided visual search. *Journal of Neurophysiology*, *80*(6), 2918–2940.

Chelazzi, L., Miller, E. K., Duncan, J., & Desimone, R. (1993). Article. *Nature*, *363*, 345–347. doi:10.1038/363345a0

Desimone, R., & Duncan, J. (1995). Neural mechanisms of selective visual attention. *Annual Review of Neuroscience*, *18*, 193–222. doi:10.1146/annurev.ne.18.030195.001205

Duncan, J., & Humphreys, G. W. (1989). Visual search and stimulus similarity. *Psychological Review*, *96*(3), 433–458. doi:10.1037/0033-295X.96.3.433

Friston, K. (2009). The free-energy principle: A rough guide to the brain? *Trends in Cognitive Sciences*, *13*(7), 293–301. doi:10.1016/j.tics.2009.04.005

Friston, K., Mattout, J., & Kilner, J. (2011). Action understanding and active inference. *Biological Cybernetics*, *104*, 137–160. doi:10.1007/s00422-011-0424-z

Grill-Spector, K., & Henson, R. (2006). Repetition and the brain: Neural models of stimulus-specific effects. *Trends in Cognitive Sciences*, *10*(1), 14–23. doi:10.1016/j.tics.2005.11.006

Hinton, G. E., & Salakhutdinov, R. R. (2006). Reducing the dimensionality of data with neural networks. *Science*, *313*(5786), 504–507. doi:10.1126/science.1127647

Hopfield, J. J. (1982). Neural networks and physical systems with emergent collective computational abilities. *Proceedings of the National Academy of Sciences of the United States of America*, *79*(8), 2554–2558. doi:10.1073/pnas.79.8.2554

Hyvärinen, A., Hurri, J., & Hoyer, P. O. (2009). *Natural image statistics*. Berlin, Germany: Springer-Verlag. doi:10.1007/978-1-84882-491-1

Igelnik, B., Tabib-Azar, M., & LeClair, S. R. (2001). A net with complex weights. *IEEE Transactions on Neural Networks*, *12*(2). doi:10.1109/72.914521

Itti, L., & Koch, C. (2001). Computational modelling of visual attention. *Nature Reviews. Neuroscience*, *2*(3), 194–203. doi:10.1038/35058500

Luck, S. J., Chelazzi, L., Hillyard, S. A., & Desimone, R. (1997). Neural mechanisms of spatial selective attention in areas V1, V2, and V4 of macaque visual cortex. *Journal of Neurophysiology*, *77*(1), 24–42.

Olshausen, B. A., & Field, D. J. (1996). Emergence of simple-cell receptive field properties by learning a sparse code for natural images. *Nature*, *381*, 607–609. doi:10.1038/381607a0

Rao, R. P., & Ballard, D. H. (1999). Predictive coding in the visual cortex: A functional interpretation of extra-classical receptive field effects. *Nature Neuroscience*. doi:10.1038/4580

Reynolds, J. H., & Desimone, R. (1999). The role of neural mechanisms of attention in solving the binding problem. *Neuron*, *24*(1), 19–29. doi:10.1016/S0896-6273(00)80819-3

Rifkin, R., & Klautau, A. (2004). In defense of one-vs-all classification. *Journal of Machine Learning Research*, *5*, 101–141.

Rosenblatt, F. (1958). The perceptron: A probabilistic model for information storage and organization in the brain. *Psychological Review*, *65*(6), 386–408. doi:10.1037/h0042519

Rumelhart, D. E., & McClelland, J. L. (1986). Parallel distributed processing: Explorations in the microstructure of cognition. *Foundations*, 1.

Schmidhuber, J. (1992). Learning complex, extended sequences using the principle of history compression. *Neural Computation*, *4*(2), 234–242. doi:10.1162/neco.1992.4.2.234

Spratling, M. W., & Johnson, M. H. (2004). A feedback model of visual attention. *Journal of Cognitive Neuroscience*, *16*(2), 219–237. doi:10.1162/089892904322984526

Treue, S., & Martinez-Trujillo, J. C. (1999). Feature-based attention influences motion processing gain in macaque visual cortex. *Nature*, *399*(6736), 575–579. doi:10.1038/21176

Tsotsos, J. K. (1990). Article. *Journal of Behavioral and Brain Science*, *13*, 423–445. doi:10.1017/S0140525X00079577

Usher, M., & Niebur, E. (1996). Modeling the temporal dynamics of IT neurons in visual search: A mechanism for top-down selective attention. *Journal of Cognitive Neuroscience*, *8*(4), 311–327. doi:10.1162/jocn.1996.8.4.311

Vapnik, V. N. (1995). *The nature of statistical learning theory*. New York, NY: Springer-Verlag.

Williams, R. J., & Zipser, D. (1994). Gradient-based learning algorithms for recurrent networks and their computational complexity. In *Backpropagation: Theory, architectures & applications*. Hillsdale, NJ: Erlbaum.

Zeiler, M. D., Kirshnan, D., Taylor, G. W., & Fergus, R. (2010). *Deconvolutional networks*. Computer Vision & Pattern Recognition CVPR.

Chapter 13
Numerical Version of the Non–Uniform Method for Finding Point Estimates of Uncertain Scaling Constants

Natalia D. Nikolova
Nikola Vaptsarov Naval Academy, Bulgaria

Kiril I. Tenekedjiev
Nikola Vaptsarov Naval Academy, Bulgaria

ABSTRACT

The chapter focuses on the analysis of scaling constants when constructing a utility function over multi-dimensional prizes. Due to fuzzy rationality, those constants are elicited in an interval form. It is assumed that the decision maker has provided additional information describing the uncertainty of the scaling constants' values within their uncertainty interval. The non-uniform method is presented to find point estimates of the interval scaling constants and to test their unit sum. An analytical solution of the procedure to construct the distribution of the interval scaling constants is provided, along with its numerical realization. A numerical procedure to estimate p_{value} of the statistical test is also presented. The method allows making an uncertainty description of constants through different types of probability distributions and fuzzy sets.

INTRODUCTION

Quantitative decision analysis is based on subjective statistics (Jeffrey, 2004) and utility theory (Von Neumann & Morgenstern, 1947). It has its main objective to provide guidance to a rational choice of an alternative from the side of the decision maker

(DM). The concept of rational decision making lies on sets of axioms, which prescribe a way to model decision problems, measure preferences (by utilities) and uncertainty (by probabilities), and at a final step – balance this quantitative data according to expected utility (French & Insua, 2001; von Neumann & Morgenstern, 1947).

A major step in the decision analysis process is to construct an adequate model of consequenc-

DOI: 10.4018/978-1-4666-3942-3.ch013

es, which follows from the objectives of the DM in the particular problem. The adopted approach is to represent consequences as vectors, whose coordinates (attributes) measure the degree to which the consequence complies with the DM's goals. Generally, there are many objectives, hence many vector coordinates to measure these. Therefore the default structure of consequences is a d-dimensional (multi-dimensional) vector $\vec{x} = (x_1, x_2, ..., x_d)$, whose coordinates X_i (the attributes) measure different aspects in the problem that are important for the DM. Let's denote the set of all prizes as X. Then $\vec{x}$ in the set of prizes, is a subset of the d-dimensional Euclidean space.

There are three types of attribute independence which facilitate the process of constructing a utility function over $\vec{x}$. The most important one from a practical stand point is utility independence (Keeney & Raiffa, 1993). Let's divide the set of attributes $\{X_1, X_2, ..., X_d\}$ into the greatest possible number of mutually utility independent fundamental vector attributes $Y_1, Y_2, ..., Y_n$ that are $n \in \{2,3,...,d\}$ non-empty non-overlapping subsets. Each Y_i is a system of random variables with an arbitrary realization $\vec{y}_i$ and then prizes in X may be presented as $\vec{x} = (\vec{y}_1, \vec{y}_2, ..., \vec{y}_n)$. Mutual utility independence allows to decompose the multi-dimensional utility function to fundamental utility functions over groups of fundamental vector attributes $Y_1, Y_2, ..., Y_n$. Mutual utility independence allows constructing a normalized fundamental utility function $u_i(.)$ over each fundamental vector attribute Y_i: $u(\vec{x}) = f[u_1(\vec{y}_1), u_2(\vec{y}_2), ..., u_n(\vec{y}_n)]$. The importance of each vector attribute for the overall preferences of the DM over the multi-dimensional prizes is given by their scaling constants.

In a sense, one's preferences over individual attributes have to be scaled into preferences over the entire object. This is not a trivial problem because of the computational difficulties that arise in the process of elicitation and utilization of the

information regarding the scaling constants. Additionally, finding adequate point estimates of the latter is preceded by the answer to the qualitative question of what the type of the utility function is – either additive or multiplicative. This problem is equivalent to that of defining whether the sum of the constants equals to one or not. What is most difficult is that an answer to this question should be given before point estimates are available.

The scaling constants are subjectively elicited in a process of analysis of fictitious consequences (called corner consequences, whose fundamental vector attributes are set to their worst levels except for the i-th attribute, which is set to its best level) (Keeney & Raiffa, 1993). The sum of k_i shows whether the utility function is additive:

$$u = u(\vec{x}) = \sum_{i=1}^{n} k_i u_i(\vec{y}_i)$$

(if they sum to one) or multiplicative:

$$u = u(\vec{x}) = \frac{1}{K_y} \prod_{i=1}^{n} [K_y k_i u_i(\vec{y}_i) + 1] - \frac{1}{K_y}$$

(if they do not sum to one), where K_y is called a general scaling constant, and depends on the values of the scaling constants.

Any process of subjective elicitation of quantities in decision analysis is based on solving preferential equations (and so are scaling constants) (Nikolova & Tenekedjiev, 2010). In Nikolova, Shulus, Toneva, and Tenekedjiev (2005), the relative preference of the DM over the objects in those equations can be described by three fuzzy sets. As a result each preferential equation has an interval rather than a point estimate as a solution, which breaches some of the rationality requirements of utility theory. Therefore, real decision making is only based on bounded rationality, referred to as fuzzy rationality (Nikolova et al., 2005). The theory of fuzzy rationality is a generalization of classical utility theory, which tries to unify the normative rationality with the fuzziness of real preferences in the measurement process.

Fuzzy rationality strongly affects the analysis of scaling constants, which are also presented as interval estimates. So even though it is possible to know for sure the values of some constants, practically speaking, those are always assessed subjectively as uncertainty intervals $k_i \in [k_{d,i}; k_{u,i}]$, for $i=1, 2,\ldots, n$. Then a question arises of how to find the sum of the constants, which cannot be answered in a straightforward way before point estimates $\hat{k}_i$, for $i=1, 2,\ldots, n$ are identified.

The works (Tenekedjiev & Nikolova, 2008; Nikolova, 2007) presented and implemented a uniform method for estimation of interval scaling constants. The method assumes uniform distribution of constants within their uncertainty intervals. The method is developed as an analytical procedure, and its numerical and simulation realizations are also elaborated.

This chapter further develops the theory of multi-dimensional utility by offering a new approach to the problem of interval scaling constants and the assessment of their sum. Here, a new task is formulated – it is assumed that the DM is willing to provide (either in a probabilistic or in a fuzzy form) additional information regarding the values of the scaling constants within their uncertainty interval. The solution of this task is called non-uniform method. It proposes several representations of uncertainty, grouped into two main forms – probability distributions and fuzzy sets – described in detail in the Appendix. At a next stage, this chapter discusses how to construct the distribution of the scaling constants sum, offering an analytical solution and its numerical realization. Finally, a hypothesis test is applied to judge whether the sum equals to one or not, and a numerical procedures to estimate the p_{value} of the statistical test is elaborated. A numerical example shows the implementation of the non-uniform method, and also offers initial comparison with

the uniform method. Initial findings regarding the non-uniform method were proposed in Nikolova, Mednikarov, and Tenekedjiev (2012).

BACKGROUND

The fact that scaling constants have only imprecise estimates and thus are likely to influence the construction of the utility function is a familiar problem. The research literature assumes that the type of the utility function (either multiplicative or additive) is known, and the way the constants affect the ranking of the alternatives is analyzed via sensitivity analysis. The available approaches for sensitivity analysis may be roughly distributed into two groups.

In the first group, the user (the decision maker) gives point estimates to the constants, and the decision analyst approaches the sensitivity of the selected alternative against those point estimates. The main rationale behind this is that the point estimates of the user are not precise. For example, the work Barron and Schmidt (1985) searches for that set of generated point estimates that is closest in a least-square sense to those derived from the user. In such a way the best alternative, resulting from those estimates, may be replaced by another alternative. The authors only stress an additive model. The work Rinquest (1997) summarizes the results for the additive model and introduces the so-called L_p metric that accounts for the differences between the two sets of constants. This metric allows to take into account the weight of the attributes and to use generalized distances. The same analysis is being conducted in Nishizaki and Katagiri (2004) over a multiplicative model, again with the use of the L_p metric. In all papers listed above, the tasks are formalized using a linear programming problem. The same ideas are also employed in Wolters and Mareschal (1995), where a minimal modification of the scaling constants is searched so that the given alternative is ranked first.

The simulation analysis of Butler, Jia, and Dyer (1997) also belongs to that first group. It uses two simulation models – random weight and rank order weights – to analyze the sensitivity of the decision against the scaling constants as a whole.

The second group of approaches asks from the user to define interval estimates and tries to find the sensitivity within the framework of those estimates. The work Jimenes, Rios-Insua, and Mateos (2003) claims that the interval estimates originate from the fact that it is hard for the DM to precisely estimate the subjective probabilities. This work proposes a decision support system, which uses a simulation respond distribution weights simulation method of Butler et al. (1997) to assess the influence of the constant over the ranking of alternatives. The work Nishizaki and Katagiri (2004) proposes a computational method, based on a genetic algorithm, which solves a nonlinear optimization problem for the eventual existence of rank reversal of alternatives in the case of interval scaling constants.

There is another group of methods that aim at defining point estimates of interval scaling constants. The naive method, proposed in French (1993) is commonly applied in practice. It uses midpoints of the uncertainty intervals as point estimates. If the sum differs from 1 by a small quantity, then it is assumed to be 1, and the utility function is additive. Otherwise, the utility function is multiplicative. A disadvantage of that method is that it does not account for the uncertainty of the estimates since it uses only the midpoints of the uncertainty intervals. To overcome this disadvantage, the work Nikolova (2007) for the first time tries to answer the qualitative question of whether the sum equals to one or not (thus determining the type of model of utility – multiplicative or additive), and only after that searches for the point estimates of the constants. There, a simulation realization of the developed uniform method is proposed, where the main assumption is that each scaling constant is uniformly distributed in its uncertainty interval. Finding point estimates of the constant is then brought down to the construction of the distribution and to a two-tail statistical test for singularity of their sum. The result of the test defines the value of the point estimates, i.e. if the sum is one then point estimates are normalized, otherwise midpoints of the uncertainty intervals are used as point estimates.

The analytical version of the uniform method is presented in Tenekedjiev and Nikolova (2008), and is based on the same assumption but the distributions of the partial sum of the constants are gradually build by interpolation on analytically estimated nodes. An original numerical procedure for calculation of p_{value} of a two-tail test for unity of the constants' sum is also proposed, which takes into account the interpolated nature of the constants sum's distribution.

The main drawback of the uniform method is that it does not account for possible information regarding the relative likelihood of the constants' values within their uncertainty interval. In some cases such information might be available from the user, who wishes to provide it as she feels that the end points in the uncertainty interval are less likely than some in the midsections. There are two main interpretations of such information.

The first interpretation is the probabilistic one. Sometimes the user is willing to provide the CDF (the cumulative distribution function) for the constants within their uncertainty interval. Furthermore, the uncertainty interval itself might be resulting from such information. There are at least three obvious ways to formalize this information:

1. A less demanding approach is to provide only the most likely value in the uncertainty interval, and perhaps (if possible) the quantile indices for the lower and upper margin of the uncertainty interval. The distribution might be constructed so that its borders coincide with the limits of the uncertainty interval, following the ideas in the Matlab's Statistical toolbox extension, called QAP (Tenekedjev, Nikolova, & Dimitrakiev, 2004).

2. In the form of quantile value–quantile index pairs, where the lowest and the highest possible evaluated quantiles by the user serve as the borders of the distribution (which is normalized).

3. Through a user-defined function which lies within the lower and upper bound of the uncertainty interval, its definite integral equals to one, and is nonnegative within the uncertainty interval.

The second possible interpretation is the fuzzy one. As long as the user tries to evaluate values within their uncertainty interval, it is quite possible that the only information she can provide is a normalized fuzzy set with degree of membership to the true value with support from $k_{d,i}$ to $k_{u,i}$. Again, there are several ways to formalize the fuzzy set:

1. The less demanding approach is to use triangular fuzzy number, whose degrees of membership are zero at the extremes of the interval, and have a unit value in the point $k_{max,I}$, defined by the user;

2. It is possible to employ trapezoidal fuzzy set, where the user should define the values $k_{max,d,i}$, and $k_{max,u,i}$. Both values are within the uncertainty interval;

3. It is possible to use sequence of pairs "constant values–degree of membership" to the fuzzy set of the true value;

4. It is possible to employ a user-defined function, that is nonnegative for all values from the uncertainty interval.

If any of the two types of information is employed, then it is possible to generate the distribution of the sum of the constants using risk analysis (Hertz & Thomas, 1983), as it was done in Nikolova (2007). In the case of fuzzy interpretation, the degree of membership may be normalized so that its integral equals to one, and therefore may be used as a PDF (probability density function) for the generation of pseudo-real constants. The

value of p_{value} for the singularity of the constants' sum may be found using the procedure in Nikolova (2007). The whole procedure to be presented in this work shall be called non-uniform method. The example to be given shall compare the naive and the uniform method with the non-uniform method.

REPRESENTATION OF THE NON-UNIFORM METHOD

This section presents the analytical essence of the non-uniform method, as well as its numerical interpretation.

Construction of the Distribution Law of the Scaling Constants' Sum in a Non-Trivial Case

Let $k_{d,i}$ and $k_{u,i}$ be respectively the left and the right margin of the uncertainty interval for the scaling constant k_i, whereas its best point estimate is $k_{best,i}$. If at least one of uncertainty intervals is with non-zero length, then the scaling constants may be renumbered in descending order of the length of their uncertainty intervals, where the following conditions hold:

$$k_i \in \left[k_{d,i}; k_{u,i}\right], \text{ for } i = 1,\ 2,\ldots,n,$$
$$k_{u,i} - k_{d,i} \geq k_{u,i+1} - k_{d,i+1}, \text{ for } i = 1,\ 2,\ldots,n-1,$$
$$0 \leq k_{d,i} < k_{u,i} \leq 1, \text{ for } i = 1,\ 2,\ldots,m,$$
$$k_{d,i} \leq k_{best,i} \leq k_{u,i}, \text{ for } i = 1,\ 2,\ldots,m,$$
$$k_{d,i} = k_{best,i} = k_{u,i}, \text{ for } i = m+1, m+2,\ldots,n,$$
$$\text{if } m < n$$
$$0 < m \leq n, n > 1.$$

$$(1)$$

The problem is to determine whether $k_1 + k_2 + \ldots + k_n = 1$, and then find point estimates of the constants $\hat{k}_i$, for $i = 1, 2, \ldots, n$.

A total of $3n$ auxiliary constants are introduced:

$$a_i = \sum_{r=1}^{i} k_{d,r}, \quad \text{for } i = 1, 2, \ldots, n, \qquad (2)$$

$$b_i = \sum_{r=1}^{i} k_{u,r}, \quad \text{for } i = 1, 2, \ldots, n, \qquad (3)$$

$$h_i = \sum_{r=1}^{i} k_{best,r}, \quad \text{for } i = 1, 2, \ldots, n, \qquad (4)$$

as well as a n auxiliary variables

$$y_i = \sum_{j=1}^{i} k_j, \quad \text{for } i = 1, 2, \ldots, n. \qquad (5)$$

It is assumed that each unknown constant is distributed in its uncertainty interval with density $f_{k_i}(k_i)$ for $i=1, 2, \ldots, m$. It is worth investigating the case when the following non-triviality conditions hold:

$$\begin{aligned} m &> 0, \\ a_n &< 1, \qquad\qquad (6) \\ b_n &> 1. \end{aligned}$$

Then it is necessary to construct the distribution law of the random variable y_n, which is the sum of all scaling constants. It allows analyzing statistical hypotheses for the value of the scaling constants' sum.

Analytical Construction of the Distribution Law of y_n in a Non-Trivial Case

It is convenient to build the distribution law of y_i in PDF form. Let the density of y_i be denoted $f_{y_i}(.)$, and its non-zero section be in the closed interval $[a_i; b_i]$. To answer the question of whether the sum of constants equal to one or not, it is necessary to estimate $f_{y_n}(.)$, which can be done

using $f_{y_m}(.)$ since the difference between y_n and y_m is a fixed value:

$$f_{y_n}(y_n) = \begin{cases} f_{y_m}(y_n - \sum_{j=m+1}^{n} k_{d,j}), & \text{if } m \in \{1, 2, \ldots, n-1\} \\ f_{y_m}(y_n), & \text{if } m = n \end{cases} \qquad (7)$$

Then the task is brought down to the construction of $f_{y_m}(.)$.

Case 1.1: m=1

The task is solved, since $y_1 = k_1$, $a_1 = k_{d,1}$, $b_1 = k_{u,1}$, and $f_{y_1}(y_1) = f_{k_1}(k_1)$.

Case 1.2: m>1

Now $f_{y_m}(.)$ shall be constructed recurrently, by solving $(m-1)$ sub-tasks: "Construct $f_{y_i}(.)$ using the defined $f_{y_{i-1}}(.)$ and $f_{k_i}(.)$, for $i=2, 3, \ldots, m$.". The following recurrent dependencies hold:

$$\begin{aligned} y_i &= y_{i-1} + k_i, \quad \text{for } i = 2, 3, \ldots, m, \\ a_i &= a_{i-1} + k_{d,i}, \quad \text{for } i = 2, 3, \ldots, m, \qquad (8) \\ b_i &= b_{i-1} + k_{u,i}, \quad \text{for } i = 2, 3, \ldots, m. \end{aligned}$$

The first recurrent procedure shows that the value of $f_{y_i}(y_i)$ shall be proportional to the integral on y_{i-1} of all products $f_{y_{i-1}}(y_{i-1}) f_{k_i}(y_i - y_{i-1})$:

$$f_{y_i}(y_i) \sim \int_{-\infty}^{+\infty} f_{y_{i-1}}(y_{i-1}) f_{k_i}(y_i - y_{i-1}) dy_{i-1} = \varphi_{y_i}(y_i),$$

$$\text{for} \quad y_i \in [a_i; b_i] \qquad (9)$$

The sub-integral quantity is different than zero under the following conditions:

$$\begin{vmatrix} y_{i-1} \geq a_{i-1} \\ y_{i-1} \leq b_{i-1} \\ y_i - y_{i-1} \geq k_{d,i} \\ y_i - y_{i-1} \leq k_{u,i} \\ y_{i-1} \geq \max\{a_{i-1}, y_i - k_{u,i}\} = y_{i-1}^d(y_i) \\ y_{i-1} \leq \min\{b_{i-1}, y_i - k_{d,i}\} = y_{i-1}^u(y_i) \end{vmatrix} \Rightarrow \begin{vmatrix} y_{i-1} \geq a_{i-1} \\ y_{i-1} \geq y_i - k_{u,i} \\ y_{i-1} \leq b_{i-1} \\ y_{i-1} \leq y_i - k_{d,i} \end{vmatrix} \Rightarrow$$

$$\tag{10}$$

Figure 1 presents an example of the defined limits at $i=8$.

The required $f_{y_i}(.)$ may be found by normalizing $\varphi_{y_i}(.)$, so that the area between the function and the abscissa equals to one:

$$f_{y_i}(y_i) = \frac{\varphi_{y_i}(y_i)}{\int_{a_i}^{b_i} \varphi_{y_i}(y_i) dy_i}, \quad \text{for } i = 2, 3, \dots, m. \tag{11}$$

Numerical Construction of the Distribution Law of y_n in a Non-Trivial Case

The analytical dependencies from the previous section may be numerically approximated. Let the distributions of the variables k_i and y_i be in a

Figure 1. Integration limits in the sub-task "construct $f_{y_8}(.)$ using $f_{y_7}(.)$ and $f_{k_8}(.)$", at $a_7=0.8$, $b_7=1.8$, $k_{d,8}=0.1$ and $k_{u,8}=0.5$

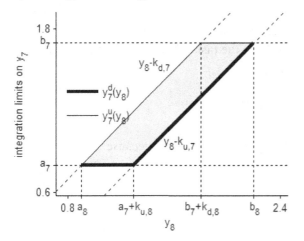

general histogram form $f_{k_i}(.)$ and $\hat{f}_{y_i}(.)$ as piecewise linear interpolations of the corresponding PDF, with possible discontinuities at each node.

Let's describe $f_{k_i}(.)$ with $(2.Nk_i -2)$ nodes: $\{(k_j^{(i)}, f_j^{(i,krt)}) \mid j=1, 2,\dots, Nk_i-1\}$ and $\{(k_j^{(i)}, f_j^{(i,klf)}) \mid j=2, 3,\dots, Nk_i\}$. The following condition holds:

$$Nk_i > 1 \tag{12}$$

$$0 \leq k_1^{(i)} < k_2^{(i)} < \dots < k_{Nk_i}^{(i)} \leq 1 \tag{13}$$

$$f_j^{(i,krt)} \geq 0, \text{for } j = 1, 2,\dots, Nk_i - 1 \tag{14}$$

$$f_j^{(i,klf)} \geq 0, \text{for } j = 2, 3,\dots, Nk_i \tag{15}$$

$$\sum_{j=1}^{Nk_i-1} \frac{f_{j+1}^{(i,krt)} + f_j^{(i,klf)}}{2}\left(k_{j+1}^{(i)} - k_j^{(i)}\right) = 1 \tag{16}$$

$$\left(f_1^{(i,krt)}\right)^2 + \left(f_2^{(i,klt)}\right)^2 > 0 \tag{17}$$

$$\left(f_{Nk_i-1}^{(i,krt)}\right)^2 + \left(f_{Nk_i}^{(i,klt)}\right)^2 > 0 \tag{18}$$

Then the PDF of the variable k_i would be as shown in Box 1.

According to (17) and (18):

$$k_{d,i} = k_1^{(i)} \tag{20}$$

$$k_{u,i} = k_{Nk_i}^{(i)} \tag{21}$$

As long as some of the nodes ordinates in (19) can be equal, the determination of $k_{best,i}$ is not so trivial. It is estimated by the following algorithm.

Algorithm 1. Algorithm to Estimate the Best Point Estimate $k_{best,i}$ for k_i Using $f_{k_i}(.)$

1. Form a set of Nk maximal PDF values of $f_{k_i}(.)$:

Box 1.

$$
f_{k_i}(k)=
\begin{cases}
0, & \text{if } k < k_1^{(i)}\\[4pt]
f_1^{(i,krt)}, & \text{if } k = k_1^{(i)}\\[8pt]
\dfrac{(k - k_j^{(i)})\, f_{j+1}^{(i,krt)}+(k_{j+1}^{(i)} - k)\, f_j^{(i,klf)}}{k_{j+1}^{(i)} - k_j^{(i)}}, & \text{if } k_j^{(i)} < k < k_{j+1}^{(i)}\ ,\ \text{ for } j=1,2,...,Nk_i - 1\\[12pt]
\dfrac{f_j^{(i,klf)} + f_j^{(i,krt)}}{2}, & \text{if } k = k_j^{(i)}\ ,\ \text{ for } j=2,3,...,Nk_i - 1\\[10pt]
f_{Nk_i}^{(i,klf)}, & \text{if } k = k_{Nk_i}^{(i)}\\[6pt]
0, & \text{if } k_{Nk_i}^{(i)} < k
\end{cases}
\tag{19}
$$

$$ft_1 = f_1^{(i,krt)}$$

$$ft_j = \max\left\{ f_j^{(i,krt)},\, f_j^{(i,klf)} \right\},$$
$$\text{for} \quad j = 2, 3, ..., Nk_i + 1$$

$$ft_{Nk_i} = f_{Nk_i}^{(i,klf)};$$

2. Find the maximal value of the ordinates of $f_{k_i}(.)$:

$$f_{max} = \max\left\{ ft_1,\ ft_2, ..., ft_{Nk_i} \right\}$$

3. Count the nodes of $f_{k_i}(.)$ with ordinates equal to $f_{max,i}$:

$$Mb = \sum_{\substack{j=1 \\ ft_j = f_{max}}}^{Nk_n} 1$$

4. Estimate $k_{best,i}$ as the mean value of the abscissas of all nodes which have maximal ordinates:

$$k_{best,i} = \left(\sum_{\substack{j=1 \\ ft_j = f_{max}}}^{Nk_n} k_j^{(i)} \right) / Mb$$

Let's describe $\hat{f}_{y_i}(.)$ with $(2.Ny_i -2)$ nodes: $\{(y_j^{(i)}, f_j^{(i,yrt)}) \mid j=1,2,...,Ny_i-1\}$ and $\{(y_j^{(i)}, f_j^{(i,ylf)}) \mid j=2, 3,..., Ny_i\}$. The following condition holds:

$$y_1^{(i)} < y_2^{(i)} < ... < y_{Ny_i}^{(i)} \tag{22}$$

$$f_j^{(i,yrt)} \geq 0,\ \text{for } j = 1,\ 2,..., Ny_i - 1 \tag{23}$$

$$f_j^{(i,ylf)} \geq 0, \text{for } j = 2,\ 3,..., Ny_i \tag{24}$$

$$\sum_{j=1}^{Ny_i - 1} \frac{f_{j+1}^{(i,yrt)} + f_j^{(i,ylf)}}{2}\left(y_{j+1}^{(i)} - y_j^{(i)} \right) = 1 \tag{25}$$

Then the PDF of the variable $y_i = k_1 + k_2 + ... + k_i$ would be as shown in Box 2.

The nodes of $\hat{f}_{y_n}(.)$ may be easily calculated using the nodes of $\hat{f}_{y_m}(.)$, since the difference between y_n and y_m is a fixed value:

Then the task is brought down to finding the nodes of $\hat{f}_{y_m}(.)$.

Case 2.1: m=1

The problem is solved because $\hat{f}_{y_1}(.)$ coincides with $f_{k_i}(.)$:

Box 2.

$$\hat{f}_{y_i}(y) = \begin{cases} 0, & \text{if } y < y_1^{(i)} \\ f_1^{(i,yrt)}, & \text{if } y = y_1^{(i)} \\ \dfrac{(y - y_j^{(i)})\, f_{j+1}^{(i,yrt)} + (y_{j+1}^{(i)} - y)\, f_j^{(i,ylf)}}{y_{j+1}^{(i)} - y_j^{(i)}}, & \text{if } y_j^{(i)} < y < y_{j+1}^{(i)}, \\ & \text{for } j=1,\,2,...,\,Ny_i - 1 \\ \dfrac{f_j^{(i,ylf)} + f_j^{(i,yrt)}}{2}, & \text{if } y = y_j^{(i)}, \\ & \text{for } j=2,\,3,...,\,Ny_i - 1 \\ f_{Ny_i}^{(i,ylf)}, & \text{if } y = y_{Ny_i}^{(i)} \\ 0, & \text{if } y_{Ny_i}^{(i)} < y \end{cases} \qquad (26)$$

Box 3.

$$\begin{cases} Ny_n = Ny_m \\ y_j^{(n)} = \begin{cases} y_j^{(m)} + \displaystyle\sum_{j=m+1}^{n} k_{d,j}, & \text{if } m < n \\ y_j^{(m)}, & \text{if } m = n \end{cases} & , \text{ for } j = 1,2,...,Ny_n \\ f_j^{(n,ylf)} = f_j^{(m,ylf)} & , \text{ for } j = 1,2,...,Ny_n \\ f_j^{(n,yrt)} = f_j^{(m,yrt)} & , \text{ for } j = 1,2,...,Ny_n \end{cases} \qquad (27)$$

$$\begin{cases} Ny_1 = Ny_1 \\ y_j^{(1)} = k_j^{(1)} & \text{,for } j=1,\,2,...,Ny_1 \\ f_j^{(1,yrt)} = f_j^{(1,krt)} & \text{, for } j=1,\,2,...,Ny_1 - 1 \\ f_j^{(1,ylf)} = f_j^{(1,klf)} & \text{,for } j=2,\,3,...,Ny_1 \end{cases} \qquad (28)$$

Case 2.2: *m>1*

Now the nodes of $\hat{f}_{y_m}(.)$ shall be found recurrently by solving $(m-1)$ sub-tasks: "Find the nodes of $\hat{f}_{y_i}(.)$, using the defined nodes of $\hat{f}_{y_{i-1}}(.)$ and $f_{k_i}(.)$, for $i=2,\,3,...,\,m$". Each sub-task may be solved according to the algorithm below, where $\psi_{y_i}(.)$ is a continuous piecewise linear approximation of the function $\varphi_{y_i}(.)$ defined by Equation (9).

Algorithm 2. Algorithm to Find the Nodes of $\hat{f}_{y_i}(.)$ Using Defined Nodes of $\hat{f}_{y_{i-1}}(.)$ and $f_{k_i}(.)$

1. Choose Ny_i as an integer satisfying the condition $Ny_i \geq Ny_{i-1}$
2. Calculate the limits of the non-zero section of $f_{y_i}(.)$:

$$a_i = y_1^{(i-1)} + k_{d,i},$$

$$b_i = y_{N_{i-1}}^{(i-1)} + k_{u,i};$$

3. Choose the abscissas of the nodes uniformly distributed in the interval $[a_i; b_i]$:

$$y_j^{(i)} = a_i + (b_i - a_i)(j-1)/(Ny_i - 1) , \quad \text{for } j=1, 2,..., Ny_i$$

4. Set to zero the ordinates of the endmost nodes of the piece-wise linear function $\psi_{y_i}(.)$ whose N_i nodes $\{(y_j^{(i)}, \psi_j^{(i)}) \mid j=1, 2, ..., Ny_i\}$ have equal abscissas with the nodes of $\hat{f}_{y_i}(.)$:

$$\psi_1^{(i)} = 0, \quad \psi_{N_i}^{(i)} = 0.$$

5. For j, such that $2 \le j \le (N_i+1)/2$, calculate $\psi_j^{(i)}$ following the next steps:

   a. Calculate the lower and upper limit of the definite integral at $y_j^{(i)}$:

$$c = y_{i-1}^d(y_j^{(i)}) = \begin{cases} y_1^{(i-1)}, & \text{if } y_j^{(i)} \le y_1^{(i-1)} + k_{u,i} \\ y_j^{(i)} - k_{u,i}, & \text{if } y_j^{(i)} > y_1^{(i-1)} + k_{u,i} \end{cases}$$

$$d = y_{i-1}^u(y_j^{(i)}) = \begin{cases} y_j^{(i)} - k_{d,i}, & \text{if } y_j^{(i)} \le y_{N_{i-1}}^{(i-1)} + k_{d,i} \\ y_{N_{i-1}}^{(i-1)}, & \text{if } y_j^{(i)} > y_{N_{i-1}}^{(i-1)} + k_{d,i} \end{cases}$$

b. Count the nodes of $\hat{f}_{y_{i-1}}(.)$ with abscissas between c and d:

$$My = \sum_{\substack{k=1 \\ c<y_k^{(i-1)}<d}}^{N_{i-1}} 1 ;$$

c. If $My>0$, then find the first index of a node with abscissa between c and d:

$$j_{min} = \arg\{ \min_{\substack{j \\ c<y_j^{(i-1)}<d}} y_j^{(i-1)}\};$$

d. Form a set of $(My+2)$ values for y_{i-1}:

$$yt_1 = c;$$

$$yt_{jt} = y_{k_{min}+jt-2}^{(i-1)} \quad , \text{for } jt=2, 3,..., My+1$$

$$yt_{My+2} = d;$$

e. Calculate the values of the function $\hat{f}_{y_{i-1}}(.)$ at yt_{jt}, for $jt=1, 2,..., My+2$ as shown in Box 4.

f. Form a set of $(My+2)$ values for k_i:

Box 4.

$$fyt_{jt} = \begin{cases} 0, & \text{if } yt_{jt} < y_1^{(i-1)} \\ f_1^{(i-1,yrt)}, & \text{if } yt_{jt} = y_1^{(i-1)} \\ \dfrac{(yt_{jt} - y_j^{(i-1)}) f_{j+1}^{(i-1,yrt)} + (y_{j+1}^{(i-1)} - yt_{jt}) f_j^{(i-1,ylf)}}{y_{j+1}^{(i-1)} - y_j^{(i-1)}}, & \text{if } y_j^{(i-1)} < yt_{jt} < y_{j+1}^{(i-1)} , \\ & \text{for } j=1, 2,..., Ny_{i-1} - 1 \\ \dfrac{f_j^{(i-1,ylf)} + f_j^{(i-1,yrt)}}{2}, & \text{if } yt_{jt} = y_j^{(i-1)} , \\ & \text{for } j=2, 3,..., Ny_{i-1} - 1 \\ f_{Ny_{i-1}}^{(i-1,ylf)}, & \text{if } yt_{jt} = y_{Ny_{i-1}}^{(i-1)} \\ 0, & \text{if } y_{Ny_{i-1}}^{(i-1)} < yt_{jt} \end{cases}$$

Box 5.

$$
fkt_{jt} = \begin{cases}
0, & \text{if } kt_{jt} < k_1^{(i)} \\[2mm]
f_1^{(i,krt)}, & \text{if } kt_{jt} = k_1^{(i)} \\[2mm]
\dfrac{(kt_{jt} - k_j^{(i)})\, f_{j+1}^{(i,krt)} + (k_{j+1}^{(i)} - kt_{jt})\, f_j^{(i,klf)}}{k_{j+1}^{(i)} - k_j^{(i)}}, & \text{if } k_j^{(i)} < kt_{jt} < k_{j+1}^{(i)}\ , \\[2mm]
& \quad \text{for } j=1, 2,..., Nk_i - 1 \\[2mm]
\dfrac{f_j^{(i,klf)} + f_j^{(i,krt)}}{2}, & \text{if } kt_{jt} = k_j^{(i)}\ , \\[2mm]
& \quad \text{for } j=2, 3,..., Nk_i - 1 \\[2mm]
f_{Nk_i}^{(i,klf)}, & \text{if } kt_{jt} = k_{Nk_i}^{(i)} \\[2mm]
0, & \text{if } k_{Nk_i}^{(i)} < kt_{jt}
\end{cases}
$$

$$kt_{jt} = y_j^{(i)} - yt_{jt} \quad , \text{for } jt=1, 2, 3,..., My + 2$$

    g.   Calculate the values of the function $f_{k_i}(.)$ at kt_{jt}, for $jt=1, 2,..., My+2$ as shown in Box 5.

    h.   Calculate the integral:

$$\psi_j^{(i)} = \int_c^d \hat{f}_{y_{i-1}}(y_{i-1})\, f_{k_i}(y_i - y_{i-1})\, \mathrm{d}y_{i-1}$$

as a sum of the areas of the trapeziums with different heights:

$$\psi_j^{(i)} = \sum_{jt=1}^{My+1} \frac{fyt_{jt+1} fkt_{jt+1} + fyt_{jt} fk_{jt}}{2}\left(yt_{jt+1} - yt_{jt}\right)$$

6.   Calculate the area between $\psi_{y_i}(.)$ and the abscissa as a sum of the areas of the trapeziums with equal heights:

$$S = \frac{\left(\psi_1^{(i)} + \psi_{N_i}^{(i)} + 2\displaystyle\sum_{j=2}^{N_i} \psi_j^{(i)}\right)\left(y_{N_i}^{(i)} - y_1^{(i)}\right)}{2(N_i - 1)}$$

7.   Normalize the nodes of $\psi_{y_i}(.)$ so that the area between the new function $\hat{f}_{y_i}(.)$ and the abscissa equals to one:

$$f_j^{(i)} = \psi_j^{(i)} / S\ , j=1, 2, ..., N_i.$$

8.   Set the PDF $\hat{f}_{y_i}(.)$ in general histogram form:

$$\begin{aligned}
f_j^{(i,yrt)} &= f_j^{(i)} \quad , \text{for } j = 1, 2,..., Ny_1 - 1 \\
f_j^{(i,ylf)} &= f_j^{(i)} \quad , \text{for } j = 2, 3,..., Ny_1
\end{aligned}$$

Numerical Estimation of p_{value}

If the non-triviality conditions (6) hold, then it is impossible to say whether the sum of the scaling constants equals to one or not. Nikolova (2007) proposes to use a two-tail statistical test with a null hypothesis "the sum of the scaling constants equals to one" (H_0: y_n=1) and alternative hypothesis "the sum of scaling constants is not equal to one" (H_1: $y_n \neq 1$). At a level of significance α and calculated p_{value} (i.e. probability to reject H_0 that is true, or the type I error of the test), H_0 is rejected and H_1 is accepted if $p_{value} \leq \alpha$, or H_0 fails to be rejected if $p_{value} > \alpha$ (Hanke & Reitsch, 1991). It is necessary to assess p_{value}. Nikolova (2007) proves an analytical dependence of p_{value} and the density $f_{y_n}(.)$ of the form:

$$
p_{value} = \begin{cases} 2\int_{a_n}^{1} f_{y_n}(y)\mathrm{d}y & \text{if } \int_{a_n}^{1} f_{y_n}(y)\mathrm{d}y < 0.5 \\ 2 - 2\int_{a_n}^{1} f_{y_n}(y)\mathrm{d}y & \text{if } \int_{a_n}^{1} f_{y_n}(y)\mathrm{d}y \geq 0.5 \end{cases}
$$

(29)

Dependence (29) may be numerically approximated. Let $\hat{f}_{y_n}(.)$ be the general histogram approximation of $f_{y_n}(.)$ with $(2* Ny_n - 2)$. Then the integral in (29) may be approximated by

$$
\int_{a_n}^{1} f_{y_n}(y)\mathrm{d}y \approx \int_{a_n}^{1} \hat{f}_{y_n}(y)\mathrm{d}y
$$

(30)

The value of p_{value} may be estimated using the following algorithm.

Algorithm 3. Algorithm for Numerical Estimation of p_{value} in a Non-Trivial Case

1. Count the nodes of $\hat{f}_{y_n}(.)$ with abscissas smaller than 1:

$$
Mp = \sum_{\substack{j=1 \\ y_j^{(n)} < 1}}^{Ny_n} 1\,;
$$

2. Calculate the value of $\hat{f}_{y_n}(.)$ in 1 as shown in Box 6.

3. Calculate $s = \int_{a_n}^{1} \hat{f}_{y_n}(y)\mathrm{d}y$ as a sum of the areas of trapeziums with different heights as shown in Box 7.

4. Approximate p_{value} by

$$
\hat{p}_{value} = \begin{cases} 2s, & \text{if } s < 0.5 \\ 2 - 2s, & \text{if } s \geq 0.5 \end{cases}
$$

Trivial cases for the value of the constants' sum are analyzed in Nikolova (2007), where defining p_{value} does not require the construction of the distribution law of y_n. If $a_n = b_n = 1$, then $p_{value} = 1$ and H_0 fails to be rejected. If $a_n = b_n \neq 1$, $a_n < b_n \leq 1$, or $1 \leq a_n < b_n$, then $p_{value} = 0$ and H_0 is rejected.

Point estimates of the scaling constants are defined depending on the result of the test, following (31), where $\beta = (h_n - 1)/(h_n - a_n)$ and $\gamma = (b_n - 1)/(b_n - h_n)$ as shown in Box 8.

Box 6.

$$
\hat{f}_{y_n}(1) = \begin{cases} 0, & \text{if } 1 < y_1^{(n)} \\ f_1^{(n,yrt)}, & \text{if } 1 = y_1^{(n)} \\ \dfrac{(1 - y_j^{(n)})\, f_{j+1}^{(n,yrt)} + (y_{j+1}^{(n)} - 1)\, f_j^{(n,ylf)}}{y_{j+1}^{(n)} - y_j^{(n)}}, & \begin{array}{l} \text{if } y_j^{(n)} < 1 < y_{j+1}^{(n)}\,, \\ \text{for } j=1, 2,..., Ny_n - 1 \end{array} \\ \dfrac{f_j^{(n,ylf)} + f_j^{(n,yrt)}}{2}, & \begin{array}{l} \text{if } 1 = y_j^{(n)}\,, \\ \text{for } j=2, 3,..., Ny_n - 1 \end{array} \\ f_{Ny_n}^{(n,ylf)}, & \text{if } 1 = y_{Ny_n}^{(n)} \\ 0, & \text{if } y_{Ny_n}^{(n)} < 1 \end{cases}
$$

Box 7.

$$s = \int\limits_{a_n}^{1} \hat{f}_{y_n}(y)\mathrm{d}y = \begin{cases} \dfrac{\left(\hat{f}_{y_n}(1)+f_1^{(n,yrt)}\right)(1-y_1^{(n)})}{2} & , \text{if } Mp = 1 \\[4mm] \dfrac{\displaystyle\sum_{j=1}^{Mp-1}(f_j^{(n,ylt)} + f_{j-1}^{(n,yrt)})(y_j^{(n)} - y_{j-1}^{(n)})}{2} & , \text{if } Mp \geq 2 \\[2mm] + \dfrac{\left(\hat{f}_{y_n}(1)+f_{Mp}^{(n,yrt)}\right)(1-y_{Mp}^{(n)})}{2} \end{cases}$$

Box 8.

$$\hat{k}_i = \begin{cases} \beta k_{d,i} + (1-\beta)k_{best,i} & , \text{if } H_0 \text{ fails to be rejected and } h_n > 1 \\ \gamma k_{best,i} + (1-\gamma)k_{u,i} & , \text{if } H_0 \text{ fails to be rejected and } h_n < 1 \\ k_{best,i} & , \text{if } H_1 \text{ is accepted or } h_n = 1 \end{cases} \qquad (31)$$

Numerical Example

The procedures, algorithms and plotting accompanying the non-uniform method were embodied into original program functions in MATLAB R2012a. The software is available free of charge upon request from the authors.

A numerical example shall be analyzed, where the DM needs to rank alternatives with eleven-dimensional consequences $\vec{x} = (x_1, x_2, \ldots, x_{11})$ with $d=11$ attributes. The objective is to construct an utility function over the consequences. The DM has established mutual utility independence between the attributes, and constructed eleven one-dimensional utility functions $u_i(x_i)$, for $i=1, 2, \ldots,$ 11. The DM has solved eleven preferential equations as in Nikolova and Tenekedjiev (2010) and elicited the uncertainty intervals for each of the constants as follows: 1) first constant – [0.07; 0.3]; 2) second constant – [0.05; 0.05]; 3) third constant – [0.1; 0.5]; 4) fourth constant – [0.02; 0.25]; 5) fifth constant – [0.1; 0.53]; 6) sixth constant – [0; 0.78]; 7) seventh constant – [0; 0.32]; 8) eighth constant – [0.02; 0.38]; 9) ninth constant – [0.05;

0.55]; 10) tenth constant – [0; 0.6]; 11) eleventh constant – [0.1; 0.36]. Assume that the DM has provided additional information for the uncertainty in the defined uncertainty intervals, corresponding to the example cases given in Appendix 1, as follows: 1) first constant – user defined continuous FS as Fig. A10; 2) second constant – crisp set as Fig. A11; 3) third constant – triangular FS as Fig. A7; 4) fourth constant – uniform PDF as Fig. A6; 5) fifth constant – trapezoidal FS as Fig. A8; 6) sixth constant – generalized triangular PDF as Fig. A2; 7) seventh constant – truncated normal PDF as Fig. A5; 8) eighth constant – generalized histogram as Fig. A1; 9) ninth constant – linearly interpolated PDF as Fig. A4; 10) tenth constant – QAP CDF as Fig. A3; 11) eleventh constant – linearly interpolated FS as Fig. A9. This example is rather artificial. In practice, one would expect that the DM would select one of the methods, given in Appendix 1, and would use it to describe each one of the constants. The choice of a method depends entirely on the preferences of the DM.

Utility Function Over all Constants

Using the non-uniform method over all the constants, it was calculated that $\hat{p}_{value} \approx 1.81e\text{-}7$. Then a null hypothesis H_0 (stating that the sum of the constants equals to one) is rejected at a significance level of $\alpha = 0.05$ and H_1 is accepted (stating that the sum of the constants is not equal to one) since $\hat{p}_{value} \approx 1.81e\text{-}7 << 5e\text{-}2 = \alpha$. The distribution of the scaling constants' sum is given on Figure 2. The estimates of the scaling constants, according to (31), are as follows: $\hat{k}_1 = 0.4$, $\hat{k}_2 = 0.3$, $\hat{k}_3 = 0.19$, $\hat{k}_4 = 0.45$, $\hat{k}_5 = 0.45$, $\hat{k}_6 = 0.4$, $\hat{k}_7 = 0.145$, $\hat{k}_8 = 0.2$, $\hat{k}_9 = 0.135$, $\hat{k}_{10} = 0.151$, $\hat{k}_{11} = 0.05$. The value of the general constant is $K = -0.9657$. Finally, the multi-dimensional utility function would be multiplicative:

$$u = u(\vec{\mathbf{x}}) = \frac{1}{K} \prod_{i=1}^{11} [K\hat{k}_i u_i(x_i) + 1] - \frac{1}{K}$$

Similar results would be derived if the uniform method was employed, i.e. using only the interval estimates of the constants without additional information. Then, H_0 is also rejected ($p_{value} = 4.65e\text{-}7$). There is a slight difference in the point estimates of the scaling constants, as follows: $\hat{k}_1^{um} = 0.185$, $\hat{k}_2^{um} = 0.05$, $\hat{k}_3^{um} = 0.3$, $\hat{k}_4^{um} = 0.135$, $\hat{k}_5^{um} = 0.315$, $\hat{k}_6^{um} = 0.44$, $\hat{k}_7^{um} = 0.46$, $\hat{k}_8^{um} = 0.195$, $\hat{k}_9^{um} = 0.3$, $\hat{k}_{10}^{um} = 0.3$, $\hat{k}_{11}^{um} = 0.23$. The value of the general constant is $K^{um} = -0.9658$. Finally, the multi-dimensional utility function would be multiplicative:

$$u = u(\vec{\mathbf{x}}) = \frac{1}{K^{um}} \prod_{i=1}^{11} [K^{um}\hat{k}_i^{um} u_i(x_i) + 1] - \frac{1}{K^{um}}$$

Although both methods generate multiplicative utility function, the non-uniform method has an advantage in terms of better estimates of the scaling constants.

Figure 2. CDF and PDF of the sum of all scaling constants using the non-uniform method

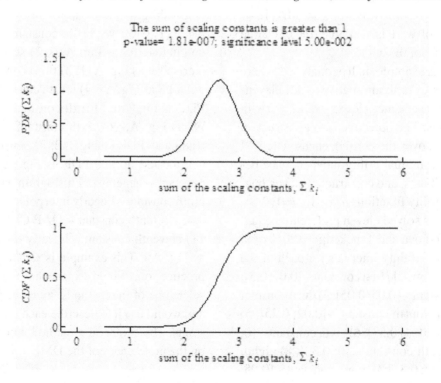

Utility Function Over Reduced Set of Constants

Two reduced sets of the constants shall be analyzed for the purpose of comparison of the non-uniform and uniform methods.

IV.2.1

Let's assume that the analyzed prizes are five-dimensional, consisting of the first five attributes. Thus, the analysis focuses only on the first five constants. This in fact means that the vector of prizes is five-dimensional, because the DM neglects the coordinates after the sixth. The individual utility functions $u_i(x_i)$ are the same as in IV.1, for $i=1,2,\ldots,5$.

Using the non-uniform method over the constants, it was calculated that $\hat{p}_{value} \approx 0.882$. Then

the null hypothesis H_0 fails to be rejected at a significance level of $\alpha = 0.05$ since $\hat{p}_{value} \approx 0.882 >> 0.05 = \alpha$ (Figure 3). The estimates of the scaling constants are as follows: $\hat{k}_1 = 0.1332$, $\hat{k}_2 = 0.05$, $\hat{k}_3 = 0.334$, $\hat{k}_4 = 0.1097$, $\hat{k}_5 = 0.373$. Finally, the multi-dimensional utility function would be additive:

$$u(\vec{\mathbf{x}}) = \sum_{i=1}^{5} k_i u_i(x_i).$$

Using the uniform method over the constants, it was calculated that $\hat{p}_{value} \approx 0.9413$. Then the null hypothesis H_0 fails to be rejected at a significance level of $\alpha = 0.05$ since $\hat{p}_{value} \approx 0.9413 >> 0.05 = \alpha$ (Figure 4). The estimates of the scaling constants are as follows: $\hat{k}_1^{um} = 0.1877$, $\hat{k}_2^{um} = 0.05$, $\hat{k}_3^{um} = 0.3047$, $\hat{k}_4^{um} = 0.1377$, $\hat{k}_5^{um} = 0.32$.

Figure 3. CDF and PDF of the sum of first to fifth scaling constants using the non-uniform method

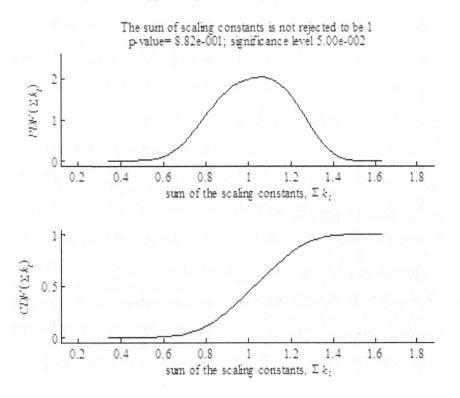

Figure 4. CDF and PDF of the sum of first to fifth scaling constants using the uniform method

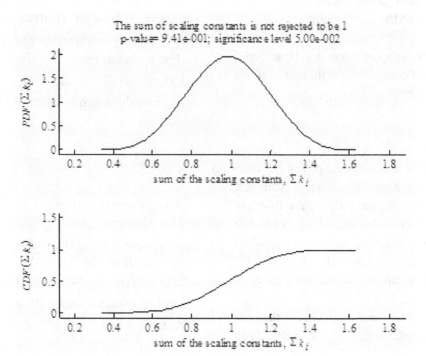

Finally, the multi-dimensional utility function would be additive:

$$u(\vec{\mathbf{x}}) = \sum_{i=1}^{5} k_i^{um} u_i(x_i).$$

As it can be seen, in this case both methods give equal qualitative results under slightly different constants.

IV.2.2

Let's assume that the analyzed prizes are six-dimensional, consisting of attributes 3, 4, 2, 5, 6, and 11. In that sense, the prize vector is $\vec{\mathbf{t}}(t_1, t_2, \ldots, t_6)$, where $t_1 = x_3$, $t_2 = x_4$, $t_3 = x_2$, $t_4 = x_5$, $t_5 = x_6$, $t_6 = x_{11}$. The individual utility functions are $v_1(t_1) = u_3(x_3) = u_3(t_1)$, $v_2(t_2) = u_4(x_4) = u_4(t_2)$, $v_3(t_3) = u_2(x_2) = u_2(t_3)$, $v_4(t_4) = u_5(x_5) = u_5(t_4)$, $v_5(t_5) = u_6(x_6) = u_6(t_5)$, $v_6(t_6) = u_{11}(x_{11}) = u_{11}(t_6)$.

Using the non-uniform method over the constants, it was calculated that $\hat{p}_{value} \approx 0.0475$. Then the null hypothesis H_0 is rejected at a significance level of $\alpha = 0.05$ since $\hat{p}_{value} \approx 0.0475 < 0.05 = \alpha$ (Figure 5). The estimates of the scaling constants are as follows: $\hat{k}_{t,1} = \hat{k}_3 = 0.4$, $\hat{k}_{t,2} = \hat{k}_4 = 0.45$, $\hat{k}_{t,3} = \hat{k}_2 = 0.4$, $\hat{k}_{t,4} = \hat{k}_5 = 0.2$, $\hat{k}_{t,5} = \hat{k}_6 = 0.135$, $\hat{k}_{t,6} = \hat{k}_{11} = 0.05$. The value of the general constant $K_t = -0.774$. Finally, the multi-dimensional utility function would be multiplicative:

$$u = u(\vec{\mathbf{t}}) = \frac{1}{K_t} \prod_{i=1}^{6} [K_t \hat{k}_{t,i} v_i(t_i) + 1] - \frac{1}{K_t}$$

Using the uniform method over the constants, it was calculated that $\hat{p}_{value} \approx 0.0909$. Then the null hypothesis H_0 fails to be rejected at a significance level of $\alpha = 0.05$ since $\hat{p}_{value} \approx 0.0909 > 0.05 = \alpha$ (Figure 6). The estimates of the scaling constants are as follows: $\hat{k}_{t,1}^{um} = \hat{k}_3^{um}$

Figure 5. CDF and PDF of the sum of scaling constants 3, 4, 2, 5, 6, and 11 using the non-uniform method

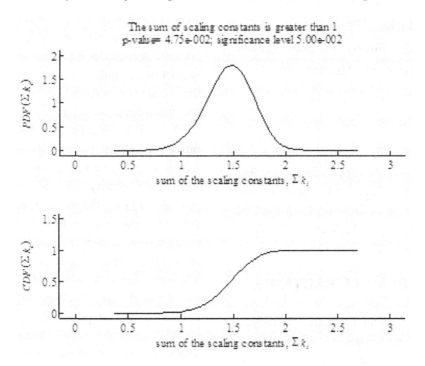

Figure 6. CDF and PDF of the sum of scaling constants 3,4,2,5,6, and 11 using the uniform method

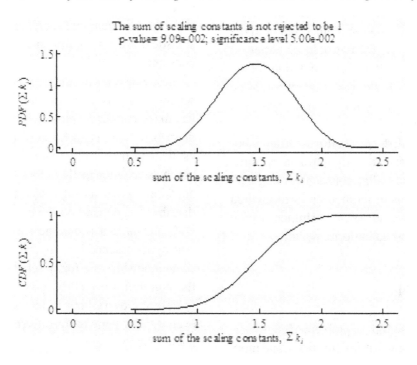

=0.206, $\hat{k}_{t,2}^{um} = \hat{k}_4^{um}$ =0.081, $\hat{k}_{t,3}^{um} = \hat{k}_2^{um}$ =0.05, $\hat{k}_{t,4}^{um} = \hat{k}_5^{um} = 0.214$, $\hat{k}_{t,5}^{um} = \hat{k}_6^{um} = 0.2802$, $\hat{k}_{t,6}^{um} = \hat{k}_{11}^{um}$ =0.1689. Finally, the multi-dimensional utility function would be additive:

$$u(\vec{\mathbf{t}}) = \sum_{i=1}^{6} k_{t,i}^{um} v_i(t_i).$$

It is evident that the additional information employed by the non-uniform method regarding the uncertainty of the constants allows to correctly define the type of preferences of the DM to multiplicative, instead of additive.

FUTURE RESEARCH DIRECTIONS

Being a novel approach in the multi-dimensional utility theory, the non-uniform method requires further analysis, testing in a variety of case studies, verification and approbation of its procedures. It is important to mention here that it is rather unlikely that a DM would use the distribution and the fuzzy set representation of uncertainty in the same time. Thus, the focus would be either on the distributional type of representation, or on the fuzzy set one. In the first case, it might be expected that the DM would use one or two types of representation.

Further research should also focus on the elaboration of other forms of description of uncertainty, associated with the scaling constants. Along with that, other versions of the non-uniform method should also be investigated, in a similar fashion to the earlier proposed uniform method.

CONCLUSION

This chapter focused on the problem of constructing multi-dimensional utility functions, and more precisely – on the work with scaling constants and definition of their sum. The main concern

was the interval form in which scaling constants were elicited in the presence of fuzzy rationality. Therefore a procedure was necessary to find their appropriate point estimates and test whether their sum of one or not. The latter defines the form of the overall multi-dimensional utility function over the multi-dimensional prizes.

A novel element of this work was the discussion on the uncertainty description of scaling constants, which was proposed to be done by two groups of forms – probability distributions and fuzzy sets. A total of 11 such forms were presented. Analytical and numerical versions of the non-uniform method to construct the distribution law of the sum of interval scaling constants were presented and formalized. A numerical procedure to find p-value in the statistical test for unit sum of the constants was also presented.

A numerical example compared the non-uniform and the uniform method for estimation of scaling constants. As the data shows, the non-uniform method provides a more precise estimation of the scaling constants points estimates, which in turn guarantees higher precision of the statistical test for significance of the sum of the constants.

In any case, the uncertainty associated with the scaling constants within their uncertainty intervals has fuzzy character regardless of the way it was described. This is so because the most precise estimate of probability that can be derived using rational elicitation methods for solving preferential equations, gives an interval estimate. All other distributions depend on the interpretation of the DM, and in that sense the subjective information by its essence is a special case of a degree of membership to a fuzzy set. The freedom that the non-uniform method gives, allows the DM to describe everything in terms of probabilities even if fuzzy logic is considered unacceptable as a whole in that setup.

REFERENCES

Barron, H., & Schmidt, C. P. (1988). Sensitivity analysis of additive multiattribute value models. *Operations Research, 36*, 122–127. doi:10.1287/opre.36.1.122

Butler, J., Jia, J., & Dyer, J. (1997). Simulation techniques for the sensitivity analysis of multi-criteria decision models. *European Journal of Operational Research, 103*, 531–546. doi:10.1016/S0377-2217(96)00307-4

French, S. (1993). *Decision theory: An introduction to the mathematics of rationality*. UK: Ellis Horwood.

French, S., & Insua, D. R. (2000). *Statistical decision theory*. UK: Arnold.

Hanke, J. E., & Reitsch, A. G. (1991). *Understanding business statistics*. USA: Irwin.

Hertz, D., & Thomas, H. (1983). *Risk analysis and its applications*. New York: John Wiley.

Jeffrey, R. (2004). *Subjective probability – the real thing*. Cambridge, UK: Cambridge University Press. doi:10.1017/CBO9780511816161

Jimenez, A., Rios-Insua, S., & Mateos, A. (2003). A decision support system for multiattribute utility evaluation based on imprecise assignment. *Decision Support Systems, 36*, 65–79. doi:10.1016/S0167-9236(02)00137-9

Keeney, R. L., & Raiffa, H. (1993). *Decisions with multiple objectives: Preference and value tradeoffs*. Cambridge, MA: Cambridge University Press.

Nikolova, N. D. (2007). Uniform method for estimation of interval scaling constants. *Engineering and Automation Problems, 1*, 79–90.

Nikolova, N. D., Mednikarov, B., & Tenekedjiev, K. (2012). Analytical version of the non-uniform method for analyzing uncertain scaling constants. In *Proc. International Conference Auomatics and Informatics*, Bulgaria: 3-7 October, Sofia (in print).

Nikolova, N. D., Shulus, A., Toneva, D., & Tenekedjiev, K. (2005). Fuzzy rationality in quantitative decision analysis. *Journal of Advanced Computational Intelligence and Intelligent Informatics, 9*(1), 65–69.

Nikolova, N. D., & Tenekedjiev, K. (2010). Fuzzy rationality and parameter elicitation in decision analysis. *International Journal of General Systems. Special Issue on Intelligent Systems, 39*(5), 539–556.

Nishizaki, I., & Katagiri, H. (2004). Sensitivity analysis incorporating fuzzy evaluation for scaling constants of multiattribute utility functions in multiplicative form. *The International Conference on Multiple Criteria Decision Making MCDM* (pp. 132-140). Canada: Whistler, B. C.

Ringuest, J. L. (1997). L-metric sensitivity analysis for single and multi-attribute decision analysis. *European Journal of Operational Research, 98*, 563–570. doi:10.1016/S0377-2217(96)00177-4

Tenekedjiev, K., & Nikolova, N. D. (2008). Justification and numerical realization of the uniform method for finding point estimates of interval elicited scaling constants. *Fuzzy Optimization and Decision Making, 7*(2), 119–145. doi:10.1007/s10700-008-9027-0

Tenekedjiev, K., Nikolova, N. D., & Dimitrakiev, D. (2004). Quantile-approximated distribution toolbox for technical diagnostics and reliability applications. *Annual Proceeding of Technical University in Varna* (pp. 233–244). Bulgaria: Varna.

Von Neumann, J., & Morgenstern, O. (1947). *Theory of games and economic behavior* (2nd ed.). USA: Princeton University Press.

Wolters, W. T. M., & Mareschal, B. (1995). Novel types of sensitivity analysis for additive MCDM methods. *European Journal of Operational Research*, *81*, 281–290. doi:10.1016/0377-2217(93) E0343-V

KEY TERMS AND DEFINITIONS

Additive Utility Function: A form of the multi-dimensional utility function that is a linear combination of the individual utility functions over the attributes, and applies when there is utility independence and the sum of scaling constants equals to one.

Alternatives: A set of prizes and the probability associated with them.

Decision Maker: The person who has the right to choose among the alternatives.

Fuzzy-Rational Decision Making: Decision analysis process based on interval estimates of any quantity, elicited by the decision maker, caused by finite discriminating abilities; the decisions are not completely rational due to violation of the transitivity requirements of preferences, described by fuzzy sets.

General Scaling Constant: An auxiliary variable that is a function of the point estimates of the scaling constants; if the sum of the scaling constants is one, then the general scaling constant equals to zero, otherwise it takes non-zero values over -1.

Multi-Dimensional Prizes: Consequences of the actions of the decision maker, which comprise of several attribute values.

Multiplicative Utility Function: A special case of a multi-dimensional utility function that is not additive but for which utility independence holds, and the sum of the scaling constants is not one.

Scaling Constant: A number from zero to one that weighs the relative importance of a given attribute in the multi-dimensional utility function.

Utility Function: A numerical function that measures the preferences of the decision maker over the prizes, and whose expected value determines the preferences over the alternatives.

Utility Independence: A case, where the preferences of the decision maker over the entire prize depend only on the individual utility functions over the attributes, and the scaling constants.

APPENDIX: UNCERTAINTY DESCRIPTIONS OF THE SCALING CONSTANTS

Although there are numerous methods we have formalized just two types of uncertainty descriptions: probability distribution and fuzzy set, which are by far the most popular. Whenever we talk about the constant k_i and its description, the index i would be omitted in this appendix, since each description refers to a separate constant, so confusion would not be possible.

AI. Uncertainty Description by a Probability Distribution

The PDF of the scaling constant is build out of the given parameters. The limits of its non-zero section determine the margins of the uncertainty interval for the scaling constant. Its best point estimates is determined as the mean value of the nodes of the distribution. The PDF of the scaling constant is approximated by piecewise linear function by introducing sufficient additional nodes into any nonlinear section. The piecewise linear PDF is presented in a general histogram form. The appendix presents 6 convenient methods for describing the probability distribution of a scaling constant. Three of those methods use the normal distribution. Let X be a normally distributed random variable with mean value μ, and standard deviation σ. Let's denote the PDF, the CDF, and the inverse CDF of X respectively with $f_{x,norm}\left(x,\mu,\sigma\right)$, $F_{x,norm}\left(x,\mu,\sigma\right)$, and $F_{x,norm}^{-1}\left(\alpha,\mu,\sigma\right)$. If x_α is the α-quantile of X, the following dependencies hold:

$$\int_{-\infty}^{x_\alpha} f_{x,norm}\left(x,\mu,\sigma\right)\mathrm{d}x = \alpha$$

$$F_{x,norm}\left(x_\alpha,\mu,\sigma\right) = \alpha$$

$$F_{x,norm}^{-1}\left(\alpha,\mu,\sigma\right) = x_\alpha$$

If Z is a normally distributed random variable with $\mu_z=0$, and $\sigma_z=1$, then its α-quantile is denoted by z_α. The following holds:

$$\int_{-\infty}^{z_\alpha} f_{x,norm}\left(x,0,1\right)\mathrm{d}x = \alpha$$

$$F_{x,norm}\left(z_\alpha,0,1\right) = \alpha$$

$$F_{x,norm}^{-1}\left(\alpha,0,1\right) = z_\alpha$$

The variable X can be normalized into the variable Z by the dependence $z=(x-\mu)/\sigma$. Then the PDF, the CDF, and the inverse CDF of z are functions with one parameter:

$$f_{z,norm}\left(z\right) = f_{x,norm}\left(\left(x-\mu\right)\big/\sigma,0,1\right)$$

$$F_{z,norm}\left(z\right) = F_{x,norm}\left(\left(x-\mu\right)\big/\sigma,0,1\right) = F_{x,norm}\left(x,\mu,\sigma\right)$$

$$F_{z,norm}^{-1}\left(\alpha\right) = z_{\alpha} = \left(x_{\alpha}-\mu\right)/\sigma = \left(F_{x,norm}^{-1}\left(\alpha,\mu,\sigma\right)-\mu\right)/\sigma$$

AI.1. Generalized Histogram Distribution of a Scaling Constant

The basic form of distribution is the generalized histogram. It is a piece-wise linear interpolations of PDF, with possible discontinuities at each node. The expressive power of the generalized histogram allows a decent approximation of almost any density using comparatively small amount of nodes.

The PDF $f_k(.)$ of the scaling constant k is approximated with ($2.Nk$ -2) nodes: $\{(k_j, f_j^{(krt)}) \mid j=1, 2,\ldots, Nk\text{-}1\}$ and $\{(k_j, f_j^{(krt)}) \mid j=2, 3,\ldots, Nk\}$. The conditions for the description are given with formulae (12 - 18). The PDF in generalized form is shown by (19). The margins of the uncertainty interval are given by (20) and (21). The best point estimate of k is calculated using Algorithm 1.

For example, assume that the DM has defined the following parameters for the required nodes of the scaling constant k_8 in a given task: $\{(0.02, 4.5), (0.12, 6), (0.17, 1.5), (0.37, \text{NaN})\}$, and $\{(0.02, \text{NaN}), (0.12, 5.5), (0.17, 6), (0.37, 0.5)\}$. Then the resulting generalized histogram PDF and its corresponding CDF are as shown in Figure 7.

Figure 7. Generalized histogram PDF and its corresponding CDF for the scaling constant k_8

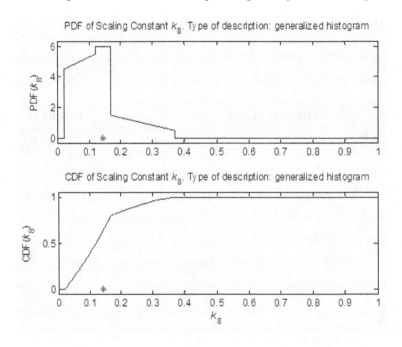

AI.2. Generalized Triangular Distribution of a Scaling Constant

The generalized triangular distribution is defined by the DM by the following parameters:

1. α, β – quantile indices, such that $0 \leq \alpha < \beta \leq 1$.
2. k_{α}, k_{β} – quantiles of the distribution. If $k_{\alpha} = 0$, then $\alpha = 0$. If $k_{\beta} = 1$, then $\beta = 1$.
3. k_{mode}, which is the mode of the distribution, where $0 \leq k_{\alpha} < k_{mode} < k_{\beta} \leq 1$.

The PDF of the generalized triangular distribution is triangular in its midsection, and proportional to the normal distribution at the tails. The overall PDF function is derived as a continuous function. It is possible to elaborate the following algorithm to derive the generalized triangular distribution.

Algorithm A1. Algorithm for Construction of the Generalized Triangular Density

1. If $\alpha = 0$, then put $f_1 = f(k_{\alpha}) = 0$ and go to step 6.
2. Find the parameters of the normal distribution N_1, such that $\mu_1 = k_{mode}$, and its α – quantile is k_{α}, thus $\sigma_1 = f\left(k_{mode}, k_{\alpha}, \alpha\right)$. Then $F_1(k) = \text{CDF}(k, \mu_1, \sigma_1)$, and the density $f_1(k) = \text{PDF}(k, \mu_1, \sigma_1)$.
3. Calculate $\alpha_0 = F_1(0)$.
4. Rescale the left tail of the density by the coefficient $f_1^{cor}(k) = f_1(k)\dfrac{\alpha}{\alpha - \alpha_0}$ for $k \in [0; k_{\alpha}]$.
5. Define the density in the left tail as $f_{left} = f_1^{cor}(k) = f_1(k_{\alpha})\dfrac{\alpha}{\alpha - \alpha_0}$.
6. If $\beta = 1$, the put $f(k_{\beta}) = f_2 = 1$ and go to step 11.
7. Find the parameters of the normal distribution N_2, such that $\mu_2 = k_{mode}$, and its β – quantile is k_{β}, thus $\sigma_2 = \left(k_{\beta} - k_{mode}\right)/z_{\beta}$, where $\sigma_2 = \left(k_{\beta} - k_{mode}\right)/z_{\beta}$ Then $F_2(k) = \text{CDF}(k, \mu_2, \sigma_2)$, and the density $f_2(k) = \text{PDF}(k, \mu_2, \sigma_2)$.
8. Calculate $\beta_1 = F_2(1)$.
9. Rescale the right tail of the density by the coefficient $f_2^{cor}(k) = f_2(k)\dfrac{1 - \beta}{\beta_1 - \beta}$ for $k \in [k_{\beta}; 1]$.
10. Define the density in the right tail as $f_{right} = f_2^{cor}(k_{\beta}) = f_2(k_{\beta})\dfrac{1 - \beta}{\beta_1 - \beta}$.
11. Find $f(k_{mode}) = f_{mode} = \dfrac{2\beta - 2\alpha + f_{left}\left(k_{mode} - k_{\alpha}\right) - f_{right}\left(k_{\beta} - k_{mode}\right)}{f_{left} - f_{right}}$, which follows from the unity of the area under the density curve.
12. Construct the generalized triangular density using the following dependence:

$$f(k) = \begin{cases} f_1^{cor}(k) & k \in [0; k_\alpha] \\ \dfrac{(k - k_\alpha) f_{mode} + (k_{mode} - k) f_{left}}{k_{mode} - k_\alpha} & k \in [k_\alpha; k_{mode}] \\ \dfrac{(k_\beta - k) f_{mode} + f_{right}(k - k_{mode})}{k_\beta - k_{mode}} & k \in [k_{mode}; k_\beta] \\ f_2^{cor}(k) & k \in [k_\beta; 1] \end{cases}$$

13. If $\alpha = 0$, then $k_d = k_\alpha$. Otherwise, $k_d = 0$.
14. If $\beta = 1$, then $k_u = k_\beta$. Otherwise, $k_u = 1$.
15. The best point estimate k_{best} of the scaling constant k is defined by the following rule:
    a. if $f_{mode} > f_1$, and $f_{mode} > f_2$, then $k_{best} = k_{mode}$;
    b. if $f_{mode} = f_1$, and $f_{mode} > f_2$, then $k_{best} = (k_{mode} + k_\alpha)/2$;
    c. if $f_{mode} > f_1$, and $f_{mode} = f_2$, then $k_{best} = (k_{mode} + k_\beta)/2$;
    d. if $f_{mode} = f_1 = f_2$, then $k_{best} = (k_\alpha + k_\beta)/2$.

An additional condition is needed here, namely that $f_{mode} \geq \max\{f_{left}, f_{right}\}$.

For example, assume that the DM has defined the following parameters for the constant k_6 in a decision problem: $k_\alpha = 0.1$, $k_\beta = 0.5$. $k_{mode} = 0.4$, $\alpha = 0.05$, $\beta = 0.8$. Then the resulting generalized triangular density and corresponding CDF would be as shown on Figure 8a. If the DM has defined the following parameters for a constant k_{12} in a decision problem: $k_\alpha = 0.1$, $k_\beta = 0.5$. $k_{mode} = 0.4$, $\alpha = 0$, $\beta = 1$, then the triangular shape of the distribution is evident from Figure 8b. If the DM has defined the following parameters for a constant k_{12} in a decision problem: $k_\alpha = 0.1$, $k_\beta = 0.5$. $k_{mode} = 0.4$, $\alpha = 0.1$, $\beta = 1$, then the triangular shape of the distribution is evident from Figure 8c. If the DM has defined the following parameters for a constant k_{12} in a decision problem: $k_\alpha = 0.1$, $k_\beta = 0.5$. $k_{mode} = 0.4$, $\alpha = 0$, $\beta = 0.9$, then the triangular shape of the distribution is evident from Figure 8d.

AI.3. Quantile Approximated Distribution of a Scaling Constant

A common case in quantitative assessment of uncertainty is to construct a CDF by approximation on a set of estimated quantiles. Assume that for the case of assessment of scaling constants, a DM has defined estimates of the quantiles $k_{\alpha_1}, k_{\alpha_2}, \ldots, k_{\alpha_m}$ ($i = 1, 2, \ldots, m$) at the corresponding quantile indices $\alpha_1, \alpha_2, \ldots, \alpha_m$ of the distribution of the constant k. Here, $k_{\alpha_1} \leq k_{\alpha_2} \leq \ldots \leq k_{\alpha_m}$, and $0 \leq \alpha_1 < \alpha_2 < \ldots < \alpha_m \leq 1$. Then it is possible to adopt the quantile-approximated (QAP) procedure for construction of CDFs presented in Tenekedjiev et al. (2004). If $\alpha_1 > 0$ and $\alpha_m < 1$, then the QAP approach uses a technique similar to that described in Algorithm 1 to approximate the tails of the distribution (under the first and above the last quantiles).

Figure 8. (a) Generalized triangular PDF and its corresponding CDF for the scaling constant k_6 with k_α =0.1, k_β =0.5. k_{mode}=0.4, α =0.05, β =0.8. (b) Generalized triangular PDF and its corresponding CDF for the scaling constant k_{12} with k_α =0.1, k_β =0.5. k_{mode}=0.4, α =0, β =1. (c) Generalized triangular PDF and its corresponding CDF for the scaling constant k_{12} with k_α =0.1, k_β =0.5. k_{mode}=0.4, α =0.1, β =1. (d) Generalized triangular PDF and its corresponding CDF for the scaling constant k_{12} with k_α =0.1, k_β =0.5. k_{mode}=0.4, α =0, β =0.9.

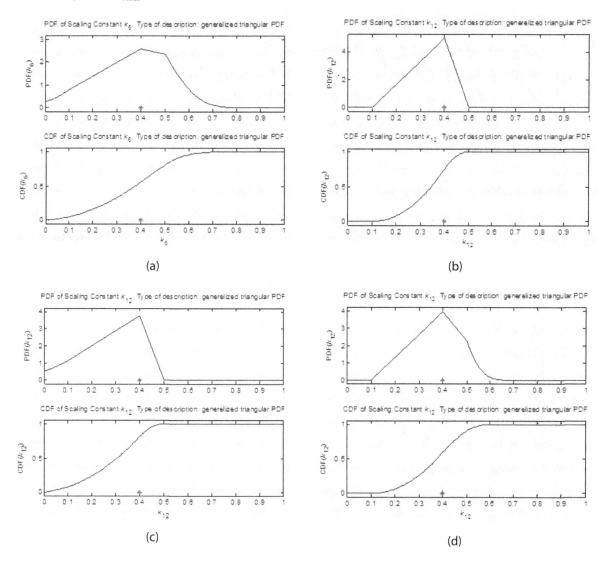

(a)　　　　　　　　　　　　　　　(b)

(c)　　　　　　　　　　　　　　　(d)

Algorithm A2. Construction of the QAP Density

1. If α_1 >0 and/or α_m <1, and α_i ≠ 0.5 (i=1,2,...,m), then find the median k_{med}=$k_{0.5}$, using linear interpolation on the available quantile estimates.
2. If α_1 =0, then put $f(k_{\alpha_1})$=f_1=0 and go to step 7.

3. Find the parameters of the normal distribution N_1, such that $\mu_1 = k_{med}$, thus $\sigma_1 = f\left(k_{med}, k_{\alpha_1}, \alpha_1\right)$. Then $F_1(k) = \text{CDF}(k, \mu_1, \sigma_1)$, and the density $f_1(k) = \text{PDF}(k, \mu_1, \sigma_1)$.

4. Calculate $\alpha_0 = F_1(0)$.

5. Rescale the left tail of the density by the coefficient $f_1^{cor}(k) = f_1(k)\dfrac{\alpha_1}{\alpha_1 - \alpha_0}$ for $k \in \left[0; k_{\alpha_1}\right]$.

6. Define the density in the left tail as $f_{left} = f_1^{cor}(k) = f_1\left(k_{\alpha_1}\right)\dfrac{\alpha_1}{\alpha_1 - \alpha_0}$.

7. If $\alpha_m = 1$, then put $f(k_{\alpha_m}) = f_2 = 1$ and go to step 12.

8. Find the parameters of the normal distribution N_2, such that $\mu_2 = k_{med}$, thus $\sigma_2 = f\left(k_{med}, k_{\alpha_m}, \alpha_m\right)$. Then $F_2(k) = \text{CDF}(k, \mu_2, \sigma_2)$, and the density $f_2(k) = \text{PDF}(k, \mu_2, \sigma_2)$.

9. Calculate $\alpha_{end} = F_2(1)$.

10. Rescale the right tail of the density by the coefficient $f_2^{cor}(k) = f_2(k)\dfrac{1 - \alpha_m}{\alpha_{end} - \alpha_m}$ for $k \in \left[k_{\alpha_m}; 1\right]$.

11. Define the density in the right tail as $f_{right} = f_2^{cor}(k) = f_2\left(k_{\alpha_m}\right)\dfrac{1 - \alpha_m}{\alpha_{end} - \alpha_m}$.

12. Find $f\left(k_{med}\right) = f_{med} = \dfrac{2\alpha_m - 2\alpha_1 + f_{left}\left(k_{med} - k_{\alpha_1}\right) - f_{right}\left(k_{\alpha_m} - k_{med}\right)}{f_{left} - f_{right}}$, which follows from the

unity of the area under the density curve.

13. Construct the generalized QAP density using the following dependence:

$$
f(k) = \begin{cases}
f_1^{cor}(k) & k \in \left[0; k_1^-\right] \\[2mm]
\dfrac{\alpha_2 - \alpha_1}{k_{\alpha_2} - k_{\alpha_1}} & k \in \left[k_{\alpha_1}^+; k_{\alpha_2}^-\right] \\[2mm]
\dots & \dots \\[2mm]
\dfrac{\alpha_m - \alpha_{m-1}}{k_{\alpha_m} - k_{\alpha_{m-1}}} & k \in \left[k_{\alpha_{m-1}}^+; k_{\alpha_m}^-\right] \\[2mm]
f_2^{cor}(k) & k \in \left[k_{\alpha_m}^+; 1\right]
\end{cases}
$$

where $k_i^- = \lim\limits_{k \to k_i^+} k$, $k_i^+ = \lim\limits_{k \to k_i^-} k$, $i = 1, 2, \ldots, m$.

14. If $\alpha_1 = 0$, then $k_d = k_{\alpha_1}$. Otherwise, $k_d = 0$

15. If $\alpha_m = 1$, then $k_u = k_{\alpha_m}$. Otherwise, $k_u = 1$.

16. The best point estimate k_{best} of the scaling constant k is defined by the following rule:
    a. if $f_{med} > f_1$, and $f_{med} > f_2$, then $k_{best} = k_{med}$;
    b. if $f_{med} = f_1$, and $f_{med} > f_2$, then $k_{best} = (k_{med} + k_{\alpha_1})/2$;
    c. if $f_{med} > f_1$, and $f_{med} = f_2$, then $k_{best} = (k_{med} + k_{\alpha_m})/2$;
    d. if $f_{med} = f_1 = f_2$, then $k_{best} = (k_\alpha + k_\beta)/2$.

For example, assume that the DM has identified the following quantiles: k_{α_1} =0.02, k_{α_2} =0.12, k_{α_3} =0.17, k_{α_4} =0.19, k_{α_5} =0.21, k_{α_6} =0.31, k_{α_7} =0.42, at the corresponding quantile indices $\alpha_1 = 0.02, \alpha_2 = 0.2, \alpha_3 = 0.4, \alpha_4 = 0.5, \alpha_5 = 0.6, \alpha_6 = 0.8, \alpha_7 = 0.95$ for the scaling constant k_{10}. Then the resulting QAP distribution (PDF and CDF) would be as shown on Figure 9a. In case the first and last quantile indices are respectively $\alpha_1 = 0, \alpha_7 = 1$, then the resulting QAP distribution (PDF and CDF) for the scaling constant k_{13} would be as shown on Figure 9b.

AI.4. Linearly Interpolated PDF of a Scaling Constant

Here $f_k(.)$ is described with Nk nodes: $\{(k_j, f_j^{(k)}) \mid j = 1, \ 2, ..., Nk\}$. The following condition holds:

$$Nk > 1 \tag{1}$$

$$0 \le k_1 < k_2 < ... < k_{Nk} \le 1 \tag{2}$$

$$f_j^{(k)} \ge 0, \ \text{for} \, j = 1, \ 2, ..., Nk \tag{3}$$

$$\sum_{j=1}^{Nk-1} \frac{f_{j+1}^{(k)} + f_j^{(k)}}{2}\left(k_{j+1} - k_j\right) = 1 \tag{4}$$

Figure 9. QAP CDF and PDF for the scaling constant k_{10}, defined by the distribution quantiles k_{α_1} =0.02, k_{α_2} =0.12, k_{α_3} =0.17, k_{α_4} =0.19, k_{α_5} =0.21, k_{α_6} =0.31, k_{α_7} =0.42, at the quantile indices: a) $\alpha_1 = 0.02$, $\alpha_2 = 0.2$, $\alpha_3 = 0.4$, $\alpha_4 = 0.5$, $\alpha_5 = 0.6$, $\alpha_6 = 0.8$, $\alpha_7 = 0.95$; b) $\alpha_1 = 0$, $\alpha_2 = 0.2$, $\alpha_3 = 0.4$, $\alpha_4 = 0.5$, $\alpha_5 = 0.6$, $\alpha_6 = 0.8$, $\alpha_7 = 1$

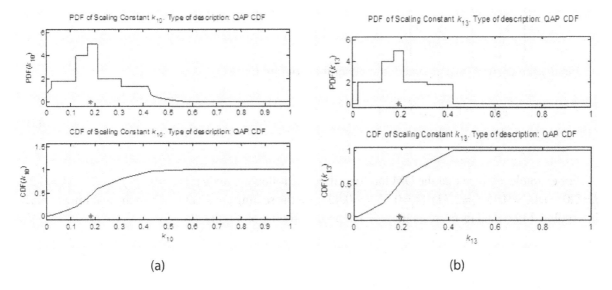

(a)   (b)

$$\left(f_1^{(k)}\right)^2 + \left(f_2^{(k)}\right)^2 > 0 \tag{5}$$

$$\left(f_{Nk-1}^{(k)}\right)^2 + \left(f_{Nk}^{(k)}\right)^2 > 0 \tag{6}$$

Then the PDF of the variable k would be

$$f_k(k) = \begin{cases} 0, & \text{if } k < k_1 \\ f_1^{(k)}, & \text{if } k = k_1 \\ \dfrac{(k - k_j)\, f_{j+1}^{(k)} + (k_{j+1} - k)\, f_j^{(k)}}{k_{j+1} - k_j}, & \text{if } k_j < k \le k_{j+1}, \text{ for } j = 1, 2, \dots, Nk - 1 \\ 0, & \text{if } k_{Nk} < k \end{cases} \tag{7}$$

According to Equation 5 and Equation 6:

$$k_d = k_1 \tag{8}$$

$$k_u = k_{Nk} \tag{9}$$

As long as some of the nodes ordinates in Equation 7 can be equal, the determination of $k_{best,i}$ is done in two steps:

1. Find the maximal value of the ordinates of $f_k(.)$: $f_{\max} = \max\left\{ f_1^{(k)},\, f_2^{(k)}, \dots, f_{Nk}^{(k)} \right\}$;
2. Estimate k_{best} as the mean value of the abscissas of all nodes which have maximal ordinates:

$$k_{best} = \left(\sum_{\substack{j=1 \\ ft_j = f_{\max}}}^{Nk} k_j \right) \Bigg/ \left(\sum_{\substack{j=1 \\ ft_j = f_{\max}}}^{Nk} 1 \right)$$

Finally the derived $f_k(.)$ is stated into general histogram form:

$$\left| \begin{aligned} f_j^{(krt)} &= f_j^{(k)} &&, \text{ for } j = 1, 2, \dots, Nk - 1 \\ f_j^{(krt)} &= f_j^{(k)} &&, \text{ for } j = 2, 3, \dots, Nk \end{aligned} \right. \tag{10}$$

For example, assume that the DM has identified the following nodes: $\{(k_1 = 0.05, f_1 = 1.25), (k_2 = 0.25, f_2 = 2.083), (k_3 = 0.45, f_3 = 2.91), (k_4 = 0.55, f_4 = 0.42)\}$ for the scaling constant k_9. Then the resulting linearly interpolated PDF and its corresponding CDF area as shown on Figure 10.

Figure 10. Linearly interpolated PDF and its corresponding CDF for the scaling constant k_9, defined by the nodes $\{(k_1=0.05, f_1=1.25), (k_2=0.25, f_2=2.083), (k_3=0.45, f_3=2.91), (k_4=0.55, f_4=0.42)\}$.

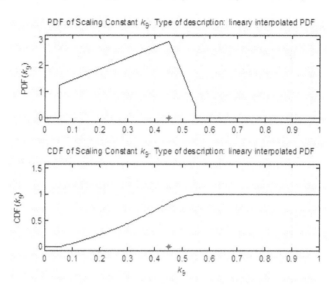

AI.5. Truncated Normal Distribution of a Scaling Constant

The density of a scaling constant may be assumed to be normally distributed according to a normal distributional law $N(\mu, \sigma)$. In this case, the DM needs to define the distribution mean value and standard deviation. However, by default the normal distribution applies for an interval of the variable $(-\infty; +\infty)$, whereas in the same time a scaling constant is only in position to take values in the closed interval [0; 1]. Therefore, the truncated normal density should be introduced, where the variable is limited to values within the interval [0; 1], and the area under the density curve is rescaled so that it still equals to one. The following algorithm applies here:

Algorithm A3. Construction of Truncated Normal Density

1. Construct the initial density of the scaling constant as a normal density $f_0(k)=N(k, \mu, \sigma)$.

2. Calculate $\int_0^1 f(k)\,\mathrm{d}k = I$.

3. Rescale $f_0(k)$ to $f(k)$ so that $f(k)=f_0(k)/I$. for $k \in [0;1]$.

For example, assume that the DM has identified the parameters $\mu=0.3$, $\sigma=0.2$ of a normal distribution of the scaling constant k_7 in a given decision problem. The corresponding truncated normal distribution, following Algorithm A3, is given on Figure 11.

Figure 11. Truncated normal PDF and its corresponding CDF for the scaling constant k_7, defined by the normal density function $f_0(k)=N(k, 0.3, 0.2)$

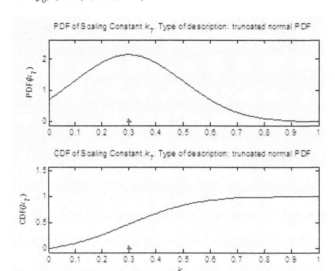

AI.6.Uniform PDF Distribution of a Scaling Constant

In the uniform case, each constant is uniformly distributed within its uncertainty interval:

$$
\begin{aligned}
&k_i \in \left[k_{d,i}; k_{u,i}\right], \ \text{for} \ i = 1, \ 2, \ldots, n, \\
&k_{u,i} - k_{d,i} \geq k_{u,i+1} - k_{d,i+1}, \text{for} \ i = 1, \ 2, \ldots, n-1, \\
&0 < k_{d,i} < k_{u,i} < 1, \text{if} \ i = 1, \ 2, \ldots, m, \\
&k_{d,i} = k_{u,i}, \text{if} \ i = m+1, m+2, \ldots, n, \\
&0 \leq m \leq n
\end{aligned}
\tag{11}
$$

Thus, for each constant, the DM needs to define the lower and upper bounds $k_{d,i}$ and $k_{u,i}$. Figure 12 shows the uniformly distributed constant $k_4 \in [0.02; 0.25]$, and its corresponding CDF, derived by integration of the uniform PDF.

AII. Uncertainty Description by a Fuzzy Set

Let's define the fuzzy set of the possible values of a scaling constant. The degree of membership of this fuzzy set is build out of the given parameters, and a normalized fuzzy set is obtained. The best point estimate of the constant is determined as the mean value of the $\alpha - cut$ for $\alpha = 1$. The limits of its support determine the margins of the uncertainty interval for the scaling constant. The degree of membership of the normalized fuzzy set is divided by its area under the curve. The resulting function is interpreted as the PDF of the scaling constant. The PDF of the scaling constant is approximated by piecewise linear function by introducing sufficient additional nodes into any nonlinear section. The piecewise linear PDF is presented in a general histogram form. We have developed 5 convenient methods for describing the fuzzy set of the possible values of a scaling constant.

Figure 12. Uniform PDF an its corresponding CDF for the scaling constant $k_4 \in [0.02; 0.25]$

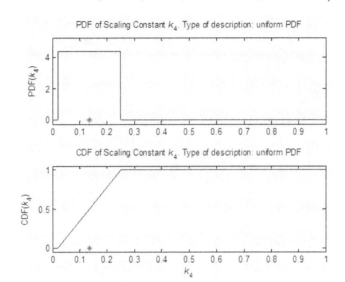

AII.1.Triangular Fuzzy Set Description of a Scaling Constant

In order to define the triangular fuzzy set, the DM needs to define the points k_d, k_u, and k_{mode}, which are similar in meaning as the points k_α, k_β and k_{mode} from the generalized triangular distribution case in section AI.2. The PDF of the scaling constant is found by dividing the degree of membership by its area under the curve. For example, if the DM has defined that $k_d=0.1$, $k_u=0.5$ and $k_{mode}=0.4$ for the scaling constant k_3, then its membership function, and corresponding PDF and CDF would be as shown on Figure 13.

AII.2. Trapezoidal Fuzzy Set Description of a Scaling Constant

The membership function here takes the form of a trapezium, and the DM needs to define four values k_a, k_b, k_c, and k_d, as well as the degrees of membership of the inner two points. The PDF of the scaling constant is found by dividing the degree of membership by its area under the curve. For example, if the DM has defined that $k_a=0.1$, $k_b=0.15$, $k_c=0.45$, and $k_d=0.53$, with values of the membership function in the inner points respectively 0.6 and 1 for the scaling constant k_5 in a given task, then its membership function, and corresponding PDF and CDF would be as shown on Figure 14.

AII.3. Linearly Interpolated Fuzzy Set Description of a Scaling Constant

The membership function is described by a set of Nk nodes $\{(k_j, \mu_j^{(k)}) \mid j=1, 2,..., Nk\}$ as in section AI.4. The PDF of the scaling constant is found by dividing the degree of membership by its area under the curve. For example, assume that the DM has defined the following nodes of the membership function for the scaling constant k_{11} in a given task: $\{(0.1, 0.4); (0.2; 1); (0.24, 0.94); (0.35, 0.5); (0.36, 0.3)\}$, then its membership function, and corresponding PDF and CDF would be as shown on Figure 15.

Figure 13. Membership function, PDF and CDF of the scaling constant k₃ represented by a triangular fuzzy set

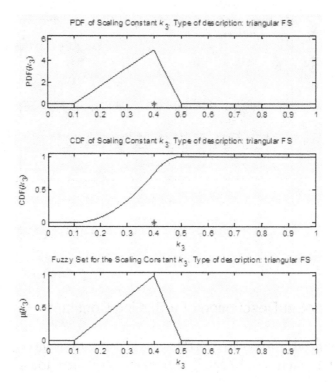

Figure 14. Membership function, PDF and CDF of the scaling constant k₅ represented by a trapezoidal fuzzy set

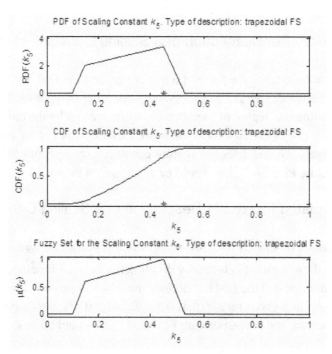

Figure 15. Membership function, PDF and CDF of the scaling constant k_{11} represented by a linearly interpolated fuzzy set

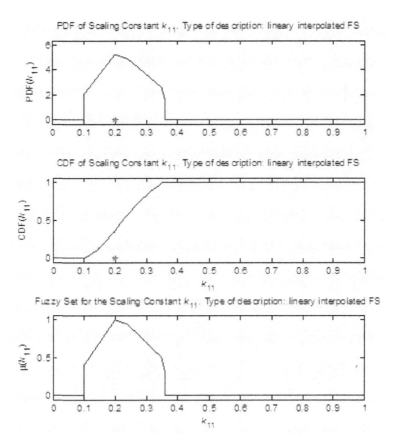

AII.4. User Defined Description of a Continuous Fuzzy Set of a Scaling Constant

In a similar fashion to a uniformly distributed uncertainty, for the case of continuous fuzzy set the DM only defines the boundaries of the possible values of the scaling constant. The PDF of the scaling constant is found by dividing the degree of membership by its area under the curve. For example, if the DM has defined the bounds 0.07 and 0.3 for the interval of values of the scaling constant k_1 from a given task, then the membership function, and the resulting PDF and CDF might be as shown on Figure 16.

AII.5. Crisp Set Description of a Scaling Constant

This is the only case, where there is no uncertainty associated with the values of the scaling constant from the side of the DM. Therefore, the crisp set is defined by a single value for the scaling constant, denoted as k_s. Then it is true that $k_d = k_u = k_{best} = k_s$. The crisp set description may be viewed as a singular case of discrete distribution. Therefore, only CDF can be defined, whereas PDF is impossible to construct.

For example, if the DM has defined the value $k_s = 0.05$ for the scaling constant k_2, then its CDF would take the form, presented on fig. A11.

Figure 16. Membership function, PDF and CDF of the scaling constant k₁ represented by a user defined continuous fuzzy set

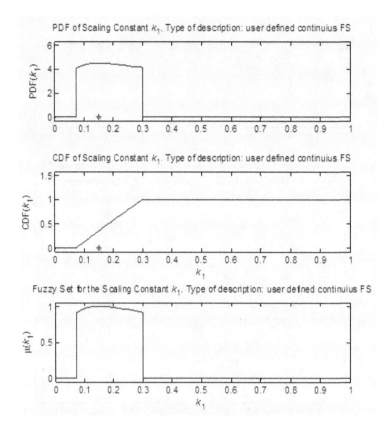

Figure 17. CDF of the crisp set description of the scaling constant k₂

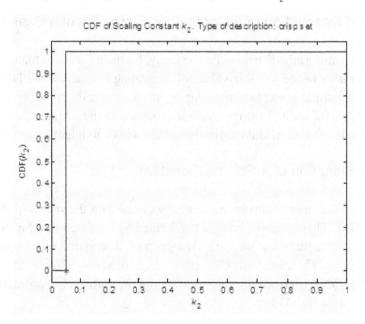

Chapter 14
Widely Linear Estimation with Geometric Algebra

Tohru Nitta
National Institute of Advanced Industrial Science and Technology (AIST), Japan

ABSTRACT

This chapter reviews the widely linear estimation for complex numbers, quaternions, and geometric algebras (or Clifford algebras) and their application examples. It was proved effective mathematically to add $\mathbf{x}^*$, the complex conjugate number of $\mathbf{x}$, as an explanatory variable in estimation of complex-valued data in 1995. Thereafter, the technique has been extended to higher-dimensional algebras. The widely linear estimation improves the accuracy and the efficiency of estimation, then expands the scalability of the estimation framework, and is applicable and useful for many fields including neural computing with high-dimensional parameters.

INTRODUCTION

Suppose a problem to determine the relationship between two kinds of samples as

$$\mathbf{x} = \left(x_1, \cdots, x_N\right)^T$$

and y, where T expresses transposition, obtained from a certain system as that for determining a relationship between a long-term interest rate and a gold bullion price. Assume linear relationship between the two samples, i.e.,

$$y = \sum_{k=1}^{N} a_k x_k$$

In this case, what is necessary is merely to determine a real-valued coefficient vector

$$\mathbf{a} = \left(a_1, \cdots, a_N\right)^T$$

by any means. Here, y can be estimated from $\mathbf{x}$ using parameter $\mathbf{a}$ thus obtained.

Samples $\mathbf{x}$, y, and parameter $\mathbf{a}$ are all real values in the above-mentioned problem. However, it is necessary to treat complex-valued data with Fourier transform and wavelet transformation, for example, in fields such as communica-

DOI: 10.4018/978-1-4666-3942-3.ch014

Widely Linear Estimation with Geometric Algebra

tions, image processing, and speech processing. For cases where numbers other than complex numbers are used, it is also necessary to treat two-dimensional data as one unit.

x has been used conventionally as an explanatory variable in such cases. It was pointed out recently that there are cases in which sufficient estimates cannot be acquired. Moreover, it was proved effective mathematically to add $\mathbf{x}^*$, the complex conjugate number of **x**, as an explanatory variable. This technique causes the improvement of the accuracy and the efficiency of estimation, then expands the scalability of the estimation framework, and is applicable and useful for neuro-computing. This chapter describes this widely linear estimation for complex numbers, quaternions, and Clifford numbers (Dorst, Fontijne & Mann, 2007).

BACKGROUND

First, a technique to treat real-valued data is described. Assume a case in which a true value denoted by a real-valued random variable $y \in \mathbf{R}$ is estimated from an observed value denoted by a real-valued random vector $\mathbf{x} \in \mathbf{R}^N$, where $\mathbf{R}$ is the set of real numbers and N is a natural number. Then consider an estimated value $\hat{y}$ expressed as follows:

$$\hat{y} = \mathbf{h}^T \mathbf{x} \tag{1}$$

where $\mathbf{h} \in \mathbf{R}^N$. The problem is to find a parameter $\mathbf{h} \in \mathbf{R}^N$ that minimizes mean square error $E|y-\hat{y}|^2$. Such a framework is designated as (real-valued) linear mean square estimation.

The (real-valued) least mean square (LMS) algorithm is often used to obtain a parameter $\mathbf{h} \in \mathbf{R}^N$ that minimizes mean square error $E|y-\hat{y}|^2$ (Widrow & Hoff, 1960; Widrow, 1966; Farhang-Boroujeny, 1999; Sayed, 2003). The LMS

algorithm is often adopted for an adaptive filter by virtue of its simplicity and robustness. The online adaptive function of an adaptive filter is suitable for signals in the steady-state. For that reason, it is applied to noise reduction, signal processing of radar and sonar, channel equalizers of mobile phones, echo removal, etc. Weight in an LMS algorithm is updated using the following equation. At iteration (time step) k,

$$\mathbf{w}(k+1) = \mathbf{w}(k) + \mu \cdot e(k) \cdot \mathbf{x}(k) \tag{2}$$

where **w** is a real-valued weight vector which corresponds to $\mathbf{h} \in \mathbf{R}^N$ in Equation (1), μ denotes the step size, e represents an error between the desired value and the actual value, and **x** stands for an input vector. If the step size μ is chosen to be very small, then the LMS algorithm converges very slowly. Contrarily, if μ is large, then it converges faster, but is less stable.

COMPLEX-VALUED WIDELY LINEAR ESTIMATION

This section describes complex-valued widely linear estimation.

Complex-Valued Linear Mean Square Estimation

First, consider a model that extends real-valued linear mean square estimation described in the BACKGROUND to complex numbers. Assume a case in which a true value denoted by a complex-valued random variable $y \in \mathbf{C}$ is estimated from an observed value denoted by a complex-valued random vector $\mathbf{x} \in \mathbf{C}^N$, where **C** is the set of complex numbers. Then assume an estimated value $\hat{y}_L$ expressed as

$$\hat{y}_L = \mathbf{h}^H \mathbf{x} \tag{3}$$

294

where $\mathbf{h} \in \mathbf{C}^N$, and H represents complex conjugate transposition. The problem is to find a complex-valued parameter $\mathbf{h} \in \mathbf{C}^N$ that minimizes mean square error $E\left|y - \hat{y}_L\right|^2$. Such a framework is referred to as complex-valued linear mean square estimation.

The complex-valued LMS algorithm extends the LMS algorithm described in the BACKGROUND to complex numbers supposing processing of complex-valued / two-variable signals in digital communication, chaos mapping, vector field, etc. (Widrow, McCool, & Ball, 1975). Weight in the complex-valued LMS algorithm is updated using the following equation. At iteration (time step) k,

$$\mathbf{w}(k+1) = \mathbf{w}(k) + \mu \cdot e(k) \cdot \mathbf{x}(k) \tag{4}$$

where $\mathbf{w}$ is a complex-valued weight vector which corresponds to $\mathbf{h} \in \mathbf{C}^N$ in Equation (3), μ denotes the step size, e represents an error between the desired value and the actual value, and $\mathbf{x}$ stands for an complex-valued input vector.

Complex-Valued Widely Linear Mean Square Estimation

Next, complex-valued widely linear mean square estimation is described. The point of this framework of estimation is adding a complex conjugate term as an explanatory variable by which the estimation accuracy and the efficiency is improved compared with that of the complex-valued linear mean square estimation described in the previous section.

An estimated value $\hat{y}$ expressed as follows is considered:

$$\hat{y} = \mathbf{h}^H \mathbf{x} + \mathbf{g}^H \mathbf{x}^* \tag{5}$$

where $\mathbf{g}, \mathbf{h} \in \mathbf{C}^N$, and $v^* \overset{def}{=} a - ib$ is the complex conjugate of

$$v = a + ib \in \mathbf{C}$$

The problem is to find complex-valued parameters $\mathbf{g}, \mathbf{h} \in \mathbf{C}^N$ that minimize mean square error $E\left|y - \hat{y}\right|^2$. An important difference from complex-valued linear mean square estimation described in the previous section is that a complex conjugate term $\mathbf{x}^*$ is added as an explanatory variable. This causes the improvement of the accuracy and the efficiency of estimation, and then expands the scalability of the estimation framework.

Picinbono et al. proved mathematically that an estimated error by complex-valued widely linear mean square estimation is smaller than the estimated error by the usual complex-valued linear mean square estimation (Picinbono & Chevalie, 1995):

$$E\left|y - \hat{y}_L\right|^2 \geq E\left|y - \hat{y}\right|^2,$$

where the equality holds only in exceptional cases.

It can be inferred intuitively from Figure 1 that the complex-valued widely linear estimation is superior to the conventional linear estimation method. The samples of complex-valued random variable x and y are axisymmetric for a straight line represented by a broken line in the figure. It is therefore difficult to estimate the sample of y by performing rotation, reduction, or expansion of the sample of x about the origin. Nevertheless, inversion of the sample of x about the real axis, i.e., assuming it as the sample of conjugate complex-valued random variable x^*, allows y to be estimated by rotation, reduction, and expansion about the origin.

Properness of a Complex-Valued Random Vector

This section describes the properness of a complex-valued random vector closely related to complex-valued widely linear mean square estimation described in the previous section. Intuitively, the

Figure 1. Example demonstrating effectiveness of complex-valued widely linear estimation. Samples of complex-valued random variable x and y are axisymmetric about the broken line.

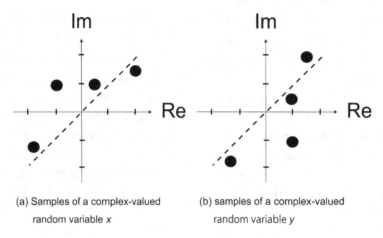

(a) Samples of a complex-valued random variable *x*

(b) samples of a complex-valued random variable *y*

properness is a concept to categorize complex-valued data. Any complex-valued data can be classified into two categories: proper and improper. The proper complex-valued data depicted in the complex plane are rotational invariant. That is, the shape of the data does not change when arbitrary rotations are applied to the data around the origin. In contrast, the improper complex-valued data are rotational variant. Mathematically, such a situation can be represented by the covariance matrix as described below. Conventional statistical methods used in the complex-valued domain had not taken account of improper complex-valued data. Advent of statistical methods that can treat improper complex-valued data could lead to the improvement of accuracy and efficiency of the methods, and expand their scalability.

This chapter assumes the mean vector of a random vector as $\mathbf{0}$ for simplicity. Generally, the covariance matrix of a real-valued random vector $\mathbf{x} \in \mathbf{R}^N$ is given as $E[\mathbf{xx}^T]$. The covariance matrix of a complex-valued random vector $\mathbf{x} \in \mathbf{C}^N$ is given as $E[\mathbf{xx}^H]$. This covariance matrix $E[\mathbf{xx}^H]$ has been used in many applications treating a complex-valued random vector. As a matter of fact however, this does not thoroughly represent the second-order statistics of a

complex-valued random vector $\mathbf{x}$ (Picinbono, 1996). It is necessary to take a pseudo-covariance matrix $E[\mathbf{xx}^T]$ into consideration to express second order statistics appropriately. Consider an augmented complex-valued random vector $\underline{\mathbf{x}} = [\mathbf{x} \quad \mathbf{x}^*]^T$. Its augmented covariance matrix $\underline{R}_{xx}$ is given as

$$\underline{R}_{xx} \overset{def}{=} E[\underline{\mathbf{x}}\underline{\mathbf{x}}^H] = \begin{pmatrix} R_{xx} & \tilde{R}_{xx} \\ \tilde{R}_{xx}^* & R_{xx}^* \end{pmatrix} \qquad (6)$$

where

$$R_{xx} \overset{def}{=} E[\mathbf{xx}^H],$$

$$\tilde{R}_{xx} \overset{def}{=} E[\mathbf{xx}^T]$$

Equation 6 includes both a covariance matrix $E[\mathbf{xx}^H]$ and a pseudo-covariance matrix $E[\mathbf{xx}^T]$. Accordingly, an augmented complex-valued random vector $\underline{\mathbf{x}} = [\mathbf{x} \quad \mathbf{x}^*]^T$ can express second-order statistics perfectly. A specific term properness is designated to explain the above explicitly.

Definition 1: A complex-valued random vector $\mathbf{x} \in \mathbf{C}^N$ is proper when $E[\mathbf{x}\mathbf{x}^T] = \mathbf{0}$, otherwise it is improper when $E[\mathbf{x}\mathbf{x}^T] \neq \mathbf{0}$.

The conventional linear estimation suffices for a proper complex-valued random vector, while widely linear estimation is effective for an improper complex-valued random vector.

As an example, assume a complex-valued random variable $x = u + iv \in \mathbf{C}$ obeying complex-valued normal distribution, where the average is 0, variance $R_{\mathrm{xx}} = E|\mathbf{x}|^2$, and pseudo-variance

$$\tilde{R}_{\mathrm{xx}} = E\left[\mathbf{x}^2\right] = \rho R_{\mathrm{xx}}$$

ρ is a complex-valued correlation coefficient of x and x^*, and satisfies $|\rho| < 1$. ρ is also a measure for estimating the degree of properness. The schematic diagram of the probability density function of a complex-valued random variable x is shown in Figure2. Figure 2(a) presents a proper case ($\rho = 0$), while Figure 2(b) expresses an improper case:

$$\rho = 0.8 \exp\left[i3\pi / 2\right]$$

Probability is uniform along a concentric circle (ellipse). Properness is also referred to as circularity. This term derives from the fact that the whole shape of the schematic diagram of a probability density function is invariant by rotation centering on the origin, as shown in Figure 2(a). See Schreier and Scharf (2010) for details.

QUATERNION WIDELY LINEAR ESTIMATION

This section addresses quaternion widely linear estimation, which is the natural extension of the complex-valued widely linear estimation described in the previous section. Quaternion is an extension of complex number, a four-dimensional number expressed as

$$v = a + ib + jc + kd \in \mathbf{Q}$$

where $\mathbf{Q}$ represents the set of quaternions (Hamilton, 1899), and has been recognized as a useful

Figure 2. Schematic diagram of the probability density function of a complex-valued random variable $x = u + iv$ obeying complex-valued normal distribution. The average is 0, variance $R_{\mathrm{xx}} = E|\mathbf{x}|^2$, and pseudo-variance $\tilde{R}_{\mathrm{xx}} = E\left[\mathbf{x}^2\right] = \rho R_{\mathrm{xx}}$. The same probability is denoted on a concentric circle (ellipse).

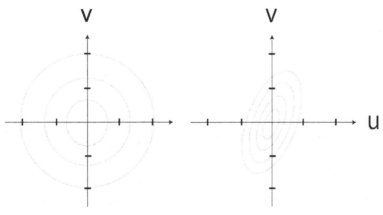

(a) A proper case (ρ=0)   (b) An impoper case (ρ=0.8exp[i3π/2])

tool in science and technology. Needs for an adaptive filter for multidimensional signals have emerged because of recent progress in environmental science, robot engineering, and biomedicine. The quaternion LMS estimation is required in such a trend.

Quaternion Linear Mean Square Estimation

First, quaternion linear mean square estimation is described. Assume a case in which a true value denoted by a quaternion random variable $y \in \mathbf{Q}$ is estimated from an observed value denoted by a quaternion random vector $\mathbf{x} \in \mathbf{Q}^N$. Then consider an estimated value $\hat{y}_L$ expressed as follows:

$$\hat{y}_L = \mathbf{h}^H \mathbf{x} \tag{7}$$

where $\mathbf{h} \in \mathbf{Q}^N$, and H expresses quaternion conjugate transpose. The problem is to find a quaternion parameter $\mathbf{h} \in \mathbf{Q}^N$ that minimizes mean square error $E|y - \hat{y}_L|^2$. Such a framework is designated as the quaternion linear mean square estimation.

Quaternion Widely Linear Mean Square Estimation

Next, quaternion widely linear mean square estimation is explained. Assume an estimated value $\hat{y}$ expressed as

$$\hat{y} = \mathbf{h}^H \mathbf{x} + \mathbf{g}^H \mathbf{x}^* \tag{8}$$

where $\mathbf{g}, \mathbf{h} \in \mathbf{Q}^N, H$ is quaternion conjugate transpose, and

$$v^* \overset{def}{=} a - ib - jc - kd$$

is the quaternion conjugate of:

$$v = a + ib + jc + kd \in \mathbf{Q}$$

The difference from the quaternion linear mean square estimation described in the previous section is that a conjugate quaternion term $\mathbf{x}^*$ is added as an explanatory variable. As the case of the complex-valued widely linear mean square estimation, this improves the accuracy and the efficiency of estimation compared with that of the quaternion linear mean square estimation described in the previous section, and then expands the scalability of the estimation framework. The problem is to find quaternion parameters $\mathbf{g}, \mathbf{h} \in \mathbf{Q}^N$ that minimize mean square error $E|y - \hat{y}|^2$.

Took et al. first proposed quaternion widely linear mean square estimation (Took & Mandic, 2009). They formulated quaternion widely linear mean square estimation with the framework of a quaternion adaptive filter, and proposed a learning algorithm applied thereto, referred to as the augmented quaternion least mean square algorithm.

Nitta proved mathematically that an estimated error acquired with quaternion widely linear mean square estimation is less than that with usual quaternion linear mean square estimation (Nitta, 2011):

$$E|y - \hat{y}_L|^2 \geq E|y - \hat{y}|^2,$$

where the equality holds in exceptional cases only. This result was verified using a method for the complex-valued widely linear estimation described by Picinbono et al. (Picinbono & Chevalie, 1995).

Properness of a Quaternion Random Vector

This section discusses the properness of a quaternion random vector, a natural extension of the properness of a complex-valued random vector described in Section Properness of a Complex-Valued Random Vector.

Vakhania first discussed the properness of a quaternion random vector (Vakhania, 1999). It was defined as the invariance of a probability density function under a certain special rotation. Then Amblard et al. defined it as the invariance under arbitrary rotation (Amblard & Bihan, 2004). This chapter presents an explanation based on reference Buchholz and Bihan (2008) in which the definition of reference Amblard and Bihan (2004) is provided briefly.

There are two levels in the definition of properness of a quaternion random vector.

$\mathbf{C}^{\eta}$ -Properness

Definition 2: Let η be a pure unit quaternion, whose real part is 0 and magnitude is unity. Then a quaternion random vector $\mathbf{x} \in \mathbf{Q}^N$ is $\mathbf{C}^{\eta}$ -proper.

$$\stackrel{def}{\Longleftrightarrow} \mathbf{x} \stackrel{d}{=} \exp\left[\eta\theta\right] \cdot \mathbf{x}$$

holds for any $\theta \in \mathbf{R}$ where $\stackrel{d}{=}$ implies "identical probability distribution." A quaternion random vector which is not $\mathbf{C}^{\eta}$ -proper is $\mathbf{C}^{\eta}$ -improper.

Intuitively, this implies that a random vector $\exp\left[\eta\theta\right] \cdot \mathbf{x}$ obtained by rotating a quaternion random vector $\mathbf{x}$ around one axis η obeys the same probability distribution as $\mathbf{x}$. Consider the case of $\eta = i$ by contrast with Definition 1. When a $\mathbf{C}^i$ -proper quaternion random vector

$$\mathbf{x} = \mathbf{x}_0 + i\mathbf{x}_1 + j\mathbf{x}_2 + k\mathbf{x}_3$$

is expressed using Cayley-Dickson notation, i.e., $\mathbf{x}^{(1)} + \mathbf{x}^{(2)}j$ where

$$\mathbf{x}^{(1)} = \mathbf{x}_0 + i\mathbf{x}_1,$$

$$\mathbf{x}^{(2)} = \mathbf{x}_2 + i\mathbf{x}_3$$

Then

$$E[\mathbf{x}^{(1)}\mathbf{x}^{(1)T}] = E[\mathbf{x}^{(2)}\mathbf{x}^{(2)T}]$$
$$= E[\mathbf{x}^{(1)}\mathbf{x}^{(2)H}] = 0$$

$\mathbf{H}$ -Properness

Definition 3: A quaternion random vector $\mathbf{x} \in \mathbf{Q}^N$ is $\mathbf{H}$ -proper.

$$\stackrel{def}{\Longleftrightarrow} \mathbf{x} \stackrel{d}{=} \exp\left[\eta\theta\right] \cdot \mathbf{x}$$

for any pure unit quaternion η , whose real part is 0 and magnitude is unity, and any $\theta \in \mathbf{R}$. A quaternion random vector that is not $\mathbf{H}$ -proper is $\mathbf{H}$ -improper.

Intuitively, this implies that a random vector $\exp\left[\eta\theta\right] \cdot \mathbf{x}$ obtained by rotating a quaternion random vector $\mathbf{x}$ around any axis η obeys the same probability distribution as $\mathbf{x}$. Consider this case by contrast with definition 1. When a $\mathbf{H}$ -proper quaternion random vector

$$\mathbf{x} = \mathbf{x}_0 + i\mathbf{x}_1 + j\mathbf{x}_2 + k\mathbf{x}_3$$

is expressed using Cayley-Dickson notation, i.e., $\mathbf{x}^{(1)} + \mathbf{x}^{(2)}j$, where

$$\mathbf{x}^{(1)} = \mathbf{x}_0 + i\mathbf{x}_1,$$

$$\mathbf{x}^{(2)} = \mathbf{x}_2 + i\mathbf{x}_3,$$

then

$$E[\mathbf{x}^{(1)}\mathbf{x}^{(1)T}] = E[\mathbf{x}^{(2)}\mathbf{x}^{(2)T}]$$
$$= E[\mathbf{x}^{(1)}\mathbf{x}^{(2)H}] = E[\mathbf{x}^{(1)}\mathbf{x}^{(2)T}] = 0$$

For example, signals handled by a vector sensor include those with the properness mentioned above (Buchholz & Bihan, 2008). Next we assume two discrete signals. If polarized, the signals can be expressed as a $\mathbf{C}^{\eta}$-proper quaternion random vector, otherwise if not polarized, they can be expressed as a $\mathbf{H}$-proper quaternion random vector.

Quaternion Widely Linear Estimation Using Involution

This section introduces a quaternion widely linear mean square estimation extended using involution (Took & Mandic, 2010). Generally, involution is mapping that has itself as its inverse mapping:

$$f^{-1}(x) = f(x)$$

for any x.

Define the following three involutions for a quaternion

$$q = q_a + iq_b + jq_c + kq_d \in \mathbf{Q}:$$

$$q^i = -iqi = q_a + iq_b - jq_c - kq_d \qquad (9)$$

$$q^j = -jqj = q_a - iq_b + jq_c - kq_d \qquad (10)$$

$$q^k = -kqk = q_a - iq_b - jq_c + kq_d \qquad (11)$$

The conjugate quaternion of q is

$$q = q_a - iq_b - jq_c - kq_d,$$

in which its three imaginary terms are all negative, whereas an involution quaternion has any two negative terms of the three. Then, let a quaternion random vector $\mathbf{x} \in \mathbf{Q}^N$ be an observed value, and let a quaternion random variable $y \in \mathbf{Q}$ be a true value. Then assume an estimated value $\hat{y}$ as

$$\hat{y} = \mathbf{h}^H \mathbf{x} + \mathbf{g}^H \mathbf{x}^* + \mathbf{u}^H \mathbf{x}^{i*} + \mathbf{v}^H \mathbf{x}^{j*} \qquad (12)$$

where $\mathbf{g}, \mathbf{h}, \mathbf{u}, \mathbf{v} \in \mathbf{Q}^N$. Difference from quaternion widely linear mean square estimation introduced in Section Quaternion Widely Linear Mean Square Estimation is that involution quaternion terms $\mathbf{x}^{i*}$ and $\mathbf{x}^{j*}$ are added as explanatory variables. Since Equation (12) contains more information on quaternion statistics than Equation (8), this brings out further improvement of the accuracy and the efficiency of estimation compared with that of the quaternion widely linear mean square estimation described in Section Quaternion Widely Linear Mean Square Estimation, and then leads to further expansion of the scalability of the estimation framework. The problem is to find quaternion parameters $\mathbf{g}, \mathbf{h}, \mathbf{u}, \mathbf{v} \in \mathbf{Q}^N$ that minimize mean square error $E|y - \hat{y}|^2$.

Took et al. formulated quaternion widely linear mean square estimation using the involution quaternion described above with the framework of a quaternion adaptive filter, proposed the augmented involution quaternion LMS algorithm applied thereto, and evaluated its performance by simulation (see Section Application Examples).

Ujang, Took, and Mandic (2011) proposed a quaternion widely linear mean square estimation in which Equation (12) was modified into

$$\hat{y} = \mathbf{h}^H \mathbf{x} + \mathbf{g}^H \mathbf{x}^{i*} + \mathbf{u}^H \mathbf{x}^{j*} + \mathbf{v}^H \mathbf{x}^{k*} \qquad (13)$$

Furthermore, they adopted a quaternion function locally regular as an activation function. In quaternion neuro-computing to date, real-valued nonlinear functions f_a, f_b, f_c, f_d have been applied separately to four terms of a quaternion

$$q = q_a + iq_b + jq_c + kq_d$$

as

$$f(q) = f_a(q_a) + if_b(q_b) + jf_c(q_c) + kf_d(q_d) \qquad (14)$$

where f is designated as a split-type activation function. An earlier study (Ujang, Took & Mandic, 2011) was the first to employ non-split-type activation functions, such as $\tanh : \mathbf{Q} \to \mathbf{Q}$. A quaternion function

$$f : \mathbf{Q} \to \mathbf{Q}, q = q_a + iq_b + jq_c + kq_d \mapsto f(q)$$

is regular when the following Cauchy-Riemann-Feuter (CRF) condition is satisfied:

$$\frac{\partial f}{\partial q_a} + i\frac{\partial f}{\partial q_b} + j\frac{\partial f}{\partial q_c} + k\frac{\partial f}{\partial q_d} = 0. \qquad (15)$$

This is equivalent to the quaternion version of Cauchy-Riemann equations in the complex analysis. Because quaternion functions satisfying the CRF condition are only linear functions and constants, non-linearity cannot be introduced using regular quaternion functions as the activation functions of a quaternion neuron. However, a quaternion function that is not regular as a quaternion function but locally regular (Leo & Rotelli, 2003) can be used as an activation function to assure nonlinearity. Ujang et al. compared quaternion widely linear mean square estimation to which the above-mentioned local regularity was introduced with conventional methods, such as quaternion neural network using a split-type activation function (Arena, Fortuna, Muscato, & Xibilia, 1998) and quaternion adaptive filter using a split-type activation function (Ujang, Took, & Mandic, 2010) by simulation. Results show superior learning convergence speed and prediction performance of the former.

CLIFFORD WIDELY LINEAR ESTIMATION

This section describes Clifford widely linear estimation, which is the generalization of complex-valued widely linear estimation and quaternion widely linear estimation (Nitta, 2011).

Consider a Clifford algebra $Cl_{p,q}$. Assume a case in which a true value denoted by a Clifford random variable $y \in Cl_{p,q}$ is estimated from an observed value denoted by a Clifford random vector $\mathbf{x} \in Cl_{p,q}^N$. Then assume an estimated value $\hat{y}_L$ expressed as

$$\hat{y}_L = \mathbf{h}^H \mathbf{x} \qquad (16)$$

where $\mathbf{h} \in Cl_{p,q}^N$, and where H expresses the Clifford conjugate transpose. The problem is to find a Clifford-valued parameter $\mathbf{h} \in Cl_{p,q}^N$ that minimizes the mean square error $E|y - \hat{y}_L|^2$. Such a framework is designated as Clifford linear mean square estimation.

The Clifford conjugate is defined as follows: Let $e_0, \cdots, e_n$ be the basis of $\mathbf{R}^{n+1}$. For any $x \in Cl_{p,q}$, let

$$x = [x]_0 + [x]_1 + \cdots + [x]_n \qquad (17)$$

where $[x]_k$ is constructed by unifying all terms such as $e_{i_1} e_{i_2} \cdots e_{i_k}$, which comprise k items selected from $e_0, \cdots, e_n$, and aligned. Then a Clifford conjugate $x^* \in Cl_{p,q}$ is given as

$$x^* = [x]_0 - [x]_1 - [x]_2 + [x]_3 + [x]_4 - \cdots \qquad (18)$$

Next, Clifford widely linear mean square estimation is described. Consider an estimated value $\hat{y}$ expressed as

$$\hat{y} = \mathbf{h}^H \mathbf{x} + \mathbf{g}^H \mathbf{x}^* \qquad (19)$$

where $\mathbf{g}, \mathbf{h} \in Cl_{p,q}^N$, and v^* is the Clifford conjugate of $v \in Cl_{p,q}$. The salient difference from the Clifford linear mean square estimation described above is that a Clifford conjugate term $\mathbf{x}^*$ is added as an explanatory variable. The problem is to find Clifford-valued parameters $\mathbf{g}, \mathbf{h} \in Cl_{p,q}^N$ that minimize mean square error $E\left| y - \hat{y} \right|^2$.

APPLICATION EXAMPLES

Application examples of complex-valued and quaternary widely linear estimation are introduced.

Complex-valued widely linear estimation was proposed in an earlier report of the literature (Brown & Crane, 1969; Gardner, 1993) as effective under limited conditions. Brown et al. demonstrated that the SN ratio was double that of the usual matched filter, by employing complex-valued widely linear estimation for a matched filter. Furthermore, it was shown that a mean square error is halved under some limited conditions compared with the usual linear filter, in the case of the common linear filter (Brown & Crane, 1969). Gardner applied complex-valued widely linear estimation to the cyclic Wiener filter that generalized the Wiener filter, which treats complex time series data (Gardner, 1993).

The application of the complex-valued independent component analysis (Complex ICA), a technique for separating complex-valued signals, includes wireless communications, radars, MRI data analysis, electroencephalograms, and face recognition. Generally, signal sources handled with independent component analysis (ICA) are classified to the following two categories according to their applicable fields: super-Gaussian, with probability distribution having a sharp peak and a large skirt, and sub-Gaussian, with flat probability distribution less variant around

the origin, but taking very small values at both ends. Especially in the case of complex-valued data, signal sources are further divided into those which are proper or improper. Complex-valued fast fixed point algorithm (c-FastICA) (Bingham & Hyvarinen, 2000) has been used best to solve a complex-valued ICA problem. However its assumption that treating complex-valued data is proper has prevented it from handling improper data. Novey et al. extended c-FastICA so that it could respond also to improper signal sources by applying complex-valued widely linear estimation (Novey & Adali, 2008).

Complex-valued widely linear estimation has also been applied to communications (Gerstacker, Schober, & Lampe, 2003; Schober, Gerstacker, & Lampe, 2004).

The prediction performance of the augmented quaternion LMS algorithm was estimated using computer simulation. The Lorentz attractor, which is a three-dimensional nonlinear system, was used originally for modeling atmospheric turbulence, but is also employed for modeling laser behavior, electric generators, and water wheels today. The performance of the augmented quaternion LMS algorithm was evaluated by regarding three variables of the Lorentz attractor as pure quaternions, whose real part is 0. The augmented quaternion LMS algorithm demonstrated better prediction performance than with the (usual) quaternion LMS algorithm and LMS algorithm not using widely linear estimation.

The augmented quaternion LMS algorithm was also applied to short-term wind forecast in a three-dimensional space, which plays an important role in renewable energy, air pollution models, and aircraft safety. Three-dimensional wind data were expressed with pure quaternions. Experimental results have indicated that the augmented quaternion LMS algorithm is superior to the (usual) quaternion LMS algorithm and complex-valued LMS algorithm, which processes three-dimensional information with two complex-valued LMSs. Furthermore, another experiment revealed the same result, in which a quartet of data consisting of three-dimensional wind data with thermal data added (data fusion) were expressed with quaternions.

Experiments for a **H**-proper autoregressive model demonstrated comparable performance by usual quaternion LMS not using a conjugate quaternion, augmented quaternion LMS (Section Quaternion Widely Linear Mean Square Estimation), and augmented involution quaternion LMS. However, applying augmented involution quaternion LMS to a **H**-improper four-dimensional Saito circuit and a short-term wind prediction problem (wind velocity and temperature in three-dimensional space are fused as a quaternion) revealed the learning speed and prediction performance of augmented involution quaternion LMS surpassing usual quaternion LMS not using a conjugate quaternion and augmented quaternion LMS (Section Quaternion Widely Linear Mean Square Estimation).

Short-Term Wind Forecasting

Mandic et al. built a model that expressed the data of the two-dimensional wind data with complex numbers, and proposed a technique to conduct short-term wind prediction using complex-valued widely linear estimation (Mandic, Javidi, Goh, Kuh, & Aihara, 2009). The modeling and prediction of wind are requirements for the efficient operation of a wind turbine, and are also important for the optimum allocation of energy supplied from a wind park. Moreover, short-term prediction is necessary to protect wind turbines from damage, and to control their vibration. Since wind velocity and direction affect wind turbines simultaneously, independent prediction thereof might exaggerate an error. Therefore, it is more preferred to express wind data as complex numbers (Figure 3).

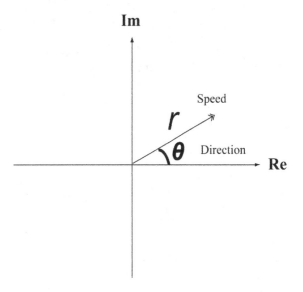

Figure 3. A complex-valued representation of wind data.

A wind predictor is implemented using a complex-valued finite impulse response (FIR) filter to which complex-valued widely linear estimation is applied. Forecasting of more than one step ahead is implemented in the recursive method where at time k the predictor predicts all the intermediate values up to $(k + T)$ steps ahead by using the previously estimated values at

$$k + 1, \cdots, k + T - 1$$

(Wan, 1993). The complex-valued FIR filter is shown in Figure 4. The error signal at time k is given by

$$e(k) = d(k) - y(k)$$

where $d(k)$ is the desired response, and $y(k)$ is the output given by

$$y(k) = \mathbf{x}(k)^T \mathbf{w}(k) \qquad (20)$$

Figure 4. Linear adaptive finite impulse response filter.

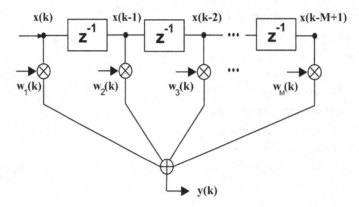

where

$$\mathbf{x}(k) = \left[x(k), \cdots, x(k - M + 1) \right]^{T}$$

denotes the complex-valued input signal vector,

$$\mathbf{w}(k) = \left[w_1(k), \cdots, w_M(k) \right]^{T}$$

the complex-valued weight vector, and M the number of tap inputs. The weight update rule can be obtained using the general complex-valued stochastic gradient method as

$$\mathbf{w}(k + 1) = \mathbf{w}(k) + \mu \cdot e(k) \cdot \mathbf{x}(k)^{*} \qquad (21)$$

where μ is the step size, and z^{*} is the complex conjugate of a complex number z. This is the complex-valued gradient descent based least mean square (CLMS) algorithm.

Mandic et al. extended the complex-valued FIR filter described above to the widely linear framework (called augmented complex-valued least mean square (ACLMS) algorithm) in order to fully utilize the available information within the data. The error signal at time k is given by

$$e(k) = d(k) - y(k)$$

where $d(k)$ is the desired response, and $y(k)$ is the output given by

$$y(k) = \left(\mathbf{x}^{a}(k) \right)^{T} \mathbf{w}^{a}(k) \qquad (22)$$

where

$$\mathbf{x}^{a}(k) = \left[\mathbf{x}(k), \mathbf{x}(k)^{*} \right]^{T}$$

denotes the augmented complex-valued input signal vector, and

$$\mathbf{w}^{a}(k) = \left[w_1(k), \cdots, w_M(k), w_1(d)^{*}, \cdots, w_M(k)^{*} \right]^{T}$$

the augmented complex-valued weight vector. The augmented complex-valued LMS (ACLMS) weight update rule can be rewritten as

$$\mathbf{w}^{a}(k + 1) = \mathbf{w}^{a}(k) + \mu \cdot e(k) \cdot \left(\mathbf{x}^{a}(k) \right)^{*} \qquad (23)$$

This is the widely linear version of the complex-valued LMS algorithm.

One of the two experiments described in Mandic, Javidi, Goh, Kuh, and Aihara (2009) is introduced here where the data obtained from the

Iowa (USA) Department of Transport were used. Table 1 shows the input data which are the average wind data for 1h, 3h and 6h. The data were normalized to zero mean and unit variance. The initial weights were chosen randomly. The following two performance measures were used: the error mean B and the coefficient of multiple determination r (Drossu & Obradovic, 1996).

$$B = \frac{1}{T} \sum_{\alpha=1}^{T} \left| x_\alpha - \hat{x}_\alpha \right| \tag{24}$$

$$r^2 = 1 - \frac{\sum_{\alpha=1}^{T} \left| x_\alpha - \hat{x}_\alpha \right|^2}{\sum_{\alpha=1}^{T} \left| x_\alpha - \overline{x}_\alpha \right|^2} \tag{25}$$

where T is the number of samples, x_α is the actual signal value, $\hat{x}_\alpha$ is the forecasted value,

and $\overline{x}_\alpha$ is the mean of the data. The error mean B is used to measure whether the predictor is biased. The coefficient of multiple determination r for which the values are close to unity indicates perfect prediction. Table 2 shows the simulation result of six steps ahead prediction for wind data. In all cases the predictors using the ACLMS algorithm reveals their excellent performance compared with the predictors using the standard CLMS algorithm, both in terms of bias and prediction accuracy.

FUTURE RESEARCH DIRECTIONS

Studies of widely linear estimation using Clifford algebra have just started, and future deployment including the handling of improperness is anticipated. Its potential for fusion with various high-dimension neural networks is also expected (Nitta, 2009).

CONCLUSION

This chapter reviews widely linear estimation in a high-dimension domain. The study of widely linear estimation about complex numbers started in 1969, and has remained active since the 1990s. Related studies of the quaternion domain were apparently initiated by Vakhania in 1999, and have been conducted actively during these last several years with rapid development.

Table 1. Statistical properties of the wind data sets. (© 2009, Elsevier.).

	1h	3h	6h
Cumulative samples	1200	1200	1200
Minimum speed (m/s)	0	0	0
Maximum speed (m/s)	13.0582	12.2865	11.4663
Mean speed (m/s)	3.2905	3.2905	3.2905
Standard deviation (m/s)	2.3387	2.2653	2.1520

Table 2. Performance measures for 1-, 3- and 6-h average of wind data for six steps ahead prediction. (© 2009, Elsevier.).

	1h		3h		6h	
Algorithm	CLMS	ACLMS	CLMS	ACLMS	CLMS	ACLMS
B	0.088934	0.073271	0.074041	0.018205	0.1107	0.062436
r	0.1149	0.3081	0.14988	0.32099	0.1258	0.4657

REFERENCES

Amblard, P.-O., & Le Bihan, N. (2004). On properness of quaternion valued random variables. In *Proc. IMA Conference on Mathematics in Signal Processing* (pp. 23-26). Cirencester, U. K.

Arena, P., Fortuna, L., Muscato, G., & Xibilia, M. G. (1998). *Neural networks in multidimensional domain, Lecture Notes in Control and Information Sciences 234.* Springer. doi:10.1007/BFb0047683

Bingham, E., & Hyvarinen, A. (2000). A fast fixed-point algorithm for independent component analysis. *International Journal of Neural Systems, 10*, 1–8.

Brown, W. M., & Crane, R. B. (1969). Conjugate linear filtering. *IEEE Transactions on Information Theory, 15*(4), 462–465. doi:10.1109/TIT.1969.1054330

Buchholz, S., & Le Bihan, N. (2008). Random vectors with values in quaternion Hilbert spaces. *International Journal of Neural Systems, 18*(2), 75–85. doi:10.1142/S0129065708001403

DeLeo, S., & Rotelli, P. P. (2003). Quaternionic analyticity. *Applied Mathematics Letters, 16*(7), 1077–1081. doi:10.1016/S0893-9659(03)90097-8

Dorst, L., Fontijne, D., & Mann, S. (2007). *Geometric algebra for computer science.* Elsevier.

Drossu, R., & Obradovic, Z. (1996). Rapid design of neural networks for time series prediction. *IEEE Computational Science & Engineering, 3*(2), 78–89. doi:10.1109/99.503317

Farhang-Boroujeny, B. (1999). *Adaptive filters theory and applications.* New York: Wiley.

Gardner, W. A. (1993). Cyclic wiener filtering: Theory and method. *IEEE Transactions on Communications, 41*(1), 151–163. doi:10.1109/26.212375

Gerstacker, H., Schober, R., & Lampe, A. (2003). Receivers with widely linear processing for frequency-selective channels. *IEEE Trans. Comuunications, 51*(9), 1512–1523. doi:10.1109/TCOMM.2003.816992

Hamilton, W. (1899). *Elements of quaternions* (2nd ed.). London, UK: Longmans, Green, & Company.

Mandic, D. P., Javidi, S., Goh, S. L., Kuh, A., & Aihara, K. (2009). Complex-valued prediction of wind profile using augmented complex statistics. *Renewable Energy, 34*(1), 196–201. doi:10.1016/j.renene.2008.03.022

Nitta, T. (Ed.). (2009). *Complex-valued neural networks: Utilizing high-dimensional parameters.* Pennsylvania: Information Science Reference. doi:10.4018/978-1-60566-214-5

Nitta, T. (2011). Widely linear processing of hypercomplex signals. In B.-L. Lu, L. Zhang and J. Kwok (Eds.), *Proc. Int. Conf. on Neural Information Processing (ICONIP2011), Shanghai, China, Nov. 13-17, Part I (Lecture Notes in Computer Science), No. 7062* (pp. 519-525).

Novey, M., & Adali, T. (2008). On extending the complex FastICA algorithm to noncircular sources. *IEEE Transactions on Signal Processing, 56*(5), 2148–2154. doi:10.1109/TSP.2007.911278

Picinbono, B. (1996). Second-order complex random vectors and normal distribution. *IEEE Transactions on Signal Processing, 44*(10), 2037–2040. doi:10.1109/78.539051

Picinbono, B., & Chevalie, P. (1995). Widely linear estimation with complex data. *IEEE Transactions on Signal Processing, 43*(8), 2030–2033. doi:10.1109/78.403373

Sayed, A. H. (2003). *Fundamentals of adaptive filtering.* New York: Wiley IEEE Press.

Schober, R., Gerstacker, W. H., & Lampe, L. H.-J. (2004). Data-aided and blind stochastic gradient algorithm for widely linear MMSE MAI suppression for DS-CDMA. *IEEE Transactions on Signal Processing, 52*(3), 746–756. doi:10.1109/TSP.2003.822359

Schreier, P. J., & Scharf, L. L. (2010). *Statistical signal processing of complex-valued data - the theory of improper and noncircular signals.* Cambridge University Press. doi:10.1017/CBO9780511815911

Took, C. C., & Mandic, D. P. (2009). The quaternion LMS algorithm for adaptive filtering of hypercomplex processes. *IEEE Transactions on Signal Processing, 57*(4), 1316–1327. doi:10.1109/TSP.2008.2010600

Took, C. C., & Mandic, D. P. (2010). A quaternion widely linear adaptive filter. *IEEE Transactions on Signal Processing, 58*(8), 4427–4431. doi:10.1109/TSP.2010.2048323

Ujang, B. C., Took, C. C., & Mandic, D. P. (2010). Split quaternion nonlinear adaptive filtering. *Neural Networks, 23*(3), 426–434. doi:10.1016/j.neunet.2009.10.006

Ujang, B. C., Took, C. C., & Mandic, D. P. (2011). Quaternion-valued nonlinear adaptive filtering. *IEEE Transactions on Neural Networks, 22*(8), 1193–1206. doi:10.1109/TNN.2011.2157358

Vakhania, N. N. (1999). Random vectors with values in quaternion Hilbert spaces. *Theory of Probability and Its Applications, 43*(1), 99–115. doi:10.1137/S0040585X97976696

Wan, E. (1993). Time series prediction using a neural network with embedded tapped delay-lines. *Predicting the future and understanding the past. SFI studies in* the science of complexity, 195-217.

Widrow, B. (1966). *Adaptive filters I: Fundamentals. Rep. SEL-66-126(TR-6764-6).* Stanford, CA: Stanford Electronic Laboratories.

Widrow, B., & Hoff, M. E. (1960). Adaptive switching circuits. *IRE WESCON Convention Record, Part 4,* 96-104.

Widrow, B., McCool, J., & Ball, M. (1975). The complex LMS algorithm. *Proceedings of the IEEE, 63,* 719–720. doi:10.1109/PROC.1975.9807

ADDITIONAL READING

Hirose, A. (Ed.). (2003). *Complex-valued neural networks.* Singapore: World Scientific Publishing.

Hirose, A. (2006). Complex-valued neural networks. In *Series on studies in computational intelligence (Vol. 32).* Springer-Verlag.

Igelnik, B., Tabib-Azar, M., & LeClair, S. R. (2001). A net with complex weights. *IEEE Transactions on Neural Networks, 12*(2), 236–249. doi:10.1109/72.914521

Mandic, D. P., & Goh, V. S. L. (2009). *Complex valued nonlinear adaptive filters.* John Wiley & Sons, Ltd. doi:10.1002/9780470742624

Nitta, T. (1997). An extension of the back-propagation algorithm to complex numbers. *Neural Networks, 10*(8), 1392–1415. doi:10.1016/S0893-6080(97)00036-1

Nitta, T. (2004). Orthogonality of decision boundaries in complex-valued neural networks. *Neural Computation, 16*(1), 73–97. doi:10.1162/08997660460734001

Nitta, T. (2008). The uniqueness theorem for complex-valued neural networks with threshold parameters and the redundancy of the parameters. *International Journal of Neural Systems, 18*(2), 123–134. doi:10.1142/S0129065708001439

Nitta, T. (2011). Ability of the 1-n-1 complex-valued neural network to learn transformations. In Igelnik, B. (Ed.), *Computational modeling and simulation of intellect: Current state and future perspectives* (pp. 566–596). USA: Pennsylvania, Information Science Reference. doi:10.4018/978-1-60960-551-3.ch022

Sommer, G. (Ed.). (2001). *Geometric computing with Clifford algebras*. Springer-Verlag.

KEY TERMS AND DEFINITIONS

Artificial Neural Network: A network composed of artificial neurons. Artificial neural networks can be trained to find nonlinear relationships in data.

Axisymmetric: Symmetric in respect to an axis.

Complex Number: A number of the form $a + ib$ where a and b are real numbers, and i is the imaginary unit such that $i^2 = -1$. a is called the *real part*, and b the *imaginary part*.

Complex-Valued Neural Network: An artificial neural network whose learnable parameters are complex numbers. Complex-valued neural network can learn complex-valued patterns in a natural way.

Estimation: A method for figuring out a set of objects quantitatively.

Explanatory Variable: A variable which is used to explain or to predict changes in the values of another variable.

Geometric Algebra (Clifford Algebra): 2^n-dimensional associative algebra that embraces real numbers, complex numbers and quaternions. Geometric algebra allows the processing of geometric entities like points, lines and so on. Clifford algebra is named after the British mathematician William K. Clifford.

Polarized Signal: A signal that has a direction in which it oscillates as it propagates.

Quaternion: A number of the form $a + ib + jc + kd$ where a, b, c and d are real numbers, and i, j, k are the imaginary units such that $i^2 = j^2 = k^2 = -1$. a is called the *real part*, and the other three terms the *imaginary part*.

SN Ratio (Signal to Noise Ratio): A measurement of the level of a signal as compared to the level of noise that is present in that signal. If the incoming signal strength in microvolts is V_s, and the noise level in microvolts is V_n, then the SN ratio is given by $20 \log_{10} \left(V_s / V_n \right)$. SN ratio is usually expressed in decibels (dB).

Compilation of References

Aarts, E. (1989). Simulated annealing: An introduction. *Statistica Neerlandica*, *43*(1), 31–52. doi:10.1111/j.1467-9574.1989.tb01245.x.

Achler, T., Vural, D., & Amir, E. (2009). Counting objects with biologically inspired regulatory-feedback networks. In *Proceedings of the 2009 IEEE International Joint Conference on Neural Networks*. ACM/IEEE.

Achler, T. (2011). Non-oscillatory dynamics to disambiguate pattern mixtures. In Rao, R., & Cecchi, G. A. (Eds.), *Relevance of the time domain to neural network models*. New York, NY: Springer.

Achler, T. (2012). *Towards bridging the gap between pattern recognition & symbolic representation within neural networks. Neural-Symbolic Learning & Reasoning*. AAAI.

Achler, T., & Bettencourt, L. (2011). *Evaluating the contribution of top-down feedback and post-learning reconstruction. Biologically Inspired Cognitive Architectures*. AAAI.

Agarwal, S. (2002). *Spectral clustering toolbox*. Retrieved from http://homes.cs.washington.edu/~sagarwal/code.html

Agrawal, R., Imielinski, T., & Swami, A. (1993). Mining association rules between sets of items in large databases. In *Proceedings of the 1993 ACM-SIGMOD International Conference on Management of Data* (pp. 207-216). New York, NY: ACM Press.

Aha, D., & Bankert, R. L. (1995). A comparative evaluation of sequential feature selection algorithms. In *Proceedings of the Fifth International Workshop on Artificial Intelligence and Statistics* (pp. 1-7). Springer-Verlag.

Ahmadinejad, S. H., Jalili, S., & Abadi, M. (2011). A hybrid model for correlating alerts of known and unknown attack scenarios and updating attack graphs. *Computer Networks*, *55*(9), 2221–2240. doi:10.1016/j.comnet.2011.03.005.

Aizerman, M. A., Braverman, E. A., & Rozonoer, L. (1964). Theoretical foundations of the potential function method in pattern recognition learning. *Automation and Remote Control*, *25*, 821–837.

Albert, A. E., & Gardner, L. A. (1967). *Stochastic approximation and nonlinear regression. MIT Press Research Monograph, 42*. Cambridge, MA: MIT Press.

Albus, J. (1975). A new approach to manipulator control: The Cerebellar model articulation controller. *Transactions of the American Society of Mechanical Engineers. Journal of Dynamic Systems, Measurement, and Control*, *97*, 220–227. doi:10.1115/1.3426922.

Allen, D. E., Powell, R. J., & Singh, A. K. (2012). Machine learning and short positions in stock trading strategies. Handbook of Short Selling, pp. 467-478.

Alon, A., Barkai, D., Notterman, A., Gish, K., Ybarra, S., Mack, D., & Levine, A. J. (1999). Broad patterns of gene expression revealed by clustering analysis of tumor and normal colon tissues probed by oligonucleotide arrays. In *Proceedings of the Proc. Natl. Acad. Sci.* (pp. 6745–6750). PNAS.

Álvarez-Estévez, D., Sánchez-Maroño, D., Alonso-Betanzos, A., & Moret-Bonillo, V. (2011). Reducing dimensionality in a database of sleep EEG arousals. *Expert Systems with Applications*, *38*(6), 7746–7754. doi:10.1016/j.eswa.2010.12.134.

Amblard, P.-O., & Le Bihan, N. (2004). On properness of quaternion valued random variables. In *Proc. IMA Conference on Mathematics in Signal Processing* (pp. 23-26). Cirencester, U. K.

Amine, A., Elakadi, A., Rziza, M., & Aboutajdine, D. (2009). GA-SVM and mutual information based frequency feature selection for face recognition. *Journal of Computer Science*.

Amiri, F., Rezaei Yousefi, M., Lucas, C., Shakery, A., & Yazdani, N. (2011). Mutual information-based feature selection for intrusion detection systems. *Journal of Network and Computer Applications*, 1184–1199. doi:10.1016/j.jnca.2011.01.002.

Ammann, P., Wijesekera, D., & Kaushik, S. (2002). Scalable, graph-based network vulnerability analysis. In *Proceedings of the 9th ACM conference on computer and communications security* (pp. 217-224). New York, NY: ACM.

Arabic, P., Hubert, L. J., & De Soete, G. (1996). *Complexity theory: An introduction for practitioners of classification* (pp. 199–233). Clustering and Classification.

Arena, P., Fortuna, L., Muscato, G., & Xibilia, M. G. (1998). *Neural networks in multidimensional domain, Lecture Notes in Control and Information Sciences 234.* Springer. doi:10.1007/BFb0047683.

Arnol'd, V. I. (1957). On functions of three variables. *Transactions of the American Mathematical Society*, 2(28), 51–54.

Astrom, K., & Wittenmark, J. B. (1994). *Adaptive Control.* Boston, MA: Addison-Wesley.

Auld, T., & Moore, A. W. (2007). Bayesian neural networks for Internet traffic classification. *IEEE Transactions on Neural Networks*, 18(1), 223–239. doi:10.1109/TNN.2006.883010 PMID:17278474.

Baraniuk, R., & Wakin, M. (2006). Random projections of smooth manifolds. *Foundations of Computational Mathematics*.

Barbakh, W., & Fyfe, C. (2008). Online clustering algorithms. *International Journal of Neural Systems*, 18(3), 185–194. doi:10.1142/S0129065708001518 PMID:18595148.

Barron, H., & Schmidt, C. P. (1988). Sensitivity analysis of additive multiattribute value models. *Operations Research*, 36, 122–127. doi:10.1287/opre.36.1.122.

Beaubouef, T., & Petry, F. (1994). Rough querying of crisp data in relational databases. In *Third Int. Workshop on Rough Sets and Soft Computing (RSSC'94)* (pp. 34-41). Higher School of Economics.

Beaubouef, T., Petry, F., & Buckles, B. (1995). Extension of the relational database and its algebra with rough set techniques. *Computational Intelligence*, 11, 233–245. doi:10.1111/j.1467-8640.1995.tb00030.x.

Behring, C., Bracho, M., Castro, M., & Moreno, J. A. (2000). An algorithm for robot path planning with cellular automata. In S. Bandini and T. Worsch (Eds.), *Fourth international conference on cellular automata for research and industry: Theoretical and practical issues on cellular automata* (pp. 11-19). London, UK: Springer-Verlag.

Bellmann, M., Schmalz, T., & Blumentritt, S. (2010). Comparative biomechanical analysis of current microprocessor-controlled prosthetic knee joints. *Archives of Physical Medicine and Rehabilitation*, 91, 644–652. doi:10.1016/j.apmr.2009.12.014 PMID:20382300.

Bellman, R. (1957). *Dynamic programming.* Princeton, NJ: Princeton University Press.

Bergantz, D., & Barad, H. (1988). Neural network control of cybernetic limb prostheses. *IEEE International Conference on Engineering in Medicine and Biology Society* (Vol. 3, pp. 1486–1487). IEEE.

Beringer, J., & Hüllermeier, E. (2006). Online clustering of parallel data streams. *Data & Knowledge Engineering*, 58(2), 180–204. doi:10.1016/j.datak.2005.05.009.

Bichot, N. P., Rossi, A. F., & Desimone, R. (2005). Parallel and serial neural mechanisms for visual search in macaque area V4. *Science*, 308(5721), 529–534. doi:10.1126/science.1109676 PMID:15845848.

Bingham, E., & Hyvarinen, A. (2000). A fast fixed-point algorithm for independent component analysis. *International Journal of Neural Systems*, 10, 1–8. PMID:10798706.

Bitmead, R., & Anderson, B. (1980). Lyapunov techniques for the exponential stability of linear difference equations with random coefficients. *IEEE Transactions on Automatic Control*, *25*(4), 782–787. doi:10.1109/TAC.1980.1102427.

Blanco, R. (2004). Gene selection for cancer classification using wrapper approaches. *International Journal of Pattern Recognition and Artificial Intelligence*, *18*, 1373–1390. doi:10.1142/S0218001404003800.

Boilot, P. (2003). Electronic noses inter-comparison, data fusion and sensor selection in discrimination of standard fruit solutions. *Sensors and Actuators. B, Chemical*, *88*(1), 80–88. doi:10.1016/S0925-4005(02)00313-1.

Bolón-Canedo, V., Peteiro-Barral, D., Alonso-Betanzos, A., Guijarro-Berdiñas, B., & Sánchez-Maroño, N. (2011). Scalability analysis of ANN training algorithms with feature selection. *Lecture Notes in Artificial Intelligence*, 84-93.

Bolón-Canedo, V., Sánchez-Maroño, N., & Alonso-Betanzos, A. (2010). On the effectiveness of discretization on gene selection of microarray data. *International Joint Conference on Neural Networks*, (pp. 3167-3174). ACM/IEEE.

Bolón-Canedo, V., Sánchez-Maroño, N., & Alonso-Betanzos, A. (2010). Feature selection and classification in multiple class datasets. An application to KDD cup 99 dataset. *Expert Systems with Applications*, 5947–5957.

Bolón-Canedo, V., Sánchez-Maroño, N., & Alonso-Betanzos, A. (2011). An ensemble of filters and classifiers for microarray data classification. *Pattern Recognition*, *45*, 531–539. doi:10.1016/j.patcog.2011.06.006.

Bordes, A., Bottou, L., & Gallinari, P. (2009). SGD-QN: Careful quasi-Newton stochastic gradient descent. *Journal of Machine Learning Research*, *10*, 1737–1754.

Bosc, P., & Pivert, O. (2001). On some fuzzy extensions of association rules. In *Proceedings of IFSA-NAFIPS 2001* (pp. 1104–1109). Piscataway, NJ: IEEE Press. doi:10.1109/NAFIPS.2001.944759.

Braun, J. (2009). *An application of Kolmogorov's superposition theorem to function reconstruction in higher dimensions*. (Unpublished Doctoral Dissertation). Rheinischen Friedrich-Wilhelms-Universiät, Bonn, Germany.

Braun, J., & Griebel, M. (2007). On a constructive proof of Kolmogorov's superposition theorem. *Constructive Approximation*.

Breiman, L. (2001). Random forests. *Machine Learning*, *45*(1), 5–32. doi:10.1023/A:1010933404324.

Bronshtein, I. N., Semendiaev, K. A., & Hirsch, K. A. (2007). *Handbook of mathematics*. New York, NY: Springer.

Brown, W. M., & Crane, R. B. (1969). Conjugate linear filtering. *IEEE Transactions on Information Theory*, *15*(4), 462–465. doi:10.1109/TIT.1969.1054330.

Bruce, J. R. (2006). *Real-time motion planning and safe navigation in dynamic multi-robot environments*. (Unpublished doctoral dissertation). Carnegie Mellon University.

Buchholz, S., & Le Bihan, N. (2008). Random vectors with values in quaternion Hilbert spaces. *International Journal of Neural Systems*, *18*(2), 75–85. doi:10.1142/S0129065708001403 PMID:18452243.

Buckles, B., & Petry, F. (1982). A fuzzy representation for relational data bases. *International Journal of Fuzzy Sets and Systems*, *7*, 213–226. doi:10.1016/0165-0114(82)90052-5.

Buck, R. C. (1975). Approximate functional complexity. *Bulletin of the American Mathematical Society*, *81*(6). doi:10.1090/S0002-9904-1975-13938-3.

Buck, R. C. (1979). Approximate complexity and functional representation. *Journal of Mathematical Analysis and Applications*, *70*, 280–298. doi:10.1016/0022-247X(79)90091-X.

Butler, J., Jia, J., & Dyer, J. (1997). Simulation techniques for the sensitivity analysis of multi-criteria decision models. *European Journal of Operational Research*, *103*, 531–546. doi:10.1016/S0377-2217(96)00307-4.

Cai, Y., Cercone, N., & Han, J. (1991). Attribute-oriented induction in relational databases. In Piatetsky-Shapiro, G., & Frawley, J. (Eds.), *Knowledge discovery in databases* (pp. 213–228). Boston, MA: MIT Press.

Calisi, D. (2009). *Mobile robots and vehicles motion systems: A unifying framework*. (Unpublished doctoral dissertation). Sapienza Universita di Roma.

Can, F. (1993). Incremental clustering for dynamic information processing.[TOIS]. *ACM Transactions on Information Systems*, *11*(2), 43–164. doi:10.1145/130226.134466.

Can, F., & Ozkarahan, E. A. (1990). Concepts and effectiveness of the covercoefficient-based clustering methodology for text databases.[TODS]. *ACM Transactions on Database Systems*, *15*(4), 483–517. doi:10.1145/99935.99938.

Carpenter, G. A., & Grossberg, S. (1987). A massively parallel architecture for a self-organizing neural pattern-recognition machine. *Computer Vision Graphics and Image Processing*, *37*(1), 54–115. doi:10.1016/S0734-189X(87)80014-2.

Carter, C., & Hamilton, H. (1998). Efficient attribute-oriented generalization for knowledge discovery from large databases. *IEEE Transactions on Knowledge and Data Engineering*, *10*, 193–208. doi:10.1109/69.683752.

Caruana, R., & Freitag, D. (1994). Greedy attribute selection. In *Proceedings of the Eleventh International Conference on Machine Learning* (pp. 28-36). Burlington, MA: Morgan Kaufmann Publishers.

Casimir, R., Boutleux, E., Clerc, G., & Yahoui, A. (2006). The use of features selection and nearest neighbors rule for faults diagnostic in induction motors. *Engineering Applications of Artificial Intelligence*, 169–177. doi:10.1016/j.engappai.2005.07.004.

Cauwenberghs, G., & Poggio, T. (2001). Advances in neural information processing systems: *Vol. 13. Incremental and decremental support vector machine learning* (pp. 409–123). Cambridge, MA: MIT Press.

Chang, Y.-C., & Chen, B.-S. (2000). Robust tracking designs for both holonomic and nonholonomic constrained mechanical systems. *Fuzzy Systems*, *8*(1), 46–66. doi:10.1109/91.824768.

Chang, Y.-C., & Chen, B.-S. (2005). Intelligent robust tracking controls for holonomic and nonholonomic mechanical systems using only position measurements. *IEEE Transactions on Fuzzy Systems*, *13*(4), 491–507. doi:10.1109/TFUZZ.2004.840125.

Chelazzi, L., Duncan, J., Miller, E. K., & Desimone, R. (1998). Responses of neurons in inferior temporal cortex during memory-guided visual search. *Journal of Neurophysiology*, *80*(6), 2918–2940. PMID:9862896.

Chelazzi, L., Miller, E. K., Duncan, J., & Desimone, R. (1993). Article. *Nature*, *363*, 345–347. doi:10.1038/363345a0 PMID:8497317.

Chen, H., Sun, D., Yang, J., & Chen, J. (2010). Localization for multirobot formations in indoor environment. *IEEE/ASME Transactions on Mechatronics*, *15*(4), 561–574. doi:10.1109/TMECH.2009.2030584.

Chen, J., Huang, H., Tian, S., & Qu, Y. (2009). Feature selection for text classification with Naïve Bayes. *Expert Systems with Applications*, 5432–5435. doi:10.1016/j.eswa.2008.06.054.

Chen, X., Ye, Y., Xu, X., & Huang, J. (2012). A feature group weighting method for subspace clustering of high-dimensional data. *Pattern Recognition*, *45*, 434–446. doi:10.1016/j.patcog.2011.06.004.

Chidlovskii, B., & Lecerf, L. (2008). *Scalable feature selection for multi-class problems. Machine Learning and Knowledge Discovery in Databases, (5211)* (pp. 227–240). New York, NY: Springer. doi:10.1007/978-3-540-87479-9_33.

Chin, T., Machida, K., Sawamura, S., Shiba, R., Oyabu, H., & Nagakura, Y. et al. (2006). Comparison of different microprocessor controlled knee joints on the energy consumption during walking in trans-femoral amputees: Intelligent knee prosthesis (IP) versus C-leg. *Prosthetics and Orthotics International*, *30*, 73–80. doi:10.1080/03093640500533414 PMID:16739783.

Chivers, H., Clark, J., Nobles, P., Shaikh, S., & Chen, H. (2010). Knowing who to watch: Identifying attackers whose actions are hidden within false alarms and background noise. *Information Systems Frontiers*, 1–18.

Chopra, B., Bhambri, V., & Krishan, B. (2005). Implementation of data mining techniques for strategic CRM issues. *International Journal of Computer Technology and Applications*, *2*(4), 879–883.

Chu, M., Ingols, K., Lippmann, R., Webster, S., & Boyer, S. (2010). Visualizing attack graphs, reachability, and trust relationships with NAVIGATOR. In *Proceedings of the Seventh International Symposium on Visualization for Cyber Security (VizSec '10)* (pp. 22-33). New York, NY: ACM.

Ciric, M., Ignjatovic, J., & Bogdanovi, S. (2007). Fuzzy equivalence relations and their equivalence classes. *International Journal of Fuzzy Sets and Systems, 158*(12), 1295–1313. doi:10.1016/j.fss.2007.01.010.

Claasen, T., & Mecklenbraeuker, W. (1985). Adaptive techniques for signal processing in communications. *IEEE Communications Magazine, 23*, 8–19. doi:10.1109/MCOM.1985.1092451.

Clark, K., Tyree, J., Dawkins, J., & Hale, J. (2004). Quantitative and qualitative analytical techniques for network security assessment. *IEEE Workshop on Information Assurance and Security* (pp. 321-328). West Point, NY: IEEE.

Clark, K., Tyree, S., Dawkins, J., & Hale, J. (2007). Guiding threat analysis with threat source models. *Information Assurance and Security Workshop* (pp. 321-328). IEEE.

Cortes, C., & Vapnik, V. (1995). Support vector networks. *Machine Learning, 20*, 273–297. doi:10.1007/BF00994018.

Cover, T. M. (1965). Geometrical and statistical properties of systems of linear inequalities with applications in pattern recognition. *IEEE Transactions on Electronic Computers, 14*, 326–334. doi:10.1109/PGEC.1965.264137.

Cover, T., & Hart, P. (1967). Nearest neighbor pattern classification. *IEEE Transactions on Information Theory, 13*(1), 21–27. doi:10.1109/TIT.1967.1053964.

Crammer, K., Dekel, O., Keshet, J., Shalev-Shwartz, S., & Singer, Y. (2006). Online passive-aggressive algorithms. *Journal of Machine Learning Research, 7*, 551–585.

Crooka, J. N., Edelman, D. B., & Thomas, L. C. (2007). Recent developments in consumer credit risk assessment. *European Journal of Operational Research*, 1447–1465. doi:10.1016/j.ejor.2006.09.100.

Crotti, M., Dusi, M., Gringoli, F., & Salgarelli, L. (2007). Traffic classification through simple statistical fingerprinting. *ACM IGCOMM CCR, 37*(1).

Crovella, M. E., & Bestavros, A. (1997). Self-similarity in World Wide Web traffic: Evidence and possible causes. *IEEE/ACM Transactions on Networking, 5*, 835–846. doi:10.1109/90.650143.

Dacier, M., Deswarte, Y., & Kaâniche, M. (1996). Quantitative assessment of operational security: Models and tools. *LAAS Research Report 96493*.

Das, A. S., Datar, M., Garg, A., & Rajaram, S. (2007). Google news personalization: Scalable online collaborative filtering. In *Proceedings of the 16th international conference on World Wide Web* (pp. 271-280). ACM.

Dasgupta, A., Drineas, P., & Harb, B. (2007). Feature selection methods for text classification. *Proceedings of the 13th ACM SIGKDD International Conference on Knowledge Discovery and Data Mining*, (pp. 230-239).

Dash, M., & Liu, A. (1997). Feature selection for classification. *Intelligent Data Analysis, 1*(3), 1–12.

Dash, M., & Liu, H. (2003). Consistency-based search in feature selection. *Artificial Intelligence*, 155–176. doi:10.1016/S0004-3702(03)00079-1.

Davenport, M., Duarte, M., Wakin, M., Laska, J., Takhar, D., Kelly, K., & Baraniuk, R. (2007). The smashed filter for compressive classification and target recognition. In *Proceedings of SPIE (Vol. 6498)*. SPIE. doi:10.1117/12.714460.

Dayan, P. (1999). Unsupervised learning. In Wilson, R. A., & Keil, F. (Eds.), *The MIT Encyclopedia of the Cognitive*. Cambridge, MA: MIT Press.

Dean, J., & Ghemawat, S. (2010). System and method for efficient large-scale data processing.

Dean, J., & Ghemawat, S. (2008). MapReduce: Simplified data processing on large clusters. *Communications of the ACM, 51*(1), 107–113. doi:10.1145/1327452.1327492.

DeLeo, S., & Rotelli, P. P. (2003). Quaternionic analyticity. *Applied Mathematics Letters, 16*(7), 1077–1081. doi:10.1016/S0893-9659(03)90097-8.

Dellon, B., & Matsuoka, Y. (2007). Prosthetics, exoskeletons, and rehabilitation. *IEEE Robotics & Automation Magazine, 14*, 30–34. doi:10.1109/MRA.2007.339622.

Deluzio, K. (2011, May). *Gait analysis*. Retrieved from http://me.queensu.ca/people/deluzio/GaitAnalysis.php

Desimone, R., & Duncan, J. (1995). Neural mechanisms of selective visual attention. *Annual Review of Neuroscience*, *18*, 193–222. doi:10.1146/annurev.ne.18.030195.001205 PMID:7605061.

Desrochers, M. (1990). A classification scheme for vehicle routing and scheduling problems. *European Journal of Operational Research*, *46*(3), 322–332. doi:10.1016/0377-2217(90)90007-X.

Diel, C., & Cauwenberghs, G. (2003). SVM incremental learning, adaptation and optimization. In *Proceedings of the International Joint Conference on Neural Networks (IJCNN)* (vol. 4, pp. 2685—2690). ACM/IEEE.

Ding, C., & Peng, H. (2003). Minimum redundancy feature selection from microarray gene expression data. *Proceedings of the IEEE Conference on Computational Systems Bioinformatics*, (pp. 523-528).

d'Ocagne, M. (1899). *Traite de Nomographie*. Paris, France.

Donoho, D. (2006). Compressed sensing. *IEEE Transactions on Information Theory*, *52*(4), 1289–1306. doi:10.1109/TIT.2006.871582.

Dorigo, M., & Gambardella, L. (1997). Ant colonies for the traveling salesman problem. *Bio Systems*, *43*(2), 73–81. doi:10.1016/S0303-2647(97)01708-5 PMID:9231906.

Dorst, L., Fontijne, D., & Mann, S. (2007). *Geometric algebra for computer science*. Elsevier.

Dosen, S., & Popovic, D. (2008). Accelerometers and force sensing resistors for optimal control of walking of a hemiplegic. *IEEE Transactions on Bio-Medical Engineering*, *55*, 1973–1984. doi:10.1109/TBME.2008.919715 PMID:18632360.

Doss, R. (1977). A superposition theorem for unbounded continuous functions. *Transactions of the American Mathematical Society*, *233*, 197–203. doi:10.1090/S0002-9947-1977-0582781-1.

Dredze, M., Crammer, K., & Pereira, F. (2008). Confidence-weighted linear classification. In *ICML, ACM International Conference Proceeding Series* (vol. 307, pp. 264–271).

Drossu, R., & Obradovic, Z. (1996). Rapid design of neural networks for time series prediction. *IEEE Computational Science & Engineering*, *3*(2), 78–89. doi:10.1109/99.503317.

Du, D., Simon, D., & Ergezer, M. (2009). Oppositional biogeography-based optimization. *IEEE Conference on Systems, Man, and Cybernetics* (pp. 1035-1040). San Antonio, TX.

Dubes, A. K., & Jain, R. C. (1998). *Algorithms for clustering data*. New York, NY: Prentice-Hall.

Duda, R., Hart, P., & Stork, D. (2001). *Pattern Classification* (2nd ed.). Hoboken, NJ: John Wiley & Sons.

Dudoit, S., Fridlyand, J., & Speed, T. (2002). Comparison of discrimination methods for the classification of tumors using gene expression data. *Journal of the American Statistical Association*, *97*(457), 77–87. doi:10.1198/016214502753479248.

Duncan, J., & Humphreys, G. W. (1989). Visual search and stimulus similarity. *Psychological Review*, *96*(3), 433–458. doi:10.1037/0033-295X.96.3.433 PMID:2756067.

El Akadi, A., Amine, A., El Ouardighi, A., & Aboutajdine, D. (2010). A two-stage gene selection scheme utilizing mRMR filter and GA wrapper. *Knowledge and Information Systems*, *26*(3), 487–500. doi:10.1007/s10115-010-0288-x.

Elsley, R. (1990, June). Adaptive control of prosthetic limbs using neural networks. *International Joint Conference on Neural Networks* (Vol. 2, pp. 771–776). IEEE.

Engel, Y., Mannor, S., & Meir, R. (2004). The kernel recursive least-squares algorithm. *IEEE Transactions on Signal Processing*, *52*(8), 2275–2285. doi:10.1109/TSP.2004.830985.

Ergezer, M., & Simon, D. (2011). Oppositional biogeography-based optimization for combinatorial problems. *IEEE Congress On Evolutionary Computation* (pp.1496-1503). New Orleans, LA.

Ester, M. (1996). A density-based algorithm for discovering clusters in large spatial databases with noise. *2nd International Conference Knowledge Discovery and Data Mining* (pp. 226-231). Menlo Park, CA.

Everitt, B. S., Landau, S., & Leese, M. (2001). *Cluster analysis*. London, UK: Arnold.

Evesham, H. A. (1982). *Nomography*. Boston, MA: Docent Press.

Fan, J., & Fan, Y. (2008). High dimensional classification using features annealed independence rules. *Annals of Statistics*, *36*(6), 2605–2637. doi:10.1214/07-AOS504 PMID:19169416.

Farhang-Boroujeny, B. (1999). *Adaptive filters theory and applications*. New York: Wiley.

Farhangi, H. (2010). The path of the smart grid. *IEEE Power and Energy Magazine*, *8*, 18–28. doi:10.1109/MPE.2009.934876.

Fawcett, T. (2006). An introduction to ROC analysis. *Pattern Recognition Letters*, *27*, 861–874. doi:10.1016/j.patrec.2005.10.010.

Feng, J. B., Lin, I. C., Tsai, C. S., & Chu, Y. P. (2006). Reversible watermarking: Current status and key issues. *International Journal of Network Security*, *2*(3), 161–171.

Fisher, D. (1987). Knowledge acquisition via incremental conceptual clustering. *Machine Learning*, *2*(2), 139–172. doi:10.1007/BF00114265.

Fleuret, F. (2004). Fast binary feature selection with conditional mutual information. *Journal of Machine Learning Research*, *5*, 1531–1555.

Forman, G. (2003). An extensive empirical study of feature selection metrics for text classification. *Journal of Machine Learning Research*, *3*, 1289–1305.

Forman, G. (2008). Feature selection for text classification. In Liu, H., & Motoda, H. (Eds.), *Computational methods of feature selection*. London, UK: Chapman & Hall.

Fortune, S. (1992). Voronoi diagrams and Delaunay triangulations. In Du, D., & Hwang, F. K. (Eds.), *Euclidean geometry and computers* (pp. 193–233). Singapore: World Scientific Publishing Co. doi:10.1142/97898143 55858_0006.

Fowlkes, C., Belongie, S., & Malik, J. (2001). Efficient spatiotemporal grouping using the Nystrom method. In *Proc. IEEE Conf. Comput. Vision and Pattern Recognition* (pp. 231-238). IEEE.

Fox, B., & McMahon, M. (1991). Genetic operators for sequencing problems. In Rawlin, G. (Ed.), *Foundations of genetic algorithms 1* (pp. 284–300). San Mateo, CA: Morgan Kaufmann.

French, S. (1993). *Decision theory: An introduction to the mathematics of rationality*. UK: Ellis Horwood.

French, S., & Insua, D. R. (2000). *Statistical decision theory*. UK: Arnold.

Fridman, B. L. (1967). Improvement in the smoothness of functions in the Kolmogorov superposition theorem. *Soviet Mathematics Dokladi, 8*(6).

Friedman, C. A., Huang, J., & Sandow, S. (2004). A financial approach to machine learning with applications to credit risk. In *Proceedings of IMA Workshop of Financial Modeling*. New York, NY: Springer.

Frigault, M., Wang, L., Anoop, S., & Jajodia, S. (2008). Measuring network security using dynamic bayesian network. In *Proceedings of the 4th ACM workshop on Quality of protection (QoP '08)* (pp. 23-30). New York, NY: ACM.

Friston, K. (2009). The free-energy principle: A rough guide to the brain? *Trends in Cognitive Sciences*, *13*(7), 293–301. doi:10.1016/j.tics.2009.04.005 PMID:19559644.

Friston, K., Mattout, J., & Kilner, J. (2011). Action understanding and active inference. *Biological Cybernetics*, *104*, 137–160. doi:10.1007/s00422-011-0424-z PMID:21327826.

Gailey, R., Allen, K., Castles, J., Kucharik, J., & Roeder, M. (2008). Review of secondary physical conditions associated with lower limb amputation and long-term prosthesis use. *Journal of Rehabilitation Research and Development*, *45*, 15–29. doi:10.1682/JRRD.2006.11.0147 PMID:18566923.

Galindo, J., & Tamayo, P. (2000). Credit risk assessment using statistical and machine learning: Basic methodology and risk modeling applications. *Journal of Comparative Economics*, *15*(2).

Gao, Y., Fan, J., Xue, X., & Jain, R. (2006). Automatic image annotation by incorporating feature hierarchy and boosting to scale up SVM classifiers. *Proceedings of the 14th annual ACM international conference on multimedia*, (pp. 901-910).

Garcia, D., Hall, L., Goldgof, D., & Kramer, K. (2006). A parallel feature selection algorithm from random subsets. *In Proceedings of the 17th European Conference on Machine Learning.*

Gardner, W. A. (1993). Cyclic wiener filtering: Theory and method. *IEEE Transactions on Communications, 41*(1), 151–163. doi:10.1109/26.212375.

Garrido, S., Moreno, L., Blanco, D., & Jurewicz, P. (2011). Path planning for mobile robot navigation using voronoi diagram and fast marching. *International Journal of Robotics and Automation, 2,* 154–176.

Gentile, C. (2001). A new approximate maximal margin classification algorithm. *Journal of Machine Learning Research, 2,* 213–242.

Gerdelan, A., & Reyes, N. (2006a, February). A novel hybrid fuzzy a star robot navigation system for target pursuit and obstacle avoidance. In *1st Korean-New Zealand joint workshop on advance of computational intelligence methods and applications* (pp. 75-79). Auckland, New Zealand: Auckland University of Technology.

Gerdelan, A., & Reyes, N. (2006). Synthesizing adaptive navigational robot behaviour using a hybrid fuzzy a star approach. In B. Reusch (Ed.), 9th Dortmund fuzzy days: Computational intelligence, theory and applications (pp. 699-710). Berlin, Germany: Springer-Verlag.

Gerdelan, A., & Reyes, N. (2009). Towards a generalised hybrid path-planning and motion control system with auto-calibration for animated characters in 3D environments. In M. Köppen, N. Kasabov, & G. Coghill (Eds.), *15th International Conference on Neural Information Processing: Advances in neuro-information processing* (Vol. 5506, pp. 1079-1086). New York, NY: Springer.

Gerstacker, H., Schober, R., & Lampe, A. (2003). Receivers with widely linear processing for frequency-selective channels. *IEEE Trans. Comuunications, 51*(9), 1512–1523. doi:10.1109/TCOMM.2003.816992.

Gevaert, O. (2006). Predicting the prognosis of breast cancer by integrating clinical and microarray data with bayesian networks. *Bioinformatics (Oxford, England), 22,* 184–190. doi:10.1093/bioinformatics/btl230 PMID:16873470.

Girosi, F., & Poggio, T. (1989). Representation properties of networks: Kolmogorov's theorem is irrelevant. *Neural Computation, 1,* 465–469. doi:10.1162/neco.1989.1.4.465.

Golmohammadi, S. K., Azadeh, A., & Gharehgozli, A. (2006). Action selection in robots based on learning fuzzy cognitive map. In *Proceedings of IEEE International Conference on Industrial Informatics,* (pp. 731-736). IEEE.

Gong, S. (2010). *An efficient collaborative recommendation algorithm based on item clustering* (pp. 381–387). Advances in Wireless Networks and Information Systems. doi:10.1007/978-3-642-14350-2_48.

Gordon, A. (1999). *Classification.* Boca Raton, FL: Chapman & Hall, CRC.

Grill-Spector, K., & Henson, R. et al. (2006). Repetition and the brain: Neural models of stimulus-specific effects. *Trends in Cognitive Sciences, 10*(1), 14–23. doi:10.1016/j.tics.2005.11.006 PMID:16321563.

Gropp, W., Luskand, E., & Skjellum, A. (1999). *Using MPI: Portable Parallel Programming with the Message-Passing Interface.* Cambridge, MA: MIT Press.

Grossman, R., Kamath, C., Kegelmeyer, P., & Kumar, V. (2001). *Data mining for scientific and engineering applications.* Boston, MA: Kluwer Publishers. doi:10.1007/978-1-4615-1733-7.

Grzymala-Busse, J. (1991). *Managing uncertainty in expert systems.* Boston, MA: Kluwer Academic Publishers. doi:10.1007/978-1-4615-3982-7.

Guile, G., & Wenjia, W. (2008). Boosting for feature selection for microarray data analysis. *IEEE International Joint Conference on Neural Networks IJCNN 2008,* (pp. 2559-2563).

Gu, J., Ding, X., Wang, S., & Wu, Y. (2010). Action and gait recognition from recovered 3-D human joints. *IEEE Transactions on Systems, Man, and Cybernetics. Part B, Cybernetics, 40,* 1021–1033. doi:10.1109/TSMCB.2010.2043526 PMID:20388599.

Guo, B., Damper, R., Gunn, S., & Nelson, J. (2008). A fast separability-based feature-selection method for high-dimensional remotely sensed image classification. *Pattern Recognition, 41,* 1653–1662. doi:10.1016/j.patcog.2007.11.007.

Gutin, G., Yeo, A., & Zverovich, A. (2002). Traveling salesman should not be greedy: Domination analysis of greedy-type heuristics for the TSP. *Discrete Applied Mathematics, 117*, 81–86. doi:10.1016/S0166-218X(01)00195-0.

Guyon, I. (2008). Practical feature selection: From correlation to causality. In Fogelman-Soulie, F., Perrotta, D., Piskorski, J., & Steinberger, R. (Eds.), *Mining Massive Data Sets for Security.*

Guyon, I., Gunn, S., Nikravesh, M., & Zadeh, L. (2006). *Feature extraction. Foundations and applications (Vol. 207).* Berlin, Germany: Springer-Verlag. doi:10.1007/978-3-540-35488-8.

Guyon, I., Weston, J., Barnhill, S., & Vapnik, V. (2002). Gene selection for cancer classification using support vector machines. *Journal of Machine Learning, 46*(1-3), 389–422. doi:10.1023/A:1012487302797.

Hajnayeb, A., Ghasemloonia, A., Khadem, S., & Moradi, M. (2011). Application and comparison of an ANN-based feature selection method and the genetic algorithm in gearbox fault diagnosis. *Expert Systems with Applications,* 10205–10209. doi:10.1016/j.eswa.2011.02.065.

Hale, E., Yin, W., & Zhang, Y. (2007). *A fixed-point continuation method for `1-regularized minimization with applications to compressed sensing.* CAAM Technical Report TR07-07. Rice University.

Hall, M. (1999). *Correlation-based feature selection for machine learning.* (Doctoral Dissertation). The University of Waikato, New Zealand.

Ham, F. M., Rekab, K., Acharyya, R., & Lee, Y. C. (2008). Infrasound signal classification using parallel RBF neural networks. *International Journal of Signal and Imaging Systems Engineering, 1*(¾), pp. 155-167.

Ham, F. M., & Acharyya, R. (2007). A universal neural network-based infrasound event classifier. In Chen, C. H. (Ed.), *Signal and image processing for remote sensing.* New York, NY: Taylor & Francis Group. doi:10.1201/9781420066678.ch3.

Ham, F. M., & Kostanic, I. (2001). *Principles of neuro-computing for science and engineering.* New York, NY: McGraw-Hill Higher Education.

Hamilton, W. (1899). *Elements of quaternions* (2nd ed.). London, UK: Longmans, Green, & Company.

Han, J. (1994). Towards efficient induction mechanisms in database systems. *Theoretical Computer Science, 133,* 361–385. doi:10.1016/0304-3975(94)90194-5.

Han, J., & Kamber, M. (2006). *Data mining: Concepts and techniques* (2nd ed.). San Diego, CA: Academic Press.

Hanke, J. E., & Reitsch, A. G. (1991). *Understanding business statistics.* USA: Irwin.

Haralick, R., Shanmugan, K., & Its'hak, D. (1973). Textural Features for Image Classification. *IEEE Transactions on Systems, Man, and Cybernetics, SMC-3*(6), 610–621. doi:10.1109/TSMC.1973.4309314.

Hartney, C. J. (2012, July). Security risk metrics: An attack graph-centric approach. (Unpublished Master's thesis). The University of Tulsa.

Hart, P., Nilsson, N., & Raphael, B. (1968). A formal basis for the heuristic determination of minimum cost paths. *IEEE Transactions of Systems Science and Cybernetics, 4*(2), 100–107. doi:10.1109/TSSC.1968.300136.

Hartung, F., & Kutter, M. (1999). Multimedia watermarking techniques. *Proceedings of the IEEE, 87*(7), 1079–1107. doi:10.1109/5.771066.

Hawrylak, P. J., Cain, J. T., & Mickle, M. H. (2007). Analytic modeling methodology for analysis of energy consumption for ISO 18000-7 RFID networks. *International Journal of Radio Frequency Identification Technology and Applications, 1*(4), 371–400. doi:10.1504/IJRFITA.2007.017748.

Hawrylak, P. J., Cain, J. T., & Mickle, M. H. (2009). Analysis methods for sensor networks. In Misra, S., Woungang, I., & Misra, S. C. (Eds.), *Guide to wireless sensor networks* (pp. 635–658). New York, NY: Springer. doi:10.1007/978-1-84882-218-4_25.

Hawrylak, P. J., Louthan, G., Daily, J., Hale, J., & Papa, M. (2011). Attack graphs and scenario driven wireless computer network defense. In Onwubiko, C., & Owens, T. (Eds.), *Situational awareness in computer network defense: Principles, methods and applications* (pp. 284–301). Hershey, PA: IGI Global.

Haykin, S. (2002). *Adaptive Filter Theory* (4th ed.). New York, NY: Prentice Hall.

He, C., Liu, C., Li, Y., & Tao, J. (2010). Intelligent gear fault detection based on relevance vector machine with variance radial basis function kernel. *IEEE/ASME International Conference on Advanced Intelligent Mechatronics (AIM)*, (pp. 785-789).

Hecht-Nielsen, R. (1987). Kolmogorov's mapping neural network existence theorem. In *Proceedings of the IEEE International Conference on Neural Networks III* (pp. 11-13). IEEE.

Hecht-Nielsen, R. (1990). *Neurocomputing*. New York, NY: Eddison-Wesley Publishing Company.

Herbster, M. (2001). Learning additive models online with fast evaluating kernels. In *Proceedings of the 14th Annual Conference on Computational Learning Theory* (pp. 444–460). New York, NY: Springer.

Herlocker, J. L., Konstan, J. A., Terveen, L. G., & Riedl, J. T. (2004). Evaluating collaborative filtering recommender systems. *ACM Transactions on Information Systems*, *22*(1), 5–53. doi:10.1145/963770.963772.

Hernan, S., Lambert, S., Ostwald, T., & Shostack, A. (2006, November). Uncover security design flaws using the STRIDE approach. *MSDN Magazine*.

Hertz, D., & Thomas, H. (1983). *Risk analysis and its applications*. New York: John Wiley.

Hilbert, D. (1900). *Mathematische probleme* (pp. 253–297). Gottingen: Nachrichten Akademi der Wissenschaften.

Hilderman, R., Hamilton, H., & Cercone, N. (1999). Data mining in large databases using domain generalization graphs. *Journal of Intelligent Information Systems*, *13*(3), 195–234. doi:10.1023/A:1008769516670.

Hinton, G. E., & Salakhutdinov, R. R. (2006). Reducing the dimensionality of data with neural networks. *Science*, *313*(5786), 504–507. doi:10.1126/science.1127647 PMID:16873662.

Holland, J. (1975). *Adaptation in natural and artificial systems*. Ann Arbor, MI: The University of Michigan Press.

Hong, S.-W., Shin, S.-W., & Ahn, D.-S. (2001). Formation control based on artificial intelligence for multi-agent coordination. In *International Symposium on Industrial Electronics* (vol.1, pp. 429 -434). IEEE.

Hopfield, J. J. (1982). Neural networks and physical systems with emergent collective computational abilities. *Proceedings of the National Academy of Sciences of the United States of America*, *79*(8), 2554–2558. doi:10.1073/pnas.79.8.2554 PMID:6953413.

Howard, M., & Leblanc, D. (2003). *Writing secure*. Redmond, WA: Microsoft Press.

Hua, J., Tembe, W., & Dougherty, E. (2009). Performance of feature-selection methods in the classification of high-dimension data. *Pattern Recognition*, *42*(3), 409–424. doi:10.1016/j.patcog.2008.08.001.

Huang, G.-B., Saratchandran, P., & Sundararajan, N. (2005). A generalized growing and pruning RBF (GGAP-RBF) neural network for function approximation. *IEEE Transactions on Neural Networks*, *16*(1), 57–67. doi:10.1109/TNN.2004.836241 PMID:15732389.

Huang, J., Cai, Y., & Xu, X. (2007). A hybrid genetic algorithm for feature selection wrapper based on mutual information. *Pattern Recognition Letters*, *28*(13), 1825–1844. doi:10.1016/j.patrec.2007.05.011.

Huang, W., Nakamori, Y., & Wang, S. Y. (2004). Forecasting stock market movement direction with support vector machine. *Computers & Operations Research*. doi:10.1016/j.cor.2004.03.016.

Hu, Y., & Jeon, B. (2006). Reversible visible watermarking and lossless recovery of original images. *IEEE Transactions on Circuits and Systems for Video Technology*, *16*(11), 1423–1429. doi:10.1109/TCSVT.2006.884011.

Hu, Y., Kwong, S., & Huang, J. (2006). An algorithm for removable visible watermarking. *IEEE Transactions on Circuits and Systems for Video Technology*, *16*(1), 129–133. doi:10.1109/TCSVT.2005.858742.

Hyunsoo, K., Howland, P., & Park, H. (2005). Dimension reduction in text classification with support vector machines. *Journal of Machine Learning Research*, *6*, 37–53.

Hyvärinen, A., Hurri, J., & Hoyer, P. O. (2009). *Natural image statistics*. Berlin, Germany: Springer-Verlag. doi:10.1007/978-1-84882-491-1.

Igelnick, B., & Parikh, N. (2003). Kolmogorov's spline network. *IEEE Transactions on Neural Networks, 14,* 725–733. doi:10.1109/TNN.2003.813830 PMID:18238055.

Igelnik, B. (2009). Kolmogorov's spline complex network and adaptative dynamic modeling of data. In complex-valued neural networks: Utilizing high dimensional parameters (pp. 56-78). Hershey, PA: IGI Global.

Igelnik, B., Pao, Y.-H., & LeClair, S. R. (1999). The ensemble approach to neural-network learning and generalization. *IEEE Transactions on Neural Networks, 10*(1), 19–30. doi:10.1109/72.737490 PMID:18252500.

Igelnik, B., & Parikh, N. (2003). Kolmogorov's spline network. *IEEE Transactions on Neural Networks, 14*(4), 725–733. doi:10.1109/TNN.2003.813830 PMID:18238055.

Igelnik, B., Tabib-Azar, M., & LeClair, S. R. (2001). A net with complex weights. *IEEE Transactions on Neural Networks, 12*(2), 236–249. doi:10.1109/72.914521 PMID:18244381.

Iizuka, N., Oka, M., Yamada-Okabe, H., Nishida, M., Maeda, Y., & Mori, N. et al. (2003). Oligonucleotide microarray for prediction of early intrahepatic recurrence of hepatocellular carcinoma after curative resection. *Lancet, 9361*(361), 923–929. doi:10.1016/S0140-6736(03)12775-4 PMID:12648972.

Ingols, K., Chu, M., Lippmann, R., Webster, S., & Boyer, S. (2009). Modeling modern network at-tacks and countermeasures using attack graphs. *Computer Security Applications Conference* (pp. 117-126). IEEE.

Ingols, K., Lippmann, R., & Piwowarski, K. (2006). Practical attack graph generation for network defense. In *Proceedings of the 22nd Annual Computer Security Applications Conference* (pp. 121-130). Washington, DC: IEEE Computer Society.

Inza, I. (2004). Filter versus wrapper gene selection approaches in DNA microarray domains. *Artificial Intelligence in Medicine, 31,* 91–103. doi:10.1016/j.artmed.2004.01.007 PMID:15219288.

Isard, M., Budiu, M., Yu, Y., Birrell, A., & Fetterly, D. (2007). Dryad: Distributed data-parallel programs from sequential building blocks. *ACM SIGOPS Operating Systems Review, 41*(3), 59–72. doi:10.1145/1272998.1273005.

Ishibashi, K., Hatano, K., & Takeda, M. (2008). Online learning of approximate maximum p-norm margin classifiers with biases. In *Proceedings of the 21st Annual Conference on Learning Theory* (vol. 1599, pp. 154–161).

Itti, L., & Koch, C. (2001). Computational modelling of visual attention. *Nature Reviews. Neuroscience, 2*(3), 194–203. doi:10.1038/35058500 PMID:11256080.

Jain, A. K. (2010). Data clustering: 50 years beyond k-means. *Pattern Recognition Letters, 31*(8), 651–666. doi:10.1016/j.patrec.2009.09.011.

Jain, A. K., Murty, M. N., & Flynn, P. J. (1999). Data clustering: A review. *ACM Computing Surveys, 31*(3), 264–323. doi:10.1145/331499.331504.

Jang, J., Sun, C., & Mizutani, E. (1997). *Neuro-fuzzy and soft computing: A computational approach to learning and machine intelligence*. Upper Saddle River, NJ: Prentice Hall. doi:10.1109/TAC.1997.633847.

Jardine, A. K. S., Lin, D., & Banjevic, D. (2006). A review on machinery diagnostics and prognostics implementing condition-based maintenance. *Mechanical Systems and Signal Processing, 20,* 1483–1510. doi:10.1016/j.ymssp.2005.09.012.

Jaszkiewicz, A. (2002). Genetic local search for multiobjective combinatorial optimization. *European Journal of Operational Research, 137*(1), 50–71. doi:10.1016/S0377-2217(01)00104-7.

Jayasiri, A., Mann, G., & Gosine, R. (2011). Behavior coordination of mobile robotics using supervisory control of fuzzy discrete event systems. *IEEE Transactions on Systems, Man, and Cybernetics. Part B, 41*(5), 1224–1238.

Jeffrey, R. (2004). *Subjective probability – the real thing*. Cambridge, UK: Cambridge University Press. doi:10.1017/CBO9780511816161.

Jianjiang, L., Tianzhong, Z., & Zhang, Y. (2008). Feature selection based on genetic algorithm for image annotation. *Knowledge-Based Systems, 21,* 887–891. doi:10.1016/j.knosys.2008.03.051.

Jimenez, A., Rios-Insua, S., & Mateos, A. (2003). A decision support system for multiattribute utility evaluation based on imprecise assignment. *Decision Support Systems*, *36*, 65–79. doi:10.1016/S0167-9236(02)00137-9.

Jin, C., & Yang, C. (2011). Integrating hierarchical feature selection and classifier training for multi-label image annotation. *Proceedings of the 34th International ACM SIGIR Conference on Research and Development in Information Retrieval*.

Jirapech-Umpai, T., & Aitken, S. (2005). Feature selection and classification for microarray data analysis. Evolutionary methods for identifying predictive genes. *Bioinformatics (Oxford, England)*, *6*(148).

Johansson, J., Sherrill, D., Riley, P., Bonato, P., & Herr, H. (2005). A clinical comparison of variable-damping and mechanically passive prosthetic knee devices. *American Journal of Physical Medicine & Rehabilitation*, *84*, 563–575. doi:10.1097/01.phm.0000174665.74933.0b PMID:16034225.

Johnson, D., & McGeoch, L. (1997). The traveling salesman problem: A case study in local optimization. In Aarts, E., & Lenstra, J. (Eds.), *Local search in combinatorial optimization* (pp. 215–310). New York, NY: John Wiley & Sons.

Kacprzyk, J. (1999). Fuzzy logic for linguistic summarization of databases. In *Proc.8th Int'l Conf. on Fuzzy Systems* (pp. 813-818). IEEE.

Kalanovic, V., Popovic, D., & Skaug, N. (2000). Feedback error learning neural network for trans-femoral prosthesis. *IEEE Transactions on Rehabilitation Engineering*, *8*, 71–80. doi:10.1109/86.830951 PMID:10779110.

Kalman, R. E. (1960). A new approach to linear filtering and prediction problems. *Transactions of the ASME-Journal of Basic Engineering, Series D*, *82*, 35–45.

Kanan, H., & Faez, K. (2008). An improved feature selection method based on ant colony optimization (ACO) evaluated on face recognition system. *Applied Mathematics and Computation*, 716–725. doi:10.1016/j.amc.2008.05.115.

Karagiannis, T., Papagiannaki, K., & Faloutsos, M. (2005, August). BLINC: Multilevel traffic classification in the dark. In *SIGCOMM'05: Proceedings of the 2005 Conference on Applications, Technologies, Architectures and Protocols for Computer Communications* (pp. 229-240). Philadelphia, PA.

Katakis, I., Tsoumakas, G., & Vlahavas, I. (2006). Dynamic feature space and incremental feature selection for the classification of textual data streams. *ECML PKDD Workshop on Knowledge Discovery from Data Streams*, (pp. 107-116).

Katakis, I., Tsoumakas, G., & Vlahavas, I. (2008). *Incremental clustering for the classification of concept-drifting data streams*. Retrieved from http://www.researchgate.net/publication/228980443_Incremental_Clustering_for_the_Classification_of_Concept-Drifting_Data_Streams?ev=prf_pub

Keeney, R. L., & Raiffa, H. (1993). *Decisions with multiple objectives: Preference and value tradeoffs*. Cambridge, MA: Cambridge University Press.

Khandani, A. E., Kim, A. J., & Lo, A. W. (2010). Consumer credit-risk models via machine-learning algorithms. *Journal of Banking & Finance*, *34*, 2767–2787. doi:10.1016/j.jbankfin.2010.06.001.

Kim, J., & Oh, J. (2001). Development of an above knee prosthesis using MR damper and leg simulator. In *Proceedings of the 2001 IEEE International Conference on Robotics & Automation* (pp. 3686–3691). IEEE.

Kim, J.-H. (2012). *Federation of International Robot-soccer Association*. Korea Advanced Institute of Science and Technology (KAIST). Retrieved May 25, 2012, from http://www.fira.net/

Kim, J.-H., Kim, K.-C., Kim, D.-H., Kim, Y.-J., & Vadakkepat, P. (1998). Path planning and role selection mechanism for soccer robots. In *IEEE International Conference on Robotics and Automation* (Vol. 4, pp. 3216-3221). IEEE.

Kim, Y., Kim, U., Jung, M., Kang, W., & Noh, Y. (2009). Mining association rules for RFID data with concept hierarchy. In *Proceedings of the 11th international conference on Advanced Communication Technology* (Vol. 2, pp. 1002-1006). Piscataway, NJ: IEEE Press.

Kim, Y.-H., & Kim, J.-H. (2009) Multiobjective quantum-inspired evolutionary algorithm for fuzzy path planning of mobile robot. In *Proceedings of the Eleventh Congress on Evolutionary Computation* (pp. 1185-1192). IEEE.

Kim, J.-H., Kim, Y.-H., Choi, S.-H., & Park, I.-W. (2009). Evolutionary multiobjective optimization in robot soccer system for education. *IEEE Computational Intelligence Magazine*, 2, 31–41.

King, B. (1967). Step-wise clustering procedures. *Journal of the American Statistical Association*, 86–101. doi:10.1080/01621459.1967.10482890.

Kira, K., & Rendell, L. A. (1992). A practical approach to feature selection. *Proceedings of the 9th International Conference on Machine Learning*, (pp. 249-256). Burlington, MA: Morgan Kaufmann Publishers Inc.

Kirk, J. (2007). *Traveling salesman problem - genetic algorithm*. Retrieved April 1, 2012, from: http://www.mathworks.com/matlabcentral/fileexchange/13680

Kirpatrick, S., Gelatt, C., & Vecchi, M. (1983). Optimization by simulation annealing. *Science*, 220, 671–680. doi:10.1126/science.220.4598.671 PMID:17813860.

Kivinen, J., Smola, A. J., & Williamson, R. C. (2002). Advances in neural information processing systems: *Vol. 14. Online learning with kernels* (pp. 785–792). Cambridge, MA: MIT Press.

Kivinen, J., Smola, A. J., & Williamson, R. C. (2004). Online learning with kernels. *IEEE Transactions on Signal Processing*, 52(8), 2165–2176. doi:10.1109/TSP.2004.830991.

Kohavi, R., & John, G. (1997). Wrappers for feature subset selection. *Artificial Intelligence*, 97(1-2), 273–324. doi:10.1016/S0004-3702(97)00043-X.

Kohavi, R., & Provost, F. (1998). 'Glossary of Terms', special issue on applications of machine learning and the knowledge discovery process. *Machine Learning*, 30, 271–274. doi:10.1023/A:1017181826899.

Koh, H., & Tan, G. (2005). Data mining applications in healthcare. *Journal of Healthcare Information Management*, 19(2), 64–72. PMID:15869215.

Kolmogorov, A. N. (1957). On the representation of continuous functions of many variables by superposition of continuous functions of one variable and addition. *Transactions of the American Mathematical Society*, 2(28), 55–59.

Komorowski, J., Pawlak, Z., & Polkowski, L. (1999). Rough sets: A tutorial. In Pal, S., & Skowron, A. (Eds.), *Rough fuzzy hybridization: A new trend in decision-making* (pp. 3–98). Singapore: Springer-Verlag.

Koperski, K., & Han, J. (1995). Discovery of spatial association rules in geographic information databases. In *Proceedings of 4th International Symposium on Large Spatial Databases* (pp. 47-66). Berlin, Germany: Springer-Verlag.

Köppen, M., & Yoshida, K. (2002). Universal representation of image functions by their Sprecher construction. *Soft Computing as Transdisciplinary Science and Technology*, 202-210.

Köppen, M. (2002). Lecture Notes in Computer Science: *Vol. 140. On the training of a Kolmogorov network*. Berlin, Germany: Springer-Verlag. doi:10.1007/3-540-46084-5_77.

Kubica, J., Singh, S., & Sorokina, D. (2012). Parallel large-scale feature selection. In Bekkerman, R., Bilenko, M., & Langford, J. (Eds.), *Scaling Up Machine Learning: Parallel and Distributed Approaches*. Cambridge, MA: Cambridge University Press.

Kulkarni, J., Gaine, W., Buckley, J., Rankine, J., & Adams, J. (2005). Chronic low back pain in traumatic lower limb amputees. *Clinical Rehabilitation*, 19, 81–86. doi:10.1191/0269215505cr819oa PMID:15704512.

Kumar, V., Grama, A., Gupta, A., & Karypis, G. (1994). *Introduction to parallel computing*. Redwood City, CA: The Benjamin/Cummings Publishing Company.

Kurková, V. (1991). Kolmogorov's theorem is relevant. *Neural Computation*, 3, 617–622. doi:10.1162/neco.1991.3.4.617.

Kwong, R. H., & Johnston, E. W. (1992). A variable step size LMS algorithm. *IEEE Transactions on Signal Processing*, 40(7), 1633–1642. doi:10.1109/78.143435.

Lazarescu, M., Turpin, A., & Venktest, S. (2002). An application of machine learning techniques for the classification of glaucomatous progression. In *Proceedings of the Joint IAPR International Workshop on Structural, Syntactic, and Statistical Pattern Recognition* (pp. 243–251).

Le, T. H. N., Nguyen, K. H., & Le, H. B. (2010). Literature survey on image watermarking tools, watermark attacks and benchmarking tools. *Second International Conferences on Advances in Multimedia (MMEDIA)* (pp. 67-73). IEEE.

LeCun, Y., Bottou, L., Orr, G. B., & Müller, K.-R. (1998). Efficient backprop. In Orr, G., & Muller, K. (Eds.), *Neural networks: Tricks of the trade* (pp. 9–50). New York, NY: Springer. doi:10.1007/3-540-49430-8_2.

Lee, K. (2001). Mining generalized fuzzy quantitative association rules with fuzzy generalization hierarchies. In *Proceedings of IFSA-NAFIPS 2001* (pp. 2977-2982). Piscataway NJ: IEEE Press.

Lee, S., Choi, J., Plataniotis, K., & Ro, Y. (2010). Color component feature selection in feature-level fusion based color face recognition. *IEEE International Conference on Fuzzy Systems (FUZZ)*, (pp. 1-6).

Lee, D.-H., & Kim, J.-H. (2009). Motivation and context-based multi-robot architecture for dynamic task, role and behavior selections. In *Fira 2009* (pp. 161–170). New York, NY: Springer. doi:10.1007/978-3-642-03983-6_20.

Lee, D.-H., Na, K.-I., & Kim, J.-H. (2010). Task and role selection strategy for multi-robot cooperation in robot soccer. In *Fira roboworld congress* (pp. 170–177). New York, NY: Springer. doi:10.1007/978-3-642-15810-0_22.

Lee, D., & Kim, M. (1997). Database summarization using fuzzy ISA hierarchies. *IEEE Transactions on Systems, Man, and Cybernetics - part B*, *27*(1), 68–78. doi:10.1109/3477.552186.

Lee, J., Lee, J., Park, M., & Song, S. (2005). An extensive comparison of recent classification tools applied to microarray data. *Computational Statistics & Data Analysis*, *48*(4), 869–885. doi:10.1016/j.csda.2004.03.017.

Lee, S.-M., Kim, J.-H., & Myung, H. (2011). Design of interval type-2 fuzzy logic controllers for flocking algorithm. In *IEEE international conference on fuzzy systems* (pp. 2594–2599). IEEE.

Lei, Y., He, Z., & Zi, Y. (2009). Application of an intelligent classification method to mechanical fault diagnosis. *Expert Systems with Applications*, 9941–9948. doi:10.1016/j.eswa.2009.01.065.

Leni, P.-E. (2011). *Nouvelles méthodes de traitement de signaux multidimensionnels par décomposition suivant le théorème de Superposition de Kolmogorov.* (Doctoral Dissertation). Université de Bourgogne, Le Creusot, France.

Leni, P.-E., & Fougerolle, Y. D., Truchetet, F. (2008). Kolmogorov superposition theorem and its application to multivariate function decomposition and image representation. *IEEE Conference on Signal-Image Technology & Interned-Based Systems*. Bali, Indonesia.

Leni, P.-E., Fougerolle, Y. D., & Truchetet, F. (2009). Kolmogorov superposition theorem and wavelet decomposition for image compression. *Lecture Notes in Computer Science*, *5807*, 43–53. doi:10.1007/978-3-642-04697-1_5.

Leni, P.-E., Fougerolle, Y. D., & Truchetet, F. (2011). The Kolmogorov spline network for image processing. In Igelnik, B. (Ed.), *Computational Modeling and Simulation of Intellect: Current State and Future Perspectives* (pp. 25–51). Hershey, PA: IGI Global. doi:10.4018/978-1-60960-551-3.ch002.

Li, K., Yao, F., & Liu, R. (2011). An online clustering algorithm. In *Eighth International Conference on Fuzzy Systems and Knowledge Discovery (FSKD)* (vol. 2, pp. 1104–1108).

Liang, N.-Y., Huang, G.-B., Saratchandran, P., & Sundararajan, N. (2006). A fast and accurate online sequential learning algorithm for feedforward networks. *IEEE Transactions on Neural Networks*, *17*, 1411–1423. doi:10.1109/TNN.2006.880583 PMID:17131657.

Liao, Q., Striegel, A., & Chawla, N. (2010). Visualizing graph dynamics and similarity for enterprise network security and management. In *Proceedings of the Seventh International Symposium on Visualization for Cyber Security (VizSec '10)* (pp. 34-45). New York, NY: ACM.

Li, B., Zhang, P., Tian, H., Mi, S., Liu, D., & Ren, G. (2011). A new feature extraction and selection scheme for hybrid fault diagnosis of gearbox. *Expert Systems with Applications*, 10000–10009. doi:10.1016/j.eswa.2011.02.008.

Linden, G., Smith, B., & York, J. (2003). Amazon.com recommendations: Item-to-item collaborative filtering. *IEEE Internet Computing*, 76–80. doi:10.1109/MIC.2003.1167344.

Linquan, Y., Zhongwen, L., Zhonghua, T., & Weixian, L. (2008). Path planning algorithm for mobile robot obstacle avoidance adopting belzier curve based on genetic algorithm. In *IEEE Conference on Decision and Control* (pp. 3286-3289). IEEE.

Lippmann, R., Ingols, K., & Scott, C. (2006). Validating and restoring defense in depth using attack graphs. *Military Communications Conference (MILCOM)* (pp. 1-10). IEEE.

Lippmann, R., & Ingols, K. (2005). *An annotated review of past papers on attack graphs*. Lexington, MA: Massachusetts Institute of Technology, Lincoln Laboratory.

Li, T., Zhang, C., & Ogihara, M. (2004). A comparative study of feature selection and multiclass classification methods for tissue classification based on gene expression. *Bioinformatics (Oxford, England)*, 20(15), 2429–2437. doi:10.1093/bioinformatics/bth267 PMID:15087314.

Little, S., & Ruger, S. (2009). Conservation of effort in feature selection for image annotation. *IEEE Workshop on Multimedia Signals Processing*, (pp. 5-7).

Liu, H., & Motoda, H. (1998). *Feature extraction, construction and selection: A data mining perspective*. New York, NY: Springer. doi:10.1007/978-1-4615-5725-8.

Liu, T. Y., & Tsai, W. H. (2010). Generic lossless visible watermarking - A new approach. *IEEE Transactions on Image Processing*, 19(5), 1224–1235. doi:10.1109/TIP.2010.2040757 PMID:20089476.

Liu, W., Park, I., Wang, Y., & Principe, J. C. (2009). Extended kernel recursive least squares algorithm. *IEEE Transactions on Signal Processing*, 57(10), 3801–3814. doi:10.1109/TSP.2009.2022007.

Liu, W., Pokharel, P., & Principe, J. C. (2008). The kernel least-mean-square algorithm. *IEEE Transactions on Signal Processing*, 56(2), 543–554. doi:10.1109/TSP.2007.907881.

Liu, W., & Príncipe, J. C. (2008). Kernel affine projection algorithms. *EURASIP Journal on Advances in Signal Processing*, 56(2), 12.

Li, Y., & Long, P. M. (2002). The relaxed online maximum margin algorithm. *Machine Learning*, 46(1-3), 361–387. doi:10.1023/A:1012435301888.

Logg, C., & Cottrell, L. (2003, October). Characterization of the traffic between SLAC and the internet. Retrieved from http://www.slac.stanford.edu/comp/net/slacnetflow/html

López, F., Torres, M., Batista, B., Pérez, J., & Moreno-Vega, M. (2006). Solving feature subset selection problem by a parallel scatter search. *European Journal of Operational Research*, 169(2), 477–489. doi:10.1016/j.ejor.2004.08.010.

Lorentz, G. G. (1962). Metric entropy, widths, and superpositions of functions. *The American Mathematical Monthly*, 69(6), 469–485. doi:10.2307/2311185.

Lorentz, G. G. (1966). *Approximation of functions*. New York, NY: Holt, Rinehart and Winston.

Loscalzo, S., Yu, L., & Ding, C. (2009). Consensus group stable feature selection. In *KDD '09: Proceedings of the 15th ACM SIGKDD international conference on Knowledge discovery and data mining* (pp. 567-576). ACM.

Louthan, G. (2011, November). *Hybrid attack graphs for modeling cyber physical systems security*. (Unpublished Master's thesis). The University of Tulsa.

Lozano-Pérez, T., & Kaelbling, L. (2005). *Massachusetts Institute of Technology Open CourseWare: Artificial intelligence*. Retrieved May 25, 2012, from http://ocw.mit.edu/courses/electrical-engineering-and-computer-science/6-034-artificial-intelligence-spring-2005/

Lozovyy, P., Thomas, G., & Simon, D. (2011). Biogeography-based optimization for robot controller tuning. In Igelnik, B. (Ed.), *Computational modeling and simulation of intellect: Current state and future perspectives* (pp. 162–181). Hershey, PA: IGI Global. doi:10.4018/978-1-60960-551-3.ch007.

Lu, Y., Cohen, I., Zhou, X., & Tian, Q. (2007). Feature selection using principal feature analysis. *Proceedings of the 15th international conference on Multimedia,* (pp. 301-304). New York, NY: ACM.

Luck, S. J., Chelazzi, L., Hillyard, S. A., & Desimone, R. (1997). Neural mechanisms of spatial selective attention in areas V1, V2, and V4 of macaque visual cortex. *Journal of Neurophysiology, 77*(1), 24–42. PMID:9120566.

MacQueen, J. (1967). Some methods for classification and analysis of multivariate observation. In *Proceedings of the Fifth Berkeley Symposium on Mathematical Statistics and Probability* (vol. 1, pp. 281-297). Berkeley, CA: University of California Press.

Ma, J., Theiler, K., & Perkins, S. (2003). Accurate on-line support vector regression. *Neural Computation, 15,* 2683–2703. doi:10.1162/089976603322385117 PMID:14577858.

Malerba, D., Lisi, F., Appice, A., & Sblendorio, F. (2002). Mining spatial association rules in census data: A relational approach. *Research in Official Statistics, 5*(1), 19–44.

Manadhata, P. K., & Wing, J. M. (2011). An attack surface metric. *IEEE Transactions on Software Engineering, 37*(3), 371–386. doi:10.1109/TSE.2010.60.

Mandic, D. P., Javidi, S., Goh, S. L., Kuh, A., & Aihara, K. (2009). Complex-valued prediction of wind profile using augmented complex statistics. *Renewable Energy, 34*(1), 196–201. doi:10.1016/j.renene.2008.03.022.

Mandic, D., & Chambers, J. (2002). *Recurrent neural networks for prediction: Learning algorithms, architectures and stability.* Hoboken, NJ: John Wiley and Sons.

Mannini, A., & Sabatini, A. M. (2011). On-line classification of human activity estimation of walk-run speed from acceleration data using support vector machines. In *Proccedings of IEEE Egineering in Medicine & Biology Society* (pp. 3302–3305). New York, NY: ACM. doi:10.1109/IEMBS.2011.6090896.

Mao, H.-D., & Zhang, W.-M. (2007). An approach for network security analysis using logic exploitation graph. In *7th IEEE International Conference on Computer and Information Technology* (pp. 761-766). IEEE.

Maron, O., & Lozano-Perez, T. (1998). A framework for multiple instance learning. *Neural Information Processing Systems, 10.*

Martin, M. (2002). On-line support vector machine regression. In *Proceedings of the 13th European Conference on Machine Learning (ECML'02)* (In Lecture Notes in Artificial Intelligence 2430, pp. 282-294). Berlin, Germany: Springer-Verlag.

Martin, M. (2002). *On-line support vector machines for function approximation. Technical Report.* Catalonia, Spain: Universitat Politècnica de Catalunya, Departament de Llengatges i Sistemes Informàtics.

Mathewos, B., Carvalho, M., & Ham, F. M. (2011, October). Network traffic classification using a parallel neural network classifier architecture. In *CSIIRW '11: Proceedings of the 7th Annual Workshop on Cyber Security and Information Intelligence Research.* New York, NY.

Matos, F., Batista, L., & Poel, J. (2008). Face recognition using DCT coefficients selection. *Proceedings of the 2008 ACM symposium on Applied computing,* (pp. 1753-1757).

Mayyas, K., & Aboulnasr, T. (1997). Leaky LMS algorithm: MSE analysis for Gaussian data. *IEEE Transactions on Signal Processing, 45*(4), 927–934. doi:10.1109/78.564181.

Mazumdar, D., Mitra, S., & Mitra, S. (2010). *Evolutionary-rough feature selection for face recognition. Transactions on rough sets XII* (pp. 117–142). New York, NY: Springer. doi:10.1007/978-3-642-14467-7_7.

McDonald, C., Smith, D., Brower, R., Ceberio, M., & Sarkodie-Gyan, T. (2007, June). Determination of human gait phase using fuzzy inference. In *IEEE International Conference on Rehabilitation Robotics,* (pp. 661–665). IEEE.

Meier, J.D., Mackman, A., Dunner, M., Vasireddy, S., Escamilla, R., & Murukan, A. (2003, June). *Improving Web application security: Threats and countermeasures roadmap.* Redmond, WA: Microsoft Press.

Mendel, J. (2007). Type-2 fuzzy sets and systems: An overview. *IEEE Comp. Intell Mag., 2*(10), 20–29.

Menger, K. (1932). *Kurventheorie.* Berlin, Germany: Teubner Verlag.

Meyer, P., Schretter, C., & Bontempi, G. (2008). Information-theoretic feature selection in microarray data using variable complementarity. *IEEE Journal of Selected Topics in Signal Processing*, 2(3), 261–274. doi:10.1109/JSTSP.2008.923858.

Mian, A. (2011). Online learning from local features for video-based face recognition. *Pattern Recognition*, 44(5), 1068–1075. doi:10.1016/j.patcog.2010.12.001.

Michalski, R. (1980). Knowledge acquisition through conceptual clustering: A theoretical framework and an algorithm for partitioning data into conjunctive concepts. *Journal of Policy Analysis and Information Systems*, 4(3), 219–244.

Miller, H., & Han, J. (2001). Geographic data mining and knowledge discovery: An overview. In Miller, H. J., & Han, J. (Eds.), *Geographic data mining and knowledge discovery* (pp. 3–32). London, UK: Taylor and Francis. doi:10.4324/9780203468029_chapter_1.

Milligan, G. W., & Cooper, M. C. (1985). An examination of procedures for determining the number of clusters in a data set. *Psychometrika*, 50(2), 159–179. doi:10.1007/BF02294245.

Mitchell, M. (1998). *An introduction to genetic algorithms*. Cambridge, MA: MIT Press.

Modan, M., Peles, E., Halkin, H., Nitzan, H., Azaria, M., & Gitel, S. et al. (1998). Increased cardiovascular disease mortality rates in traumatic lower limb amputees. *The American Journal of Cardiology*, 82, 1242–1247. doi:10.1016/S0002-9149(98)00601-8 PMID:9832102.

Mo, H., & Xu, L. (2010). Biogeography migration algorithm for traveling salesman problem. In Tan, Y., Shi, Y., & Tan, K. (Eds.), *Advances in swarm intelligence* (pp. 405–414). Beijing, China: Springer. doi:10.1007/978-3-642-13495-1_50.

Moon, B. S. (2001). An explicit solution for the cubic spline interpolation for functions of a single variable. *Applied Mathematics and Computation*, 117, 251–255. doi:10.1016/S0096-3003(99)00178-2.

Moore, A., & Papagiannaki, K. (2005, April). Toward the accurate identification of network applications. In *Proc. Passive and Active Measurement Workshop*. Boston, MA.

Moore, D., Keys, K., Koga, R., Lagache, E., & Claffy, K. C. (2001, December). The CoralReef software suite as a tool for system and network administrators. In *LISA'01: Proceedings of the 15th USENIX Conference on Systems Administration* (pp. 133- 144). San Diego, CA.

Moore, A. W., & Zuev, D. (2005). Internet traffic classification using Bayesian analysis techniques. *SIGMETRICS Performance Evaluation Review*, 33, 50–60. doi:10.1145/1071690.1064220.

Moore, A. W., & Zuev, D. (2005). *Discriminators for use in flow based classification. Technical report*. Cambridge: Intel Research.

Nagumo, J. I., & Noda, A. (1967). A learning method for system identification. *IEEE Transactions on Automatic Control*, 12(3), 282–287. doi:10.1109/TAC.1967.1098599.

Nakamura, M., Mines, R., & Kreinovich, V. (1993). Guaranteed intervals for Kolmogorov's theorem (and their possible relation to neural networks). *Interval Computations*, 3, 183–199.

Nanda, S., & Majumdar, S. (1992). Fuzzy rough sets. *Fuzzy Sets and Systems*, 45, 157–160. doi:10.1016/0165-0114(92)90114-J.

National Vulnerability Database. (2012). Website. Retrieved Aug. 22, 2012, from http://nvd.nist.gov/

Nayak, R., Jain, L., & Ting, B. (2001). Artificial neural networks in biomedical engineering: A review. *Proceedings of the 1st Asian-Pacific Congress on Computational Mechanics* (pp. 887–892). Amsterdam, The Netherlands: Elsevier Science Limited.

Nguyen, H., & Walker, E. (2005). *A first course in fuzzy logic* (3rd ed.). Boca Raton, FL: CRC press.

Nguyen-Tuong, D., & Peters, J. (2011). Incremental online sparsification for model learning in real-time robot control. *Neurocomputing*, 74(11), 1859–1867. doi:10.1016/j.neucom.2010.06.033.

Nikolova, N. D., Mednikarov, B., & Tenekedjiev, K. (2012). Analytical version of the non-uniform method for analyzing uncertain scaling constants. In *Proc. International Conference Auomatics and Informatics*, Bulgria: 3-7 October, Sofia (in print).

Nikolova, N. D. (2007). Uniform method for estimation of interval scaling constants. *Engineering and Automation Problems, 1*, 79–90.

Nikolova, N. D., Shulus, A., Toneva, D., & Tenekedjiev, K. (2005). Fuzzy rationality in quantitative decision analysis. *Journal of Advanced Computational Intelligence and Intelligent Informatics, 9*(1), 65–69.

Nikolova, N. D., & Tenekedjiev, K. (2010). Fuzzy rationality and parameter elicitation in decision analysis. *International Journal of General Systems. Special Issue on Intelligent Systems, 39*(5), 539–556.

Ning, P., & Xu, D. (2003). Learning attack strategies from intrusion alerts. In *Proceedings of the 10th ACM conference on Computer and communications security (CCS '03)* (pp. 200-209). New York, NY: ACM.

Ning, P., Cui, Y., & Reeves, D. S. (2002). Constructing attack scenarios through correlation of intrusion alerts. In V. Atluri (Ed.), *Proceedings of the 9th ACM conference on Computer and communications security (CCS '02)* (pp. 245-254). New York, NY: ACM.

Ning, P., Cui, Y., Reeves, D. S., & Xu, D. (2004). Techniques and tools for analyzing intrusion alerts. *ACM Transactions on Information and System Security, 7*(2), 274–318. doi:10.1145/996943.996947.

Nishizaki, I., & Katagiri, H. (2004). Sensitivity analysis incorporating fuzzy evaluation for scaling constants of multiattribute utility functions in multiplicative form. *The International Conference on Multiple Criteria Decision Making MCDM* (pp. 132-140). Canada: Whistler, B. C.

NIST. (2010, August). *Guidelines for Smart Grid Cyber Security* (NISTIR 7628). National Institute of Standards.

Nitta, T. (2011). Widely linear processing of hypercomplex signals. In B.-L. Lu, L. Zhang and J. Kwok (Eds.), *Proc. Int. Conf. on Neural Information Processing (ICONIP2011), Shanghai, China, Nov. 13-17, Part I (Lecture Notes in Computer Science), No. 7062* (pp. 519-525).

Nitta, T. (Ed.). (2009). *Complex-valued neural networks: Utilizing high-dimensional parameters*. Pennsylvania: Information Science Reference. doi:10.4018/978-1-60566-214-5.

Noel, S., & Jajodia, S. (2004). Managing attack graph complexity through visual hierarchical aggregation. In *Proceedings of the 2004 ACM workshop on visualization and data mining for computer security (VizSEC/DMSEC '04)* (pp. 109-118). New York, NY: ACM.Noel, S., Robertson, E., & Jajodia, S. (2004). Correlating intrusion events and building attack scenarios through attack graph distances. *20ᵗʰ Annual Computer Security Applications Conference* (pp. 350-359). IEEE.

Noel, S., Jajodia, S., Wang, L., & Singhal, A. (2010). Measuring security risk of networks using attack graphs. *International Journal of Next-Generation Computing, 1*(1), 135–147.

Novey, M., & Adali, T. (2008). On extending the complex FastICA algorithm to noncircular sources. *IEEE Transactions on Signal Processing, 56*(5), 2148–2154. doi:10.1109/TSP.2007.911278.

Oliver, I., Smith, D., & Holland, J. (1987). A study of permutation crossover operators on the traveling salesman problem. *2nd International Conference on Genetic Algorithm and their application* (pp. 224-230).

Olshausen, B. A., & Field, D. J. (1996). Emergence of simple-cell receptive field properties by learning a sparse code for natural images. *Nature, 381*, 607–609. doi:10.1038/381607a0 PMID:8637596.

Ortalo, R., Deswarte, Y., & Kaâniche, M. (1999). Experimenting with quantitative evaluation tools for monitoring operational security. *IEEE Transactions on Software Engineering, 25*(5), 633–650. doi:10.1109/32.815323.

Ostrand, P. A. (1965). Dimension of metric spaces and Hilbert's problem 13. *Bulletin of the American Mathematical Society, 71*(4), 619–622. doi:10.1090/S0002-9904-1965-11363-5.

O'Toole, A., Valentin, D., & Abdi, H. (1993). A low dimensional representation of faces in the higher dimensions of the space. *Journal of the Optical Society of America, series A, 10*, 405–411. doi:10.1364/JOSAA.10.000405.

Ovchinnikov, S. (1991). Similarity relations, fuzzy partitions and fuzzy orderings. *International Journal of Fuzzy Sets and Systems, 40*, 107–126. doi:10.1016/0165-0114(91)90048-U.

Ozeki, K., & Umeda, T. (1984). An adaptive filtering algorithm using an orthogonal projection to an affine subspace and its properties. *Electronics and Communications in Japan, 67-A*(5), 19–27.

Pamula, J., Jajodia, S., Ammann, P., & Swarup, V. (2006). A weakest-adversary security metric for network configuration security analysis. In *Proceedings of the 2nd ACM workshop on Quality of protection (QoP '06)* (pp. 31-38). New York, NY: ACM.

Pappas, I., Popovic, M., Keller, T., Dietz, V., & Morari, M. (2001). A reliable gait phase detection system. *IEEE Transactions on Neural Systems and Rehabilitation Engineering, 9*, 113–125. doi:10.1109/7333.928571 PMID:11474964.

Paredes, E. S. (2007). Atlas of mammography (3rd ed.). Alphen aan den Rijn, The Netherlands: Wolters Kluwer (Health).

Park, J., Tyan, H. R., & Kuo, C. (2006). Internet traffic classification for scalable QoS provision. In *2006 IEEE International Conference on Multimedia and Expo* (pp. 1221-1224). Toronto, Ontario, Canada.

Park, J.-H., Kim, J.-H., Ahn, B.-H., & Jeon, M.-G. (2006). A selection scheme for excluding defective rules of evolutionary fuzzy path planning. In *Pacific Rim International Conference in Artificial Intelligence* (pp. 747-756). New York, NY: Springer.

Park, J.-H., Stonier, D., Kim, J.-H., Ahn, B.-H., & Jeon, M.-G. (2007). Recombinant rule selection in evolutionary algorithm for fuzzy path planner of robot soccer. In *Proceedings of the 29th annual German Conference on Artificial Intelligence: KI'06* (pp. 317-330). Berlin, Germany: Springer-Verlag.

Pawlak, Z. (1984). Rough sets. *International Journal of Man-Machine Studies, 21*, 127–134. doi:10.1016/S0020-7373(84)80062-0.

Pawlak, Z. (1991). *Rough sets: Theoretical aspects of reasoning about data*. Norwell, MA: Kluwer Academic Publishers.

Paxson, V. (1994, August). Empirically derived analytic models of wide-area TCP connections. *IEEE/ACM Transactions on Networking, 2*, 316–336. doi:10.1109/90.330413.

Peng, H., Long, F., & Ding, C. (2005). Feature selection based on mutual information: Criteria of max-dependency, max-relevance, and min-redundancy. *IEEE Transactions on Pattern Analysis and Machine Intelligence, 27*(8), 1226–1238. doi:10.1109/TPAMI.2005.159 PMID:16119262.

Peng, Y., Wu, Z., & Jiang, J. (2010). A novel feature selection approach for biomedical data classification. *Journal of Biomedical Informatics, 43*(1), 15–23. doi:10.1016/j.jbi.2009.07.008 PMID:19647098.

Perez-Freire, L., Comesana, P., Troncoso-Pastoriza, J. R., & Perez-Gonzalez, F. (2006). Watermarking security: A survey. *Lecture Notes in Computer Science, 4300*, 41–73. doi:10.1007/11926214_2.

Perkins, S., & Theiler, J. (2003). Online feature selection using grafting. *Proceedings of the Twentieth International Conference on Machine Learning (ICML)* (pp. 592-599). Washington, DC: ACM Press.

Perkins, S., Lacker, K., & Theiler, J. (2003). Grafting: Fast, incremental feature selection by gradient descent in function space. *Journal of Machine Learning Research, 3*, 1333–1356.

Peteiro-Barral, D., Guijarro-Berdinas, B., & Perez-Sanchez, B. (2011). Dealing with "very large" datasets. An overview of a promising research line: Distributed learning. In *Proceedings of the 3rd International Conference on Agents and Artificial Intelligence* (Vol. 1, pp. 476-481). New York, NY: Springer.

Petry, F. (1996). *Fuzzy databases: Principles and application*. Norwell, MA: Kluwer Academic Publishers. doi:10.1007/978-1-4613-1319-9.

Petry, F. (2011). Data discovery approaches for vague spatial data. In Igelnik, B. (Ed.), *Computational modeling and simulation of intellect* (pp. 342-360). Hershey, PA: IGI Global. doi:10.4018/978-1-60960-551-3.ch014.

Petry, F., & Yager, R. (2008). Evidence resolution using concept hierarchies. *IEEE Transactions on Fuzzy Systems, 16*(2), 299–308. doi:10.1109/TFUZZ.2007.895966.

Petry, F., & Zhao, L. (2009). Data mining by attribute generalization with fuzzy hierarchies in fuzzy databases. *Fuzzy Sets and Systems, 160*(15), 2206–2223. doi:10.1016/j.fss.2009.02.014.

Philips, C., & Swiler, L. (1998). A graph-based system for network-vulnerability analysis. In *Proceedings of the 1998 Workshop on New Security Paradigms* (pp. 71-79). New York, NY: ACM.

Piazza, P. (2002). Health alerts to fight bioterror. *Security Management, 46*(5), 40.

Picinbono, B. (1996). Second-order complex random vectors and normal distribution. *IEEE Transactions on Signal Processing, 44*(10), 2037–2040. doi:10.1109/78.539051.

Picinbono, B., & Chevalie, P. (1995). Widely linear estimation with complex data. *IEEE Transactions on Signal Processing, 43*(8), 2030–2033. doi:10.1109/78.403373.

Plackett, R. (1950). Some theorems in least squares. *Biometrika, 37*(1/2), 149–157. doi:10.2307/2332158 PMID:15420260.

Pohle, C., & Spiliopoulou, M. (2002). Building and exploiting ad hoc concept hierarchies for Web log analysis. In *Proceedings of the 4th International Conference on Data Warehousing and Knowledge Discovery* (pp. 83-93). London, UK: Springer-Verlag.

Pontil, M., & Verri, A. (1997). Properties of support vector machines. *Neural Computation, 10*, 955–974. doi:10.1162/089976698300017575 PMID:9573414.

Poon, P., & Carter, J. (1995). Genetic algorithm crossover operators for ordering applications. *Computers & Operations Research, 22*(1), 135–147. doi:10.1016/0305-0548(93)E0024-N.

Porto-Díaz, I., Bolón-Canedo, V., Alonso-Betanzos, A., & Fontenla-Romero, O. (2011). A study of performance on microarray datasets for a classifier based on information theoretic learning. *Neural Networks, 24*(8), 888–896. PMID:21703822.

Quinlan, J. R. (1986). Induction of decision trees. *Machine Learning, 1*(1), 81–106. doi:10.1007/BF00116251.

Qu, J., & Zuo, M. J. (2012). An LSSVR-based algorithm for online system condition prognostics. *Expert Systems with Applications, 39*(5), 6089–6102. doi:10.1016/j.eswa.2011.12.002.

Rafalski, E. (2002). Using data mining and data repository methods to identify marketing opportunities in healthcare. *Journal of Consumer Marketing, 19*(7), 607–613. doi:10.1108/07363760210451429.

Ralaivola, L., & d'Alche-Buc, F. (2001). Incremental support vector machine learning: A local approach. In *International Conference on Artificial Neural Networks (ICANN 2001)* (pp. 322–330). Berlin, Germany: Springer-Verlag.

Ramadan, R., & Abdel-Kader, R. (2009). Face recognition using particle swarm optimization-based selected features. *International Journal of Signal Processing, Image Processing and Pattern Recognition*, 51-65.

Ramsbrok, D., Berthier, R., & Cikuer, M. (2007). Profiling attacker behavior following SSH compromises. *Dependable Systems and Networks, 2007. DSN'07. 37th Annual IEEE/IFIP International Conference*, (pp. 199-124). IEEE.

Rao, R. P., & Ballard, D. H. (1999). Predictive coding in the visual cortex: A functional interpretation of extra-classical receptive field effects. *Nature Neuroscience*. doi:10.1038/4580 PMID:10195184.

Raschia, R., & Mouaddib, N. (2002). SAINTETIQ: A fuzzy set-based approach to database summarization. *Fuzzy Sets and Systems, 129*, 37–162. doi:10.1016/S0165-0114(01)00197-X.

Reinelt, G. (1991). TSPLib - A traveling salesman problem library. *ORSA Journal on Computing, 3*, 376–384. doi:10.1287/ijoc.3.4.376.

Reyes, N., & Dadios, E. (2004). Dynamic colour object recognition. *Journal of Advanced Computational Intelligence, 8*, 29–38.

Reynolds, J. H., & Desimone, R. (1999). The role of neural mechanisms of attention in solving the binding problem. *Neuron, 24*(1), 19–29. doi:10.1016/S0896-6273(00)80819-3 PMID:10677024.

Rifkin, R., & Klautau, A. (2004). In defense of one-vs-all classification. *Journal of Machine Learning Research, 5*, 101–141.

Ringuest, J. L. (1997). L-metric sensitivity analysis for single and multi-attribute decision analysis. *European Journal of Operational Research*, *98*, 563–570. doi:10.1016/S0377-2217(96)00177-4.

Ritchey, R., & Ammann, P. (2000). Using model checking to analyze network vulnerabilities. In *Proceedings of the 2000 IEEE Symposium on Research on Security and Privacy* (pp. 156-165). Washington, DC: IEEE Computer Society.

Romero, E., Barrio, I., & Belanche, L. (2007). Incremental and decremental learning linear support vector machines. In *International Conference on Artificial Neural Networks (ICANN 2007)* (Part I, LNCS 4668, pp. 209-218). Berlin, Germany: Springer.

Rosenblatt, F. (1958). The perceptron: A probabilistic model for information storage and organization in the brain. *Psychological Review*, *65*(6), 386–408. doi:10.1037/h0042519 PMID:13602029.

Roughan, M., Sen, S., Spatscheck, O., & Duffield, N. (2004). Class-of-service mapping for QoS: A statistical signature-based approach to IP traffic classification. In *Internet Measurement Conference.* ACM.

Ruiz, R. (2006). Incremental wrapper-based gene selection from microarray data for cancer classification. *Pattern Recognition*, *39*, 2383–2392. doi:10.1016/j.patcog.2005.11.001.

Rumelhart, D. E., & McClelland, J. L. (1986). Parallel distributed processing: Explorations in the microstructure of cognition. *Foundations*, *1*.

Sadeghi, A. R. (2008). *The marriage of cryptography and watermarking - beneficial and challenging for secure watermarking and detection* (pp. 2–18). Digital Watermarking. doi:10.1007/978-3-540-92238-4_2.

Saeys, Y., Abeel, T., & Peer, Y. (2008). Robust feature selection using ensemble feature selection techniques. *European conference on Machine Learning and Knowledge Discovery in Databases-Part II*, (pp. 313-325).

Saeys, Y., Inza, I., & Larrañaga, P. (2007). A review of feature selection techniques in bioinformatics. *Bioinformatics (Oxford, England)*, *23*(19), 2507–2517. doi:10.1093/bioinformatics/btm344 PMID:17720704.

Sagan, H. (1994). *Space-filling curves*. New York, NY: Springer-Verlag. doi:10.1007/978-1-4612-0871-6.

Saha, D. (2008). Extending logical attack graphs for efficient vulnerability analysis. In *Proceedings of the 15th ACM conference on Computer and communications security (CCS '08)* (pp. 63-74). New York, NY: ACM.

Sampat, M. P., Bovik, A. C., Markey, M. K., Whitman, G. J., & Stephens, T. W. (2006). Toroidal gaussian filters for detection and extraction of properties of spiculated masses. *IEEE International Conference on Acoustics, Speech, and Signal Processing* (pp. 610-621). IEEE.

Sayed, A. H. (2003). *Fundamentals of Adaptive Filtering*. Hoboken, NJ: Wiley–IEEE Press.

Schmidhuber, J. (1992). Learning complex, extended sequences using the principle of history compression. *Neural Computation*, *4*(2), 234–242. doi:10.1162/neco.1992.4.2.234.

Schneier, B. (1999, December). Attack trees: Modeling security threats. *Dr. Dobb's Journal*, 21-29.

Schober, R., Gerstacker, W. H., & Lampe, L. H.-J. (2004). Data-aided and blind stochastic gradient algorithm for widely linear MMSE MAI suppression for DS-CDMA. *IEEE Transactions on Signal Processing*, *52*(3), 746–756. doi:10.1109/TSP.2003.822359.

Schreier, P. J., & Scharf, L. L. (2010). *Statistical signal processing of complex-valued data - the theory of improper and noncircular signals*. Cambridge University Press. doi:10.1017/CBO9780511815911.

Segal, A., Orendurff, M., Klute, G., McDowell, M., Pecoraro, J., Shofer, J., & Czerniecki, J. (2006). Kinematic and kinetic comparisons of transfemoral amputee gait using C-Leg and Mauch SNS prosthetic knees. *Journal of Rehabilitation Research and Development*, *43*, 857–870. doi:10.1682/JRRD.2005.09.0147 PMID:17436172.

Sen, S., Spatscheck, O., & Wang, D. (2004, May). Accurate, scalable in network identification of P2P traffic using application signatures. In *WWW 2004*, New York, NY.

Seroussi, R., Gitter, A., Czerniecki, J., & Weaver, K. (1996). Mechanical work adaptations of above-knee amputee ambulation. *Archives of Physical Medicine and Rehabilitation, 77*, 1209–1214. doi:10.1016/S0003-9993(96)90151-3 PMID:8931539.

Seshadri, A. (2006). *Traveling salesman problem (TSP) using simulated annealing.* Retrieved April 1, 2012, from http://www.mathworks.com/matlabcentral/fileexchange/9612-traveling-salesman-problem-tsp-using-simulated-annealing

Setia, L., & Burkhardt, H. (2006). Feature selection for automatic image annotation. *Lecture Notes in Computer Science, 4174*, 294–303. doi:10.1007/11861898_30.

Seymour, R., Engbretson, B., Kott, K., Ordway, N., Brooks, G., & Crannell, J. et al. (2007). Comparison between the C-leg microprocessor-controlled prosthetic knee and non-microprocessor control prosthetic knees: a preliminary study of energy expenditure, obstacle course performance, and quality of life survey. *Prosthetics and Orthotics International, 31*, 51–61. doi:10.1080/03093640600982255 PMID:17365885.

Shepitsen, A., Gemmell, J., Mobasher, B., & Burke, R. (2008). Personalized recommendation in social tagging systems using hierarchical clustering. In *Proceedings of the ACM conference on Recommender systems* (pp. 259-266). New York, NY: ACM.

Sheyner, O., Haines, J., Jha, S., Lippmann, R., & Wing, J. M. (2002). Automated generation and analysis of attack graphs. In *Proceedings of the 2002 IEEE Symposium on Security and Privacy* (pp. 273-284). IEEE.

Shi, J., & Malik, J. (2000). Normalized cuts and image segmentation. *IEEE Transactions on Pattern Analysis Intelligence, 22*(8).

Shiotani, S., Fukuda, T., & Shibata, T. (1995). A neural network architecture for incremental learning. *Neurocomputing, 9*(2), 111–130. doi:10.1016/0925-2312(94)00061-V.

Sigaud, O., Salaün, C., & Padois, V. (2011). On-line regression algorithms for learning mechanical models of robots: A survey. *Robotics and Autonomous Systems, 59*(12), 1115–1129. doi:10.1016/j.robot.2011.07.006.

Simon, D. (2008). Biogeography-based optimization. *IEEE Transactions on Evolutionary Computation, 12*(6), 702–713. doi:10.1109/TEVC.2008.919004.

Singh, J., Garg, P., & De, A. N. (2009). Watermarking of unified multimedia data types, audio and image. *Annual IEEE India Conference (INDICON)* (pp. 1-4). IEEE.

Singh, S., Kubica, J., Larsen, S., & Sorokina, D. (2009). *Parallel large scale feature selection for logistic regression* (pp. 1172–1183). SIAM.

Slowinski, R. (1992). A generalization of the indiscernibility relation for rough sets analysis of quantitative information. *Rivista di Matematica per le Scienze Economiche e Sociali, 15*(1), 65–78. doi:10.1007/BF02086527.

Sokal, P. S. (1973). *Numerical taxonomy.* San Francisco, CA: Freeman WH and Co..

Somol, P., Grim, J., & Pudil, P. (2011). Fast dependency-aware feature selection in very-high-dimensional pattern recognition. *IEEE International Conference on System, Man and Cybernetics (SMC)*, (pp. 502-509).

Souza, J., Matwin, S., & Japkowicz, N. (2006). Parallelizing feature selection. *Journal of Algorithmica, 45*(3), 433–456. doi:10.1007/s00453-006-1220-3.

Spratling, M. W., & Johnson, M. H. (2004). A feedback model of visual attention. *Journal of Cognitive Neuroscience, 16*(2), 219–237. doi:10.1162/089892904322984526 PMID:15068593.

Sprecher, D. A. (1965). On the structure of continuous functions of several variables. *Transactions of the American Mathematical Society, 115*(3), 340–355. doi:10.1090/S0002-9947-1965-0210852-X.

Sprecher, D. A. (1972). A survey of solved and unsolved problems in superposition of functions. *Journal of Approximation Theory, 6*, 123–134. doi:10.1016/0021-9045(72)90069-X.

Sprecher, D. A. (1993). A universal mapping for Kolmogorov's superposition theorem. *Neural Networks, 6*, 1089–1094. doi:10.1016/S0893-6080(09)80020-8.

Sprecher, D. A. (1996). A numerical implementation of Kolmogorov's superpositions. *Neural Networks, 9*(5), 765–772. doi:10.1016/0893-6080(95)00081-X PMID:12662561.

Sprecher, D. A. (1997). A numerical implementation of Kolmogorov's superpositions II. *Neural Networks, 10*(3), 447–457. doi:10.1016/S0893-6080(96)00073-1.

Sprecher, D. A. (2002). Space-filling curves and Kolmogorov superpositions-based neural networks. *Neural Networks, 15*, 57–67. doi:10.1016/S0893-6080(01)00107-1 PMID:11958490.

Sprecher, D. A., & Draghici, S. (2002). Space-filling curves and Kolmogorov superposition-based neural networks. *Neural Networks, 15*(1), 57–67. doi:10.1016/S0893-6080(01)00107-1 PMID:11958490.

Srinivasan, P. (1991). The importance of rough approximations for information retrieval. *International Journal of Man-Machine Studies, 34*, 657–671. doi:10.1016/0020-7373(91)90017-2.

Statnikov, A., Aliferis, C., Tsamardinos, I., Hardin, D., & Levy, S. (2005). A comprehensive evaluation of multicategory classification methods for microarray gene expression cancer diagnosis. *Bioinformatics (Oxford, England), 21*(5), 631–643. doi:10.1093/bioinformatics/bti033 PMID:15374862.

Stoian, V., & Ivanescu, M. (2008). In Zemliak, A. (Ed.), *Frontiers in robotics, automation and control* (pp. 111–132). New York, NY: Intechopen.

Sugumaran, V., Muralidharan, V., & Ramachandran, K. (2007). Feature selection using decision tree and classification through proximal support vector machine for fault diagnostics of roller bearing. *Mechanical Systems and Signal Processing*, 930–942. doi:10.1016/j.ymssp.2006.05.004.

Sugumaran, V., & Ramachandran, K. (2011). Fault diagnosis of roller bearing using fuzzy classifier and histogram features with focus on automatic rule learning. *Expert Systems with Applications*, 4901–4907. doi:10.1016/j.eswa.2010.09.089.

Sun, R., Yang, B., Peng, L., Chen, Z., Zhang, L., & Jing, S. (2010). Traffic classification using probabilistic neural networks. *International Conference on Natural Computation* (Vol. 4, pp. 1914-1919).

Sun, Y., Todorovic, S., & Goodison, S. (2008). A feature selection algorithm capable of handling extremely large data dimensionality. *SIAM International Conference on Data Mining*, (pp. 530-540).

Suresh, S., & Sundararajan, N. (2012). An on-line learning neural controller for helicopters performing highly nonlinear maneuvers. *Applied Soft Computing, 12*(1), 360–371. doi:10.1016/j.asoc.2011.08.036.

Su, X., & Khoshgoftaar, T. M. (2009). A survey of collaborative filtering techniques. *Advances in Artificial Intelligence*. doi:10.1155/2009/421425.

Syed, N. A., Liu, H., & Sung, K. K. (1999). Incremental learning with support vector machines. In *Proceedings of the Workshop on Support Vector Machines at the International Joint Conference on Artificial Intelligence—IJCAI-99*. Burlington, MA: Morgan Kaufmann.

Tan, P., Steinbach, M., & Kumar, V. (2005). *Introduction to data mining*. Boston, MA: Addison Wesley.

Tao, G., & Michalewicz, Z. (1998). Inver-over operator for the TSP. Parallel problem solving from nature V, pp. 803–812.

Tax, D. M. J., & Laskov, P. (2003). Online SVM learning: From classification to data description and back. In C. Molina, T. Adali, J. Larsen, M. Van Hulle, S. Douglas, and J. Rouat (Eds.), *Proceedings of IEEE 13th Workshop on Neural Networks for Signal Processing (NNSP'03)*, pp. 499–508. IEEE.

Taylor, Y., Xu, H., Lee, R., & Ramadge, P. J. (2011). Online kernel SVM for real-time fMRI brain state prediction. In *Proceedings of the International Conference on Acoustics, Speech and Signal Processing*, 2040–2043. ACM/IEEE.

Tedesco, G., & Aickelin, U. (2008). Real-time alert correlation with type graphs. *Lecture Notes in Computer Science, 5352*, 173–187. doi:10.1007/978-3-540-89862-7_16.

Templeton, S., & Levitt, K. (2001). A requires/provides model for computer attacks. In *Proceedings of the 2000 workshop on new security paradigms* (pp. 31-38). New York, NY: ACM.

Tenekedjiev, K., Nikolova, N. D., & Dimitrakiev, D. (2004). Quantile-approximated distribution toolbox for technical diagnostics and reliability applications. Annual Proceeding of Technical University in Varna (pp. 233–244). Bulgaria: Varna.

Tenekedjiev, K., & Nikolova, N. D. (2008). Justification and numerical realization of the uniform method for finding point estimates of interval elicited scaling constants. *Fuzzy Optimization and Decision Making*, 7(2), 119–145. doi:10.1007/s10700-008-9027-0.

Tibshirani, R. (1996). Regression shrinkage and selection via the lasso. *Journal of the Royal Statistical Society. Series B. Methodological*, 58(1), 267–288.

Tibshirani, R., Walther, G., & Hastie, T. (2001). Estimating the number of clusters in a data set via the gap statistic. *Journal of the Royal Statistical Society. Series B, Statistical Methodology*, 63(2), 411–423. doi:10.1111/1467-9868.00293.

Tidwell, T., Larson, R., Fitch, K., & Hale, J. (2001). Modeling Internet attacks. In *Proceedings of the 2001 IEEE workshop on information assurance and security* (Vol. 59). IEEE.

Took, C. C., & Mandic, D. P. (2009). The quaternion LMS algorithm for adaptive filtering of hypercomplex processes. *IEEE Transactions on Signal Processing*, 57(4), 1316–1327. doi:10.1109/TSP.2008.2010600.

Took, C. C., & Mandic, D. P. (2010). A quaternion widely linear adaptive filter. *IEEE Transactions on Signal Processing*, 58(8), 4427–4431. doi:10.1109/TSP.2010.2048323.

Treue, S., & Martinez-Trujillo, J. C. (1999). Feature-based attention influences motion processing gain in macaque visual cortex. *Nature*, 399(6736), 575–579. doi:10.1038/21176 PMID:10376597.

Tsai, H. M., & Chang, L. W. (2007). A high secure reversible visible watermarking scheme. In *IEEE International Conference on Multimedia and Expo* (pp. 2106-2109). ISBN 1424410169

Tsai, H. M., & Chang, L. W. (2010). Secure reversible visible image watermarking with authentication. *Signal Processing Image Communication*, 25(1), 10–17. doi:10.1016/j.image.2009.11.002.

Tsotsos, J. K. (1990). Article. *Journal of Behavioral and Brain Science*, 13, 423–445. doi:10.1017/S0140525X00079577.

Ujang, B. C., Took, C. C., & Mandic, D. P. (2010). Split quaternion nonlinear adaptive filtering. *Neural Networks*, 23(3), 426–434. doi:10.1016/j.neunet.2009.10.006 PMID:19926443.

Ujang, B. C., Took, C. C., & Mandic, D. P. (2011). Quaternion-valued nonlinear adaptive filtering. *IEEE Transactions on Neural Networks*, 22(8), 1193–1206. doi:10.1109/TNN.2011.2157358 PMID:21712159.

Usher, M., & Niebur, E. (1996). Modeling the temporal dynamics of IT neurons in visual search: A mechanism for top-down selective attention. *Journal of Cognitive Neuroscience*, 8(4), 311–327. doi:10.1162/jocn.1996.8.4.311.

Vachhani, L., Mahindrakar, A., & Sridharan, K. (2011). Mobile robot navigation through a hardware-efficient implementation for control-law-based construction of generalized voronoi diagram. *IEEE/ASME Transactions on Mechatronics*, 16(6), 1083–1095. doi:10.1109/TMECH.2010.2076825.

Vainer, I., Kraus, S., Kamimka, G., & Slovin, H. (2010). Obtaining scalable and accurate classification in large-scale spatio-temporal domains. *Knowledge and Information Systems*.

Vakhania, N. N. (1999). Random vectors with values in quaternion Hilbert spaces. *Theory of Probability and Its Applications*, 43(1), 99–115. doi:10.1137/S0040585X97976696.

Valades, G. P. (2011). *Patent 7925065B2*. Washington, DC: US Patent Office.

Valdes, A., & Skinner, K. (2001). Probablistic alert correlation. In *Recent advances in intrusion detection, lecture notes in computer science* (pp. 54–68). Heidelberg, Germany: Springer-Valdeg. doi:10.1007/3-540-45474-8_4.

Van den Ham, H., Moerland, R., Reinders, M., & Vergaegh, W. (2009). A sensitivity analysis of microarray feature selection and classification under measurement noise. *IEE International Workshop on Genomic Signal Processing and Statistics GENSIPS 2009*, (pp. 1-4).

Vapnik, V. N. (1995). *The nature of statistical learning theory*. New York, NY: Springer-Verlag.

Varga, A. (2001). The OMNeT++ discrete event simulation system. In *Proceedings of the European Simulation Multiconference*. IEEE.

Varga, A., & Hornig, R. (2008). An overview of the OMNeT++ simulation environment. In *Proceedings of the 1st International Conference on Simulation Tools and Techniques for Communications, Networks and Systems* (pp. 1-10). ACM.

Varol, H., Sup, F., & Goldfarb, M. (2010). Multiclass real-time intent recognition of a powered lower limb prosthesis. *IEEE Transactions on Bio-Medical Engineering*, *57*, 542–551. doi:10.1109/TBME.2009.2034734 PMID:19846361.

Vašák, J., & Madarasz, L. (2010). Adaptation of fuzzy cognitive maps - a comparison study. *Acta Polytechnica Hungarica*, *7*(3), 109–122.

Verron, S., Tiplica, T., & Kobi, A. (2008). Fault detection and identification with a new feature selection based on mutual information. *Journal of Process Control*, 479–490. doi:10.1016/j.jprocont.2007.08.003.

Vituskin, A.G. (1977). On representation of functions by means of superpositions and related topics. *L'enseignement Mathématique, 2nd Series XXIII*(3-4), 255-320.

Vituskin, A. G. (1954). On the 13th problem of Hilbert. *Doklady Akademii Nauk*, *95*, 701–704.

Von Neumann, J., & Morgenstern, O. (1947). *Theory of games and economic behavior* (2nd ed.). USA: Princeton University Press.

Walach, E., & Widrow, B. (1984). The least mean fourth (LMF) adaptive algorithm and its family. *IEEE Transactions on Information Theory*, *40*(2), 275–283. doi:10.1109/TIT.1984.1056886.

Wan, E. (1993). Time series prediction using a neural network with embedded tapped delay-lines. *Predicting the future and understanding the past. SFI studies in* the science of complexity, 195-217.

Wang, H. (2007). *Solving symmetrical and symmetrical TSP base on ant colony algorithm*. Retrieved April 1, 2012, from http://www.mathworks.com/matlabcentral/fileexchange/14543

Wang, L., Singhal, A., & Jajodia, S. (2007). Toward measuring network security using attack graphs. In *Proceedings of the 2007 ACM workshop on Quality of protection (QoP '07)* (pp. 49-54). New York, NY: ACM.

Wang, L., Islam, T., Long, T., Singhal, A., & Jajodia, S. (2008). An attack graph-based probabilistic security metric. In *Data and Applications Security XXII* (pp. 283–296). New York, NY: Springer. doi:10.1007/978-3-540-70567-3_22.

Wang, L., & Khan, L. (2006). Automatic image annotation and retrieval using weighted feature selection. *Multimedia Tools and Applications*, *29*(1), 55–71. doi:10.1007/s11042-006-7813-7.

Wang, L., Liu, A., & Jajodia, S. (2006). Using attack graphs for correlating, hypothesizing, and predicting intrusion alerts. *Computer Communications*, *29*(15), 2917–2933. doi:10.1016/j.comcom.2006.04.001.

Wang, L., Noel, S., & Jajodia, S. (2006). Minimum-cost network hardening using attack graphs. *Computer Communications*, *29*(18), 3812–3824. doi:10.1016/j.comcom.2006.06.018.

Wang, L., Yao, C., Singhal, A., & Jajodia, S. (2008). Implementing interactive analysis of attack graphs using relational databases. *Journal of Computer Security*, *16*(4), 419–437.

Wang, Y. (2005). Gene selection from microarray data for cancer classification. A machine learning approach. *Computational Biology and Chemistry*, *29*, 37–46. doi:10.1016/j.compbiolchem.2004.11.001 PMID:15680584.

Wei, D., Chan, H., Petrick, N., Sahiner, B., Helvie, M., Adler, D., & Goodsitt, M. (1997). False-positive reduction technique for detection of masses on digital mammograms: Global and local multiresolution texture analysis. *Medical Physics*, *24*(6), 903–914. doi:10.1118/1.598011 PMID:9198026.

Widrow, B., & Hoff, M. E. (1960). Adaptive switching circuits. In *Proceedings of IRE WESCON Convention* (vol. 4, pp. 96–104). Los Angeles, CA: Institute of Radio Engineers.

Widrow, B. (1966). *Adaptive filters I: Fundamentals. Rep. SEL-66-126(TR-6764-6)*. Stanford, CA: Stanford Electronic Laboratories.

Widrow, B., McCool, J., & Ball, M. (1975). The complex LMS algorithm. *Proceedings of the IEEE, 63*, 719–720. doi:10.1109/PROC.1975.9807.

Widrow, B., & Steams, S. D. (1985). *Adaptive signal processing*. Englewood Cliffs, NJ: Prentice-Hall.

Williamson, R., & Andrews, B. (2001). Detecting absolute human knee angle and angular velocity using accelerometers and rate gyroscopes. *Medical & Biological Engineering & Computing, 39*, 294–302. doi:10.1007/BF02345283 PMID:11465883.

Williams, R. J., & Zipser, D. (1994). Gradient-based learning algorithms for recurrent networks and their computational complexity. In *Back-propagation: Theory, architectures & applications*. Hillsdale, NJ: Erlbaum.

Wilmot, T. (2011, August). *Intelligent controls for a semi-active hydraulic prosthetic knee*. (Master's Thesis). Cleveland State University. Retrieved from http://www.csuohio.edu/engineering/ece/research/ thesis.html

Wilmot, T., Rarick, R., Bogert, A., Szatmary, S., Samorezov, S., Smith, W., & Simon, D. (2013). *Biogeography based optimization for hydraulic prosthetic knee control*. (Submitted for publication). Retrieved from http://embeddedlab.csuohio.edu/BBO

Wilson, E., & Hilferty, M. (1931). The distribution of chi-squared. *Proceedings of the National Academy of Sciences*, (pp. 684-688). Washington.

Witten, I., & E., F. (2005). *Data mining: Practical machine learning tools and techniques* (2nd ed.). San Francisco, CA: Morgan Kaufmann.

Wolters, W. T. M., & Mareschal, B. (1995). Novel types of sensitivity analysis for additive MCDM methods. *European Journal of Operational Research, 81*, 281–290. doi:10.1016/0377-2217(93)E0343-V.

WordNet. (2012). Website. Retrieved from wordnet.princeton.edu

Wu, X., Yu, K., Wang, H., & Ding, W. (2010). Online streaming feature selection. *Proceedings of the 27th International Conference on Machine Learning, ICML*.

Wu, F., Wang, T., & Lee, J. (2010). An online adaptive condition-based maintenance method for mechanical systems. *Mechanical Systems and Signal Processing, 24*(8), 2985–2995. doi:10.1016/j.ymssp.2010.04.003.

Xu, R., & Wunsch, D. (2005). Survey of clustering algorithms. *IEEE Transactions on Neural Networks, 16*(3), 645–678. doi:10.1109/TNN.2005.845141 PMID:15940994.

Yager, R. (1991). On linguistic summaries of data. In Piatesky-Shapiro, G., & Frawley, J. (Eds.), *Knowledge Discovery in Databases* (pp. 347–363). Boston, MA: MIT Press.

Yager, R., & Petry, F. (2006). A multicriteria approach to data summarization using concept ontologies. *IEEE Transactions on Fuzzy Systems, 14*(6), 767–780. doi:10.1109/TFUZZ.2006.879954.

Yang, J., Zhang, D., Yong, X., & Yang, J. (2005). Two-dimensional discriminant transform for face recognition. *Pattern Recognition*, 1125–1129. doi:10.1016/j.patcog.2004.11.019.

Yang, Y., Sun, X., Yang, H., & Li, C. T. (2008). Removable visible image watermarking algorithm in the discrete cosine transform domain. *Journal of Electronic Imaging, 17*(3), 033008. doi:10.1117/1.2952843.

Yang, Y., Sun, X., Yang, H., Li, C. T., & Xiao, R. (2009). A contrast-sensitive reversible visible image watermarking technique. *IEEE Transactions on Circuits and Systems for Video Technology, 19*(5), 656–667. doi:10.1109/TCSVT.2009.2017401.

Yeh, C. Y., Huang, C. W., & Lee, S. J. (2011). A multiple-kernel support vector regression approach for stock market price forecasting. *Expert Systems with Applications, 38*(3), 2177–2186. doi:10.1016/j.eswa.2010.08.004.

Yetisenler, C., & Ozkurt, A. (2006). Multiple robot path planning for robot soccer. In *Proceedings of the 14th Turkish Conference on Artificial Intelligence and Neural Networks* (pp. 11–23). New York, NY: Springer.

Yeung, K., & Bumgarner, R. (2003). Multiclass classification of microarray data with repeated measurements: Application to cancer. *Genome Biology, 4*(R83). PMID:14659020.

Yin, W., & Zhang, Y. (2008). Extracting salient features from less data via L1-minimization. *SIAG/OPT Views-and-News, A Forum for the SIAM Activity Group on Optimization, 19*, 11-19.

Yingwei, L., Sundararajan, N., & Saratchandran, P. (1998). Performance evaluation of a sequential minimal radial basis function (RBF) neural network learning algorithm. *IEEE Transactions on Neural Networks, 9*(2), 308–318. doi:10.1109/72.661125 PMID:18252454.

Yip, S. K., Au, O., Ho, C. W., & Wong, H. M. (2006). Lossless visible watermarking. *IEEE International Conference on Multimedia and Expo* (pp. 853-856). IEEE.

Younus, A., & Yang, B. (2012). Intelligent fault diagnosis of rotating machinery using infrared thermal image. *Expert Systems with Applications*, 2082–2091. doi:10.1016/j.eswa.2011.08.004.

Yu, L., & Liu, H. (2003). Feature selection for high-dimensional data: A fast correlation-based filter solution. *Proceedings of The Twentieth International Conference on Machine Learning*, (pp. 856-863).

Yu, L., & Liu, H. (2004). Efficient feature selection via analysis of relevance and redundancy. *Journal of Machine Learning Research, 5*, 1205–1224.

Zadeh, L. (1970). Similarity relations and fuzzy orderings. *Information Sciences, 3*, 177–200. doi:10.1016/S0020-0255(71)80005-1.

Zahedi, S., Sykes, A., Lang, S., & Cullington, I. (2005). Adaptive prosthesis – a new concept in prosthetic knee control. *Robotica, 23*, 337–244. doi:10.1017/S0263574704001365.

Zander, S., Nguyen, T.T.T., & Armitage, G. (2005, March/April). Self-learning IP traffic classification based on statistical flow characteristics. *Passive & Active Measurement Workshop (PAM) 2005,* Boston, USA.

Zecevic, G. (1998). Web based interface to scada system. In *Power System Technology. Proceedings. POWERCON '98. 1998 International Conference* (Vol. 2, pp. 1218–1221).

Zeiler, M. D., Kirshnan, D., Taylor, G. W., & Fergus, R. (2010). *Deconvolutional networks*. Computer Vision & Pattern Recognition CVPR.

Zemke, S. (2002). On developing a financial prediction system: Pitfalls and possibilities. In *Proceedings of DMLL Worshop at ICML 2002*. ICML.

Zhang, C., Ruan, J., & Tan, Y. (2011). An incremental feature subset selection algorithm base on boolean matrix in decision system. *Journal of Convergence Information Technology*, 16-23.

Zhang, Y., & Ren, L. (2010). Two feature selections for analysis of microarray data. *IEEE Fifth International Conference on Bio-Inspired Computing: Theories and Applications BIC-TA 2010*, (pp. 1259-1262).

Zhang, J., Pu, J., Chen, C., & Fleischer, R. (2010). Low-resolution gait recognition. *IEEE Transactions on Systems, Man, and Cybernetics. Part B, Cybernetics, 40*, 986–996. doi:10.1109/TSMCB.2010.2042166 PMID:20199936.

Zhang, K., Li, Y., Scarf, P., & Ball, A. (2011). Feature selection for high-dimensional machinery fault diagnosis data using multiple models and Radial Basis Function networks. *Neurocomputing*, 2941–2952. doi:10.1016/j.neucom.2011.03.043.

Zhang, Y., Ding, C., & Li, T. (2008). Gene selection algorithm by combining ReliefF and mRMR. *BMC Genomics, 9*(Suppl 2), S27. doi:10.1186/1471-2164-9-S2-S27 PMID:18831793.

Zhao, Z., & Liu, H. (2007). Searching for interacting features. *Proceedings of International Joint Conference on Artificial Intelligence*, (pp. 1157-1161).

Zhao, Z., & Liu, H. (2012). *Spectral feature selection for data mining*. Boca Ratón, FL: CRC Press, Taylor & Francis Group.

Zhou, J., Heckman, M., Reynolds, B., Carlson, A., & Bishop, M. (2007). Modeling network intrusion detection alerts for correlation. *ACM Transactions on Information and System Security, 10*(1). doi:10.1145/1210263.1210267.

About the Contributors

Boris Igelnik received MS degree in electrical engineering from the Moscow Electrical Engineering Institute of Communication, MS degree in mathematics from the Moscow State University, and PhD degree in Electrical Engineering from the Institute for Problems of Information Transmission, Academy of Sciences USSR, Moscow, Russia and the Moscow Electrical Engineering Institute of Communication. He is Chief Scientist at the BMI Research, Inc., Richmond Heights (Cleveland), OH, USA. His current research interests are in the areas of computational and artificial intelligence, digital signal processing, image processing, adaptive control, robotics, and computational models of intellect. Boris Igelnik is a Senior Member of IEEE.

Jacek M. Zurada received his MS and PhD degrees (with distinction) in electrical engineering from the Technical University of Gdansk, Poland. He is Director of Computational Intelligence Lab, University of Louisville, Louisville, KY, USA. His current research interests are in the areas of neural networks, computational intelligence, data mining, image processing and VLSI circuits. He is a Member of Polish Academy of Sciences and Fellow of IEEE. Dr. Zurada has been elected IEEE VP Technical Activities 2014.

* * *

Tsvi Achler is interested in how the brain may use top-down feedback during recognition. He received his Bachelor degrees from UC Berkeley in Electrical Engineering and Computer Science. He received a MD and a PhD in Neuroscience from the University of Illinois at Urbana-Champaign. He is associated with the Synthetic Visual Cognition Group at the Los Alamos National Labs and IBM Research Almaden.

Amparo Alonso-Betanzos received the Ph.D. degree for her work in the area of medical expert systems in 1988 at the University of Santiago de Compostela. Later, she was a postdoctoral fellow in the Medical College of Georgia, Augusta. She is currently a Full Professor in the Department of Computer Science, University of A Coruña. Her main current areas are intelligent systems, machine learning and feature selection.

Andre Barczak is a senior lecturer in computer science at Massey University in New Zealand. He has a bachelor of engineering and a master of engineering from University of Campinas (Brazil). He completed his PhD in computer science at Massey University in 2007. His research interests are mainly in computer vision (feature extraction, object detection and recognition) and artificial intelligence (machine learning). The list of research publications includes about 45 papers in international conferences and journals.

Theresa Beaubouef since earning a Ph.D. in computer science from Tulane University in 1994 has held positions with the Naval Research Laboratory and Xavier University, and is currently a professor at Southeastern Louisiana University. Her research interests include the areas of uncertainty in databases, spatial databases, and data mining. In 2007 she was awarded her university's President's Award for Excellence in Research.

Verónica Bolón-Canedo received her B.S. degree in Computer Science from University of A Coruña, Spain, in 2008. She received her M.S. degree in 2010 and is currently a Ph.D. student in the Department of Computer Science at the same university. Her research interests include machine learning and feature selection.

Marco M. Carvalho is an Associated Professor at the Florida Institute of Technology, and a Research Scientist at the Institute for Human and Machine Cognition. He graduated in Mechanical Engineering at the University Brasilia (UnB – Brazil), where he also completed his M.Sc. in Mechanical Engineering with specialization in dynamic systems. Marco Carvalho also holds a M.Sc. in Computer Science from the University of West Florida and a Ph.D. in Computer Science from Tulane University, with specialization in Machine Learning and Data Mining. Dr. Carvalho currently leads the Intelligent Communication and Information Systems Laboratory at Florida Tech, and is the Principal Investigator of several research projects in the areas of cyber security, information management and communication systems. He also servers as an associate editor to the IEEE Transactions on Systems, Man, and Cybernetics--Part B: Cybernetics.

Dawei Du was born in Jinan, China, on February 20, 1984. He received the B.S. degree from South-Central University of Nationalities, Wuhan, China, the M.S. degree from Cleveland State University, Cleveland. He is working toward the Ph.D. degree in Cleveland State University, Cleveland. He is a member of the Embedded Control Systems Research Laboratory. His current research interests include evolutionary computation, optimal control and Kalman filtering.

Diego Fernández-Francos received the B.Eng. and M.Sc. in Computer Science degrees from University of A Coruña, Spain, in 2010 and 2011. He is currently a Ph.D. student in the Department of Computer Science at the same university. His research interests include novelty detection, predictive maintenance and condition monitoring of machinery.

Oscar Fontenla-Romero was born in Ferrol, Spain, in 1974. He received his B.S., M.S. and Ph.D. degrees in computer science from the University of A Coruña, in 1997, 1998, and 2002, respectively. He works as an Associate Professor at the Department of Computer Science of University of A Coruña since 2004. He was a Visiting Researcher with the Computational NeuroEngineering Laboratory, University of Florida, Gainesville. His research interests include statistical and mathematical aspects of learning, kernel machines and neural networks and their applications to data mining, signal processing and system identification.

Yohan D. Fougerolle received the MS degree in electrical engineering from the University of Burgundy, Dijon, France, in 2002, and the Ph.D from the same university in 2005. Since 2007, he is an assistant professor in the department of Electrical Engineering, at the University of Burgundy, Le Creusot, France. His research interests include 3D digitization, solid modeling, surface reconstruction, and image processing.

Bertha Guijarro-Berdiñas obtained her Ph.D. in Computer Science in 1998 from University of A Coruña (Spain). She is currently a Full Professor at the Department of Computer Science of this University and member of the Laboratory of R&D in Artificial Intelligence (LIDIA- UDC). Dr. Guijarro's main research interests are in both applied and theoretical aspects of machine learning (big data learning, distributed learning, efficient learning), knowledge-based systems and knowledge engineering. She has participated in more than 30 research projects funded by European, national and regional agencies, as well as in diverse agreements with companies; also she has patented a system for fetal monitoring and diagnosis, and has published more than 70 publications in the field of Artificial Intelligence.

John Hale is a Professor in the Tandy School of Computer Science and a faculty researcher in the Institute for Information Security at The University of Tulsa. He received his Bachelor of Science in 1990, Master of Science in 1992 and doctorate degree in 1997, all in computer science from the University of Tulsa. Dr. Hale has overseen the development of one of the premier information assurance curricula in the nation while at iSec. In 2000, he earned a prestigious National Science Foundation CAREER award for his education and research initiatives at iSec. His research interests include cyber attack modeling, analysis and visualization, enterprise security management, secure operating systems, distributed system verification and policy coordination.

Fredric M. Ham received his PhD in electrical engineering from Iowa State University. He has been a faculty member at Florida Tech since 1988 and is currently the Dean of Engineering. He is a Fellow of IEEE, SPIE and INNS. He is past president of the International Neural Network Society (INNS) (2007–2008), and served on the INNS Board of Governors from 2009-2011. From 1977-1978 he worked for Shell Oil as a Geophysicist, and from 1980-1988 he was a Staff Engineer at Harris Corporation in Melbourne, Florida, where he worked in the Systems Analysis Group (he performed the error analysis for the control algorithms for the Hubble Space Telescope); and the Large Space Structures Controls Group. Dr. Ham has over 100 technical publications and is author of the textbook: Principles of Neurocomputing for Science and Engineering, McGraw-Hill, 2001. His research interests include neural networks, tactical infrasound systems, adaptive signal processing and biosensors.

Bereket M. Hambebo is a Graduate Research Assistant at Florida Institute of Technology working towards his PhD d. He received his B.Sc. degree in Electrical Engineering from Bahir Dar University, Ethiopia, and his M.Sc. degree in Electrical Engineering from Florida Institute of Technology. Bereket is currently part of the Information Professing Laboratory, and Intelligent Communication and Information Systems Laboratory, where is conducts researches in infrasound signal processing and cellular communications. His research interests include wireless communications, channel modeling, and machine learning and applications.

Jonathan Hamm is studying for his B.S. in Computer Science from Tandy School of Computer Science at The University of Tulsa. His research interests are in the areas of computer security and network model acquisition.

Michael Haney received his B.S. in Mathematics from the University of Kentucky in 1998. He is currently studying for his Masters of Science in Computer Science from the Tandy School of Computer Science at The University of Tulsa. His research interests are in the field of intrusion detection systems (IDSs) and Situation Awareness.

Chris Hartney received his BS in Computer Science with a Mathematics minor from The University of Tulsa in 2010. He received his Masters of Science in Computer Science from the Tandy School of Computer Science at The University of Tulsa in 2012. His research is focused on network based attack graphs. His Master's Thesis was titled "Security Risk Metrics: An Attack Graph-Centric Approach". He has presented attack graph related research at the Tulsa Research Colloquium in 2012, Cyber Security and Information Intelligence Research Workshop in 2011, and the Annual Computer Security Applications Conference in 2010.

Peter J. Hawrylak is an Assistant Professor in the Electrical Engineering department at The University of Tulsa (TU), is chair of the AIM RFID Experts Group (REG), and chair of the Healthcare Initiative (HCI) sub-group of the AIM REG. Dr. Hawrylak is a member of The University of Tulsa's Institute for Information Security (iSec), which is a NSA (U.S. National Security Agency) Center of Excellence. Peter has seven (7) issued patents in the RFID space. Peter's research interests are in the areas embedded system security, radio frequency identification (RFID), the Internet of Things, embedded systems, and low power wireless systems. He is Associate Editor of the International Journal of Radio Frequency Identification Technology and Applications (IJRFITA) journal published by InderScience Publishers, which focuses on the application and development of RFID technology.

Pierre-Emmanuel Leni received in 2007 the master degree in electrical engineering from the University of Burgundy in Dijon, France. He pursued his Ph.D. degree at the Le2i laboratory, UMR CNRS 5158, in Le Creusot, France. He is currently a research engineer in the Chrono-Environment laboratory, in Montbéliard, France. His research interests include neural networks, functional representation, and image processing, particularly image compression.

Alexandra Manevitch was born in Arkhangelsk, Russia, in 1971. She received the M.Sc. degree in Radio Physical Science and Engineering from the Saint-Petersburg State Technical University, Saint-Petersburg, Russia, in 1994, and Ph.D. degree in Applied Science from the Hebrew University of Jerusalem, Jerusalem, Israel, in 2004. Her research interests include Object Recognition, Image Processing, Computer Vision, and Data Analysis. Her industrial research experience included the Nanonics Imaging Ltd (Israel), Siemens AG, Computer Aided Detection (Israel), and Intel, Video Processing Group (Israel).). She is coauthor of two US patents.

David Martínez-Rego was born in Ferrol, Spain, in 1984. He received his M.S. degree in computer science from the University of A Coruña, in 2008. He works as research staff, with a FPU grant of the Ministerio de Ciencia e Innovación, at the Department of Computer Science of University of A Coruña since 2009. His current research interests include theoretical works on neural networks, predictive maintenance and learning optimization.

Natalia Danailova Nikolova is an Associated Professor at the Dept. of Information Technologies of N. Vaptsarov Naval Academy, Varna, Bulgaria. She has a background in management sciences (MBA in 2003), and holds a PhD degree in quantitative decision analysis. Over the past 12 years she has performed active research in scientific areas like fuzzy-rational decision analysis, simulation-based risk analysis, subjective statistics, simulation modeling. She is a member of IEEE, SIPTA, IFAC, IAMU.

Tohru Nitta received the B.S. degree in mathematics, M.S. and Ph.D. degrees in information science from University of Tsukuba, Japan, in 1983, 1985, and 1995 respectively. From 1985 to 1990, he was with NEC Corporation and engaged in research on expert systems. He joined the Electrotechnical Laboratory, Agency of Industrial Science and Technology, Ministry of International Trade and Industry in 1990. He is currently a Senior Research Scientist in National Institute of Advanced Industrial Science and Technology (former Electrotechnical Laboratory), Japan. He was also with Department of Mathematics, Graduate School of Science, Osaka University as an Associate Professor from 2000 to 2006, and as a Professor from 2006 to 2008 (additional post). His research interests include complex adaptive systems such as neural networks.

Beatriz Pérez-Sánchez was born in A Coruña, Spain, in 1980. She received her Ph.D. degree in Computer Science from the University of A Coruña in 2010. She works as an Assistant Professor at the Department of Computer Science of this University since 2007 and is member of the Laboratory of R&D in Artificial Intelligence. Her current research interests are in both applied and theoretical works of neural networks and and learning optimization.

Diego Peteiro-Barral received his B.S. degree in Computer Science from University of A Coruña, Spain, in 2008. He received his M.S. degree in 2010 and is currently a Ph.D. student in the Department of Computer Science at the same university. His research interests include large-scale learning and distributed learning.

Frederick E. Petry received BS and MS degrees in physics and a Ph.D. in computer science from Ohio State University in 1975. He is currently a computer scientist in the Naval Research Laboratory, Stennis Space Center Mississippi and was on the faculty of University of Alabama in Huntsville, Ohio State University and Tulane University. Dr. Petry has over 350 scientific publications including 130 journal articles/book chapters and 8 books written or edited. He is an IEEE Fellow, Fellow of the International Fuzzy Systems Association and an ACM Distinguished Scientist. In 2002 he was chosen as the outstanding researcher of the year in Tulane University School of Engineering and received the Naval Research Laboratory's Berman Research Publication awards in 2004, 08 and 10.

Iago Porto-Díaz received his B.S. degree in Computer Science from University of A Coruña, Spain, in 2008. He received his M.S. degree in 2010 and is currently a Ph.D. student in the Department of Computer Science at the same university. His research interests include machine learning and feature selection.

Napoleon H. Reyes is a Senior Lecturer in Computer Science at Massey University, Auckland, New Zealand. He is a recipient of a High Distinction award in Computer Science at De La Salle University, Manila, Philippines, for completing his PhD with a cumulative GPA of 4.0/4.0 in 2004. Having been educated also as a Physicist (B.Sc. in Physics), and an artist by heart, Dr. Reyes has rich and diverse research interests, ranging from artificial intelligence in path-planning, control and machine learning, to color processing. Over the years, he has served as an academic in Computer Science, Physics and Electronics and Communications Engineering. His teaching repertoire includes artificial intelligence, object-oriented programming, computer networks, internet programming and introductory physics laboratory courses. He has published over 40 research works, including international conferences and journals. In addition, he has served as workshop chair, invited keynote speaker and special session chair for international conferences.

Noelia Sánchez-Maroño received a Ph.D. degree for her work in the area of functional and neuronal networks in 2005 at the University of A Coruña. She is currently teaching at the Department of Computer Science in the same university. Her current research areas include agent-based modeling, machine learning and feature selection.

Dan Simon received his BS from Arizona State University, his MS from the University of Washington, and his PhD from Syracuse University, all in Electrical Engineering. He has 14 years of industrial experience in various industries, including aerospace, automotive, biomedical, process control, and software engineering, and continues his relationship with industry through regular consulting. He joined Cleveland State University in 1999 and has been a Professor in the Electrical and Computer Engineering Department since 2008. His teaching and research interests include control theory, computer intelligence, and embedded systems. His research has been supported by the NASA Glenn Research Center, the Cleveland Clinic Foundation, the National Science Foundation, and several industrial organizations. He has written over 80 refereed publications, and is the author of the books Optimal State Estimation (John Wiley & Sons, 2006) and Evolutionary Optimization Algorithms (John Wiley & Sons, 2013).

Peter Sinčák is the Head of the Center for Intelligent Technologies and Program Director of the Artificial Intelligence branch at Technical University of Košice, Slovakia. He is also the Vice-President of the Slovak AI Society, and since 2009-2012, he was the Executive Director of Košice IT Valley, comprising of 20 IT companies in the region. In addition, he is an active member of IEEE, CIS and RAS. Dr. Sinčák finished his PhD in 1992, at the Czech Academy of Science, Czech Republic. His primary interests are in computational intelligence, learning systems and distributed intelligence, and he has contributed over 70 publications in these fields.

William Smith recently retired after working at the Cleveland Clinic Foundation for over 30 years. Before joining the Cleveland Clinic, he worked as an aerospace engineer at TRW, a machine tool engineer at Warner and Swasey, and as a machinist for several organizations. Dr. Smith has published extensively on blood pump devices and technology, and holds a number of patents for medical devices. His current work involves both blood pumping systems and orthopedic devices. Dr. Smith's research has been funded by the National Institutes of Health, the Department of Defense, the Whitaker Foundation and private industry. He has collaborated with many small businesses on a large number of successful SBIR grant applications. Dr. Smith obtained his PhD in engineering from Cleveland State University.

David Sprecher is a mathematician with emphasis in approximation theory, function complexity and representations of functions of several variables. He began his studies in mathematics at the Hebrew University, and graduate studies at Columbia University, and earned his Ph.D. from the University of Maryland at College Park. His scientific work includes articles published in mathematics and neural network journals, an Elements of Real Analysis book published by Academic Press and Dover, five elementary books on mathematics published by Harper and Row, and over five hundred reviews published in Mathematical Reviews and Zentrablatt fur mathematic. He was on the faculties of the University of Maryland, Syracuse University, and the University of California at Santa Barbara, where he is Professor Emeritus.

Inna Stainvas is currently a Senior Researcher at Advanced Research Center Israel, General Motors. Her research interests include 3D Object Recognition, Computer Vision, Image Processing and Machine Learning. She received her Ph. D. from Tel-Aviv University in March 2000. Her dissertation was devoted to face recognition using a hybrid recognition/reconstruction neural network architecture. From 2000-2003, she was employed as a Postdoctoral Research Fellow in The Neural Computing Research Group (NCRG) at Aston University, UK. During her Postdoctoral position she specialized in application of probabilistic models to pollution detection in sea surface (Blue Water Project). She is coauthor of two US patents.

Teo Susnjak has a master's degree with distinction in Computer Science from Massey University, as well as a PhD focusing on machine learning since 2012. Prior to his academic career, Dr. Susnjak was a Tennis Professional, representing New Zealand in the Davis Cup. He has experience working in the engineering industry as a machine learning analysts and developer for computer vision tasks. He has recently been appointed as a lecturer in Information Technology at Massey University, teaching software engineering principles and methodologies. His primary research interests involve artificial intelligence topics such as machine learning and expert systems, together with computer vision applications.

Steve Szatmary graduated summa cum laude from Baldwin-Wallace College in 1990 with a bachelor of science in mathematics and computer science. He is a co-recipient of the 1996 American Society of Nondestructive Testing's Outstanding Paper Award for Research in Nondestructive Evaluation during his time working as a contractor for NASA Lewis Research Center (now NASA Glenn). More recently, he has worked in the areas of systems engineering for Multi-Dimensional Imaging and UNIX and Linux systems administration for MTD Products and the Cleveland Museum of Art. He is currently pursuing a master's degree in electrical engineering with emphasis in computer engineering at Cleveland State University.

Kiril Ivanov Tenekedjiev is a Full Professor at the Dept. of Information Technologies of N. Vaptsarov Naval Academy, Varna,Bulgaria. He is a mechanical engineer (1986), and holds a PhD in statistical pattern recognition (1994) and DSc in quantitative decision analysis (2004). He supervises a decision making and risk analysis competitive research team. He was a Fulbright Visiting Scholar in 2007-2008, as well as a visiting scientist at the EC Joint Research Center (2003). He participated and/or coordinated 28 international scientific projects and some 11 national ones. Over the past 22 years he has performed active research in scientific areas like fuzzy-rational decision analysis, simulation-based risk analysis, subjective statistics, simulation modeling, statistical pattern recognition, mathematical modeling, epidemiological modeling, modeling of biochemical reactions, etc. He is an IEEE Senior Member, as well as member of SIPTA, IFAC, IAMU.

George Thomas is a senior electrical engineering undergraduate student at Cleveland State University. His industrial experience includes the design and prototype assembly of a GSM-based remote data acquisition system for solar power plant installations as an intern for IndigoSolar. He is currently working on the design of consumer electronic devices for personal computers with Innovative Developments Inc., a small entrepreneurial company. George has worked as a research assistant in the embedded control systems research laboratory at CSU since 2009. His work in this lab involves embedded systems, control systems, and soft computing. George is also currently in an accelerated master's degree program in electrical engineering at Cleveland State University.

Frédéric Truchetet was born in Dijon, France, on October 13, 1951. He received the master degree in physics at Dijon University, France, in 1973 and a Ph.D. in electronics at the same University in 1977. He was for two years with Thomson-CSF as a research engineer. He is currently "Professeur des Universités" in Le2i, UMR CNRS 5158, vice president of the Université de Bourgogne and expert/advisor for French Ministry of Research. His research interests are focused on image processing for artificial vision inspection and particularly on wavelet transform, multiresolution edge detection and image compression. He is member IEEE and SPIE.

Ján Vaščák is an Assistant Professor in Artificial Intelligence at Technical University of Košice, Slovakia. His professional career is connected with computational intelligence, especially with fuzzy logic and self-learning means for adaptive systems, including neural networks and evolutionary algorithms, too. He utilizes them in robotics, mainly in problems of control, navigation and decision making for cooperative tasks with the support of multi-agent systems. Dr. Vaščák has published more than 90 research works, including international conferences, journals as well as book chapters. He has been as an invited keynote speaker and program committee member for several international conferences and meetings.

Tim Wilmot graduated from Cleveland State University with both a BA in physics and a BS in electrical engineering in 2010, and with a MS in electrical engineering in 2011. His masters degree was attained through an accelerated masters program, and he received the 2009-2010 outstanding senior award from the electrical and computer engineering department at Cleveland State University as an undergraduate. Tim previously held a co-op position at Saint-Gobain Crystals where he worked on material characterization, testing, and patent research for imaging applications. He now works at Belcan SEED, where he develops control systems and interfaces for robots and other automation applications.

Index